1994

THE MODERN LIBRARY

of the World's Best Books

▶▶▶

THE POEMS, PROSE
AND PLAYS OF
ALEXANDER PUSHKIN

>>

The publishers will be pleased to send upon request, an illustrated folder setting forth the purpose and scope of THE MODERN LIBRARY, *and listing each volume in the series. Every reader of books will find titles he has been looking for, handsomely printed, in unabridged editions, and at an unusually low price.*

>>

≫≫≫≫≫≫≫≫≫≫≫≫≫≫≫≫≫≫≫≫≫≫≫≫≫≫≫≫≫≫≫≫≫≫≫≫≫

THE POEMS,

PROSE AND PLAYS OF

ALEXANDER PUSHKIN

≫≫≫≫≫≫≫≫≫≫≫≫≫≫≫≫≫≫≫≫≫≫≫≫≫≫≫≫≫≫≫≫≫≫≫≫≫≫

Selected and Edited, with an Introduction

BY AVRAHM YARMOLINSKY

≫≫≫≫≫≫≫≫≫≫≫≫≫≫≫≫≫≫≫≫≫≫≫≫≫≫≫≫≫≫≫≫

THE MODERN LIBRARY

NEW YORK

Natalie Duddington's translation of Pushkin's "The Captain's Daughter"
included in this volume is taken from Everyman's Library.

THE MODERN LIBRARY

IS PUBLISHED BY

RANDOM HOUSE, INC.

BENNETT A. CERF · DONALD S. KLOPFER · ROBERT K. HAAS

Manufactured in the United States of America
By H. Wolff

CONTENTS

v

V. PROSE

The Works of
ALEXANDER PUSHKIN

NOTE

The verse translations, with few exceptions, keep to Pushkin's metre and rhyme-scheme. In particular it should be noted that the version of *Eugene Onegin* is strictly faithful to the form of the original. The date placed at the end of each piece refers to the year when it was composed. In some instances it has seemed desirable to indicate as well the year when it was first published. Aside from *Eugene Onegin*, the contents of each section are arranged chronologically.

INTRODUCTION

I

A QUARTER of a century after Pushkin's death a Russian critic wrote: "Pushkin is our all." The nihilists were a dissenting voice, but with this exception, the acclaim of the poet as the supreme embodiment of the national genius has been universal. In time it became usual for his compatriots to regard him as the peer of the foremost artists of the West, ranking with Shakespeare, Michelangelo, Beethoven. If the rest of the world has not been persuaded to accept this estimate, it allows that Pushkin is a literary figure not to be ignored. And yet abroad he is the least appreciated, as he is the least known, of the major Russian authors. The reason for this is not far to seek. His chief medium was verse, and, furthermore, verse that singularly resists translation, since it is lacking in imagery and is innocent of intellection, relying for its magic on precision, clarity, and a verbal felicity as palpable as it is difficult to convey. There is something in Pushkin's poetry, irrespective of its substance, as Tschaikovsky observed, which enables it to penetrate to the depths of the soul—that something is its music.

The transvaluation of values that came about with the revolution, in altering the approach to Pushkin, served only to enhance his reputation and his popularity. The coming centenary of his death has brought out the fact that both Soviet Russia and the Dispersion are eager to claim him for their own. To the émigrés he is a kind of palladium, the symbol of the nation's cultural tradition, now temporarily in eclipse, and the pledge of its renewal. To those at home in the new

regime he is equally a national figure, in fact, has officially been proclaimed such, but with a difference.

In 1899, on the occasion of the celebration of the one
hundredth anniversary of Pushkin's birth, an underground revolutionary organization issued a leaflet in
which it repudiated him on the grounds that "he was
never a friend of the people, but a friend of the Czar,
the gentry, the bourgeoisie." Such an attitude is now
regarded as dangerously purblind. The new society,
seeing itself as the heir of all the ages, accepts him as a
precious part of its patrimony. In connection with the
centenary, active efforts are being made to bring the
poet to the attention of the masses. Millions of copies
of his works are being printed both in the original and
in the various languages of the Union. Critics are busy
commenting on them, graphic artists are illustrating
them, composers are setting them to music, producers
are staging his plays, and his tales in dramatic form,
and for some time a Pushkin hour has been an ob-
ligatory feature of radio programs. His writings are
looked upon as the proper pabulum for youth, and as
the model for young authors. Under the hammer and
sickle, as under the double-headed eagle, exegesis and
research center upon the poet's life and works, so that
the already monumental body of Pushkin scholarship
grows apace.

The new Russia, as did the old, reveres in him the
greatest poet of the nation, the man who shaped the
literary language and fathered its literature. But it jus-
tifies delight in him in new ways. He is found to be as
congenial with the present social order as he was formerly felt to be with the old. Pushkin has always been
the object of a cult, and by the same token a figure
around whom legends clung. Today, in its cruder
form, the legend runs that he was a rebel poet, whose
valiant Muse never ceased to do battle against tyranny,

and who perished at the hands of an assassin, the tool of a reactionary clique. More responsible interpreters represent him as one who, though not a man of the masses, felt with them by reason of his deep humanity, and had their emancipation at heart; as a writer whose work possessed a buoyant, life-affirming quality expressive of the attitude of a rising social class; as an author who progressed from a personal lyricism to an objective, realistic art; as a good European, a citizen of the world, a Renaissance man with universal interests; as a free spirit, unhampered by skepticism and mysticism, rejoicing in the clear light of reason, and combating, however indirectly, the powers of darkness.

The foreign reader, in making his response to Pushkin, has one advantage over the poet's compatriots: the innocency of the eye. True, what meets this eye is only a pale reflection of the original. Nevertheless, the verse and prose chosen for this volume will, it is hoped, enable the outsider to discover for himself something of the enchantment that Pushkin has exercised over his countrymen. The essay that follows is not so much a critical appraisal as a bare outline of Pushkin's story. The work may have more meaning when one knows a little of the man behind it.

II

ALEXANDER SERGEYEVICH PUSHKIN was born on June 6 (May 26, O.S.), 1799, in Moscow. On his father's side, he came of an old, well-connected family, which had long been living beyond its means. Through his mother he was descended from "the Negro of Peter the Great," Ibrahim Hannibal, who seems to have been the son of an Ethiopian princeling. Hannibal married a Balto-German gentlewoman, by whom he had eleven children, one of them being Pushkin's maternal grandfather. The poet was rather proud of his six-century-old lineage, and he also liked to refer to his African origin, on one occasion speaking with sympathy of the fate of those he called "my brother Negroes." Whether or not this exotic strain in his heredity had anything to do with his sensual temperament and his keen feeling for rhythm must remain a matter of conjecture.

Like most of the gentry, the Pushkins were more Gallic than Russian in their culture. French was spoken in the home, the children's tutors were apt to be French, and so were the books on the library shelves. Their contents were the intellectual fare of little Alexander, an impulsive, rather precocious child with a phenomenal memory. The home atmosphere was not unfavorable to the boy's literary interests. Among the people who came to the house were prominent men of letters. The father dabbled in French verse, and one of the uncles had something of a reputation as an author. Even the servants wooed the Muse. His knowledge of the vernacular and his intimacy with native folklore Pushkin owed chiefly to them, since they had charge of him most of the time. The parents were fashionable, pleasure-loving people, and the mother, "the beautiful Creole," was rather flighty. Neither took much interest in the four children they had brought into the world, least of all in Alexander. He seems to have formed no emotional ties either with his father or his mother. At heart he remained all his life a free spirit, hampered by his weaknesses rather than encumbered by pieties, filial or other.

At the age of twelve the boy entered the Lyceum, at Tsarskoe Selo (now Detskoe Selo), the Russian Versailles. This exclusive boarding-school, intended to form future bureaucrats, was housed in a wing of the Great Palace and enjoyed the Emperor's special protection.

On the teaching staff were some men of note, and the
French instructor, curiously enough, was a brother of
Marat. The curriculum included, besides the human-
ities, some courses in political economy and natural
law, but the goal of this education was the gentleman
rather than the scholar. Pushkin spent six unbroken
years in this genial establishment, where he formed enduring friendships. In fact, his schoolmates stood him
in lieu of family and home. An indifferent student, he
profited chiefly by his reading of Voltaire and of the
gayer and more elegant poets of the French Enlightenment. He also dipped into the Latin classics, though,
as he confessed later, he preferred Apuleius to Cicero.

Literature was in vogue at the Lyceum. Pushkin
could hardly recall the time when he was not writing
verse, first in French, then in the vernacular. His earliest work in Russian was a long poem modeled on *La
Pucelle d'Orléans*. Naturally, he contributed to the
manuscript magazines edited by the pupils. He turned
out a solemn ode now and then, but for the most part
he scribbled anacreontic lyrics, epistles and wistful
elegies, madrigals and pastorals, all derivative stuff,
but couched in an unusually fluent and graceful style.
The epigrams which he tossed off early won him the
reputation of a wicked wit. He had just turned fifteen
when he leaped into print with a poem. While still at
school he began to be considered the hope of Russian
literature by a group of advanced young writers who
met occasionally to poke fun at their stodgy elders.
Never did recognition come more easily to an author.

The erotic strain in Pushkin's early verse was more
than a literary manner. He was as premature in love as
in letters. His amatory career began while he was still
wearing the schoolboy's blue uniform with the red
collar. He is said to have shared the manly pleasures of
the hussars stationed in the town. His contacts with

these officers may have encouraged both the libertine and the liberal in him, for the army was then the seat of opposition, as the universities were to be in a later generation. Moreover, the Lyceum was near enough to the palace for familiarity to breed contempt. The school publications sometimes contained shafts directed against the august person of the Emperor himself.

Upon graduation from the Lyceum, in June, 1817, Pushkin received a nominal appointment in the Foreign Office. The hot-blooded youth promptly began to sow his wild oats with zest. He drank, gambled, fought duels, attended the ballet—and the ballerinas—and, above all, was "a martyr to sensual love," with dire consequences to his health and rather slender purse. If we are to credit a poem of this period, this "hideous descendant of Negroes" pleased "youthful beauty" by "the shameless fury of desire." All these distractions did not hinder him from composing verse. He was beginning to write from experience, and his style was taking shape. In those days, however, he was best known for his saucy epigrams aimed at high dignitaries of Church and State, including the Czar, and as the author of a few civic poems deploring the evils of serfdom, extolling liberty and fulminating against tyranny. A certain section of the cultivated public was then agitated by the political unrest which led to the formation of secret societies and was to culminate in the conspiracy of December, 1825, so that sallies against the existing regime were apt to be warmly received. It is noteworthy that his radicalism went hand in hand with an advocacy of the rule of law, as against an arbitrary autocracy.

He was also working on and off at *Ruslan and Ludmila,* a long narrative poem. It was completed in March, 1820, and published three months later. In itself this playful tale of a princess snatched away from

the bridal chamber by a magician and eventually rescued by a knight, was a puerile performance, but its
appearance was something of an event. The republic of
Russian letters, then a diminutive country indeed, had
for some time been split into two hostile camps. The
conservatives, led by a pedant who was a vice-admiral
and who was to become Minister of Education, sought
to rid the literary language of foreign elements and
preserve its traditional connection with the archaic
tongue of the Church books. They championed the
dignified and decorous classicism of the preceding century. A school of younger and more gifted writers
adopted "the new style." They sought to modernize
and secularize the language, bringing it nearer to the
speech of polite society. They cultivated a less solemn
variety of classicism and were receptive to romantic
influences. Pushkin's poem, severely attacked by the
die-hards, was a shining example of the new poetics
and contributed to the triumph of the progressives.
The common reader was charmed by its light tone and
felicitous lines. For years Pushkin was known as "the
singer of Ruslan and Ludmila." Glinka's opera was to
enhance the popularity of the tale.

III

WHEN the little book in its colored paper cover made
its appearance, its author was no longer in the capital.
The previous month he had been transferred to the
South to serve under General Inzov, the administrator
of the colonies set up in the sparsely populated provinces of New Russia. This was deportation in disguise.
Early in 1820, Pushkin had been driven to the thought
of suicide by the rumor that he had been subjected to
the intolerable indignity of a flogging by the police.
Apparently imagining that overt punishment would
rehabilitate him, he behaved in a provoking manner,

thus forcing the authorities to take steps against him.

He was leaving Petersburg in a mood of mingled rage and relief. He had wearied of dissipation, and exile came as a release. He carried with him a letter in which the Foreign Minister recommended him to his new superior in these terms: "Deprived of filial attachment, he could have only one sentiment: a passionate desire for independence . . . . There is no excess in which this young man has not indulged, as there is no perfection which he cannot attain by the high excellence of his talents." The letter further stated that the culprit "solemnly promised to renounce [his errors] forever," and that his future now depended on the success of the General's "good counsels."

General Inzov did not burden the *enfant terrible* either with counsels or official duties. Instead, he lodged and boarded him, gave him frequent leaves, lent him money, and when he was forced to put him under domestic arrest for his escapades, visited the prisoner and entertained him with talk of the Spanish revolution. Pushkin stayed for a while at Yekaterino-slav (now Dnepropetrovsk) and for two years at Kishinev. There is a story that he joined a camp of gypsies and wandered with them over the steppes of Southern Bessarabia. It is certain that he traveled with some aristocratic friends in the Northern Caucasus and in the Crimea, spending several sunny weeks on their estate, which was situated on the enchanted southern coast of the peninsula. He spent equally happy weeks on another friend's estate near Kiev, where he came in touch with several men who were to play a leading part in the Decembrist conspiracy. Here his time was divided between "demagogical discussions," as he put it, and champagne dinners. There were few but charming women, including the beautiful and complaisant hostess. He continued to fall in love with all the pretty women in sight, although at least one of his flames believed at this time that his sole devotion was to the Muse.

At first he rather enjoyed his new situation. A man with his literary upbringing could not but delight in the classical associations which clung to that outer fringe of the Mediterranean world where fate had cast him. He liked to think of himself as a second Ovid lost among barbarians. But before long, exile began to pall. There was the boredom and the penury, the absence of civilized amusements, like the theatre, the lack of intellectual companionship and of creature comforts. Such lines as "I've lived to bury my desires" would point to moods of utter dejection. As his stay in the "accursed town" of Kishinev lengthened, he chafed more and more under the burden of his banishment. He soon slipped back into his old dissipated habits. In other ways, too, he proved unregenerate. His poem, "The Dagger," written in 1821, to celebrate the slaying of Caesar and of Kotzebue, is on a par with the boldest political lyrics of his earlier days. To an extent, his puerile bravado, his impudent escapades, his sartorial extravagances, his cynicism, were now a protest against the constituted authorities, of whom he felt himself to be the victim.

He drew a breath of relief when, in the summer of 1823, he was ordered to join the staff of Count Vorontzov, Governor General of New Russia, at Odessa. The busy, picturesque seaport contrasted favorably with the dusty landlocked Bessarabian city. For a while he enjoyed the sun and the sea, and, among other amenities, the Italian opera, the theatre, and the oysters at Otton's. But he was soon complaining about his "stifling Asiatic jail" and forming plans of escape.

A new trouble was now added to the old ones: he did not get on with his superior. The Governor Gen-

eral had little regard for the genius of his humble sub-
ordinate. He began by offering him patronage, which
the touchy poet found insulting. Then the Count attempted to force him to perform his official duties.
Pushkin was outraged; he was not a Government
clerk, but a professional author. True, he received an
annual salary of 700 rubles, but he considered this a
convict's keep rather than a civil servant's emolument.
He tendered his resignation.

Count Vorontzov had for some time been making
efforts to rid himself of the troublesome fellow. He
may have been partly moved by jealousy, for Pushkin
had fallen in love with the Countess, among others.
And then the authorities got hold of a letter of his, in
which he said he was taking "lessons in pure atheism"
from a deaf Englishman, and that the doctrine, though
disagreeable, was "most plausible." Real punishment
was in order. He was expelled from the service and
ordered to betake himself to the family estate at Mikhailovskoye, in the province of Pskov, and to live there
indefinitely under the surveillance of the police and the
ecclesiastical authorities. The disguised banishment
was now an open one. He shook the dust of Odessa
from his feet in August, 1824.

The four years spent in the South enriched his experience and stimulated his growth as a writer. Working as he did by fits and starts, he managed to produce
a considerable amount of verse. Literature was beginning to count as a source of income for a man constantly in need of money. Some of his lyrics reveal the
influence of André Chénier. His verse shows more
clearly the effect of his reading of Byron, with whose
work he became acquainted during this period. There
was much in Pushkin's situation to feed a romantic
malaise and a romantic revolt against the conventions
of society.

Byron's imprint is clearly recognizable in the verse narratives that he was then writing. "The Caucasian Prisoner," the earliest of the so-called Southern Poems, is the story of a Circassian girl who falls in love with a Russian prisoner and drowns herself after helping him to escape. Another has to do with the love of a Tartar khan for a Polish princess, his prisoner, and her death in the harem at the hand of a rival. "The Gypsies" relates the story of a young man who, fleeing civilization, joins a gypsy camp, kills his rival for the favors of Zemphira, and herself as well, and is expelled from the tribe. "The Brother Robbers," like so many works of the period, remained unfinished, and is indeed a mere fragment of what was to be a long tale about outlaws. These poems contain remote echoes of Rousseauism (Pushkin was a reader of Jean-Jacques), and exhibit that sensitiveness to nature in its more exotic aspects, that mood of aristocratic misanthropy and world-weary *tristesse,* that are associated with Byronism.

Among the longer pieces completed in the South was "The Gavriliad," which is believed to have been written in 1821, during Passion Week. It is a bawdy burlesque of the Annunciation, which manages to be blasphemous and ribald in a bland, graceful eighteenth-century manner. Ever since the Lyceum days Pushkin had occasionally lapsed into risqué verse.

His romanticism did not go very deep. He was not a rebel by nature, but by force of circumstance. He managed to patch up a peace with life, and as he sobered down, his writings came to take on a realistic character. Some of the ideas and predilections that he retained through life, indicate, however, that, for all his kinship with the eighteenth century, he belonged to a romantic generation. To contemporaries, at least, he was "the Byron of Russia." He was described as such by an Englishman writing from St. Petersburg on Christmas Eve, 1829.

IV

ARRIVING in Mikhailovskoye in August, 1824, the poet found himself in the bosom of his family. The homecoming was scarcely like the return of the prodigal. The elder Pushkin undertook to assist the local marshal of the nobility in exercising official surveillance over the young man, which involved, among other forms of espionage, opening his correspondence. As a result there were violent scenes, after one of which the father made the charge that Alexander had raised his hand against him. Pushkin was in despair: a fortress jail, a monastic prison, would be better than this domestic hell. Fortunately, the father put an end to the intolerable situation by removing himself and the rest of the family to another estate, thus leaving the field clear to his unnatural son.

The latter remained alone in the shabby little manor-house, surrounded by Grandfather Hannibal's old-fashioned furniture. For company he depended partly on the servants and especially on his old nurse, who would entertain him with folk-tales during the long winter evenings. He lived in the house like a guest, taking no interest in the affairs of the estate. He walked, and rode horseback a good deal, visited the country fairs, and liked to mingle with the beggars who chanted the Russian equivalent of spirituals at the gates of the local monastery. He avoided the gentry, except for one neighboring estate where there was a houseful of women. He played whist with the lady of the house, teased one of her daughters, and flirted with another. Eventually both the mother and the elder daughter fell in love with him and quarreled over him. He was himself infatuated with a niece, a married woman. In a famous lyric elicited by the affair he described her as "the genius of pure beauty," but several years later in a private communication, in which he casually announced his conquest of the lady, he spoke of her as a "Babylonian harlot." He also had an affair with a serf girl, which resulted in her pregnancy. Whether the child was actually born, and if so, what became of it, is one of the few things concerning the poet which the legion of Pushkinists have so far been unable to ferret out.

For the first time he had a chance to work steadily, free from the usual distractions. Always keenly aware of the gaps in his education, he read a great deal, particularly in Russian history, and he wrote. He began by completing "The Gypsies." He had brought from Odessa another unfinished manuscript: the first two chapters of a novel in verse, *Eugene Onegin,* which he had begun at Kishinev. Since he was, as usual, in great need of money, he issued them in two separate volumes, and went on with the tale at his leisure. To the list of his long narrative poems he added "Count Nulin," a skit in which he amused himself by parodying "The Rape of Lucrece."

The lyrics of this period illustrate the breadth of the poet's sympathies. He took pleasure in adapting foreign material and he liked to set his stage with properties from other times and countries. On one occasion he spoke of himself as the Minister of Foreign Affairs on the Russian Parnassus. He turned into Russian several stanzas from *Orlando Furioso,* paraphrased some verses of "The Song of Songs," and composed a group of poems on themes borrowed from the *Koran.* It is possible that at the end of his stay at Mikhailovskoye he wrote "The Prophet," suggested by a passage in Isaiah. This lyric bodies forth the romantic notion of the poet as the divinely inspired *vates.* Generations of

Russian readers have felt it to be one of the most superb examples of noble utterance in the language.

During his rustic captivity Pushkin made a new departure in composing what he described as "a romantic tragedy," *Boris Godunov*. It was completed in the late autumn of 1825. He is said to have written a comedy in French at the age of twelve, and he never ceased to take the liveliest interest in the theatre. There is a dramatic element in his narrative poems, particularly in "The Gypsies." That he should next attempt a play in verse, was a logical step. *Boris Godunov* is a dramatic chronicle dealing with the initial phase of Russia's Troubled Times, at the close of the sixteenth century. It is not, however, a work of political import. The upheavals of the period merely supply the material for a drama of personal ambition. The principle of autocracy is not called in question—both the elective Czar and the Pretender speak and act in its name. The treatment of the collective character, "the People," is typical of an age when even extremists looked askance at the idea of a popular rising. The dramatist attributes to the populace a deep-seated moral instinct, but he sees it also as easily misguided, unconscious of its might, a blind, unpredictable, somewhat dangerous giant.

In writing his play Pushkin hoped to give the native stage a new orientation. The theatre in Russia had been dominated since its inception by French classicism. He believed that "the popular laws" of Elizabethan drama suited the Russian temperament better than "the courtly habit" of Racine's tragedy. Accordingly, he deliberately patterned his work on "the system of our father, Shakespeare." He read the plays, be it noted, in a French translation. In *Boris Godunov* the Aristotelian unities are disregarded; the action does not revolve around a single hero; tragedy and comedy are commingled, and occasionally colloquial prose intrudes upon the stately blank verse. Blank verse itself was frowned upon as not sufficiently dignified and was indeed soon to be literally outlawed by the directors of the Imperial theatres.

Pushkin did not influence Russian dramaturgy as he had hoped. In fact, he did not even make a real contribution to the native repertory. He produced not a Shakespearean piece, but a series of loosely connected scenes, dramatically ineffective and difficult to stage. Although the censor reported favorably on *Boris Godunov,* finding that the spirit of the whole was "monarchistic," the text was withheld from publication until 1831, and the first attempt to produce the play, which was made nearly forty years later, proved a failure. It remained a closet piece, and as such is held in high esteem because of its magnificent poetry. Its stage reputation it owes to the fact that it furnished the libretto for Musorgsky's opera as edited by Rimsky-Korsakov.

The writing of the play gave Pushkin a sense of accomplishment. Further, his life at Mikhailovskoye offered other satisfactions. It held the simple pleasures that he described in the fourth chapter of *Eugene Onegin.* And yet this charming spot was, after all, but a prison, and his days were "fettered days." This banishment was more irksome than the earlier one. Again the thought of expatriation haunted him; he would settle in Western Europe; he would flee to Greece, to America. Before the end of the first lonely year he was petitioning the emperor to allow him to go abroad for his health. Instead, he was permitted to visit the neighboring town of Pskov.

On November 19 (O.S.), 1825, Alexander I died. For a while there was uncertainty as to which of his two brothers was his legitimate successor. The secret

societies, of which there were two, decided to take advantage of the confusion and carry out a military *coup
d'état,* to the end of establishing a constitutional mon-
archy or possibly a republican government. It is said
that when the news of the Emperor's death and the
rumor of the rising reached Pushkin, he decided, on
the spur of the moment, to rush to Petersburg. He had
not been a member of either of the societies; it may be
that his friends who did belong considered him too
flighty to be counted on, or that they wished to spare
him the danger, or perhaps his own prudence prevailed. Besides, his enthusiasm for liberty had cooled.
It is probable, however, that had he been in the capital,
he would have joined the insurgents on the impulse of
the moment. The fact is that the exile did not break
bonds. On the eve of the rising he was completing his
neat and frivolous "Count Nulin," and he spent the
fateful December fourteenth as though it were any
other day. He was safe at Mikhailovskoye during the
subsequent months when the Decembrists were being
rounded up and tried, and he was still there when, on
July 13 (O.S.), five of the rebels, with one of whom he
was fairly intimate, were hanged.

The failure of the conspiracy could not but sober
him further. He was now inclined to regard the existing order as a "necessity." He sincerely wished to make
his peace with the government. An influential friend
advised him to be patient, lie low, and write well-intentioned pieces like *Boris Godunov,* for although the
authorities knew he was not implicated, manuscript
copies of his poems had been found in the possession
of most of the conspirators. He obeyed, fuming inwardly at his protracted isolation, and tried to concen-
trate on *Eugene Onegin.* In May he petitioned the
new Czar for permission to reside in Moscow or
Petersburg, or to go abroad, assuring his monarch that

he had no intention of opposing "the accepted order."
Some days later he was writing to a friend that if freedom were restored to him, he would not remain in
Russia another month, adding: "We live in a sad age,
but when I picture to myself London, railways, steam
boats, English reviews, or Paris theatres and brothels,
ken Mikhailovskoye bores and enrages

ame and went and still there was no
situation. Finally, early in September a
ment courier arrived in Pskov to escort
w in great haste. Was he to be clapped
ike so many of his friends, deported to
did not know that the government had
favorable report on him from a special
ad investigated him. On reaching the
in was immediately taken to see the Em-
what passed between the poet and the
t known. The outcome was that Push-
ent was brought to an abrupt end.

not it is true that, on being questioned
Pushkin said frankly that, had he been in
e would have appeared on the Senate
he rebels, it is certain that he promised to
ject thereafter. There is little doubt that
sincerely admired Nicholas as a man and
is greatness as a ruler and a patriot.
his release from Mikhailovskoye, Push-
memoir on popular education, at the
. Here he expressed the hope that those
e ideas of the conspirators had come to
d that the brothers and friends of those
hed would perceive the necessity of the
d forgive it in their hearts. On the mar-
inal manuscript Pushkin twice drew a
ive men hanging from it. He may have

wanted Nicholas to believe that he forgave him for the hangings. But his true feelings were more probably expressed in his noble "Message to Siberia," written about the same time. He slipped this poem into the hands of the wife of one of the Decembrists who was leaving town to rejoin her husband in exile.[1] In the days that followed the first anniversary of the hangings, Pushkin wrote the lyric "Arion," which carried an allusion to himself as the only survivor of the shipwrecked generation represented by the Decembrists, and later in the year he said a kind word about them in his usual commemorative poem on the opening of the Lyceum. If he had not shared their efforts and could not now sympathize with their intention, he admired their courage and compassionated their fate.

V

"GENTLEMEN, permit me to introduce a new Pushkin; please forget the old one." Thus the Czar is said to have presented the poet to a group of courtiers after the interview with him. But the change of heart that the Emperor discerned in Pushkin did not visibly affect his habits. After the audience, he stayed on in Moscow, basking in his newly acquired freedom and in his fame. His reputation was at its height, and he was being lionized by aristocratic hostesses. Soon he was again leading the disorderly irresponsible life of a gay bachelor. In fact, he was listed by the Moscow police as a notorious gambler. Once more he was burning the candle at both ends, but not with the same

[1] A poem written by one of the exiles in reply to this message enjoyed great popularity in revolutionary circles. Therein "the bard" is assured that the Decembrists are proud of their chains and live in the faith that

> Our grievous labors were not all in vain;
> A flame will yet be kindled from the spark.

The last line was the motto of *The Spark*, an underground journal edited by Lenin.

pleasure. He was beginning to pay the price of his precocity and his excesses. So often his days left an ashen taste in his mouth. The note of regret for wasted years recurs in his poems. The lyric, "Casual Gift," which he wrote on his twenty-ninth birthday, is expressive of a bleak mood which was now assailing him more frequently.

He lived in Petersburg, lodging in a shabby hotel room, but he made frequent visits to his friends in Moscow. He was on the move a great deal, driven by restlessness and distress of mind. Sustained work was difficult. He wrote more easily during the long vacations in the country, which he took chiefly in autumn, his favorite season, staying either with friends or on one of the family estates. To a certain extent his mode of life exemplified his theory of the nature of the poet. According to his lyric, "Poet" (1827), the bard, as long as Apollo does not summon him, may lead the despicable existence of a worldling and a trifler, but when the divine call reaches him, his soul rouses like an awakened eagle, and "savage and sullen," he flees in search of the proud solitude that Nature alone can offer.

He could escape to the country, but he was not permitted to go abroad, and occasionally even his trips to the provinces were frowned upon. Nominally he enjoyed the special protection of the Emperor, who undertook to be the sole censor of his writings. The tutelage turned out to be anything but a blessing. The Czar appointed Count Benckendorff, chief of the Gendarmerie, to act as go-between and as the poet's official mentor. Benckendorff assumed that the Czar's protégé would make no move without his knowledge, and when Pushkin failed to live up to his expectations, lectured him like a schoolboy. Some months after Pushkin's interview with the Czar, Benckendorff was writing to his imperial master: "Just the same, he [Pushkin] is pretty much of a good-for-nothing, but if we succeed in directing his pen and his talk, it will be useful."

In April, 1828, when war with Turkey broke out, he asked permission to join the army, but was refused. Grand Duke Constantine Pavlovich wrote to Benckendorff that the poet was guided not by patriotism, but by the desire to infect the young officers with his "immoral principles." He applied for leave to go abroad, and was again refused. That he was, in spite of everything, still a suspect character, was brought home to him with particular vividness when the police discovered in the possession of a certain army officer a manuscript poem of his with an inscription seeming to show that it referred to the Decembrist revolt. Although Pushkin explained that the lines had been written before the conspiracy, the State Council eventually made him sign a paper declaring that he would submit all his writings to preliminary censorship, and subjected him to secret police surveillance. As a matter of fact, he had never ceased to be under such surveillance. At the time when this sentence was passed (summer of 1828) he had another lawsuit on his hands. Three serfs had complained to the Metropolitan that their master was undermining their religious faith by reading them "The Gavriliad." Pushkin did not scruple to deny his authorship of the poem, but to no avail. The charge, which was a serious matter, was dropped only at the personal intervention of the Emperor, to whom the poet had addressed a confidential letter, presumably confessing his authorship and offering his apologies for having perpetrated the piece.

In what Pushkin wrote during these years there was little to give the authorities cause for suspicion. Indeed, in his forceful if ill-constructed long poem, "Poltava"

(1828), he celebrates imperial Russia as Virgil did imperial Rome. The traitor, Mazeppa, plotting the
Ukraine's secession from Muscovy, is a villain out of
melodrama, while Peter, the victor of Poltava, and
symbol of the rising empire, is pictured as a demi-god.
One or two of his lyrics go so far as to express the
poet's devotion to his sovereign, and on the occasion
of the Polish rebellion of 1830-31, he spoke in the unmistakable accents of a nationalist and a patriot. For
the rest, the social motif is muted in his verse. It is upon the emotional commonplaces in which the personal
lyric is rooted that his shorter poems dwell. There are
among them manifestoes of an aristocratic aestheticism. With Horatian disdain of the mob and its utili-
tarian preoccupations, he declares that the poet is born
not to traffic in the marketplace or engage in life's
battles, but

> *for inspiration,*
> *For sweet sounds and for prayers.*

This aestheticism carries an emphasis on the poet's
independence, which in itself was an implicit protest
against the tyrannical paternalism that was strangling
Russia. If only now and then, his dissidence and his
democratic leanings do crop out in his lyrics, notably
in "Secular Power." Whatever its purport, his verse
was like a breath of pure air in the stagnant atmosphere of oppression.

While he was not precisely "a new Pushkin," the
years were exercising a restraining effect on both his
work and his conduct. At the close of the sixth chapter
of *Eugene Onegin,* written toward the end of his stay
at Mikhailovskoye, he had already said good-bye to
his youth. He felt that he was past his noon. It was
time for him to settle down. He ran after women as
before, but now with the notion of matrimony at the
back of his head—he who had said that marriage emas-

culates the soul! In the winter of 1828, at a ball in Moscow, he was introduced to Natalie Goncharova, a
sixteen-year-old girl of rare beauty. Then, as usual, he
was more or less involved emotionally with several
married and unmarried women, including "the bronze
Venus," of whom his poem "Portrait" is an idealized
sketch, and a young girl whom he had once called his
demon and whom he seriously considered marrying.
Nevertheless, Natalie made a deep impression on him.
The next spring he saw her again, and forthwith proposed to her. Since his return from banishment he had
made several moves toward matrimony, but for one
reason or another they had come to nothing. This time
he received an evasive reply. He wrote to the girl's
mother (the father was in an insane asylum) to thank
her for allowing him to hope, and the same day—it
was May 1 (O.S.), 1829—he started off on a long trip.

He went to the Caucasus, that romantic land which
he had first visited a decade earlier, but this time he
traveled into the heart of the country and further
south. One day he came to the frontier and beheld, for
the first time in his life, foreign land. His mount
forded the river that formed the border line, and
carried him onto the Turkish shore. But, alas! the territory had just been conquered by Paskevich's troops.
It was Pushkin's lot never to escape from the im-
mensities of Russia. He was now near the front—the
war was still going on—and having obtained permission to visit his brother, who was in active service, he
joined the army and had a taste of military life. Indeed,
he took part in at least one engagement in the informal
capacity of "half-soldier, half-tourist," as he described
himself. By autumn he was back in Moscow, where he
had to take a lecture from Benckendorff, whom he
had failed to apprise of his moves. His account of this
trip, is, next to his diary and letters, the most import-

ant of his autobiographical writings. His Caucasian impressions are reflected in a group of lyrics written about this time.

The distractions of his travels did not erase the image of Natalie from his mind. For her part, she was extremely chilly. He left Moscow, tried to work, and again applied for leave to go abroad or to join a mission to China. The authorities remained adamant. The early spring found him again in Moscow, and on Easter Sunday he proposed once more, and this time was accepted. It was only fitting, a friend wrote to him in congratulating him on the event, that the foremost romantic poet should marry the foremost romantic beauty of his generation.

Hectic months followed. Pushkin was marrying into a family which was living on the last crumbs of a fortune accumulated in the preceding century by a textile manufacturer who had been elevated to the ranks of the gentry. His future mother-in-law, a grasping, meddlesome, bigoted woman, soon decided that she had made a bad bargain, and kept on postponing the wedding. She obviously repented having promised her daughter, now a celebrated beauty, to this scribbler with an uncertain income, who was, moreover, under a cloud politically. To placate the Goncharovs on the latter score, Pushkin obtained a statement from Benckendorff to the effect that, far from being a political suspect, he was a protégé of the Emperor. He also bestirred himself to raise money. He wished to pay off his gambling debts, which were considerable, and to assure his immediate future, at least. His father settled on him an estate near Boldino, in the province of Nizhny Novgorod, so that he was now a landed proprietor and the owner of two hundred male "souls." He mortgaged his property forthwith, a good part of the proceeds going to his future mother-in-law, who demanded it, so that Natalie might have a dowry. The money was spent chiefly on the bride's trousseau.

It is doubtful if at this time he saw her as she was: an empty-headed, frivolous girl, without education, intellectual interests or even manners, whose accomplishments were limited to dancing, embroidering and a little French. He must, however, have had no illusions about her feelings toward him. At most, she was impressed with his fame. Himself, he had, like Mme. Goncharova, his misgivings. He was thirty, and Natalie was his one hundred and thirteenth love, as he said half in earnest, half in jest (the year before his betrothal he jotted down in a girl's album a list of his flames, and the catalogue came to thirty-seven items). In spite of a passion for Natalie which allowed him to idealize her as his "Madonna," and to declare that he would sacrifice his freedom and his pleasure for her sake, more and more often he found himself thinking of the cares of matrimony and the delights of single blessedness.

In the early autumn he went off to Boldino to take formal possession of his estate and with the hope of doing some work in the country. Just before his departure, Mme. Goncharova had made a particularly distressing scene, and he had written to Natalie that she was free. As for himself, he added, he would either marry her or not marry at all.

"You cannot imagine," he wrote to a friend on arriving in Boldino, "what a joy it is to have fled far from one's fiancée and to start writing verse." The verse he wrote that autumn includes some of his most famous lyrics, such as "Elegy," "Abandoning an Alien Country," "Verses Written During a Sleepless Night," "Autumn" (early version), and "The Demons," that matchless, untranslatable evocation of a snowstorm. In one of the lyrics he sketches sharply the prosy, de-

pressing background of his days. Cholera having
broken out, he was detained at Boldino, virtually a
prisoner, until early in December. Neither this nor the
uncertainty about his status as a fiancé seems to have
interfered with his writing. Those months, perhaps
because of their total lack of distraction, were his most
fruitful season. He worked on *Eugene Onegin,* putting the finishing touches to Chapters VII and VIII,
and starting a new chapter, which was to remain a
fragment. He also polished off "The Cottage in Kolomna," a narrative poem in that light vein which the
poet never ceased to cultivate. It is a farcical piece, a
trifle in the Gallic manner, delightful for its humor
and its technical felicity, and unusual in that it deals
with the life of the lower middle class in the capital.

The harvest of those months included also four short
plays. With the exception of *The Feast in Time of
Plague,* which is largely a rendering of parts of John
Wilson's *City of the Plague,* they are original pieces
modeled on "the dramatic scenes" of Pushkin's English contemporary, Barry Cornwall (Bryan Waller
Procter). *The Covetous Knight, Mozart and Salieri,* and *The Stone Guest* are objective psychological
studies of three of the original sins: greed, envy, lust.
The foreign setting (medieval France, Germany,
Spain) is barely indicated, the interest centering on the
temperamental drive which the protagonist embodies.
These scenes are written in blank verse, but the style
is nearer ordinary speech than is the blank verse of
Boris Godunov. Pushkin could have said with Cornwall: "One object that I had in view, when I wrote
these scenes, was to try the effect of a more natural
style than that which has for a long time prevailed in
our dramatic literature." *Mozart and Salieri,* the only
one of his dramatic compositions staged during his
lifetime (in 1832), met with no success.

"The years to rugged prose constrain me," Pushkin had written at the end of the sixth chapter of *Eugene Onegin*, composed toward the close of his rustic exile. He had previously tried his hand at criticism, but it was only the year that followed his release from Mikhailovskoye that he turned to imaginative prose with "The Negro of Peter the Great." This story of the unfortunate marriage of Pushkin's Ethiopian ancestor was conceived on a large scale, but after completing the first six chapters, he abandoned it. The fragment is of considerable interest as an early character study of a Negro and also as a piece of historical fiction, couched in a style reminiscent of pre-romantic French prose. As in "Poltava," Peter is idealized, but in a more sober fashion. Having given up the revolutionary velleities of his youth, Pushkin pinned his faith to the westernization of Russia, and thus became an admirer of the ruler who sought so vigorously to remake the empire in the image of Europe.

It was during his seclusion at Boldino that he turned out his first finished piece of prose, *The Tales of Belkin*. It should be remembered that as a poet Pushkin had a certain tradition to build upon and depart from, while as a prose writer he was more truly a pioneer. His performance here calls for an historic rather than an aesthetic evaluation. It is less significant intrinsically than as the foundation of a tradition. He broke new ground both in his use of the language and in his creative response to the life around him. At one time he said that he would like to see the literary language preserve "a kind of Biblical ribaldry," adding that simplicity and coarseness suited the Russian tongue better than "European finicalness and French refinement." His own style has the clarity without meanness that Aristotle praised. He found it difficult to forego elegance, but in *The Tales of Belkin* he escaped the rhetoric of his few predecessors.

Here he looked away from historical issues and personages and attempted to deal impersonally with contemporary life as lived by people in moderate circumstances. The author chooses to conceal himself behind the pretended story-teller, who is the merest lay figure. In these stories each character is firmly drawn against his social background, but the tales do not exhibit the imaginative power or possess the psychological significance which would raise them much above the plane of the anecdote. They make agreeable reading, but they bear the same relation to the fiction of Pushkin's successors that a pen-and-ink sketch does to an oil painting.

At last he had to abandon his leisure and the literary activities it allowed. Back in Moscow he somehow made it up with the Goncharovs, but soon new quarrels started. He spent New Year's Eve with gypsy singers. A week before his wedding he was writing to a friend that he had decided to get married because it was the usual thing, but he was doing it "without rapture, without boyish enchantment," and he would be surprised if the future held any joy for him. He embarrassed the friends whom he entertained on the eve of the ceremony by his extreme dejection. He was cheerful on the day of the wedding, February 18 (O. S.), 1831, but it is said that during the ceremony several incidents occurred which the bridegroom, who was very superstitious, interpreted as evil omens.

VI

AFTER some unexpectedly happy weeks in Moscow, the young couple settled at Tsarskoe Selo, the scene of Pushkin's schooldays. He hoped that they might live there quietly and cheaply, but he was to be severely disappointed. With the arrival of the Court in the summer, Pushkin found himself singled out for special notice by the Emperor. He was given a sinecure in the Foreign Office which carried with it a salary of 5000 rubles. Natalie too seems to have found favor in the Czar's eyes, much to her husband's annoyance. While she gave herself wholly to the social whirl into which they were now caught up, he resented the havoc that the round of gaieties played with his work.

All that he produced during these months was a couple of folk-tales in verse and a few lyrics. In the autumn, always his most fertile season, he finally wrote finis to *Eugene Onegin*. He had begun the novel in the ebullient days of his youth, conceiving it as a satirical verse narrative in the Byronic manner. He had been returning to the manuscript on and off for eight years, and not unnaturally, the piece bears the impress of the changes that life wrought in the author. It is a variable work, passing readily from grave to gay, from the cynical to the sentimental, always avoiding rhetoric and occasionally rising to poetry of a high order. There are some passages that are flat and unprofitable, but the verse always charms one by its technical felicity. A genial, spontaneous performance, the narrative makes room for all manner of digressions, the author moving in and out of the picture at will, introducing his friends when he pleases, and freely bringing into the text echoes of and allusions to the work of his contemporaries. In no other piece did he write himself down so fully, nor did any other exhibit his genius so comprehensively and effectively. Pushkin's successors were not to write their fictions in verse, but they owed to him an awareness of men and women in their social setting, a feeling for the minutiae of life in town and country, an interest in character, for all of which *Eugene Onegin* is remarkable and which make it the fountainhead of the Russian novel. The opera that Tschaikovsky based upon it added to its enormous popularity.

In addition to the text as Pushkin presented it to the public when it first appeared in its entirety, in 1833, there exist fragments of a chapter that was to describe Onegin's travels in Russia. He intended to have it follow Chapter VII, so as to make less abrupt the transition from Tatyana, the provincial girl, to Tatyana, the *grande dame*. Pushkin also began writing a chapter in which the hero, after having been repulsed by Tatyana, falls in with the Decembrists. He composed as many as sixteen stanzas, but fearing that they would get him into trouble with the authorities, he destroyed them, preserving only the first four lines of each, and those in cipher. The opening quatrain is an acidulous thumbnail sketch of Alexander I:

A monarch weak and also cunning,
A fop gone bald, toil's arrant foe,
Whom fame had, by strange chance, been sunning,
Was then our ruler, as you know.

During the months at Tsarskoe Selo, when he first came into closer contact with Nicholas, Pushkin may have had a better opinion of Alexander's successor, but his illusions were not to be long-lived. When winter came, he followed the Court to Petersburg, where he was to spend most of his time during the half dozen years that remained to him, his trips to the country being rarer than in his bachelor days. He was married a little over a year when his wife presented him with a daughter, and she bore him a son the year following, but the cares of motherhood nowise lessened her eagerness for the more glittering side of society life. The poet found himself reduced to accepting the rôle of the husband of a prima donna. He spent his time escorting the dazzling Natalie to interminable balls, dutifully swallowing ices and suppressing yawns. He was attracted by other women, including one of his sisters-in-law, and occasionally he sought entertainment in the fashion of his bachelor days, but if he aroused his wife's jealousy, on the whole he was a devoted husband, and one who had ample reason to be jealous on his own account. He was annoyed by the attentions shown his coquettish wife and irritated by the company of aristocratic knaves and fools into which he was thrown. As he did not always conceal his sentiments, he made enemies in high places.

Pushkin's sinecure allowed him free access to the archives. He took advantage of it to engage in historical research and indeed was thought of as an official historiographer. The past had always attracted him, perhaps because he felt himself less restricted in dealing with it. The subject he finally chose to investigate was the Pugachov rebellion, the bloody jacquerie which swept across Eastern Russia under Catherine the Great. In the latter part of 1833 he escaped from the hateful social round, spending several months in a tour of the Pugachov country.

He had barely returned when the new year brought him an insulting gift in the shape of an appointment to the post of Gentleman of the Bedchamber, an honor usually accorded younger men. Pushkin was certain that this rank had been conferred on him so that his wife might attend Court balls without impropriety. The poet was now a courtier. He hated his uniform, and referred to it as a jester's motley. He hated the Court, and called it a cess-pool. Nevertheless, he wore the uniform and he attended the Court functions. Furthermore, he accepted a subvention from the Czar in order to publish his history of the Pugachov rebellion. Financially, his affairs were going from bad to worse. His father having become completely insolvent, he accepted the burden of managing the family estates. He had no means of securing money save by his pen. In order to write, he needed the leisure and the peace that the life he was living denied him. But Natalie would not think of burying herself in the provinces, nor could he offend the Czar by running off to the country. It was a vicious circle. To add to his vexations, he discovered that his letters to his wife were being opened by the police.

He must put an end to this intolerable dependence, for which, after all, he had himself to thank. In June, 1834, he made an ineffectual attempt to resign from the service, which only humiliated him further. A year later he made another effort to free himself from his entanglement. This time he pointed out to the Czar that during his married life he had incurred debts amounting to 60,000 rubles, and pleaded for a four years' leave of absence, so that in retirement he might be free to write, and thus mend his fortunes. He had to accept a four months' leave and a sum of 35,000 rubles which was only nominally a loan. The Czar thought it safer to keep the poet under his eye. The more Pushkin struggled, the more firmly he became enmeshed. The financial assistance was of little help. Living beyond his means, he was reduced to pawning his valuables, and he owed money even to his own valet. He was aging. He was irritable. Work was more difficult than ever. The year 1835 was particularly sterile. He had no paucity of ideas, but he kept passing from one thing to another, unable to finish anything. The one piece he had to show for his labor was a medley of prose and verse, "Egyptian Nights," in itself the merest fragment. The critics were burying him. Was he indeed played out?

His productivity was diminished during these years. But his finest prose work was just ahead of him, and it was not long since he had written some of his most powerful verse. One thinks of "The Bronze Horseman," technically one of his supreme works, which he composed in less than a month in the autumn of 1833. Like "Poltava," it celebrates Peter the Great. Incidentally, it is a paean to the city that he had erected on the marshes in defiance of Nature and as proof of his indomitable will. Yet the poet sees not only the greatness of the man who represents Russia's manifest destiny, but also the pitiableness of the small individual crushed by Leviathan. The vain revolt of the elements, symbolized by the Neva flooding the city, is paralleled by the equally futile threats that the crazed little clerk launches at Peter's statue. In the end the reader's feelings are divided between sympathy for the helpless clerk and admiration of the mighty Czar. Whether or not the censors found such sympathy subversive, they held the piece to be objectionable, and indeed it became accessible in unexpurgated form only in the present century.

And then there were his verse renderings of folk tales, which are among the most precious literary heirlooms of the nation. Pushkin had always been interested in the songs and stories of the unlettered peasantry, and had a keen ear for the peculiar turns of folk speech. This gift, combined with his humor and his craftsmanship, allow these five fairy-tales to rank with his best work. "The Tale of the Pope and His Workman, Baldà" is the gem of the collection, but "The Tale of the Golden Cockerel" is better known because of Rimsky-Korsakov's opera, *Coq d'Or,* which is based upon it. It may be of interest to note that Pushkin derived the story of the magic weathercock from a chapter in Washington Irving's *Alhambra,* a

French translation of which was in his library. About this time, notably in 1832-3, Pushkin also wrote "The Songs of the Western Slavs," which testify to his delight in folk balladry. Many of these pieces are free versions of poems by Prosper Mérimée which he passed off as Serbian folk songs. In spite of their spurious origin, Pushkin's Songs have the authenticity of poetry.

In his final period his chief medium was prose. "The Queen of Spades," written in 1833-4, might have been included among *The Tales of Belkin,* yet it has more body and much greater psychological depth. If there is filiation in literature, this story may be regarded as the humble ancestor of Dostoyevsky's subtle masterpiece, *Crime and Punishment.* "Dubrovsky," an earlier tale, introduces the note, somewhat muffled it is true, of protest against injustice, which was to be echoed so resonantly by later writers, beginning with the author of *A Sportsman's Sketches.* The story is far less important as a Russian variation on the Robin Hood theme than as the earliest story about rural Russia in which the iniquity of the courts and the evils of serfdom are so presented as to suggest that something may be wrong with the system. Perhaps because he realized that it could never pass the censors, Pushkin was content to leave the story, as it has come down to us, in the rough.

The piece that gives Pushkin's measure as a prose writer is "The Captain's Daughter," practically the last thing that he published. It bears the same relation to his prose that *Eugene Onegin* does to his verse. A piece of historical fiction which resurrects the age of Catherine, it interweaves a family chronicle with an account of the Pugachov rising. The story of young Grinyov's love affair and marriage is a tale such as Pushkin had said he would compose when, in defiance of Apollo, he ceased to speak the language of the gods.

One can understand why Tolstoy considered it the poet's greatest achievement. Rudimentary and occasionally melodramatic though it is, it has, in its small way, some of the qualities of *War and Peace:* the balance, the soundness, the affirmative attitude. It has too the best character drawing that Pushkin ever did, and is couched throughout in a chaste and simple style which has been a happy influence upon generations of Russian writers.

Pushkin casts a kind of glamor over the figure of the impostor, Pugachov, in this novel. Instinctively he sides with the daring rebel, be it the peasant leader of a jacquerie, or an outlawed gentleman, as in the case of Dubrovsky, or an heroic bandit like Kirdjali in the story of that name. Yet the social implications of the rebellion, which forms the background of "The Captain's Daughter," are slurred over, the most realistic details of the conflict occurring in a portion of the story that was omitted from the final text. Here, as in his scholarly study of the rising, Pushkin's viewpoint is inevitably that of a representative of the class against which Pugachov had taken up arms. "Heaven save us," he has his narrator exclaim, "from seeing a Russian rebellion, senseless and ruthless." In another place he interrupts the narrative to remind his reader that the best and most lasting changes are those which result from a gradual improvement in manners and customs.

In his last years he felt more strongly than ever that the country stood to gain nothing from a violent upheaval. He had the inclinations of a liberal, and his sympathies were with the downtrodden, but he had his doubts about democracy and on at least one occasion he spoke with great scorn of the American experiment. Government by gentlemen, a kind of enlightened absolutism, was not without its appeal for him.

He could exalt the free individual, bowing to none, living at his own sweet will, admiring Nature and the arts, and having no care to meddle with such matters as the making of wars and the imposition of taxes. This naïve attitude is expressed in some detail in a didactic poem which is among his last. In another lyric, however, written at about the same time, indifference gives way to indignation against what he calls "secular power." And when he came to sum up his life-work (in "Unto Myself I Reared a Monument"), he spoke not as the aesthete who is above the battle, but rather as a humane libertarian, basing his claim to enduring renown on the fact that with his lyre he had roused kindly sentiments and in a cruel age had "celebrated freedom."

VII

THE BEGINNING of 1836 brought the distressed poet a ray of hope. He had long been wanting to publish a magazine, and after much delay he was at length permitted to do so. The enterprise, he thought, might prove quite profitable, enabling him to pay off his debts and free himself from his embarrassing dependence on the Czar's bounty. It was his intention to establish, with *The Contemporary*, a solid periodical, at once a literary miscellany and a journal of ideas, head and shoulders above the public prints of the day. He took for his pattern the English periodicals, such as the *Edinburgh Review*. He knew that he could count on the support of a group of authors, some of them young men like Gogol, but chiefly writers of the older generation. Naturally, he was to be not only the editor, but a contributor as well, writing special articles and drawing upon his unpublished work.

Though he was engaged in the highest type of journalism, Pushkin felt that his undertaking exposed him

to all manner of indignities. He had therefore to safe-
guard the more carefully the venerable name he was
bequeathing to his children, of whom there were now
four. It was the devil's doing, he wrote to his wife
about this time, that he, a man with talent and a soul,
had been born in Russia. He was now more touchy
than ever on the subject of his honor. In May he barely
avoided a duel with a gentleman who had been over-
heard talking frivolously with Natalie. She was then
giving him another and more serious cause for anxiety.
Already in the winter of 1835-6, which was a particularly brilliant season, gossip was coupling her name
with that of a certain Georges d'Anthès. This dashing
young officer of the Guards was a French émigré who
was soon to be adopted by Baron Heckeren, the Dutch
Ambassador to the Russian Court. Although Pushkin
trusted his wife, her coquetry and the young man's
persistent attentions created a trying situation.

The summer was a dismal one. The review proved
a sore disappointment. There was not a sufficient public for a serious quarterly such as he was issuing. Moreover, some readers felt that he was no longer in the
literary vanguard. The money that was needed so badly failed to materialize and, what with the censorship
and the work connected with the magazine, it was
only a source of vexation. His debts were mounting
and the demands made on him by his relatives were
increasing. Furthermore, when autumn came, he had
to forego his customary retreat to the country. He
was unable to work, and he was in a state of irritability which was doubtless aggravated by jealousy of
d'Anthès. The latter, in pursuing Natalie, had the help
of his adoptive father, who seems to have played the
part of pander while spreading rumors to the effect
that Natalie was having a liaison with the Emperor.

Scandal-mongers were eager to enlarge upon the Push-kins' quarrels and infidelities.

On November 4 (O.S.), Pushkin received an anonymous letter informing him that the Most Serene Order of Cuckolds had elected him coadjutor to the Grand Master, as well as historiographer. It was plain that the purpose of the communication was to insinuate that the new member of the Order had the Czar to thank for his horns. Pushkin's first step was to make an ineffectual attempt to repay the loan he had received from the Czar, as a preliminary to severing his relations with the Court. Assuming that Baron Heckeren was responsible for the letter, he then challenged d'Anthès to a duel. The challenge was accepted, but Pushkin withdrew it on learning that a match had been arranged between his sister-in-law, Catherine Goncharova, and his opponent. When pressed to do so, Pushkin declared that in proposing to Catherine, d'Anthès was acting as a man of honor, but privately he held to the belief that the marriage was a cowardly dodge to avoid the duel and perhaps intended as a cover for clandestine relations with Natalie. There is some reason to believe that d'Anthès had previously had a liaison with Catherine and that there was urgent cause for hurrying the nuptials, which occurred on January 10 (O.S.), 1837.

After the wedding d'Anthès continued to press his attentions upon his newly acquired sister-in-law, acting with a boldness that was bound to provoke Push-kin, and aided as before by Heckeren. An anonymous letter informing Pushkin that his wife had had a rendezvous with d'Anthès incited him to write a violently abusive letter to the old baron. As a result, d'Anthès challenged Pushkin to a duel, which took place on February 8 (January 27 O.S.), 1837. His opponent was only slightly wounded, but Pushkin was seriously hurt. Two days later death freed him from Benckendorff's officiousness, from the Czar's burdensome generosity, from the pangs caused by Natalie's careless frivolity, from malice and intrigue, espionage and calumny, from his own crippling weaknesses. He loved life too well, however, to have welcomed the bullet which gave him his romantic congé. And although he made a Christian end, one cannot be certain that he had the comfort of a belief in an afterlife. Yet he achieved immortality, of the kind that poets desire—"on the lips of living men."

AVRAHM YARMOLINSKY

Lyrics and Ballads

Old Man

(*After Marot*)

I am no more the ardent lover
Who caused the world such vast amaze:
My spring is past, my summer over,
And dead the fires of other days.
Oh, Eros, god of youth! your servant
Was loyal—that you will avow.
Could I be born again this moment,
Ah, with what zest I'd serve you now!

[1815]

To Chaadayev

Not long we basked in the illusion
Of love, of hope, of quiet fame;
Like morning mists, a dream's delusion,
Youth's pastimes vanished as they came.
But still, with strong desires burning,
Beneath oppression's fateful hand,
The summons of the fatherland
We are impatiently discerning;
In hope, in torment, we are turning
Toward freedom, waiting her command—
Thus anguished do young lovers stand
Who wait the promised tryst with yearning.
While freedom kindles us, my friend,
While honor calls us and we hear it,
Come: to our country let us tend
The noble promptings of the spirit.
Comrade, believe: joy's star will leap

Upon our sight, a radiant token;
Russia will rouse from her long sleep;
And where autocracy lies, broken,
Our names shall yet be graven deep.

[1818]

To N. N.

From Aesculapius escaping,
I'm lean and shaven, but alive;
His cruel paw no more torments me,
And there is hope that I may thrive.
Now health, the light friend of Priapus,
And sleep, are entering my door,
And in my plain and crowded corner
Repose becomes my guest once more.
Then humor this poor convalescent,
You too—he longs to see again
Your face, you lawless carefree creature,
You, Pindus' lazy citizen,
True son of Freedom and of Bacchus,
Who worships Venus piously,
A masterhand at every pleasure.
From Petersburg society,
Its chilly charms, its idle bustle,
Its clacking tongues that nothing stills,
Its various and endless boredom,
I'm summoned by the fields and hills,
The shady maples in the garden,
The bank of the deserted burn,
The liberties the country offers.
Give me your hand. I will return
At the beginning of October:
We'll drink together once again,
And o'er our cups with friendly candor

Discuss a dozen gentlemen—
We'll talk of fools and wicked gentry,
And those with flunkeys' souls from birth,
And sometimes of the Czar of Heaven,
And sometimes of the one on earth.

[1819]

Gay Feast

I love the festive board
Where joy's the one presiding,
And freedom, my adored,
The banquet's course is guiding.
When "Drink!" half-drowns the song
That only morning throttles,
When wide-flung is the throng,
And close the jostling bottles.

[1819]

A Nereid

Below the dawn-flushed sky, where the green billow
    lies
Caressing Tauris' flank, I saw a Nereid rise.
Breathless for joy I lay, hid in the olive trees,
And watched the demi-goddess riding the rosy seas.
The waters lapped about her swan-white breast and
    young,
As from her long soft hair the wreaths of foam she
    wrung.

[1820]

Grapes

I shall not miss the roses, fading
As soon as spring's fleet days are done;
I like the grapes whose clusters ripen
Upon the hillside in the sun—
The glory of my fertile valley,
They hang, each lustrous as a pearl,
Gold autumn's joy: oblong, transparent,
Like the slim fingers of a girl.

[1820]

"I've Lived to Bury My Desires"

I've lived to bury my desires,
And see my dreams corrode with rust;
Now all that's left are fruitless fires
That burn my empty heart to dust.

Struck by the storms of cruel Fate
My crown of summer bloom is sere;
Alone and sad I watch and wait,
And wonder if the end is near.

As conquered by the last cold air,
When winter whistles in the wind,
Alone upon a branch that's bare
A trembling leaf is left behind.

[1821]

The Lay of the Wise Oleg

Wise Oleg to the war he hath bounced him again,
  The Khozars have awaken'd his ire;
For rapine and raid, hamlet, city, and plain
  He gives over to falchion and fire.
In mail of Byzance, with his host in the rear,
The Prince pricks along on his faithful destrer.

From the darksome fir-forest, to meet that array,
  Forth paces a gray-haired magician:
To none but Perun did that sorcerer pray,
  Fulfilling the prophet's dread mission:
His life he had wasted in penance and pain:—
And beside that enchanter Oleg drew his rein.

"Now rede me, enchanter, beloved of Perun,
  The good and the ill that's before me;
Shall my foes find a cause for rejoicing right soon
  When the earth of the grave is piled o'er me?
Unfold all the truth; fear me not; and for meed,
Choose among them—I give thee my best battle-steed."

"Oh, enchanters they care not for prince or for peer,
  And gifts are but needlessly given;
The wise tongue ne'er stumbleth for falsehood or fear,
  'Tis the friend of the councils of Heaven!
The years of the future are clouded and dark,
Yet on thy fair forehead thy fate I can mark:

"Remember now firmly the words of my tongue:
  The warrior delighteth in glory;
On the gate of Byzantium thy buckler is hung,
  Thy conquests are famous in story;
Thou holdest dominion o'er land and o'er sea,
And the foe views with envy thy great destiny:

"Not the rage of the deep with its treacherous wave,
    At the stroke of the hurricane-hour—
Not the knife of the coward, the sword of the brave,
    To undo thee shall ever have power:
Within thy strong harness no wound shalt thou know,
A guardian attends thee where'er thou dost go.

'Thy steed fears not labor, nor danger, nor pain,
    His lord's lightest accent he heareth,
Now still, though the arrows fall round him like rain,
    Across the red field he careereth;
He fears not the winter, he fears not to bleed—
Yet thy death-wound shall come from thy good battle-
        steed!"

Oleg smiled a moment, but yet on his brow,
    In his eye, thought and sorrow were blended;
In silence he leaned on his saddle and slow
    The Prince from his courser descended;
And as though from a friend he were parting with
        pain,
He strokes his broad neck and his dark flowing mane.

"Farewell then, my comrade, fleet, faithful, and bold!
    We must part—such is Destiny's power:
Now rest thee—I swear, in thy stirrup of gold
    No foot shall be set, from this hour.
Farewell! we've been comrades for many a year—
My squires, now I pray ye, come take my destrer.

"The softest of carpets his horse-cloth shall be:
    And lead him away to the meadow;
On the choicest of corn he shall feed daintily,
    He shall drink of the well in the shadow."
Then straightway departed the squires with the steed,
And to valiant Oleg a fresh courser they lead.

Oleg and his comrades are feasting, I trow;
    The mead-cups are merrily clashing:

Their locks are as white as the glimmering snow
  When the sun on the grave-mound is flashing:
They talk of old times, of the days of their pride,
And the frays where together they struck side by side.

"But where," quoth Oleg, "is my good battle-horse?
  My mettlesome charger—how fares he?
Is he playful as ever, as fleet in the course?
  His age and his freedom how bears he?"
They answer and say: on the hill by the stream
He has long slept the slumber that knows not a dream.

Oleg bent his head and in thought knit his brow:
  "What hath all thy magic effected?
A false lying dotard, Enchanter, art thou:
  Thy counsels I should have rejected.
My horse might have borne me till now, but for thee."
Then the bones of his charger Oleg wished to see.

Oleg rode with Igor the Prince at his side,
  Behind him his spearmen were serried;
And there on a slope by the Dnieper's swift tide
  Lay the bones of his charger, unburied:
They are washed by the rain, the dust o'er them is cast,
And above them the feather-grass waves in the blast.

Then the Prince set his foot on the courser's white
    skull;
  Saying: "Sleep, my old friend, in thy glory!
Thy lord hath outlived thee, his days are nigh full:
  At his funeral feast, red and gory,
'Tis not thou 'neath the axe that shall redden the sod,
That my dust may be pleasured to quaff thy brave
    blood.

"And I am to find my destruction in *this?*
  My death in a skeleton seeking?"
From the skull of the courser a snake, with a hiss,

Crept forth, as the hero was speaking:
Round his legs, like a ribbon, it twined its black ring;
And the Prince shriek'd aloud as he felt the keen sting.

The mead-cups are foaming, they circle around;
   At Oleg's mighty death-feast they're ringing;
Prince Igor and Olga they sit on the mound;
   The warriors the death-song are singing:
And they talk of old times, of the days of their pride,
And the frays where together they struck side by side.

                          [1822]

The Coach of Life

Though often somewhat heavy-freighted,
The coach rolls at an easy pace;
And Time, the coachman, grizzly-pated,
But smart, alert—is in his place.

We board it lightly in the morning
And on our way at once proceed.
Repose and slothful comfort scorning,
We shout: "Hey, there! Get on! Full speed!"

Noon finds us done with reckless daring,
And shaken up. Now care's the rule.
Down hills, through gulleys roughly faring,
We sulk, and cry: "Hey, easy, fool!"

The coach rolls on, no pitfalls dodging.
At dusk, to pains more wonted grown,
We drowse, while to the night's dark lodging
Old coachman Time drives on, drives on.

                          [1823]

"With Freedom's Seed"

"Behold, a sower went forth to sow."

With freedom's seed the desert sowing,
I walked before the morning star;
From pure and guiltless fingers throwing—
Where slavish plows had left a scar—
The fecund seed, the procreator;
Oh, vain and sad disseminator,
I learned then what lost labors are . . .
Graze if you will, you peaceful nations,
Who never rouse at honor's horn!
Should flocks heed freedom's invocations?
Their part is to be slain or shorn,
Their dower the yoke their sires have worn
Through snug and sheeplike generations.

[1823]

Epigrams

On Count M. S. Vorontozov

I

Half hero and half ignoramus,
What's more, half scoundrel, don't forget.
But on this score the man gives promise
That he will make a whole one yet.

[1824]

II

Though soporific not a little,
He's so pugnacious, you would think
That with a mad dog's foaming spittle
This critic thins his opiate ink.

[1824 (?)]

"Beneath Her Native Skies"

Beneath her native skies she languished and she
     drooped,
   And now she has at last departed;
Perchance the fair young ghost a moment o'er me
     stooped,
   A shadow broken-hearted.

But 'twixt us twain is drawn a line I may not cross.
   How strange seems now the old devotion!
Indifferent lips were those that told me of my loss,
   I heard of it without emotion.

So that is she who set my careless heart afire,
   And whom I loved with tender sadness,
Toward whom I strained, consumed with anguish and
     desire,
   Who brought me to the verge of madness!

Where is the pain, and where the love that hurt me
     most?
   Sweet memories awhile outlive you,
But not for long, you credulous poor ghost—
   I've no remorse, no tears to give you.

                                        [1825 (?)]

Winter Evening

   Storm-clouds dim the sky; the tempest
   Weaves the snow in patterns wild;
   Like a beast the gale is howling,
   And now wailing like a child;
   On the worn old roof it rustles
   The piled thatch, and then again

Like a traveler belated
Knocks upon the window-pane.

Sad and dark our shabby cottage,
Indoors not a sound is heard;
Nanny, sitting at the window,
Can't you give me just a word?
What is wrong, dear? Are you wearied
By the wind, so loud and rough?
Or the buzzing of your distaff—
Has that set you dozing off?

Let us drink, dear old companion,
You who shared my sorry start;
Get the mug and drown our troubles;
That's the way to cheer the heart.
Sing the ballad of the titmouse
Who beyond the seas was gone,
Or the song about the maiden
Fetching water just at dawn.

Storm-clouds dim the sky; the tempest
Weaves the snow in patterns wild;
Like a beast the gale is howling,
And now wailing like a child.
Let us drink, dear old companion,
You who shared my sorry start;
Get the mug and drown our troubles;
That's the way to cheer the heart.

[1825]

The Prophet

Athirst in spirit, through the gloom
Of an unpeopled waste I blundered,
And saw a six-winged seraph loom
Where the two pathways met and sundered.

He laid his fingers on my eyes:
His touch lay soft as slumber lies,—
And like an eagle's, his crag shaken,
Did my prophetic eyes awaken.
Upon my ears his fingers fell
And sound rose—stormy swell on swell:
I heard the spheres revolving, chiming,
The angels in their soaring sweep,
The monsters moving in the deep,
The green vine in the valley climbing.
And from my mouth the seraph wrung
Forth by its roots my sinful tongue;
The evil things and vain it babbled
His hand drew forth and so effaced,
And the wise serpent's tongue he placed
Between my lips with hand blood-dabbled;
And with a sword he clove my breast,
Plucked out the heart he made beat higher,
And in my stricken bosom pressed
Instead a coal of living fire.
Upon the wastes, a lifeless clod,
I lay, and heard the voice of God:
"Arise, oh, prophet, watch and hearken,
And with my Will thy soul engird,
Roam the gray seas, the roads that darken,
And burn men's hearts with this, my Word."

[1826]

Message to Siberia

Deep in the Siberian mine,
Keep your patience proud;
The bitter toil shall not be lost,
The rebel thought unbowed.

The sister of misfortune, Hope,
In the under-darkness dumb
Speaks joyful courage to your heart:
The day desired will come.

And love and friendship pour to you
Across the darkened doors,
Even as round your galley-beds
My free music pours.

The heavy-hanging chains will fall,
The walls will crumble at a word;
And Freedom greet you in the light,
And brothers give you back the sword.

[1827]

Arion

We numbered many in the ship,
Some spread the sails, some pulled, together,
The mighty oars; 'twas placid weather.
The rudder in his steady grip,
Our helmsman silently was steering
The heavy galley through the sea,
While I, from doubts and sorrows free,
Sang to the crew . . . When suddenly,
A storm! and the wide sea was rearing . . .
The helmsman and the crew were lost.
No sailor by the storm was tossed
Ashore—but I, who had been singing.
I chant the songs I loved of yore,
And on the sunned and rocky shore
I dry my robes, all wet and clinging.

[1827]

Three Springs

Three springs in life's immense and joyless desert
Mysteriously rise and hurry on;
The spring of youth, unsteady and rebellious,
Bubbling and seething, tosses, boils, is gone;
Life's exiles at the bright Castalian fountain
Drink draughts more pure, more heady than the first;
But 'tis the deep, cold wellspring of oblivion
That slakes most sweetly ecstasy and thirst.

[1827]

Remembrance

When noisy day no more assails the ears of men,
    And on the silent city slowly
Night's pallid shadow falls, while after toil again
    The wage of sleep repays them wholly—
Then in the hush my hours drag out their dismal
        course,
    No peace my weary vigils bring me:
But through the listless night the serpents of remorse
    With piercing fangs more shrewdly sting me;
Obsessed by seething dreams, the over-burdened soul
    Can neither bear its pain, nor cure it;
In silence Memory unwinds her lengthy scroll
    Before me, and I must endure it.
And loathing it, I read the record of the years,
    I curse and tremble like one baited;
For all my bitter groans, for all my bitters tears,
    The lines are not obliterated.

[1828]

"Casual Gift"

(*May 26, 1828*)

Casual gift, oh, gift inutile,
Life, why wert thou given me?
Why should fate thus grant us futile
Terms of doomed mortality?

Did a cruel power fashion
Beings for itself to flout?
Who thus storms my soul with passion?
Who thus fills my mind with doubt?

Goal, there can be none before me,
Empty-hearted, idle-willed.
Life's monotony rolls o'er me,
Tired with longings unfulfilled.

[1828]

"The Man I Was of Old"

Tel j'étais autrefois et tel je suis encor.

The man I was of old, that man I still remain:
Lighthearted, soon in love. You know, my friends,
　　'tis vain
To think I can behold the fair without elation,
And timid tenderness and secret agitation.
Has love not played with me and teased me quite
　　enough?
In Cytherea's nets, wrought of such sturdy stuff,
Like a young hawk have I not struggled long and
　　striven?
Unchastened by the pangs whereby I have been driven,
Unto new idols I my old entreaties bring . . .

[1828]

The Upas Tree

Within the desert, like a scar,
On wastes the heat has desolated,
Like a dread sentry an antiar,
From all the world stands isolated.

Nature, who made the thirsting plains,
Upon a day of anger bore it,
And root and branch and inmost veins,
With foulest poison did she store it.

Down through the bark the poison drips,
To melt as noontide sunlight quickens,
But when the sun at evening dips,
Into transparent pitch it thickens.

No bird upon those boughs draws breath,
No tiger nears—the tempest solely
Dares run upon that tree of death,
And then flies onward, poisoned wholly.

And if its foliage be bedewed
By some stray cloud above it roaming,
The rain from poisoned branches spewed
Falls on the sands with venom foaming.

But by a man a man was sent
To the antiar: a look commanded.
He brought the venom virulent
Back from the tree that Fate had branded.

He brought the deathy pitch, and yet
Besides a withered bough he carried.
In chilly drops the dreadful sweat
Poured from his face; his look was harried.

Upon a bed of bast he lay,
The stricken bearer of disaster,

And perished that he might obey
His calm unconquerable master.

And in the pitch the mighty Czar
His arrows soaked without contrition,
And to his neighbors near and far
He sped the couriers of perdition.

[1828]

Portrait

When she, the fiery-souled, appears,
O women of the North, among you,
It is a brilliant challenge flung you,
Your fixed conventions, worldly fears;
She flies against them, bright and daring,
And spends herself, and falling, scars,
Like an anarchic comet flaring
Among the calculated stars.

[1828]

"Lovely Youth"

Camp on the Euphrates

Lovely youth, when war-drums rattle
Be not ravished: seal your ears;
Do not leap into the battle
With the crowd of mountaineers.
Well I know that death will shun you,
And that where the sabres fly
Azrael will look upon you,
Note your beauty, and pass by!
But the war will be unsparing:
You, I fear, must suffer harm—
Lose your timid grace of bearing,
Lose your shy and languid charm.

[1829]

"I Loved You Once"

I loved you once, nor can this heart be quiet:
For it would seem that love still lingers here;
But do not you be further troubled by it;
I would in no wise hurt you, oh, my dear.

I loved you without hope, a mute offender;
What jealous pangs, what shy despairs I knew!
A love as deep as this, as true, as tender,
God grant another may yet offer you.

[1829]

"Here's Winter"

Here's winter. Far from town, what shall we do? I
    question
The servant bringing in my morning cup of tea:
"How is the weather—warm? Not storming? The
    ground's covered
With feathery fresh snow? Come, is it best to be
Astride a horse at once, or rather, until dinner,
Shall we stay in and thumb the neighbor's old re-
    views?"
The snow is fresh and fine. We rise, and mount our
    horses,
And trot through fields whose gleam the early light
    renews.
We carry whips; the dogs run close behind our stir-
    rups;
With careful eyes we search the snow, we scour the
    plain
For tracks, ride round and round, and tardily at twi-
    light,
After we've missed two hares, at last turn home again.

How jolly! Evening comes: without, the storm is
      howling;
The candle-light is dim. The heart is wrenched with
      pain.
Slow drop by drop I drink my boredom's bitter poison.
I try a book. The eyes glide down the page,—in vain:
My thoughts are far away . . . and so I close the
      volume,
Sit down, take up my pen; I force my Muse to say
Some incoherent words, but harmony is wanting,
Sounds do not chime together . . . where now is my
      sway
Over my rhyme? I can't control this curious hand-
      maid:
The verse is shapeless, cold, so lame it cannot walk.
So I dismiss the Muse: I am too tired to quarrel.
I go into the parlor where I hear them talk
About the sugar-works, about the next election;
The hostess, like the weather, frowns, her only arts
Are plying rapidly her long steel knitting-needles,
Or telling people's fortunes by the king of hearts.
What boredom! Thus the days go by, in lonely se-
      quence!
But if, while I play draughts on a gray evening,
Into our dreary village a closed sledge or carriage
Some unexpected guests should oddly chance to bring:
Say, an old woman and two girls, her two young
      daughters
(Tall, fair-haired creatures, both), the place that was
      so dull,
So God-forsaken, all at once is bright and lively,
And suddenly, good heavens! life grows rich and full!
Attentive sidelong looks by a few words are followed,
There's talk, then friendly laughter, and songs when
      lamps are lit,
And after giddy waltzes there come languid glances,

There's whispering at table, sly and ready wit;
Upon the narrow stairs a lingering encounter;
When twilight falls, a girl steals from her wonted
    place
And out onto the porch, bare-throated, chest uncov-
    ered,—
The wind is up, the snow blows straight into her face!
But never mind! Our fair is heedless of the snow-
    storm.
Unhurt in northern blasts the Russian rose will blow.
How hotly burns a kiss in keen and frosty weather!
How fresh a Russian girl abloom in gusts of snow!

                        [1829]

Stanzas

Along the noisy streets I wander,
A church invites me, it may be,
Or with mad youths my time I squander,
And still these thoughts are haunting me:

This year will fly, the next will follow
As fast, and all whom you see here
Eternity will swifty swallow;
For some the hour is drawing near.

When I behold a lone oak thriving,
I think: when I age and decay,
This patriarch will be surviving,
As it survived my fathers' day.

If I caress a babe, I'm thinking
Thus soon: Farewell! I must make room
For you, and out of sight be sinking—
My time to fade is yours to bloom.

Each day, each year in thought addressing,
I ask in turn as it goes past

How it will be remembered, guessing
Which will be reckoned as my last.

And when fate strikes, where will it find me?
In battle, on the road, at sea?
Will that near valley be assigned me
Where my cold clay at home may be?

The witless body's unaffected,
Nor recks where it decays, 'tis clear,
Yet in my heart I have elected
To rest near places once held dear.

At the grave's portals, unrepining
May young life play, and where I lie
May heedless Nature still be shining
With beauty that shall never die.

[1829]

To the Poet

Thou shalt not, poet, prize the people's love.
The noise of their applause will quickly die;
Then shalt thou hear the judgment of the fool
And chilling laughter from the multitude.
But stand thou firm, untroubled and austere;
Thou art a king and kings must live alone.
Thine own free spirit calls to thee; pass on,
Make perfect the fair blossom of thy dreams,
Nor ask for praises of achievement won.
Praise lives within; 'tis thou that art the judge,
And thine the strictest judgment of them all.
Art thou content? Then leave the herd to howl;
Leave them to spit upon thine altar fires
And on the dancing incense of thy shrine.

[1830]

Madonna

Not by old masters, rich on crowded walls,
My house I ever sought to ornament,
That gaping guests might marvel while they leant
To connoisseurs with condescending drawls.
Amidst slow labors, far from garish halls,
Before one picture I would fain have spent
Eternity: where the calm canvas thralls
As though the Virgin and the Saviour bent
From regnant clouds, the Glorious and the Wise,
The meek and hallowed, with unearthly eyes,
Beneath the palm of Zion, these alone . . .
My wish is granted: God has shown thy face
To me; here, my Madonna, thou shalt throne:
Most pure exemplar of the purest grace.

[1830]

Elegy

The mirth, now dead, that once was madly bubbling,
Like fumes of last night's cups is vaguely troubling;
Not so the griefs that to those years belong:
Like wine, I find, with age they grow more strong.
My path is bleak—before me stretch my morrows:
A tossing sea, foreboding toil and sorrows.
And yet I do not wish to die, be sure;
I want to live—think, suffer, and endure;
And I shall know some savor of elation
Amidst the cares, the woes, and the vexation:
At times I shall be drunk on music still,
Or at a moving tale my eyes will fill,
And, as sad dusk folds down about my story,
Love's farewell smile may shed a parting glory.

[1830]

"My Critic, Rosy-Gilled"

My critic, rosy-gilled, who are so quick to offer
Our gloomy Muse affront, you plump, pot-bellied
    scoffer,
Come here, I beg, sit down, and have a little nip;
Together we may get the better of the hyp.
Behold the view: a row of wretched huts, and ponder
The black earth of the plain that slopes behind them
    yonder;
Above the hovels hang low clouds, thick-massed and
    gray.
But the bright meadows, friend, the dark woods—
    where are they?
Where is the stream? Beside the low fence in the court
Two trees rejoice the eye; they're of a meager sort,
Such pitiable things, the two of them together,
And one is stripped quite bare by autumn's rainy
    weather,
The other's yellow leaves wait, sopping, to be strewn
On puddles by the wind that will be raging soon.
There's not a living cur. True, here a peasant trudges
Across the empty court, and at his heels two drudges.
The coffin of a child beneath his arm, no hat
Upon his head—he calls to the priest's lazy brat
To bid his dad unlock the church—"You've legs to
    run with!
Be quick! We're late—high time the funeral were
    done with!"

"Why do you frown, my friend?" "You've kept this
    up too long;
Can't you amuse us with a merry sort of song?"

"Where are you off to now?" "To Moscow, I am
    setting

Out for the birthday ball." "But are you quite for-
getting
That we are quarantined? The cholera's with us.
Come, cool your heels here, as in the grim Caucasus
Your humble servant did—there's nothing else to do
now.
Well, brother, you don't scoff: so you've got the hyp
too now!"

[1830]

"For One Last Time"

For one last time I am embracing
Your image, all but lost to me;
The heart is eager to be tracing
A dream that time will be effacing,
And dwells upon love's memory.

Our years roll onward, ever changing;
They change, and we change in the end—
Far from your poet you are ranging,
And darkness like the grave's, estranging,
Has rapt you from that passionate friend.

This heart its leave of you has taken;
Accept, my distant dear, love's close,
As does the wife death leaves forsaken,
As does the exile's comrade, shaken
And mute, who clasps him once, and goes.

[1830]

Verses Written
During a Sleepless Night

Sleep evades me, there's no light:
Darkness wraps the earth with slumber,
Only weary tickings number

The slow hours of the night.
Parca, chattering woman-fashion,
Night, that offers no compassion,
Life, that stirs like rustling mice—
Why encage me in your vise?
Why the whispering insistence—
Are you but the pale persistence
Of a day departed twice?
What black failures do you reckon?
Do you prophesy or beckon?
I would know whence you are sprung,
I would study your dark tongue . . .

[1830]

On the Translation of the Iliad

Sacred, sonorous, is heard the long-muted speech of
    the Hellenes;
  Shaken, my soul knows thee near, shade of the
    mighty old man.

[1830]

"Abandoning an Alien Country"

Abandoning an alien country,
You sought your distant native land;
How could I stop the tears at parting
When sorrow was beyond command?
With hands that momently grew colder
I tried to hold you, wordlessly
I begged that our farewells, our anguish,
Might be prolonged eternally.

But from the bitter kiss and clinging
You tore away your lips; and from
The gloomy land of lonely exile

To a new country bade me come.
You said: "When we are reunited,
Beneath a sky of endless blue,
In the soft shadow of the olives,
Then, lip to lip, I'll solace you."

But yonder, where the blue is radiant,
And where the olives from the shore
Cast tender shadows on the waters,
You fell asleep, to wake no more.
The funeral urn, alas, is holding
Your beauty and your sorrow now,
But the sweet kiss of our reunion . . .
I wait—I hold you to your vow.

[1830]

Work

Here is the long-bided hour: the labor of years is
    accomplished.
Why should this sadness unplumbed secretly weigh on
    my heart?
Is it, my work being done, I stand like a laborer, use-
    less,
One who has taken his pay, a stranger to tasks that
    are new?
Is it the work I regret, the silent companion of mid-
    night,
Friend of the golden-haired Dawn, friend of the gods
    of the hearth?

[1830]

"When in My Arms"

When in my arms your slender beauty
Is locked, O you whom I adore,
And from my lips, between the kisses,
Love's tender words delight to pour,
In silence from my tight embraces
Your supple form you gently free,
And with a skeptic's smile, my dear one
You mockingly reply to me;
The sad tradition of betrayal
You have remembered all too well;
You listen dully, scarcely heeding
A syllable of what I tell.
I curse the zeal, the crafty ardors,
I curse the criminal delight
Of youth, and the appointed meetings,
The garden trysts in the hushed night;
I curse the whispered lovers' discourse,
The magic spells that lay in verse,
The gullible young girls' caresses,
Their tears, their late regrets I curse.

[1831]

"No, Never Think"

No, never think, my dear, that in my heart I treasure
The tumult of the blood, the frenzied gusts of pleasure,
Those groans of hers, those shrieks: a young Bac-
chante's cries,
When writhing like a snake in my embrace she lies.

And wounding kiss and touch, urgent and hot, en-
  gender
The final shudderings that consummate surrender.

How sweeter far are you, my meek, my quiet one—
By what tormenting bliss is my whole soul undone
When, after I have long and eagerly been pleading,
With bashful graciousness to my deep need conceding,
You give yourself to me, but shyly, turned away,
To all my ardors cold, scarce heeding what I say,
Responding, growing warm, oh, in how slow a fash-
  ion,
To share, unwilling, yet to share at last my passion!
          [1832 (?)]

Autumn

(*Fragment*)

"What does not enter then my drowsy mind . . . ?"
             Derzhavin

I

October comes at last. The grove is shaking
The last reluctant leaves from naked boughs.
The autumn cold has breathed, the road is freezing—
The brook still sounds behind the miller's house,
But the pond's hushed; now with his pack my neigh-
  bor
Makes for the distant field—his hounds will rouse
The woods with barking, and his horse's feet
Will trample cruelly the winter wheat.

II

This is my time! What is the Spring to me?
Thaw is a bore: mud running thick and stinking—
Spring makes me ill: my mind is never free
From dizzy dreams, my blood's in constant ferment.
Give me instead Winter's austerity,
The snows under the moon—and what is gayer
Than to glide lightly in a sleigh with her
Whose fingers are like fire beneath the fur?

III

And oh, the fun, steel-shod to trace a pattern
In crystal on the river's glassy face!
The shining stir of festivals in winter!
But there's a limit—nobody could face
Six months of snow—even that cave-dweller,
The bear, would growl "enough" in such a case.
Sleigh-rides with young Armidas pall, by Jove,
And you turn sour with loafing by the stove.

IV

Oh, darling Summer, I could cherish you,
If heat and dust and gnats and flies were banished.
These dull the mind, the heart grows weary, too.
We, like the meadows, suffer drought: thought withers
Drink is our only hope, and how we rue
Old woman Winter, at whose funeral banquet
Pancakes and wine were served, but now we hold
Memorial feasts of ices, sweet and cold.

V

They say ill things of the last days of Autumn:
But I, friend reader, not a one will hear;
Her quiet beauty touches me as surely

As does a wistful child, to no one dear.
She can rejoice me more, I tell you frankly,
Than all the other seasons of the year.
I am a humble lover, and I could
Find, singularly, much in her that's good.

VI

How shall I make it clear? I find her pleasing
As you perhaps may like a sickly girl,
Condemned to die, and shortly, who is drooping
Without a murmur of reproach to hurl
At life, forsaking her—upon her paling
Young lips a little smile is seen to curl.
She does not hear the grave's horrific yawn.
Today she lives—tomorrow she is gone.

VII

Oh, mournful season that delights the eyes,
Your farewell beauty captivates my spirit.
I love the pomp of Nature's fading dyes,
The forests, garmented in gold and purple,
The rush of noisy wind, and the pale skies
Half-hidden by the clouds in darkling billows,
And the rare sun-ray and the early frost,
And threats of grizzled Winter, heard and lost.

VIII

Each time that Autumn comes I bloom afresh;
For me, I find, the Russian cold is good;
Again I go through life's routine with relish:
Sleep comes in season, and the need for food;
Desire seethes—and I am young and merry,
My heart beats fast with lightly leaping blood.
I'm full of life—such is my organism
(If you will please excuse the prosaism).

IX

My horse is brought; far out onto the plain
He carries his glad rider, and the frozen
Dale echoes to his shining hooves, his mane
Streams in the keen wind like a banner blowing,
And the bright ice creaks under him again.
But day soon flickers out. At the forgotten
Hearth, where the fire purrs low or leaps like wind,
I read, or nourish long thoughts in my mind.

X

And I forget the world in the sweet silence,
While I am lulled by fancy, and once more
The soul oppressed with the old lyric fever
Trembles, reverberates, and seeks to pour
Its burden freely forth, and as though dreaming
I watch the children that my visions bore,
And I am host to the invisible throngs
Who fill my reveries and build my songs.

XI

And thoughts stir bravely in my head, and rhymes
Run forth to meet them on light feet, and fingers
Reach for the pen, and the good quill betimes
Asks for the foolscap. Wait: the verses follow.
Thus a still ship sleeps on still seas. Hark: Chimes!
And swiftly all hands leap to man the rigging,
The sails are filled, they belly in the wind—
The monster moves—a foaming track behind.

XII

It sails, but whither is it our ship goes? . . .

                                    [1833]

Funeral Song

God be your guide on the long rough way!
No fear, praise God, that you go astray.
The night is clear and the moon is up.
Set down, set down the empty cup.

The bullet is quick and fever slow;
You died as you lived—free.
Your foe fled when he'd struck the blow;
But your son was swift as he.

Brother, do not forget us now,
And when, somehow, you meet,
Greet our father for me, and bow,
Bow down before his feet.

Tell him my wound is already healed,
The pains are past and done;
Tell him when I came back from the field
My wife had borne me a son.

For grandfather's sake we named him Yan:
He is a clever lad,
Already he wields a yataghan
And his rifle-shot's not bad.

My daughter lives at Lisgora: she
Has not tired of the man she wed;
Tvark long since went down to the sea—
You'll learn if he's living or dead.

God be your guide on the long rough way!
No fear, praise God, that you go astray.
The night is clear and the moon is up.
Set down, set down the empty cup.

[1833]

" . . . I Visited Again"

        . . . I visited again
That corner of the earth where once I spent,
In placid exile, two unheeded years.
A decade's gone since then—and in my life
There have been many changes—in myself,
Who from the general law am not exempt,
There have been changes, too—but here once more
The past envelops me, and suddenly
It seems that only yesterday I roamed
These groves.

       Here stands the exile's cottage, where
I lived with my poor nurse. The good old woman
Has passed away—no longer do I hear
Through the thin wall her heavy tread as she
Goes on her busy rounds.

        Here is the hill
Upon whose wooded crest I often sat
Unstirring, staring down upon the lake—
Recalling, as I looked, with melancholy,
Another shore, and other waves I knew . . .
Among the golden meadows, the green fields,
It stretches its blue breadth, the same still lake:
A fisherman across its lonely waters
Is rowing now, and dragging in his wake
A wretched net. Upon the sloping shores
Are scattered hamlets—and beyond them there
A mill squats crookedly—it scarcely stirs
Its wings in this soft wind . . .

        Upon the edge
Of the ancestral acres, on the spot
Where the rough road, trenched by the heavy rains,

Begins its upward climb, three pine-trees rise—
One stands apart, and two are close together,
And I remember how, of moonlight nights,
When I rode past, their rustling greeted me
Like a familiar voice. I took that road,
I saw the pines before me once again.
They are the same, and on the ear the same
Familiar whisper breaks from shaken boughs,
But at the base, beside their aged roots
(Where I remembered only barrenness),
Has sprung a fair young grove, and I observe
A verdant family; the bushes crowd
Like children in their shadow. And apart,
Alone as ever, their glum comrade stands,
Like an old bachelor, about whose feet
There stretches only bareness as before.
I hail you, race of youthful newcomers!
I shall not witness your maturity,
When you shall have outgrown my ancient friends,
And with your shoulders hide their very heads
From passers-by. But let my grandson hear
Your wordless greeting when, as he returns,
Content, light-hearted, from a talk with friends,
He too rides past you in the dark of night,
And thinks, perhaps, of me.

[1835]

"'Tis Time, My Friend"

'Tis time, my friend, 'tis time! The heart for rest is
            crying—
The days go by, each hour bears off as it is flying
A shred of our existence—we two, we plan to live,
But death may come, how soon? And joy is fugitive.

Not happiness, but peace and freedom may be granted
On earth: this is my hope, who by one dream am
      haunted—
A weary slave, I plan escape before the night
To the remote repose of toil and pure delight.

[1836 (?)]

Secular Power

When the supreme event had at long last transpired,
And God upon the cross in agony expired,
On either side the Tree two looked on one another:
One, Mary Magdalene, and one, the Virgin Mother—
      In grief two women stood.
But now whom do we see beneath the holy rood,
As though it were the porch of him who rules the
      city—
Not here the holy twain, borne down by pain and
      pity,
But, shakos on their heads and bayonet in hand,
Beside the crucifix two bristling sentries stand.
Are they set here to guard the cross as 'twere State
      cargo?
Is it on mice or thieves you thus lay an embargo?
Would you add dignity unto the King of kings?
What honor do you think your patronage thus brings,
You mighty of the earth, what help by you is rendered
To Him who's crowned with thorns, to Him who
      freely tendered
His body to the scourge, without complaint or fear,
The Christ who had to bear the cross, the nails, the
      spear?
Fear you the mob's affront to Him who won remission,

Whose death has saved the race of Adam from perdi-
    tion?
Is it to keep the way for strolling gentry clear
That thus the common folk are not admitted here?
                            [1836]

"Pure Men, and Women Too"

Pure men, and women too, all of the world unspotted,
That they might reach the heights to holy saints
    allotted,
That they might fortify the heart against life's stress,
Composed such prayers as still comfort us and bless.
But none has ever stirred in me such deep emotions
As that the priest recites at Lententide devotions;
The words which mark for us that saddest season rise
Most often to my lips, and in that prayer lies
Support ineffable when I, a sinner, hear it:
"Thou, Lord of all my life, avert Thou from my spirit
Both idle melancholy and ambition's sting,
That hidden snake, and joy in foolish gossiping.
But let me see, O God, my sins, and make confession,
So that my brother be not damned by my transgression,
And quicken Thou in me the breath and being of
Both fortitude and meekness, chastity and love."
                            [1836]

"In Vain I Seek to Flee"

In vain I seek to flee to Zion's lofty height:
Rapacious sin pursues, alert to watch my flight;
'Tis thus, with nostrils thrust in yielding sandy hol-
    lows,
The shy deer's pungent spoor the hungry lion follows.
                            [1836]

"When, Lost in Thought"

When, lost in thought, I roam beyond the city's
    bounds
And find myself within the public burial-grounds,
The fashionable tombs behind the railing squatting,
Where the great capital's uncounted dead are rotting,
All huddled in a swamp, a crowding, teeming horde,
Like greedy guests that swarm about a beggar's board;
Officials' sepulchers, and merchants', too, all fizzles:
The clumsy products of inexpert, vulgar chisels,
Inscribed in prose and verse with virtues, service, rank,
Outlandish ornaments displayed on either flank;
A widow's fond lament for an old cuckold coffined;
The urns screwed from their posts by thieves; the
      earth that's softened
And slippery, where graves are gaping dark and wide
To welcome tenants who next day will move inside—
All this brings troubled thoughts; I feel my spirits fail
    me
As I survey the scene, and evil blues assail me.
One wants to spit and run!
                        But what calm pleasure lies—
When rural autumn sheds its peace from evening
    skies—
In seeing the churchyard, where, solemnly reposing
Among their ancestors, the country dead are dozing!
There, unadorned, the graves have ample elbow-room;
At midnight no pale thief creeps forth to rob the tomb;
The peasant sighs and says a prayer as he passes
The time-worn stones o'ergrown with yellowed moss
      and grasses;
No noseless angels soar, no blowsy Graces here,
No petty pyramids or idle urns appear;

But a broad oak above these dignified graves brooding
Bestirs its boughs in music. . .

[1836]

"Unto Myself I Reared a Monument"

Exegi monumentum
Unto myself I reared a monument not builded
By hands; a track thereto the people's feet will tread;
Not Alexander's shaft is lofty as my pillar
    That proudly lifts its splendid head.

Not wholly shall I die—but in the lyre my spirit
Shall, incorruptible and bodiless, survive—
And I shall know renown as long as under heaven
    One poet yet remains alive.

The rumor of my fame will sweep through vasty
    Russia,
And all its peoples speak this name, whose light shall
    reign
Alike for haughty Slav, and Finn, and savage Tungus,
    And Kalmuck riders of the plain.

I shall be loved, and long the people will remember
The kindly thoughts I stirred—my music's brightest
    crown,
How in this cruel age I celebrated freedom,
    And begged for ruth toward those cast down.

Oh, Muse, as ever, now obey your God's command-
    ments,
Of insult unafraid, to praise and slander cool,
Demanding no reward, sing on, but in your wisdom
    Be silent when you meet a fool.

[1836]

NOTES

To Chaadayev—Pushkin was at school when he met Pyotr Chaadayev, who was then an officer in a hussar regiment stationed at Tsarskoe Selo. Eventually Chaadayev gave up the liberalism of his youth and turned mystic. In middle life he published a series of essays in which he denied the greatness of his country and in consequence was officially declared insane. See also note to *Eugene Onegin,* Ch. I, stanza xxv, 1. 5.

"With Freedom's Seed"—"This is my last liberal raving," Pushkin wrote in a letter from Odessa, dated Dec. 1 (O.S.), 1823, alluding to his poem on the death of Napoleon. "I have given up all that, and the other day I wrote an imitation of the parable by that moderate democrat, Jesus Christ." The poem, "With Freedom's Seed," is transcribed therewith. In a rough draft of this letter he said that he had written his "imitation" as he looked about him and cast a glance at Western Europe. The early twenties witnessed the triumph of political reaction on the continent.

Epigram I—This shaft was directed against Pushkin's superior at Odessa.

Winter Evening—The "Nanny" of this poem is Pushkin's old nurse, Arina, his companion during his confinement at Mikhailovskoye. Another reference to her occurs in the poem, "I visited again."

The Prophet—Cf. Isaiah VI, 1-10.

Message to Siberia—This poem, addressed to the Decembrists, was published posthumously.

"Casual Gift"—May 26, 1828, was Pushkin's twenty-ninth birthday.

"The Man I Was of Old"—The epigraph is from André Chénier.

Verses Written During a Sleepless Night—It is believed that Zhukovsky, the editor of this posthumously published lyric, is responsible for the last line, and that as Pushkin originally wrote it, it ran simply: "I seek your meaning."

On the Translation of the Iliad—The translation referred to was made by Nikolay Gnedich, who devoted seventeen years to the task.

Work—Probably occasioned by the completion of *Eugene Onegin*.

"No, Never Think"—This lyric, which was published posthumously, may have been written in 1830, in which case the lady is not, as has been thought, the poet's wife.

Funeral Song—One of the "Songs of the Western Slavs," adapted by Pushkin from Mérimée's literary forgery, *La Guzla*, in the belief that it was genuine. Mérimée attributed this piece to Hyacinthe Maglanovich, an Illyrian minstrel, who was a figment of his imagination.

Secular Power—The reference is to The Crucifixion, a canvas by K. P. Bryullov, exhibited in Petersburg in 1836; sentries were placed about it to keep off the crowd.

"Pure Men, and Women Too"—The prayer referred to was composed by St. Ephraim the Syrian, who flourished in the fourth century.

II

Narrative Poems

POLTAVA

(From Canto III)

The East is bright with dawn. Already
From field and hill the cannon roars.
The purple smoke in swirl and eddy
Toward a cloudless heaven soars
To meet the beams that morning pours.
The ranks are closed. The marksmen scatter—
They lie awhile in ambush yet.
The balls go rolling, bullets spatter,
And coldly slants the bayonet.
The Swede, long crowned with Victory's favors,
Tears through the trench-fire, nor wavers.
The frantic cavalry in force
Rides forth—the infantry, impassive,
With solid tread and firm front massive
Moves forward to support the horse.
And here the battlefield is burning,
And there with fatal thunder lours;
But now the tide of war is turning,
And fortune, it is plain, is ours.
Rebuffs from every quarter meeting,
The troops are strewn about the field;
Rosen goes through the pass, retreating,
And fiery Schlippenbach must yield.
We crowd the Swedes, about them rattles
The din of war; their banners shake,
Beclouded, as the God of Battles
Sheds grace on every move we make

93

Then, like the voice of Heaven, urging
The victors, Peter's voice sounds clear:
"Now, with God's help, to work!" And here,
His favorites about him surging,
Comes Peter from the tent. His eyes
Dart fire, his face commands surrender,
His steps are swift. The tempest's splendor
Alone with Peter's splendor vies.
He goes. They bring his charger, panting;
High-strung, yet ready to obey,
He scents the fire of the fray
And quivers. Now with eyeballs slanting,
Into the dust of war he fares,
Proud of the rider that he bears.

Noon nears. The blazing heat bores deeper.
The battle rests—a tired reaper.
The Cossack steeds, paraded, shine.
The regiments fall into line.
No martial music is redounding,
And from the hills the hungry roar
Of the calmed cannon breaks no more.
And lo! across the plain resounding,
A deep "Hurrah!" rolls from afar:
The regiments have seen the Czar.

                                    [1828]

THE BRONZE HORSEMAN

A Petersburg Tale, 1833

FOREWORD

The occurrence related in this tale is based on fact. The details of the flood are taken from the journals of the day. The curious may consult the account composed by V. I. Berkh.[1]

INTRODUCTION

There, by the billows desolate,
He stood, with mighty thoughts elate,
And gazed; but in the distance only
A sorry skiff on the broad spate
Of Neva drifted seaward, lonely.
The moss-grown miry banks with rare
Hovels were dotted here and there
Where wretched Finns for shelter crowded;
The murmuring woodlands had no share
Of sunshine, all in mist beshrouded.
And thus He mused: "From here, indeed
Shall we strike terror in the Swede;
And here a city by our labor
Founded, shall gall our haughty neighbor;
'Here cut'—so Nature gives command—
'Your window [2] through on Europe; stand
Firm-footed by the sea, unchanging!'
Ay, ships of every flag shall come
By waters they had never swum,
And we shall revel, freely ranging."

95

A century—and that city young,
Gem of the Northern world, amazing,
From gloomy wood and swamp upsprung,
Had risen, in pride and splendor blazing.
Where once, by that low-lying shore,
In waters never known before
The Finnish fisherman, sole creature,
And left forlorn by stepdame Nature,
Cast ragged nets—today, along
Those shores, astir with life and motion,
Vast shapely palaces in throng
And towers are seen: from every ocean,
From the world's end, the ships come fast,
To reach the loaded quays at last.
The Neva now is clad in granite
With many a bridge to overspan it;
The islands lie beneath a screen
Of gardens deep in dusky green.
To that young capital is drooping
The crest of Moscow on the ground,
A dowager in purple, stooping
Before an empress newly crowned.

  I love thee, city of Peter's making;
I love thy harmonies austere,
And Neva's sovran waters breaking
Along her banks of granite sheer;
Thy traceried iron gates; thy sparkling,
Yet moonless, meditative gloom
And thy transparent twilight darkling;
And when I write within my room
Or lampless, read—then, sunk in slumber,
The empty thoroughfares, past number,
Are piled, stand clear upon the night;
The Admiralty spire is bright;
Nor may the darkness mount, to smother
The golden cloudland of the light,

For soon one dawn succeeds another
With barely half-an-hour of night.
I love thy ruthless winter, lowering
With bitter frost and windless air;
The sledges along Neva scouring;
Girls' cheeks—no rose so bright and fair!
The flash and noise of balls, the chatter;
The bachelor's hour of feasting, too;
The cups that foam and hiss and spatter,
The punch that in the bowl burns blue.
I love the warlike animation
On playing-fields of Mars; to see
The troops of foot and horse in station,
And their superb monotony;
Their ordered, undulating muster;
Flags, tattered on the glorious day;
Those brazen helmets in their lustre
Shot through and riddled in the fray.
I love thee, city of soldiers, blowing
Smoke from thy forts: thy booming gun;
—A Northern empress is bestowing
Upon the royal house a son!
Or when, another battle won,
Proud Russia holds her celebration;
Or when the Neva breaking free
Her dark blue ice bears out to sea
And scents the spring, in exultation.

　Now, city of Peter, stand thou fast,
Foursquare, like Russia; vaunt thy splendor!
The very element shall surrender
And make her peace with thee at last.
Their ancient bondage and their rancors
The Finnish waves shall bury deep
Nor vex with idle spite that cankers
Our Peter's everlasting sleep!
　There was a dreadful time, we keep

Still freshly on our memories painted;
And you, my friends, shall be acquainted
By me, with all that history:
A grievous record it will be.

PART I [3]

O'er darkened Petrograd there rolled
November's breath of autumn cold;
And Neva with her boisterous billow
Splashed on her shapely bounding wall
And tossed in restless rise and fall
Like a sick man upon his pillow.
'Twas late, and dark had fallen; the rain
Beat fiercely on the window-pane;
A wind that howled and wailed was blowing.
   'Twas then that young Yevgeny [4] came
Home from a party—I am going
To call our hero by that name,
For it sounds pleasing, and moreover
My pen once liked it—why discover
The needless surname?—True, it may
Have been illustrious in past ages,
—Rung, through tradition, in the pages
Of Karamzin; and yet, today
That name is never recollected,
By Rumor and the World rejected.
Our hero—somewhere—served the State;
He shunned the presence of the great;
Lived in Kolomna; for the fate
Cared not of forbears dead and rotten,
Or antique matters long forgotten.
   So, home Yevgeny came, and tossed
His cloak aside; undressed; and sinking
Sleepless upon his bed, was lost
In sundry meditations—thinking
Of what?—How poor he was; how pain

And toil might some day hope to gain
An honored, free, assured position;
How God, it might be, in addition
Would grant him better brains and pay.
Such idle folk there were, and they,
Lucky and lazy, not too brightly
Gifted, lived easily and lightly;
And he—was only in his second
Year at the desk.
                    He further reckoned
That still the ugly weather held;
That still the river swelled and swelled;
That almost now from Neva's eddy
The bridges had been moved already;
That from Parasha he must be
Parted for some two days, or three.
And all that night, he lay, so dreaming,
And wishing sadly that the gale
Would bate its melancholy screaming
And that the rain would not assail
The glass so fiercely. . . . But sleep closes
His eyes at last, and he reposes.
  But see, the mists of that rough night
Thin out, and the pale day grows bright;
That dreadful day!—For Neva, leaping
Seaward all night against the blast
Was beaten in the strife at last,
Against the frantic tempest sweeping;
And on her banks at break of day
The people swarmed and crowded, curious,
And reveled in the towering spray
That spattered where the waves were furious.
But the wind driving from the bay
Dammed Neva back, and she receding
Came up, in wrath and riot speeding;
And soon the islands flooded lay.

Madder the weather grew, and ever
Higher upswelled the roaring river
And bubbled like a kettle, and whirled
And like a maddened beast was hurled
Swift on the city. All things routed
Fled from its path, and all about it
A sudden space was cleared; the flow
Dashed in the cellars down below;
Canals up to their gratings spouted.
Behold Petropol floating lie
Like Triton in the deep, waist-high!

   A siege! the wicked waves, attacking
Climb thief-like through the windows; backing,
The boats stern-foremost smite the glass;
Trays with their soaking wrappage pass;
And timbers, roofs, and huts all shattered,
The wares of thrifty traders scattered,
And the pale beggar's chattels small,
Bridges swept off beneath the squall,
Coffins from sodden graveyards—all
Swim in the streets!
. . . . And contemplating
God's wrath, the folk their doom are waiting.
All will be lost; ah, where shall they
Find food and shelter for today?

   The glorious Emperor, now departed,
In that grim year was sovereign
Of Russia still. He came, sick-hearted,
Out on his balcony, and in pain
He said: "No czar, 'tis sure, is master
Over God's elements!" In thought
He sat, and gazed on the disaster
Sad-eyed, and on the evil wrought;
For now the squares with lakes were studded,
Their torrents broad the streets had flooded,
And now forlorn and islanded

The palace seemed. The Emperor said
One word—and see, along the highways
His generals [5] hurrying, through the byways!
From city's end to end they sped
Through storm and peril, bent on saving
The people, now in panic raving
And drowning in their houses there.
  New-built, high up in Peter's Square
A corner mansion then ascended;
And where its lofty perron ended
Two sentry lions stood at guard
Like living things, and kept their ward
With paw uplifted. Here, bare-headed,
Pale, rigid, arms across his breast,
Upon the creature's marble crest
Sat poor Yevgeny. But he dreaded
Nought for himself; he did not hear
The hungry rollers rising near
And on his very footsoles plashing,
Feel on his face the rainstorm lashing,
Or how the riotous, moaning blast
Had snatcht his hat. His eyes were fast
Fixt on one spot in desperation
Where from the deeps in agitation
The wicked waves like mountains rose,
Where the storm howled, and round were driven
Fragments of wreck. . . .   There, God in Heaven!
Hard by the bay should stand, and close,
Alas, too close to the wild water,
A paintless fence, a willow-tree,
And there a frail old house should be
Where dwelt a widow, with a daughter
Parasha—and his dream was she!
His dream—or was it but a vision,
All that he saw? Was life also
An idle dream which in derision

Fate sends to mock us here below?
   And he, as though a man enchanted
And on the marble pinned and planted,
Cannot descend, and round him lie
Only the waters. There, on high,
With Neva still beneath him churning,
Unshaken, on Yevgeny turning
His back, and with an arm flung wide,
Behold the Image sit, and ride
Upon his brazen horse astride!

PART II

   But now, with rack and ruin sated
And weary of her insolence
And uproar, Neva, still elated
With her rebellious turbulence,
Stole back, and left her booty stranded
And unregarded. So a bandit
Bursts with his horde upon a village
To smash and slay, destroy and pillage;
Whence yells, and violence, and alarms,
Gritting of teeth, and grievous harms
And wailings; then the evildoers
Rush home; but dreading the pursuers
And sagging with the stolen load
They drop their plunder on the road.
   Meanwhile the water had abated
And pavements now uncovered lay;
And our Yevgeny, by dismay
And hope and longing agitated,
Sore-hearted to the river sped.
But still it lay disquieted
And still the wicked waves were seething
In pride of victory, as though
A flame were smoldering below;
And heavily was Neva breathing

Like to a horse besprent with foam
Who gallops from the battle home.
   Yevgeny watches, and descrying
By happy chance a boat, goes flying
To hail the ferryman; and he,
Unhired and idle, willingly
Convoys him for a threepence, plying
Through that intimidating sea.
The old tried oarsman long contended
With the wild waters; hour by hour,
Sunk in the trough, the skiff descended
Mid rollers, ready to devour
Rash crew and all—at last contriving
To make the farther shore.
                   Arriving,
Yevgeny—evil is his lot!—
Runs to the old familiar spot
Down the old street,—and knows it not.
All, to his horror, is demolished,
Leveled or ruined or abolished.
Houses are twisted all awry,
And some are altogether shattered,
Some shifted by the seas; and scattered
Are bodies, flung as bodies lie
On battlefields. Unthinkingly,
Half-fainting, and excruciated,
Yevgeny rushes on, awaited
By destiny with unrevealed
Tidings, as in a letter sealed.
   He scours the suburb; and discerning
The bay, he knows the house is near;
And then stops short; ah, what is here?
Retreating, and again returning,
He looks—advances—looks again.
'Tis there they dwelt, the marks are plain;
There is the willow. Surely yonder

The gate was standing, in the past;
Now, washt away! No house!—O'ercast
With care, behold Yevgeny wander
For ever round and round the place,
And talk aloud, and strike his face
With his bare hand. A moment after,
He breaks into a roar of laughter.

   The vapors of the night came down
Upon the terror-stricken town,
But all the people long debated
The doings of the day, and waited
And could not sleep. The morning light
From pale and weary clouds gleamed bright
On the still capital; no traces
Now of the woes of yesternight!
With royal purple it effaces
The mischief; all things are proceeding
In form and order as of old;
The people are already treading,
Impassive, in their fashion, cold,
Through the cleared thoroughfares, unheeding;
And now official folk forsake
Their last night's refuge, as they make
Their way to duty. Greatly daring,
The huckster now takes heart, unbaring
His cellar, late the prey and sack
Of Neva—hoping to get back
His heavy loss and wasted labor
Out of the pockets of his neighbor.
The drifted boats from each courtyard
Are carried.
          To a certain bard,
A count, a favorite of heaven
To one Khvostov, the theme was given
To chant in his immortal song
How Neva's shores had suffered wrong.
   But my Yevgeny, poor, sick fellow!—

Alas, the tumult in his brain
Had left him powerless to sustain
Those shocks of terror. For the bellow
Of riotous winds and Neva near
Resounded always in his ear;
A host of hideous thoughts attacked him,
A kind of nightmare rent and racked him,
And on he wandered silently;
And as the week, the month, went by,
Never came home. His habitation,
As time ran out, the landlord took,
And leased the now deserted nook
For a poor poet's occupation.
   Nor ever came Yevgeny home
For his belongings; he would roam,
A stranger to the world; his ration
A morsel tendered in compassion
Out of a window; he would tramp
All day, and on the quay would camp
To sleep; his garments, old and fraying,
Were all in tatters and decaying.
And the malicious boys would pelt
The man with stones; and oft he felt
The cabman's whiplash on him flicking;
For he had lost the skill of picking
His footsteps—deafened, it may be,
By fears that clamored inwardly.
So, dragging out his days, ill-fated,
He seemed like something miscreated,
No beast, nor yet of human birth,
Neither a denizen of earth
Nor phantom of the dead.

Belated

One night, on Neva wharf he slept.
Now summer days toward autumn crept;
A wet and stormy wind was blowing,
And Neva's sullen waters flowing

Plashed on the wharf and muttered there
Complaining—beat the slippery stair
As suitors beat in supplication
Unheeded at a judge's door.
In gloom and rain, amid the roar
Of winds—a sound of desolation
With cries of watchmen interchanged
Afar, who through the darkness ranged—
Our poor Yevgeny woke; and daunted,
By well-remembered terrors haunted,
He started sharply, rose in haste,
And forth upon his wanderings paced;
—And halted on a sudden, staring
About him silently, and wearing
A look of wild alarm and awe.
Where had he come? for now he saw
The pillars of that lofty dwelling
Where, on the perron sentineling,
Two lion-figures stand at guard
Like living things, keep watch and ward
With lifted paw. Upright and glooming,
Above the stony barrier looming,
The Image, with an arm flung wide,
Sat on his brazen horse astride.[6]
    And now Yevgeny, with a shiver
Of terror, felt his reason clear.
He knew the place, for it was here
The flood had gamboled, here the river
Had surged; here, rioting in their wrath,
The wicked waves had swept a path
And with their tumult had surrounded
Yevgeny, lions, square—and Him
Who, moveless and aloft and dim,
Our city by the sea had founded,
Whose will was Fate. Appalling there
He sat, begirt with mist and air.
What thoughts engrave His brow! what hidden

Power and authority He claims!
What fire in yonder charger flames!
Proud charger, whither art thou ridden,
Where leapest thou? and where, on whom,
Wilt plant thy hoof?—Ah, lord of doom
And potentate, 'twas thus, appearing
Above the void, and in thy hold
A curb of iron, thou sat'st of old
O'er Russia, on her haunches rearing!
  About the Image, at its base,
Poor mad Yevgeny circled, straining
His wild gaze upward at the face
That once o'er half the world was reigning.
His eye was dimmed, cramped was his breast,
His brow on the cold grill was pressed,
While through his heart a flame was creeping
And in his veins the blood was leaping.
He halted sullenly beneath
The haughty Image, clenched his teeth
And clasped his hands, as though some devil
Possessed him, some dark power of evil,
And shuddered, whispering angrily,
"Ay, architect, with thy creation
Of marvels. . . . Ah, beware of me!"
And then, in wild precipitation
He fled.
         For now he seemed to see
The awful Emperor, quietly,
With momentary anger burning,
His visage to Yevgeny turning!
And rushing through the empty square,
He hears behind him as it were
Thunders that rattle in a chorus,
A gallop ponderous, sonorous,
That shakes the pavement. At full height,
Illumined by the pale moonlight,
With arm outflung, behind him riding

See, the bronze horseman comes, bestriding
The charger, clanging in his flight.
All night the madman flees; no matter
Where he may wander at his will,
Hard on his track with heavy clatter
There the bronze horseman gallops still.

Thereafter, whensoever straying
Across that square Yevgeny went
By chance, his face was still betraying
Disturbance and bewilderment.
As though to ease a heart tormented
His hand upon it he would clap
In haste, put off his shabby cap,
And never raise his eyes demented,
And seek some byway unfrequented.

A little island lies in view
Along the shore; and here, belated,
Sometimes with nets a fisher-crew
Will moor and cook their long-awaited
And meager supper. Hither too
Some civil servant, idly floating,
Will come upon a Sunday, boating.
That isle is desolate and bare;
No blade of grass springs anywhere.
Once the great flood had sported, driving
The frail hut thither. Long surviving,
It floated on the water there
Like some black bush. A vessel plying
Bore it, last spring, upon her deck.
They found it empty, all a wreck;
And also, cold and dead and lying
Upon the threshold, they had found
My crazy hero. In the ground
His poor cold body there they hurried,
And left it to God's mercy, buried.

[1833]
[PUBLISHED POSTHUMOUSLY 1837]

NOTES

[1] The work referred to is *A Detailed Historical Account of all the Floods that Occurred in St. Petersburg*, by V. N. Berkh—Pushkin was mistaken about the author's patronymic—St. Petersburg, 1826.

EDITOR'S NOTE

[2] Algarotti has somewhere said: *"Pétersbourg est la fenêtre, par laquelle la Russie regarde en Europe."*

AUTHOR'S NOTE

Francesco Algarotti, a friend of Voltaire's, left an account of a trip to Russia he made in 1739: *Letters from Count Algarotti to Lord Hervey and the Marquis Scipio Maffei, Containing the State of the Trade, Marine, Revenues, and Forces of the Russian Empire,* translated from the Italian, in two vols., London, 1769. In his letter dated Petersburg, June 30, 1739, occurs this passage: "I am at length going to give you some account of this new city, of the great window lately opened in the north, thro' which Russia looks into Europe."

EDITOR'S NOTE

[3] Mickiewicz, in one of his best poems, "Oleszkiewicz," has in most beautiful lines described the day preceding the Petersburg flood. It is only a pity that his description is inaccurate. There was no snow—the Neva was not covered with ice. Our description is more correct, although it has none of the brilliant colors of the Polish poet.

AUTHOR'S NOTE

Oleszkiewicz, painter, mystic, and friend of Mickiewicz, in this poem appears at night in a boat on the Neva,

hears the storm rising, and forebodes the flood that is coming on the morrow. He also, under the palace walls,
apostrophizes the sleepless czar, Alexander I, not, like
Pushkin, as a benevolent and sorrowing monarch, but
from the Polish standpoint, as one in whose soul the evil
principle has prevailed: "God will shake the steps of the
Assyrian throne."

TRANSLATOR'S NOTE

[4] The Russian form of Eugene.

[5] Count Miloradovich and Adjutant-General Benckendorff.

AUTHOR'S NOTE

[6] See description of the monument in Mickiewicz. It is
borrowed from Ruban, as Mickiewicz himself observes.

AUTHOR'S NOTE

The reference is to "Pomnik Piotra Wielkiego," by the
great Polish poet and patriot.

EDITOR'S NOTE

EUGENE ONEGIN

A Novel In Verse

Pétri de vanité il avait encore plus de cette espèce
d'orgueil qui fait avouer avec la même indifférence les
bonnes comme les mauvaises actions, suite d'un senti-
ment de supériorité, peut-être imaginaire.

Tiré d'une lettre particulière

Dedication

Not with a notion of delighting
Proud worldlings, but to pleasure you,
For friendship's sake would I were writing
A nobler page, more fine and true,
Worthy of him I am addressing,
Whose days are living poetry—
Affection's pledge, indeed, expressing
Your dreams, your high simplicity.
No matter—ah, but look with favor
Upon the chapters in your hand,
Half-grave, half-gay, and with a flavor
Of what is common, what is grand;
To this were fribbling hours devoted,
Late nights, yes, and a facile art;
Fruit of spoiled years, or green and tart,
The mind's reflections coldly noted,
The bitter insights of the heart.

III

Chapter One

Makes haste to live and cannot wait to feel.
K. Vyazemsky

"My uncle's shown his good intentions
By falling desperately ill;
His worth is proved; of all inventions
Where will you find one better still?
He's an example, I'm averring;
But, God, what boredom—there, unstirring,
By day, by night, thus to be bid
To sit beside an invalid!
Low cunning must assist devotion
To one who is but half-alive:
You puff his pillow and contrive
Amusement while you mix his potion;
You sigh, and think with furrowed brow—
'Why can't the devil take you now?'"

II

'Tis thus the gay dog's thoughts are freighted,
As through the dust his horses fare,
Who by the high gods' will is fated
To be his relative's sole heir.
You knew Ruslan and fair Ludmila;
For this new hero prithee feel a
Like fellowship, as I regale
You, readers, with another tale:
Onegin, meet him, born and nourished
Where old Neva's gray waters flow,
Where you were born, or, as a beau,
It may be, in your glory flourished.
I moved there also for a while,
But find the North is not my style.

III

A man of rank, his worthy father
Would always give three balls a year;
He lived in debt, and did not bother
To keep his hopeless ledgers clear.
Fate guarded Eugene, our young waster;
While in due time *Monsieur* replaced her,
At first *Madame* controlled the child;
The charming lad was rather wild.
Monsieur l'Abbé, a Frenchman, seedy,
Thought sermons fashioned to annoy;
He spared the rod to spoil the boy,
And in a voice polite but reedy
Would chide him, would forgive him soon,
And walk him in the afternoon.

IV

When Eugene reached the restless season
Of seething hopes and giddy play,
And melancholy minus reason,
Monsieur was sent upon his way.
Now my Onegin, keen as brandy,
Went forth, in dress—a London dandy,
His hair cut in the latest mode;
He dined, he danced, he fenced, he rode.
In French he could converse politely,
As well as write; and how he bowed!
In the mazurka, 'twas allowed,
No partner ever was so sprightly.
What more is asked? The world is warm
In praise of so much wit and charm.

V

Since but a random education
Is all they give us as a rule,
With us, to miss a reputation
For learning takes an utter fool.
Onegin, wiseacres aplenty
Pronounced most learned, though not yet twenty,
And some harsh judges found, forsooth,
A very pedant in the youth.
In talk he showed true talent, swerving
About with great felicity,
On weighty matters carefully
The silence of the sage preserving,
And with the spark of a *bon mot*
He set the ladies' eyes aglow.

VI

Since Latin's held not worth attention,
His knowledge of the tongue was slight:
Of Juvenal he could make mention,
Decipher epigraphs at sight,
Quote Virgil, not a long selection,
And always needing some correction,
And in a letter to a friend
Place a proud *vale* at the end.
He had no itch to dig for glories
Deep in the dust that time has laid,
He let the classic laurel fade,
But knew the most amusing stories
That have come down the years to us
Since the dead days of Romulus.

VII

The art of verse, that lofty pleasure,
He never mastered, never knew
Trochaic from iambic measure,
In spite of all we tried to do.
Theocritus and Homer bored him;
If true delight you would afford him
You'd give him Adam Smith to read.
A deep economist, indeed,
He talked about the wealth of nations;
The state relied, his friends were told,
Upon its staples, not on gold—
This subject filled his conversations.
His father listened, frowned, and groaned,
And mortgaged all the land he owned.

VIII

All Eugene knew is past relating,
But for one thing he had a bent,
And I am not exaggerating
His principal accomplishment;
From early youth his dedication
Was to a single occupation;
He knew one torment, one delight
Through empty day and idle night:
The science of the tender passion
That Ovid sang, that brought him here,
And closed his turbulent career
In such a brief and tragic fashion—
Ovid, who here, so far from Rome,
Found in the steppes an exile's home.

IX—X

He early played the fond deceiver,
And feigned the pang of jealousy,
Rejoiced the fair one but to grieve her,
Seemed sunk in gloom, or bold and free,
Would turn quite taciturn with languor,
Then flash with pride and flame with anger,
Show rapture or indifference,
Or burn with sudden eloquence!
The letters that he wrote so neatly,
So easily, with passion seethed;
One thing alone he loved, he breathed;
He could forget himself completely.
His eyes, how tender, quick and clear,
Or shining with the summoned tear!

XI

He knew the ruses that would brighten
The eyes of the ingenuous young;
He could pretend despair, to frighten,
Or use the adulator's tongue;
He'd catch the moment of emotion,
And out of an old-fashioned notion
The strait-laced innocent beguile
With skill and passion, touch and smile.
He would implore the shy confession,
Catch the first stirrings of the heart,
Secure a tryst with tender art,
And at the following sweet session
Would, tête-à-tête, where no one heard,
Instruct the fair without a word.

XII

'Twas early he learned how to flutter
The heart of the confirmed coquette!
What biting words the rogue would utter
Of those he wished her to forget!
None was so quick as he at trapping
A rival, or to catch him napping.
You men who lived in wedded bliss
Remained his friends, I grant you this.
The married rakes, no longer naughty,
Would show him every friendliness;
Suspicious age could do no less,
Nor yet the cuckold, stout and haughty,
Whose satisfactions were, through life,
Himself, his dinner, and his wife.

XIII—XV

After an evening's dissipations
He will lie late, and on his tray
Find notes piled high. What? Invitations?
Three ladies mention a soirée,
Here is a ball, and there a party;
His appetite for pleasure's hearty—
Where will my naughty lad repair?
For he is welcome everywhere.
Meanwhile, in morning costume, gaily
Donning his wide-brimmed Bolivar,
He joins the throng on the *boulevard*,
To promenade, as all do daily,
Until Breguet's unsleeping chime
Announces it is dinner-time.

XVI

At dusk a sleigh's the thing, and calling:
"Make way! Make way!" along they fly.
Upon his beaver collar falling,
Like silver dust the snowflakes lie.
Talon's his goal, no hesitating:
His friend [Kaverin] must be waiting.
He comes: a cork pops, up it goes,
The vintage of the comet flows.
A bleeding roastbeef's on the table,
And truffles, luxury of youth,
French dishes for the gourmet's tooth,
And Strasbourg pies, imperishable;
Here's every dainty that you please:
Gold pines, and live Limburger cheese.

XVII

Glass after glass is drained in drenching
The hot fat cutlets; you would say
They've raised a thirst there is no quenching.
But now it's time for the ballet.
The theatre's wicked legislator,
Who unto every fascinator
In turn his fickle flattery brings,
And boasts the freedom of the wings,
Onegin flies to taste the blisses
And breathe the free air of the stage,
To praise the dancer now the rage,
Or greet a luckless Phèdre with hisses,
Or call the actress he preferred
Just for the sake of being heard.

XVIII

Oh, land of boundless fascination!
There bold Fonvizin, freedom's friend,
Sped shafts of satire at the nation,
Knyazhnin played ape there without end,
Semyonova there wrought her magic
With Ozerov's grave lines and tragic.
Katenin at a later day
Revived the grandeur of Corneille;
There Shakovskoy brought noisy laughter
With his sardonic comedies;
Didelot enjoyed his victories
Upon those very boards thereafter.
Where, in the shadow of the wings,
My youth fled by, remembrance clings.

XIX

My goddesses! How shall I trace you?
I sadly call on each sweet name.
Can others ever quite replace you?
And you, can you remain the same?
Oh, once again will you be singing
For me? Shall I yet see you winging
Your way in soulful flight and free,
My fair Russian Terpsichore?
Or must I with dull glances follow
Strange faces mid the painted set,
And having stared through my lorgnette
At the gay spectacle turned hollow,
Observe it with a yawn at last,
And silently recall the past?

XX

The theatre's full, the boxes glitter,
The stalls are seething, the pit roars,
The gallery claps and stamps, atwitter;
The curtain rustles as it soars;
A fairy light about her playing,
The magic of the bow obeying,
A crowd of nymphs around her—lo!
Istomina on lifted toe.
One foot upon the floor is planted,
The other slowly circles, thus,
Then wafted as by Eolus
She flies, a thing of down, enchanted;
Now serpentine she twists and wheels,
And now she leaps and claps her heels.

XXI

The house rocks with applause; undaunted,
And treading toes, between the chairs
Onegin presses; with his vaunted
Aplomb, he lifts his eye-glass, stares
Askance at fair, unwonted faces,
Remarks the jewels and the laces,
And notes complexions, with a sneer
Briefly surveying every tier.
He bows to sundry friends; his mocking
Slow eyes come last to rest upon
The lighted stage, and with a yawn
He sighs: "They're past the age—it's shocking!
I've haunted the ballet—what for?
Even Didelot becomes a bore."

XXII

The imps and cupids, quick as monkeys,
Upon the boards still flutter free,
While in the lobby sleepy flunkeys
Are guarding fur-coats faithfully;
Within, you hear the feet still pounding,
The coughs, the shouts and hisses sounding.
The noses blown, and without pause,
Above it all, the wild applause.
The carriage horses, chilled with waiting,
Impatient, twitch beneath the lamp,
The coachmen round the bonfires tramp,
Their masters wearily berating.
But our Onegin's out of range
Of curses: he's gone home to change.

XXIII

Shall I depict less with a prudent
Than with a quite impartial pen
The cabinet where fashion's student
Is dressed, undressed, and dressed again?
What London haberdashers hallow
We buy with timber and with tallow:
'Tis here, to please a lavish whim,
With all a dandy's mind can limn,
And all that Paris in her passion
For the most costly merchandise
So elegantly can devise
To tempt the sporting man of fashion.
Observe his closet well, and gage
Thereby our eighteen-year-old sage.

XXIV

Here's bronze and china in profusion,
And Turkish pipes of amber rare,
And, for the senses' sweet confusion,
Perfumes in crystal cut with care;
Steel files and combs of various guises,
And brushes, thirty shapes and sizes,
That teeth and nails may both be served,
Are here, with scissors straight and curved.
Rousseau (forgive me if I chatter)
Could not conceive how pompous Grimm
Dared clean his nails in front of him—
The lofty madcap!—but no matter:
In this case it is not too strong
To call that friend of freedom wrong.

XXV

A man of sense, I am conceding,
Can pay attention to his nails;
Why should one quarrel with good breeding?
With most folk, custom's rule prevails.
My Eugene was [Chadayev] second:
With every jealous word he reckoned,
No rung would suit him but the top—
In dress a pedant and a fop.
To prink and preen he'd ask no urging,
But spend three hours before the glass,
Till from his dressing-room he'd pass,
Like Venus' very self emerging
When as a man at masquerade
The frivolous great goddess played.

XXVI

Now having given due attention
To a toilette you must admire,
The learned world would have me mention
Each detail of our friend's attire.
One takes a risk in such discussion,
Because there are no words in Russian
For *trousers, dress-coat,* and for *vest;*
But then, it puts me to the test,
For as it is, my style is peppered
With foreign words; their frequency
I trust that you will pardon me;
With French it's spotted like a leopard—
Although I've glanced at, in times gone,
The Academic lexicon.

XXVII

But never mind, let's rather hurry
Off to the ball as is required,
Whither Onegin in a flurry
Is dashing in the cab he hired.
Along dark streets wrapped deep in slumber
Gay carriages, a goodly number,
Shed rainbow lights across the snow
From their twin lanterns as they go.
With lampions bright on sills and ledges
The splendid mansion shines and gleams,
And silhouetted by the beams,
Across the pane a shadow edges:
The profile that a move will blur
Of lovely lady, modish sir.

XXVIII

Straight past the porter, like an arrow
Our hero took the marble stair,
But then he paused, and with his narrow
White hand he swiftly smoothed his hair,
And entered. Here the throng is trooping;
The orchestra's already drooping;
A gay mazurka holds the crowd;
The press is thick, the hubbub loud.
The Horse Guard's spurs clank as he dances;
And hand meets hand, and hearts beat high;
The ladies' little feet fly by,
Pursued in flight by flaming glances;
While wildly all the fiddles sing
To drown the jealous whispering.

XXIX

When I knew ardor and elation,
On balls I also used to dote:
There one can make a declaration,
And cleverly convey a note.
Husbands esteemed, to you I tender—
Your honor's most astute defender—
My services in time of need:
My earnest counsels prithee heed.
And guard your daughters more severely,
You mothers, as your own once did,
Or else—or else—, else God forbid!
Hold your lorgnette up, watch them nearly.
These warnings in your ears are dinned
Because it's long since I have sinned.

XXX

Obeying folly's least suggestion,
How much of life I spent in vain,
And yet, were morals not in question,
I'd live through every ball again.
I love fierce youth, my private passion
Is the shrewd elegance of fashion,
The crowd whose sparkle nothing dims,
The little feet and lovely limbs;
Search Russia through, you'll scarce discover
Three pairs of truly pretty feet.
Ah, once how fast my heart would beat
When two feet tripped toward their lover!
I'm sad and cold, yet they can start
In dreams a tumult in my heart.

XXXI

When will you lose remembrance of them?
Where go, you madman, to forget?
Ah, little feet, how I did love them!
Now on what flowers are they set?
In Orient luxury once cherished,
The trace you left has long since perished
From Northern snows: you loved to tread
Upon voluptuous rugs instead.
It was for you that I neglected
The call of fame, for you forgot
My country, and an exile's lot—
All thoughts, but those of you, rejected.
Brief as your footprints on the grass,
The happiness of youth must pass.

XXXII

Diana's breast, the face of Flora,
Are charming, friends, but I would put
Them both aside and only for a
Glimpse of Terpsichore's sweet foot.
Prophetic of a priceless pleasure,
A clue to joys beyond all measure,
Its classic grace draws in its wake
Desires that are too keen to slake.
Where'er it goes, I am its lover:
When on the grass in Spring it's pressed,
Or by the fireplace set at rest,
At table, 'neath the damask cover,
Crossing the ballroom's polished floor,
Or climbing down the rocky shore.

XXXIII

Well I remember waves in riot
Before a storm; I wanted, too,
Thus to rush forth, then lapse in quiet
There at her feet, as they would do.
The billows covered them with kisses,
My lips were envious of their blisses!
No, when with youth and love on fire,
I did not ache with such desire
To brush the shy lips of a maiden
Or touch to flame a rosy cheek,
Or with such urgent ardor seek
To kiss the breast with languor laden;
No, passion never wrought for me
The same consuming agony.

XXXIV

With sighs I think, bemused adorer,
Aghast at time's swift slipping sands,
How once I held her stirrup for her,
And caught that foot in these two hands;
Again imagination's kindled,
The heart that thought its fires had dwindled
Flames up, the embers glow again
With sudden passion, sudden pain . . .
But in their praises why be stringing
Anew the garrulous fond lyre?
The haughty creatures may inspire
Our songs, but are not worth the singing.
Their looks enchant, their words are sweet,
And quite as faithless as their feet.

XXXV

And what of my Onegin? Drowsing,
He's driven from the ball to bed:
The drum is heard, the city's rousing,
For Petersburg's no sleepyhead.
The peddler plods, the merchant dresses,
While into town the milkmaid presses,
Bearing her jar o'er creaking snows;
And to his stand the cabby goes.
The cheerful morning sounds awaken;
The shutters open; chimneys spout;
The baker's wicket opens out,
A loaf is proffered, coins are taken,
A white cap shows, all in a trice:
The baker's German and precise.

XXXVI

The ball's wild gaiety was wearing,
So turning morning into night,
To darkness' kind abode repairing,
Now sleeps the scion of delight.
By afternoon he will be waking,
He'll then resume till day is breaking
The merry and monotonous round,
And then once more till noon sleep sound.
But was true joy to Eugene granted
Then, in the flower of his youth?
Was pleasure *happiness* in sooth
'Mid all the conquests that he vaunted?
When in the banquet-hall he beamed
Was he the carefree soul he seemed?

XXXVII

No, soon the world began to bore him,
The senses soon grew blunt and dull,
In vain the belles might clamor for him,
He found the fairest faces null;
Seduction ceased to be amusing,
And friendship's claims he was refusing,
Because he could make no *bon mot*,
Could not wash down with *Veuve Cliquot*
The beefsteak and the Strasbourg patty
When his poor head began to ache;
And though he was an ardent rake,
An exquisite both bold and natty,
The time came when he quite abhorred
Even the pistol and the sword.

XXXVIII

But there's no need that I dissemble
His illness—name it how you choose,
The English *spleen* it may resemble,
'Twas in a word the Russian blues.
He spared us, true, one piece of folly;
Although he grew more melancholy,
Was bored with everything he tried,
He did stop short of suicide.
Soft glance, nor welcome sweetly caroled,
Nor cards, nor gossip, chased his gloom;
He'd stroll into the drawing-room
Surly and languid as Childe Harold.
A wanton sigh was not worth mention:
Nothing attracted his attention.

XXXIX—XLII

He first abandoned you, capricious
Great ladies, of whom he'd been fond;
Indeed, today there is a vicious
Ennui pervading the *haut monde*.
Perhaps some lady may find matter
In Say and Bentham for her chatter,
But the discussions I have heard,
Though innocent, are quite absurd.
If you have any mind to flirt, you
Are turned by one cool glance to ice,
So pious are they, so precise,
And so inflexible their virtue.
They are so clever, so serene,
The sight of them produces spleen.

XLIII

You also, youthful belles, belated
O'er Petersburg's dark pavements borne
In dashing cabs, you too were fated
To learn my Eugene's air of scorn.
To stormy gaiety a traitor,
Onegin now decides he'll cater
To an ambitious author's whims:
His door he locks, his lamp he trims.
He yawns, for serious labor tries him,
His page is empty as can be,
The pen makes mock of such as he,
And so the bumptious guild denies him;
And I can't say the clique is wrong
To which, God help me, I belong.

XLIV

At length our hollow-hearted hero
A worthy course of action finds:
The sum of all his thoughts is zero,
And so he'll rifle keener minds;
A shelf of books he's been perusing,
But who does that is only choosing
Between a rascal and a bore;
He's read and read, and pray, what for?
Old fogies all, chained to tradition,
The newcomers but ape the old;
Behind the curtain's funeral fold
He soon consigns them to perdition.
He's done with women, and it looks
As though he's surely done with books.

XLV

The *beau monde's* burdensome conventions
I too had dropped, and found him then—
As bored as I with vain inventions—
The most congenial of men.
His way of dreaming, willy-nilly,
His sharp intelligence and chilly,
I liked, and his peculiar pose;
I was embittered, he morose.
We both had played with passion, early
We both had wearied of the game;
The hearts of both now spurned the flame
And had grown ashen-cold and surly;
And both, though young, could but await
Men's malice and the stroke of Fate.

XLVI

One who has lived and thought, grows scornful,
Disdain sits silent in his eye;
One who has felt, is often mournful,
Disturbed by ghosts of days gone by:
He can no longer be enchanted,
No respite to his heart is granted—
Remembering the past, perforce
He is the victim of remorse.
All this lends charm to conversation,
And though the talk of my young friend
At first disturbed me, in the end
I listened, not without elation,
To his sharp judgments, sullen wit,
And epigrams that scored a hit.

XLVII

Of quiet summer nights, how often,
When with diaphanous pale light
O'er the Neva the sky would soften
And the smooth waters, mirror-bright,
Would fail to show Diana gleaming,
We yielded to delicious dreaming,
Recalling in the soft sweet air
Many a distant love-affair—
The pleasures relished, triumphs thwarted;
Like prisoners released in sleep
To roam the forests, green and deep,
We were in reverie transported,
And carried to that region where
All life before us still lay fair.

XLVIII

Onegin leaned above the river
Upon the granite parapet,
As did the bard—yet not aquiver
With ecstasy, but with regret.
Here one heard naught but echoes, dying,
From distant streets where cabs were flying,
And sentinel to sentinel
Sounding the cry that all was well;
Alone a lazy boatman lifted
His oars above the drowsy stream;
A horn rang out, as in a dream;
A song across the waters drifted;
But Tasso's murmured octaves are,
By night, in dalliance, sweeter far.

XLIX

Oh, waters of the Adriatic!
Oh, Brenta! I shall yet rejoice
When once again, inspired, ecstatic,
I hear the magic of your voice,
Sacred to scions of Apollo!
No bard was keen as I to follow
The strains of Albion's proud lyre
Extolling you in tones of fire!
Once free, and night will find me gloating
Upon a fair Venetian face,
Within the gondola's embrace
In golden languor vaguely floating;
And she will learn my knowledge of
The tongue of Petrarch and of love.

L

'Tis time to loose me from my tether;
I call on freedom—naught avails:
I pace the beach, await good weather,
And beckon to the passing sails.
When, wrapped in storm, shall I be battling
The billows, while the shrouds are rattling,
And roam the sea's expanse, unpent,
Quit of the shore's dull element?
'Tis time to seek the southern surges
Beneath my Afric's sunny sky,
And, there at home, for Russia sigh,
Lamenting in new songs and dirges
The land that knew my love, my pain,
Where long my buried heart has lain.

LI

The pair of us had planned to wander,
On foreign scenes to feast our eyes;
But I am here and he is yonder:
Fate had arranged it otherwise.
Upon the death of his dear father
The creditors began to gather,
And Eugene, when he saw these sirs—
Each man must do as he prefers—
Because he hated litigation
Surrendered his inheritance;
He thought it no great loss—perchance
He had some other expectation?
Had Eugene, from a little bird,
Of his old uncle's illness heard?

LII

Indeed, he soon received a letter
Which told him that his uncle lay
Too ill for hopes of getting better,
And had his last farewells to say.
Eugene perused the sad epistle;
Thoughts of the future made him whistle;
He caught the post with eager haste,
But soon was yawning while he raced:
He knew the task would sorely try him
For (as I've said) there he must sit
And fawn and play the hypocrite.
But when he comes they notify him
His uncle's in his coffin laid:
His debt to nature has been paid.

LIII

The servants gave him all assistance,
The house hummed like a hive of bees
With friends and foes come from a distance
Just to enjoy the obsequies.
The dead man buried, they were able
To do full justice to the table,
And, feeling they had done their best,
Gravely departed priest and guest.
Here was Onegin, then, possessing
His stables, forests, streams and land,
He who could never understand
An ordered way of life, confessing
His early years were all a waste,
And this routine was to his taste.

LIV

Two days he found it quite diverting:
The meadows' solitary look,
The shady thickets' cool, begirting
The purling of a gentle brook;
The third day interest abated
And he was not the least elated
By grove and stream and field and steep—
They only sent him off to sleep.
For though the country boasts no palace,
No card-game, poetry, or ball,
Its pleasures, like the city's, pall,
He noted with accustomed malice.
A shadow, or a wife, pursues
As he was followed by the blues.

LV

I like a life of country quiet;
There may the lyre sound clear and free,
There fancies bloom and dreams run riot—
It suits my Muse as it suits me.
At peace, it is my artless pleasure
To wander by the lake at leisure,
In solitude without a flaw,
And *far niente* is my law.
Each morning I awake proposing
Another day without an aim;
I have no care for flighty fame;
I hardly read, I'm often dozing.
Was it not thus I long since spent
My youth in slothful sweet content?

LVI

To love and idleness devoted,
To flowery field and village sport,
With pleasure I have often noted
That I am not Onegin's sort;
Let no sly reader be so daring—
Onegin's traits with mine comparing—
And no calumnious friend so pert
As some time later to assert
That here, for all the world to know it,
I've drawn a likeness perfectly:
A portrait of none else but me,
Like Byron, pride's consummate poet;
As though there were a tacit ban
On writing of another man.

LVII

Poets, it is my observation,
Indulge in lovers' dreams with ease;
I too made it my occupation
To play with tender reveries.
First memory would trace the features,
In secret, of dear distant creatures,
And the rare magic of the Muse
The breath of life would then infuse.
The mountain maid, untamed, inspiring,
The prisoned girls of the Salgir,
'Twas thus I sang them—both were dear.
Now my companions are inquiring:
"In all the jealous crowd, what she
Commands your tender minstrelsy?

LVIII

"Whose glances, quickening emotion,
Caressingly repaid your song?
To whom did your confessed devotion,
To whom your pensive verse belong?"
To no one, friends, you must believe me:
I loved, and nothing could relieve me.
That man alone knows blessedness
Who is inspired in his distress:
For thus he brings his passion's fuel
To poetry's exalted flame;
And when consoled by art—and fame,
Like Petrarch, he finds love less cruel.
But, feeling the blind archer's sting,
I was a dolt and could not sing.

LIX

The Muse has come, and love departed,
The darkened mind is clear again;
And as of old I mix, free-hearted,
Feeling and thought with music's strain·
I write, and longing is diminished;
Beside the stanza all unfinished
No more the casual pen is led
To sketch a woman's legs or head.
Cold ashes hide no smoldering ember;
I have no tears, in spite of grief;
The storms which shook it like a leaf
Soon, soon my soul will not remember:
Then what a poem I'll contrive
In cantos numbering twenty-five!

LX

The plan I had no pains to settle,
The hero's named, the work's begun;
My novel finds me in good fettle
And I've completed Chapter One.
I've scanned the pages most severely,
The errors are a trifle merely,
And those I do not greatly rue;
I'll give the censorship its due,
Let critics wreak their indignation
Upon the finished product then;
Neva, oh, offspring of my pen,
Shall greet you. Go, my dear creation:
Be sentenced by a crooked jury
And earn me fame and sound and fury.

Chapter Two

O rus!

Horace

O Rus!

I

The village where Onegin's leisure
But left him bored to a degree
Would ravish one who prized the treasure
Of innocent felicity.
The mansion, by a hill well hidden,
Where winds and tempests were forbidden,
And near a stream, stood calm and proud,
Surveying fallow land and plowed.
Beyond, the plain, with hamlets dotted,
And chequered brown and gold and green,
A halcyon bucolic scene,
With roaming flocks was lightly spotted;
While in the garden's lavish shade
The contemplative dryads played.

II

The mansion from its firm foundation
Up to its roof was past all praise,
Expressing the discrimination,
The noble taste of bygone days.
The stove with colored tiles, appealing
If out of date, the lofty ceiling,
Ancestral portraits in the gloom
And damask of the drawing-room—
All this is now outworn and faded,
The glory's gone, I know not why;
But the sad ruin brought no sigh
From Eugene: he was far too jaded—
In time-worn halls and those that just
Had been refurbished, yawn he must.

III

The room where the old man berated
His housekeeper for forty years,
Killed flies, and snugly rusticated,
Is now our hero's, it appears.
The furnishings are plain and stable,
The floor is oak; two chests, a table,
A down-stuffed couch are all, I think,
And nowhere is a spot of ink.
Onegin searched the cupboards, finding
Liqueurs, a ledger, applejack,
And tucked away, an almanac
For 1808 without a binding:
The old man had no time to look
Into a more exacting book.

IV

Alone among his new possessions,
At first Eugene began to dream
Of making certain grand concessions
And setting up a new regime;
For the corvée he substituted
Light quit-rent, and the slave, well suited
Because there was not much to pay,
Blessed the new master every day.
Not so his calculating neighbor
Who thought our Eugene was a gull;
Another neighbor tapped his skull:
Why thus dispense with lawful labor?
The youth was called on every hand
A faddist and a firebrand.

V

The neighbors promptly called and twaddled
Of this and that, to his distress;
Hence oft he had his stallion saddled
At the back porch in readiness,
That he, when wheels were within hearing,
Might dash away as they were nearing.
The gentry all cried out in scorn,
This insult was not to be borne.
"Onegin is a boor, a mason;
He leaves the ladies' hands unkissed;
Drinks wine in tumblers," it was hissed;
"He never puts a civil face on,
Says, 'yes' and 'no,' but never 'sir.'"
In this opinion all concur.

VI

Another landowner come newly
To his estate about this time
Was also picked to pieces duly,
For gossip is not held a crime.
Vladimir Lensky, handsome, youthful,
A Kantian, unspoiled and truthful,
Whose soul was shaped in Göttingen,
And who could wield the poet's pen.
From misty Germany, Vladimir
Had brought the fruits of learning's tree:
An ardent faith in liberty,
The spirit of an oddish dreamer,
Rapt eloquence in speech and song,
And curls as black as they were long.

VII

Unspoiled by the vain show and fleeting
Of this cold world, his soul would bless
With equal warmth a comrade's greeting
And a shy maiden's pure caress.
His heart the nest of fond illusion,
In worldly dazzle and confusion
The hopeful youth was quick to find
Much to enchant his virgin mind.
His doubts were never past the curing,
In reverie they would dissolve;
Life was a riddle he would solve,
He found it puzzling but alluring;
He racked his brains, and still believed
That miracles could be achieved.

VIII

A kindred soul, he held, was burning
To be united to his own,
And day by day in pensive yearning
It waited on, for him alone;
He held that loyal friends and steady
To save his honor stood quite ready
To suffer prison, and would fly
At once the slanderer to defy.
He held that some by Fate were chosen
. . . .
. . . .
. . . .
. . . .
. . . .

IX

He early knew the agitation
Of love for virtue, sore regret,
The stir of noble indignation,
Hope of a name none might forget.
He was none of your poetasters,
Goethe and Schiller were his masters,
Beneath their sky he plucked his lyre,
His spirit knew their lyric fire.
And, fortune's darling, in his rhyming
He paid the Muses honor due;
His sentiments were fine and true,
His music therewith sweetly chiming;
His were the dreams that move the heart
And his the charm of simple art.

X

The theme from which he ne'er departed
Was love: he sang it late and soon,
Serene as maidens simple-hearted,
As infant slumbers, as the moon
In the unruffled heavens shining;
He sang of parting and repining;
The mystic, wistful hours of night;
Of distance, promising delight;
He sang the rose, romantic flower;
And lands remote, where on the breast
Of silence he had lain at rest
And let his tears unheeded shower;
He sang life's bloom and early blight:
His nineteenth year was scarce in sight.

XI

Eugene alone was framed to measure
The gifts the newcomer possessed;
The local gentry's round of pleasure
Could scarce inspire young Lensky's zest.
He fled their noisy conversation
And found their prudent talk vexation:
All kin and kennels, crops and wine;
Here not a wit was found to shine
(Not with fine words are parsnips buttered);
No syllable of sentiment,
No grace, no flash of merriment,
Lay hid in all the prose they uttered,—
No *savoir vivre,* no hint of verse;
And when their wives talked, it was worse.

XII

Lensky was thought an eligible,
A wealthy youth and handsome too;
There *was* something intelligible
About this common rustic view;
The talk would turn with strange persistence
Upon the bachelor's sad existence;
All wish to see their daughters wed
To this half-Russian, German-bred.
The samovar, that blest invention,
Is brought, and Dunya pours his tea;
And next the girl's guitar we see;
They whisper: "Dunya, pay attention!"
And Dunya squeaks (would she were dumb!)
"Into my golden chamber, come!"

XIII

Of course young Lensky felt no yearning
For marriage bond or marriage bell;
Instead of that, our friend was burning
To know Onegin really well.
They met; except that both were human,
They were unlike as any two men:
As rock and wave, or ice and flame,
Or prose and verse—in naught the same.
So different, first they bored each other,
Then liking grew: they met each day
On horseback; such close friends were they
They clung as brother clings to brother.
Thus people, frankly I confess,
Grow fond—out of sheer idleness.

XIV

Such faithful friendship as my hero's
Is in these parlous days unknown;
We think all other people zeros,
And integers: ourselves alone.
We're all Napoleons, we're certain—
On sentiment we draw the curtain;
Two-legged millions are our tools;
Emotion is for clowns and fools.
Eugene, more tolerant than many,
Yet, as a rule, despised mankind;
Exceptions may be hard to find
But there's no rule that has not any:
He scorned most men (not everyone),
Esteemed emotion, feeling none.

XV

He listened to young Lensky, smiling:
The poet's ardent speech, the mind
So immature and so beguiling,
The fiery glance, he could but find
A novelty framed to divert him;
He thought: I must not disconcert him
By mocking glance or chilly word,
Such bliss is transient, if absurd;
Since time, without my interference,
Will cure the lad, for good or ill,
Let him believe in wonders still
And credit the world's fair appearance;
Youth's fever is its own excuse
For ravings that it may induce.

XVI

In deep reflection, hot discussion,
Their meetings passed; in turn they spoke
Of foreign history and Russian,
Of prejudice's ancient yoke,
Of good and evil, and of science,
Of destiny and its defiance,
Of that dread mystery, the grave;
Their judgment both men freely gave.
The poet in his exaltation
Would cite a verse he had by heart,
Some fragment of his Northern art,
And clinch the point with a quotation.
Though Eugene lent a willing ear,
He found the matter not too clear.

XVII

The passions, though, concerned more often
Our talkative young eremites;
Onegin's mocking voice would soften
As he depicted their delights;
He sighed, no longer subject to them:
Most blessed is he who never knew them,
And blessed the man who rids him of
Their pangs! and he, remote from love,
Who never longed and never hated,
Who, yawning, with his friends and wife,
In gossip finds the spice of life,
All jealous thoughts evaporated—
The happy man who took no chance
At cards with his inheritance!

XVIII

When we seek refuge, growing colder,
Beneath the prudent flag of peace,
When passion's fires no longer smolder,
And all their wayward stirrings cease,
And when we find our old devotion
No more a reason for emotion,
And its late sequel as absurd,
We yet attend upon the word
That trembles with another's passion;
The heart recalls its ancient scars,
As one who fought forgotten wars
Reviews the past in wistful fashion:
A veteran who never fails
To hang upon the young bloods' tales.

XIX

But fiery youth cannot dissemble
Its love or anger, grief or joy;
It all pours forth from lips that tremble
With the avowals of a boy.
Wearing a look of self-possession,
Onegin heard the sweet confession
His friend unburdened himself of—
He was a veteran in love.
Freely the poet spoke and truly,
His heart was pure, his conscience clear;
Onegin was allowed to hear
In full the tender story duly,
A tale of sentiment not new,
These many years, to me, or you.

XX

He loved as people love no longer
Whose hearts the years at length anneal;
His was the love of poets, stronger
Than other men are doomed to feel:
He knew one constant inspiration,
And not long years of separation,
Nor distance, changed his earnest mood
Or brought his longing quietude.
Not hours when he fulfilled the duties
That poets owe unto the Muse,
Nor studies such as pedants choose,
Nor noisy games, nor foreign beauties,
Could alter Lensky's virgin soul
Where love burned like a living coal.

XXI

When scarce a lad, his heart was captured—
A heart that had not felt a pang—
By little Olga, and, enraptured,
He watched her as she played and sang;
And one would find the children roaming
Together in the forest gloaming;
The fathers, indeed all, could see
Their marriage was a certainty.
Watched fondly, in seclusion growing,
The charming and ingenuous maid
Bloomed like a flower in the shade;
A lily of the valley blowing
In the thick grass where none can see,
Unknown to butterfly and bee.

XXII

The poet's earliest elation
Young Olga was the first to stir;
She was his lyre's first inspiration,
His virgin lyric was of her.
But now adieu, oh, golden playtime!
He loved the dark and shunned the daytime,
And craved the forest's shady boon,
The silent stars, the brooding moon—
The moon, the lampion of heaven,
To which we vowed our walks apart,
Whose secret solace on the heart
Would drop so tenderly at even . . .
Though now a light of no repute,
The street-lamps' pallid substitute.

XXIII

As grateful as a kiss, as simple
As Lensky's life that knew no guile,
Was gentle Olga—in her dimple
One saw the cheerful morning smile;
Her sky-blue eyes, her cheeks like roses,
Her flaxen hair, her graceful poses,
Her voice, were such as they portray
In all the novels of the day.
There was a time when the portrayal
Was one that I found exquisite,
But now I am fed up with it;
Dear reader, pardon the betrayal;
And I shall speak, if you allow,
About her older sister now.

XXIV

Though it suggests a peasant's hovel,
Tatyana was her sister's name:
For the first time in any novel
It humbly asks romantic fame.
Why not? You can have no objection,
Though it is true your recollection
Of syllables so musical
Is bound up with the servants' hall,
With olden days and doddering nurses:
We can't please the fastidious,
For there's a lack of taste in us,
And in our names (and in our verses);
Enlightenment makes such as we
No finer, but just finicky.

XXV

Tatyana was her name then—granted.
She would not win you by her face,
She lacked her sister's charm, and wanted
Her rosy innocence and grace.
No, silent, wild, and melancholy,
And swift to flee from fun and folly,
Shy as the doe who runs alone,
She seemed a stranger to her own.
To fondle either parent never
Was our morose Tatyana's way,
And as a child she'd romp and play
With other children scarcely ever,
But by the window she would brood
The whole day through in solitude.

XXVI

Since infancy her only pleasure
Was reverie; she wreathed with dream
The placid course of rustic leisure;
Her tender fingers sewed no seam,
Nor was she found with head inclining
O'er her embroidery, designing
In colored silks a pattern fit
To make a guest exclaim at it.
The will to rule is seen thus early:
The child while still at play prepares
For all her future social cares
And the polite world's hurly-burly.
And tells her doll with anxious thought
The maxims her mamma has taught.

XXVII

But even then, and more's the pity,
Tatyana had no doll at all
To gossip to about the city
And what the fashions were that fall.
She was not one of those who glories
In mischief, but horrific stories
Enchanted her while yet a child,
In winter when the nights were wild.
And when the little girls collected
To tag each other, or to roam
The woods, Tatyana stayed at home,
By solitude nowise dejected;
Her dreamy mood did not consort
With laughter and with noisy sport.

XXVIII

Tatyana might be found romancing
Upon her balcony alone
Just as the stars had left off dancing,
When dawn's first ray had barely shown;
When the cool messenger of morning,
The wind, would enter, gently warning
That day would soon be on the march,
And wake the birds in beech and larch.
In winter, when night's shade encloses
More lingeringly half the world,
And in the misty moonlight furled,
The lazy Orient longer dozes,
Roused at her wonted hour from rest,
By candle-light she rose and dressed.

XXIX

She found in a romantic story
All one might care to be or know;
Living the chapters through, she'd glory
In Richardson as in Rousseau.
Her father saw no harm in reading
(He was a decent chap, conceding
He lived in quite another age);
But then he never read a page.
He did not know that books could say things
To move you even while you slept;
He thought the tomes his daughter kept
Beneath her pillow, empty playthings;
While, on the other hand, his wife
Held Richardson as dear as life.

XXX

The lady's lasting admiration
The novelist had long since won;
She had not read with fascination
Of Lovelace or of Grandison,
But she had heard of them a dozen
Or more times from her Moscow cousin,
Princess Aline, when she was young,
And when, besides, her heart was wrung:
She was affianced, but her mother
Had made the choice, 'twas not her own;
Her heart was filled with one alone,
For, sad to say, she loved another:
A Grandison attached to cards,
A beau, a sergeant of the Guards.

XXXI

She followed, as he did, the fashion;
On elegance her mind was bent.
But what availed her urgent passion?
They married her *sans* her consent.
Her prudent husband, to distract her,
Off to the country promptly packed her,
Hoping her grief might thus abate;
They settled down on his estate,
Where she, with God knows who for neighbors,
At first but wept and tore her hair,
Spoke of divorce in her despair,
Then plunged into domestic labors:
Content, since habit, more or less,
Is surrogate for happiness.

XXXII

Kind habit soothed her sorrow sweetly,
Until a great discovery
Consoled the lady quite completely,
And grief changed to serenity.
Between her hours of toil and leisure
The good wife took her husband's measure,
And kept him underneath her rule.
She did the overseeing; cool
And resolute, she shipped the peasant
For army service; kept the books;
She pickled mushrooms with her cooks;
Slapped servant-girls who were unpleasant;
And steamed herself on Saturday—
Her spouse had not a word to say.

XXXIII

Time was when she would be composing
An album verse with tender mien;
She used a sing-song voice; and, posing,
Praskovya she would call "Pauline";
She pinched her waist with tightened laces,
Affected a most nasal "n";
But years went rolling by, and then
She lost her Frenchy airs and graces:
The album and the corset vanished,
The tender verse, Princess Pauline;
She said "Akulka" for Céline;
The nasal twang she also banished,
And wore—her last defences down—
A mob-cap and a dressing-gown.

XXXIV

But her good husband loved her dearly,
And trusted her with house and pelf,
And never looked at her too nearly—
He wore a dressing-gown himself;
His life, that knew no cares or labors,
Rolled by in peace; at times, the neighbors
Some friendly family—at eve,
Dropped in to gossip, laugh, or grieve
Together, o'er some simple matter;
And time would pass, and there would be
Young Olga coming to make tea,
And put a finis to their chatter;
They'd sup, then time for sleep drew nigh,
And so the guests would say good-bye.

XXXV

They loved the good old ways, and wallowed
At Carnival in savory cheer,
Eating the pancakes custom hallowed;
They took communion twice a year;
At Christmas, carols were their pleasure;
They liked to tread a country measure;
At Whitsun, when the populace
Yawned through the long thanksgiving mass,
They too were of their duties heedful,
And on the lovage dropped a tear,
Holding their pious habits dear;
As men need air, they found *kvass* needful,
Liked hearty guests who ate and drank,
And served each course to them by rank.

XXXVI

And so they aged, like all things mortal,
And in due time the husband passed
Submissive through the grave's dark portal,
And wore the funeral wreath at last.
A tender father, a good master,
His passing came as a disaster
To friend and child and faithful wife;
He'd led a kind and simple life;
He died a short hour before dinner.
His epitaph is plain as he;
Graved on the monument you see:
"Dmitry Larin, a poor sinner,
God's servant, and a brigadier,
Come to eternal rest, lies here."

XXXVII

Come home again, young Lensky duly
Beheld the bed where all must lie,
And by those ashes, mourning truly,
Paid them the tribute of a sigh.
"Alas, poor Yorick!" he lamented,
"Once in those arms I lay contented,
And took his medal for a toy
When I was but a tiny boy!
He hoped that in good time I'd marry
His Olga. I can hear him say:
'May I but live to see the day!
When we were young, we did not tarry.' "
And Lensky, grieving honestly,
Wrote, on the spot, an elegy.

XXXVIII

And there he also wrote another
Upon the patriarchal dust,
And wept his father and his mother . . .
Alas! by God's strange will we must
Behold each generation flourish,
And watch life's furrows briefly nourish
The perishable human crop,
Which ripens fairly, but to drop;
And where one falls, another surges . . .
The race of men recks nothing, save
Its reckless growth: into the grave
The grandfathers it promptly urges.
Our time will come when it is due,
Our grandchildren evict us too.

XXXIX

Meanwhile, forget all toil and trouble,
Take what is offered of delight.
I know that life is but a bubble,
My fondness for it is but slight;
I am deceived by no illusion;
But I salute hope's shy intrusion,
And sometimes in my heart I own
I would not leave the world, unknown.
I have no faith in its requiting
My labors, yet perhaps this name
May wear the laurel-crown of fame,
And yet win luster from my writing;
One line, held in the memory,
May speak, like a fond friend, of me.

XL

My words may move some unborn lover;
My stanza, saved by jealous fate,
It may be Lethe will not cover;
Ah, yes, at some far distant date,
When I am gone, and cannot know it,
The cordial words: "There was a poet!"
Some dunce may yet pronounce as he
Points out my portrait unctuously.
Such are the bard's gratifications;
My thanks, friend, you will not refuse,
You venerator of the Muse
Who will recall my poor creations,
You who will smooth in after days
With kindly hand the old man's bays.

Chapter Three

Elle étoit fille, elle étoit amoureuse.

Malfilâtre

I

"These poets! What! another visit?"
"Good-bye, Onegin, I must go."
"I shan't detain you; but where is it
You spend your time, I'd like to know?"
"These evenings? At the Larins'." "Splendid.
But, Lord, before the evening's ended
How is it that you do not fall
Asleep from boredom?" "Not at all."
"I cannot grasp it. I'll be betting
Here's what you find there (am I right?):
The guests are greeted with delight;
You have a Russian family setting,
With tea and jam, and endless tattle
About the weather, flax, and cattle . . ."

II

"I see no harm in that; I'm grateful."
"But it's a bore, my friend, that's clear."
"Your fashionable world is hateful;
I find the plain home circle dear,
Where I can . . ." "Ah, another pretty
Bucolic piece! Good Lord, have pity!
Well, must you go now? Not so fast!
When shall I meet the girl at last
Whom you have found so interesting?
I'd like to see with my own eyes
Your Phyllis, whom you idolize.
Pray introduce me." "You are jesting."
"No." "Gladly." "When?" "At once. You'll see
How very welcome you will be."

III

"Let's go."
               The friends, without delaying,
Dashed off; arrived; and heartily
Were greeted, with almost dismaying
Old-fashioned hospitality.
The table shone with wax; they handed
The saucers of preserve about,
Set huckleberry syrup out,
Just as the social rites demanded.
....
....
....
....
....
....

IV

They travel homeward quickly, choosing,
For it is late, the shortest way;
And reader, you are not refusing
To overhear what they may say.
"Well, now, Onegin. Yawning?" "Merely
A habit, Lensky." "Oh, but clearly,
You're bored." "As ever. But I mark
That we are driving in the dark.
Be quick! Drive on!" he bids the peasant;
"This silly landscape! Never mind;
Your Madam Larina's, I find,
A nice old woman, plain but pleasant.
That huckleberry syrup will,
I've a suspicion, make me ill.

V

"But tell me, which one is Tatyana?"
"She sat beside the window. She
Is like the poet's maid, Svetlana,
Given to mournful reverie."
"You love the younger? Curious creature!"
"Why do you say so?" "Not a feature
Of Olga's looks alive to me.
Her sister tempts the Muse, not she.
Your Olga's face, so round and blooming,
Is like Van Dyck's Madonna. Fie!
Or like, up in the silly sky,
That silly moon you see there looming."
Vladimir made a dry response
And then sat silent for the nonce.

VI

The neighbors, pleasantly diverted,
Asked what Onegin's visit meant,
And one and all of them exerted
Themselves to find out his intent.
Tatyana's match was all the rumor;
They gossiped on, in high good humor,
If there was carping comment, too;
And there were those who said they knew
The plans to have been consummated.
But that the wedding was deferred
Because they lacked—hadn't one heard?—
The rings that the new mode dictated.
Of Lensky's troth there was no chatter:
His wedding was a settled matter.

VII

Tatyana listened with vexation
To gossip; but her heart would fill
With a strange, secret exultation;
She conned the talk against her will;
A thought was born, and grew, unbidden;
Thus grows a seed the earth has hidden
When springtime's sun shines warm above:
The time had come—she was in love.
Long since her dreams had set her yearning
And coveting the fatal food;
Long since with sweet disquietude
Had her shy wistful heart been burning;
And freighted with a youthful gloom
Her soul was waiting . . . ah, for whom?

VIII

He came. And her eyes opened. Quaking,
She whispered to herself: 'Tis he!
Alas, in dreams, asleep or waking,
From thoughts of him she is not free;
All speaks of him, but to confound her;
His magic presence hovers round her;
And so from idle talk she flies,
And from the servants' anxious eyes.
Plunged into sadness beyond measure,
When guests arrive she pays no heed,
But wishes them away with speed,
And curses their unwelcome leisure;
She hates their having come at all,
Their endlessly protracted call.

IX

Now with what eager concentration
She reads the sweet romance, and how
Discovers a new fascination
In its seductive figments now!
The creatures fancy animated:
Werther, to be a martyr fated,
Malek-Adhel and de Linar,
St. Preux, the rival of Wolmar,
And Grandison, who leaves us sleeping,
The matchless bore—on these she mused;
And all, our tender dreamer fused
Into one image, her heart leaping
As fancy in the lot would trace
Onegin's form, Onegin's face.

X

And so her quick imagination
Reveals herself in every scene;
She is the novelist's creation:
Julie, Clarissa, or Delphine;
She wanders with imagined lovers
Through silent woods, and she discovers
Her dreams in every circumstance
Of some imported wild romance.
Another's joy her heart possesses,
Another's grief is hers to rue,
And in her mind a *billet-doux*
To her dear hero she addresses.
The hero we're intent upon,
However, was no Grandison.

XI

There was a time when the impassioned
Romancer, having settled on
A noble style of writing, fashioned
The pattern of a paragon.
His soul by highest motives guided,
The darling object was provided
With a fine mind and handsome face;
His enemies were always base.
This ever-rapturous hero, burning
With pure devotion, knew no bliss
So exquisite as sacrifice;
And to the final pages turning,
You'd find the way of vice was hard,
And virtue won its due reward.

XII

But now all minds are fogged and cloudy,
We're put to sleep by moral tales;
We like romances not too rowdy
Wherein agreeable vice prevails.
The British Muse's wild invention
Lays claim to the young girl's attention;
Dark Melmoth fills her with delight;
The Vampire wrecks her sleep at night;
She loves the secrets that environ
The Corsair or the Wandering Jew;
Strange Jean Sbogar enchants her too.
By a most happy whim, Lord Byron
Has clothed a hopeless egoism
In saturnine romanticism.

XIII

All this is futile, and you know it,
My friends. Perhaps, by heaven's decree,
I shall yet cease to be a poet;
Another demon seizing me,
I shall defy the dread Apollo,
Content in my old age to follow
The fashion of an older day:
Write prose, and take the humbler way;
I'll tell no ghostly tales, or gory,
Or paint the villain's agony;
A simple Russian family
Will be the subject of my story,
And love's delicious dream, and, too,
The customs that our fathers knew.

XIV

The father's simple words repeating,
Or the old uncle's, I shall tell
Next of the children's breathless meeting,
Where lindens hide the lovers well;
Of jealous pangs, and separation,
And tears of reconciliation
After they've quarreled once again;
I'll bring them to the altar then . . .
I shall recall the tongue of longing,
The languors of a distant day,
When at my mistress' feet I lay
And to my lips the words came thronging;
The lover's language, the sweet vow,
Of which I've lost the habit now.

XV

Tatyana, dear Tatyana! Weeping,
I share the scalding tears you drop:
Your fate is put into the keeping
Of a most tyrannous young fop.
And you, my dear, are doomed to perish;
But first, what dark delight you cherish,
What dazzling hopes awhile are yours,
As you discover life's allures,
And drink desire's sweet poisoned potion.
You dwell in dreams, and you persist
In fancying a happy tryst
In every nook, with strange emotion;
And everywhere that you may turn
Your marked seducer you discern.

XVI

Her grief into the garden taking,
Tatyana goes, impelled by love.
She drops her eyes, her heart is aching,
Her languor will not let her move.
Her eyes shine, and her breath has dwindled,
Her chest heaves, and her cheeks are kindled
With flame that fails as it appears;
There is a roaring in her ears . . .
Night falls; the moon, already riding
Aloft, the whole of heaven sees;
The nightingale's keen melodies
Pour from the boughs where she is hiding.
Sleepless, Tatyana would converse
In gentle whispers with her nurse.

XVII

"I cannot sleep, nurse; it is stifling!
Open the window; come, sit here."
"What ails you, Tanya?" "Oh, it's trifling,
I'm bored; tell me a story, dear."
"A story?" asked the good old woman,
"Of maids and creatures superhuman?
Ah, yes, I knew such old wives' tales,
But I grow old, and memory fails;
How sad it is to be forgetting!
I've fallen on black days, my dear—
I lose the thread, my mind's not clear,
It is no wonder I am fretting . . ."
"But, nurse, you still can tell me of
Your own young days. Were you in love?"

XVIII

"What notions! You may find it blameless,
But in my youth no one engaged
In talk of love. It was thought shameless—
My mother-in-law would have raged."
"But you were married, nurse," said Tanya,
"How was it?" "By God's will, my Vanya
Was but a boy, if truth were told,
And I was just thirteen years old.
The marriage-broker kept on pressing
The matter for a fortnight; oh,
What tears I shed you do not know,
The day my father gave his blessing;
They loosed my braids, and singing low
Led me to church. I had to go.

XIX

"I lived, by strangers quite surrounded,
My husband's folk . . . But do you hear?"
"Ah, nurse, nurse darling, I am hounded
By longing. I am ill, I fear:
I want to cry, to sob—oh, nursey!"
"My child, you're ill! The Lord have mercy!
God grant it's nothing! Welladay!
How can I help you, only say!
I'll sprinkle you with holy water,
You have a fever . . ." "Fever, no:
I . . . I'm in love," she murmured low.
The nurse replied: "God save you, daughter!"
And crossed the girl, and as she made
The sign with shaking hand, she prayed.

XX

"I am in love," poor Tanya uttered
The words again with stifled moan.
"Dear, you are ill," the old nurse muttered.
"I am in love; leave me alone."
Meanwhile, the moon her silver duty
Performing, lit the girl's pale beauty,
And with a somber splendor shone
On her loose hair, her tears, and on
The bench where the old nurse was seated
In kerchief and long gown of wool,
Before her charge, whose eyes were full,
Whose posture was of one defeated.
And while the world in silence slept,
The moon her magic vigil kept.

XXI

The moon's enchantment so obsessed her,
Her soul to distant regions fled,
And then a sudden thought possessed her . . .
"Go, leave me, nurse," Tatyana said,
"Move up the table, give me paper,
And pen; good night." Her single taper
Is the benign and silent moon;
Alone, Tatyana broods, and soon
Propped on her elbow, she is writing,
Thinking of Eugene all the while.
A young girl's ardor, clear of guile,
Breathes through the words she is inditing.
The letter's ready to be sent;
For whom, Tatyana, is it meant?

XXII

I have known women, stern and rigid,
Great ladies, far too proud to fall,
As pure as winter, and as frigid;
I understood them not at all.
I marveled at their iron virtue,
Their freezing glances framed to hurt you,
And sooth, I fled these haughty belles
Upon whose brows methought was hell's
Inscription written: "Ye surrender
All hope, for aye, who enter here."
They like to fill a man with fear,
And shun the heart that would be tender.
By the Neva it may be you
Have seen such ladies, not a few.

XXIII

And where the faithful suitor hovers,
I have seen other belles who bent
A glance upon their urgent lovers,
Self-centered and indifferent.
And what was my amazement, finding
They sought to make love's ties more binding
By an assumed austerity;
And fright but bred fidelity;
At least, if pity seemed to soften
Their voices, and their words were kind,
Young love, because it is so blind,
Would grow more ardent very often,
And the fond fool would then pursue
The unconcerned beloved anew.

XXIV

Why is Tatyana an offender?
Is it because she cannot deem
Deceit exists, but clings with tender
Simplicity to her young dream?
Is it because her love is artless,
And she, not knowing men are heartless,
Obeys her feelings *sans* demur?
Or because Heaven gifted her
With fiery imagination,
With rebel will and lively mind,
And with a heart for love designed,
A spirit brooking no dictation?
And can you not forgive, if she
Shows passion's volatility?

XXV

Not like a cool coquette who tenders
Her heart, and when she likes, withdraws,
Tatyana like a child surrenders
Herself to love and all its laws.
She does not argue: by delaying
We win the game that we are playing,
And raise love's value cleverly;
First let us prick his vanity
With hope, then prove it an illusion,
Raise doubts that leave his heart perplexed,
With jealousy revive it next,
And thus reduce him to confusion;
Lest, sick of pleasure, momently
The sly thrall struggle to be free.

XXVI

But I foresee a fresh objection,
And I confess I am perplexed:
Could Russia pardon my defection
Should I not give the letter's text
In Russian? And the task's infernal.
Tatyana read no Russian journal,
She did not speak the language well
And found it rather hard to spell;
And so of course the girl decided
To write in French . . . What's to be done?
For lady never, no, not one,
Her love in Russian has confided;
Our native tongue turns up its nose
At mere epistolary prose.

XXVII

They say the ladies should read Russian,
But though the arguments are keen,
I cannot suffer the discussion—
To find a Moscow magazine
In those white hands would be distressing!
The fair ones, whom you were addressing
With flattering pen and heart aglow,
Were all of them, as well you know,
My poet friends, inclined to stammer
When they employed the mother-tongue;
We loved them, though, when we were young
For just those little slips of grammar;
The foreign tongue is native to
Those lovely lips; is it not true?

XXVIII

To see a pedant in a bonnet!
A scholar in a yellow shawl!
Pray God I do not come upon it
Where guests disperse, or at a ball!
I hate red lips that are unsmiling,
And likewise do not find beguiling
The sound of Russian when correct;
Slight errors have a choice effect.
Perhaps, heeding the journals' clamor,
The younger beauties will declare
That poetry is their affair,
And will accustom us to grammar;
But as for me . . . my loving praise
Is for the good old-fashioned ways.

XXIX

My heart will as of old be shaken,
Touched by the careless twittering,
The phrasing, awkward or mistaken,
Of some attractive little thing.
I am not given to repentance—
French turns will please me in a sentence
As do the sins of years long fled
Or light verse that our fathers read.
Enough. 'Tis time that I presented
The letter to you quite intact.
By God! I wish I could retract.
Was ever harder task invented?
Parny's sad tenderness is now
No more the vogue, you will allow.

XXX

Singer of feasts and tender sorrow,
If only you were with me still,
I might indeed make bold to borrow
Your magic music and your skill:
Your version of Tatyana's letter
Would be in every way far better
Than anything that I could do—
I bow and cede my rights to you . . .
But no, our paths have separated.
To praises unaccustomed grown,
Beneath the Finnish sky, alone,
Among sad cliffs he moves. I'm fated
To mourn his absence, and in vain,
He does not even guess my pain.

XXXI

Tatyana's letter lies before me,
I treasure it most piously;
These artless lines can never bore me,
They touch the springs of reverie.
Who taught her how to be so lavish
With ardent words, and how to ravish
The heart with virgin tenderness?
Where did she learn this wild excess?
Love's discourse, perilous, delicious,
She knew, I wonder how. I fear
The version of it given here
Is like a copy pale and vicious,
Or like an air from Freischütz played
By someone awkward and afraid.

Tatyana's Letter to Onegin

I write you, and my act is serving
As my confession. Why say more?
I know of what I am deserving—
That you should scorn me, or ignore.
But for my wretched fate preserving
A drop of pity, you'll forebear
To give me over to despair.
I first resolved upon refraining
From speech: you never would have learned
The secret shame with which I burned,
If there had been a hope remaining
That I should see you once a week
Or less, that I should hear you speak,
And answer with the barest greeting,

But have one thing, when you were gone,
One thing alone to think upon
For days, until another meeting.
But you're unsociable, they say,
The country, and its dulness, bore you;
We . . . we don't shine in any way,
But have a warm, frank welcome for you.

Why did you come to visit us?
Here in this village unfrequented,
Not knowing you, I would not thus
Have learned how hearts can be tormented.
I might (who knows?) have grown contented,
My girlish dreams forever stilled,
And found a partner in another,
And been a faithful wife and mother,
And loved the duties well fulfilled.

Another! . . . No, I could have given
My heart to one, and one alone!
It was decreed . . . the will of Heaven
Ordains it so: I am your own.
All my past life has had one meaning—
That I should meet you. God on High
Has sent you, and I shall be leaning
On your protection till I die . . .
You came in dreams: I feared to waken,
I loved your image even then;
I trembled at your glance, and when
You spoke, my very soul was shaken.
Only a dream? It could not be!
The moment that I saw you coming,
I burned, my pulses started drumming,
And my heart whispered: it is he!
Yes, deep within I had the feeling,
When at my tasks of charity,

Or when, the world about me reeling,
I looked for peace in prayer, kneeling,
That silently you spoke to me.
Just now, did I not see you flitting
Through the dim room where I am sitting,
To stand, dear vision, by my bed?
Was it not you who gently gave me
A word to solace and to save me:
The hope on which my heart is fed?
Are you a guardian angel to me?
Or but a tempter to undo me?
Dispel my doubts! My mind's awhirl;
Perhaps this is a mad delusion,
The folly of a simple girl:
Fate plans a different conclusion . . .
So be it! Now my destiny
Lies in your hands, for you to fashion;
Forgive the tears you wring from me,
I throw myself on your compassion . . .
Imagine: here I am alone,
With none to understand or cherish
My restless thoughts, and I must perish,
Stifled, in solitude, unknown.
I wait: when once your look has spoken,
The heart once more with hope will glow,
Or a deserved reproach will show
The painful dream forever broken!

Reread I cannot . . . I must end . . .
The fear, the shame, are past endurance . . .
Upon your honor I depend,
And lean upon it with assurance . . .

XXXII

Tatyana moans, and as she shivers
The letter shakes; she heaves a sigh;
Upon her tongue the wafer quivers—
Both tongue and seal are pink, are dry.
Her nightgown slips from off her shoulder,
And her head sinks. The dawn grows bolder,
And soon the east will be alight;
The moon is fading with the night;
The lifting mist reveals the pleasant
Pale valley and the silver stream;
The first shy rays begin to gleam;
The shepherd's horn awakes the peasant;
'Tis morning; all the world's astir:
It makes no difference to her.

XXXIII

Dawn's air is sweet, she does not feel it,
She sits with downcast head, too lax
To take the letter up and seal it
With her neat monogram in wax.
The old gray nurse thinks she is napping
And enters softly without rapping,
Upon her tray a steaming cup:
"Come now, my child, it's time: get up.
But you're already dressed! God save me,
You are an early bird! Last night
I left you in a dreadful fright;
But never mind the turn you gave me;
I see the pain has left no trace;
A poppy could not match your face."

XXXIV

"Ah, nurse, I know you won't refuse me."
"Of course not, darling, only say . . ."
"Don't think . . . but really . . . don't accuse me . .
Do me this favor, nurse, I pray."
"God knows how gladly, only say it . . ."
"Then bid your grandson—don't delay it—
Carry this letter secretly
To O . . . our neighbor. Oh, but he
Must breathe no word, must never mention
My name . . ." "Yes, but to whom, my dear?
I must be growing dull, I fear,
Although indeed I paid attention.
We have so many neighbors, I
Could scarcely count them, should I try."

XXXV

"How dull-witted you are, nurse, truly!"
"The mind grows blunt as one grows old;
Age comes to all, my darling, duly.
The master had no need to scold
When I was young—a mere suggestion . . ."
"Ah, nurse, your mind is not in question.
What difference does that make to me?
It is my letter, don't you see,
My letter to Onegin." "Bless me,
Do not be cross because I fail
To grasp things . . . But you're growing pale;
Tanya, my dear, your looks distress me."
"Oh, it is nothing, nurse, I know.
Be sure you have your grandson go."

XXXVI

The day is done: he's not replying,
Another day: he still is dumb;
Dressed early, shadow-pale, and sighing,
She waits: when will the answer come?
Then Olga's suitor paid a visit.
"Has he forgotten us—what is it?
Where is your friend?" the hostess said;
Tatyana trembled and grew red.
"Something detained him. He intended
To come today, and without fail.
Perhaps what kept him was the mail,"
Thus Lensky his good friend defended.
Tatyana looked as though she heard
A black reproach in every word.

XXXVII

At dusk the samovar is gleaming
Upon the table, piping hot;
And as it hisses, gently steaming,
The vapor wreathes the china pot.
Now Olga sits before it, filling
The lustrous tea-cups, never spilling
A drop of the dark fragrant stream;
A serving-lad hands round the cream.
Apart, Tatyana can but linger
Beside the window; on the pane
She breathes again and yet again,
And in the mist her little finger
Describes in pensive tracery
The hallowed letters O and E.

XXXVIII

But her soul aches, and nothing pleases,
Her eyes betray her with a tear.
The sudden sound of hoofs! . . . She freezes.
Now nearer! Galloping . . . and here
Is Eugene! By another portal
Tatyana leaps like nothing mortal
From porch to court, and shadow-light
She flies, she flies, nor in her flight
Looks backward; lightning-like she rushes
On past the bright parterre, the lawn,
The grove, the bridge, the lake, and on,
And fleeing, breaks the lilac-bushes,
And gains the brookside, breathing fast,
Where, on a rustic bench at last

XXXIX

She falls . . .
                "He's here! Eugene!" she panted;
"Oh, God, what can he think of me?"
Her anguished heart some peace was granted
By a dark hope of what might be.
Tatyana burned and shivered, asking:
"He's coming?" But in silence basking,
The country round about was still,
Save for the chorus on the hill
Where the maids sang to keep from cheating
The masters of the berry-crop.
They dared not let their voices drop:
For if they sing, they can't be eating
(A shrewd command that perfectly
Proves rustic ingenuity!).

Maids' Song

Merrily, my laughing ones,
Maidens, come and trip it now,
Come and form a circle and
Foot it neatly on the green!
Girls, strike up a melody,
Sing a song, a happy song,
Sing and bring a dashing lad
Hither to our frolic and
When he comes, ah, when he comes,
When we see him nearing us,
Fly, my darlings, run away,
Pelt the lad with cherries ripe,
Cherries and red raspberries,
Fling him currants ripe and red.
Eavesdroppers, be off, away!
Not for you our songs are sung,
Do not spy upon our games,
Come away, girls, come away!

XL

Tatyana hears the chorus sounding,
But heedlessly; she cannot school
Her shaken heart to stop its pounding,
Or wait for her hot cheeks to cool.
But still she pants, her terror growing,
And hotter yet the blush is glowing
Upon her shamed and flaming cheeks;
Thus a poor moth imprisoned seeks
To free its wings, and frantic, pushes
Against the palm that holds it tight;
Thus a gray hare will quake with fright
Glimpsing behind the distant bushes
A crouching huntsman, ill-concealed,
And stop defenceless in the field.

XLI

At last she rose, and gently sighing
She sought the path, but as she turned,
Before her, there was no denying,
Eugene himself with eyes that burned
Stood like a threatening apparition;
As though she feared an inquisition
She halted, like one scorched by fire.
But what was further to transpire
After this unexpected meeting,
I cannot say; I've talked so long
That I am feeling far from strong;
Forgive me, then, for thus retreating.
Just now a walk would suit me best.
In time I shall relate the rest.

Chapter Four

La morale est dans la nature des choses.

Necker

I—VII

A woman's love for us increases
The less we love her, sooth to say—
She stoops, she falls, her struggling ceases;
Caught fast, she cannot get away.
Once lechery that took its pleasure
And boasted, bold beyond all measure,
And never loved where it desired,
Was all the art of love required.
In this important sport the jaded
Old monkeys of another age
Were proper people to engage;
Now Lovelace's renown is faded,
Gone with the styles we do not use,
With proud perukes and red-heeled shoes.

VIII

Who would not weary of evasion,
And of repeating platitudes,
Of holding forth with great persuasion
On themes to which none now alludes,
Of finding worn-out prejudices,
That even thirteen-year-old misses
Would scarcely call intelligent,
The subject of an argument?
Who would not tire of threats and rages,
Entreaties, vows, and foolish fears,
Deceit and gossip, rings and tears,
Of letters running to six pages,
Mammas and aunts who pry and peer,
And friendly husbands' heavy cheer?

IX

Thus Eugene thought with melancholy.
In his first youth he was the prey
Of many a wild fit of folly,
And never said his passions nay.
A pampered boy, allured by pleasure,
Then disappointed beyond measure,
Wearied by what he had desired,
By facile conquest swiftly tired,
At noisy gatherings and after,
In silence, hearing still the faint
Sad murmur of the soul's complaint,
And covering a yawn with laughter—
He killed eight years thus like a dunce—
The flower of life that blooms but once.

X

Allured by neither looks nor station,
His courting now was minus zest;
Refused—he soon found consolation;
Betrayed—he took a welcome rest.
Though he pursued, the chase was palling;
Both love and malice scarce recalling,
Ladies he left he never missed.
Thus, for an evening game of whist,
A guest comes, an indifferent player;
Sits down; the game is done—he goes;
Drives home to take his night's repose,
His mood no gloomier, no gayer;
Not knowing in the morning where
When evening comes he will repair.

XI

But our Onegin's heart was stricken
When Tanya's tender message came;
Its girlish fire began to quicken
A swarm of thoughts exempt from blame.
Again her pale face looms before him,
Her melancholy eyes adore him—
And as on these his fancy dwelt,
Onegin a pure rapture felt.
Perchance he briefly knew the fever
That thrilled him in the days gone by,
And yet her trust he'd not belie,
He would not play the base deceiver.
But to the garden let us race
Where Tanya met him face to face.

XII

Two minutes passed with neither speaking,
Then he came up to her and said:
"You wrote me. There is no use seeking
To disavow it now. I read
A pure love's innocent effusion;
Your candor filled me with confusion;
I read a shy, confiding word,
And feelings, long quiescent, stirred;
I would not praise you, but sincerely
I would requite sincerity;
You may expect no less from me;
Your frank avowal touched me nearly.
Hear my confession, then, I pray,
And you shall judge me as you may.

XIII

"If I were one of those who rather
Enjoy staid domesticity,
If as a husband and a father
The kindly fates had fancied me,
Where should I seek a dearer treasure?
If for a moment I found pleasure
In cosy scenes of fireside life,
You, you alone would be my wife.
This is no rhetoric I'm using:
Finding my youthful dream come true—
All candor and all grace in you,
You are the helpmeet I'd be choosing:
A pledge of every loveliness,
And I'd be happy . . . more or less!

XIV

"I must confess, though loth to hurt you,
I was not born for happiness;
I am unworthy of your virtue;
I'd bring you nothing but distress.
My conscience speaks—pray let me finish;
My love, first warm, would soon diminish,
Killed by familiarity;
Our marriage would mean misery.
Then you will weep, but who supposes
Your grief will bring me to remorse?
I shall lose patience then, of course:
Hymen will choose no other roses
To make the path before our feet,
Alas, too thorny to be sweet.

XV

"What is there more to be lamented
Than this: a household where the wife
Whose spouse has left her, discontented,
Grieves for the wretch throughout her life,
While the dull husband, fully knowing
Her worth, each year more sullen growing,
And jealous in a frigid way,
Can only curse his wedding-day!
And I am such. Was it naught better
Than that you sought, poor innocent,
When writing that intelligent,
That ardent and most charming letter?
The cruel fates have surely not
Designed for you so sad a lot!

XVI

"His days and dreams what man recovers?
Never shall I my soul renew . . .
I feel, if not indeed a lover's,
More than a brother's love for you.
Be patient, then, as with a brother:
One cherished fancy for another
A girl will more than once forego,
As every spring the saplings show
New leaves for those the tempests scatter.
So Heaven wills it. Your young soul
Will love again. But self-control,
My dear, is an important matter:
Though I was worthy your belief,
Impulsiveness may lead to grief."

XVII

So Eugene preached and Tanya listened,
Scarce breathing, making no replies,
And blinded by the tears that glistened
Unheeded in her great dark eyes.
He offered her his arm. Despairing,
With drooping head and languid bearing
(Mechanically, as they say),
Tatyana took her silent way
Homeward, along the kitchen-garden;
And when they entered, arm in arm,
The company could see no harm
And nothing to remark or pardon;
For rustic freedom thus delights,
As does proud Moscow, in its rights.

XVIII

In this affair our friend was tested
And behaved well, you will agree;
Thus once again he manifested
His soul's innate nobility;
Though there are people, most malicious,
Who called him everything that's vicious
And had no word for him but blame—
Both friends and foes (they're all the same).
We need the wit that nature gave us
To face our foes as all men must,
But from the ones we love and trust,
From our good friends, may Heaven save us!
These friends! 'twas not for nothing that
They came into my mind so pat.

XIX

My meaning? Nothing. My intention
Is but to lull dark thoughts to sleep.
But *in parenthesis* I mention:
There is no calumny so deep,
Born of a liar in an attic,
There is no notion so erratic,
No fancy of a worldly mob,
No coarse *mot* of a witty snob,
That will not be ten times repeated
To decent folk, and with a smile,
By your good friend, all without guile,
And not a single word deleted;
But he will back you while you live,
He loves you . . . as a relative!

XX

H'm, h'm! dear reader, pray apprise me,
Are all your relatives quite well?
You might be pleased—if so, advise me—
To have your humble servant tell
What the word *relatives* embraces.
It means the people to whose faces
We show at all times due respect,
And whom we kiss as they expect,
And visit at the Christmas season,
Unless indeed we send a card
In token of our warm regard,
Lest they should miss us beyond reason
All during the ensuing year.
And so God grant them health and cheer!

XXI

If friends and kin are undeserving,
You may rely upon the fair,
And firmly count upon preserving
Their love, though tempests fill the air.
Oh, yes. But there's the whirl of fashion,
And then the wayward course of passion,
And the opinion of the town . . .
The sex, of course, is light as down.
And while a husband is respected
By any wife who's virtuous,
By words and looks insidious
The faithful one is soon affected:
For woman is a tender fool,
And love is but the devil's tool.

XXII

On whom shall we bestow affection,
And whom shall we confide in, pray?
In whom discover no defection?
Who will assent to all we say?
Who will not seek our faults to flout us?
Who will not spread vile lies about us?
Who will not weary us, with speed?
Who will supply our every need?
It is a phantom you are chasing,
And vainer labor there is none—
Love your own self and so have done!
This estimable friend embracing,
You prove you know, beyond a doubt,
Dear reader, what you are about.

XXIII

What of the tryst, then, so ill-fated?
Alas, it is not hard to guess!
The pains of love still agitated
The soul so shy of happiness;
The promise of her spring was blighted,
But love grew greater, unrequited;
She could but peak and pine and weep,
And night would find her far from sleep.
Lost like a muted sound and vanished,
Her virgin calm is of the past;
Poor Tanya's youth is fading fast,
And health and hope and joy are banished:
Thus darkly drives the storm that shrouds
The blithest dawn in sullen clouds.

XXIV

Tatyana's bloom is all but faded;
She sighs, she pines both day and night!
And all distraction finds her jaded,
She looks on nothing with delight.
The neighbors' heads and tongues are wagging:
"High time she wed!" But I am dragging
My story out, and it is wrong
To dwell on sorry things so long.
Now let me speak of something jolly,
Portraying happy love for you;
Yet bidding the poor girl adieu,
I am assailed by melancholy;
Forgive me: Tanya, from the start,
Has held the first place in my heart.

XXV

From hour to hour yet more enraptured
By the young Olga's winning ways,
Vladimir was completely captured
And found his chains a thing to praise.
Always together, now they're sitting
In her room while the light is flitting;
Or in the morning, arm in arm,
The two explore the garden's charm.
And think of it! So timid is he,
That only once in a great while,
Emboldened by his Olga's smile,
And with love's sweet confusion dizzy,
He dares to trifle with a tress
Or kiss the hem of her dear dress.

XXVI

Sometimes he reads to Olga, trying
To choose such moral tales as might
Have passages on nature vying
With those Chateaubriand could write;
And certain pages (fabrications,
A snare to maids' imaginations)
He passes over in a rush
And not without a tell-tale blush.
At whiles, upon their elbows leaning,
In grave seclusion as is fit,
Above the chess-board they will sit,
And ponder each move's secret meaning,
Till Lensky, too absorbed to look,
With his own pawn takes his own rook.

XXVII

If he goes home, his dreams still linger
About his Olga; it may be,
Having her album there to finger,
He decorates it earnestly:
In ink or colors he is sketching
A rustic view that she found fetching,
A tomb, a temple vowed to love,
A lyre that bears a little dove;
Or on the sheet another wrote on,
A sweet remembrance to ensure,
Below that other's signature
He writes a verse for her to dote on—
A passing thought's enduring trace
That time and change may not erase.

XXVIII

Of course you've often seen that treasure,
The album of a country miss,
Scrawled over by her friends at leisure
With blotted rhyme and criss-cross kiss—
Where spelling has been sadly spited,
And an eternal friendship plighted
In hacked as well as hackneyed verse
That could not very well be worse.
On the first page there's this confection:
"Qu'écrirez-vous sur ces tablettes?"
Beneath it: *"t. à. v.* Annette";
And on the last page this reflection:
"You are the one that I adore,
Who loves you more may write yet more."

XXIX

Here you will find as decoration
Two hearts, a torch, and flow'rs, be sure,
And many a solemn protestation
Of loves that *to the grave* endure;
But for my part I do not mind
Inscribing albums of this kind:
I know there'll be a warm reception
Of any nonsense I set down,
And critics later, with a frown,
Or else a smile that's pure deception,
Will not debate and ponder it,
And search my nonsense for some wit.

XXX

But you, chance volumes that in Hades
Once graced the devil's own abode,
You tomes wherewith resplendent ladies
Torment the rhymesters *à la mode,*
You handsome albums decorated
By what Tolstoy's fine brush created,
Or graced by Baratynsky's pen,
May Heaven blast your page, amen!
When a fine lady seeks to win me
Her well-bound quarto to inscribe,
I fain would write a diatribe—
A mocking demon stirs within me
And prompts something satirical;
But they demand a madrigal!

XXXI

No smart conceits does Lensky fashion
For Olga's album—not a bit!
His lyrics breathe a candid passion,
There is no sparkle here of wit;
Dear Olga is his only matter,
Her looks, her words—he does not flatter.
But with the living truth aglow,
His verses like a river flow.
Thus you, Yazykov, when affection
For God knows whom inspired your soul,
Let the sonorous stanzas roll;
And your remarkable collection
Of elegies at some far date
Will tell the story of your fate.

XXXII

But hush! Our sternest critic rises
And bids us cast away the wreath
Of elegy that he despises,
And throws this challenge in our teeth:
"Stop crying, stop this tiresome quacking
About the self-same thing, this clacking
About the past, what's done and gone;
Enough, sing other tunes, move on!"
"Correct; you'll bring for our inspection
The classic trumpet, sword, and mask;
You'll bid us free, to speed our task,
The frozen funds of intellection—
Eh, friend?" But no, attend again:
"Write odes, odes only, gentlemen,

XXXIII

"As in the old days poets wrote them—
That ancient glory still shines bright . . ."
"What! only solemn odes? Just quote them:
They're duller than the things we write.
Recall Dmitriyev's castigation;
Why should you have such veneration
For all that musty rhetoric,
While our sad rhymesters earn a kick?"
"Ah, but the elegy is flighty,
Inane and petty, while the ode
Travels how different a road—
Its aim is high, its meaning mighty . . ."
I'll not debate the point. Ye gods!
Why set two ages thus at odds?

XXXIV

Admiring glory, loving freedom,
Vladimir too had odes to write,
But seeing Olga wouldn't read 'em,
The lovelorn boy ignored them quite.
Lives there a poet who rehearses
To his dear charmer his own verses?
They say that life does not afford
A more magnificent reward.
How blessed the lover who is granted
The chance to read his modest songs
To her to whom his heart belongs,
And watch her, languidly enchanted!
How blessed, indeed . . . though she might choose
Something more certain to amuse.

XXXV

The things that I concoct in lonely
Long hours, the melodies I mend,
I read not to the crowd, but only
To my old nurse, my childhood's friend;
Or after dinner I may vary
The boredom: nabbing the unwary
Good neighbor who's dropped in on me.
I choke him with a tragedy;
Or else (joking aside) while strolling
Beside my quiet lake, beset
By tiresome rhymes and vain regret,
I frighten the wild ducks by rolling
My tuneful stanzas forth till they
Take off, and smoothly soar away.

XXXVI—XXXVII

And now what of Onegin? Truly
I fear, friends, lest your patience fail:
His daily occupations duly
I shall, to pleasure you, detail.
As hermits live who hope for heaven
He lived—in summer rose at seven;
And lightly clad, though airs were chill,
Walked to the stream below the hill;
Gulnare's bold singer emulating,
He swam this Hellespont anew,
Then dipped into some vile review,
Keeping his morning coffee waiting,
And next he dressed . . .

XXXVIII—XXXIX

A book, a walk where shadows flitted
And brooklets murmured pleasantly,
And, if a black-eyed girl permitted,
Sometimes a kiss as fresh as she,
A lively horse, but not too restive,
A dinner that was rather festive,
Therewith a bottle of light wine,
And solitude—this was, in fine,
Onegin's holy life; unheeding,
He let the summer season fly,
Nor reckoned days as they went by,
No other entertainment needing,
Forgetting friends and city ways
And tedious planned holidays.

XL

Our northern summer, swiftly flying,
Is southern winter's travesty;
And even as we are denying
Its passage, it has ceased to be.
More often now the sun was clouded;
The sky breathed autumn, somber, shrouded;
Shorter and shorter grew the days;
Sad murmurs filled the woodland ways
As the dark coverts were denuded;
Now southward swept the caravan
Of the wild geese, a noisy clan;
And mists above the meadows brooded;
A tedious season they await
Who hear November at the gate.

XLI

The hazy dawn commences coldly,
The silent fields, abandoned, wait,
And on the highway marches boldly
The wolf beside his hungry mate.
The horse who scents him snorts and quivers,
The traveler observes and shivers
And dashes uphill and is gone;
Now from the shed at crack of dawn
The herd no longer drives his cattle,
Nor calls them, noons, for mustering;
Indoors, the maid will softly sing
Above her spinning-wheel's low rattle;
Her work the crackling matchwood lights,
The friend of wintry cottage nights.

XLII

The frosts begin to snap, and gleaming
With silver hoar, the meadows lie . . .
(The reader waits the rhyme-word: beaming,
Well, take it, since you are so sly!).
The icy river shows a luster
That fine parquet can never muster,
And on their skates the merry boys
Now cut the ice with scraping noise;
Down to the waterfront there stumbles
A clumsy goose, and thinks to put
Into the stream her red-webbed foot,
But stepping forth she slips and tumbles;
The first gay snowflakes spin once more
And drop in stars upon the shore.

XLIII

What, in the country, when it's dreary,
Can a man do? Go walking there?
This is the season eyes grow weary,
Beholding bareness everywhere.
On the bleak steppe go horseback-riding?
Yes, but your horse will soon be sliding,
His worn shoe slipping on the ice,
And he will throw you in a trice.
Stay indoors, by a book befriended?
Here's Pradt and Scott. You do not think
You care to? Check accounts, or drink,
Till somehow the long evening's ended,
And so the morrow passes, too—
Your winter is cut out for you.

XLIV

Onegin, like Childe Harold, scorning
All labor, took to pensive ways;
An icy bath begins his morning,
And then at home all day he stays
Alone, and sunk in calculation,
He finds sufficient occupation
In billiards, with a good blunt cue
And ivory balls, not more than two.
But as the rural dusk advances
The game he can at last forget;
Beside the fire a table's set,
He waits: and up a troika prances,
His roans bring Lensky to the door;
Come, it is time to dine once more.

XLV

The pail is brought, the ice is clinking
Round old Moët or Veuve Cliquot;
This is what poets should be drinking
And they delight to see it flow.
Like Hippocrene it sparkles brightly,
The golden bubbles rising lightly
(The image, why, of this and that:
I quote myself, and do it pat).
I could not see it without gloating,
And once I gave my meager all
To get it, friends, do you recall?
How many follies then were floating
Upon the magic of that stream—
What verse, what talk, how fair a dream!

XLVI

But this bright sibilant potation
Betrays my stomach, and although
I love it still, at the dictation
Of prudence now I drink Bordeaux.
Aÿ is risky, if delicious;
It's like a mistress, gay, capricious,
Enchanting, sparkling, frivolous,
And empty—so it seems to us . . .
But you, Bordeaux, I always treasure
As a good comrade, one who shares
Our sorrows and our smaller cares,
And also our calm hours of leisure,
One whose warm kindness has no end—
Long live Bordeaux, the faithful friend!

XLVII

The fire is out; the ashes, shifting,
Have dimmed the golden coal; half-seen,
A thread of smoke is upward drifting;
The hearth breathes warmth, and all's serene;
Up through the flue the pipe-smoke passes;
Upon the table gleam the glasses,
Their rapid bubbles hissing still;
The shadows creep across the sill.
(A friendly glass, and friendly chatter
I've always thought well suited to
The hour called *"entre chien et loup,"*
The reason doesn't really matter.)
But let us rather now inquire
What's said beside the fading fire.

XLVIII

"Well, how are the young ladies faring?
Your Olga? And Tatyana too?"
"Pour me a little more, be sparing . . .
Hold on, old fellow, that will do . . .
The family is well; they send you
Regards. But Olga, oh, my friend, you
Should see how lovely she has grown!
Such shoulders I have never known!
And what a throat! And what a spirit! . . .
Let's call some time. Take my advice;
You looked in at the house just twice
And never after that went near it.
But I'm a dunce! They bade me say
You are to come, and named the day."

XLIX

"I?" "Yes, a birthday celebration—
Taytana's—comes next Saturday.
You have her mother's invitation
And Olenka's. Why say them nay?"
"Oh, there will be a dreadful babble,
And such a crowd, a perfect rabble . . ."
"No, nobody! You're quite secure,
Only the family, I'm sure.
Oblige me! Is it such hard labor?"
"Agreed." "Now that is good of you!"
He said, and found his words the cue
To drink a toast to his fair neighbor,
Then fell again to talking of
His precious Olga: such is love!

L

The day was set, his heart elated;
When but a fortnight more had fled
He'd greet the hour so long awaited,
The secrets of the nuptial bed;
And dreaming of his exultation
He never thought of the vexation
That Hymen brings, the grief and pain,
And the cool yawns that come amain.
While we, with married life not smitten,
Are certain that it only means
A series of fatiguing scenes,
Such stuff as Lafontaine has written . . .
Ah, my poor Lensky, he was made
For such a life, I am afraid.

LI

Beloved . . . or such was his conviction,
He was in bliss. Indeed, thrice blessed
Is he who can believe a fiction,
Who, lulling reason, comes to rest
In the soft luxury of feeling,
Like a poor sot to shelter reeling
Or (since it's ugly to be drunk)
An insect in a flower sunk;
But wretched is the man who never
Can be surprised, who is not stirred
By a translated move or word,
Who cannot feel: he is too clever,
Whose heart experience has chilled,
Whose raptures are forever stilled.

Chapter Five

Be thou spared these fearful dreams,
Thou, my sweet Svetlana.

Zhukovsky

I

That year was extraordinary,
The autumn seemed so loth to go;
Upon the third of January,
At last, by night, arrived the snow.
Tatyana, still an early riser,
Found a white picture to surprise her:
The courtyard white, a white parterre,
The roofs, the fence, all molded fair;
The frost-work o'er the panes was twining;
The trees in wintry silver gleamed;
And in the court gay magpies screamed;
While winter's carpet, softly shining,
Upon the distant hills lay light,
And all she looked on glistened white.

II

Here's winter! . . . The triumphant peasant
Upon his sledge tries out the road;
His mare scents snow upon the pleasant
Keen air, and trots without a goad;
The bold *kibitka* swiftly traces
Two fluffy furrows as it races;
The driver on his box we note
With his red belt and sheepskin coat.
A serf-boy takes his dog out sleighing,
Himself transformed into a horse;
One finger's frostbitten, of course,
But nothing hurts when you are playing;
And at the window, not too grim,
His mother stands and threatens him.

III

Such vulgar scenes as these despising,
You may dismiss them as unfit
For verse—it would not be surprising,
There's little here that's exquisite.
Another, at a god's dictation,
Described with frenzied inspiration
First snow, and delicately wrote
Of wintry pleasures; you will dote
Upon those lines of his commending
The glories of these frosty days,
Like secret promenades in sleighs;
But I, my friend, am not contending
With you, nor yet with you who spin
Fine tales about your fair young Finn.

IV

Tanya, though she could give no reason,
Was yet a thorough Russian; hence
She loved the Russian winter season
And its cold white magnificence:
The hoar-frost in the sun a-shimmer,
And sleighing, and, when light grew dimmer,
The snows still gleaming softly pink,
And the long evenings black as ink.
Yuletide they duly celebrated
As custom bade: with charm and spell
The maids would gleefully foretell
To the young ladies what was fated,
And promised them each year again
A soldier spouse and a campaign.

V

Tanya with simple faith defended
The people's lore of days gone by;
She knew what dreams and cards portended,
And what the moon might signify.
She quaked at omens; all around her
Were signs and warnings to confound her—
Her heart assailed, where'er she went
By some obscure presentiment.
Upon the stove the cat elected
To wash his face with careful paw,
And purr the while: Tatyana saw
At once that guests might be expected.
If on the left she would espy
A slender crescent riding high,

VI

Her face would pale, her body quivered.
And when a star dropped down the sky
And into golden fragments shivered,
She'd watch its flight with anxious eye,
And hurriedly before it perished
Confide to it the wish she cherished.
If she encountered, unaware,
A black-frocked monk, or if a hare
Should cross her path while she was walking,
She would go stumbling down the road,
In dread of what this might forebode;
She fancied ghosts behind her stalking,
And terror-stricken would await
The blow of a malignant fate.

VII

And yet she found it no affliction—
Her terror held a secret charm:
Since nature, fond of contradiction,
Allows a zest to our alarm.
Now Yule-tide brings its fun and folly.
The young tell fortunes, all are jolly,
For carefree youth knows no regret,
Life's vista gleams before it yet.
The aged, at the grave's grim portal,
Through spectacles, with failing eyes,
Tell fortunes, too, but otherwise:
The joys they knew have all proved mortal.
No matter: lisping like a child,
Hope lies to them, and they're beguiled.

VIII

Tatyana stares in fascination,
Seeing the molten wax assume
A shape wherein imagination
Prefigures joy to come, or doom;
Now from the dish where they are lying
The rings are plucked; each maiden, sighing,
Seeks omens in the song they sing;
This ditty sounds for Tanya's ring:
"There peasants, rich beyond all measure,
Can shovel silver with a spade;
We sing about a lucky maid,
For glory will be hers, and treasure!"
The tune, however, threatens her;
Pussy is what the girls prefer.

IX

A frosty night; the heavens muster
A starry host of choiring spheres
That shine with an harmonious luster . . .
Tatyana in the court appears,
And, careless of the cold, is training
A mirror on the moon, now waning;
The image trembling in the glass
Is but the wistful moon's, alas! . . .
The crunch of snow . . . a step approaches;
Straight to the stranger Tanya speeds,
Her tender voice is like a reed's,
And rash the question that she broaches:
"Your name is—what?" He passes on,
But first he answers: "Agafon."

X

Tanya prepared for fortune-telling
As her good nurse would have her do:
And in the bath-house, not the dwelling,
They set a table laid for two;
But she took fright, our shy Tatyana;
I, too, recalling poor Svetlana,
As suddenly grew timorous,
So fortune-telling's not for us.
Tanya, her silken belt untying,
Undressed at last and went to bed.
Sweet Lel now hovers o'er her head,
And one may find a mirror lying
Beneath her pillow. Darkness keeps
All secrets safe. Tatyana sleeps.

XI

She dreams. And wonders are appearing
Before her now, without a doubt:
She walks across a snowy clearing,
There's gloom and darkness all about;
Amid the snowdrifts, seething, roaring,
A torrent gray with foam is pouring;
Darkly it rushes on amain,
A thing the winter could not chain;
By a slim icicle united,
Two slender boughs are flung across
The waters, where they boil and toss;
And by this shaking bridge affrighted,
The helpless girl can do no more
Than halt bewildered on the shore.

XII

She chides the waters that impede her,
But naught avails her girlish wrath;
No helping hand is near to lead her
Across in safety to the path;
A snowdrift stirs, it falls asunder:
Just fancy who appears from under!
A shaggy bear! At Tanya's cry
The creature bellows in reply
As his repellent aid he proffers;
The frightened maiden gathers strength
And puts her little hand at length
Upon the sharp-clawed paw he offers,
And steps across; her blood congeals:
The bear is marching at her heels.

XIII

Look back she dare not: fear would blind her;
She hurries, but the dreadful shape
Of her rough lackey is behind her,
In vain she struggles to escape;
Forward, with groan and grunt he lunges,
And into the deep forest plunges;
In still and somber beauty stand
The pines, their boughs on every hand
Tufted with snow; the stars are shining
Through lofty tree-tops everywhere;
Birch, linden, aspen, all are bare;
The road is lost and past divining,
The rapids and the underbrush
Deep drifted in the snowy hush.

XIV

Into the woods, pursued, she presses;
The snow is reaching to her knee;
A branch leans down to snare her tresses,
To scratch her neck, and stubbornly
Plucks at the ear-rings she is wearing,
Her trinkets rudely from her tearing;
Her small wet slipper's next to go,
All covered with the brittle snow;
She drops her handkerchief, and shivers,
Afraid to stop: the bear is near;
She dare not lift, for shame and fear,
Her trailing skirt, with hand that quivers;
She runs, he follows on and on;
She can no more, her strength is gone.

XV

She falls into the snow; alertly
The shaggy monster seizes her,
And in his arms she lies inertly,
She does not breathe, she does not stir;
Along the forest path he crashes,
And to a humble cottage dashes:
Crowding, the trees about it grow,
And it is weighted down with snow;
One window glimmers bright and rosy,
Within, a noisy clatter swells;
The bear says: "Here my gossip dwells,
Come warm yourself where it is cozy;"
And doing with her as he will,
He lays her down upon the sill.

XVI

Recovered, Tanya, pale and shrinking,
Looks round: the bear is gone, at least;
She hears wild shouts and glasses clinking
As at a mighty funeral feast;
The noise is queer and terrifying.
With caution through the key-hole spying
She sees . . . Why, who would credit it?
About the table monsters sit!
One is a horned and dog-faced creature,
One has a cock's head plain to see,
And there's a witch with a goatee,
A dwarf, whose tail is quite a feature,
A haughty skeleton, and that
Is half a crane and half a cat.

XVII

More horrors: here a lobster riding
A spider; here a red-capped skull
A goose's snaky neck bestriding—
Most fearful and most wonderful!
A wind-mill all alone is whirling,
Its wings with crazy motions twirling;
They bark and whistle, sing and screech,
To horse's stamp and human speech!
And in the crowd that filled the hovel,
Aghast, Tatyana recognized
The dreaded one, the dearly prized:
The very hero of our novel!
Onegin sits and drinks a health,
And glances at the door by stealth.

XVIII

His slightest move is overawing;
He drinks: with greedy howls they swill;
He laughs, and they are all guffawing;
He frowns, and everyone is still;
It's plain that here he is the master.
No longer fearful of disaster,
But curious, as maidens are,
Tatyana sets the door ajar . . .
A sudden gust of wind surprises
The crowd of house-sprites, blowing out
The lights, bewildering the rout;
With flashing eyes Onegin rises
And scrapes his chair along the floor;
All rise; he marches to the door.

XIX

Consumed with terror, Tanya, quaking,
Would fly the place: she cannot stir;
For all the efforts she is making,
No single sound escapes from her;
Eugene flings wide the door: defenseless,
The poor girl stands there, almost senseless;
She hears the raucous laughter swell
And sees the gaping fiends of hell:
The horns and hoofs, the whiskered faces,
The tails and tusks and bloody jaws,
The crooked trunks, the gleaming claws,
The bony hands, the sly grimaces;
All point to her, and all combine
In shouting fiercely: "Mine! She's mine!"

XX

"She's mine!" cries Eugene, stern and daring;
They vanish, claimed by the unknown;
The chilly dark the girl is sharing
With Eugene, and with him alone.
His gentle touch nowise dismays her,
As on a shaky bench he lays her,
And on her shoulder leans his head;
When suddenly they're visited
By Lensky and his love; light flashes;
Eugene berates them, rolls his eyes,
And lifts his hand as who defies
Unbidden guests; the scene abashes
Tatyana, and with failing breath,
The maiden lies there, pale as death.

XXI

The quarrel grows; Onegin quickly
Leaps for a knife, and Lensky falls;
The fearful shadows gather thickly;
A horrid shout assails the walls
And leaves the little hovel shaking . . .
Tatyana, terror-struck, is waking . . .
Her dear familiar room shows plain,
And through the frosty window-pane
The dawn shines ruddy; Olga rushes
In to her sister, swallow-light;
Her rosy cheeks are not less bright
Than in the north Aurora's blushes.
"Tell me your dream," all breathlessly
She cries: "Whom, Tanya, did you see?"

XXII

But, every interruption spurning,
She lies as though she has not heard,
Her book in hand, and slowly turning
Page after page, says not a word.
Although her book has no pretensions
To holding poets' sweet inventions,
Deep truths, or well-drawn scenes—yet not
Racine or Virgil, Walter Scott,
Or Seneca's, or Byron's pages,
Or Fashion Journal, could enthrall
As did this author: chief of all
Diviners and Chaldean sages.
This Martin Zadeka, it seems,
Was *the* interpreter of dreams.

XXIII

It happened that a peddler tendered
This learned opus one fine day
To Tanya, and therewith surrendered
A prize that chanced to come his way:
Malvine—because the set was broken
Three-fifty was the price bespoken,
And in exchange he took as well
Volume the third of Marmontel,
Two Petriads, and a collection
Of fables, and a grammar too.
She thumbed her Martin till he knew
No rival in the girl's affection . . .
He offered solace and delight,
And slept beside her every night.

XXIV

The dream alarms her, and not knowing
What hidden meaning in its lies,
She searches for a passage showing
What such a nightmare signifies.
Some clue the index may afford her,
Where, set in alphabetic order,
She finds: abyss, ape, bear, bridge, cave,
Dirk, door, eclipse, fir, ghost, ice, knave,
Etcetera. The glosses vex her,
Her growing doubts they cannot still.
She fears the dream bodes only ill,
And yet the auguries perplex her.
The dream pervades her mournful moods,
And so for days poor Tanya broods.

XXV

But lo! from out the morning valley
The rosy dawn brings forth the sun,
And with good cheer and merry sally
The name-day feast is soon begun.
The guests are early in arriving,
Whole families of neighbors driving
Up to the steps, in coach and shay,
Calash, kibitka, crowded sleigh.
The hall is packed to suffocation,
The parlor's crowded; barking pugs,
And girls who kiss with laughs and hugs,
Increase the din of celebration;
Guests bow and scrape within the door,
And nurses scream and children roar.

XXVI

Beside his wife, that chubby charmer,
Plump Pustyakov strides heavily;
Here comes Gvozdin, a first-rate farmer
Whose peasants live in beggary;
The two Skotinins, gray as sages,
Line up with children of all ages:
From two to thirty, in a row;
Here's Petushkov, a rural beau;
My cousin, sleepy-eyed Buyanov,
Down in his hair, with visored cap
(I'm certain that you know the chap);
The old fat counselor, Flyanov,
A gossip, glutton, clown, and cheat,
Who likes a bribe as much as meat.

XXVII

Among the crush of people passes,
Leading his offspring, Kharlikov;
With them, a red-wigged man in glasses:
The wit Triquet, late of Tambov.
His pocket burns: it holds a treasure,
A song he brings for Tanya's pleasure.
All children know the melody:
Réveillez-vous, belle endormie.
The verses came—but who would know it?—
From a moth-eaten almanac;
He rescued them, and with the knack
That argues a resourceful poet,
Eliminated *belle Nina,*
Inserting: *belle Tatiana.*

XXVIII

Behold! from town arrives—what rapture!
The company commander, whom
Each rural mother hopes to capture,
The idol of all maids in bloom.
His news sets girlish hearts to drumming:
A regimental band is coming!
The colonel's sending it. A ball!
Upon each other's necks they fall,
Anticipating this distraction.
But dinner's served, and arm in arm
The couples to the table swarm;
Tanya's the center of attraction.
They cross themselves, their heads incline,
Then buzzing, all sit down to dine.

XXIX

Awhile all conversation ceases;
They chew. The pleasant prandial chink
Of plates and silverware increases,
The touching glasses chime and clink.
The feast goes on, but soon thereafter
The room grows loud with talk and laughter
And none can hear his neighbor speak,
They chortle, argue, shout and squeak.
And while they all are in high feather,
The door swings wide, and Lensky's here,
Onegin too. "At last, oh, dear!"
The hostess cries. Guests squeeze together
Move plates and chairs with ready glee,
And seat the two friends hastily.

XXX

They face Tatyana, who is paler
Than is the moon one sees at dawn;
With the emotions that assail her
She trembles like a hunted fawn;
Her darkening eyes she never raises;
With stormy passion's heat she blazes;
She suffocates; she scarcely hears
The two friends' greetings; and the tears
Are all but flowing; her heart flutters,
The poor thing nearly swoons; she's ill.
But now her reason and her will
Prevail. Two words she softly mutters,
And that between her teeth, to greet
These guests, and somehow keeps her seat

XXXI

Eugene had long abominated
High tragedy and swoons and tears,
And girlish fits of nerves he hated:
He'd suffered from such things for years.
The feast he was quite unprepared for,
'Twas not the sort of thing he cared for;
And having noted, in a pet,
That poor Tatyana was upset,
He dropped his eyes in irritation
And sulked, and swore that he would trim
His friend for thus misleading him;
Now soothed by this anticipation,
He set his mind to work with zest,
Caricaturing every guest.

XXXII

Eugene was not alone in noting
Tatyana's trouble; but each eye
Was at that moment busy gloating
Upon a succulent fat pie
(Alas, too salty), and observing
A pitch-sealed bottle they were serving
As a fit sequel to the roast:
Wine of the Don, to drink a toast.
And then appeared a row of glasses,
Each long and narrow as your waist,
Zizi, that asks to be embraced;
My soul's fair crystal, what surpasses
Your charm? My verses sang your praise;
You made me drunk in other days.

XXXIII

Released from the damp cork, the bottle
Pops; the wine fizzes; and Triquet,
Whom silence was about to throttle,
With dignity brings forth his lay.
The gathering, affected by it
Before it's heard, is grave and quiet.
Tatyana, breathless, cannot stir;
Triquet turns, with his sheet, to her,
And sings, off key. The song is greeted
With shouts and plaudits. Tanya now
Is forced to curtsey, to his bow.
Though great, the poet's not conceited,
His toast rings out the first of all,
Then he presents the madrigal.

XXXIV

All greeted and congratulated
Tatyana, who spoke each one fair;
Eugene, as he his turn awaited,
Observed the girl's embarrassed air,
Her sad fatigue, her helpless languor,
And pity took the place of anger.
He bowed to her without a word,
But somehow his mere look averred
Deep tenderness; perhaps he meant it,
Or else he may, deliberately,
Have played a prank in coquetry,
Or somehow couldn't quite prevent it,
But tenderness his look *did* show,
And Tanya's heart began to glow.

XXXV

The chairs shoved backward scrape the flooring;
All crowd into the drawing-room
Like bees that from the hive are pouring
Into a meadow sweet with bloom.
The feast makes every move a labor
And neighbor wheezes unto neighbor.
The ladies sit beside the fire;
The girls, off by themselves, conspire;
Green tables are set up, alluring
The gamblers, worthy men and bold:
Ombre and Boston claim the old,
And more play whist, whose fame's enduring—
A most tedious family,
All greedy boredom's progeny.

XXXVI

The whist-players are lion-hearted:
They've played eight rubbers at a stretch,
Eight times changed places since they started;
They stop because the servants fetch
The tea. I note the hour, or nearly,
By dinner, tea, and supper merely.
Off in the country we can say
What time it is with no Breguet
Except the stomach; I may mention
In passing that my stanzas speak
Of feasts and sundry foods and eke
Of corks, with much the same attention
That to such matters Homer pays,
Who's had three thousand years of praise.

XXXVII—XXXIX

But here is tea: the girls demurely
Their steaming cups have barely stirred
When sweetly through the doors and surely
Bassoon and flute at once are heard.
Because the tune is so diverting,
His cup of tea with rum deserting,
The local Paris: Petushkov,
Comes up to carry Olga off,
And Lensky—Tanya; Karhlikova,
A virgin of ripe years, accepts
Triquet; next follow two adepts:
Buyanov leads off Pustyakova;
The ballroom summons one and all,
Thus brilliantly begins the ball.

XL

At the beginning of my story
I thought to paint (see Chapter One)
A northern ball in all its glory,
A thing Albani might have done;
But yielding to a dream's distraction,
I reminisced of the attraction
That ladies' feet have had for me.
Oh, I have erred sufficiently
In tracking you! I should be moving
On other paths, since youth is spent,
And grow, with time, intelligent,
My style and my affairs improving,
And, if my novel is to thrive,
Free from digressions Chapter Five.

XLI

Like giddy youth forever swirling
In dizzy circles round and round,
The waltz sends tireless couples twirling
To flute and viol's merry sound.
Revenge approaches, so, concealing
A smile, Onegin is appealing
To Olga. First they spin about,
Then he suggests they sit one out,
And chats of this and that politely;
A moment, and the pair once more
Are waltzing round the dancing-floor.
All wonder whether they see rightly;
And staring in dismayed surprise,
Lensky can scarcely trust his eyes.

XLII

Now the mazurka's strains are sounding.
Of old the ballroom used to shake
To the mazurka; with the pounding
Of heels the stout parquet would quake,
And window-sashes rattled loudly.
Not now: we, like the ladies, proudly
And smoothly glide on polished boards;
But the provincial town affords
A place for the old-fashioned splendor:
The leaps, the heels, the whiskers fair,
Are just the same as what they were;
The country to the past is tender,
Nor bends to fashion's tyrannies:
The modern Russian's worst disease.

XLIII—XLIV

My lively cousin now advancing,
Presents the charming sisters both
To Eugene, who at once goes dancing
Away with Olga, nothing loth;
He leads her, nonchalantly gliding,
And in an attitude confiding,
His head above her fondly bent,
Whispers an outworn compliment,
And presses her soft hand—elation
Inflames the girl's conceited face;
My Lensky's fury grows apace;
He waits with jealous indignation
The end of the mazurka, and
For the cotillion begs her hand.

XLV

She cannot. No? But why? She's given
Onegin the cotillion. Lord!
What does he hear? She dared . . . He's driven
To think the girl that he adored
Is but a flirt. Though she is barely
Out of her swaddling-clothes, she's fairly
Accomplished as a vile coquette!
Such treachery who could forget?
Poor Lensky cannot bear his sorrow.
He curses women's whims with force,
Goes out at once, demands a horse,
And dashes off. Before the morrow
A brace of pistols and two balls
Will square accounts, whoever falls.

Chapter Six

Là sotto giorni nubilosi e brevi
Nasce una gente a cui l'morir non dole.

Petrarch

I

Revenge was something of a pleasure,
But Eugene, now his friend was gone,
Was bored again beyond all measure;
Olenka too began to yawn,
By her dull partner's mood infected;
And as she looked about, dejected,
For Lensky, the cotillion seemed
To her a tiresome thing she dreamed.
It's over. Having supped, the gentry
Are glad at last to take a rest:
A place is found for every guest
'Twixt the maid's attic and the entry,
And gratefully to bed they creep;
Eugene alone goes home to sleep.

II

All's hushed: within the parlor, sighing
And snoring, heavy Pustyakov
Beside his heavy mate is lying.
Gvozdin, Buyanov, Petushkov,
And Flyanov, somewhat ill, encumber
The dining-room: on chairs they slumber.
Upon the floor Triquet we view
In flannels and a night-cap too.
The girls with Olga and Tatyana
Are settled: they are fast asleep;
But at her window, fain to weep,
Poor Tanya, lighted by Diana,
Stares out upon the shadowed lea:
There is no sleep for such as she.

III

Once more Tatyana's heart is drumming;
Delight is mingled with distress
As she reviews Onegin's coming
And his brief look of tenderness—
And then, with Olga, how he acted!
She puzzles till she is distracted,
And jealous longing frets the maid—
As though a chilly hand were laid
Upon her heart, as though a rumbling
Black chasm were gaping at her feet . . .
"But ruin at his hands is sweet,"
Says Tanya, "Nay, I am not grumbling:
Complaint will make my pain no less.
He cannot give me happiness."

IV

Proceed, my tale! Here's matter for ye,
Good readers: a new face arrives.
Five versts away from Krasnogorye,
Our Lensky's village, lives and thrives,
'Mongst thinkers who are few and cloudy,
Zaretzky, once a jolly rowdy,
A gambler who won all the stakes,
A tavern tribune, chief of rakes,
But now a kind and simple father,
Albeit still a bachelor,
A good landed proprietor,
A friend in need, as you will gather—
Even a man of honor: thus
The times improve, and better us!

V

Time was when all the world was vying
In praise of his base hardihood;
He hit an ace, there's no denying,
At fifteen feet: his aim was good.
One day when leading his battalion,
He fell from off his Kalmuck stallion
Drunk as an owl, into a trench,
And so was captured by the French—
A precious pledge! The man was guided
By honor's dictates, was indeed
A modern Regulus; at need
He'd suffer bonds again, provided
That at Very's on credit he
Could drain each morning bottles three.

VI

He well knew how to set you laughing,
Made game of fools, and being bent
On secret or on open chaffing,
Could hoodwink the intelligent;
Though on occasion like a duffer
This clever jester had to suffer,
And for the pranks he liked to play
Took punishment once in a way.
He liked debate, and sometimes rudely
And sometimes neatly made retort,
And shrewdly held his peace; in sport
Would start a quarrel quite as shrewdly,
To have two friends at daggers drawn
And send them, armed, from bed at dawn,

VII

Or into concord gently shame them,
To earn a luncheon from the two,
And later privately defame them
With a gay jest and words untrue.
Sed alia tempora! Such jolly
Pranks (like love's dream, another folly)
Belong to youth, with youth are fled.
And my Zaretzky, as I said,
Beneath the shade of his acacias
Has found a refuge from the blast
And lives like a true sage at last,
Plants cabbages like old Horatius,
And raises fowls, while at his knee
The children learn their A-B-C.

VIII

He was no fool; and Eugene, ready
To praise his mind if not his heart,
Admired his judgment, always steady,
And found his comments sane and smart.
He often paid a call, surmising
A welcome; it was not surprising
For Eugene to behold him there
That morning, gay and debonair.
He barely spoke; his urgent mission
Zaretzky was not one to shirk—
At once he offered with a smirk
A note of Lensky's composition;
Onegin took the letter to
The window, where he read it through.

IX

The poet, swift in thought and action,
With most polite and cool address,
Herein demanded satisfaction,
For honor could require no less.
The messenger was not kept waiting:
Onegin without hesitating
Replied as though he little cared
What came of it: "Always prepared."
On hearing this, Zaretzky started
To go: he had no wish to stay,
And he was busy anyway,
And so without more words, departed;
But left alone, Onegin sighed,
With his own self dissatisfied.

X

And rightly: for Onegin, sitting
In judgment on himself could be
Severe, and he was not acquitting
Himself, even in privacy.
First: he accused himself of mocking
Young timid love, and that was shocking.
Second: the poet was a fool,
But at eighteen that is the rule;
And holding him in such affection
Eugene should not have been so rash,
Not thus have sought to cut a dash,
Nor shown a fighter's predilection,
But, like a man of worth and sense,
Have acted with intelligence.

XI

Had he been quicker in revealing—
Instead of bristling at the start—
That he was yet a man of feeling,
He'd have disarmed the youthful heart.
"Too late," he thinks. "And then that vicious
Old duelist can be malicious:
He thrust his nose in right away,
And he would have a deal to say . . .
Of course, one should reward his gabble
With scorn; yet smiles upon the lips
Of fools, and slyly whispered quips . . . "
Lo! the opinion of the rabble
Is honor's mainspring, I'll be bound—
The thing that makes the world go round.

XII

The poet, with impatience burning,
Sits home, awaiting the reply;
And here the gossip is returning
With solemn gait and sparkling eye.
The young Othello is delighted!
He feared that he had not incited
The rogue, who somehow would escape
By a sly dodge or ready jape.
He savors the few words that settle
His doubts: for meet they surely will
At dawn tomorrow, near the mill;
Then let each man be on his mettle:
They'll cock the trigger and let fly,
Their mark the temple or the thigh.

XIII

Each hour of torment added fuel
To Lensky's wrath: he would not see
The base coquette before the duel;
He marked the time, and presently
He waved his hand, as one who'd rue it
And was at Olga's ere he knew it!
He was convinced the fickle fair
Would be dismayed to see him there;
But no!—straight down the steps to meet him
Unhesitatingly she ran,
Bewildering the wretched man,
And turned a joyful face to greet him
In the same carefree lively way
As upon any other day.

XIV

"Why did you leave," the maiden asked him,
"So very early yesterday?"
Deeply disturbed as thus she tasked him,
Poor Lensky scarce knew what to say.
His jealousy and his vexation
Were banished by her animation,
Her look, so candid and serene,
Her sweet simplicity of mien! . . . .
He gazes, and his heart is riven:
She loves him still; and in remorse,
He now repents him of the course
He took, and fain would be forgiven;
He trembles, cannot say a word,
His heart leaps up, his soul is stirred.

XV—XVII

In Olga's presence poor Vladimir
Ignores what happened yesterday,
And full of grief the wistful dreamer
Broods over all he dare not say:
"From threatened ruin I'll retrieve her,
I shall not suffer the deceiver
To tempt with tender word and sigh
The youthful heart; I will defy
The poisonous vile worm that mumbles
The lily-stem, and withers so
The bud that just begins to blow,
But ere 'tis open, fades and crumbles."
These proud reflections all portend:
I'll have a duel with my friend.

XVIII

Had he but known the wounding sorrow
That burdened my Tatyana's heart!
Had Tanya known that on the morrow
Fresh grief would cause a keener smart—
Could she but have foreseen the meeting
And the two friends for death competing,
She then, as love has power to do,
Might have united them anew!
But none as yet came near divining
Her passion, not by chance or skill;
Eugene was apt at keeping still;
In secret Tanya was repining;
The nurse alone might well have guessed,
But she was slow of wit at best.

XIX

All evening Lensky was distracted,
A glum, and next a merry man;
But nurselings of the Muse have acted
Like this since first the world began;
With frowning brow he would be sitting
At the spinet, then swiftly quitting
The music, he would whisper low
To Olga: "I am happy—no?"
But it is late, he should be leaving;
His heart is all but crushed with pain,
And as he says farewell again
He feels that it must break with grieving.
She looks at him in some dismay.
"What ails you?" "Nothing." So—away.

XX

At home his pistols claimed attention;
He looked them over, boxed them right,
Undressed, and opened—need I mention?—
Schiller, of course, by candle-light.
But ever sadder, ever fonder,
He has a single thought to ponder:
He seems to see his Olga there
Unutterably dear and fair.
Inspired by tender melancholy,
Vladimir shuts the book, and then
There pours in torrents from his pen
Verse full of amatory folly,
Which he declaims with ecstasy
Like Delwig drunk in company.

XXI

By chance, these verses have not perished;
I have them here for you to see:
"Oh, golden days, my springtide cherished,
Ah, whither, whither did you flee?
The day to come, what is it bearing?
In vain into the darkness staring
I try to glimpse it; but I trust
The law of Fate is ever just.
From the drawn bow the arrow leaping
May pass me by or pierce me through;
Yet all is well—each has its due:
The hour for waking and for sleeping;
The day of busy cares is blessed,
And blessed the darkness bringing rest.

XXII

"The ray of dawn will shine tomorrow,
And day will brighten wold and wave,
When I, mayhap, past joy and sorrow,
Shall know the secrets of the grave,
And Lethe's sluggish tide will swallow
The poet, and the world will follow
His course no more; but, oh, most dear,
Will you not come to shed a tear
Upon the urn, and think: 'Ill-fated!
He loved me, and the dawn of life
With its unseasonable strife
To me alone he dedicated! . . .'?
Dear friend, before this heart is numb—
Your spouse awaits; come to me, come! . . ."

XXIII

His strain was languid, dark (romantic,
We call it--if no trace I find
Of such a manner, I'm pedantic,
And how it strikes me, never mind).
The poet did not think of stopping
Until, near dawn, his head was dropping
Upon "ideal"—modish word—
And sleep at last her boon conferred;
But scarce did consciousness forsake him
When into the hushed study came
His neighbor, calling out his name,
Not hesitating to awake him.
"Get up," he cried, "Past six, I vow,
Onegin's waiting for us now."

XXIV

He erred; for Eugene, hardy sinner,
Was sleeping, heedless of the clock;
The shades of night are growing thinner,
And Lucifer's hailed by the cock;
Onegin sleeps and does not worry.
The sun appears, a brief snow-flurry
Is gaily whirling overhead,
And still our Eugene lies abed
In cosy comfort, sleeping sweetly.
At last he rouses, opens wide
His drowsy eyes, and draws aside
The bed-curtains; awake completely,
He marks the hour with some dismay:
He must be off without delay.

XXV

Responding to his hasty ringing,
In runs his valet, prompt Guillot,
His dressing-gown and slippers bringing,
And hands him linen white as snow.
With utmost speed Onegin dresses,
And bids his servant, since time presses,
Prepare with him to leave the place
At once, and bear the weapon-case.
The sledge awaits. He does not tarry:
He's in, and flying to the mill.
They come. Quite unaffected still,
He gives his man the arms to carry
(Lepage's work), and has him tie
The horses to an oak near by.

XXVI

Upon the dam leaned Lensky; waiting,
The while Zaretzky with a sneer
Upon the mill-stone dissertating
Was quite the rustic engineer.
Onegin comes, apologizing.
Zaretzky, not at all disguising
Surprise, asks: "Where's your second, pray?"
A classicist in such a fray,
And sentimentally devoted
To method, he would not allow
That one be potted anyhow,
But by rule only, and he doted
Upon the good old-fashioned ways
(A bias worthy of our praise).

XXVII

"My second?" Eugene said, "Permit me:
My worthy friend, Monsieur Guillot.
If fault there be, you will acquit me
Of making such a choice, I know;
He is, though not renowned or quoted,
An honest fellow, be it noted.
Zaretzky bit his lip, quite vexed,
Onegin turned to Lensky next:
"Well, shall we start?" The young Othello
Responded: "Why should we delay?"
Behind the mill they went straightway.
Zaretzky and the *honest fellow*
Went off and talked in solemn wise;
The foes stood by, with downcast eyes.

XXVIII

The foes! How long had they been parted
By this most black and vengeful mood?
How long since they were happy-hearted,
And sharing leisure, thoughts, and food,
And doings, in a friendly fashion?
But now, the prey of evil passion,
Like those whom an old feud inflames,
As in a nightmare each one aims
At slaughter, with a heart of leather . . .
Were it not better, if before
Those gentle hands were stained with gore
A laugh would bring the pair together?
But worldly quarrels breed the dread
Of worldly scorn, and thus are fed.

XXIX

The pistols gleam, held straight and steady;
The hammers on the ramrods knock;
The bullets are crammed down already;
One hears the clicking of a cock.
Into the pan the powder's sifted,
The jagged flint still harmless, lifted.
Behind a stump among the trees
Guillot is standing, ill at ease.
Their gestures marked by firm decision,
The enemies their mantles doff.
And now Zaretzky measures off
Thirty-two paces with precision;
At either end the two friends stand,
Each with a weapon in his hand.

XXX

"Approach!" How calm and cold their faces
As the two foes, with even tread,
Not aiming yet, advance four paces,
Four steps toward a narrow bed.
First Eugene, still advancing duly,
Begins to raise his pistol coolly.
Now five steps more the pair have made,
And Lensky, firm and unafraid,
Screws up his eye and is preparing
To take aim also—but just then
Onegin fires . . . oh, hapless men,
Such is the guerdon of your daring!
The fatal hour is past recall;
The poet lets his pistol fall,

XXXI

His hand upon his breast lays lightly,
And drops. His clouded eyes betray
Not pain, but death. Thus, sparkling whitely
Where the quick sunbeams on it play,
A snowball down the hill goes tumbling
And sinks from sight, soon to be crumbling.
Onegin, frozen with despair,
Runs to the poor youth lying there,
And looks, and calls him . . . But no power
Avails to rouse him: he is gone.
The poet in the very dawn
Of life has perished like a flower
That by a sudden storm was drenched;
Alas! the altar-fire is quenched.

XXXII

He did not stir, but like one dreaming
He lay most strangely there at rest.
The blood from the fresh wound was steaming:
The ball had pierced clean through the breast.
A moment since, this heart was quickened
By poetry and love, or sickened
By hate and dread, and strongly beat
With dancing blood, with living heat.
But now, 'tis as a house forsaken,
Where all is silent, dark and drear,
The shutters closed, the windows blear
With chalk. No knock can ever waken
The lady of the house: she's fled—
Where to, God knows; she never said.

XXXIII

'Tis pleasant with a wicked sally
To make a man feel like an ass,
To see him, baited, turn and rally,
And glance, unwilling, in the glass,
Ashamed to own his every feature;
'Tis yet more pleasant if the creature
Should howl absurdly: "It is I!"
And yet more pleasant, on the sly
To make his noble coffin ready:
A proper distance to allow,
Then, aiming at his pallid brow,
To hold the pistol straight and steady;
But yet the pleasure's dulled if he
Is launched into eternity.

XXXIV

Suppose your pistol-shot has ended
A comrade's promising career,
One who, by a rash glance offended,
Or by an accidental sneer,
During a drunken conversation
Or in a fit of blind vexation
Was bold enough to challenge you—
Will not your soul be filled with rue
When on the ground you see him, stricken,
Upon his brow the mark of death,
And watch the failing of his breath,
And know that heart will never quicken?
Say, now, my friend, what will you feel
When he lies deaf to your appeal?

XXXV

Onegin grips his pistol tightly,
His heart with sore repentance filled,
Beholding Lensky. "Well?" Forthrightly
The neighbor now declares: "He's killed."
He's killed! The fearful affirmation
Makes Eugene quake with consternation.
He calls for help, in misery;
And in the sleigh most carefully
The frozen corpse Zaretzky places,
To take the awful cargo home.
The horses scent the dead, and foam
Is slobbered over bit and traces,
As, sped like arrows from the bow,
They gallop snorting o'er the snow.

XXXVI

Friends, for the poet you are grieving:
Cut off before his hopes could bloom;
The world of glory thus bereaving,
He came, unripe, unto the tomb!
Where is the burning agitation,
Where is the noble aspiration,
The thoughts of youth so high and grave,
The tender feelings and the brave?
Where are the storms of love and longing,
The thirst for knowledge, toil, and fame,
The dread of vice, the fear of shame,
And you, bright phantoms round him thronging,
You, figments of sweet reverie,
You, dreams of sacred poesy?

XXXVII

Mayhap he would have been reputed,
Or gloriously served the world;
Mayhap the lyre so early muted
Beneath his fingers would have hurled
A mighty music down the ages.
Perchance he would have earned the wages
By worldly approbation paid.
Or it may be his martyred shade
Bore to the grave to sleep forever
A holy secret, and a voice
To make the soul of man rejoice
Is lost to us, and he shall never
Be thrilled upon Elysian ways
To hear a people's hymn of praise.

XXXVIII—XXXIX

Perchance a humble lot awaited
The poet, and he may, forsooth,
Like many others have been fated
To lose his ardor with his youth.
He might have altered and deserted
The Muse—to marriage been converted,
And worn in comfort, far from town,
Horns and a quilted dressing-gown;
He might have learned that life was shabby
At bottom, and, too bored to think,
Have been content to eat and drink,
Had gout at forty, fat and flabby;
He might have gone to bed and died
While doctors hemmed and women cried.

XL

Whate'er was to befall Vladimir,
One thought must fill your heart with pain:
The lover, poet, pensive dreamer,
Alas! by a friend's hand was slain.
There is the spot if you would know it:
Left of the village where the poet
Once dwelt, two pines are intertwined—
Below you see the river wind
That waters well the nearby valley.
The women mowing oft repair
To plunge their tinkling pitchers there,
And there the weary ploughmen dally.
Beside that stream with shadows laced
A simple monument is placed.

XLI

Near by (when springtime rains have peppered
The fields with droplets once again),
Weaving his shoe of bast, the shepherd
Sings of the Volga fishermen;
And the young city miss who's facing
A summer in the country, racing
Across the meadowland alone,
Will halt her horse beside the stone,
Tug at the leather rein, and turning
Her gauzy veil aside to see
The simple lines there graven, she
Will feel her heart with pity burning,
And as she reads, the tears will rise
To mist her wide and tender eyes.

XLII

And plunged in sorry thought, more slowly
On through the field the girl will ride,
The while her wistful spirit wholly
With Lensky's fate is occupied;
"And what of Olga?" is her query:
"Was all her life thereafter dreary?
Or was the time of sorrow brief?
Where did her sister take her grief?
Where is the saturnine betrayer,
The smart coquettes' smart enemy,
The exile from society
Who was the fair young poet's slayer?"
In time, my readers, you shall hear
It all, in detail, never fear,

XLIII

Not now. I love my hero truly,
And shall return to him, I vow,
All his concerns recounting duly,
But that is not my pleasure now.
The years to rugged prose constrain me,
No more can careless rhymes detain me,
And I admit, in penitence,
I court the Muse with indolence.
No more I find it quite so pressing
To soil the sheets with flying quill;
But other fancies, dark and chill,
And other cares, severe, distressing,
In festive crowds, in solitude,
Upon my dreaming soul intrude.

XLIV

By new desires I am enchanted,
New sorrows come, my heart to fret;
The hopes of old will not be granted,
The olden sorrows I regret.
Ah, dreams! where has your sweetness vanished?
Where's youth (the rhyme comes glibly) banished?
And is the vernal crown of youth
Quite withered now in very truth?
Can the sad thought with which I flirted
In elegiac mood, at last
Be fact, and can my spring be past
(As I in jest so oft asserted)?
Will it no more return to me?
Shall I be thirty presently?

XLV

The afternoon of life is starting,
I must admit the sorry truth.
Amen: but friendly be our parting,
My frivolous and merry youth!
My thanks for all the hours of gladness,
The tender torments, and the sadness,
The storm and strife, the frequent feast;
For all your great gifts and your least,
My thanks. Alike in peace and riot
I found you good, and I attest
I tasted all your joys with zest;
Enough! My soul is calm and quiet
As on another road I fare,
To rest from loads I used to bear.

XLVI

Let me look back. Farewell, then, bowers
Where I would loll, without a goal,
But lulled by the fond dream that dowers
With joy the contemplative soul!
And you, oh, youthful inspiration,
Come, rouse anew imagination—
Upon the dull mind's slumbers break,
My little nook do not forsake;
Let not the poet's heart know capture
By sullen time, and soon grow wry
And hard and cold, and petrify
Here in the world's benumbing rapture,
This pool we bathe in, friends, this muck
In which, God help us, we are stuck.

Chapter Seven

Moscow, Russia's darling daughter,
Where's your equal to be found?

Dmitriyev

How can one not love Moscow, pray?

Baratynsky

Speak ill of Moscow! There's your traveler!
Where will you find a better place, good sir?
Oh, yes, what's far away, that we prefer!

Griboyedov

I

From nearby hills the snow, already
Obeying the spring sun's commands,
Flows down in muddy streams and steady
Into the flooded meadowlands.
Still half asleep, nature is meeting
The year's bright dawn with gentle greeting.
The heavens glow with azure light.
The naked woods surprise the sight,
A delicate green down assuming.
The bee deserts her waxen cell
To gather tribute from the dell.
Soon the dry valleys will be blooming;
The cattle low; the nightingale
Has thrilled by night the silent dale.

II

Ah, spring, fair spring, the lovers' season,
How sad I find you! How you flood
My soul with dreams that challenge reason,
And with strange languor fill my blood!
My stricken heart cries out and fails me
When once the breath of spring assails me,
Although its touch be soft as fleece,
While I lie lapped in rural peace!
Is it that I was born to languish,
And all that sparkles, triumphs, sings,
Is alien to my breast, and brings
No gift but weariness and anguish
To one whose soul has perished, and
Who sees the dark on every hand?

III

Or is it that we fail to cherish
The tender leaves, but in the spring
Mourn those that autumn doomed to perish,
The while we hear the woodland sing?
Or are our thoughts in truth so cruel
That nature's season of renewal
But brings to mind our fading years
That no hope of renewal cheers?
Or it may be that we are taken
In our poetic reverie
Far back to a lost spring, and we,
By dreams of a far country shaken,
Recall with pain the vanished boon:
A night of magic, and a moon . . .

IV

Kind drones, and you who wisely savor
Your pleasures with a taste more keen,
And you who bask in fortune's favor,
And you, skilled pupils of Levshin,
You rustic Priams, and you gentle
Fair ladies who are sentimental—
Spring calls you to the verdant soil,
To sunny gardens' fragrant toil;
The time of tempting nights approaches,
When every walk fresh wonders yields;
Then, hurry, hurry to the fields!
Have your own horses pull your coaches,
Or post-horses, if thus inclined,
But fast or slow, leave town behind!

V

And you, my reader, wise and witty,
In your imported carriage, pray
Desert at last the restless city
Where winter-long you were so gay;
And while my wanton muse rejoices
We'll listen to the forest voices,
Upon the nameless river's shore
In that same hamlet where of yore
My Eugene through the winter tarried,
An idle, cheerless recluse, near
Young Tanya, whom I still hold dear,
Poor dreamer whom he sadly harried;
But where no more one meets his face . . .
And where he left a lasting trace.

VI

Within the hill-encircled valley
Come seek the stream that slowly goes
Through meadowland and linden alley,
On down to where the river flows.
The nightingale, this season's lover,
There sings all night; wild roses cover
The bank; one hears a gentle spring;
And where two pines their shadows fling
A gravestone tells its mournful story.
The passer-by may read it clear:
"Vladimir Lensky slumbers here,
Who early found both death and glory,
In such a year, at such an age;
Take rest, young poet, as thy wage."

VII

Upon a trailing branch suspended
Above this modest urn there hung
A wreath, that by the breeze befriended
Caressed the tomb o'er which it swung.
There, when the tardy moon was shining,
Two girls would come, and sadly twining
Their arms about each other, creep
To the low grave, to sit and weep.
But now . . . the tombstone and its story
Are quite forgot. The path is now
O'ergrown. No wreath hangs on the bough;
Alone the shepherd, weak and hoary,
As erstwhile comes, to hum an air
And plait his humble footgear there.

VIII—X

Poor Lensky! Olga's heart was laden
With sorrow, but her tears were brief.
Alas! a young and lively maiden
Can scarce be faithful to her grief.
Another captured her attention,
Another's amorous invention
Soon found a way to soothe her pain;
An uhlan wooed her, not in vain;
She loves an uhlan with devotion . . .
Already, 'neath the bridal crown,
Before the altar, head cast down,
She stands, suffused with shy emotion,
Her lowered eyes agleam the while,
And on her lips a careless smile.

XI

Poor Lensky! Past the grave's grim portal,
Was the sad singer shocked to learn
That Olga's love, alas, was mortal,
And did his shade in sorrow yearn?
Or, lulled by Lethe's quiet flowing,
And blissful still, since all unknowing,
By nothing stirred, where all is dim,
Is this world shut for aye to him?
Oblivion is waiting for us
Beyond the grave, yes, at the end
The voice of mistress, foe, and friend,
Is hushed. Alone the angry chorus
Of heirs is heard, indecently
Disputing your small legacy.

XII

Not long the Larin house was waking
To Olga's voice: away she went,
Since now her uhlan was betaking
Himself back to his regiment.
The poor old lady, broken-hearted,
Wept o'er her daughter as they parted,
And seemed about to faint and fall;
But Tanya had no tears at all;
And yet her face was pale and clouded
As that of one beneath a spell.
When all went out to say farewell,
And round the loaded carriage crowded,
She too at length came forth, and nigh
The couple stood, to say good-bye.

XIII

As one who through a fog is peering,
Tatyana watched them drive away
Till they were out of sight and hearing. . . .
She is alone, alack-a-day!
The comrade upon whom she doted,
Her dove, her confidante devoted,
Is snatched away from her by Fate
Who best knows how to separate.
She has no aim, no occupation,
But like a shadow moves about,
Or on the garden gazes out . . .
But nothing offers consolation,
Nor eases tears too long suppressed,
Nor soothes the ache within her breast.

XIV

Tatyana's solitude adds fuel
To her vain passion day by day;
Her heart speaks ever of the cruel
Onegin, also far away.
She will not see him, the betrayer;
Nay, she must hate her brother's slayer.
The poet is no more . . . his lot
Was to be readily forgot.
Though he was brave, though he was gifted,
His bride was soon content to be
Another's, and his memory
Like smoke across the azure drifted;
Two hearts, one may perhaps believe,
Yet grieve for him . . . But wherefore grieve?

XV

By the still stream, with dusk descending,
One heard the crickets' slender choir.
The dancers from the green were wending.
On the far bank the smoky fire
Built by the fishermen was flaring.
Now through the open meadow faring,
Where moonlight silvered shrub and stone,
Tatyana, dreaming, walked alone.
She clambered up a hill, commanding
A village view she seemed to know,
A garden river-girt, and lo!
Near by, she saw the mansion standing.
Tanya surveys it with a start,
And faster, faster throbs her heart.

XVI

A trespasser may hope for pardon.
"I am not known here. He is gone . . .
I might just see the house and garden,"
She thinks, uncertain, and goes on.
Her mind with agitation seething,
Downhill she trudges, scarcely breathing.
She looks about in puzzled sort,
And enters the deserted court.
The dogs attack her, all but biting
The stranger. At her frightened cry,
Out from the house the serf-boys fly,
A noisy brood. Not without fighting,
They chase the dogs away, alert
Lest the young lady should be hurt.

XVII

"The manor-house," says Tanya, shyly,
"I should most dearly like to see."
At once the children run off spryly
To ask Anisya for the key.
Anisya surely won't ignore them:
Yes, now the door is opened for them,
And Tanya enters. Here her prince,
Our hero, lived not so long since.
She looks about, with heart that flutters:
A cue rests on the table-top,
Upon the couch, a riding-crop.
She walks ahead. The old crone mutters:
"The fireplace, miss, please look at it—
'Twas here the master used to sit.

XVIII

"With the late Lensky almost nightly
He dined here. What fine gentlemen!
Please follow me," she said politely.
"Here you will find the master's den.
He took his coffee here, and rested,
The steward came here when requested;
Here, mornings, he would read his book . .
This too was the old master's nook;
Of Sundays, putting on his glasses,
It was his pleasure quietly
To play a game of cards with me,
Beside the window. So life passes . . .
May his soul now be with the blest,
And in the grave his bones have rest!"

XIX

Tatyana thrills with pain and pleasure
At everything she gazes on;
Each object seems a priceless treasure,
Commemorating one who's gone;
She looks, half soothed and half excited,
First at the desk, with lamp unlighted,
The pile of books no longer read,
Then at the rug that decks the bed,
The haughty portrait of Lord Byron,
The view into the moonlit night,
And likes the pallid evening light
That shows a statuette of iron:
The arms are crossed—a well-known pose—
The hat is cocked. the brow morose.

XX

In the smart sanctum, all a-quiver,
Tatyana, spell-bound, lingers still.
But it is late. Above the river,
The grove's asleep. The wind blows chill.
The dale is dark and vapor-ridden.
Behind a hill the moon is hidden;
And pleasant though it is to roam,
The fair young pilgrim must go home.
Pretending calmness, Tanya quitted
The room, though not without a sigh,
And pleading first that by-and-by
She might return; yes, if permitted,
Although the house was empty, she
Would make the den her library.

XXI

She halted at the gate-way, telling
The housekeeper a slow good-bye;
And came to the abandoned dwelling
Next day before the sun was high.
Into the silent study, setting
Aside all timid thoughts, forgetting
The world without, Tatyana crept,
And there she stayed, and wept, and wept.
The volumes at long last succeeding
In catching Tanya's eye, she took
A glance at many a curious book,
And all seemed dull. But soon the reading
Absorbed the girl, and she was thrown
Headlong into a world unknown.

XXII

Onegin's taste for books had vanished
Long since, but notice if you please
That there were works he never banished
From his affection; they were these:
Lord Byron's tales, which well consorted
With two or three bright-backed imported
Romances, upon every page
Exhibiting the present age,
And modern man's true soul divulging:
A creature arid, cold, and vain,
Careless of others' joy and pain,
In endless reverie indulging,
One whose embittered mind finds zest
In nothing, but can never rest.

XXIII

Some pages held a sharp incentive
To reading, where a finger-nail
Had marked the place; and, more attentive,
Tatyana scanned them without fail.
She noted, trembling and excited,
What passage, what remark delighted
Onegin, what shrewd line expressed
A thought in which he acquiesced.
She found the margins most appealing:
The pencil-marks he made with care
Upon the pages everywhere
Were all unconsciously revealing:
A cross, a question-mark, a word—
From these the man might be inferred.

XXIV

So Tanya bit by bit is learning
The truth, and, God be praised, can see
At last for whom her heart is yearning
By Fate's imperious decree.
A danger to all lovely ladies,
Is he from Heaven or from Hades?
This strange and sorry character,
Angel or fiend, as you prefer,
What is he? A mere imitation,
A Muscovite in Harold's cloak,
A wretched ghost, a foreign joke
But with a new interpretation,
A lexicon of snobbery
And fashion, or a parody?

XXV

Has she the answer to the riddle
And has she found *the word?* She lets
The time run on, and in the middle
Of her researches quite forgets
She should go home, where guests are waiting
And where indeed of her they're prating.
"What's to be done? She's not a child,"
The mother groans. "It drives me wild;
I've married off my younger daughter,
Tatyana should be settled, too.
But, heavens, what am I to do
When she can only throw cold water
On every single suitor's hopes?
All day she roams the woods and mopes."

XXVI

"In love with someone?" "But who is it?
Buyanov's hand she has refused,
And Petushkov's. We had a visit
From the hussar, Pykhtin, who used
As many wiles as I could mention
To win her—showed her such attention!
She must accept at last, I thought,
But no! the whole thing came to naught."
"You'll have to take her to the city—
To Moscow: it's the brides' bazaar;
That's where the eligibles are!"
"Not on my income, more's the pity!"
"But for a season it will do;
If not, my dear, I'll see you through."

XXVII

By this delightful counsel guided,
The mother fell to figuring
Expenses, and therewith decided
A Moscow winter was the thing.
The news gives Tanya little pleasure.
To let the worldlings take the measure
Of her demure provincial ways,
Revealing to their haughty gaze
Her dowdy frocks, and to their mercies
Her countrified simplicity
Of speech, and earn the mockery
Of Moscow beaus and Moscow Circes!
Oh, horror! Better far to stay
Safe in the woodland, hid away.

XXVIII

She rises as the morning flushes
With rosy light the eastern skies,
And off into the fields she rushes,
To say, with sorrow in her eyes:
"Farewell, you dear and peaceful valleys,
Familiar hills, familiar alleys,
You woodlands where I used to roam,
Farewell, you friendly skies of home;
Kind, cheerful nature, it is bitter
To leave such quiet haunts as these
For worldly shows and vanities,
The crowd, the hubbub, and the glitter!
And why? What am I striving for?
What does my future hold in store?"

XXIX

Her walks are longer, she will dally
Beside a stream, or on a hill,
And find, wherever she may sally
Some charming spot to hold her still.
Among her groves and meadows ranging,
Her fondness for them never changing,
She speaks to them as to old friends.
But all too soon the summer ends,
And golden autumn is arriving.
Pale nature shudders, tempest-tossed,
Decked out as for a holocaust . . .
The north wind breathes and bellows, driving
The clouds before him—can it be?
Winter. the sorceress, 'tis she!

XXX

In many guises she comes flying:
Upon the oak her tufts are hung;
About the hills and meadows lying,
Her billowy soft rugs are flung;
A touch, and the sharp cliffs are beveled,
The river and its banks are leveled;
Frost glistens. Mother Winter's arts
Are dazzling, and rejoice our hearts.
But Tanya does not share our pleasure,
And heedless of the winter fun,
She does not sniff the cold, or run
To the low roof to fetch her measure
Of snow, and wash her face and chest.
She glances at the road, distressed.

XXXI

The day upon which they intended
To leave, is gone; they let time slip
Away, while the old sleigh was mended
And re-upholstered for the trip.
The three *kibitkas* customary
Are crammed with all that's necessary:
With chairs and chests and casseroles,
With jams and featherbeds and bowls,
With cocks in cages (these one slaughters
In town), with pots and pans and gear
Of all sorts; finally you hear
A noise off in the servants' quarters
Of loud farewells and crying maids;
And now they bring out eighteen jades,

XXXII

And while the breakfast is preparing
They hitch them to the master's sleigh;
The maids and coachmen vie in swearing;
The loads on the *kibitkas* sway.
The bearded old postilion's mounted—
His nag has ribs that might be counted.
The servants gather at the gates
For the good-byes; the turn-out waits.
The ladies enter; now it's gliding
Away, the good old sleigh, at last.
"Farewell, the days of peace are past;
You haunts where I might stay in hiding,
Farewell! Forever, or for years?"
Tatyana cannot stop her tears.

XXXIII

Enlightenment may be belated
With us, but grows apace; indeed,
Philosophers have calculated
Five centuries are all we need
To have our roads completely mended,
And the improvement will be splendid!
For all through Russia there will run
Highways to make the country one.
We shall have arched, cast-iron bridges
And tunnels under water, too,
And if that's not enough to do,
We'll split apart the mountain ridges,
And not a station will be known
Without a tavern of its own.

XXXIV

Just now our roads are bad for coaches;
Forgotten bridges rot and sink;
And at the stations lice and roaches
Refuse to let you sleep a wink;
There are no inns. In a cold cottage
You scarce can get a dish of pottage:
The menu hangs there, in plain sight,
But just to tease your appetite;
While with his clumsy Russian hammer
The rustic cyclop labors, daft,
At Europe's dainty handicraft,
And blesses, as he halts his clamor,
The ruts and ditches that abound
Wherever there is Russian ground.

XXXV

But journeys made in wintry weather
Are far too pleasant to seem long.
The highroad, leveled altogether,
Runs smoothly as a hackneyed song.
Our dapper coachmen are astounding,
Our troikas tireless, forward bounding,
Mile-posts rejoice the idle eye,
They look like fenceposts, flashing by.
But Tanya's mother, not ignoring
The cost of post-horses, was glad
To use her own, and hence they had
To rest the nags: the halts were boring,
And Tanya found the journey bleak.
They had to travel for a week.

XXXVI

The goal is there before them. Blazing
Like fire, the gilded crosses rise
Above the domes of Moscow, dazing
With splendor unaccustomed eyes.
Ah, friends, how I rejoiced, beholding
The terraced scene, the view unfolding
Of park and palace, dome and spire,
With every church in bright attire.
How often, sick with separation,
My thoughts in exile turned to you,
Oh, Moscow, Moscow! I would view
You in my fond imagination . . .
Moscow: those syllables can start
A tumult in the Russian heart!

XXXVII

There the Petrovsky Palace, hiding
Its splendor among ancient trees,
Stands grim and grand, morosely priding
Itself upon its memories.
For here, Napoleon, elated
With his last victory, awaited
In vain a Moscow on her knees
To tender him the Kremlin keys.
But it was not capitulation
My Moscow offered Bonaparte—
No feast, no gift to warm his heart:
But she prepared a conflagration.
From here he watched with thoughtful eyes
The fierce flames reddening the skies.

XXXVIII

You witness of that fallen glory,
Farewell, proud palace! But why wait?
On with the journey and the story!
The columns of the city gate
Gleam white; the sleigh, more swift than steady,
Bumps down Tverskaya Street already.
Past sentry-boxes now they dash,
Past shops and lamp-posts, serfs who lash
Their nags, huts, mansions, monasteries,
Parks, pharmacies, Bohkarans, guards,
Fat merchants, Cossacks, boulevards,
Old women, boys with cheeks like cherries,
Lions on gates with great stone jaws,
And crosses black with flocks of daws.

XXXIX-XL

So to their destination straightway
They traveled, but a dull hour passed
Before they halted at a gateway
Off in a narrow lane, at last.
They'd come to an old aunt, now failing—
For four long years she had been ailing.
A Kalmuck, spectacled and worn,
Flings wide the door; his caftan's torn,
He holds a stocking he was mending;
Upon the parlor sofa lies
The princess, and her feeble cries
Of welcome are indeed heart-rending.
The two old women weep, embrace,
And soon their tongues begin to race.

XLI

"*Princesse!*" "Pachette! I can't believe it!"
"Yes, after all these years, Aline!"
"How long do you remain?" "Conceive it!"
"Sit down, *mon ange!*" "My dear *Cousine!*"
"It's like a novel . . . life's so chancey . . ."
"And this is my Tatyana." "Fancy!
Come here, my dear. Why, this seems all
A dream . . . *Cousine*, do you recall
Your Grandison?" "I can't remember—
My Grandison? Oh, Grandison!
Where is he? Yes, I know the one."
"He lives in Moscow. Last December
It was he came to visit me.
His son was married recently.

XLII

"The other . . . But we've time tomorrow,
N'est-ce pas, for all we want of talk?
We'll show off Tanya. To my sorrow,
I can't go out: I cannot walk—
My legs betray me . . . But it's tiring
To travel, you must be desiring
As I am, too, a little rest:
We'll go together . . . Oh, my chest! . . .
Just think, this joy, I can't endure it,
Let alone grief . . . I have no strength . . .
My dear, when old age comes at length
It's misery, and who can cure it?"
At that she could no longer hide
Her weakness, and she coughed and cried.

XLIII

Tatyana cannot but be grateful
To the kind invalid, and yet
She finds the city cold and hateful,
And does not cease to pine and fret.
Behind the strange bed's silken curtain
She lies for hours, with sleep uncertain;
And the poor girl is roused betimes
Each morning by the Moscow chimes,
The call to early labors dinning;
Out of the window she may stare—
She will not find her meadows there,
When the deep shades of night are thinning:
She sees a court she does not know,
A kitchen and a fence below.

XLIV

There is a dinner-party daily
Where Tanya's met with "oh-s" and "ah-s,"
Her wistful languor greeted gaily
By grandmammas and grandpapas.
The relatives—and there are dozens—
Are cordial to the country cousins,
And all exclaim delightedly
And offer hospitality.
"How Tanya's grown! Why, how long is it
Since you were christened? Gracious sakes!
I boxed your ears! I gave you cakes!"
She hears it all at every visit.
In chorus the old ladies cry:
"Dear me, the years have just flown by!"

XLV

They do not change, depend upon it,
But keep to their familiar ways:
Princess Yelena wears the bonnet
Of tulle she wore in other days;
Lukerya Lvovna still paints thickly,
Lubov Petrovna lies as quickly,
Ivan Petrovich ne'er was keen,
Semyon Petrovich is as mean,
Aunt Pelageya still possesses
Monsieur Finemouche, friend of the house,
And the same pom, and the same spouse,
The well-known clubman, who, God bless us,
Is just as deaf and just as meek,
And gorges seven days a week.

XLVI

Their daughters, after due embraces,
Examine Tanya silently
From head to foot, and Moscow's Graces
Are quite perplexed by such as she:
They find her odd—so unaffected,
So countrified, a bit dejected,
A namby-pamby, colorless
And thin, but pretty, more or less;
Yet soon they let down their defences,
Invite her, kiss her, press her hands,
Fluff up her hair as style commands,
And murmur sing-song confidences,
Relating with romantic art
The girlish secrets of the heart,

XLVII

Reciting all their hopes with candor,
Their conquests and their pranks with glee;
Embellished with a little slander,
The simple talk flows readily.
Then they demand in compensation
That she should offer a narration
Of her own heart's shy hopes and fears;
But Tanya, dreaming, hardly hears,
And does not pay the least attention,
But listens with an absent smile,
And guards in silence all the while
The secret she will never mention,
The treasure none can ever guess,
The source of tears and happiness.

XLVIII

The parlor hums with conversation,
In which Tatyana ought to share
She thinks, but it is sheer vexation
To hear the vulgar chatter there.
Such people with each day grow duller,
Their very slander has no color;
And every query, every tale,
Their news, their gossip—all are stale.
The hours go by: they do not waken;
No witty thought occurs, no word
Even by accident is heard
Whereby the mind or heart is shaken.
Oh, empty world! Oh, stupid folk
Who neither crack nor are a joke!

XLIX

Viewed by the archive youths who cluster
At any gathering or dance,
The poor young girl does not pass muster—
They eye our heroine askance.
One clownish fellow, idly leaning
Against a door, remarks with meaning
That she's ideal—he must jot
A poem to her on the spot.
Once Vyazemsky sat down beside her
When he was calling on an aunt
Where entertainment was but scant;
And an old gentleman espied her,
Asked who she was, set straight his wig,
And gave his neighbor's ribs a dig.

L

But where Melpomene's bold gesture
Displays to the indifferent crowd
The tawdry glitter of her vesture,
The while she howls both long and loud;
Where Thalia as she's gently napping
Is heedless of the friendly clapping;
And where the youthful galaxy
Admires alone Terpsichore
(As was the case, upon my honor,
In our time too, in days of old),
The proud lorgnettes the ladies hold
Were in no instance trained upon her,
Nor, from the loge and the parterre,
The eyeglass of the connoisseur.

LI

They take her to the Club for dances.
The rooms are thronged and hot and gay.
The blare, the lights, the shining glances,
The couples as they whirl away,
The lovely ladies' filmy dresses,
The balcony where such a press is,
The young and hopeful brides-to-be,
Confound the senses suddenly.
Here dandies now in the ascendant
Show off their impudence, their vests,
Their monocles that rake the guests.
And here hussars on leave, resplendent
And thunderous, flock eagerly:
They come, they conquer, and they flee.

LII

The stars of night are fair and many,
The Moscow belles are many, too.
Yet brighter shines the moon than any
Of her companions in the blue.
But she in whom my thoughts are rooted,
Before whom my bold lyre is muted,
'Mid maids and matrons seems to glide
Like to the moon in lonely pride.
How heavenly, as she advances,
Her motion, in pure splendor dressed!
What languor fills her lovely breast!
What languor in her magic glances!
But now, enough, have done; for you
Have paid to folly what's her due.

LIII

They waltz, they bow, they curtsey, flitting
About: a noisy laughing host . . .
While unobserved, Tatyana's sitting
Between two aunts, beside a post,
And stares unseeing, in no hurry
To join the hateful worldly flurry.
She stifles here . . . her heart is sore,
And turns to what is hers no more:
The country life, the rustic hovels,
The lonely thicket where a stream
Is all abubble and agleam,
Her flowers, her romantic novels,
And most, the linden-shaded ways
Where *he* had met her ravished gaze.

LIV

Thus far away her thoughts are flying;
The world, the ball, are both forgot,
When a great general, espying
The girl, stands rooted to the spot.
The aunts, of one thing only thinking,
Each to the other slyly winking,
Together nudge Tatyana and
Each whispers from behind her hand:
"Look quickly to the left." But balking
She asks: "The left? What's there to see?"
"Just look . . . that man . . . he's one of three
In uniform . . . Now he is walking
Away, his profile may be seen . . ."
"Who? That fat general, you mean?"

LV

Tatyana's brilliant catch discerning,
We think good wishes are the things.
But it is time I was returning
To him of whom indeed I sing . . .
And by the way, now that I mention
The subject, give me your attention:
Of my young friend I sing, and of
His whims; O hover thou above
My labors—bless them with thy beauty,
Thou epic Muse! Upon my way
Be thou my staff, nor let me stray.
Enough. Though late, I've done my duty,
To classicism doffed my hat:
Here's the exordium. That's that!

Chapter Eight

Fare thee well, and if for ever
Still for ever fare thee well.

Byron

I

When, a Lyceum lad, I flourished,
And roamed its gardens at my ease,
On Apuleius gladly nourished,
While Cicero could scarcely please;
When in the springtime I would dally
To watch the swans in some dim valley
And hear, above the lake, their cries,
The Muse first shone before my eyes.
My student cell grew bright with treasures
Such as the Muse alone can bring;
Thither she came to sport and sing
Of youthful pranks and childish pleasures.
And of the glorious days of old,
Of all the dreams the heart can hold.

II

And the world smiled upon her, pressing
On us the favors that men crave;
We won good old Derzhavin's blessing
Upon the threshold of his grave.

III

And I, all discipline refusing,
Took wilful passion for my guide;
My path was what the crowd was choosing;
The lively Muse was at my side
At giddy feasts and wild discussions,
And when, at midnight, madcap Russians,
We scared patrols with blatant noise;
She shared our banquets, crowned our joys—
Like a Bacchante at the revels,
Sang for the guests across the wine,
And ardently this Muse of mine
Was wooed by passionate young devils.
My flighty friend made quite a stir,
In short, and I was proud of her.

IV

But this gay circle I deserted,
And fled afar . . . She followed me.
How often, by her tales diverted
As I fared onward gloomily,
I heard her friendly accents soften;
And on Caucasian cliffs how often,
Like pale Lenore, by moonlight she
Would gallop side by side with me!
How oft on the dark shores of Tauris
She bade me hear the waters sing,
The Nereids' low murmuring,
The sounding waves' eternal chorus,
And the deep seas His praise rehearse
Who fathered the vast universe.

V

The feasts where wealth and wit were squandered,
The dazzling capital, forgot—
To sad Moldavia she wandered,
And in that far and savage spot
Among the tents of nomads moving,
Full soon my errant Muse was proving
As wild as they: forsook her songs
For the wild steppes' barbaric tongues,
The language of the gods rejected . . .
Then all is changed. For lo! she veers,
And as a rural miss appears
Within my garden, unexpected;
There, wistful-eyed, behold her stand,
With a French volume in her hand.

VI

And now for the first time I'm bringing
My Muse to a superb soirée;
And jealous fears my heart are stinging
As I her rustic charms survey.
Past thick-ranked guests, aristocratic,
Renowned, resplendent, diplomatic,
Fine ladies, military fops,
She glides; and now serenely stops,
And, seated, eagerly is eyeing
The glitter of the noisy press,
The flash of wit, the flouncing dress,
The gallants for their hostess vying,
The ladies, each a picture when
Framed somberly by gentlemen.

VII

She likes the talk of haughty sages
Pursued with so much elegance;
And the assorted ranks and ages,
And pride that ever looks askance.
But in a corner who is standing,
The throng with a mute eye commanding?
He seems, indeed, an alien here,
To whom these faces all appear
But tiresome ghosts. Can we unmask him?
And does his somber aspect mean
Offended vanity or spleen?
Why is he here? Who is he? Task him!
Can it be Eugene? Truly? . . . Aye!
"When did he get here, by the bye?

VIII

"Has he grown tame at last, and mellow?
Or does he follow his old bent
And as of yore play the odd fellow?
Pray whom now does he represent?
Would he be Melmoth or Childe Harold,
Or as a Quaker go appareled,
A bigot seem—a patriot—
A cosmopolitan—or what?
To a new pose will he be goaded,
Or in the end will he just be
A decent chap—like you and me?
I say: give up a style outmoded.
It's time he ceased to be a show . . ."
"Ah, then you know him?" "Yes, and no."

IX

"Then why upbraid him thus severely?
Is it because we like to sit
Upon the judgment-seat, or merely
Because rash ardor and quick wit
Are found absurd or else offensive
By those whose parts are not extensive?
Is it because intelligence
Loves elbow-room and thrusts us hence?
Or is stupidity malicious—
And trifles of importance to
Important folk, and is it true
That only mediocrity
Befits and pleases you and me?"

X

Blessèd is he who could be merry
And young in youth; blessèd is he
Who ripened, like good port or sherry,
As years went by, and readily
Grew worldly-wise as life grew chilly,
Gave up his dreams as wild and silly:
At twenty to the fashion bred,
At thirty profitably wed,
Quite free of all his debts at fifty,
Obtaining, with himself to thank,
First glory, and then wealth and rank,
All in good time, serene and thrifty—
Of whom 'twas said throughout his span:
X. is an admirable man.

XI

But oh, how deeply we must rue it,
That youth was given us in vain,
That we were hourly faithless to it,
And that it cheated us again;
That our bright pristine hopes grew battered,
Our freshest dreams grew sear, and scattered
Like leaves that in wet autumn stray,
Wind-tossed, and all too soon decay.
It's maddening to see before you
A row of dinners, dull and sure,
Find life a function to endure,
Go with the solemn folk who bore you,
For all their views and passions not,
At heart, giving a single jot.

XII

The gossips ever are malicious,
And it is very hard to bear
When they proclaim you odd or vicious,
Dub you a rogue, which is unfair,
Or else my demon—condemnation
Enough to kill a reputation.
Onegin (I return to him),
Having, to satisfy a whim,
Dispatched his friend, and had his pleasure,
And, with no aim on which to fix,
Having attained to twenty-six—
Blasé, grown tired of empty leisure,
Without affairs, or rank, or wife,
Found nothing fit to fill his life.

XIII

Thus he grew restless and decided
That he must have a change of scene
(A plaguey wish by which are guided
The few who relish toil and teen).
He left his rustics to their tillage,
Abandoning his pleasant village,
The fields' and forests' solitude
Where still the bloody ghost pursued.
And started on his aimless cruising,
By one emotion only stirred;
Till travel, as you'll have inferred,
Ceased, like all else, to be amusing.
So he returned, took Chatzky's cue,
And forthwith to a ball he flew.

XIV

And now the guests, exchanging glances,
And whispering, make quite a stir:
A lady down the room advances,
A haughty general after her.
She is not hurried, is not chilly,
Nor full of idle chat and silly;
She lacks the look of snobbishness,
The cold pretensions to success,
The little tricks that are affected
By ladies in society . . .
Hers is a still simplicity.
She seems the image quite perfected
Of *comme il faut*—Shishkov, berate
Me if you must: I can't translate.

XV

The ladies all pressed closer to her;
Old women smiled as she went by;
Men, while they did not dare pursue her,
Bowed lower, sought to catch her eye;
Young girls, in passing, hushed their chatter;
The general, since such tributes flatter
An escort much, puffed out his chest
And raised his nose above the rest.
She was no beauty: that were fiction
To utter, yet she'd not a trace,
From head to foot, in form or face,
Of what, in fashionable diction
And in high London circles, they
Term *vulgar*. To my great dismay,

XVI

Although I find it so expressive,
The word is one I can't translate:
Its vogue—since we are not progressive,
And the word's new—should not be great.
For epigrams it would be splendid . . .
But here's our lady unattended.
All nonchalance and charm and grace,
She at a table took her place
Beside that most superb of creatures,
Fair Nina Voronskaya, who
Presents to the Neva a view
Of Cleopatra, but whose features,
However dazzling to the sight,
Cannot eclipse her neighbor's quite.

XVII

"Can it, indeed," thinks Eugene, "can it
Be she? It is . . . But no . . . And yet . . .
To come, as from another planet,
From that dull hole . . ." And his lorgnette
Repeatedly and almost grimly
Is trained on her whose features dimly
Remind him of a face forgot.
"Forgive me, Prince, but can you not
Say who it is that now the Spanish
Ambassador is speaking to?
She's wearing raspberry." "Yes, you
Have been away! Before you vanish
Again, you'll meet her, 'pon my life!"
"But tell me who she is." "My wife."

XVIII

"Well, that is news—couldn't be better!
You're married long?" "Two years." "To whom?"
"A Larina." "Tanya?" "You've met her?"
"I am their neighbor." "Come, resume
Your friendship." At this invitation
The prince's comrade and relation
Now met his spouse. The princess gazed
At him . . . And if she was amazed,
And if the sudden sight dismayed her,
And if her soul was deeply stirred,
No look, no tremor, not a word
In any small degree betrayed her:
Her manner was what it had been
Before, her bow was as serene.

XIX

Not only did she fail to shiver,
Turn pale or blush, as one distressed . . .
Her eyebrows did not even quiver,
Nor yet were her soft lips compressed.
Not all Onegin's observation
Could show him an approximation
To Tanya of the days that were;
He wanted to converse with her
And . . . could not. Now she spoke, inquiring
When he had come, and if, of late,
He'd had a glimpse of his estate;
Then, with a look that showed her tiring,
Begged that her husband suffer her
To leave . . . Our Eugene could not stir.

XX

Can it be that Tatyana truly
Whom, at the start of our romance,
Quite tête-à-tête he'd lectured duly
(You will recall the circumstance)?
How noble was the tone he'd taken;
The spot itself was God-forsaken.
Can this be she who long since wrote—
He has it still—a touching note,
A letter heartfelt, artless, candid;
That little girl . . . is it a dream?
That little girl he did not deem
It wrong to scorn when pride commanded—
Can it be she who only now
Showed him so cold and calm a brow?

XXI

He quits the rout, and, meditating,
Drives home; and so at last to bed:
Thoughts sad and sweet still agitating
The sleepless fellow's heart and head.
He wakes to find a note—that's pleasant:
The prince invites him to be present
At a soirée. "God! to see her! . . .
I'll go!" And he does not defer
The polite "yes" that is behooving.
Is he bewitched? It's very droll.
By what is his cold torpid soul
Now stirred? Is it vexation moving
The man? Or vanity, forsooth?
Or love, the grave concern of youth?

XXII

He counts the slow hours, vainly trying
To hurry them: he cannot wait.
The clock strikes ten: he's off, he's flying,
And suddenly he's at the gate.
He goes in to the princess, quaking;
Tatyana is alone; but making
An effort to converse with her,
He finds that no remarks occur
To him; and thereby sadly daunted,
Onegin fumbles as he seeks
To answer when the lady speaks.
By one persistent thought he's haunted.
He does not cease his stubborn stare:
She sits with an untroubled air.

XXIII

The husband enters: the appalling
Bleak tête-à-tête concludes; he cheers
His friend Onegin by recalling
The pranks and jokes of former years.
The guests, arriving, hear their laughter.
The talk is seasoned well thereafter
With the coarse salt of malice, while
Light nothings, spoken without guile
And without foolish affectation,
Give way in turn to common sense:
Not deep or learned or intense,
But reasonable conversation,
That does not frighten anyone
With a too wanton kind of fun.

XXIV

Here the patricians congregated,
Here fashionables would repair,
The dolts that must be tolerated,
The faces one meets everywhere;
Here, bonneted and wearing roses,
And with the malice time imposes,
Were ladies of a certain age,
And prim young misses looking sage;
Here an ambassador was weighing
Affairs of state, and over there
An ancient, with perfumed gray hair,
Was jesting subtly and displaying
The fine keen wit of yesteryear
Which nowadays seems somewhat queer.

XXV

Here was a man who had a weakness
For epigrams, and was annoyed
By too-sweet tea, the ladies' meekness,
The tone the gentlemen employed,
A talked-of novel, rather hazy,
A monogram he found too mazy,
The lies that journals perpetrate,
The war, the snow-fall, and his mate.

....
....
....
....
....
....

XXVI

And here too was [Prolasov], stunted
In soul, of all the guests the least
Admired—in sketching whom you blunted
Your wicked pencils, oh, St. Priest!
While in the doorway took his station—
As perfect as an illustration—
A ballroom tyrant, tightly laced,
Mute, motionless, and cherub-faced;
And there a traveler from a distance,
A brazen fellow, starched and proud,
With studied ways amused the crowd
That scarce had heard of his existence,
And though he met with no rebuff,
The guests' sly glances were enough.

XXVII

But Eugene's sole preoccupation
Was with Tatyana—not, forsooth,
The poor shy girl whose adoration
Of him had filled his simple youth,
But the proud princess, cold and serious,
The queen, aloof, remote, imperious,
Of the magnificent Neva.
Oh, humans, like your first mamma,
Ancestral Eve, you find delightful
Not what you have, but what you see
Afar: the serpent and the tree
Seduce you, though the cost be frightful.
Forbidden fruits alone entice—
Without them, there's no paradise.

XXVIII

How changed Tatyana is! How truly
She knows her rôle! With none to thank—
Tutored by her own wit—she duly
Bears the proud burden of her rank!
Who, in this cool majestic woman,
The ballroom's ruler, scarcely human,
Would dare to seek that gentle girl?
And he had set her heart awhirl!
When nights were dark and she, forsaken
By Morpheus, her dark eyes would rest
Upon the moon, and her young breast
By virginal desires was shaken,
Then in a dream that naught could dim
She'd walk life's humble road with him.

XXIX

To love all ages owe submission;
To youthful hearts its tempests bring
The very boon they would petition,
As fields are blest by storms of spring:
The rain of passion is not cruel,
But bears refreshment and renewal—
There is a quickening at the root
That bodes full flowers and honeyed fruit.
But at the late and sterile season,
At the sad turning of the years,
The tread of passion augurs tears:
Thus autumn gusts deal death and treason,
And turn the meadow to a marsh
And leave the forests gaunt and harsh.

XXX

Alas, our poor Onegin's smitten:
Tatyana fills his every thought;
His heart is by such anguish bitten
As only passion can have wrought.
He does not heed the mind's reproaches,
But, rain or shine, each day his coach is
Before her door; he waits for her;
No shadow could be faithfuller.
He knows delight when he's adjusting
The boa on her shoulders, and
When his hot fingers touch her hand,
Or when through liveried throngs he's thrusting
A way for her; he's happy if
He may pick up her handkerchief.

XXXI

She does not heed; and sore it grieves him
To note how little she is stirred;
With perfect freedom she receives him;
When guests are there, she says a word
Or bows to him—a cold convention;
At times she pays him no attention;
She has no trace of coquetry—
It's frowned on in society.
But though Onegin's peace forsake him
And his cheek pale, she does not see
Or does not care; and all agree
Consumption yet may overtake him.
He's sent to doctors, the Neva's
Best leeches send him to the spas.

XXXII

But he refuses; he's preparing
To meet his fathers speedily;
Tatyana shows no sign of caring
(Such is the sex, you will agree);
And he, reluctant to surrender,
Still clings to hope, though it be slender,
And far too wretched to be meek
He pens, with trembling hand and weak,
A missive eloquent of passion.
He did not value letters much,
And rightly, but his pain was such
That write he must, and in this fashion—
Perhaps 'twill please you if I quote
The very words Onegin wrote.

Onegin's Letter to Tatyana

All is foreseen: when I confess
My mournful secret you will shun me:
And the grave eyes that have undone me
Will look with scorn on my distress!
Indeed what can I hope for, after
You know the truth? What is the use
Of speech? For what malicious laughter
Do I thus give you an excuse?

We met by chance; I, though perceiving
Affection's spark in you, believing
Myself mistaken, did not dare
To let the tender habit seize me;
Although my freedom did not please me,
The loss of it I could not bear.
And one thing more put us asunder—
Poor Lensky fell . . . that luckless day,
From all the heart holds dear, my blunder
Forced me to tear my heart away;
An alien, roving unrestricted,
I took this peace, this liberty,
For happiness. Good God! I see
How justly now I am afflicted.

No, to be with you constantly;
To follow you with deep devotion;
And with enamored eyes to see
Each smile of yours, each glance, each motion;
To listen to you, late and soon;
To know you: spirit tuned to spirit;
In torment at your feet to swoon—
Were bliss; and death? I should not fear it!

It may not be: without relief,
I drag myself about; time's hasting,
And it is precious, being brief:
Yet in vain boredom I am wasting
The hours allotted me by Fate,
And oh, they are a weary weight!
My days are counted: I've had warning;
But to endure I need one boon—
I must be certain in the morning
Of seeing you by afternoon. . . .

I fear lest in my supplication
You should perceive with eye severe
A trick worthy of detestation;
Already your reproach I hear.
If you but knew how agonizing
It is to parch with hot desire,
By mental effort tranquilizing
The blood that burns with frantic fire;
To long to clasp your knees, and, throbbing
With anguish, pour out at your feet
Appeal, complaint, confession, sobbing
The wretched story out, complete,—
And longing thus, be forced to meet you
With a feigned chill in look and voice,
Converse at ease, seem to rejoice,
And with a cheerful eye to greet you!—

So be it; but I had to speak;
Now I am at your mercy, guided
But by your will; my fate's decided;
And I have learned how to be meek.

XXXIII

There is no answer to his letter;
A second, and a third he sends,
Alas, these missives fare no better.
Then, at a party he attends
He comes upon her, as he enters.
How firmly her attention centers
On all but him! She never sees
Onegin, but she seems to freeze
As he comes near; it's no illusion:
Upon her wrath her lips are sealed.
Onegin watches her, congealed:
Where is compassion, where confusion?
Is there a sign of tears? No trace!
Mute anger only marks her face . . .

XXXIV

Yes, and the fear of the impression
The world would gain if it should learn
About her early indiscretion . . .
No more my Eugene could discern . . .
All hope is gone! He leaves, and curses
His madness—and again immerses
Himself so deep in it that he
Once more forsakes society.
Now in his study he bethought him
Of days long past, when he had been
A giddy fop, and cruel spleen
Had chased him and had quickly caught him,
And locked him in a corner where
The lonely gloom was hard to bear.

XXXV

Again a book was his sole crony—
He read at will: Gibbon, Rousseau,
Chamfort and Herder and Manzoni,
Madame de Staël, Bichat, Tissot;
Devoured Stendhal, the arrant skeptic,
And Fontenelle, acute, eupeptic;
And Russians too he would peruse:
He was not one to pick and choose.
He read miscellany and journal,
The magazines that like to scold
Us all, and where I now am told
That my performance is infernal,
Though once they praised my magic pen:
E sempre bene, gentlemen.

XXXVI

What of it? Though his eyes were busy,
His mind was ever far away;
With whirling thoughts his soul grew dizzy,
And dreams and musings far from gay.
The page he read could scarcely bore him,
Because, between the lines before him,
Another set of lines transpired
Of which Onegin never tired.
These were the secret fond traditions
Of intimacies of the past,
And rootless dreams that could not last,
Vague threats, predictions, and suspicions,
A fairy tale that lasts the night,
Or letters that a girl might write.

XXXVII

And as he reads, both thought and feeling
Are lulled to sleep, and readily
Imagination is unreeling
Its parti-colored pageantry.
The first clear picture is disclosing
A youth, who on the snow seems dozing;
As Eugene stares his heart is chilled
To hear a voice cry: "Well? He's killed."
He sees forgotten foes, malicious
Detractors, cowardly and vile,
And cruel traitresses who smile,
And old companions, dull and vicious;
A country house he next may see—
She's at the window—always she! . . .

XXXVIII

Thus sunk in reveries, he nearly
Went raving mad or worse: became
A poet—this were paying dearly
For dreams, and would have been a shame.
But by some influence despotic,
Call it magnetic or hypnotic,
My brainless pupil almost learned
The way a Russian verse is turned.
He looked the poet, when he'd let a
Long evening pass, while he would sit
Beside the fire and hum to it
"*Idol mio*" or "*Benedetta*,"
Until the flames blazed up anew
Fed by his slipper or review.

XXXIX

The days speed by; before you know it
New warmth has melted winter's chain;
But he has not become a poet,
He did not die or go insane.
And now, at spring's bright invitation,
He quits his place of hibernation—
Close as a marmot would require—
The double windows, the snug fire;
And one fine morning finds him flying
Past the Neva in a swift sleigh;
On the streaked ice the sunbeams play;
Upon the streets the snow is lying,
By thaw and grimy steps defaced.
But whither in such anxious haste

XL

Does Eugene drive? Yes, I suspected
You knew the answer—as you say:
This same odd fellow, uncorrected,
To his Tatyana makes his way.
Looking too corpselike to be nobby,
He walks into the empty lobby.
Each room he finds unoccupied.
Here is a door—he flings it wide,
And halts in sudden deep confusion;
What sight thus fills him with dismay?
The princess, pale, in négligé,
Pores o'er a letter, in seclusion;
Her cheeks rests on her hand, and she
Is weeping, weeping quietly.

XLI

Her voiceless grief was past disguising;
In that swift moment one could see
The former Tanya, recognizing
Her in the princess readily!
As Eugene, by regrets distracted,
Fell at her feet, his heart contracted;
She shuddered, mute; her lovely eyes
Betrayed no anger, no surprise
As she surveyed him . . . His dejected
And healthless look, his dumb remorse—
These spoke to her with silent force.
And in her soul was resurrected
The simple girl whose dreams, whose ways,
Whose heart belonged to other days.

XLII

She does not raise him, leaves him kneeling;
Nor from his greedy lips withdraws
Her passive hands; her pain concealing,
She gazes at him without pause . . .
What are her reveries unspoken?
The silence at long last is broken
As she says gently: "Rise; have done.
I must say candid words or none.
Onegin, need I ask you whether
You still retain the memory
Of that lost hour beneath the tree
When destiny brought us together?
You lectured me, I listened, meek;
Today it is my turn to speak.

XLIII

"Then I was younger, maybe better,
Onegin, and I loved you; well?
How did you take my girlish letter?
Your heart responded how? Pray, tell!
Most harshly: there was no disguising
Your scorn. You did not find surprising
The plain girl's love? Why, even now,
I freeze—good God!—recalling how
You came and lectured me so coldly—
Your look that made my spirit sink!
But for that sermon do not think
I blame you . . . For you acted boldly,
Indeed, you played a noble rôle:
I thank you from my inmost soul . . .

XLIV

"Then, far from Moscow's noise and glitter,
Off in the wilds—is it not true?—
You did not like me . . . That was bitter,
But worse, what now you choose to do!
Why do you pay me these attentions?
Because society's conventions,
Deferring to my wealth and rank,
Have given me prestige? Be frank!
Because my husband's decoration,
A soldier's, wins us friends at Court,
And all would relish the report
That I had stained my reputation—
'Twould give you in society
A pleasant notoriety?

XLV

"I cannot help it: I am weeping . . .
If you recall your Tanya still,
One thought I would that you were keeping
In mind: that if I had my will,
I would prefer your harsh cold fashion
Of speech to this insulting passion,
To these long letters and these tears.
My childish dreams, my tender years,
Aroused your pity then . . . You're kneeling
Here at my feet. But dare you say
In truth what brought you here today?
What petty thought? What trivial feeling?
Can you, so generous, so keen,
Be ruled by what is small and mean?

XLVI

"To me, Onegin, all these splendors,
The tinsel of unwelcome days,
The homage that the gay world tenders,
My handsome house and my soirées—
To me all this is naught. This minute
I'd give my house and all that's in it,
This giddy play in fancy-dress,
For a few books, a wilderness
Of flowers, for our modest dwelling,
The scene where first I saw your face,
Onegin, that familiar place,
And for the simple churchyard, telling
Its tale of humble lives, where now
My poor nurse sleeps beneath the bough . . .

XLVII

"And happiness, before it glided
Away forever, was so near! . . . .
But now my fate is quite decided.
I was in too much haste, I fear;
My mother coaxed and wept; the sequel
You know; besides, all lots were equal
To hapless Tanya . . . Well, and so
I married. Now, I beg you, go.
I know your heart; I need not tremble,
Because your honor and your pride
Must in this matter be your guide.
I love you (why should I dissemble?)
But I became another's wife;
I shall be true to him through life."

XLVIII

She went. Onegin stood forsaken,
Stood thunderstruck. He could not stir.
By what a storm his heart was shaken:
What pride, what grief, what thoughts of her!
But are those stirrups he is hearing?
Tatyana's husband is appearing.
At this unlucky moment, we
Must leave my hero, ruefully,
For a long time . . . indeed, forever.
Together we have traveled far.
Congratulations! Now we are
Ashore at last, and our endeavor
Accomplished in the end. Three cheers!
You'll grant it's time to part, my dears.

XLIX

Whoever you may be, my reader,
Ally or enemy, attend
The words of this most earnest pleader:
Pray say farewell as to a friend.
Whatever in these careless stanzas
You seek: be it extravaganzas
Of memory, or welcome rest,
A living picture, or a jest,
Or merely some mistakes in grammar,
God grant you find some trifle here
To earn a smile, a dream, a tear,
Or rouse a journalistic clamor.
And now, since I've no more to tell,
I take my leave of you—farewell.

L

You too, farewell, my curious neighbor,
And you, my fair ideal, too,
And you, small fruit of eager labor:
My little book. With you I knew
The truest source of inspiration:
The world's oblivious animation,
And talk that brighten's friendship's ways.
How many swiftly flitting days
Have passed since in a hazy vision
I first saw young Tatyana glide
With her Onegin at her side—
Ere yet the crystal with precision
Had shown to my enchanted glance
The vista of a free romance!

LI

But those good friends who were insistent
That the first strophes should be read
To them . . . alas, some now are distant,
Some are no more, as Saadi said.
Onegin's portrait has been finished,
But, lacking them, the joy's diminished;
And she—she who for Tanya posed . . .
How many chapters Fate has closed!
Blesséd is he who leaves the glory
Of life's gay feast ere time is up,
Who does not drain the brimming cup,
Nor read the ending of the story,
But drops it without more ado,
As, my Onegin, I drop you.

NOTES

PUSHKIN provided his text with a number of notes, only some of which it seemed necessary to reproduce here. To assist the foreign reader, several others have been added by the editor.

Dedication, addressed to Pyotr Alexandrovich Pletnyov.

Chapter I

STANZA II, LINE 5. Ruslan and Ludmila: hero and heroine of Pushkin's first narrative poem.

LINE 14. Written during the author's Southern exile.
STANZA IX. In preparing the text for the press Pushkin occasionally omitted one or more stanzas, or left one unfinished, indicating the gap either by dots or by giving merely the number of the stanza. Whatever moved him to make these omissions, and fear of censorship seems to have been a minor factor, he did not go to the trouble of re-numbering the stanzas. He may have wished thus to tease the reader's imagination.
STANZA XV, LINE 13. Breguet: a repeater which took its name from a famous watch-maker of the period.
STANZA XVI, LINE 5. Talon: a well-known restaurateur.
AUTHOR'S NOTE

LINE 6. Kaverin: the name of this friend of Pushkin's did not figure in the early editions of the text, but is found in the manuscript.
LINE 8. There was an exceptionally fine vintage in

1811, a year which was also marked by the appearance of a comet.

STANZA XVIII. Fonvizen and Knyazhnin were eighteenth-century playwrights, the first a satirist of a liberal temper, the second having the reputation of "the Russian Racine." Semyonova, an actress who played Shakespearean rôles and acted in the tragedies written by Ozerov, a dramatist who belonged to the generation that preceded Pushkin's. Katenin, a friend of Pushkin's, translated French tragedies, while Shakhovskoy was a prolific author of comedies; both men were somewhat older than Pushkin. Didelot was a French choreographer established in Russia.

STANZA XX, LINE 8. Istomina: a celebrated *ballerina;* she danced in a ballet, arranged by Didelot, based on Pushkin's poem, "The Caucasian Prisoner."

STANZA XXIV, LINE 12. To this passage Pushkin attached a note in which, after quoting some relevant lines from Rousseau's *Confessions*, he wrote: "Grimm was in advance of his age. Nowadays, throughout enlightened Europe, nails are cleaned with a special little brush."

STANZA XXV, LINE 5. Chadayev (Chaadayev); the name of another friend of Pushkin's which also figures only in the manuscript: the Russian Beau Brummel; the Russian Ambassador to France is supposed to have said that Chadayev should be exhibited in every capital so as to show the Europeans *"un russe parfaitement comme il faut."*

STANZA XLII. This entire ironic stanza is nothing but subtle praise of our fair compatriots. Thus Boileau, in the guise of reproach, lauds Louis XIV. Our ladies combine enlightenment with amiability and strict moral purity with that Oriental charm which so captivated Mme. de Staël.

AUTHOR'S NOTE

STANZA XLVIII, LINE 3. The bard: Muravyov.
STANZA XLIX, LINE 7. The reference is to Byron.

STANZA L, LINE 3. The beach: written at Odessa, on the
Black Sea, when the author was in quasi-exile.

LINE 10. On his mother's side, the author is of African
origin. His great-grandfather, Abram Petrovich Annibal,
at the age of eight was kidnapped from the shores of
Africa and taken to Constantinople. The Russian envoy
rescued him and sent him as a gift to Peter the Great,
who had him baptized at Wilno. His brother went to
Constantinople and afterwards to St. Petersburg, offering
a ransom for him, but Peter I did not agree to return
his godson. Till a very advanced age Annibal remembered Africa, his father's luxurious life, his nineteen
brothers. He was himself the youngest boy; he remembered how they would be brought to their father, their
hands tied behind their backs, while he alone was free,
swimming where the fountains of the paternal home
were playing; he also remembered his favorite sister,
Lagan, who, at a distance, swam after the ship in which
he was being carried off.

At the age of eighteen, Annibal was sent by the Czar
to France, where he began his service in the Regent's
army; he returned to Russia with a split head and the
rank of lieutenant in the French army. From then on he
never left the Emperor's side. In Anna's reign, Annibal,
who had incurred Bühren's personal enmity, was transferred to Siberia under a specious pretext. Wearied by
the lack of companionship and the inclemency of the
climate, he returned to Petersburg without leave and
went straight to his friend, Münnich. Münnich was
amazed and advised him to go into hiding immediately.
Annibal retired to his estates, where he lived throughout the remaining years of Anna's reign, nominally considered to be serving in Siberia. Empress Elizabeth, on
ascending the throne, showered him with favors. He retired from service with the rank of General-in-Chief,
and died in Catherine's reign at the age of ninety-two.
(In time we expect to publish a complete biography of
him.)

In Russia, where, for lack of historical memoirs, the

remembrance of remarkable men soon vanishes, Annibal's curious life is known only from stories preserved by the family.

His son, Lieutenant General I. A. Annibal, was unquestionably among the most distinguished men of the age of Catherine (he died in 1800).

AUTHOR'S NOTE

STANZA LVII, LINES 9-10. The reference is to the heroines of two of Pushkin's narrative poems: "The Prisoner of the Caucasus," and "The Fountain of Bakhchi-Saray."

Chapter II

STANZA V, LINE 9. A mason: freemason; the term carried with it a suggestion of subversive tendencies.
STANZA XXIV, LINES 2-9. Among us, euphonious Greek names, as, for example, Agafon, Filat, Fedora, Fekla, are used only by the common people.

AUTHOR'S NOTE

Chapter III

STANZA V, LINE 3. Svetlana: the heroine of a ballad by Zhukovsky, an older friend of Pushkin's.
STANZA IX, LINES 7-8. Malek-Adhel: the hero of a novel by Mme. Cottin, an eighteenth-century writer; Gustave de Linar: a character in *Valérie*, a novel by Baroness Barbara von Krüdener; St. Preux and Wolmar: characters in *La Nouvelle Héloise*, by Rousseau.
STANZA X, LINE 4. Julie: the heroine of *La Nouvelle Héloise;* Clarissa: the heroine of *Clarissa Harlowe;* Delphine: the leading character in a novel of the same name by Mme. de Staël.
STANZA XII, LINES 7-11. Melmoth: the reference is to

Maturin's *Melmoth, the Wanderer; Jean Sbogar:* a novel by Charles Nodier.

STANZA XXVII, LINE 4. In the original, the Moscow Magazine is referred to by title: *The Well-Intentioned.*

STANZA XXIX, LINE 8. The original refers explicitly to the verse of Bogdanovich, an eighteenth-century poet who aimed to amuse.

STANZA XXX. The reference is to Baratynsky, a minor poet, and a friend of Pushkin's. For some misdemeanor, he was expelled from the Corps of Pages and sent to Finland to serve as a private.

Chapter IV

STANZA VII, LINES 1-2. Here Pushkin is paraphrasing a remark he made in a letter written from Kishinev in the autumn of 1822 to his brother: *"Je vous observerai seulement que moins on aime une femme et plus on est sûr de l'avoir."*

STANZA XXX, LINE 6. Tolstoy: F. P. Tolstoy, an artist of the period.

STANZA XXXI, LINE 10. Yazykov: a lyricist contemporary with Pushkin.

STANZA XXXII. The reference is to Wilhelm Küchelbecker, a schoolmate of Pushkin's who was a minor poet and author of an essay praising the ode.

LINE 10. The emblems of the classical stage.

STANZA XXXIII, LINE 5. Ivan Dmitriev: a fabulist, author of a satire on writers of odes.

STANZA XLIII, LINE 10. Dominique de Pradt, a French prelate who was Napoleon's chaplain; his political writings were popular in Russia.

STANZA L, LINE 12. The reference is to August Lafontaine, a German writer of the period who produced one hundred and fifty sentimental novels.

Chapter V

STANZA III, LINES 5-7. See "First Snow," a poem by Prince Vyazemsky.

AUTHOR'S NOTE

LINES 13-14. See the description of the Finnish winter in Baratynsky's *Eda*.

AUTHOR'S NOTE

STANZA VIII, LINES 9-14. The first song is an omen of death, while *Pussy* foretells a wedding. Its opening lines run:

> Tom-cat calls his Puss
> To sleep on the stove.

STANZA IX. The girl is supposed to see her future husband in the mirror, and to learn his name from the stranger she accosts.

STANZA X, LINE 6. In Zhukovsky's ballad, Svetlana, the heroine makes the same preparations that Tatyana does, expecting that the mirror will reflect the image of her future husband as his spirit takes a place opposite her at the table; she falls asleep, and has a terrifying dream.

LINE 12. Lel: a Slavonic divinity, of dubious authenticity, presiding over married love.

STANZA XXII, LINE 13. With us, fortune-books are published under the imprint of Martin Zadeka, who is not their author, as B. M. Fyodorov points out.

AUTHOR'S NOTE

STANZA XXIII, LINE 5. *Malvine,* a novel by Mme. Cottin.

LINE 9. Two Petriads: poems about Peter the Great by Shirinsky-Shikhmatov and Gruzintzev.

STANZA XXVI, LINES 10-11. Buyanov: a character in a poem by Pushkin's uncle, whence the cousinship.

STANZA XXXII, LINE 11. Zizi: Yevpraxiya Wulf, a rather

plump young girl with whom Pushkin conducted a flirtation when he was confined to the family estate at Mikhailovskoye. In a letter to his brother he wrote: "The other day Yevpraxiya and I compared the sizes of our waists and found them to be identical. Consequently, either I have a girth of a fifteen-year-old girl or she has that of a twenty-five-year-old man."

STANZA XXXVI, LINE 8. See Note to Stanza XV, Chapter I.

STANZA XL, LINE 4. The reference is to Francesco Albani, an Italian painter of the seventeenth century whom Pushkin admired.

CHAPTER VI

STANZA V, LINE 13. The reference is to Very Frères, a celebrated restaurant in Paris.

STANZA XX, LINE 14. Anton Delwig, a minor poet, was a schoolmate and intimate friend of Pushkin's.

STANZA XXV, LINE 13. Lepage: a famous gunsmith.

AUTHOR'S NOTE

CHAPTER VII

STANZA IV, LINE 4. Levshin: author of many works on rural economy.

AUTHOR'S NOTE

STANZA XIX, LINES 13-14. The statuette is of Napoleon.

STANZA XXII, LINES 6-14. It is believed that one of these novels was *Adolphe* by Benjamin Constant.

STANZA XXIV, LINE 10. The reference is to Childe Harold.

STANZA XXXVII. The Petrovsky Palace, just outside of Moscow, was the place where Napoleon found refuge from the fires that were ravaging the city.

STANZA XLIX, LINE 1. The reference is to a select group of young highbrows who served in the Moscow archives of the Foreign Office.

LINE 9. The reference is presumably to Prince Peter Vyazemsky, a minor author and brilliant conversationalist, who was a life-long friend of Pushkin's.

CHAPTER VIII

STANZAS I-V are romanticized autobiography.

STANZA II, LINE 3. The reference is to the examination at the Lyceum when Pushkin, as a boy of sixteen, received, for a poem of his own composition, the congratulations of the venerable poet Derzhavin, who was among those present.

STANZA IV, LINE 7. Lenore: the heroine of Bürger's ballad of that title.

STANZA XIII, LINE 13. Chatzky: a character in Griboyedov's famous comedy, *Woe from Wit*.

STANZA XIV, LINE 13. Shishkov: a vice-admiral who held various posts, including that of Minister of Education; he was a fanatical conservative and purist in linguistic matters.

STANZA XVI. LINE 11. Nina Voronskaya; probably countess A. F. Zakrevskaya, "the bronze Venus," with whom Pushkin was at one time in love and whom he depicted in his poem, "Portrait."

STANZA XXVI, LINE 4. Count Emmanuel St. Priest was a caricaturist of the period.

STANZA XXXV, LINE 3. Chamfort: an eighteenth-century French author, best known for his aphorisms.

LINE 4. Bichat: an eighteenth-century French physiologist; Tissot: a French historian of the period.

STANZA XXXVIII, LINE 12. *Idol mio:* the first words of a refrain in a duettino by Vincenzo Gabussi; *Benedetta sia la madre:* a Venetian barcarolle.

STANZA L, LINES 1-2. The reference is to Onegin and Tatyana.

Lines 8-14. Pushkin spent eight years on the writing of *Eugene Onegin*.
Stanza LI, Line 3. This is a veiled allusion to the au thor's friends among the exiled Decembrists.

III

Folk Tales

THE TALE OF THE POPE AND
OF HIS WORKMAN BALDÀ[1]

Porridge-head
Was a pope, who is dead.
He went out a-shopping one day
To look for some wares on the way;
And he came on Baldà, who was there,
Who was going he knew not where,
And who said, "Why so early abroad, old sire?
And what dost require?"
He replied, "For a workman I look,
To be stableman, carpenter, cook;
But where to procure
Such a servant?—a cheap one, be sure!"
Says Baldà, "I will come as thy servant,
I'll be spendid, and punctual, and fervent;
And my pay for the year is—three raps on thy head;
Only, give me boiled wheat when I'm fed."
Then he pondered, that pope;
Scratched his poll, put his hope
In his luck, in the Russian *Perhaps*.
"There are raps," he bethought him, *"and* raps."
And he said to Baldà, "Let it be so;
There is profit for thee and for me so;
Go and live in my yard,
And see that thou work for me nimbly and hard."

[1] The word means blockhead. Editor's Note

315

And he lives with the pope, does Baldà,
And he sleeps on straw pallet; but ah!
He gobbles like four men,
Yet he labors like seven or more men.
The sun is not up, but the work simply races;
The strip is all ploughed, and the nag in the traces;
All is bought and prepared, and the stove is well
    heated;
And Baldà bakes the egg and he shells it—they eat it;
And the popess heaps praise on Baldà,
And the daughter just pines for Baldà, and is sad;
And the little pope calls him *papa*;
And he boils up the gruel, and dandles the lad.

But only the pope never blesses
Baldà with his love and caresses,
For he thinks all the while of the reckoning;
Time flies, and the hour of repayment is beckoning!
And scarce can he eat, drink, or sleep, for, alack,
Already he feels on his forehead the crack.
So he makes a clean breast to the popess
And he asks where the last rag of hope is.
Now the woman is keen and quick-witted
And for any old trickery fitted,
And she says, "I have found us, my master,
A way to escape the disaster:
Some impossible job to Baldà now allot,
And command it be done to the very last jot;
So thy forehead will never be punished, I say,
And thou never shalt pay him, but send him away."

Then the heart of the pope is more cheerful
And his looks at Baldà are less fearful,
And he calls him: "Come here to me, do,
Baldà, my good workman and true!

Now listen: some devils have said
They will pay me a rent every year till I'm dead.
The income is all of the best; but arrears
Have been due from those devils for three mortal years.
So, when thou hast stuffed thyself full with the wheat,
Collect from those devils my quit-rent, complete."

It is idle to jar with the pope; so he,
Baldà, goes out and sits by the sea,
And there to twisting a rope he sets
And its further end in the sea he wets.
And an ancient fiend from the sea comes out:
"Baldà, why sneakest thou hereabout?"
—"I mean with the rope the sea to wrinkle
And your cursed race to cramp and crinkle."
And the ancient then is grieved in mind:
"Oh why, oh why, art thou thus unkind?"
—"Are ye asking *why*? and have not you
Forgotten the time when the rent was due?
But now, you dogs, we shall have our joke,
And you soon will find in your wheel a spoke."
—"O dear Baldà, let the sea stop wrinkling,
And all the rent is thine in a twinkling.
I will send thee my grandson—wait awhile."
—"He is easy enough," thinks Baldà, "to beguile!"

Then the messenger imp from the ocean darted,
And to mew like a famished kitten started.
"Good morrow, Baldà, my dear muzhik!
Now tell me, what is it, this rent you seek?
We never heard of your rent—that's flat;
Why, we devils have never had worries like that!
Yet take it, no matter!—on this condition,
For such is the judgment of our commission,
So that no grievance hereafter be—

That each of us run right round the sea,
And the quickest shall have the whole of the tax.
Our folk, meanwhile, have made ready their sacks."

Then said Baldà, and he laughed so slily,
"Is this, my friend, thy device so wily?
Shall the likes of thee in rivalry
Contend with the great Baldà, with *me*?
Art thou the foe who is sent to face me?
My little brother shall here replace me."

Then goes Baldà to the nearest copse;
Catches two hares, that in sack he pops,
And returns to the sea once more,
To the devilkin by the shore.
And he grips one hare by the ear;
"Thou shalt dance to our own balalaika, my dear.
Thou, devilkin, art but young and frail;
Dost thou strive with me? thou wilt only fail;
It is time and labor lost for thee;
Outstrip my brother, and thou shalt see!
So, one, two, three, and away—now race him!"

Then off goes the imp, and the hare to chase him.
And the imp by the seashore coasted,
But the hare to the forest posted.
Now the imp has circled the seas about,
And he flies in panting, his tongue lolls out,
And his snout turns up, and he's thoroughly wet,
With his paw he towels away the sweat,
And he thinks he has settled Baldà. But there!
Baldà is stroking the brother-hare,
And repeating, "My own, my deary,
Now rest, my poor brother. for thou art weary!"
Then the imp of a heap was struck,

And tamely his tail through his legs he stuck;
At the brother-hare he glanced askew,
Said, "Wait, I will fetch the rent for you."
When he got to his grandad, "Too bad!" he said;
"Baldà—the young one—got right ahead."

Then the ancient fiend had a notion;
But Baldà made a noise and commotion,
And the ocean was vexed,
And the waters were parted next,
And the imp slipt out: " 'Tis enough, muzhik;
We will send to you all the rent you seek.
But listen; dost thou behold this stick?
Now, choose thou a mark, and take thy pick;
And the one who the stick can farthest shoot, he
Shall have the whole of the rent for booty.
Why dost thou wait? why standest cowed?
Dost thou fear to sprain thy wrist?"—" 'Tis a cloud
Up there I await. I will toss thy stick up
Right in the cloud, and will start a kick-up
For you fiends!" And again he had won, had Baldà,
And the terrified imp told his grandpapa.
And Baldà again made the waters roar
And threatened the fiends with the rope once more;
And the imp popped up again; "Why dost fuss?
If thou wilt, thou shalt have all the rent from us."

"Nay, nay," says Baldà,
"I think it is *my* turn, ha ha!
Little enemy, now the conditions to make,
And to set thee a riddle to crack.
Let us see what thy strength is. Look there
At yonder gray mare:
I dare thee to lift her
And half a mile shift her.

So, carry that mare, and the rent is thine;
But carry her not, and the whole is mine."
And the poor little imp then and there
Crawled under the mare,
And there he lay lugging her
And there he lay tugging her,
And he hoisted that mare for two paces; but falling
As he took the third, he dropped there sprawling.
Then says Baldà, "What avails to try,
Thou fool of an imp, with us to vie?
For thou, in thy arms thou couldst not rear her,
But see, between my legs I'll bear her."
And he mounted the mare, and galloped a mile,
And the dust eddied up; but the imp meanwhile
Ran scared to his grandad, and told him then
How Baldà was the winner again.

Then the devils, no help for it, rose and went
In a ring, and collected the whole of the rent,
And they loaded a sack
On Baldà, who made off with a kind of a quack.
And the pope when he sees him
Just skips up and flees him
And hides in the rear of his wife
And straddles, in fear of his life.
But Baldà hunts him out on the spot, and see!
Hands over the rent, and demands his fee.

Then the pope, poor old chap,
Put his pate up. At Rap
Number One, up he flew
To the ceiling. At Rap Number Two
The pope, the poor wretch,
Lost the power of speech.
And at Rap Number Three he was battered,

And the old fellow's wits, they were shattered.
But Baldà, giving judgment, reproached him: "Too
    keen
Upon cheapness, my pope, thou has been!"

[1831]
[UNEXPURGATED TEXT FIRST PUBLISHED 1882]

THE TALE OF
THE GOLDEN COCKEREL[1]

In a realm that shall be nameless,
In a country bright and blameless,
Lived the mighty Czar Dadon,
Second in renown to none.
Fierce and bold, he would belabor
Without scruple every neighbor.
But he fancied, as he aged,
That enough wars had been waged—
Having earned a rest, he took it.
But his neighbors would not brook it,
And they harassed the old Czar,
And they ruthlessly attacked him,
And they harried and they hacked him.
Therefore, lest his realm be lost,
He maintained a mighty host.
Though his captains were not napping,
They not seldom took a rapping:
In the south they're fortified—
From the east their foemen ride;
Mend the breach, as is commanded—
On the shore an army's landed
That has come from oversea.
Czar Dadon, so vexed was he,
Was upon the point of weeping,
Didn't find it easy sleeping.
Never was life bitterer!

[1] The libretto of Rimsky-Korsakov's opera, *Coq d'Or*, is based on
this tale.   EDITOR'S NOTE

322

So to the astrologer,
To the wise old eunuch, pleading
For his help, an envoy's speeding.
To the eunuch he bows low,
And the mage consents to go
At Dadon's behest, appearing
At the court: a sign most cheering.
In his bag, as it befell,
He'd a golden cockerel.
"Set this bird," the mage directed,
"On a pole that's soon erected;
And my golden cockerel
Will protect thee very well.
When there is no sign of riot,
He will sit serene and quiet,
But if ever there should be
Threat of a calamity,
Should there come from any quarter
Raiders ripe for loot and slaughter,
Then my golden cockerel
Will arouse: his comb will swell,
He will crow, and up and doing,
Turn to where the danger's brewing."
In return the mage is told
He shall have a heap of gold,
And good Czar Dadon instanter
Promises the kind enchanter:
"Once thy wish to me is known,
'Twill be granted as my own."

On his perch, by the Czar's orders,
Sits the cock and guards the borders—
And when danger starts to peep
He arises, as from sleep,
Crows, and ruffles up his feathers,
Turns to where the trouble gathers,

Sounds his warning clear and true,
Crying: "Cock-a-doodle-doo!
Slug-a-bed, lie still and slumber,
Reign with never care or cumber!"
And the neighbors dared not seek
Any quarrel, but grew meek:
Czar Dadon there was no trapping,
For they could not catch him napping.

Peacefully two years go by,
And the cock sits quietly.
But one day, by noises shaken,
Czar Dadon is forced to waken.
Cries a captain: "Czar and Sire,
Rise, thy children's need is dire!
Trouble comes, thy realm to shatter."
"Gentlemen, what is the matter?"
Yawns Dadon. "What do you say?
Who is there? What trouble, pray?"
Says the captain: "Fear is growing,
For the cockerel is crowing:
The whole city's terrified."
The Czar looked out and spied
The gold cockerel a-working—
Toward the east he kept on jerking.
"Quickly now! Make no delay!
Take to horse, men, and away!"
Toward the east the army's speeding
That the Czar's first-born is leading.
Now the cockerel is still,
And the Czar may sleep his fill.

Eight full days go by like magic,
But no news comes, glad or tragic:
Did they fight or did they not?
Not a word Dadon has got.

Hark! Again the cock is crowing—
A new army must be going
Forth to battle; Czar Dadon
This time sends his younger son
To the rescue of his brother.
And this time, just as the other,
The young cock grows still, content.
But again no news is sent.
And again eight days go flitting,
And in fear the folk are sitting;
And once more the cockerel crows,
And a third host eastward goes.
Czar Dadon himself is leading,
Not quite certain of succeeding.

They march on, by day, by night,
And they soon are weary, quite.
Czar Dadon, in some vexation,
Vainly seeks an indication
Of a fight: a battle-ground,
Or a camp, or funeral-mound.
Strange! But as the eighth day's ending,
We find Czar Dadon ascending
Hilly pathways, with his men—
What does his gaze light on then?
'Twixt two mountain-peaks commanding
Lo! a silken tent is standing.
Wondrous silence rules the scene,
And behold, in a ravine
Lies the slaughtered army! Chastened
By the sight, the old Czar hastened
To the tent . . . Alas, Dadon!
Younger son and elder son
Lie unhelmed, and either brother
Has his sword stuck in the other.
In the field, alackaday,

Masterless, their coursers stray,
On the trampled grass and muddy,
On the silken grass now bloody . . .
Czar Dadon howled fearfully:
"Children, children! Woe is me!
Both our falcons have been taken
In the nets! I am forsaken!"
All his army howled and moaned
Till the very valleys groaned—
From the shaken mountains darted
Echoes. Then the tent-flaps parted . . .
Suddenly upon the scene
Stood the young Shamakhan queen!
Bright as dawn, with gentle greeting
She acknowledged this first meeting
With the Czar, and old Dadon,
Like a night-bird in the sun,
Stood stock still and kept on blinking
At the maid, no longer thinking
Of his sons, the dead and gone.
And she smiled at Czar Dadon—
Bowing, took his hand and led him
Straight into her tent, and fed him
Royally, and then her guest
Tenderly she laid to rest
On a couch with gold brocaded,
By her silken curtains shaded.
Seven days and seven nights
Czar Dadon knew these delights,
And, of every scruple ridden,
Did, bewitched, what he was bidden.

Long enough he had delayed—
To his army, to the maid,
Czar Dadon was now declaring
That they must be homeward faring.

Faster than Dadon there flies
Rumor, spreading truth and lies.
And the populace have straightway
Come to meet them at the gateway.
Now behind the coach they run,
Hail the queen and hail Dadon,
And most affable they find him . . .
Lo! there in the crowd behind him
Who should follow Czar Dadon,
Hair and beard white as a swan,
And a Moorish hat to top him,
But the mage? There's none to stop him;
Up he comes: "My greetings, Sire."
Says the Czar: "What's thy desire?
Pray, come closer. What's thy mission?"
"Czar," responded the magician,
"We have our accounts to square;
Thou hast sworn, thou art aware,
For the help that I accorded,
Anything thy realm afforded
Thou wouldst grant me: my desire,
As thy own, fulfilling, Sire.
'Tis this maiden I am craving:
The Shamakhan queen." "Thou'rt raving!"
Shrieked Dadon forthwith, amazed,
While his eyes with anger blazed.
"Gracious! Hast thou lost thy senses?
Who'd have dreamed such consequences
From the words that once I said!"
Cried the Czar. "What's in thy head?
Yes, I promised, but what of it?
There are limits, and I'll prove it.
What is any maid to thee?
How dare thou thus speak to Me?
Other favors I am able
To bestow: take from my stable

My best horse, or, better far,
Henceforth rank as a boyar;
Gold I'll give thee willingly—
Half my czardom is for thee."
"Naught is offered worth desiring,"
Said the mage. "I am requiring
But one gift of thee. I mean,
Namely, the Shamakhan queen."
Then the Czar, with anger spitting,
Cried: "The devil! 'Tis not fitting
That I listen to such stuff.
Thou'lt have nothing. That's enough!
To thy cost thou hast been sinning—
Reckoned wrong from the beginning.
Now be off while thou'rt yet whole!
Take him out, God bless my soul!"
The enchanter, ere they caught him,
Would have argued, but bethought him
That with certain mighty folk
Quarreling is not a joke,
And there was no word in answer
From the white-haired necromancer.
With his sceptre the Czar straight
Rapped the eunuch on his pate;
He fell forward: life departed.
Forthwith the whole city started
Quaking—but the maiden, ah!
Hee-hee-hee! and Ha-ha-ha!
Feared no sin and was not queasy.
Czar Dadon, though quite uneasy,
Gave the queen a tender smile
And rode forward in fine style.
Suddenly there is a tinkling
Little noise, and in a twinkling,
While all stood and stared anew,
From his perch the cockerel flew

To the royal coach, and lighted
On the pate of the affrighted
Czar Dadon, and there, elate,
Flapped his wings, and pecked the pate,
And soared off . . . and as it flitted,
Czar Dadon his carriage quitted:
Down he fell, and groaned at most
Once, and then gave up the ghost.
And the queen no more was seen there:
'Twas as though she'd never been there—
Fairy-tales, though far from true,
Teach good lads a thing or two.

[1834]

IV

Dramatic Writings

BORIS GODUNOV

DRAMATIS PERSONAE[1]

BORÍS GODUNÓV, elective Czar
FEÓDOR, his son, the Czarevitch
XENIA, his daughter, the Czarevna
PRINCE SHUISKY
PRINCE VOROTÝNSKY
SHCHELKÁLOV, Secretary of the Council of Boyars
THE PATRIARCH
FATHER PÍMEN, monk and chronicler
AFANASY PUSHKIN, a nobleman
SEMYON GODUNÓV
BASMÁNOV, Commander of Godunov's army
MARGARET ⎱ foreign captains in Godunov's service
WALTER ROSEN ⎰
ROZHNÓV, a prisoner of the Pretender
MISAIL ⎱ wandering monks
VARLAAM ⎰
GRIGÓRY OTRÉPYEV, a monk, afterwards Dimitry the
    Pretender
GAVRILA PUSHKIN ⎫
PRINCE KÚRBSKY ⎬ Russian supporters of the Pretender
KHRUSHCHÓV ⎭
KARÉLA, a Cossack
SOBAŃSKI, a Polish gentleman

[1] This list does not appear in the original, and has been added for the convenience of the reader.   TRANSLATOR'S NOTE

FATHER CZERNIKOWSKI, a Jesuit

WIŚNIOWIECKI ⎫
MNISZECH ⎭ Polish magnates

MARYNA, daughter of the latter

RUZIA, Maryna's maid

MOSÁLSKY ⎫
GOLÍTSYN ⎪
MOLCHÁNOV ⎬ Boyars
SHEREFÉDINOV ⎭

The People, Boyars, a Wicked Monk, Abbot of the Chudov Monastery, two Courtiers, Hostess, two Officers, Guests, Boy at Shuisky's, the Czarevna's Nurse, a Poet, a Cavalier, a Lady, Serving-women, Russian, Polish, and German troops, a Saintly Idiot, Boys, Old Woman, the Pretender's Supporters, Court Attendants, a Peasant, a Beggar, a Guard, three Soldiers.

PALACE OF THE KREMLIN

(*February 20th, 1598*)

PRINCES SHUISKY and VOROTYNSKY

VOROTYNSKY. To keep the city's peace, that is the task
  Entrusted to us twain, but we forsooth
  Have little need to watch; Moscow is empty;
  For to the Monastery all have flocked
  After the patriarch. What thinkest thou?
  How will this trouble end?

SHUISKY.   How will it end?
  That is not hard to tell. A little more
  The multitude will groan and wail, Boris
  Pucker awhile his forehead, like a toper
  Eyeing a glass of wine, and in the end
  Will humbly of his graciousness consent
  To take the crown; and then—and then will rule us
  Just as before.

VOROTYNSKY.   And yet a month has passed
  Since, cloistered with his sister, he forsook
  The world's affairs. None hitherto hath shaken
  His purpose, not the patriarch, and not
  His boyar counselors; their tears, their prayers
  He heeds not. Deaf is he to Moscow's wail,
  To the Great Council deaf; vainly they urged
  The sorrowful nun-queen to consecrate
  Boris to sovereignty; firm was his sister,

335

Inexorable as he; methinks Boris
Inspired her with this spirit. What if our ruler
Be sick in very deed of cares of state
And hath no strength to mount the throne? What
 say'st thou?

SHUISKY. I say that then the blood of the Czarevitch
 Was shed in vain, that the poor child Dimitry
 Might just as well be living.

VOROTYNSKY.   Fearful crime!
 Is it beyond all doubt Boris contrived
 The young boy's murder?

SHUISKY.   Who besides? Who else
 Bribed Chepchugov in vain? Who sent in secret
 The brothers Bityagovsky with Kachalov?
 Myself was sent to Uglich, there to probe
 This matter on the spot; fresh traces there
 I found; the town bore witness to the crime;
 With one accord the burghers all affirmed it;
 And with a single word, when I returned,
 I could have proved the secret villain's guilt.

VOROTYNSKY. Why didst thou then not crush him?

SHUISKY.   At the time,
 I do confess, his unexpected calmness,
 His shamelessness, dismayed me. Candidly
 He looked me in the eyes; he questioned me
 Closely, and I repeated to his face
 The foolish tale himself had whispered to me.

VOROTYNSKY. An ugly business, prince.

SHUISKY.   What could I do?
 Declare all to Feodor? But the Czar
 Saw all things with the eyes of Godunov.
 Heard all things with the ears of Godunov;

Grant even that I might have fully proved it,
Boris would have denied it there and then,
And I should have been haled away to prison,
And in good time—like mine own uncle—strangled
Within the silence of some deaf-walled dungeon.
I boast not when I say that, given occasion,
No penalty affrights me. I am no coward,
But also am no fool, and do not choose
Of my free will to walk into a halter.

VOROTYNSKY. Monstrous misdeed! Listen; I warrant
   you
Remorse already gnaws the murderer;
Be sure the blood of that same innocent child
Will hinder his ascension to the throne.

SHUISKY. He'll not be balked; Boris is not so timid!
   What honor for ourselves, ay, for all Russia!
A slave of yesterday, a Tartar, son
By marriage of Maluta, of a hangman,
Himself in soul a hangman, he to don
The crown and cape of Monomakh!——

VOROTYNSKY.   You are right;
He is of lowly birth; we twain can boast
A nobler lineage.

SHUISKY.   Indeed 'tis so!

VOROTYNSKY. Let us remember, Shuisky, Vorotynsky
Are, let me say, born princes.

SHUISKY.   Born princes, truly,
And of the blood of Rurik.

VOROTYNSKY.   Listen, prince;
Then we, 'twould seem, should have the right to
   mount
Feodor's throne.

SHUISKY.   Rather than Godunov.

VOROTYNSKY. In very truth 'twould seem so.

SHUISKY.   And what then?
   If still Boris pursue his crafty ways,
   Let us contrive by skilful means to rouse
   The people. Let them turn from Godunov;
   Princes they have in plenty of their own;
   Let them from out their number choose a czar.

VOROTYNSKY. We heirs of the Varangians are many,
   But 'tis no easy thing for us to vie
   With Godunov; the people are not wont
   To recognize in us an ancient branch
   Of their old warlike masters; long already
   Have we our appanages forfeited,
   Long served but as lieutenants of the czars,
   And he hath known, by fear, and love, and glory,
   How to bewitch the people.

SHUISKY. (*Looking through a window.*) He has dared,
   That's all—while we— Enough of this. Thou seest
   Dispersedly the people are returning.
   We'll go forthwith and learn what is resolved.

THE RED SQUARE

THE PEOPLE

FIRST MAN. He is inexorable! He thrust from him
   Prelates, boyars, and Patriarch; in vain
   They prostrated themselves before Boris;
   The splendor of the throne but frightens him.

SECOND MAN. O God, who is it will rule over us?
   Oh, woe to us!

THIRD MAN.   See! the Chief Minister
  Is coming out to tell us what the Council
  Has now resolved.

THE PEOPLE.   Silence! Silence! He speaks,
  The Minister of State. Hush, hush! Give ear!

SHCHELKALOV. (*From the Red Porch.*)
  The Council have resolved for the last time
  To put to proof the power of supplication
  Upon our Ruler's mournful soul. At dawn,
  After a solemn service in the Kremlin,
  The holy Patriarch will go, preceded
  By sacred banners, with the holy ikons
  Of Don and of Vladimir; with him go
  The Council, courtiers, delegates, boyars,
  And all the pious folk of Moscow; all
  Will go once more to pray the queen to pity
  Our orphaned Moscow, and to consecrate
  Boris unto the crown. Now to your homes
  Go ye in peace: pray; and to Heaven shall rise
  The heart's petition of the orthodox.
                              (*The* CROWD *disperses.*)

THE MAIDEN FIELD

FIRST MAN. To plead with the Czarina in her cell
  Now are they gone. Thither have gone Boris,
  The Patriarch, and the boyars.

SECOND MAN.   What news?

THIRD MAN. Still is he obdurate; yet there is hope.

PEASANT WOMAN. (*With a child.*)
  Drat you! stop crying, or else the bogie-man
  Will carry you off. Drat you, drat you! stop crying!

FIRST MAN. Can't we slip through behind the fence?

SECOND MAN.   No chance!
  No chance at all! Not only is the nunnery
  Crowded; the precincts too are crammed with people.
  Look what a sight! All Moscow has thronged here.
  See! fences, roofs, and every single story
  Of the Cathedral bell tower, the church-domes,
  The crosses too are studded thick with people.

FIRST MAN. A goodly sight indeed!

ANOTHER MAN.   What is that noise?

SECOND MAN. Listen! What noise is that?—The people
    groan;
  See there! They fall like waves, row upon row—
  Again—again— Now, brother, 'tis our turn;
  Be quick, down on your knees!

THE PEOPLE. (*On their knees, groaning and wailing.*)
                                      Have pity on us,
  Our father! Oh, rule over us! Oh, be
  Father to us, and Czar!

FIRST MAN. (*Sotto voce.*) Why are they wailing?

SECOND MAN. How can we know? It's the boyars' affair.
  We are small folk.

PEASANT WOMAN. (*With child.*)
                          Now, what is this? Just when
  It ought to cry, the child is still. I'll show you!
  Here comes the bogie-man! Cry, naughty child!
    (*Throws it on the ground; the child screams.*)
  That's right, that's right!

FIRST MAN.   As everyone is crying,
  Come, brother, let us also start to cry.

ANOTHER MAN. Brother, I try my best, but can't.

FIRST MAN.   Nor I.
    Haven't you got an onion? Let us rub
    Our eyes with that.

SECOND MAN.   No; but I'll take some spittle
    To wet my eyes. What's up there now?

FIRST MAN.   Who knows?

THE PEOPLE. The crown is his! He is the rightful Czar!
    Boris consents at last!—Long live Boris!

THE KREMLIN PALACE

BORIS, PATRIARCH, BOYARS

BORIS. Thou, father Patriarch, all ye boyars!
    My soul lies bare before you; ye have seen
    With what humility and fear I took
    This mighty power upon me. Ah! how heavy
    The weight of obligation! I succeed
    The great Ivans; succeed the angel Czar!—
    Oh, righteous one, oh, sovereign father, look
    From Heaven upon the tears of thy true servants,
    Bestow on him whom thou hast loved, whom thou
    Hast raised so high on earth, bestow on him
    Thy holy blessing. May I rule my people
    In glory, and like thee be good and righteous!
    To you, boyars, I look for help. Serve me
    As ye served him, what time I shared your labors,
    Ere I was chosen by the people's will.

BOYARS. We will not from our plighted oath depart.

BORIS. Now let us go to kneel before the tombs
    Of Russia's great departed rulers. Then
    Bid all our people to a mighty feast,

All, from the nobleman to the blind beggar.
To all free entrance, all most welcome guests.
                        (*Exit, the* BOYARS *following.*)

PRINCE VOROTYNSKY. (*Stopping Shuisky.*)
    Thy guess was right.

SHUISKY.   What guess?

VOROTYNSKY.   Why, thou recallest—
    The other day, here on this very spot.

SHUISKY. No, I remember nothing.

VOROTYNSKY.   When the people
    Flocked to the Maiden Field, thou said'st——

SHUISKY.   'Tis not
    The time for recollection. There are times
    When I should counsel thee not to remember,
    But even to forget. And for the rest,
    I sought but by feigned calumny to prove thee,
    The better to discern thy secret thoughts.
    But see! the people hail the Czar—my absence
    May be remarked. I'll join them.

VOROTYNSKY.   Wily courtier!

NIGHT

Cell in the Chudov Monastery

(*The Year 1603*)

FATHER PIMEN, GRIGORY (*sleeping*)

PIMEN (*Writing by lamplight.*)
    One more, the final record, and my annals
    Are ended, and fulfilled the duty laid
    By God on me, a sinner. Not in vain
    Hath God appointed me for many years

A witness, teaching me the art of letters;
A day will come when some laborious monk
Will bring to light my zealous, nameless toil,
Kindle, as I, his lamp, and from the parchment
Shaking the dust of ages will transcribe
My chronicles, that thus posterity
The bygone fortunes of the orthodox
Of their own land may learn, will mention make
Of their great czars, their labors, glory, goodness—
And humbly for their sins, their evil deeds,
Implore the Saviour's mercy—In old age
I live anew; the past unrolls before me—
Did it in years long vanished sweep along,
Full of events, and troubled like the deep?
Now it is hushed and tranquil. Few the faces
Which memory hath saved for me, and few
The words which have come down to me—the rest
Have perished, never to return—But day
Draws near, the lamp burns low, one record more,
The last. (*He writes.*)

GRIGORY. (*Waking.*) The selfsame dream! Is 't pos-
    sible?
For the third time! Accursed dream! And ever
Before the lamp sits the old man and writes—
And not all night, 'twould seem, from drowsiness
Hath closed his eyes. I love the peaceful sight,
When, his calm soul deep in the past immersed,
He pens his chronicle. Oft have I longed
To guess what 'tis he writes of. Is 't perchance
The dark dominion of the Tartars? Is it
Ivan's grim death-dealing, the stormy Council
Of Novgorod? Is it about the glory
Of our great fatherland?—I ask in vain!
Not on his lofty brow, nor in his looks
May one perceive his secret thoughts; his aspect

Is still the same: lowly at once, and lofty—
Like to some Magistrate grown gray in office,
Calmly he contemplates alike the just
And unjust, with indifference he notes
Evil and good, and knows nor wrath nor pity.

PIMEN. Art thou awake?

GRIGORY.   Pray, honored father, give me
Thy blessing.

PIMEN.   May God bless thee on this day,
Yes, and for ever after.

GRIGORY.   All night long
Thou hast been writing and abstained from sleep,
While demon visions have disturbed my peace,
The fiend molested me. I dreamed I scaled
By winding stairs a turret, from whose height
Moscow appeared an anthill, where the people
Seethed in the squares below and pointed at me
With laughter. Shame and terror came upon me—
And falling headlong, I awoke. Three times
I dreamed the selfsame dream. Is it not strange?

PIMEN. 'Tis the young blood at play; humble thyself
By prayer and fasting, and thenceforth thy dreams
Will all be bright and airy. Even now,
If I, grown weak for want of sleep, should fail
To make my orisons of wonted length,
My senile sleep is neither calm nor sinless;
My dreams hold riotous feasts, or camps of war,
And skirmishes, the wild, insane diversions
Of youthful years.

GRIGORY.   How joyfully didst thou
Live out thy youth! The fortress of Kazan
Thou fought'st beneath, with Shuisky didst repulse
The Lithuanian host. Thou 'st seen the court,

And splendor of Ivan. Ah! happy thou!
Whilst I, from boyhood up, a wretched monk,
Was it not given to play the game of war,
To revel at the table of a czar?
Then, like to thee, would I in my old age
Have gladly from the noisy world withdrawn,
To vow myself a dedicated monk,
And in the quiet cloister end my days.

PIMEN. Complain not, brother, that the sinful world
Thou early didst forsake, that few temptations
The All-High sent to thee. Believe my words;
The glory of the world, its luxury,
Woman's seductive love, seen from afar,
Enslave our souls. Long have I lived, have taken
Delight in many things, but never knew
True bliss until that season when the Lord
Guided me to the cloister. Think, my son,
On the great czars; who loftier than they?
God only. Who dares thwart them? None. And yet
Often the golden crown became to them
A burden; for a cowl they bartered it.
The Czar Ivan sought in monastic toil
Tranquillity; his palace, filled erewhile
With haughty minions, grew to all appearance
A monastery; the very cut-throats whom
He chose for guardsmen became cowled monks
In shirts of hair; the terrible Czar appeared
A pious abbot. Here, in this very cell
(At that time Cyril, the much suffering,
A righteous man, dwelt in it; even me
God then made comprehend the nothingness
Of worldly vanities), here I beheld,
Weary of angry thoughts and executions,
The Czar; among us, meditative, quiet,
Here sat the Terrible; we motionless

Stood in his presence, while he talked with us
In tranquil tones. Thus spake he to the abbot
And to us all: "My fathers, soon will come
The longed-for day; here shall I stand before you,
Hungering for salvation; Nicodemus,
Thou Sergius, and Cyril, will accept
My holy vow; to you I soon shall come
A man accursed, here the clean habit take,
Prostrate, most holy father, at thy feet."
So spake the sovereign lord, and from his lips
The words flowed sweetly. Then he wept; and we
With tears prayed God to send His love and peace
Upon his suffering and stormy soul.—
What of his son Feodor? On the throne
He sighed for the mute hermit's peaceful life.
The royal chambers to a cell of prayer
He turned, wherein the heavy cares of state
Vexed nct his holy soul. God grew to love
The Czar's humility; in his good days
Russia was blest with glory undisturbed,
And in the hour of his decease was wrought
A miracle unheard of: at his bedside,
Seen by the Czar alone, appeared a being
Exceeding bright, with whom Feodor spake,
And he addressed him as great Patriarch—
And all around him were possessed with fear,
Musing upon the vision sent from Heaven,
Since the bless'd Patriarch was absent from
The chamber of the Czar. And when he died
The palace was with holy fragrance filled,
And like the sun his countenance shone forth—
Never again shall we see such a czar—
Oh, horrible, appalling woe! We have sinned,
We have angered God; we have chosen for our ruler
A czar's assassin.

GRIGORY.   Honored father, long
  Have I desired to ask thee of the death
  Of young Dimitry, the Czarevitch; thou,
  'Tis said, wast then at Uglich.

PIMEN.   Ay, my son,
  I well remember. God it was who led me
  To witness that ill deed, that bloody sin.
  I at that time was sent to distant Uglich
  Upon some mission. I arrived at night.
  Next morning, at the hour of holy mass,
  I heard upon a sudden a bell toll;
  'Twas the alarm bell. Then a cry, an uproar;
  Men rushing to the court of the Czarina.
  Thither I haste, and there had flocked already
  All Uglich. There I see: the young Czarevitch
  Lies slaughtered, the queen mother in a swoon
  Bowed over him, the nurse in her despair
  Wailing; and then the maddened people drag
  The treacherous nurse away. Now there appears
  Suddenly in their midst, wild, pale with rage,
  That Judas, Bityagovsky. "There's the villain!"
  The raging mob cries out, and in a trice
  He is out of sight. Straightway the people rushed
  At the three fleeing murderers; they seized
  The hiding miscreants and led them up
  To the child's corpse, yet warm; when lo! a marvel—
  The lifeless little one began to tremble!
  "Confess!" the people thundered; and in terror
  Beneath the ax the villains did confess—
  And named Boris.

GRIGORY.   When this befell, how old
  Was the poor boy?

PIMEN.   Full seven years; and now

(Since then ten years have passed—nay, more—
   twelve years)
He would have been of the same age as thou,
And would have reigned; but God deemed other-
   wise.
This is the lamentable tale wherewith
My chronicle doth end; since then I scarce
Have meddled in the world's affairs. Good brother,
Thou hast acquired the precious art of writing;
To thee I hand my task. In hours exempt
From the soul's exercise, do thou record,
And without sophistry, all things whereto
Thou shalt in life be witness: war and peace,
The sway of kings, the holy miracles
Of saints, all prophecies and heavenly omens—
For me 'tis time to rest and quench my lamp—
But hark! the matin bell. Bless, Lord, thy servants!
Hand me my crutch.

                                        (*Exit.*)

GRIGORY.   Boris, Boris, before thee
   All tremble; none dares even to remind thee
   Of what befell the hapless child; meanwhile
   In his dark cell a hermit doth set down
   A stern indictment of thee. Thou wilt not
   Escape the judgment even of this world,
   As thou wilt not escape the doom of God.

BESIDE THE MONASTERY WALL*

GRIGORY and a WICKED MONK

GRIGORY. Oh, what a weariness is our poor life,
   What misery! Day comes, day goes, and ever

* This scene was omitted by Pushkin from the published text of
the play. Here the poet uses a trochaic metre, not followed by the
translator.

                                        EDITOR'S NOTE

One sees, one hears but the same thing; one sees
Only black cassocks, hears only the bell.
Yawning by day you wander, wander, nothing
To do; you doze; the whole night long till daylight
The poor monk lies awake; and when in sleep
You lose yourself, black dreams disturb the soul;
Glad that they sound the bell, that with a crutch
They rouse you. No, I will not suffer it!
I cannot! I will jump this wall and run!
The world is great; I'll take the open road;
They'll hear of me no more.

MONK.   Truly your life
Is but a sorry one, ye hot-blooded
And wild young monks!

GRIGORY.   Would that the Khan again
Assaulted us, or Lithuania
Once more rose up in arms! Good! I would then
Cross swords with them! Or what if the Czarevitch
Should suddenly arise from out the grave,
Should cry, "Where are ye, children, faithful ser-
     vants?
Help me against Boris, against my murderer!
Seize my foe, bring him to me!"

MONK.   Enough, my friend,
Of empty talk. We cannot raise the dead.
No, clearly Fate had something else in store
For the Czarevitch— But hearken: if thy mind
Is set upon a deed, then do it.

GRIGORY.   What?

MONK. If I were young as thou, if these gray hairs
Had not already streaked my beard— Dost take me?

GRIGORY. Not I.

MONK. Hearken: our folk are dull of brain,
And credulous, and glad to be amazed
By novelties and marvels. The boyars
Remember Godunov as erst he was,
Peer to themselves; and even now the race
Of the Varangians is loved by all.
Thy years match those of the Czarevitch. If
Thou'rt firm and cunning— Dost take me now?

GRIGORY. I take thee.

MONK. Well, what say'st thou?

GRIGORY. 'Tis resolved!
I am Dimitry, the Czarevitch! I!

MONK. Thy hand, my bold young friend. Thou shalt
be Czar!

PALACE OF THE PATRIARCH

PATRIARCH, ABBOT of the Chudov Monastery

PATRIARCH. And he has run away, Father Abbot?

ABBOT. He ran away, holy Patriarch, three days ago.

PATRIARCH. Accursed rascal! What is his origin?

ABBOT. Of the family of the Otrepyevs, of the lower
nobility of Halicz; in his youth he took monastic
vows, no one knows where, lived in the Yefimievsky
monastery at Suzdal, departed thence, wandered
from one monastery to another, finally came to our
brethren at Chudov; and I, seeing that he was still
young and inexperienced, entrusted him at the out-
set to Father Pimen, a venerable ancient, kind and
humble. And he was very learned, read our chronicles, composed hymns to saints; but, it would seem,

. this learning did not come to him from the Lord God——

PATRIARCH. Ah, those learned ones! What a thing to say, "I shall be Czar in Moscow." Ah, he is a vessel of the devil! However, it is of no use even to report this to the Czar; why disquiet the sovereign, our father? It will be enough to give information about his flight to Secretary Smirnov or Secretary Yefimiev. What heresy: "I shall be Czar in Moscow!" . . . Catch, catch the tool of the devil, and let him endure perpetual penance in exile at Solovetsky. But indeed—is it not heresy, Father Abbot?

ABBOT. Heresy, holy Patriarch; downright heresy.

PALACE OF THE CZAR

TWO COURTIERS

FIRST COURTIER. Where is the sovereign?

SECOND COURTIER.   In his bed-chamber,
Where he is closeted with some magician.

FIRST COURTIER. Ay, that's the kind of intercourse he
    loves:
Magicians, sorcerers, and fortune-tellers.
Ever he seeks to dip into the future,
Just like some pretty girl. Fain would I know
What 'tis that he would learn.

SECOND COURTIER.   Well, here he comes.
Shall we not question him?

FIRST COURTIER.   How grim he looks!
                                    (*Exeunt.*)

CZAR. (*Enters.*) I have attained the highest power. Six
  years
Have I reigned peacefully; but happiness
Dwells not within my soul. Even so in youth
We greedily desire the joys of love,
But scarce have quelled the hunger of the heart
With momentary pleasure, when we grow
Cold, weary and oppressed! In vain the wizards
Promise me length of days, days of dominion
Untroubled and serene—not power, not life
Rejoice me; I forebode the wrath of Heaven
And woe. For me there is no joy. I thought
To give my people glory and contentment,
To gain their loyal love by generous gifts,
But I have put away that empty hope;
The living power is hateful to the mob—
Only the dead they love. We are but fools
When our heart shakes because the people clap
Or cry out fiercely. When our land was stricken
By God with famine, perishing in torments
The people uttered moan. I opened to them
The granaries, I scattered gold among them,
Found labor for them; yet for all my pains
They cursed me! Next, a fire consumed their homes;
I built for them new dwellings; then forsooth
They blamed me for the fire! Such is the mob,
Such is its judgment! Seek its love, indeed!
I thought within my family to find
Solace; I thought to make my daughter happy
By wedlock. Like a tempest, Death took off
Her bridegroom—and at once a stealthy rumor
Pronounced me guilty of my daughter's grief—
Me, me, the hapless father! Whoso dies,
I am the secret murderer of all;
Feodor's end I hastened, 'twas I poisoned
My sister-queen, the nun—'twas ever I!

Ah! now I feel it; naught can give us peace
Mid worldly cares, nothing save only conscience!
When clear, she triumphs over wickedness,
Over dark slander; but if she be found
To have a single stain, then misery!
With what a deadly sore the soul doth smart;
The heart, with venom filled, beats like a hammer
And dins reproach into the buzzing ears;
The head is spinning, nausea tortures one,
And bloody boys revolve before the eyes;
And one would flee, but refuge there is none!
Oh, pity him whose conscience is unclean!

TAVERN ON THE LITHUANIAN
FRONTIER

MISAIL and VARLAAM, wandering monks; GRIGORY in
secular attire; HOSTESS

HOSTESS. With what shall I regale you, my reverend
sirs?

VARLAAM. With what God sends, little hostess. Is there
no wine?

HOSTESS. As if that were possible, my fathers! I will
bring it at once.   (*Exit.*)

MISAIL. Why so glum, comrade? Here is that very
Lithuanian frontier which thou didst so wish to
reach.

GRIGORY. Until I am in Lithuania, I shall not be content.

VARLAAM. What is it that makes thee so fond of Lithuania? Here are we, Father Misail and I, sinner that
I am, now that we have escaped from the monastery,

nothing matters to us. Lithuania, Russia, a whistle,
a psaltery? It is all one to us, if only there is wine.
And here it is!

MISAIL. Well said, Father Varlaam.

HOSTESS. (*Enters.*)
There you are, my fathers. Drink, and may it do you
good.

MISAIL. Thanks, my good friend. God bless thee. (*The
monks drink.* VARLAAM *trolls a ditty: "Ah, sweetheart, sweetheart mine, Show me those eyes of thine."
To* GRIGORY.) Why dost not join in the song? Why
dost not join in the drinking?

GRIGORY. I don't wish to.

MISAIL. Everyone to his liking——

VARLAAM. But a tipsy man's in Heaven, Father Misail!
Let us drink a glass to our hostess. (*Sings: "Show
those eyes of thine."*) Still, Father Misail, when I
am drinking, then I don't like sober men; tipsiness
is one thing—but pride quite another. One who
would live as we do, is welcome. If not—then take
thyself off, away with thee; a clown is no companion
for a priest.

GRIGORY. Drink, and keep thy thoughts to thyself, Father Varlaam! * I too sometimes know how to speak

* They speak in rhymed proverb.

well.

VARLAAM. But why should I keep my thoughts to myself?

MISAIL. Let him alone, Father Varlaam.

VARLAAM. But what sort of a fasting man is he? Of his

own accord he attached himself as a companion to us; no one knows who he is, no one knows whence he comes—and yet he gives himself grand airs. (*Drinks and sings: "A young monk took orders."*)

GRIGORY. (*To* HOSTESS.) Whither leads this road?

HOSTESS. To Lithuania, my provider, to the Luyov mountains.

GRIGORY. And is it far to the Luyov mountains?

HOSTESS. Not far; you might get there by evening, but for the Czar's frontier guards, and the officers of the watch.

GRIGORY. What? Guards! What does it mean?

HOSTESS. Someone has escaped from Moscow, and orders have been given to detain and search everyone.

GRIGORY. (*Aside.*) Here's a pretty mess!

VARLAAM. Hallo, comrade! Thou'rt making up to the hostess. To be sure thou wantest no vodka, but a young woman. All right, brother, all right! Everyone has his own ways, and Father Misail and I have only one care—we drink to the bottom, we drink; turn the glass upside down, and knock on the bottom.

MISAIL. Well said, Father Varlaam.

GRIGORY. (*To* HOSTESS.) Whom do they want? Who escaped from Moscow?

HOSTESS. God knows; a thief perhaps, a robber. But here even good folks are plagued now. And what will come of it? Nothing. They'll not catch a hair of the devil; as if there were no other road into Lithuania than the highway! Just turn to the left from here, then through the pinewood follow the footpath as far as the chapel on the Chekansky brook, and then straight across the marsh to Khlopino, and thence to Zakharievo, and there any child will guide you to the Luyov mountains. The only good of these officers is to plague passers-by and rob us poor folk. (*A noise is heard.*) What's that? Ah, there they are, curse them! They are going their rounds.

GRIGORY. Hostess! is there another room in the cottage?

HOSTESS. No, my dear; I should be glad myself to hide. But they are only pretending to go their rounds; but give them wine and bread, and Heaven knows what —May they choke, the accursed ones! May——

(Enter OFFICERS.)

OFFICERS. Good health to you, hostess!

HOSTESS. You are very welcome, dear guests.

AN OFFICER. (*To another.*) Ha, there's drinking going on here; we shall get something here. (*To the* MONKS) Who are you?

VARLAAM. We—are God's old men, humble monks; we are going from village to village, and collecting Christian alms for the monastery.

OFFICER. (*To* GRIGORY.) And thou?

MISAIL. Our comrade.

GRIGORY. A layman from the suburb; I have conducted the old men as far as the frontier; from here I am going to my own home.

MISAIL. So thou hast changed thy mind?

GRIGORY. (*Sotto voce.*) Hold thy tongue.

OFFICER. Hostess, bring some more wine, and we will drink here a little and talk a little with these old men.

SECOND OFFICER. (*Sotto voce.*) Yon lad, it appears, is poor; there's nothing to be got out of him; on the other hand, the old men—

FIRST OFFICER. Be silent; we shall come to them presently—Well, my fathers, how goes it?

VARLAAM. Badly, son, badly! The Christians have now turned stingy; they love their money; they hide their money. They give little to God. A great sin has come upon the peoples of the earth. All men have become traders and publicans; they think of worldly wealth, not of the salvation of the soul. You walk and walk; you beg and beg; sometimes in three days begging will not bring you three half-pence. What a sin! A week goes by; another week; you look into your bag, and there is so little in it that you are ashamed to show yourself at the monastery. What are you to do? From very sorrow you drink away what is left; a real calamity! Ah, it is bad! It seems our last days have come——

HOSTESS. (*Weeps.*) God pardon and save us!
    (*During the course of* VARLAAM's *speech the* FIRST OFFICER *was watching* MISAIL *significantly.*)

FIRST OFFICER. Alexis! hast thou the Czar's edict with thee?

SECOND OFFICER. I have it.

FIRST OFFICER. Hand it over.

MISAIL. Why art thou staring at me?

FIRST OFFICER. This is why; from Moscow there has fled a certain wicked heretic—Grishka Otrepyev. Hast thou heard this?

MISAIL. I have not.

OFFICER. Not heard it? Very good. And the Czar has ordered to catch and hang the fugitive heretic. Dost thou know this?

MISAIL. I do not.

OFFICER. (*To* VARLAAM.) Dost know how to read?

VARLAAM. In my youth I knew how, but I have forgotten.

OFFICER. (*To* MISAIL.) And thou?

MISAIL. God has not given me wisdom.

OFFICER. Here's the Czar's edict for thee.

MISAIL. What do I want it for?

OFFICER. It seems to me that this fugitive heretic, thief, swindler, is—thou.

MISAIL. I? Good gracious! What art thou talking of?

OFFICER. Stay! Bar the doors. We shall soon get at the truth at once.

HOSTESS. O the cursèd tormentors! Even an old man they won't leave in peace!

OFFICER. Which of you here can read?

GRIGORY. (*Comes forward.*) I can read!

OFFICER. Oh, indeed! And who taught thee?

GRIGORY. Our sacristan.

OFFICER. (*Gives him the edict.*) Read it aloud.

GRIGORY. (*Reads.*) "Grigory, of the family of Otrepyev, an unworthy monk of the Chudov Monastery, has fallen into heresy, and, instructed by the devil, has dared to stir up the holy brotherhood with all manner of temptations and lawlessness. And, according to information, it appears that he, the accursed Grishka, has fled to the Lithuanian frontier."

OFFICER. (*To* MISAIL.) How can it be anyone but thou?

GRIGORY. "And the Czar has commanded to catch him——"

OFFICER. And to hang!

GRIGORY. It does not say here "to hang."

OFFICER. Thou liest. What is meant is not always put into writing. Read: to catch and to hang.

GRIGORY. "And to hang. And the years of this thief Grishka" (*looking at* VARLAAM) "are more than fifty, and he is of medium height; he has a bald head, a gray beard, a fat belly."

(*All look at* VARLAAM.)

FIRST OFFICER. My lads! Here is Grishka! Hold him! bind him! What a surprise!

VARLAAM. (*Snatching the paper.*) Hands off, you dogs! What sort of a Grishka am I? What! fifty years old, gray beard, fat belly! No, brother. You're too young to play tricks on me. I have not read for a long time and I find it hard to make out, but I shall manage to make it out, as it's a hanging matter. (*Spells it out.*) "And his age twenty." Why brother, where does it say fifty?—Do you see—twenty?

SECOND OFFICER. Yes, I remember, twenty; even so it was told us.

FIRST OFFICER. (*To* GRIGORY.) Then, evidently, you are a joker, brother.

　　(*During the reading* GRIGORY *stands with downcast head, and his hand in his bosom.*)

VARLAAM. (*Continues.*) "And in stature he is small, his chest is broad, one arm is shorter than the other, has blue eyes, red hair, a wart on his cheek, another on his forehead." Then is it not thou, my friend?

　　(GRIGORY *suddenly draws a dagger; all give way before him; he dashes through the window.*)

OFFICERS. Hold him! Hold him!

　　　　　　　　　　　　(*All run in disorder.*)

MOSCOW. SHUISKY'S HOUSE

SHUISKY. MANY GUESTS. *Supper*

SHUISKY. More wine! (*He rises; all rise after him.*)
Now, my dear guests. The final jug!
Boy, read the prayer.

BOY.　　　　　　　　　Lord of the heavens, Who art
Eternally and everywhere, accept
The prayer of us Thy servants. For our monarch,
By Thee appointed, for our pious Czar,
The autocrat of Christendom, we pray.
Preserve him in the palace, on the field
Of battle, on his nightly couch; grant to him
Victory o'er his foes; from sea to sea
May he be glorified; may all his house
Blossom with health, and may its precious branches
O'ershadow all the earth; to us, his slaves,
May he, as heretofore, be generous,

Gracious, long-suffering, and may the founts
Of his unfailing wisdom flow for us;
Raising the royal cup, Lord of the heavens,
For this we pray.

SHUISKY. (*Drinks.*) Long live our mighty sovereign!
Farewell, dear guests. I thank you that ye scorned not
My bread and salt. Good-bye, and slumber well.
(*Exeunt* GUESTS: *he conducts them to the door.*)

PUSHKIN. They've left at last; indeed, Prince Vassily
Ivanovich, I began to think that we should not succeed in getting any private talk.

SHUISKY. (*To the* SERVANTS.) You there, why do you
stand gaping? Always eavesdropping on the mas-
ters! Clear the table, and then be off.
(*Exeunt* SERVANTS.)
What is it, Afanasy
Mikhailovich?

PUSHKIN.   Marvels will never cease!
A messenger from Cracow came to-day
Sent by my nephew, young Gavrila Pushkin.

SHUISKY. Well?

PUSHKIN.   'Tis strange news my nephew writes.
The son
Of Czar Ivan the Terrible— But stay——
(*Goes to the door and examines it.*)
The royal boy slain by Boris's order——

SHUISKY. But these are no new tidings.

PUSHKIN.   Wait a little;
Dimitry lives.

SHUISKY.   So that's it! News indeed!
   Dimitry living!—really marvellous!
   And is that all?

PUSHKIN.   Pray listen to the end;
   Whoe'er he be, whether he be Dimitry
   Rescued, or else some spirit in his shape,
   Some daring rogue, some insolent pretender,
   In any case Dimitry has appeared.

SHUISKY. It cannot be.

PUSHKIN   Pushkin himself beheld him
   When first he reached the court, and through the
      ranks
   Of Lithuanian courtiers went straight
   Into the secret chamber of the king.

SHUISKY. What kind of man? Whence comes he?

PUSHKIN.   No one knows.
   'Tis known that he was Wiśniowiecki's servant;
   That to a ghostly father on a bed
   Of sickness he disclosed himself; possessed
   Of this strange secret, his proud magnate nursed
      him,
   From his sick bed upraised him, and straightway
   Took him to Sigismund.

SHUISKY.   And what say men
   Of this bold fellow?

PUSHKIN.   They say he is wise,
   Affable, cunning, pleasing to all men.
   He has bewitched the fugitives from Moscow,
   The Catholic priests see eye to eye with him.
   The king caresses him, and, it is said,
   Has promised help.

SHUISKY.   All this is such a medley
   That my head whirls. Brother, beyond all doubt
   This man is a pretender, but the danger
   Is, I confess, not slight. This is grave news!
   And if it reach the people, then there'll be
   A mighty tempest.

PUSHKIN.   Such a storm that hardly
   Will Czar Boris contrive to keep the crown
   Upon his clever head; and losing it
   Will get but his deserts! He governs us
   As did the Czar Ivan of evil memory.
   What profits it that public executions
   Have ceased, that we no longer are impaled
   And dripping blood sing hymns to Jesus Christ;
   That we no more are burnt on public squares,
   Or that the Czar no longer with his sceptre
   Rakes in the coals? Have we any assurance
   Of our poor lives? Each day disgrace awaits us;
   The dungeon or Siberia, cowl or fetters,
   And then in some lost nook at last starvation,
   Or else the halter. Where are the most renowned
   Of all our houses, where the Sitsky princes,
   Where are the Shestunovs, where the Romanovs,
   Hope of our fatherland? Imprisoned, tortured,
   In exile. Do but wait, and a like fate
   Will soon be thine. Think of it! Here at home,
   We are beset, as if by foreign foes,
   By treacherous slaves—these spies are ever ready
   For base betrayal, thieves bribed by the State.
   We hang upon the word of the first servant
   Whom we may choose to punish. Then he bethought
      him
   To bind the peasant to the land he tilled,
   Forbidding change of masters, so that thus
   The masters too are bound. Do not dismiss

An idler. Willy nilly, thou must feed him!
Presume not to entice a serf away
From his old master, or you'll find yourself
In the court's clutches—Was such an evil heard of
When Czar Ivan was reigning? Are the people
Now better off? Ask them. Let the pretender
But promise them the old free right of transfer,
Then there'll be sport.

SHUISKY.   Thou'rt right; but be advised;
Of this, of all things, for a time we'll speak
No word.

PUSHKIN.   Assuredly, keep thine own counsel.
Thou art—a person of discretion; always
I speak with thee most gladly; and if aught
At any time disturbs me, I endure not
To keep it from thee; and, in truth, thy mead
And velvet ale to-day have so untied
My tongue . . . Farewell then, prince.

SHUISKY.   Brother, farewell.
Farewell, my brother, till we meet again.
                    (*He escorts* PUSHKIN *out.*)

PALACE OF THE CZAR

The CZAREVITCH *is drawing a map.* THE
CZAREVNA. THE NURSE OF THE CZAREVNA

XENIA. (*Kisses a portrait.*) Sweet bridegroom, comely
prince, not to me wast thou given, not to thy affianced bride, but to a dark grave in a strange land.
Never shall I take comfort, ever shall I weep for thee.

NURSE. Eh, Czarevna! a maiden weeps as the dew falls;
the sun will rise, will dry the dew. Thou wilt have
another bridegroom—and handsome and affable. My

charming child, thou wilt learn to love him, thou
wilt forget thy prince.

XENIA. Nay, nurse, I will be true to him even in death.
(BORIS *enters*.)

CZAR. What, Xenia? What, my sweet one? In thy girl-
hood
Already a woe-stricken widow, ever
Bewailing thy dead bridegroom! Fate forbade me
To be the author of thy bliss. Perchance
I angered Heaven; it was not mine to compass
Thy happiness. Innocent one, for what
Art thou a sufferer? And thou, my son,
With what art thou employed? What's this?

FEODOR.   A map
Of all the land of Muscovy; our czardom
From end to end. Here you see: there is Moscow,
There Novgorod, there Astrakhan. Here lies
The sea, here the dense forest tract of Perm,
And there Siberia.

CZAR.   And what is this
Which makes a winding pattern here?

FEODOR.   That is
The Volga.

CZAR.   Very good! Here's the sweet fruit
Of learning. One can view as from the clouds
Our whole dominion at a glance; its frontiers,
Its towns, its rivers. Study, son; 'tis science
That teaches us more swiftly than experience,
Our life being so brief. Some day, and soon
Perchance, the lands which thou so cunningly
To-day hast drawn on paper, all will come
Under thy hand. Then study; and more clearly,

More steadily wilt thou see, son, before thee
The sovereign task.

(SEMYON GODUNOV *enters.*)

But there comes Godunov
Bringing reports to me. (*To* XENIA.) Go to thy chamber,
Dearest; farewell, my child; God comfort thee.

(*Exeunt* XENIA *and* NURSE.)

What news hast thou for me, Semyon Nikitich?

SEMYON G. To-day at dawn the butler of Prince Shuisky
And Pushkin's servant brought me information.

CZAR. Well?

SEMYON G. In the first place, Pushkin's man deposed
That yestermorn came to his house from Cracow
A courier, who within an hour was sent
Without a letter back.

CZAR.   Arrest the courier.

SEMYON. G. Some are already sent to overtake him.

CZAR. And what of Shuisky?

SEMYON G.   Last night he entertained
His friends: the Buturlins, both Miloslavskys,
And Saltykov, with Pushkin and some others.
They parted late. Pushkin alone remained
Closeted with his host and talked with him
And at some length.

CZAR.   For Shuisky send forthwith.

SEMYON. G. Sire, he is here already.

CZAR.   Call him hither.

(*Exit* SEMYON GODUNOV.)

Dealings with Lithuania? What means this?

I like not the rebellious race of Pushkins,
Nor must I trust in Shuisky, who's evasive,
But bold and wily—

                           (*Enter* SHUISKY.)
            Prince, a word with thee.
But thou thyself, it seems, hast business with me,
And I would listen first to thee.

SHUISKY.   Yea, sire;
  It is my duty to convey to thee
  Grave news.

CZAR.   I listen.

SHUISKY. (*Sotto voce, pointing to* FEODOR.)
                  But, sire——

CZAR.   The Czarevitch
  May learn whate'er Prince Shuisky knoweth. Speak.

SHUISKY. My liege, from Lithuania there have come
  Tidings to us——

CZAR.   Are they not those same tidings
  Which yestereve a courier bore to Pushkin?

SHUISKY. Nothing is hidden from him!—Sire, I thought
  Thou knew'st not yet this secret.

CZAR.   Let not that
  Trouble thee, prince; I fain would match thy news
  With what I know; else we shall never learn
  The actual truth.

SHUISKY.   I know this only, Sire:
  In Cracow a pretender hath appeared;
  The king and nobles back him.

CZAR.   What say they?
  And who is this pretender?

SHUISKY.   I know not.

CZAR. But wherein is he dangerous?

SHUISKY.   Verily
  Thy power, my liege, is firm; by vigilance,
  Grace, bounty, thou hast won the filial love
  Of all thy slaves; but thou thyself dost know
  The mob is thoughtless, changeable, rebellious,
  Credulous, lightly given to vain hope,
  Obedient to each momentary impulse,
  To truth deaf and indifferent; it doth feed
  On fables; shameless boldness pleaseth it.
  So, if this unknown vagabond should cross
  The Lithuanian border, Dimitry's name
  Raised from the grave will gain him a whole crowd
  Of fools.

CZAR. Dimitry's?—What?—That child's?—Dimitry's?
  Withdraw, my son.

SHUISKY.   He flushed; there'll be a storm!

FEODOR. Suffer me, Sire——

CZAR.   Impossible, Czarevitch;
  Go, go!
                                    (*Exit* FEODOR.)
          Dimitry's name!

SHUISKY.   Then he knew nothing.

CZAR. Listen: take steps this very hour that Russia
  Be fenced by barriers from Lithuania;
  That not a single soul pass o'er the border,
  That not a hare run o'er to us from Poland,
  Nor crow fly here from Cracow. Off!

SHUISKY.   I go.

CZAR. Stay!—Is it not the truth that this report
Is artfully contrived? Hast ever heard
That dead men have arisen from their graves
To question czars, legitimate czars, appointed,
Acclaimed by all the people, yea, and crowned
By the great Patriarch? Should one not laugh?
Eh? What? Why laugh'st thou not thereat?

SHUISKY.   I, Sire?

CZAR. Hark, Prince Vassily; when I learned this child
Had been—this child had somehow lost its life,
'Twas thou I sent to search the matter out.
Now by the Cross, by God I do adjure thee,
Declare to me the truth upon thy conscience:
Didst recognize the slaughtered boy, or didst
Thou find another? Answer.

SHUISKY.   Sire, I swear——

CZAR. Nay, Shuisky, swear not, but reply; was it
Indeed Dimitry?

SHUISKY.   He.

CZAR.   Consider, prince.
I promise clemency; I will not punish
With vain disgrace a lie that's of the past.
But if thou cheat me now, then by my own
Son's head I swear—an ill fate shall befall thee,
Such punishment that Czar Ivan himself
Shall shudder in his grave with horror of it.

SHUISKY. In punishment no terror lies; the terror
Doth lie in thy disfavor; in thy presence
Dare I use cunning? Could I have been so blind
That I then failed to recognize Dimitry?
Three days in the cathedral did I visit

His corpse, escorted thither by all Uglich.
Around him thirteen bodies lay of those
Slain by the people, and in them corruption
Already had set in perceptibly.
But lo! the childish face of the Czarevitch
Was bright and fresh and still as though he slept;
The deep gash had congealed not, nor the lines
Of his face even altered. No, my liege,
There is no doubt; Dimitry's in his grave.

CZAR. (*Caimly.*) Enough, withdraw.

                    (*Exit* SHUISKY.)
           I choke!—let me draw breath!
I felt it; all my blood surged to my face,
And heavily receded.—So that's why
For thirteen years together I have dreamed
Ever about the murdered child. Yes, yes—
'Tis that!—now I perceive. But who is he,
My terrible antagonist? Who is it
Opposeth me? An empty name, a shadow.
Can but a ghost tear from my back the purple,
A hollow sound make beggars of my children?
This is pure madness! What is there to fear?
Blow on this phantom—and it is no more.
So, I am fast resolved; I'll show no sign
Of fear, but let no trifle be ignored.
Ah! heavy art thou, crown of Monomakh!

CRACOW. HOUSE OF WIŚNIOWIECKI

THE PRETENDER AND FATHER CZERNIKOWSKI, A JESUIT

PRETENDER. Nay, father, it will not be hard. I know
The spirit of my people; piety
With them is not extreme, their czar's example
To them is sacred. And their tolerance

Makes them indifferent. I warrant you,
Before two years my people all, and all
The Northern Church, will recognize the power
Of Peter's Vicar.

JESUIT.   May Saint Ignatius aid thee
When other times arrive. Meanwhile, Czarevitch,
Hide in thy soul the seed of heavenly grace;
Religious duty bids us oft dissemble
Before the impious world; the people judge
Thy words, thy deeds; God only sees thy motives.

PRETENDER. Amen. Who's there?
                              (*Enter* A SERVANT.)
                         Say that we will receive them.
    (*The doors are opened; enter a crowd of Russians
    and Poles.*)
Comrades! To-morrow we depart from Cracow.
Mniszech, with thee for three days in Sambor
I'll stay. I know thy hospitable castle
Both shines in splendid stateliness, and glories
In its young mistress. There I hope to see
Charming Maryna. And ye, my friends, ye, Russians
And Lithuanians, ye who have upraised
Fraternal banners 'gainst a common foe,
Against mine enemy, yon crafty villain,
Ye sons of Slavs, speedily will I lead
Your dread battalions to the longed-for conflict.
But soft! Methinks among you I descry
New faces.

GAVRILA PUSHKIN. They have come to beg for sword
And service with your Grace.

PRETENDER.   Welcome, my lads.
Come hither friends. But tell me, Pushkin, who
Is this fine youth?

PUSHKIN.   Prince Kurbsky.

PRETENDER. (*To* KURBSKY.)   A proud name!
Art kinsman to the hero of Kazan?

KURBSKY. His son.

PRETENDER.   Doth he still live?

KURBSKY.   Nay, he is dead.

PRETENDER. A noble mind! A man of war and counsel.
But from the time when he appeared beneath
The ancient town Olgin with Lithuanians,
Hardy avenger of his injuries,
Rumor hath held her tongue concerning him.

KURBSKY. My father passed the remnant of his life
On lands bestowed upon him by Báthory;
There, in Volhynia, a peaceful hermit,
Sought consolation for himself in learning;
But quiet labor did not comfort him;
He ne'er forgot the home of his young days,
And to the end pined for it.

PRETENDER.   Hapless chieftain!
How brightly shone the dawn of his resounding
And stormy life! Glad am I, noble knight,
That now in thee his blood is reconciled
To his own country. Faults of fathers must not
Be called to mind. Peace to their graves. Approach;
Give me thy hand! Is it not strange?—the son
Of Kurbsky to the throne is leading—whom?
Whom but Ivan's own son?—All favors me;
People and fate alike.—Say, who art thou?

A POLE. Sobański, a free noble.

PRETENDER.   Praise and honor
Attend thee, child of liberty. Give him

A third of his full pay beforehand—Who
Are these? On them I recognize the garb
Of my own country. These are ours.

KHRUSHCHOV. (*Bows low.*)   Yea, Sire,
Our father; we are thralls of thine, devoted
And persecuted; we have fled from Moscow,
Disgraced, to thee our czar, and for thy sake
Are ready to lay down our lives; our corpses
Shall be for thee steps to the royal throne.

PRETENDER. Take heart, innocent sufferers. Only let me
Reach Moscow, and, once there, Boris shall settle
Some scores with me and you. What news of Mos
cow? *

KHRUSHCHOV. As yet all there is quiet. But already
The folk have got to know that the Czarevitch
Was saved; already everywhere is read
Thy proclamation. All are waiting for thee.
Not long ago Boris sent two boyars
To meet their death merely because in secret
They drank thy health.

PRETENDER.   O hapless, good boyars!
But blood for blood! and woe to Godunov!
What do they say of him?

KHRUSHCHOV.   He has withdrawn
Into his gloomy palace. He is grim
And somber. Executions loom ahead.
But sickness gnaws him. Hardly hath he strength
To drag himself along, and—it is thought—
His last hour is already not far off.

---

* The passage beginning with this last phrase, down to the line
ending "may yet prove wrong", appears only in a manuscript draft
of the play.

                                        EDITOR'S NOTE

PRETENDER. A speedy death I wish him, as becomes
A great-souled foe to wish. If not, then woe
To the miscreant!—And whom doth he intend
To name as his successor?

KHRUSHCHOV. He shows not
His purposes, but it would seem he destines
Feodor, his young son, to be our czar.

PRETENDER. His reckonings, maybe, will yet prove
wrong.
And who art thou?

KARELA. A Cossack; from the Don
Sent to thee, from the free troops, the brave chieftains
Of both the upper and lower reaches,
To look upon thy bright and royal eyes,
And tender thee their homage.

PRETENDER. Well I knew
The men of Don; I doubted not to see
The Cossack banners in my ranks. We thank
Our army of the Don. To-day, we know,
The Cossacks are unjustly persecuted,
Oppressed; but if God grant us to ascend
The throne of our forefathers, as of yore
We will reward our free and faithful Don.

POET. (*Approaches, bowing low, and taking* GRIGORY
by the hem of his caftan.)
Great prince, illustrious offspring of a king!

PRETENDER. What wouldst thou?

POET. Condescendingly accept
This poor fruit of my earnest toil.

PRETENDER. What see I?
Verses in Latin! Blest a hundredfold

The tie of sword and lyre; the selfsame laurel
Binds them in friendship. I was born beneath
A northern sky, but yet the Latin muse
To me is a familiar voice; I love
The blossoms of Parnassus, I believe
The prophecies of poets. Not in vain
The ecstasy seethes in their flaming breasts;
The deed is hallowed which is glorified
Beforehand by the poets! Approach, friend.
In memory of me accept this gift.

(*Gives him a ring.*)

When fate fulfills for me her covenant,
When I assume the crown of my forefathers,
I hope again to hear the measured tones
Of thy sweet voice, and thy inspired lay.
Musa gloriam coronat, gloriaque musam.
And so friends, till to-morrow, fare you well.

ALL. Forward! Long live Dimitry! Forward, forward!
Long live Dimitry, the great prince of Moscow!

CASTLE OF THE GOVERNOR MNISZECH IN SAMBOR *

Maryna's Dressing Room

MARYNA, RUZIA (*dressing her*), SERVING-WOMEN

MARYNA. (*Before a mirror.*) Now, is it ready? Canst
thou not make haste?

RUZIA. I pray you first to make the difficult choice;
What will you wear—the necklace made of pearls—
The emerald crescent?

---

* This scene was omitted by Pushkin from the published text of
the play. Here the blank verse yields to irregular rhymed lines.
EDITOR'S NOTE

MARYNA.   No, my diamond crown.

RUZIA. Splendid! Do you remember that you wore it
    When to the palace you were pleased to go?
    They say that at the ball your gracious highness
    Shone like the sun; men sighed, fair ladies whis-
        pered—
    'Twas then that for the first time young Chodkiewicz
    Beheld you, he who later shot himself.
    And whosoever looked on you, they say
    That instant fell in love.

MARYNA.   Make haste! Make haste!

RUZIA. At once. To-day your father counts upon you.
    'Twas not for naught the young Czarevitch saw you;
    He could not hide his rapture; wounded is he
    Already; so it only needs to deal him
    A resolute blow, and instantly, my lady,
    He'll be in love with you. 'Tis now a month
    Since, quitting Cracow, heedless of the war
    And the throne of Moscow, he has feasted here,
    Your guest, enraging Poles alike and Russians.
    Heavens! Shall I yet live to see the day?—
    Say, you will not, when to his capital
    Dimitry leads the queen of Moscow, say
    You'll not forsake me?

MARYNA   Dost thou truly think
    I shall be queen?

RUZIA.   Who, if not you? Who here
    Dares to compare in beauty with my mistress?
    The race of Mniszech never yet has yielded
    To any. You in intellect are past
    All praise—Happy the suitor whom your glance
    Honors with its regard, who wins your heart—
    Whoe'er he be, be he our king, the dauphin

Of France, or even this your poor Czarevitch,
Though who he is, and whence he comes, God
   knows!

MARYNA. He's the Czar's son, as all the world admits.

RUZIA. And yet last winter he was but a servant
   In Wiśniowiecki's house.

MARYNA.   He was in hiding.

RUZIA. I do not question it: but do you know
   What people say about him? That perhaps
   He is a deacon run away from Moscow,
   In his own parish a notorious rogue.

MARYNA. What nonsense!

RUZIA.   Oh, I do not credit it!
   I only say he ought to bless his fate
   That you have so preferred him to the others.

SERVING-WOMAN. (*Runs in.*) The guests have come aĺ
   ready.

MARYNA. There you see;
   You are prepared to chatter on till daybreak.
   Meanwhile I am not dressed——

RUZIA   Within a momenı
   'Twill be quite ready.
               (*The* WAITING-WOMEN *bustle.*)

MARYNA. (*Aside.*)   I must find out all.

CASTLE OF GOVERNOR MNISZECH
AT SAMBOR

A Suite of Lighted Rooms. Music

WIŚNIOWIECKI, MNISZECH

MNISZECH. With none but my Maryna doth he speak,
With no one else preoccupied—such doings
Seem to portend a wedding. Now confess,
Didst ever think my daughter would be queen?

WIŚNIOWIECKI. Indeed, a marvel—Mniszech, didst thou think
My servant would ascend the throne of Moscow?

MNISZECH. And what a girl, look you, is my Maryna.
I merely hinted to her: "Now, be careful!
Let not Dimitry slip"—and lo! already
He is completely tangled in her toils.
    (*The band plays a Polonaise. The* PRETENDER *and*
    MARYNA *advance as the first couple.*)

MARYNA. (*Sotto voce to* DIMITRY.) To-morrow evening
at eleven, beside
The fountain that is in the linden alley.
                    (*They part. A second couple.*)

CAVALIER. What can Dimitry see in her?

LADY.   What say you?
She is a beauty.

CAVALIER.   Yes, a marble nymph;
Eyes, lips, devoid of life, without a smile.
                    (*A fresh couple.*)

LADY. He is not handsome, but his looks are pleasing,
And one can see he is of royal birth.
                    (*A fresh couple.*)

LADY. When will the army march?

CAVALIER. When the Czarevitch
Orders it; we are ready; but 'tis clear
The lady Mniszech and Dimitry mean
To keep us prisoners here.

LADY. A pleasant durance.

CAVALIER. Truly, if you . . .
(*They part; the rooms become empty.*)

MNISZECH. We old folk dance no longer;
The gay mazurka lures us not; we press not
Nor kiss the hands of charmers—ah! my friend,
I've not forgotten the old pranks! Things now
Are not what once they were, what once they were!
Youth, I'll be sworn, is not so bold, nor beauty
So lively; everything—confess, my friend—
Has somehow become dull. So let us leave them;
My comrade, let us go and find a flask
Of old Hungarian overgrown with mould;
Let's bid my butler open an old bottle,
And in a quiet corner, *tête-à-tête,*
Let's drain a draught, a stream as thick as fat;
And while we're so engaged, let's think things over.
Let us go, brother.

WIŚNIOWIECKI. Yes, my friend, let's go.

NIGHT

The Garden. The Fountain

PRETENDER. (*Enters.*) Here is the fountain; hither will
she come.
I was not born a coward; I have seen
Death near at hand, and face to face with death

My spirit hath not blenched. A life-long dungeon
Hath threatened me, I have been close pursued,
And yet my spirit quailed not, and by boldness
I have escaped captivity. But what
Is this which now constricts my breath? What means
This overpowering tremor, or this quivering
Of tense desire? No, this is fear. All day
I have been waiting for this meeting, pondering
On all that I should say to her, how best
I might enmesh Maryna's haughty mind,
Calling her queen of Moscow. But the hour
Has come—and I remember naught, I cannot
Recall the speeches I have learned by rote;
Love puts imagination to confusion—
But something there gleamed suddenly—a rustling;
Hush—no, it was the moon's deceitful light,
It was the rustling of the breeze.

MARYNA. (*Enters.*)   Czarevitch!

PRETENDER. 'Tis she. Now all the blood in me stands
    still.

MARYNA. Dimitry! Is it thou?

PRETENDER.   Bewitching voice!
                   (*Goes to her.*)
Is it thou, at last? Is it thou I see, alone
With me, beneath the roof of quiet night?
How slowly passed the tedious day! How slowly
The glow of evening died away! How long
I've waited in the gloom of night!

MARYNA.   The hours
Are flitting fast, and time is precious to me.
I did not grant a meeting here to thee
To listen to a lover's tender speeches.

No need of words. I well believe thou lovest;
But listen; with thy stormy, doubtful fate
I have resolved to join my own; but one thing,
Dimitry, I require; I claim that thou
Disclose to me thy secret hopes, thy plans,
Even thy fears, that hand in hand with thee
I may confront life boldly—not in blindness
Of childlike ignorance, not as the slave
And plaything of my husband's light desires,
Thy speechless concubine, but as thy spouse,
And worthy helpmate of the Czar of Moscow.

PRETENDER. Oh, if it be only for one short hour,
Forget the cares and troubles of my fate!
Forget 'tis the Czarevitch whom thou seest
Before thee. O, behold in me, Maryna,
A lover, by thee chosen, happy only
In one look from thee. Listen to the prayers
Of love! Grant me to utter all wherewith
My heart is full.

MARYNA.   Prince, this is not the time;
Thou tarriest, and meanwhile the devotion
Of thine adherents cooleth. Hour by hour
Danger becomes more dangerous, difficulties
More difficult; already dubious rumors
Are current, novelty already takes
The place of novelty; and Godunov
Adopts his measures.

PRETENDER.   What is Godunov?
Is thy sweet love, my only blessedness,
Swayed by Boris? Nay, nay. Indifferently
I now regard his throne, his kingly power.
Thy love—without it what to me is life,
And glory's glitter, and the throne of Russia?
On the far steppe, in a poor mud hut, thou—

Thou wilt requite me for the kingly crown;
Thy love——

MARYNA.   For shame! Forget not, prince, thy high
And sacred destiny; thy dignity
Should be to thee more dear than all the joys
Of life and its allurements. This thou canst not
With anything compare. Not to a youth,
Enthralled, inflamed to madness by my beauty—
But to the heir of Moscow's throne I give
My hand in solemn wise, to the Czarevitch
Rescued by destiny.

PRETENDER.   Torture·me not,
Charming Maryna; say not 'twas my rank
And not myself that thou didst choose. Maryna!
Thou knowest not how sorely thou dost wound
My heart thereby. What if—O fearful doubt!—
Say, if blind destiny had not assigned me
A kingly birth; if I were not indeed
Son of Ivan, were not this boy, so long
Forgotten by the world—say, then wouldst thou
Have loved me?

MARYNA.   Thou art Dimitry, and aught else
Thou canst not be; it is not possible
For me to love another.

PRETENDER.   Nay! enough—
I have no wish to share with a dead body
A mistress who belongs to him; I have done
With counterfeiting, and will tell the truth.
Know, then, that thy Dimitry long ago
Perished, was buried—not to rise again;
And wouldst thou know what sort of man I am?
Well, I will tell thee. I am—a poor monk.

Grown weary of monastic servitude,
I pondered 'neath the cowl my bold design,
Made ready for the world a miracle—
And from my cell at last fled to the Cossacks,
To their wild hovels; there I learned to handle
Both steeds and swords; I showed myself to you,
I called myself Dimitry, and deceived
The brainless Poles. What say'st thou, proud Mary-
     na?
Art thou content with my confession? Why
Dost thou keep silence?

MARYNA.   O shame! O woe is me!
                              (*Silence.*)

PRETENDER. (*Sotto voce.*) O whither hath a fit of anger
     led me?
The happiness devised with so much labor
I have, perchance, destroyed for ever. Madman,
What have I done? (*Aloud.*) I see thou art ashamed
Of love not princely; so pronounce on me
The fatal word; my fate is in thy hands.
Decide; I wait.
                    (*Falls on his knees.*)

MARYNA.   Rise, poor impostor! Think'st thou
To please with genuflections my vain heart,
As if I were a weak, confiding girl?
You err, my friend; prone at my feet I've seen
Knights and counts nobly born; but not for this
Did I reject their prayers, that a truant monk——

PRETENDER. (*Rises.*) Scorn not the young pretender;
     noble virtues
May lie perchance in him, virtues deserving
Of Moscow's throne, even of thy priceless hand——

MARYNA. Deserving of a noose, insolent wretch!

PRETENDER. I am to blame; carried away by pride
I have deceived God and the kings—have lied
Unto the world; but it is not for thee,
Maryna, to wreak punishment upon me.
Before thee I am guiltless, do not doubt it.
No, I could not deceive thee. Thou to me
Wast the one sacred being, before thee
I dared not to dissemble; love alone,
Love, jealous, blind, constrained me to tell all.

MARYNA. What's that to boast of, madman? Who de-
    manded
Confession of thee? If thou, a nameless vagrant
Couldst wonderfully blind two nations, then
At least thou shouldst deserve thy high success,
And thy bold fraud shouldst have secured, by deep,
And lasting secrecy. Say, can I yield
Myself to thee, can I, forgetting rank
And maiden modesty, unite my fate
With thine, when thou thyself impetuously
Dost thus with such simplicity reveal
Thy shame? Because of love he blabbed to me!
I marvel wherefore thou hast not from friendship
Disclosed thyself ere now unto my father,
Or else unto our king from joy, or else
Unto Prince Wiśniowiecki from the zeal
Of a devoted servant.

PRETENDER.   I swear to thee
That thou alone wast able to extort
My heart's confession; I swear to thee that never,
Nowhere, not in the feast, not in the cup
Of folly, not in friendly confidence,
Not 'neath the knife nor tortures of the rack,
Shall my tongue give away these weighty secrets.

MARYNA. Thou swearest! Then I must believe. Believe,
Of course! But may I learn by what thou swearest?

Is it not by the name of God, as suits
The Jesuits' devout adopted son?
Or by thy honor as a high-born knight?
Or, maybe, by the royal word alone
As a king's son? Is it not so? Declare.

PRETENDER. (*Proudly.*) The phantom of the Terrible
    adopted
  Me as his son; from out the grave hath named me
  Dimitry, hath stirred up the nations round me,
  And hath consigned Boris to be my victim.
  I am Czarevitch. Enough! 'Twere shame for me
  To stoop before a haughty Polish woman.
  Farewell for ever; the bloody game of war,
  The vast cares of my destiny, will stifle,
  I hope, the pangs of love. Oh, when the heat
  Of shameful passion is o'erspent, how then
  Shall I detest thee! Now I leave thee—ruin,
  Or else a crown, awaits my head in Russia;
  Whether I meet with death as fits a soldier
  In honorable fight, or as a miscreant
  Upon the public scaffold, thou shalt not
  Be my companion, nor shalt share with me
  My fate; but it may be thou shalt regret
  The destiny thou hast refused.

MARYNA.   But what
  If I expose beforehand thy bold fraud
  To all?

PRETENDER. And dost thou truly think I fear thee?
  Will they believe a Polish maiden more
  Than Russia's own Czarevitch? Know, proud lady,
  That neither king, nor pope, nor nobles trouble
  Whether my words be true, whether I be
  Dimitry or another. What care they?
  But I provide a pretext for dispute

And war; and this is all they need; and thee,
Rebellious one, believe me, they will force
To hold thy peace. Farewell.

MARYNA   Czarevitch, stay!
At last I hear the speech not of a boy,
But of a man. It reconciles me to thee.
Prince, I forget thy mad outburst, and see
Again Dimitry. Listen; now is the time!
Awake; delay no more, lead on thy troops
Quickly to Moscow, purge the Kremlin, take
Thy seat upon the throne of Moscow; then
Send me the nuptial envoy; but, God hears me,
Until thou tread the step ascending to
The throne, until by thee Boris be vanquished,
My ears are deaf to any word of love.

                                        (*Exit.*)

PRETENDER. No—easier far to strive with Godunov,
Or to play false with courtly Jesuits,
Than with a woman. Deuce take them; they're be-
    yond
My power. She twists, and coils, and crawls, slips out
Of hand, she hisses, threatens, bites. Ah, serpent!
Serpent! 'Twas not for nothing that I trembled.
She well-nigh ruined me; but I'm resolved;
At daybreak I will put my troops in motion.

THE LITHUANIAN FRONTIER

PRINCE KURBSKY *and* PRETENDER, *both
on horseback. Troops approach the frontier*

KURBSKY. (*First to reach the frontier.*) There, there it
    is; there is the Russian frontier!
Fatherland! Holy Russia! I am thine!

With scorn from off my clothing now I shake
The foreign dust, and greedily I drink
New air; it is my native air. O father,
Thy soul hath now been solaced; in the grave
Thy bones, disgraced, thrill with a sudden joy!
Again doth flash our old ancestral sword,
This glorious sword—the dread of dark Kazan!
This good sword—servant of the czars of Moscow!
Now will it revel in its feast of slaughter,
Serving the master whom it trusts.

PRETENDER. (*Rides quietly with bowed head.*) How
 happy
Is he, how flushed with gladness and with glory
His stainless soul! Brave knight, I envy thee!
The son of Kurbsky, thou in exile nurtured,
Forgetting all the wrongs borne by thy father,
Redeeming his transgression in the grave,
Thou for the son of great Ivan art ready
To shed thy blood, to give the fatherland
Its lawful czar. Righteous art thou; thy soul
Should flame with joy.

KURBSKY.   And dost not thou likewise
 Rejoice in spirit? There lies our Russia; she
 Is thine, Czarevitch! There thy people's hearts
 Are waiting for thee, there thy Moscow waits,
 Thy Kremlin, thy dominion.

PRETENDER.   Russian blood,
 O Kurbsky, first must flow! You for the Czar
 Have drawn your swords, you are stainless; but I
  lead you
 Against your brothers; I am summoning
 Lithuania against Russia; I am showing
 To foes the longed-for way to beauteous Moscow!

But let my sin fall not on me, but thee,
Boris, the regicide! Forward! Set on!

KURBSKY. Forward! Advance! And woe to Godunov.
(*They gallop. The troops cross the frontier.*)

THE COUNCIL OF THE CZAR

THE CZAR, THE PATRIARCH AND BOYARS

CZAR. Is it possible? An unfrocked monk against us
Leads rascal troops, a truant friar dares threaten
Our august person! 'Tis time to tame the madman!
Go thou forth, Trubetskoy, and thou Basmanov;
My zealous governors need help. Chernigov
Already by the rebel is besieged;
Rescue the town and citizens.

BASMANOV.   Three months
Shall not pass, Sire, ere even rumor's tongue
Shall cease to speak of the pretender; caged
In iron, like a beast from oversea,
We'll hale him into Moscow, aye, by God.
(*Exit with* TRUBETSKOY.)

CZAR. The King of Sweden hath by envoys tendered
Me his alliance. But we have no need
To lean on foreign aid; we have enough
Of our own fighting forces to repel
The traitors and the Poles. I have refused—
Shchelkalov! Send to every governor
An edict, that he mount his steed, and press
The people into service, as of old;
The servants of the clergy likewise should
Be pressed into the service. When, of old,
The land was threatened, of their own free will
Hermits bore arms; it is not now our wish

To trouble them; no, let them pray for us;
Such is the Czar's decree, such the resolve
Of his boyars. And now a weighty question
We shall decide; ye know how everywhere
The insolent pretender hath sent forth
His artful rumors; letters everywhere,
By him distributed, have sowed alarm
And doubt; seditious whispers to and fro
Pass in the market-places; minds are seething.
We needs must cool them; gladly would I keep
From executions, but by what means and how?
That we will now determine. Holy father,
Thou first declare thy thought.

PATRIARCH.   The Blessed One,
The All-Highest, hath instilled into thy soul,
Great lord, the breath of kindness and meek pa-
  tience;
Thou wishest not perdition for the sinner,
Thou wilt wait quietly, until delusion
Shall pass away; for pass away it will,
And truth's eternal sun will dawn on all.
Thy faithful bedesman, one in worldly matters
No able judge, ventures to-day to offer
His voice to thee, This offspring of the devil,
This unfrocked monk, has well impersonated
Dimitry for the people. Shamelessly
He clothed him with the name of the Czarevitch
As with a stolen vestment. It only needs
To rip it—and he will be put to shame
By his own nakedness. The means thereto
God hath Himself supplied. Know, Sire, six years
Since then have fled; 'twas in that very year
When to the seat of sovereignty the Lord
Anointed thee—there came to me one evening
A simple shepherd, a venerable old man,

Who told me a strange secret. "In my young days,"
He said, "I lost my sight, and thenceforth knew not
Nor day, nor night, till my old age; in vain
I plied myself with herbs and secret spells;
In vain did I resort in adoration
To the great wonder-workers in the cloisters;
Bathed my dark eyes in vain with healing water
From out the holy wells. The Lord vouchsafed not
Healing to me. Then I lost hope at last,
And grew accustomed to my darkness. Even
Slumber showed not to me things visible,
Only of sounds I dreamed. Once in deep sleep
I hear a childish voice; it speaks to me:
'Arise, grandfather, go to Uglich town,
To the Cathedral of Transfiguration;
There pray over my grave. The Lord is gracious—
And I shall pardon thee.' 'But who art thou?'
I asked the childish voice. 'I'm the Czarevitch
Dimitry, whom the Heavenly Czar hath taken
Into His angel band, and I am now
A mighty wonder-worker. Go, old man.'
I woke, and pondered. What is this? Maybe
God will in very deed vouchsafe to me
Belated healing. I will go. I bend
My footsteps to the distant road. I reach
Uglich, repair unto the holy minster,
Hear mass, and, zealous soul aglow, I weep
Sweetly, as if the blindness from mine eyes
Were flowing out in tears. And when the people
Began to leave, to my grandson I said:
'Lead me, Ivan, to where the young Czarevitch
Lies buried.' The boy led me—and I scarce
Had shaped before the grave a silent prayer,
When sight illumed my eyeballs; I beheld
The light of God, my grandson, and the tomb."

That is the tale, Sire, which the old man told.
   (*General confusion. In the course of this speech*
     BORIS *several times wipes his face with his hand-*
    kerchief.)
To Uglich then I sent, where it was learned
That many sufferers had likewise found
Deliverance at the grave of the Czarevitch.
This is my counsel; to the Kremlin send
The sacred relics, place them in the Minster
Of the Archangel; clearly will the people
See then the godless villain's fraud; the fiends'
Dread might will vanish as a cloud of dust.
                        (*Silence.*)

PRINCE SHUISKY. What mortal, holy father, knoweth
   the ways
Of the All-Highest? 'Tis not for me to judge Him.
Untainted sleep and power of wonder-working
He may upon the child's remains bestow;
But vulgar rumor must dispassionately
And diligently be tested; is it for us,
In stormy times of insurrection,
To weigh so great a matter? Will men not say
That insolently we made of sacred things
A worldly instrument? Even now the people
Sway madly first this way, then that, even now
There are enough already of loud rumors;
This is no time to vex the people's minds
With aught so unexpected, grave, and strange.
I myself see 'tis needful to demolish
The rumor broadcast by the unfrocked monk;
But for this end other and simpler means
Will serve. Therefore, when it shall please thee, Sire,
I will myself appear in public places,
I will dispel and exorcise this madness,
And will expose the vagabond's vile fraud.

CZAR. So be it! My lord Patriarch, I pray thee
  Go with us to the palace, where to-day
  I must converse with thee.
          (*Exeunt; all the* BOYARS *follow them.*)

FIRST BOYAR. (*Sotto voce to another.*) Didst mark how
    pale
  Our sovereign turned, how from his face there
    poured
  A mighty sweat?

SECOND BOYAR.   I durst not, I confess,
  Uplift mine eyes, nor breathe, nor even stir.

FIRST BOYAR. Prince Shuisky's saved the day. A splendid fellow!

A PLAIN NEAR NOVGOROD-SEVERSK

(*December 21st, 1604*)

SOLDIERS. (*Run in disorder.*) Woe, woe! The Czarevitch! The Poles! There they are! There they are!
          (*Enter* CAPTAINS: MARGERET *and* WALTER ROSEN.)

MARGERET. Whither, whither? Allons! Go back!

ONE OF THE FUGITIVES. You go back, if you like, cursed
  infidel.

MARGERET. Quoi, quoi?

ANOTHER. Quack! quack! You foreign frog, you like to
  croak at the Russian Czarevitch; but we—we are
  orthodox folk.

MARGERET. Qu'est-ce à dire "orthodox?" Sacrés gueux,
  maudite canaille! Mordieu, mein Herr, j'enrage; on

dirait que sa n'a pas de bras pour frapper, sa n'a que des jambes pour foutre le camp.

ROSEN. Es ist Schande.

MARGERET. Ventre-saint gris! Je ne bouge plus d'un pas; puisque le vin est tiré, il faut le boire. Qu'en dites-vous, mein Herr?

ROSEN. Sie haben recht.

MARGERET. Tudieu, il y fait chaud! Ce diable de "Pretender," comme ils l'appellent, est un bougre, qui a du poil au cul.—Qu'en pensez-vous, mein Herr?

ROSEN. Oh, ja.

MARGERET. Hé! voyez donc, voyez donc! L'action s'engage sur les derrières de l'ennemi. Ce doit être le brave Basmanov, qui aurait fait une sortie.

ROSEN. Ich glaube das.

(Enter GERMANS.)

MARGERET. Ha, ha! voici nos allemands. Messieurs! Mein Herr, dites-leur donc de se raillier et, sacrebleu, chargeons!

ROSEN. Sehr gut. Halt! (*The* GERMANS *fall into line.*) Marsch!

THE GERMANS. (*They march.*) Hilf Gott!

(Fight. The RUSSIANS flee again.)

POLES. Victory! Victory! Glory to the Czar Dimitry!

DIMITRY. (*On horseback.*) Cease firing. We have conquered. Enough! Spare Russian blood. Cease firing.

(Trumpets and drums.)

SQUARE IN FRONT OF THE CATHEDRAL IN MOSCOW

The People

ONE MAN. Will the Czar soon come out of the cathedral?

ANOTHER. The mass is ended; now the Te Deum is going on.

FIRST MAN. What! have they already cursed *him?*

SECOND MAN. I stood in the porch and heard how the deacon cried out:—Grishka Otrepyev is anathema!

FIRST MAN. Let them curse to their heart's content; the Czarevitch has nothing to do with Otrepyev.

SECOND MAN. But they are now singing mass for the repose of the soul of the Czarevitch.

FIRST MAN. What? A mass for the dead sung for a living man? They'll suffer for it, the godless wretches!

THIRD MAN. Hist! A noise. Is it not the Czar?

FOURTH MAN. No, it is the idiot.
   (*A saintly* IDIOT *enters, in an iron cap, hung round with chains; he is surrounded by* BOYS.)

BOYS. Nick, Nick, iron nightcap! T-r-r-r-r——

OLD WOMAN. Let the saintly one alone, you young devils. Pray for me, Nick, sinner that I am.

IDIOT. Give, give, give a penny.

OLD WOMAN. There is a penny for thee; remember me in thy prayers.

IDIOT. (*Seats himself on the ground and sings:*)

> The moon sails on,
> The kitten cries,
> Nick, arise,
> Pray to God.
> (*The* BOYS *surround him again.*)

A BOY. How do you do Nick? Why don't you take off your cap?

(*Raps him on the iron cap.*)

How it rings!

IDIOT. But I have got a penny.

BOY. That's not true; now, show it.
(*He snatches the penny and runs away.*)

IDIOT. (*Weeps.*) They have taken my penny, they are hurting Nick!

THE PEOPLE. The Czar, the Czar is coming!
(*The* CZAR *comes out from the Cathedral; a* BOYAR *in front of him scatters alms among the beggars.* BOYARS.)

IDIOT. Boris, Boris! The boys are hurting Nick.

CZAR. Give him alms! What is he crying about?

IDIOT. Little children are hurting Nick . . . Have them killed, as thou hadst the little Czarevitch killed.

BOYARS. Go away, fool! Seize the fool!

CZAR. Leave him alone. Pray thou for me, poor Nick.
(*Exit.*)

IDIOT. (*Calling after him.*) No, no! It is impossible to pray for Czar Herod; the Mother of God forbids it.

SEVSK

The PRETENDER, *surrounded by his supporters*

PRETENDER. Where is the prisoner?

A POLE   Here.

PRETENDER.   Call him before me.
                          (*Enter a* RUSSIAN *prisoner.*)
    Who art thou? Speak.

PRISONER.   Rozhnov, a nobleman of Moscow.

PRETENDER. Hast long been in the service?

PRISONER.   Nigh a month.

PRETENDER. Art not ashamed, Rozhnov, that thou hast
    drawn
    The sword against me?

PRISONER.   What else could I do?
    'Twas not our wish.

PRETENDER.   Didst fight beneath the walls
    Of Seversk?

PRISONER.   'Twas two weeks after the battle
    I came from Moscow.

PRETENDER.   What of Godunov?

PRISONER. The battle's loss, Mstislavsky's wound, hath
    caused him
    Much apprehension; Shuisky he hath sent
    To take command.

PRETENDER.   But why hath he recalled
    Basmanov unto Moscow?

PRISONER.   The Czar rewarded
His services with honor and with gold.
Basmanov now sits in the council of
The Czar.

PRETENDER. The army had more need of him.
Well, how go things in Moscow?

PRISONER.   All is quiet,
Thank God.

PRETENDER.   Say, do they look for me?

PRISONER.   God knows;
They dare not talk too much there now. For some
Have had their tongues cut off, and others even
Their heads. It is a fearsome state of things—
Each day an execution. All the prisons
Are crammed. Wherever two or three foregather
In public places, instantly a spy
Worms himself in; the Czar himself examines
At leisure the informers. It is just
Sheer misery; so silence is the best.

PRETENDER. An enviable life for that Czar's people!
Well, and what of the army?

PRISONER.   What of it?
Clothed and full-fed, the army is content.

PRETENDER. But is it very large?

PRISONER.   God knows.

PRETENDER.   All told
Will there be thirty thousand?

PRISONER.   Yes; 'twill run
Even to fifty thousand.
      (*The* PRETENDER *reflects; those around him glance
      at one another.*)

PRETENDER.   Well! What say
They in your camp of me?

PRISONER.   Why, of thy grace
They say, Sire (be not wroth), that thou'rt a knave,
And yet, forsooth, a man of pluck.

PRETENDER. (*Laughing.*)   Even so
I'll prove myself to them in deed. My friends,
We will not wait for Shuisky; give you joy;
To-morrow, battle.

                                 (*Exit.*)

ALL.   Long life to Dimitry!

A POLE. To-morrow, battle! They are fifty thousand,
And we scarce fifteen thousand. He is mad!

ANOTHER. That's nothing, friend. A single Pole can
    challenge
Five hundred Muscovites.

PRISONER.   Yes, thou mayst challenge!
But when it comes to fighting, then, thou braggart,
Thou'lt run away.

POLE.   If thou hadst had a sword,
Insolent prisoner, then (*pointing to his sword*) with
    this I'd soon
Have mastered thee.

PRISONER.   A Russian can make shift
Without a sword; how like you this (*shows his fist*),
    you fool?
    (*The* POLE *looks at him haughtily and departs
      in silence. All laugh.*)

A FOREST

PRETENDER AND PUSHKIN

(In the background lies a dying horse)

PRETENDER. Ah, my poor horse! How gallantly he charged
To-day in the last battle, and when wounded,
How swiftly bore me. My poor horse!

PUSHKIN. *(To himself.)*　　　　　Well, here's
A great ado about a horse, when all
Our army's smashed to bits.

PRETENDER.　　　　　Listen! Perhaps
He's but exhausted by the loss of blood,
And will recover.

PUSHKIN.　　　Nay, nay; he is dying.

PRETENDER. *(Goes to his horse.)*
My poor horse!—what to do? Take off the bridle,
And loose the girth. Let him at least die free.
　　(He unbridles and unsaddles the horse. Some
　　POLES *enter.)*
Good evening, gentlemen! How is't I see not
Kurbsky among you? I did note to-day
How he cut through to where the fight was thickest;
Around the man, like swaying ears of corn,
The sabers flashed; but higher than the rest
His blade was brandished, and his mighty cry
Drowned all cries else. Where is my knight?

POLE.　　　　　He fell
Upon the field of battle.

PRETENDER.　　　　Honor the brave,
And peace be to his soul! How few unscathed

Are left us from the fight! Accursed Cossacks,
Traitors and miscreants, you, you it is
Have ruined us! Not even for three minutes
To keep the foe at bay! I'll teach the villains!
Every tenth man I'll hang. Brigands!

PUSHKIN. Whoe'er
Be guilty, all the same we were clean worsted,
Routed!

PRETENDER. But yet we nearly conquered. Just
When I had dealt with their front rank, the Ger-
mans
Repulsed us utterly. But they're fine fellows!
By God! fine fellows! I do love them for it.
I'll form of them an honorable troop.

PUSHKIN. Where shall we spend the night?

PRETENDER. Here, in the forest.
Why not rest here tonight? And just at daybreak
We'll take the road, and dine in Rylsk. Good night.
(*He lies down, puts a saddle under his head, and
falls asleep.*)

PUSHKIN. A pleasant sleep, Czarevitch! Smashed to bits,
Rescued by flight alone, he is as careless
As a mere child; 'tis clear that Providence
Protects him, and we, friends, must not lose heart.

MOSCOW. PALACE OF THE CZAR

BORIS. BASMANOV

ÇZAR. He's vanquished, but what profit lies in that?
We are crowned with a vain conquest; he has
mustered
Again his scattered forces, and anew

Threatens us from the ramparts of Putivl.
Meanwhile what are our heroes doing? They're
At Krom, where from its rotten battlements
A band of Cossacks braves them. There is glory!
No, I am ill content with them; thyself
I shall despatch to take command of them;
I grant command not unto birth, but brains.
Their pride of precedence, let it be wounded!
The time has come for me to hold in scorn
The murmur of a worthless well-born mob,
And quash the vicious custom.

BASMANOV.   Ay, my lord
Blessèd a hundredfold will be that day
When fire consumes the lists of noblemen
With their dissensions, their proud pedigrees.

CZAR. That day is not far off; let me but first
Subdue the insurrection of the people.

BASMANOV. Why trouble about that? The people al-
     ways
Are ready for rebellion; even so
The swift steed champs the bit; so doth a lad
Chafe at his father's ruling. But what of it?
The rider quietly controls the steed,
The father sways the son.

CZAR.   Sometimes the horse
Doth throw the rider, nor does the son at all times
Abide the father's will; we can restrain
The people only by unsleeping sternness.
So thought Ivan, sagacious autocrat
And storm-subduer; so his fierce grandson thought.
No, no, kindness is lost upon the people;
Do good—it thanks you not at all; extort

And execute—'twill be no worse for you.

(*Enter a* BOYAR.)

What now?

BOYAR.   The foreign merchants, Sire.

CZAR.   I go
To welcome them. Basmanov, wait, stay here;
I still have need to speak a word with thee.

(*Exit.*)

BASMANOV. High sovereign spirit! God grant he may
    subdue
The accurst Otrepyev; and much, still much
Of good he'll do for Russia. A great thought
Within his mind has taken birth; it must not
Be suffered to grow cold. What a career
For me when once he crushes the proud might
Of the nobility. I have no rivals
In war. I shall stand closest to the throne—
And it may chance— But what is that strange noise?

(*Alarum.* BOYARS *and* COURT-ATTENDANTS *run in
    disorder, meet and whisper.*)

ONE ATTENDANT. Fetch a physician!

ANOTHER.   Quickly to the Patriarch!

A THIRD. He calls for the Czarevitch, the Czarevitch!

A FOURTH. Call a priest!

BASMANOV.   What has happened?

A FIFTH AN SIXTH.   The Czar's ill
The Czar is dying.

BASMANOV.   Good God!

A FIFTH.   On the throne

He sat, and suddenly he fell; blood gushed
From mouth and ears.
> (*The* CZAR *is carried in on a chair. All the Czar's
> household; all the* BOYARS.)

CZAR.   Let all depart—alone
Leave the Czarevitch with me. (*All withdraw.*) I
    am dying;
Let us embrace. Farewell, my son; forthwith
Thou wilt begin to reign.—O God, my God!
Forthwith, I shall appear before Thy presence—
And now I have no time to shrive my soul.
But yet, my son, I feel thou'rt dearer to me
Than is my soul's salvation—be it so!
A subject was I born; it seemed ordained
That I should die a subject in obscurity.
Yet I attained to sovereignty; but how?
Ask not. Enough that thou art innocent.
Thou wilt reign rightfully; and I alone
Am answerable for all to God. Dear son,
Cherish no false delusion, of thy free will
Blind not thyself. Stormy the days wherein
Thou dost assume the crown. He is dangerous,
This strange pretender; with a fearful name
He is weaponed. I at last with years grown skilled
In ruling could full well put down rebellion;
They quaked with fear before me; treachery
Dared not to raise its voice; but thou, a boy,
An inexperienced ruler, how wilt thou
Govern amid the tempests, quench revolt,
Shackle sedition? But God is great! He gives
Wisdom to youth, to weakness strength.—Give ear;
Firstly, select a steadfast counselor,
Cool, of ripe years, loved of the people, honored
Mid the boyars for birth and fame—say, Shuisky.
The army craves to-day a skilful leader;

Appoint Basmanov; do not heed the murmurs
Of the boyars. Thou from thy early years
Didst sit with me in council, thou dost know
The formal course of government; change not
Procedure. Custom is the soul of states.
Of late I have been driven to restore
Bans, executions—these thou canst rescind;
And they will bless thee, as they blessed thy uncle
When he succeeded to the Terrible.
At the same time, little by little, tighten
Anew the reins of government; now slacken;
But let them not slip from thy hands. Be gracious,
Accessible to foreigners, accept
Their service trustfully. Preserve with strictness
The Church's discipline. Be taciturn;
The royal voice must never lose itself
Upon the air in vain; it must be like
A sacred bell that sounds but to announce
Some great disaster or great festival.
Dear son, thou art approaching to those years
When woman's beauty agitates our blood.
Preserve, preserve the sacred purity
Of innocence and haughty modesty;
He, who through passion has been wont to wallow
In vicious pleasures in his youthful days,
Becomes in manhood bloodthirsty and surly;
His mind untimely darkens. Of thy household
Be always head; show honor to thy mother,
But rule thy house thyself; thou art a man
And czar to boot. Be tender to thy sister—
For thou art now, alas, her sole protector.

FEODOR. (*On his knees.*) No, no; live on, my father,
    and reign long;
Without thee both the folk and we will perish.

CZAR. For me all's at an end—mine eyes grow dark,
  I feel the coldness of the grave——
    (*Enter the* PATRIARCH *and* PRELATES, *followed by
    all the* BOYARS. *The* CZARINA *is supported on
    either side; the* CZAREVNA *is sobbing.*)
                              Who's there?
  Ah, 'tis the vestment—so! the holy vows—
  The hour has struck. The Czar becomes a monk,
  And the dark sepulchre will be my cell.
  Wait yet a little, my lord Patriarch,
  I still am Czar. Listen to me boyars:
  To this my son I now commit the czardom;
  Do homage to Feodor. Basmanov, thou,
  And ye, my friends, on the grave's brink I pray you
  To serve my son with zeal and rectitude!
  As yet he is both young and uncorrupted.
  Swear ye?

BOYARS.   We swear.

CZAR.   I am content. Forgive me
  My sins and my surrenders to temptation,
  The harm I meant and that I did not mean.—
  Approach now, holy father; I am ready.
    (*The rite begins. The women, who have swooned,
    are carried out.*)

ARMY HEADQUARTERS

BASMANOV *leads in* PUSHKIN

BASMANOV. Here enter, and speak freely. So to me
  He sent thee.

PUSHKIN.   He doth offer thee his friendship
  And the next place to his in Muscovy.

BASMANOV. But even thus highly by Feodor am I
   Already raised; the army I command;
   For me he scorned nobility of rank
   And the wrath of the boyars. I swore allegiance
   To him.

PUSHKIN.   Thou'st sworn allegiance to the man
   Who lawfully succeedeth to the throne;
   Suppose that there is one whose rights are greater.

BASMANOV. Enough; tell me no idle tales! I know
   Who the man is.

PUSHKIN.   Russia and Lithuania
   Have long acknowledged him to be Dimitry;
   But, be that as it may, I don't insist.
   Perchance he is indeed the real Dimitry;
   Perchance but a pretender; only this
   I know, that soon or late Boris's son
   Will yield Moscow to him.

BASMANOV.   So long as I
   Stand by the youthful Czar, so long he will not
   Forsake the throne. We have sufficient troops,
   Thank God! With victory I will inspire them.
   And whom do you intend to send against me:
   Is it Karela, is it Mniszech? Are
   Your numbers many? You have scarce eight thou-
      sand.

PUSHKIN. Indeed thou art mistaken: they will not
   Amount even to that. I say myself
   Our army is mere trash, the Cossacks only
   Rob villages, the Poles but brag and drink;
   The Russians—what shall I say?—with thee I'll not
   Dissemble; but, Basmanov, dost thou know
   Wherein our true strength lies? Not in the army,
   Nor yet in Polish aid, but in opinion—

Yes, popular opinion. Dost remember
The triumph of Dimitry, dost remember
His peaceful conquests, when, without a blow
The docile towns surrendered, and the mob
Bound the recalcitrant leaders? Thou thyself
Wast witness; was it willingly your troops
Waged war against him? Aye, and when? Boris
Was then supreme. But would they now?—Nay, nay,
It is too late to blow on the cold embers
Of this dispute; with all thy wits and firmness
Thou'lt not withstand him. Were it not far better
If thou wouldst be the one to take the lead,
Proclaim Dimitry czar, and by that act
Bind him thy friend for ever? How thinkest thou?

BASMANOV. To-morrow thou shalt know.

PUSHKIN.   Resolve.

BASMANOV.   Farewell

PUSHKIN. Ponder it well, Basmanov.

                                   (*Exit.*)

BASMANOV.   He is right.
Everywhere treason ripens; what's to do?
Wait, that the rebels may deliver me
In bonds to this Otrepyev? Had I not better
Forestall the stormy onset of the flood,
Myself to—ah! but to forswear mine oath!
Incurring fresh disgrace from age to age!
The trust of my young sovereign to requite
With horrible betrayal! 'Tis a light thing
For a dishonored exile to be plotting
Sedition and conspiracy; but I?
Is it for me, the favorite of my lord?—
But death—but power—the people's miseries . . .
                                   (*He ponders.*)

Who's there? (*Whistles.*) A horse here!
Sound the muster-drum!

PLACE OF EXECUTION, RED SQUARE, MOSCOW

PUSHKIN *enters, surrounded by the people*

THE PEOPLE. Here cometh a boyar from the Czarevitch.
Let's hear what the boyar will tell us. Hither!
Hither!

PUSHKIN. (*On a platform.*) Townsmen of Moscow!
The Czarevitch
Bids me convey his greetings to you. (*He bows.*) Ye
know
How Divine Providence saved the Czarevitch
From the base murderer's hands; he marched to
punish
His would-be murderer, but God already
Had struck him down. All Russia hath submitted
Unto Dimitry; with sincere repentance
Basmanov hath himself led forth his troops
To swear allegiance to him. With love and peace
Dimitry comes to you. Would ye, to please
The house of Godunov, uplift a hand
Against the lawful Czar, against the grandson
Of Monomakh?

THE PEOPLE.   Not we.

PUSHKIN.   Townsmen of Moscow!
The world well knows how much ye have endured
The while the harsh usurper ruled you; ban,
Dishonor, executions, taxes, hardships,
Hunger—all these ye have experienced.
Dimitry is disposed to show you favor,

Courtiers, boyars, soldiers, and functionaries,
Merchants—and all the honest folk. And will ye
Be stubborn without reason, and in pride
Flee from his kindness? But he himself is coming
To his ancestral throne with mighty escort.
Provoke not ye the Czar to wrath, fear God,
And swear allegiance to the lawful ruler;
Humble yourselves; forthwith send to Dimitry
The Metropolitan, boyars, officials,
And chosen men, that they may all do homage
To him who is their lord and father.

> (*Exit. Clamor of the* PEOPLE.)

THE PEOPLE.   Well?
He spoke the truth. Long live our lord, Dimitry!

A PEASANT ON THE PLATFORM. Folk! To the Kremlin!
   To the Royal palace!
To bind Boris's whelp!

THE PEOPLE. (*Rushing in a crowd.*)
                    Bind, drown him! Hail
Dimitry! Crush the race of Godunov!

THE KREMLIN. HOUSE OF BORIS

A GUARD *on the Steps.* FEODOR *at a Window*

BEGGAR. Alms, for Christ's sake!

GUARD. Go away; it is forbidden to speak to the prisoners.

FEODOR. Go, old man, I am poorer than thou; thou art
at liberty.

> (XENIA, *veiled, also comes to the window.*)

ONE OF THE PEOPLE. Brother and sister—poor children,
like birds in a cage.

ANOTHER. So you've pity for them? Accursèd house!

FIRST MAN. The father was a villain, but the children are innocent.

SECOND MAN. The apple does not fall far from the apple-tree.

XENIA. Dear brother! dear brother! I think the boyars are coming to us.

FEODOR. That is Golitsyn, Mosalsky. I do not know the others.

XENIA. Ah! dear brother, my heart sinks.
  (GOLITSYN, MOSALSKY, MOLCHANOV, *and* SHEREFE-
  DINOV; *behind them three soldiers.*)

THE PEOPLE. Make way, make way; the boyars are coming.
                    (*They enter the house.*)

ONE OF THE PEOPLE. What have they come for?

ANOTHER. Most like to make Feodor Godunov swear allegiance.

A THIRD. Very like. Hark! what a noise in the house! What an uproar! They are fighting!

THE PEOPLE. Do you hear? A scream! That was a wo-man's voice. Let us go up!—The doors are locked—the cries have ceased.
  (*The doors are thrown open.* MOSALSKY *appears on the steps.*)

MOSALSKY. Good folk! Maria Godunov and her son Feodor have poisoned themselves. We have seen their dead bodies.
                    (*The* PEOPLE *are silent with horror.*)

Why are ye silent? Cry, Long live Czar Dimitry Ivanovich!

(*The* PEOPLE *are speechless.*)

[1825]

[Published 1831]

* THE COVETOUS KNIGHT *

```
  ╱      *      ╲
 ╱╶────────────╴╲
```

(*Scenes from* SHENSTONE'S *tragi-comedy,*
The Covetous Knight) [1]

SCENE I

In a tower. ALBERT *and* JEAN, *his man-servant*

ALBERT. Whatever happens, at the tournament
I shall appear. Show me the helmet, Jean.
         (JEAN *gives him the helmet.*)
Pierced through, and ruined. Quite impossible
To put it on. I'll have to get a new one.
Ah, what a stroke! That cursèd Count Delorge!

JEAN. Well, anyway, you paid him back his due;
For, after you had bounced him from his stirrups,
He lay like dead a day and night—perhaps
Is not recovered yet.

ALBERT.   He's had no loss.
His breastplate of Venetian steel is whole,
And, sure, his breast's his own, and cost him noth-
    ing—
He won't be buying another for himself.
Why didn't I take his helmet from him straight?

---

[1] This sub-title is a piece of mystification on Pushkin's part.
William Shenstone wrote no such play. This is an original work.
                            EDITOR'S NOTE

I should have done it but for fear of shame
Before the ladies and the duke. Damned Count!
Better if he had pierced my skull instead.
I need clothes too. The last time, all the knights
Were sitting there in satin and in velvet;
And I alone was wearing coat-of-mail
At the duke's table. I excused myself
By saying I had happened in by chance.
But what shall I say now? O, poverty!
How it degrades the very hearts of men!
When Count Delorge with blow of mighty lance
Pierced through my helmet and went rushing by,
And I, with head uncovered, gave the spurs
To my Emir, and like a whirlwind flew,
And threw the Count some twenty paces off,
As though he were a page, and all the ladies
Rose from their seats; and when Clotilda, too,
Hiding her face, could not restrain a cry,
And all the heralds praised my mighty stroke:
Why, not a soul among them saw the reason
For all my bravery and god-like strength!
My damaged helmet simply made me mad;
Not heroism, but avarice was the cause.
Yes, that disease is easy to be caught
By one who lives beneath my father's roof.
But how's my poor Emir?

JEAN.   He still is limping.
It's quite impossible to ride him yet.

ALBERT. There's nothing to be done; I'll buy a bay.
They don't charge much for them.

JEAN.   They don't charge much,
But well you know we haven't any money.

ALBERT. What says that good-for-nothing Solomon?

JEAN. He says, he cannot lend another groat
Unless you give him good security!

ALBERT. Security! And where can I find that?

JEAN. That's what I said.

ALBERT.   And he—

JEAN.   He sighed and shrugged.

ALBERT. Didn't you tell him that my father's rich
Himself as any Jew, and that, ere long,
I shall succeed him?

JEAN.   That I told him too.

ALBERT. And he—

JEAN.   He shrugged and sighed.

ALBERT.   What wretched luck!

JEAN. He said he'd come himself.

ALBERT.   Thank God for that.
I'll never let him go without a ransom.
                    (*Knock at the door.*)
Who's there?

                              (JEW *enters.*)

JEW.   Your humble servant.

ALBERT.   Oh, my friend!
You cursèd Jew, you honored Solomon,
Please come this way: so you, I hear, won't give
Me any credit.

JEW.   Ah, my gracious lord,
With all respect to you, I'd fain . . . but cannot.
Where can I get the money? I'm quite ruined,
Helping you lords with all my might and main.

For no one pays; and I have come to ask
If you could not pay back at least a part . . .

ALBERT. You rascal! Do you think if I had money,
I'd parley here with you? But stop, enough!
Be not so obstinate, friend Solomon,
Out with your ducats. Pay me down a hundred,
Before we search you.

JEW.   Pay you down a hundred!
Where should I get a hundred ducats?

ALBERT.   Listen:
Aren't you ashamed, denying to your friends
Your help?

JEW.   I swear to you . . .

ALBERT.   Enough, enough.
So you demand security? What nonsense!
What shall I give you for security?
A pig-skin? Had I anything to pawn,
I would have sold it long ago. You dog,
Is not my knightly word enough?

JEW.   Your word,
As long as you're alive, means much, yes, much.
The treasure-chests of Flanders' wealthy men
Your word will open like a talisman;
But if to a poor Jew like me you give it
In guarantee, and afterwards you die
(Which God forbid!) your word will then be left
In my poor hands as if it were a key
To a rich casket sunken in the deep.

ALBERT. Do you suppose my father will survive me?

JEW. Who knows? Our days are not our own to
    measure:
But yesterday a youth was flourishing
And now he's dead; and four old men must bear

His corpse on stooping shoulders to the grave.
The baron's healthy. He may live for ten
Or twenty years—or twenty-five or thirty.

ALBERT. You lying Jew! When thirty years are out,
  Why, I'll be over fifty; then what use
  Will money be to me?

JEW.   What use? Why, money,
  Always, at any age is useful to us;
  The young man seeks in it a ready servant
  And, here and there, he throws it recklessly;
  The old man sees in it a trusty friend
  And guards it like the apple of his eye.

ALBERT. My father sees in money neither friend
  Nor servant, but a master—whom he serves.
  And serves him how? Like an Algerian slave,
  Like a chained dog. Within his fireless hovel
  He lives, drinks water, eats dry crusts of bread,
  Ne'er sleeps at night, but runs about and barks.
  The gold meanwhile is sleeping in the chests
  All quietly. But hush! the day will come
  When it will serve me and forget to sleep.

JEW. Yes, at his lordship's funeral will flow
  More gold than tears. And may God make you now
  His heir as soon as possible.

ALBERT.   Amen!

JEW. But might I . . .

ALBERT.   What?

JEW.   Well, I was thinking, means
  Exist to make . . .

ALBERT.   What's that you say?

JEW.   Well—just—
  I have a friend, a little, queer old man,
  A Jew, a poor apothecary . . .

ALBERT.   Oh!
  A usurer like you? Or honester?

JEW. Oh, no, my lord, he drives a different trade:
  He makes up drops . . no, really it's a marvel
  The way they work.

ALBERT.   What use are they to me?

JEW. Pour but three drops into a glass of water—
  They have no taste or color—he who drinks,
  Without a pang of colic in his belly,
  Or pain or even nausea, will die.

ALBERT. So it's in poison that your old man traffics.

JEW. Ah—yes—in poison.

ALBERT.   What? Are you proposing
  To lend to me two hundred vials of poison
  Instead of gold—a vial for every ducat?
  Or what?

JEW.   It pleases you to laugh at me.
  I simply wished . . perhaps you might . . I thought
  It might be time the baron ceased to live.

ALBERT. Poison my father! And you dare, before
  My very face—O, seize him, Jean—you dare
  Before his very son—you dirty Jew,
  You dog, you snake, upon our gate-posts you
  Will hang straightway for this.

JEW.   My lord, I'm sorry!
  Forgive me, I was jesting.

ALBERT.   Jean, a rope!

JEW. I . . . I was jesting. Here's some money for you.

ALBERT. Begone, you dog!

(JEW goes out.)

To this I'm brought by my

Own father's avarice! The Jew could dare
Propose to me . . . Give me a glass of wine!
I'm all a-tremble . . . But, I'm still in need
Of money . . . run and stop the cursèd Jew.
And get his ducats. Yes, and fetch me here
My inkhorn . . . A receipt I'll give the rascal . . .
Don't let the Jew come here . . . No, stay a mo-
ment—
His coins will reek of poison like the pieces
Of silver Judas took . . . I asked for wine!

JEAN. There's not a drop of wine.

ALBERT.   Not even that
That Raymond sent me as a gift from Spain?

JEAN. Last night I took the last remaining bottle
To the sick blacksmith.

ALBERT.   I remember. Yes . . .
Well, give me water. What a cursèd life!
No, it's decided—to the duke I'll go
And ask for justice: let him make my father
Regard me as a son, and not a mouse
Born in a cellar.

SCENE II

(Vault)

THE BARON. As the young scapegrace bides the trysting
hour
With some corrupt enchantress or perchance
Some foolish girl seduced by him, so I

All day abide the time when I shall come
Down to my secret vault and trusty chests.
O happy day! To-day into the sixth
Of all my chests (one not yet full) my fingers
Will dribble one more handful of my gold.
It seems a trifle. Yet by trifles 'tis
That treasures grow. And somewhere I have read
That once an emperor bade his warriors take
Handfuls of earth and throw them in a heap—
And a proud hill arose, and from its height
The emperor with joy could contemplate
A verdant valley covered with white tents
And a broad sea with all its scudding ships.
So, bearing handful after handful, I
Have brought my wonted tribute to this vault,
And raised my hill—and from its crest survey
My vast domains. And who can set their bounds?
For, demon-like, I rule the world from here.
I've but to wish—a palace will arise;
Into my splendid gardens there will dance
A company of nymphs in wanton sport.
The muses too will bring to me their tribute.
Free genius will become my willing slave.
Virtue herself and toil that never sleeps
With mien submissive my reward will wait.
I've but to whistle—to my knees will creep,
Obedient and timid, bloodstained crime,
And lick my hand and look into my eyes,
And read in them the sign of my desire.
All things obey me—none do I obey;
I am above all wishes and all cares;
I know my power: and this knowledge is
Enough for me . . . (*He gazes on his gold.*)
                        It seems a trifling pile,
Yet who can sum the tale of human cares,
Deceptions, tears, entreaties, maledictions

Of which it is a ponderous deputy!
There's somewhere here an old doubloon . . . Here
   'tis.
This very day a widow gave it me;
But first a whole half-day before my window
She knelt with her three children, wailing loud.
The rain came down, and stopped, and came again,
The hypocrite ne'er budged; I could, of course,
Have driven her off, but something whispered to me,
That she was bringing what her husband owed me
And didn't want to be in jail to-morrow.
And this one? That's the one that Thibault brought.
Where did the lazy rascal ever get it?
He stole it, I suppose, or, maybe, there,
At night, upon the highway, in the wood . . .
Ah yes! If all the tears, the blood and sweat
Poured out for all that is in keeping here
Should from the bosom of the earth spring forth,
Then 'twere a second Flood—and I should drown
Within my trusty vault. But now—'tis time.
             (*He prepares to open the chest.*)
Whene'er the time comes to unlock a chest,
I fall into a trembling and a fever.
It is not fear (Oh, no! Whom should I fear?
My sword is by my side; its trusty blade
Will answer for the gold), but in the act
A strange, uncanny feeling grips my heart.
Physicians do assure us, there are people
Who find a pleasure in the act of murder.
So, when I put the key into the lock,
I feel what they must feel, the very instant
They plunge the knife into the victim—pleasure
And horror both at once. (*He opens the chest.*)
               My paradise!
        (*He drops in the coins, one by one.*)
Away you go! Enough you've roved the world,

A servant to the needs and lusts of man.
Sleep here the sleep of strength and quietude,
As in the distant heavens sleep the gods! . . .
To-day I wish to hold a mighty feast;
Before each chest I'll place a lighted candle,
And open every one, and I myself
Amidst them all shall view their shining heaps.
  (*He lights candles and opens the chests one after
  the other.*)
I am a king! . . . What magic radiance spreads!
Strong is my kingdom, and obedient to me,
My bliss is here, my honor and my glory!
I am a king! . . . But after I am dead,
Who will become its sovereign? My heir!
A youthful madcap—and a spendthrift too!
Of rakes and libertines the boon companion!
Hardly shall I be cold, when he'll come down,
This wastrel, to these peaceful, silent vaults,
With all his crew of fawning, greedy courtiers.
Stealing my keys from off my very corpse,
He'll open all my chests with peals of laughter,
And all my garnered treasure-heaps will flow
Into his pockets—satin, yes, but holey.
He'll smash the sacred vessels and he'll soak
The mud with oil that should anoint a king.
He'll squander . . . But who gave him such a
  right?
As a free gift did all this come to me,
Or in the way of sport as to a gambler
Who rattles dice, then rakes his money in?
Who knows how many bitter self-repressions,
And passions tamed, and heavy thoughts, and days
Of care, and sleepless nights all this has cost me?
Or will my son say that my heart's o'ergrown
With moss, and that I never knew desires
Nor ever felt the gnawing tooth of conscience,

Conscience, that sharp-clawed beast that scrapes and
    scrapes
About the heart, that uninvited guest,
Importunate companion, creditor
Most churlish; hag, at whose unhallowed word
The moon grows dark, and in churchyards the
    tombs
Are set a-quaking, and send forth their dead! . . .
No, build up first a fortune for yourself,
And then behold! A wretch will come and squander
All that which by your blood and sweat you won.
Oh, if I could but shield my vault from such
Unworthy eyes! If only from the grave
I could but come, and, like a guardian shade,
Sit on my chest and from all living creatures
Protect my treasures, as I guard them now! . . .

SCENE III

In the castle

ALBERT, THE DUKE

ALBERT. Believe me, Sire, that long I've stood the shame
    Of bitter poverty. The direst need
    Alone has driven me to make complaint.

DUKE. I do believe it; such a man as you,
    My noble knight, does not accuse his father
    Except the need be dire. Such knaves are rare . . .
    So set your mind at rest: I shall exhort
    Your father privately and make no scandal.
    I'm waiting for him. Long 'tis since we met.
    He was my grandsire's friend. I well remember
    When I was still a youngster, he would seat
    Me on his horse and cover me with his

Great heavy shield as with a bell.

(Looks out of the window.)

Who's this?

It isn't he?

ALBERT.   It is, my lord.

DUKE.   Then go
Into that room. I'll summon you.

(ALBERT goes out; BARON enters.)

Well, Baron,
I'm glad to see you look so hale and hearty.

BARON. I'm happy, Sire, to think my health allowed
Me—spite of age—to come at your command.

DUKE. It's very long ago we parted, Baron.
Do you remember me?

BARON.   Remember, Sire?
I see you as 'twere now. A lively youngster
You were, my lord—The duke (who's dead) would
      say
To me: "Well, Philip," (for he always called me
Philip), "What say you? Eh? In twenty years,
I do assure you, both of us will be
But drivelling dotards in that youngster's pres-
      ence . . ."
Your presence, 'twas he meant . . .

DUKE.   Well, we'll renew
Acquaintance now. My court you've quite forgot.

BARON. I'm old, my lord, what should I do at court?
You're young, festivities and tournaments
Are to your taste. But at my age I find
No pleasure in them. Yet, if God send war,
I'm ready, though it be with groans, to clamber
Once more upon my horse's back; my strength

Will still suffice to draw my ancient sword,
Albeit with trembling hand, in your defence.

DUKE. Baron, your loyal zeal is known to us;
You were my grandsire's friend; my father too
Respected you; and I have always thought you
A brave and trusty knight; but please sit down.
You've children, Baron?

BARON.   I've an only son.

DUKE. Why do I never see him at my court?
You it may bore, but both his age and station
Make it but fitting that he should attend us.

BARON. My son dislikes a noisy, worldly life;
He's of a shy and melancholy turn—
Around the castle through the woods he roves
Forever like a fawn.

DUKE.   It is not well
He grow a hermit; we'll accustom him
Straightway to revels, balls and tournaments.
Send him to me; and fix upon your son
A maintenance that doth befit his station . . .
I see you frown—the journey wearied you,
Perhaps?

BARON.   My lord, it is not weariness;
But you have much confused me. This confession
I would not make before you, but your words
Compel me to report about my son
Things which I fain would have concealed from you.
Unfortunately, Sire, he is unworthy
Of your most gracious favors and regard.
For all his youth he's spent in riotous living,
In basest vice.

DUKE. The cause of this, good Baron,
May be that he's alone. For solitude
And idleness are ruinous to youth.
Send him to us; for here he will forget
The habits that his wilding life begat.

BARON. Forgive me, gracious Sire, but really I
Am quite unable to consent to this . . .

DUKE. But why?

BARON. O! Let an old man go, my lord!

DUKE. No, I demand; reveal to me the reason
Of your refusal.

BARON. 'Gainst my son I am
Most angered.

DUKE. Wherefore?

BARON. For his wicked crime.

DUKE. But what does it consist in, tell me that?

BARON. Oh, spare me, dear my lord . . .

DUKE. 'Tis passing strange!
Are you ashamed of him?

BARON. Ashamed, indeed . . .

DUKE. But what can he have done?

BARON. He . . . he did plan
To kill me.

DUKE. Kill! To justice then shall I
Deliver him, vile felon that he is.

BARON. I shall not try to prove it, though I know
That he is simply longing for my death,

And though I know that he has made attempt
To . . . .

DUKE.　　　What?

BARON.　　　　　　To rob me.
　　　　　　　　(ALBERT *rushes into the room.*)

ALBERT.　　　　　　　　　Baron, that's a lie!

DUKE. (*To the son.*) How dare you? . . .

BARON.　　　You! You here! You dare! To me! . . .
To me, your father, dare say such a word! . . .
I lie? And that before my lord himself! . . .
To me, to me . . . Am I a knight no longer?

ALBERT. A liar's what you are!

BARON.　　　　　　　　E'en yet the thunder,
O God of justice, has not crashed! Then pick
This up, and let the sword decide between us!
　　(*Throws down his glove, his son promptly picks
　　it up.*)

ALBERT. Thanks, father, for your gift; it is the first!

DUKE. What have I seen? What is it I have witnessed?
A son takes up his aged father's challenge!
On evil days I fell when I did put
The ducal chain upon me! Silence, you,
Insensate man, and you, young tiger-cub!
Enough! (*To the son.*) Have done with this at once,
　　and give
That glove to me forthwith.
　　　　　　　　　(*Takes it away from him.*)

ALBERT. (*Aside.*)　　This is a pity!

DUKE. The way he clutched it! Out upon you, monster!
Begone; and never dare to show yourself

Before my eyes, until such time as I
Shall summon you.

(*Exit* ALBERT.)

And you, unhappy gray-beard,
Are you not filled with shame? . . .

BARON.   Forgive me, Sire . . .
I cannot stand . . . my knees are giving way . . .
I'm choking . . . choking . . . where, where are
    my keys?
My keys, my keys!

DUKE.   He's dead. O God in heaven!
What dreadful times! and ah! what dreadful hearts!

[1830]

❧ MOZART AND SALIERI ☙

SCENE I

A room

SALIERI. Men say: there is no justice upon earth.
But neither is there justice in the Heavens!
That's clear to me as any simple scale.
For I was born with a great love for art:
When—still a child—I heard the organ peal
Its lofty measures through our ancient church,
I listened all attention—and sweet tears,
Sweet and involuntary tears would flow.
Though young, I spurned all frivolous pursuits:
All studies else than music were to me
Repugnant; and with stubborn arrogance
I turned from them to dedicate myself
To music only. Hard is the first step
And tiresome the first journey. I o'ercame
Early discomfitures; and craftsmanship
I set up as a pedestal for art;
Became the merest craftsman; to my fingers
I lent a docile, cold agility,
And sureness to my ear. I stifled sounds,
And then dissected music like a corpse,
Checked harmony by algebraic rules;
And only then, tested and proved in science,
I ventured to indulge creative fancy.

I started to create—but secretly—
Not daring yet even to dream of glory.
Not seldom, having spent in silent cell
Two or three days, forgetting sleep and food,
Tasting the joy and tears of inspiration,
I threw my labors in the fire and watched
My thoughts and songs—the children of my brain—
Flame up, then vanish in a wisp of smoke . . .
What do I say? When the great Gluck appeared,
Revealing new, deep, captivating secrets—
Did I not then reject all I had learned,
All I had loved, and ardently believed,
And did I not walk bravely in his footsteps
Unmurmuring, like one who, gone astray,
Is bid by one he meets retrace his journey?
By vigorous and tense persistency,
At last, within the boundless realm of music
I reached a lofty place. At last fame deigned
To smile on me; and in the hearts of men
I found an echo to my own creation.
Then I was happy, and enjoyed in peace
My labors, my success, my fame—nor less
The labors and successes of my friends,
My fellow-workers in the art divine.
No! Never did I know the sting of envy,
Oh, never!—neither when Piccini triumphed
In capturing the ears of skittish Paris,
Nor the first time there broke upon my sense
Iphigenia's opening harmonies.
Who dares to say that ever proud Salieri
Could stoop to envy, like a loathsome snake
Trampled upon by men, yet still alive
And impotently gnawing sand and dust?
No one! . . . But now—myself I say it—now
I do know envy! Yes, Salieri envies,
Deeply, in anguish envies.—O ye Heavens!

Where, where is justice, when the sacred gift,
When deathless genius comes not to reward
Perfervid love and utter self-denial,
And toils and strivings and beseeching prayers,
But puts her halo round a lack-wit's skull,
A frivolous idler's brow? . . . O Mozart, Mozart!

                     (*Enter* MOZART.)

MOZART. Aha! You saw me enter! I was hoping
  To treat you to an unexpected jest.

SALIERI. You here! . . . How long have you been here?

MOZART.   A moment.
  I started out to see you, bringing something
  To show to you; but just as I was passing
  The inn, I heard a fiddle . . . Dear Salieri,
  In all your life you never yet have heard
  Such funny sounds! . . . A blind old fiddler there
  Was playing *"Voi che sapete."* Heavens!
  I couldn't wait, I brought the fiddler with me
  To entertain you with his artistry.
  Come in!

               (*Enter a blind* OLD MAN *with a fiddle.*)
           Now play us something out of Mozart!
(*The* OLD MAN *plays an air from "Don Juan".* MOZART
    bursts out laughing.)

SALIERI. And you can laugh?

MOZART.   Why, yes, of course, Salieri!
  And do you not laugh too?

SALIERI.   I do not, Mozart.
  I do not laugh when some poor, wretched dauber
  Besmears a masterpiece of Raphael's painting.
  I do not laugh when some grotesque buffoon
  Dishonors Dante with a parody.
  Begone, old man!

MOZART. Oh, wait! Here's something! Take it;
Drink to my health.

(*The* OLD MAN *goes out.*)
But, you, my dear Salieri,
Are not in a good mood to-day. I'll come
Another time.

SALIERI. What were you bringing me?

MOZART. Nothing—the merest trifle. One night lately,
As I was tossing on my sleepless bed,
Into my head came two or three ideas.
Today I wrote them down, and I should like
To hear your comments on them; but at present
You can't attend to me.

SALIERI. Ah, Mozart, Mozart!
When can I not attend to you? Sit down;
I'm listening!

MOZART. (*at the piano*):
Just imagine someone—well,
Let's say myself—a trifle younger, though—
In love—but not too deeply—just enamored—
I'm with some lady—or a friend—say you;
I'm cheerful . . . Suddenly a glimpse of death,
The dark descends—or something of the sort.
Now listen. (*He plays.*)

SALIERI. You were bringing *this* to me
And you could loiter at a common tavern,
To hear a blind old fiddler? God in Heaven!
Mozart, you are unworthy of yourself!

MOZART. Well, do you like it?

SALIERI. What profundity,
What boldness, and what art of composition!

You, Mozart, are a god and know it not!
I know it.

MOZART.   Bah! Really? Perhaps I am—
However it may be, my godhood's famished.

SALIERI. Listen; this evening we shall dine together—
The Golden Lion inn is where we meet.

MOZART. That's very kind. But let me just run home,
To tell my wife not to expect me back
For dinner.   (*Goes out.*)

SALIERI.   I'll await you; do not fail me.
No longer can I thwart my destiny.
For I am chosen to arrest his course.
If he lives on, then all of us will perish—
High-priests and servants of the art of music—
Not I alone with my o'ershadowed glory.
And what will it avail if Mozart live
And scale still higher summits of perfection?
Will he thereby raise art itself? No, no,
'Twill fall again, when once he disappears.
He will not leave a single heir behind.
Then what can he avail us? Like a cherub
He brings to us some songs of paradise,
And wakens in us children of the dust
A wingless longing—then he flies away!
Well, let him fly away! We'll speed his going!

This poison—my Isora's parting gift—
For eighteen years I've carried on my person,
And often since that day has life appeared
Unbearable to me. And I have sat
At table with my unsuspecting foe;
Yet never to the whisper of temptation
Have yielded, not because I am a coward,
Nor yet because I do not feel an insult,

Nor from a love of life. I always tarried.
Whenever thirst for death would torture me—
"Why die?" I asked, and mused: "Perhaps—who
    knows?
Life yet may bring to me unlooked for gifts;
The trance of genius yet may visit me
And the creative night and inspiration;
Perhaps a second Haydn may create
Great master-works . . . and I'll rejoice in them . . ."
While I was feasting with my hated guest,
"Perhaps," I thought, "a still more loathsome foe
I'll find; perhaps a still more loathsome insult
Will crash upon me from a lordly height—
Then, then your day will come, Isora's gift!"
And I was right! And I have found at last
My enemy; at last a second Haydn
Has drenched my soul with raptures all divine!
Now—is the hour! O sacred gift of love,
Today I'll pour thee into friendship's cup!

SCENE II

Private room at an inn; piano.

MOZART AND SALIERI (*At table.*)

SALIER. What makes you look so glum to-day?

MOZART.   Me? Nothing!

SALIERI. Mozart, I swear there's something on your
    mind!
    The dinner's good, the wine is excellent,
    Yet you sit silent, moping.

MOZART. I confess
My *Requiem* is on my mind.

SALIERI. Aha!
You're working at a *Requiem?* Since when?

MOZART. About three weeks. But one queer circumstance . . .
Did I not tell you?

SALIERI. No.

MOZART. Then listen now:
I came home late one night three weeks ago.
They told me that a man had called to see me.
Now, why I cannot tell, but all that night
I thought: "Who can this be? What can he want
Of me?" The following day a second time
He called again and found me not at home.
Next day, while I was playing on the floor
With my young son, I heard them summon me.
I left the room. A man, dressed all in black,
With courtly bow, commissioned me to write
A *Requiem*—and vanished. I sat down
At once and started writing. Since that hour
My man in black has never called again;
I'm glad of it; for I'd be loth to part
With my creation, though the *Requiem* now
Is finished quite. But meanwhile I . . .

SALIERI. Go on!

MOZART. I feel a bit ashamed confessing . . .

SALIERI. What?

MOZART. That day and night, my man in black gives
ne'er

A moment's peace to me. Behind me ever
He hovers like a shadow. At this moment,
It seems to me he's sitting at this table,
An uninvited guest.

SALIERI.   What childish terrors!
Dispel these idle fancies. Beaumarchais
Was always saying: "Listen, friend Salieri,
Whenever gloomy thoughts beset your mind,
Why, then uncork a bottle of champagne,
Or read *Le Mariage de Figaro*."

MOZART. Yes! Beaumarchais and you were friends, I
     know;
And wasn't it for him you wrote *Tarare*?
A glorious thing! There's one *motif* in that . . .
I keep repeating it when I am happy—
La-la, la-la . . . Ah, is it true, Salieri,
That Beaumarchais once poisoned someone?

SALIERI.   No,
I doubt it. He was quite too comical
For such a task as that!

MOZART.   He was a genius
Like you and me. But villainy and genius
Are two things than can never go together.

SALIERI. You think so?
                    (*Pours poison into* MOZART's *glass.*)
                    Well, now drink.

MOZART.   Your health, my friend,
I drink, and pledge that candid covenant
That links the names of Mozart and Salieri,
Two sons of harmony. (*Drinks.*)

SALIERI.   Stop, stop, I say,
You've drunk it all! . . . and waited not for me?

MOZART. (*Throws his napkin on the table.*)
  Well, now I've had my fill. (*Goes to the piano.*)
                 Salieri, listen,
I'll play my *Requiem*. (*Plays.*)
               What! Are you weeping?

SALIERI. Yes, these are the first tears I've ever shed.
  I feel both pain and pleasure, like a man
  Who has performed a sad and painful duty,
  Or like to one from whom the healing knife
  Has cut a suffering limb. Friend Mozart, mark not
  These tears. Continue playing, hasten thus
  To fill my soul with paradisal strains.

MOZART. If only everyone could feel the power
  Of harmony like you! But no, for then
  The world could not exist; no man would stoop
  To care about the needs of vulgar life—
  For all would give themselves to art alone.
  We are a chosen few, we happy idlers,
  Born to contemn profane utility,
  The priests of beauty—and of naught besides,
  Aren't we, Salieri?—But I feel unwell.
  Something oppresses me; I'll go and sleep.
  Farewell!

SALIERI.   Good-bye. (*Alone.*)
             You'll sleep a long sleep, Mozart.
  But was he really right? Am I no genius?
  So villainy and genius are two things
  That never go together? That's not true;
  Think but of Buonarotti . . . Or was that
  A tale of the dull, stupid crowd—and he
  Who built the Vatican was *not* a murderer?

                         1830

NOTE

The Italian composer, Antonio Salieri, was a bitter enemy of Mozart, and indeed was rumored to have caused his death by poison.

The mention, at the close, of Buonarotti is an allusion to the story that Michelangelo, in pursuit of a more realistic art, murdered the model for the Christ in his Crucifixion.

EDITOR

THE STONE GUEST

LEPORELLO.   *O statua gentilissima*
                Del gran Commendatore! . . .
                Ah, Padrone!

                                        Don Giovanni

SCENE I

DON JUAN AND LEPORELLO

DON JUAN. Here we'll await the night.—And so at last
  We've reached the portals of Madrid, and soon
  Along the well-known streets shall I be flitting,
  Mustache and brows concealed by cloak and hat.
  What think you? Could I e'er be recognized?

LEPORELLO. Ah, sure 'tis hard to recognize Don Juan!
  There are so many like him.

DON JUAN.   Do you jest?
  Well, who will recognize me?

LEPORELLO.   Why, the first
  Watchman you meet, or gypsy or drunk fiddler,
  Or your own kind—some saucy cavalier,
  With flowing cloak and sword under his arm.

DON JUAN. What matter, if I'm recognized! Provided
  I meet not with the king himself, I fear
  No other soul in all Madrid beside.

LEPORELLO. To-morrow it will reach the king's own ear
   That Don Juan is in Madrid again,
   Without authority returned from exile.
   And then what will he do?

DON JUAN.   He'll send me back.
   Dear me, they won't cut off my head, you know.
   No crime have I committed 'gainst the State!
   He sent me off for very love of me,
   In order that the murdered man's relations
   Might cease to worry me.

LEPORELLO.   Just so, just so!
   If only you had stayed there quietly!

DON JUAN. Your humble servant thanks you for the
    pleasure!
   I all but died of boredom there. What people!
   And what a land! The sky? . . . A pall of smoke;
   The women? Why, I never would exchange—
   Mark what I say, my foolish Leporello—
   The humblest peasant-girl in Andalusia
   For all their leading beauties—that I wouldn't.
   At first, indeed, these women took my fancy
   With their blue eyes and that white skin of theirs,
   Their modesty—but most, their novelty;
   But, thank the Lord, I soon had sized them up—
   Saw that 'twas sin to deal with them at all,
   There isn't any life in them—they're all
   But waxen dolls . . . whereas our girls! . . . But
    hist!
   We seem to know this place; you recognize it?

LEPORELLO. How could I fail to? I remember well
   The convent of St. Anthony. You used
   To come on visits here, and I would hold
   The horses in this grove; a cursèd duty,

I do confess! More pleasantly you spent
Your time here than did I, forsooth.

DON JUAN. (*Pensively.*)   Poor Inez!
She is no more! And how I did adore her!

LEPORELLO. Inez—the black-eyed girl? . . . Oh, I re-
member!
For three long months you courted her in vain;
'Twas only through the devil's help you won.

DON JUAN. 'Twas in July . . . at night. I used to find
Strange pleasure in her melancholy gaze
And in her ashen lips. A curious thing!
But you, it seems, did not consider her
A beauty. And, in fact, there wasn't much
Of real beauty in her. But her eyes,
Her eyes alone, her glance too . . . such a glance
I never since have met. And then her voice
Was soft and weak, as though she were not well . . .
Her husband was a rough and heartless black-
guard—
I realized too late . . . Alas, poor Inez! . . .

LEPORELLO. What of it? On her heels came others.

DON JUAN.   True!

LEPORELLO. And if we live there will be others still.

DON JUAN. E'en so.

LEPORELLO.   And now what lady in Madrid
Shall we be seeking out?

DON JUAN.   Why, whom but Laura!
I'm off to show myself to her.

LEPORELLO.   Now that's
The way to talk.

DON JUAN.   Just watch me walk straight in;
And if there's someone with her, I'll suggest
His exit through the window.

LEPORELLO.   Why, of course!
Well, now we have recovered our good spirits.
It's not for long dead women can disturb us.
But who is this that comes our way? (*Enter* MONK.)

MONK.   She will
Be here this instant. Who are you? The servants
Of Doña Anna?

LEPORELLO.   We are our own masters,
Out for a stroll.

DON JUAN.   But whom are you awaiting?

MONK. Good Doña Anna will be here to visit
Her husband's tomb, and shortly.

DON JUAN.   Doña Anna
De Solva? What? The wife of the commander
Slain by . . . the name I can't recall . . . ?

MONK.   The vile,
The dissolute, the godless Don Juan.

LEPORELLO. Oho! Well, well! The fame of Don Juan
Has even reached the peaceful convent now;
His eulogies are sung by anchorites.

MONK. Perhaps you know him?

LEPORELLO.   We? No, God forbid,
And where can he be now?

MONK.   He isn't here.
He's far away in exile.

LEPORELLO.   Thank the Lord!
The farther off the better. Would that all

Such rascals in a single sack were sewn
And thrown into the sea.

DON JUAN.   What stuff and nonsense
Is this?

LEPORELLO. Be silent: 'twas on purpose I . . .

DON JUAN. So here it was they buried the commander?

MONK. 'Twas here. And here his widow did erect
A monument to him and every day
She comes to weep, and pray that God may grant
His soul salvation.

DON JUAN.   What a curious widow!
And is the lady pretty?

MONK.   Anchorites,
Like us, should not be moved by woman's beauty;
But lying is a sin: a saint himself
Must yet admit her wondrous loveliness.

DON JUAN. The dead man had good reason to be jealous;
He kept this Doña Anna bolted up:
Not one of us e'er caught a glimpse of her.
I'd like to have a talk with her sometime.

MONK. Oh, Doña Anna never talks with men.

DON JUAN. She talks with you, good father, doesn't she?

MONK. Oh, that's a different matter—I'm a monk.
But there she is.   (*Enter* DOÑA ANNA.)

DOÑA ANNA.   Come, open, holy father.

MONK. I come, Señora; I was waiting for you.
                    (DOÑA ANNA *follows the* MONK.)

LEPORELLO. Well, what's she like?

DON JUAN.   There's nothing visible
  Of her beneath her somber widow's veil;
  I just but glimpsed a trim and narrow heel.

LEPORELLO. That's quite enough for you. Imagination
  Will in a jiffy sketch you out the rest;
  Your fancy's quicker than the painter's brush.
  The starting-point is all the same to you—
  The forehead, or the foot.

DON JUAN.   O Leporello,
  I'll get to know her.

LEPORELLO. (*to himself.*) There you have the man!
  That's the last straw! The fellow, having killed
  The husband, now would like to feast his eyes
  Upon the widow's tears! The wretch!

DON JUAN.   But see
  The dusk is on us. Ere the moon arise
  Above us and transform this inky black
  Into a glowing twilight, let us creep
  Into Madrid.

LEPORELLO.   A Spanish nobleman,
  Like any thief, awaits the night—and fears
  The moon. O Heavens! What a cursèd life!
  Ah, how much longer must I bear with him?
  My strength, in truth, is nearly at an end!

SCENE II

Room. Supper at LAURA'S.

FIRST GUEST. I swear to you, dear Laura, never yet
  Was such perfection in your acting shown!
  How thoroughly you understood your rôle!

SECOND GUEST. And with what power its meaning you
    unfolded!

THIRD GUEST. And with what art!

LAURA.   To-day, indeed, success
    Did crown my every movement, every word:
    I yielded freely to my inspiration;
    The words flowed forth, as though it was the heart,
    And not the timid memory, gave them birth.

FIRST GUEST. 'Tis true; and even now your eyes are shin-
    ing,
    Your cheeks are burning—no, your ecstasy
    Has not yet faded. Laura, let it not
    Grow cold before it bear some fruit: pray, Laura,
    Do sing us something!

LAURA.   Give me my guitar. (*Sings.*)

ALL. Ah, *brava! brava!* Wonderful! Superb!

FIRST GUEST. Our thanks, enchantress! You have cast a
    spell
    Upon our hearts. Among the joys of life,
    To love alone does music yield the prize;
    But love itself is melody. . . . Behold:
    Carlos himself, your surly guest, is touched!

SECOND GUEST. What harmonies! And how much soul
    therein!
    Who wrote the words, dear Laura?

LAURA.   Don Juan.

DON CARLOS. What? Don Juan?

LAURA.   Some time or other he,
    My loyal friend—and fickle lover—wrote them.

DON CARLOS. Your Don Juan's an atheist and a rascal;
  While you, you're but a fool.

LAURA.   Have you gone mad?
  Grandee of Spain though you may be, I'll bid
  My servants cut your throat straightway for this.

DON CARLOS. (*Gets up.*) Well, call them then.

FIRST GUEST.   No, Laura, do not do it;
  Don Carlos, don't be angered. She forgot . . .

LAURA. Forgot? That Don Juan in single combat
  Quite honorably killed his brother? True,
  'Twere better he had killed Don Carlos.

DON CARLOS.   I
  Was stupid to get angry.

LAURA.   You admit
  That you were stupid—let us make our peace.

DON CARLOS. Forgive me, Laura; it was all my fault.
  But still you know I cannot hear that name
  With equanimity.

LAURA.   Am I to blame
  If that name's on my tongue at every moment?

GUEST. Come, Laura, as a sign your anger's passed,
  Sing once again.

LAURA.   I'll sing a good-night song.
  'Tis time—for night has come. What shall I sing?
  Ah! listen. (*Sings.*)

ALL.   Charming! Matchless! How sublime!

LAURA. Good night, my friends.

GUESTS.   Good night and thanks,
      sweet Laura.
          (*They go out.* LAURA *stops* DON CARLOS.)

LAURA. You utter madman, you! Remain with me.
You took my fancy; you reminded me
Of Don Juan, the way you rated me
And set your teeth and ground them.

DON CARLOS. Lucky man!
You loved him then? (LAURA *nods.*) You loved him
deeply?

LAURA. Deeply.

DON CARLOS. And do you love him now?

LAURA. This very minute?
Why, no. I cannot love two men at once.
It's you I love at present.

DON CARLOS. Tell me, Laura,
How old are you?

LAURA. I am eighteen, my friend.

DON CARLOS. O Laura, you are young . . . and will be
young
For five or six years more. Around you men
Will throng for six years more and shower you
With flattery, with gifts and with caresses,
Divert you with nocturnal serenades,
And kill each other for you at the cross-roads
By night. But when your prime has passed, and
when
Your eyes are sunken, and their puckered lids
Grow dark, and in your tresses gray hairs glint,
And men begin to call you "an old woman,"
Well, what will you say then?

LAURA. Ah, then . . . But why
Be thinking now of that? What conversation!
Or are you always thinking things like that?
Come out upon the balcony. How calm

The sky! The air is still and warm; the night
Is odorous with lemon and with laurel;
The bright moon's shining in the dense, dark blue—
The watchmen's drawn-out cry resounds: "All's
   well!" . . .
But far away now in the north—in Paris—
Perhaps the sky is overcast with clouds,
A cold rain's falling and the wind is blowing.
But what is that to us? Now listen, Carlos:
I order you to smile at me.—That's right.

DON CARLOS. You fascinating demon! (*Knock at door.*)

DON JUAN.   Laura, ho!

LAURA. Who's there? Whose voice is that?

DON JUAN.   Unlock the door . . .

LAURA. Lord! Can it be?
                (*Opens the door, enter* DON JUAN.)

DON JUAN.   Good evening!

LAURA.   Don Juan! . . .
       (LAURA *throws herself on his neck.*)

DON CARLOS. What! Don Juan! . . .

DON JUAN.   Laura, my darling girl! . . .
                   (*Kisses her.*)
Whom have you here, my Laura?

DON CARLOS.   It is I—
Don Carlos.

DON JUAN.   What an unexpected meeting!
To-morrow I am at your service . . .

DON CARLOS.   No!
Not then—at once.

LAURA   Don Carlos, stop, I say!
You're in my house, not in the public street—
I beg you, go away.

DON CARLOS. (*Not listening to her*.) I'm waiting. Well?
Your sword is at your side.

DON JUAN.   Oh, if you have
No patience, very well. . . .   (*They fight*.)

LAURA.   Oh! oh! Juan! . . .
(*Throws herself on the bed*. DON CARLOS *falls*.)

DON JUAN. Get up, my Laura, it's all over.

LAURA.   What
Lies there? He's killed? How lovely! In my room!
And what shall I do now, you scapegrace, devil?
And how shall I dispose of him?

DON JUAN.   Perhaps
He's still alive. (*Examines the body*.)

LAURA.   Alive, forsooth! Why look,
You wretched man! You pierced him through the
     heart—
No fear, you didn't miss! No blood is flowing
From the three-cornered wound, nor is he breathing.
So what do you say now?

DON JUAN.   It can't be helped.
He asked for it himself.

LAURA.   Ah, Don Juan,
It's most annoying, really. Your old tricks! . . .
And yet you're ne'er to blame! Whence come you
     now?
How long have you been here?

DON JUAN.   I just arrived
And on the quiet—for I've not been pardoned.

LAURA. And instantly you recollected Laura?
    So far so good. But stop! I don't believe you.
    You happened to be passing through the street,
    And saw my house.

DON JUAN.   No, Laura, you can ask
    My servant Leporello. I am lodging
    Outside the city in a wretched tavern.
    For Laura's sake I'm visiting Madrid.   (*Kisses her.*)

LAURA. You are my darling! . . . Stop . . . not right
    before
    The dead man! Oh, what *shall* we do with him?

DON JUAN. Just leave him here—before the break of day,
    I'll take him out enfolded in my cloak,
    And place him on the cross-roads.

LAURA.   Only look
    That no one sees you. 'Twas a stroke of luck
    Your visit was not timed a minute sooner!
    Your friends were supping here with me. They just
    Had left. Suppose that you had found them here!

DON JUAN. How long, my Laura, have you loved him?

LAURA.   Whom?
    You must be raving.

DON JUAN.   Laura, come, confess
    How many times you've been unfaithful since
    My absence?

LAURA.   What about yourself, you scapegrace?

DON JUAN. Come, tell me . . . No, we'll talk about it
    later! . . .

SCENE III

The Commander's Monument

DON JUAN. All's for the best: for, having slain Don
    Carlos
    Without intent, in humble hermit's guise
    I've taken refuge here—and every day
    I see my charming widow, who has noticed
    Me too, I think. Until the present we
    Have stood on formal terms with one another;
    To-day, however, I shall break the ice;
    'Tis time! But how to start? "May I presume?" . . .
    Or no: "Señora" . . . Bah! whatever comes
    Into my head, I'll say spontaneously
    Like one whose serenade is improvised.
    It's time she came. Without her, I believe
    The poor commander has a tedious time.
    They've made him look a very giant here!
    What mighty shoulders! What a Hercules! . . .
    Whereas the man himself was small and puny;
    If he were here and, standing on tip-toe,
    Stretched out his arm, he could not reach his nose.
    When hard by the Escurial we met,
    He ran upon my sword-point and expired,
    Just like a dragon-fly upon a pin.
    But he was proud and fearless—and he had
    A rugged spirit. . . there she is (*Enter* DOÑA ANNA.)

DOÑA ANNA.   Again
    He's here. O father, I've distracted you
    From holy meditations. Pardon me.

DON JUAN. 'Tis I who must beseech *your* pardon, rather,
    Señora; for perhaps I am preventing
    Your grief from flowing freely as it might.

DOÑA ANNA. No, father, for my sorrow is within me.
E'en in your presence may my prayers ascend
Humbly to Heaven; and I beg you join
Your voice with mine.

DON JUAN.   I pray with Doña Anna!
A lot so happy I do not deserve!
These vicious lips of mine will never dare
Repeat your holy supplications; I
But from afar with reverence do look
On you, when, bowing silently, you spread
Your raven tresses o'er the pallid marble—
And then it seems to me that secretly
An angel has alighted on this tomb.
Within my troubled heart it is not prayers
That I find then. I stand in speechless wonder
And think—Oh! happy man, whose chilly marble
Is warmed with breath from her celestial lips
And with the tears of her great love bedewed.

DOÑA ANNA. Strange words are these!

DON JUAN.   Señora?

DOÑA ANNA.   Said to me! . . .
You have forgotten . . .

DON JUAN.   What? That I am only
A wretched hermit? That my sinful voice
Should not resound so loudly in this place?

DOÑA ANNA. It seemed to me . . . I did not understand . . .

DON JUAN. Aha! I see; you have discovered all!

DOÑA ANNA. I have discovered! What?

DON JUAN.   That I'm no monk . . .
And at your feet I humbly beg your pardon.

DOÑA ANNA. O Heavens! Pray get up! Who are you
　　then?

DON JUAN. Unhappy victim of a hopeless passion!

DOÑA ANNA. O God in Heaven! Here, before this tomb!
　　Begone! . . .

DON JUAN.　　　A minute, Doña Anna, pray
　　A single minute!

DOÑA ANNA.　　　But if someone comes! . . .

DON JUAN. The gate is locked. A single minute, pray!

DOÑA ANNA. Well, come! What is it that you wish for?

DON JUAN.　　　　　　　　　　　　　　　Death!
　　Oh, let me die this instant at your feet,
　　And let my hapless dust be buried here,
　　Not near the dust of him who's dear to you,
　　Not on this spot—not near—but some way off,
　　There—at the very threshold—at the gate,
　　That there, in passing, you might touch my grave
　　With your light foot or with your garment's hem
　　Whene'er you come to bow your curly head
　　Upon this haughty monument and weep.

DOÑA ANNA. You've surely lost your senses.

DON JUAN.　　　　　　　　　　　　　　Doña Anna,
　　To wish for death—is that a sign of madness?
　　Were I a madman, then would I be fain
　　To stay among the living, I'd have hope
　　Some day to touch your heart with tender love;
　　Were I a madman, I would spend the nights
　　Below your window and disturb your sleep
　　With serenades; I would not hide myself.
　　But, on the contrary, I'd strive to be
　　Oberved by you wherever I might go;

Were I a madman, I'd refuse to suffer
In silence . . .

DOÑA ANNA.   So you call this silence, then?

DON JUAN. Chance, Doña Anna, carried me away;
For otherwise, you never would have learned
Of this, the gloomy secret of my heart . . .

DOÑA ANNA. And have you then been long in love with
me?

DON JUAN. How long I've been in love I do not know.
But only since that hour I've known the value
Of this brief life, yes, only since that hour
I've understood what happiness could mean.

DOÑA ANNA. Begone! Begone! You are a dangerous
man.

DON JUAN. Dangerous! How?

DOÑA ANNA.   I fear to listen to you.

DON JUAN. Then I'll be silent; only do not send
Away the man to whom the sight of you
Is all the consolation he has left.
I do not entertain audacious hopes,
Make no demands upon you, but I must,
If I am still condemned to live, have leave
To see you.

DOÑA ANNA.   Go—for this is not the place
For words like these, for madness such as this . . .
To-morrow come to where I live; if you
Will swear to keep within respectful bounds,
I shall receive you—in the evening, later . . .
E'er since the hour that I became a widow
I have not seen a soul . . .

DON JUAN.   O Doña Anna!—
You angel! May God comfort you, as now
You offer balm to this unhappy soul!

DOÑA ANNA. Begone! Begone!

DON JUAN.   One minute more, I pray.

DOÑA ANNA. Well, then, 'tis I must go . . . Besides, my
    mind
Is far from prayer. You've distracted me
With all your worldly talk; my ear to such
Has long been unaccustomed.—But to-morrow
I shall receive you . . .

DON JUAN.   Even yet I cannot
Believe, I cannot trust my happiness!
To-morrow I shall see you! . . . And not here,
And not by stealth!

DOÑA ANNA.   To-morrow, yes, to-morrow.
What is your name?

DON JUAN.   Diego de Calvado.

DOÑA ANNA. Farewell, Don Diego.   (*Exit.*)

DON JUAN.   Leporello!
                (LEPORELLO *enters.*)

LEPORELLO.   What
Is now your pleasure?

DON JUAN.   Dearest Leporello!
What bliss!—"To-morrow, in the evening, later" . . .
My Leporello, yes, to-morrow! . . . So
Prepare . . . I'm happy as a child!

LEPORELLO.   So you
Conversed with Doña Anna? Maybe she

Addressed to you a gracious word or two,
Or you bestowed on her your blessing.

DON JUAN. No,
My Leporello, no! An assignation,
An assignation has she granted me!

LEPORELLO. Can it be so? O widows, you are all
The same.

DON JUAN. Oh, what a happy man am I!
I'm ready to embrace the world—or sing!

LEPORELLO. And what will the commander have to say
About all this?

DON JUAN. You think he will be jealous?
No, truly; he's a man of common sense.
And surely has grown meeker since he died.

LEPORELLO. No, see his statue there.

DON JUAN. Well, what?

LEPORELLO. It seems
As though it's looking at you angrily.

DON JUAN. My Leporello, here's a notion: go
And bid it come to-morrow to my house—
No, not to mine—I mean to Doña Anna's.

LEPORELLO. Invite the statue! Why?

DON JUAN. Well, certainly,
Not for the purpose of conversing with it.
But bid the statue come to Doña Anna's
To-morrow evening rather late and stand
On guard before the door.

LEPORELLO. Here's an odd way
To jest! And jest with whom!

DON JUAN.   Go on!

LEPORELLO.   But . . .

DON JUAN   Go!

LEPORELLO. Most excellent and beautiful of statues!
  My master, Don Juan, most humbly bids
  You come . . . Good Lord, I cannot, I'm afraid.

DON JUAN. Coward! I'll give it to you! . . .

LEPORELLO.   Very well!
  My master, Don Juan, doth bid you come
  To-morrow rather late to your wife's house
  And guard the door . . .
                                  (*The statue nods.*)
                  Oh!

DON JUAN.   What's the matter there?

LEPORELLO. Oh! Oh! Oh! Oh! I'll die!

DON JUAN.   Whatever's happened?

LEPORELLO. (*Nodding.*) The statue . . . Oh!

DON JUAN.   What's this you're doing—bowing?

LEPORELLO. No, no, not I—but it!

DON JUAN.   What fiddle-faddle
  Is this?

LEPORELLO. Then go yourself.

DON JUAN.   Well, look, you knave!
  (*To the statue.*) Commander, I do herewith bid you
    come
  Unto your widow's house, where I shall be
  To-morrow, and keep watch before the door.
  Well? Will you?   (*Statue nods again.*)
                  God!

LEPORELLO. I told you . . .

DON JUAN. Let us go.

SCENE IV

DOÑA ANNA's *Room*. DON JUAN *and* DOÑA ANNA.

DOÑA ANNA. Don Diego, I've received you; yet I fear
My melancholy conversation will
Soon bore you; wretched widow that I am,
I never can forget my loss. Like April
I mingle tears with smiles. But tell me why
Are you so silent?

DON JUAN. I'm enjoying deeply
And silently the thought that I'm alone
With charming Doña Anna—here, not there
Beside that lucky dead man's monument—
And see you now no longer on your knees
Before your marble spouse.

DOÑA ANNA. Don Diego, are
You jealous then? My husband tortures you
E'en in his grave?

DON JUAN. I ought not to be jealous:
For he was your own choice.

DOÑA ANNA. Oh no; my mother
Commanded me to marry Don Alvaro,
For we were poor and Don Alvaro rich.

DON JUAN. The lucky man! He brought but empty treasures
To set before a goddess' feet; for that
He tasted all the bliss of paradise.
If I had known you first, with utter rapture

I'd have bestowed on you my rank, my wealth,
All, everything, for but one gentle glance!
Your slave, I would have held your wishes sacred!
I would have studied all your whims, that I
Might then anticipate them, that your life
Might be one long enchantment without end!
Alas! fate has decreed quite otherwise!

DOÑA ANNA. Ah, Diego, stop! 'Tis wrong of me to listen
To you—it is forbidden me to love you:
E'en to the grave a widow must be faithful.
If only you could know how Don Alvaro
Did love me! Oh, 'tis certain Don Alvaro,
Had he been left a widower, had ne'er
Received into his house a lovelorn lady.
He would have kept his faith with spousal love.

DON JUAN. O, Doña Anna, torture not my heart
With everlasting mention of your spouse.
Pray cease from your chastisement, although I
Perhaps deserve chastisement.

DOÑA ANNA.   And pray how?
You are not bound, I think, by holy ties
To anyone? In loving me, you do
No wrong in Heaven's eyes or mine.

DON JUAN.   In yours!
O God!

DOÑA ANNA. It isn't possible you're guilty
Of any wrong to me? Or, tell me, how?

DON JUAN. No, never! . . .

DOÑA ANNA.   Diego, tell me what you mean!
You've done me wrong? But tell me, how and when?

DON JUAN. No, not for worlds!

DOÑA ANNA.   But, Diego, this is strange!
  I ask you, I demand of you . . .

DON JUAN.   No, no!

DOÑA ANNA. So this is being docile to my will!
  But what was that you said to me just now?
  That you would like to be my very slave.
  I'm getting angry, Diego; answer me,
  In what way have you wronged me?

DON JUAN.   No, I dare
  Not tell; you'd never want to look on me,
  You'd fall to hating me.

DOÑA ANNA.   No, e'en beforehand
  I pardon you, I only want to know . . .

DON JUAN. Do not desire to know this terrible,
  This deadly secret.

DOÑA ANNA.   Deadly! . . . I'm in torment:
  I'm full of curiosity—what is it?
  I didn't know you—how could you offend me?
  I have no enemies, and never had.
  The only one is he who slew my husband.

DON JUAN. (*To himself.*) The dénouement approaches!
    —Tell me now,
  Did you e'er know the wretched Don Juan?

DOÑA ANNA. I never in my life set eyes on him.

DON JUAN. But in your heart you bear him enmity?

DOÑA ANNA. As honor binds me. But you're trying now,
  Don Diego, to divert me from my question—
  I ask . . .

DON JUAN. Suppose that you should meet Don Juan?

DOÑA ANNA. I'd plunge a dagger in the villain's heart.

DON JUAN. Where is your dagger, Doña Anna? Here's
My breast.

DOÑA ANNA. O Diego! What is that you say?

DON JUAN. No Diego I—my name's Juan.

DOÑA ANNA.   O God!
No, no, it cannot be, I don't believe . . .

DON JUAN. I'm Don Juan.

DOÑA ANNA.   It isn't true.

DON JUAN.   I killed
Your husband; and have no regrets for that—
There is no trace of penitence within me.

DOÑA ANNA. What do I hear? No, no, it cannot be.

DON JUAN. I'm Don Juan, and I do love you.

DOÑA ANNA. (*Falling*.)   Where,
Where am I? Where? I'm fainting!

DON JUAN.   God in Heaven!
What's happened to her? Doña Anna, what's
The matter with you? Come, wake up, wake up,
And pull yourself together; at your feet
Your slave, your Diego kneels.

DOÑA ANNA.   Leave me alone.
(*Weakly*.) You are my enemy—you took away
From me all, all that in my life . . .

DON JUAN.   Dear creature!
I'm ready now to expiate that blow;
I only wait your order at your feet:
Command—I'll die; command—and I shall breathe
For you alone . . .

DOÑA ANNA.   So this is Don Juan?

DON JUAN. True, is it not, he's been described to you
  As an outrageous villain and a monster.
  O Doña Anna, rumor is perhaps
  Not wholly wrong; upon my weary conscience
  There weighs, perhaps, a heavy load of evil;
  I've long been an adept in lechery;
  But since I saw you first all that has changed:
  It seems to me, that I've been born anew!
  For, loving you, virtue herself I love—
  And humbly, for the first time in my life,
  Before her now I bend my trembling knees.

DOÑA ANNA. Yes, Don Juan is eloquent—I know!
  I've heard them say: he is a sly seducer,
  A very fiend. How many wretched women
  Have you destroyed?

DON JUAN.   Not one of them till now
  Was I in love with.

DOÑA ANNA.   And shall I believe
  That Don Juan at last has fallen in love,
  That I am not another of his victims!

DON JUAN. If I had wished to dupe you, do you think
  I would have thus avowed the truth or uttered
  That name that you can hardly bear to hear?
  What do you see of trick or craft in that?

DOÑA ANNA. Who knows your heart? But how could
    you come here?
  For anyone might recognize you here—
  And then your death would be inevitable.

DON JUAN. Ah, what is death? For one sweet moment's
    tryst
  I'd give my life without a murmur.

DOÑA ANNA.   How
Will you escape from here, imprudent man?

DON JUAN. (*Kissing her hand.*) And so you are con
cerned about the life
Of poor Juan! Then in your heavenly soul
There is not any hatred, Doña Anna?

DOÑA ANNA. Alas! if only I knew how to hate you!
But we must part.

DON JUAN.   When shall we meet again?

DOÑA ANNA. I do not know. Some time.

DON JUAN.   To-morrow?

DOÑA ANNA.   Where?

DON JUAN. Here.

DOÑA ANNA.   O Don Juan, how weak a heart is mine!

DON JUAN. A quiet kiss in token of forgiveness . . .

DOÑA ANNA. It's time to go.

DON JUAN.   Just one, cold, quiet kiss . . .

DOÑA ANNA. Oh, how importunate you are! Well, there!
. . . (*A knock at the door.*)
What is that knock I hear? . . . Oh, hide, Don Juan!

DON JUAN. Good-bye, until we meet again, my darling.
                          (*Goes out and runs in again.*)
Oh! . . .

DOÑA ANNA. What's the matter? Oh!
                          (*Enter the* STATUE *of the commander;*
                                  DOÑA ANNA *falls.*)

STATUE.   Your call I've answered.

DON JUAN. O God! O Doña Anna!

STATUE.   Let her be,
All's over. You are trembling, Don Juan.

DON JUAN. I? No! . . . I bade you come; I'm glad to
see you.

STATUE. Give me your hand.

DON JUAN.   Here, take it . . . Oh, how heavy
The pressure of his cold and stony hand!
Release me, let me go, let go my hand! . . .
I'm perishing—all's over—Doña Anna!
                    (*They sink into the ground.*)
                              [1830]
            [PUBLISHED POSTHUMOUSLY, 1839]

V

Prose

The Tales of the Late
IVAN PETROVITCH BELKIN

MME. PROSTAKOVA: *My dear sir, from his childhood on he
has been fond of stories.*
SKOTININ: *Mitrofan takes after me.*

The Minor

EDITOR'S FOREWORD

HAVING undertaken to arrange the publication
of the Tales of I. P. Belkin, which are herewith
offered to the public, we wished to add to these a biography, however brief, of the late author, and thereby to
satisfy, at least partly, the just curiosity of lovers of our
native letters. To that end we addressed ourselves to
Marya Alexeyevna Trafilina, the heiress of Ivan Petrovich Belkin and his nearest of kin; but unfortunately
it was impossible for her to furnish any intelligence
concerning him, inasmuch as she had never known the
deceased. She advised us to confer on the matter with
an esteemed person, who had been a friend of Ivan
Petrovich. We followed this advice, and our letter
elicited the following answer. We present it here without any changes or explanatory notes, as a precious tes-

467

timony to a noble manner of thinking and a touching friendship, and at the same time as a sufficient biographical account.

— — —, Esq.

My dear sir!

On the twenty-third of this month I had the honor of receiving your most esteemed letter of the fifteenth, in which you express your desire to secure detailed information regarding the dates of birth and death, the career in the service, the domestic circumstances, as well as the occupations and the character of the late Ivan Petrovich Belkin, my late good friend and neighbor. I take great pleasure in complying with your request, and I am here setting forth, my dear sir, all that I can recall of our talks and my own observations.

Ivan Petrovich Belkin was born of honorable and noble parents in the year 1798 in the village of Goryukhino. His late father, second-major Piotr Ivanovich Belkin, was married to Pelageya Gavrilovna, *née* Trafilina. He was a man of moderate means, modest habits, very shrewd in business matters. Their son received his elementary education from a village beadle. To this esteemed man he owed, it would seem, his interest in reading and in Russian letters. In 1815 he entered the service in a Jaeger regiment of the infantry (I do not remember the number), in which he remained until the year 1823. The deaths of his parents, which occurred almost simultaneously, caused him to retire and settle at Goryukhino, his family estate.

Having undertaken the management of the estate, Ivan Petrovich, because of his inexperience and softheartedness, soon began to neglect his property, and relaxed the strict regime established by his late parent. Having dismissed the punctual and efficient steward with whom his peasants (as is their habit) were di satisfied, he placed the management of the village in the hands of his old housekeeper, who had acquired his confidence through her ability to tell stories. This stupid old woman could not tell a twenty-five-ruble from a fifty-ruble note. She was god-mother to the children of all the peasants, and so the latter were not in fear of her. The steward they had elected indulged them to such an extent, at the same time defrauding the master, that Ivan Petrovich was forced to abolish the corvée and introduce a very moderate quit-rent. Even then, the peasants, taking advantage of his weakness, obtained a special privilege the first year, and during the next two years paid more than two-thirds of the quit-rent in nuts, huckleberries, and the like; and even so they were in arrear.

Having been a friend of Ivan Petrovich's late parent, I deemed it my duty to offer my advice to the son, too, and repeatedly I volunteered to restore the order he had allowed to fall into decay. To that end, having come to see him one day, I demanded the account books, summoned the rascally steward, and, in the presence of Ivan Petrovich, started examining them. At first the young master followed me with all possible attention and diligence, but after we had ascertained from the accounts that in the last two years the number of peasants had increased, while the quantity of fowls and cattle had considerably diminished, Ivan Petrovich was satisfied with this bit of information, and no longer listened to me, and at the very moment when my investigation and strict questioning had reduced the thievish steward to extreme embarrassment, and indeed forced him to complete silence, to my extreme mortification I heard Ivan Petrovich snoring loudly in his chair. Thenceforward I ceased to intervene in his business affairs and entrusted them (as he did himself) to the care of the Almighty.

This, however, did not injure our friendly relations to any degree; for, commiserating as I did his weakness and the ruinous negligence common to all our young noblemen, I sincerely loved Ivan Petrovich. It was indeed impossible not to like a young man so gentle and honorable. On his part, Ivan Petrovich showed respect to my years and was cordially attached to me. Until his very end he saw me nearly every day, prizing my simple conversation, although we did not resemble each other in habits, or manner of thinking, or character.

Ivan Petrovich lived in the most moderate fashion, and avoided excesses of any sort. I never chanced to see him tipsy (which in our parts may be accounted an unheard-of miracle); he had a strong leaning toward the female sex, but he was truly as bashful as a girl.[1]

Besides the tales which you are pleased to mention in your letter, Ivan Petrovich left many manuscripts, some of which are in my hands, the rest having been put by his housekeeper to various domestic uses. Thus, last winter all the windows in her own wing were pasted over with the first part of the novel which he did not complete. The above-mentioned tales were, it seems, his first effort. As Ivan Petrovich said, they are for the most part true stories, which he had heard from various persons.[2] But the names in them were almost all his own invention, while the names of the villages and hamlets were taken from our neighbor-

---

[1] Follows an anecdote, which we do not give, deeming it superfluous; we assure the reader, however, that it contains nothing prejudicial to the memory of Ivan Petrovich Belkin.

[2] Indeed, in Mr. Belkin's manuscript, there is an inscription, in the author's hand, over each tale: "Heard by me from such-and-such a person" (follow rank or title and initials of name and surname). We quote for the curious student: "The Postmaster" was told to him by Titular Counsellor A.G.N., "The Shot" by Lieutenant I. L. P., "The Undertaker" by B. V., shop-assistant, "The Snow Storm" and "Mistress into Maid" by Miss K. I. T.

hood, for which reason my village too is mentioned somewhere. This happened not because of any malicious design, but solely through lack of imagination.

In the autumn of 1828, Ivan Petrovich came down with a catarrhal fever, which took a bad turn, so that he died, in spite of the tireless efforts of our district doctor, a man very skillful, particularly in the treatment of inveterate diseases, such as bunions and the like. He died in my arms in the thirtieth year of his life, and was buried near his deceased parents in the churchyard of the village of Goryukhino.

Ivan Petrovich was of middle height, had gray eyes, blond hair, a straight nose; his complexion was fair and his face lean.

Here, my dear sir, is all I can recall regarding the manner of life, the occupations, the character and the appearance of my late neighbor and friend. In case you should think fit to make some use of my letter, I respectfully beg you not to mention my name; for much as I esteem and admire authors, I deem it superfluous, and indeed at my age unseemly, to enter their ranks.

With every expression of sincere esteem, believe me, etc.

November 16, 1830,
The village of Nenaradovo.

Considering it our duty to respect the wish of our author's esteemed friend, we signalize our deepest gratitude to him for the intelligence furnished by him, and trust that the public will appreciate his candor and good-nature.

A. P.

THE SHOT

We fought a duel.

Baratynsky

I swore to shoot him, as the code of dueling allows (It was my turn to fire).

Evening at Camp

I

WE were stationed in the town of N——. The life of an officer in the army is well known. In the morning, drill and the riding-school; dinner with the Colonel or at a Jewish restaurant; in the evening, punch and cards. In N—— there was not one open house, nor a single marriageable girl. We used to meet in each other's rooms, where all we saw was men in uniform.

One civilian only was admitted into our society. He was about thirty-five years of age, and therefore we looked upon him as an old fellow. His experience gave him great advantage over us, and his habitual sullenness, stern disposition and caustic tongue produced a deep impression upon our young minds. Some mystery surrounded his existence; he had the appearance of a Russian, although his name was a foreign one. He had formerly served in the Hussars, and with distinction. Nobody knew the cause that had induced him to retire from the service and settle in a wretched town, where he lived poorly and, at the same time, extravagantly. He always went on foot, and constantly wore a shabby black overcoat, but the officers of our regiment were ever welcome at his table. His dinners, it is true, never consisted of more than two or three dishes, prepared by a retired soldier, but the champagne flowed like water. Nobody knew what his circumstances were, or what his income was, and nobody dared to question him about them. He had a collection of books, chiefly works on military matters and novels. He willingly lent them to us to read, and never asked for their return; on the other hand, he never returned to the owner the books that were lent to him. His principal amusement was shooting with a pistol. The walls of his room were riddled with bullets, and were as full of holes as a honey-comb. A rich collection of pistols was the only luxury in the humble cottage where he lived. The skill which he had acquired with his favorite weapon was simply incredible; and if he had offered to shoot a pear off somebody's forage-cap, not a man in our regiment would have hesitated to expose his head to the bullet.

Our conversation often turned upon duels. Silvio—so I will call him—never joined in it. When asked if he had ever fought, he drily replied that he had; but he entered into no particulars, and it was evident that such questions were not to his liking. We imagined that he had upon his conscience the memory of some unhappy victim of his terrible skill. It never entered into the head of any of us to suspect him of anything like cowardice. There are persons whose mere look is sufficient to repel such suspicions. But an unexpected incident occurred which astounded us all.

One day, about ten of our officers dined with Silvio. They drank as usual, that is to say, a great deal. After dinner we asked our host to hold the bank for a game at faro. For a long time he refused, as he hardly ever played, but at last he ordered cards to be brought, placed half a hundred gold coins upon the table, and sat down to deal. We took our places around him, and the game began. It was Silvio's custom to preserve complete silence when playing. He never argued, and never entered into explanations. If the punter made a mistake in calculating, he immediately paid him the difference or noted down the surplus. We were acquainted with this habit of his, and we always allowed him to have his own way; but among us on this occasion was an officer who had only recently been transferred to our regiment. During the course of the game, this officer absently scored one point too many. Silvio took the chalk and noted down the correct account according to his usual custom. The officers, thinking that he had made a mistake, began to enter into explanations. Silvio continued dealing in silence. The officer, losing patience, took the brush and rubbed out what he considered an error. Silvio took the chalk and corrected the score again. The officer, heated with wine, play, and the laughter of his comrades, considered himself grossly insulted, and in his rage he seized a brass candlestick from the table, and hurled it at Silvio, who barely succeeded in avoiding the missile. We were filled with consternation. Silvio rose, white with rage, and with gleaming eyes, said:

"My dear sir, have the goodness to withdraw, and thank God that this has happened in my house."

None of us entertained the slightest doubt as to what the result would be, and we already looked upon our now comrade as a dead man. The officer withdrew, saying that he was ready to answer for his offense in whatever way the banker liked. The play went on for a few minutes longer, but feeling that our host was too overwrought to care for the game, we withdrew one after the other, and repaired to our respective quarters, after having exchanged a few words upon the probability of there soon being a vacancy in the regiment.

The next day, at the riding-school, we were already asking each other if the poor lieutenant was still alive, when he himself appeared among us. We put the same question to him, and he replied that he had not yet heard from Silvio. This astonished us. We went to Silvio's house and found him in the courtyard shooting bullet after bullet into an ace pasted upon the gate. He received us as usual, but did not utter a word about the event of the previous evening. Three days passed, and the lieutenant was still alive. We asked each other in astonishment: "Can it be possible that Silvio is not going to fight?"

Silvio did not fight. He was satisfied with a very lame explanation, and made peace with his assailant.

This lowered him very much in the opinion of all our young fellows. Want of courage is the last thing to be pardoned by young men, who usually look upon bravery as the chief of all human virtues, and the excuse for every possible fault. But, by degrees, everything was forgotten, and Silvio regained his former influence.

I alone could not approach him on the old footing. Being endowed by nature with a romantic imagination, I had become attached more than all the others to the man whose life was an enigma, and who seemed to me the hero of some mysterious tale. He was fond of me; at least, with me alone did he drop his customary sarcastic tone, and converse on different subjects in a simple and unusually agreeable manner. But after this unlucky evening, the thought that his honor had been tarnished, and that the stain had been allowed to remain upon it through his own fault, was ever present in my mind, and prevented me from treating him as before. I was ashamed to look at him. Silvio was too intelligent and experienced not to observe this and guess the cause of it. This seemed to vex him; at least I observed once or twice a desire on his part to enter into an explanation with me, but I avoided such opportunities, and Silvio gave up the attempt. From that time forward I saw him only in the presence of my comrades, and our former confidential conversations came to an end.

Those who live amidst the excitements of the capital have no idea of the many experiences familiar to the inhabitants of villages and small towns, as, for instance, waiting for the arrival of the post. On Tuesdays and Fridays our regimental bureau used to be filled with officers: some expecting money, some letters, and others newspapers. The packets were usually opened on the spot, items of news were communicated from one to another, and the bureau used to present a very animated picture. Silvio used to have his letters addressed to our regiment, and he was generally there to receive them.

One day he received a letter, the seal of which he broke with a look of the greatest impatience. As he read the contents, his eyes sparkled. The officers, each occupied with his own mail, did not observe anything.

"Gentlemen," said Silvio, "circumstances demand my immediate departure; I leave tonight. I hope that you will not refuse to dine with me for the last time. I shall expect you, too," he added, turning toward me. "I shall expect you without fail."

With these words he hastily departed, and we, after agreeing to meet at Silvio's, dispersed to our various quarters.

I arrived at Silvio's house at the appointed time, and found nearly the whole regiment there. All his belongings were already packed; nothing remained but the

bare, bullet-riddled walls. We sat down to table. Our
host was in an excellent humor, and his gaiety was
quickly communicated to the rest. Corks popped every
moment, glasses foamed incessantly, and, with the utmost warmth, we wished our departing friend a pleasant journey and every happiness. When we rose from
the table it was already late in the evening. After having wished everybody good-bye, Silvio took me by the
hand and detained me just at the moment when I was
preparing to depart.

"I want to speak to you," he said in a low voice.

I stopped behind.

The guests had departed, and we two were left alone.
Sitting down opposite each other, we silently lit our
pipes. Silvio seemed greatly troubled; not a trace remained of his former feverish gaiety. The intense pallor of his face, his sparkling eyes, and the thick smoke
issuing from his mouth, gave him a truly diabolical appearance. Several minutes elapsed, and then Silvio
broke the silence.

"Perhaps we shall never see each other again," said
he; "before we part, I should like to have an explanation with you. You may have observed that I care very
little for the opinion of other people, but I like you,
and I feel that it would be painful to me to leave you
with a wrong impression upon your mind."

He paused, and began to refill his pipe. I sat gazing
silently at the floor.

"You thought it strange," he continued, "that I did
not demand satisfaction from that drunken idiot
R——. You will admit, however, that since I had the
choice of weapons, his life was in my hands, while my
own was in no great danger. I could ascribe my for-
bearance to generosity alone, but I will not tell a lie.
If I could have chastised R—— without the least risk
to my own life, I should never have pardoned him."

I looked at Silvio with astonishment. Such a confession completely astounded me. Silvio continued:

"Exactly so: I have no right to expose myself to death. Six years ago I received a slap in the face, and my enemy still lives."

My curiosity was greatly excited.

"Did you not fight with him?" I asked. "Circumstances probably separated you."

"I did fight with him," replied Silvio: "and here is a souvenir of our duel."

Silvio rose and took from a cardboard box a red cap with a gold tassel and galloon (what the French call a *bonnet de police*); he put it on——a bullet had passed through it about an inch above the forehead.

"You know," continued Silvio, "that I served in one of the Hussar regiments. My character is well known to you: I am accustomed to taking the lead. From my youth this has been my passion. In our time dissoluteness was the fashion, and I was the wildest man in the army. We used to boast of our drunkenness: I outdrank the famous B——,[1] of whom D. D——[2] has sung. In our regiment duels were constantly taking place, and in all of them I was either second or principal. My comrades adored me, while the regimental commanders, who were constantly being changed, looked upon me as a necessary evil.

"I was calmly, or rather boisterously enjoying my reputation, when a young man belonging to a wealthy and distinguished family—I will not mention his name —joined our regiment. Never in my life have I met with such a fortunate fellow! Imagine to yourself youth, wit, beauty, unbounded gaiety, the most reckless bravery, a famous name, untold wealth—imagine

[1] Burtzov, an officer of the Hussars, notorious for his drinking powers and escapades.

[2] Denis Davydov, author (1781-1839).   TRANSLATOR'S NOTE

all these, and you can form some idea of the effect that he would be sure to produce among us. My supremacy was shaken. Dazzled by my reputation, he began to seek my friendship, but I received him coldly, and without the least regret he held aloof from me. I began to hate him. His success in the regiment and in the society of ladies brought me to the verge of despair. I began to seek a quarrel with him; to my epigrams he replied with epigrams which always seemed to me more spontaneous and more cutting than mine, and which were decidedly more amusing, for he joked while I fumed. At last, at a ball given by a Polish landed proprietor, seeing him the object of the attention of all the ladies, and especially of the mistress of the house, with whom I was having a liaison, I whispered some grossly insulting remark in his ear. He flamed up and gave me a slap in the face. We grasped our swords; the ladies fainted; we were separated; and that same night we set out to fight.

"The dawn was just breaking. I was standing at the appointed place with my three seconds. With indescribable impatience I awaited my opponent. The spring sun rose, and it was already growing hot. I saw him coming in the distance. He was on foot, in uniform, wearing his sword, and was accompanied by one second. We advanced to meet him. He approached, holding his cap filled with black cherries. The seconds measured twelve paces for us. I had to fire first, but my agitation was so great, that I could not depend upon the steadiness of my hand; and in order to give myself time to become calm, I ceded to him the first shot. My adversary would not agree to this. It was decided that we should cast lots. The first number fell to him, the constant favorite of fortune. He took aim, and his bullet went through my cap. It was now my turn. His life at last was in my hands; I looked at him eagerly, endeavoring to detect if only the faintest shadow of uneasiness. But he stood in front of my pistol, picking out the ripest cherries from his cap and spitting out the stones, which flew almost as far as my feet. His indifference enraged me beyond measure. 'What is the use,' thought I, 'of depriving him of life, when he attaches no value whatever to it?' A malicious thought flashed through my mind. I lowered my pistol.

" 'You don't seem to be ready for death just at present,' I said to him: 'you wish to have your breakfast; I do not wish to hinder you.'

" 'You are not hindering me in the least,' he replied, 'Have the goodness to fire, or just as you please—you owe me a shot; I shall always be at your service.'

"I turned to the seconds, informing them that I had no intention of firing that day, and with that the duel came to an end.

"I resigned my commission and retired to this little place. Since then, not a day has passed that I have not thought of revenge. And now my hour has arrived."

Silvio took from his pocket the letter that he had received that morning, and gave it to me to read. Someone (it seemed to be his business agent) wrote to him from Moscow, that a *certain person* was going to be married to a young and beautiful girl.

"You can guess," said Silvio, "who the certain person is. I am going to Moscow. We shall see if he will look death in the face with as much indifference now, when he is on the eve of being married, as he did once when he was eating cherries!"

With these words, Silvio rose, threw his cap upon the floor, and began pacing up and down the room like a tiger in his cage. I had listened to him in silence; strange conflicting feelings agitated me.

The servant entered and announced that the horses were ready. Silvio grasped my hand tightly, and we embraced each other. He seated himself in the carriage, in which there were two suitcases, one containing his pistols, the other his effects. We said good-bye once more, and the horses galloped off.

II

SEVERAL years passed, and family circumstances compelled me to settle in a poor little village of the N—— district. Occupied with farming, I continued to sigh in secret for my former active and carefree life. The most difficult thing of all was having to accustom myself to passing the spring and winter evenings in perfect solitude. Until the hour for dinner I managed to pass away the time somehow or other, talking with the bailiff, riding about to inspect the work, or going round to look at the new buildings; but as soon as it began to get dark, I positively did not know what to do with myself. The few books that I had found in the cupboards and store-rooms, I already knew by heart. All the stories that my housekeeper Kirilovna could remember, I had heard over and over again. The songs of the peasant women made me feel depressed. I tried drinking spirits, but it made my head ache; and moreover, I confess I was afraid of becoming a drunkard from mere chagrin, that is to say, the saddest kind of drunkard, of which I had seen many examples in our district. I had no near neighbors, except two or three topers, whose conversation consisted for the most part of hiccups and sighs. Solitude was preferable to their society.

Four versts from my house there was a rich estate belonging to the Countess B——; but nobody lived there except the steward. The Countess had only visited her estate once, during the first year of her married life, and then she had remained there only a month. But in the second spring of my secluded life, a report was circulated that the Countess, with her husband, was coming to spend the summer on her estate. Indeed, they arrived at the beginning of June.

The arrival of a rich neighbor is an important event in the lives of country people. The landed proprietors and the people of their household talk about it for two months beforehand, and for three years afterwards. As for me, I must confess that the news of the arrival of a young and beautiful neighbor affected me strongly. I burned with impatience to see her, and the first Sunday after her arrival I set out after dinner for the village of A——, to pay my respects to the Countess and her husband, as their nearest neighbor and most humble servant.

A lackey conducted me into the Count's study, and then went to announce me. The spacious room was furnished with every possible luxury. The walls were lined with bookcases, each surmounted by a bronze bust; over the marble mantelpiece was a large mirror; on the floor was a green cloth covered with carpets. Unaccustomed to luxury in my own poor corner, and not having seen the wealth of other people for a long time, I awaited the appearance of the Count with some little trepidation, as a suppliant from the provinces awaits the entrance of the minister. The door opened, and a handsome-looking man, of about thirty-two, entered the room. The Count approached me with a frank and friendly air: I tried to be self-possessed and began to introduce myself, but he anticipated me. We sat down. His conversation, which was easy and agreeable, soon dissipated my awkward bashfulness; and I was already beginning to recover my usual composure, when the Countess suddenly entered, and I became more confused than ever. She was indeed beautiful.

The Count presented me. I wished to appear at ease, but the more I tried to assume an air of unconstraint, the more awkward I felt. In order to give me time to recover myself and to become accustomed to my new acquaintances, they began to talk to each other, treat ing me as a good neighbor, and without ceremony. Meanwhile, I walked about the room, examining the books and pictures. I am no judge of pictures, but one of them attracted my attention. It represented some view in Switzerland, but it was not the painting that struck me, but the circumstance that the canvas was shot through by two bullets, one planted just above the other.

"A good shot, that!" said I, turning to the Count.

"Yes," replied he, "a very remarkable shot. . . . Do you shoot well?" he continued.

"Tolerably," I replied, rejoicing that the conversation had turned at last upon a subject that was familiar to me. "At thirty paces I can manage to hit a card without fail—I mean, of course, with a pistol that I am used to."

"Really?" said the Countess, with a look of the greatest interest. "And you, my dear, could you hit a card at thirty paces?"

"Some day," replied the Count, "we will try. In my time I did not shoot badly, but it is now four years since I touched a pistol."

"Oh!" I observed, "in that case, I don't mind laying a wager that Your Excellency will not hit the card at twenty paces: the pistol demands daily practice. I know that from experience. In our regiment I was reckoned one of the best shots. It once happened that I did not touch a pistol for a whole month, as I had sent mine to be mended; and would you believe it, Your Excellency, the first time I began to shoot again, I missed a bottle four times in succession at twenty paces! Our captain, a witty and amusing fellow, happened to be standing by, and he said to me: 'It is evident, my friend, that you will not lift your hand against the bottle.' No, Your Excellency, you must not neglect to practice, or your hand will soon lose its cunning. The best shot that I ever met used to shoot at least three times every day before dinner. It was as much his custom to do this, as it was to drink his daily glass of brandy."

The Count and Countess seemed pleased that I had begun to talk.

"And what sort of a shot was he?" asked the Count.

"Well, it was this way with him, Your Excellency: if he saw a fly settle on the wall—you smile, Countess, but, before Heaven, it is the truth—if he saw a fly, he would call out: 'Kuzka, my pistol!' Kuzka would bring him a loaded pistol—bang! and the fly would be crushed against the wall."

"Wonderful!" said the Count. "And what was his name?"

"Silvio, Your Excellency."

"Silvio!" exclaimed the Count, starting up. "Did you know Silvio?"

"How could I help knowing him, Your Excellency: we were intimate friends; he was received in our regiment like a brother officer, but it is now five years since I had any news of him. Then Your Excellency also knew him?"

"Oh, yes, I knew him very well. Did he ever tell you of one very strange incident in his life?"

"Does Your Excellency refer to the slap in the face that he received from some scamp at a ball?"

"Did he tell you the name of this scamp?"

"No, Your Excellency, he never mentioned his name. . . . Ah! Your Excellency!" I continued, guessing the truth: "pardon me . . . I did not know . . . could it have been you?"

"Yes, I myself," replied the Count, with a look of extraordinary distress; "and that picture with a bullet through it is a memento of our last meeting."

"Ah, my dear," said the Countess, "for Heaven's sake, do not speak about that; it would be too terrible for me to listen to."

"No," replied the Count: "I will relate everything. He knows how I insulted his friend, and it is only right that he should know how Silvio revenged himself."

The Count pushed a chair towards me, and with the liveliest interest I listened to the following story:

"Five years ago I got married. The first month—the honeymoon—I spent here, in this village. To this house I am indebted for the happiest moments of my life, as well as for one of its most painful recollections.

"One evening we went out together for a ride on horseback. My wife's horse became restive; she grew frightened, gave the reins to me, and returned home on foot. I rode on before. In the courtyard I saw a traveling carriage, and I was told that in my study sat waiting for me a man who would not give his name, but who merely said that he had business with me. I entered the room and saw in the darkness a man, covered with dust and wearing a beard of several days' growth. He was standing there, near the fireplace. I approached him, trying to remember his features.

" 'You do not recognize me, Count?' said he, in a quivering voice.

" 'Silvio!' I cried, and I confess that I felt as if my hair had suddenly stood on end.

" 'Exactly,' continued he. 'There is a shot due me, and I have come to discharge my pistol. Are you ready?'

"His pistol protruded from a side pocket. I measured twelve paces and took my stand there in that corner, begging him to fire quickly, before my wife arrived. He hesitated, and asked for a light. Candles were brought in. I closed the doors, gave orders that nobody was to enter, and again begged him to fire. He drew out his pistol and took aim. . . . I counted the seconds . . . I thought of her . . . A terrible minute passed! Silvio lowered his hand.

" 'I regret,' said he, 'that the pistol is not loaded with cherry-stones . . . the bullet is heavy. It seems to me that this is not a duel, but a murder. I am not accustomed to taking aim at unarmed men. Let us begin all over again; we will cast lots as to who shall fire first.'

"My head went round . . . I think I raised some objection. . . . At last we loaded another pistol, and rolled up two pieces of paper. He placed these latter in his cap—the same through which I had once sent a bullet—and again I drew the first number.

" 'You are devilishly lucky, Count,' said he, with a smile that I shall never forget.

"I don't know what was the matter with me, or how it was that he managed to make me do it . . . but I fired and hit that picture."

The Count pointed with his finger to the perforated picture; his face burned like fire; the Countess was whiter than her own handkerchief; and I could not restrain an exclamation.

"I fired," continued the Count, "and, thank Heaven, missed my aim. Then Silvio . . . at that moment he was really terrible. . . . Silvio raised his hand to take aim at me. Suddenly the door opens, Masha rushes into the room, and with a shriek throws herself upon my neck. Her presence restored to me all my courage.

" 'My dear,' said I to her, 'don't you see that we are joking? How frightened you are! Go and drink a glass of water and then come back to us; I will introduce you to an old friend and comrade.'

"Masha still doubted.

" 'Tell me, is my husband speaking the truth?' said she, turning to the terrible Silvio: 'is it true that you are only joking?'

" 'He is always joking, Countess,' replied Silvio: 'once he gave me a slap in the face in jest; on another occasion he sent a bullet through my cap in jest; and just now, when he fired at me and missed me, it was all in jest. And now I feel inclined to have a joke.'

"With these words he raised his pistol to take aim at me—right before her! Masha threw herself at his feet.

" 'Rise, Masha; are you not ashamed!' I cried in a rage: 'and you, sir, will you stop making fun of a poor woman? Will you fire or not?'

" 'I will not,' replied Silvio: 'I am satisfied. I have seen your confusion, your alarm. I forced you to fire at me. That is sufficient. You will remember me. I leave you to your conscience.'

"Then he turned to go, but pausing in the doorway, and looking at the picture that my shot had passed through, he fired at it almost without taking aim, and disappeared. My wife had fainted away; the servants did not venture to stop him, the mere look of him filled them with terror. He went out upon the steps, called his coachman, and drove off before I could recover myself."

The Count fell silent. In this way I learned the end of the story, whose beginning had once made such a deep impression upon me. The hero of it I never saw again. It is said that Silvio commanded a detachment of hetaerists during the revolt under Alexander Ypsilanti, and that he was killed in the battle of Skulyani.

THE SNOWSTORM

Horses dash across the slopes,
Trampling snow deep-drifted . . .
By the wayside stands a church,
Lonely cross uplifted.

. . . .

Suddenly a snowstorm flings
Tufted flakes about us,
O'er the sledge with whistling wing
Flies a crow to flout us.
Weird his cry, foreboding grief!
Gathering their forces,
Manes upraised, toward the dark
Peer the speeding horses . . .

Zhukovsky

TOWARD the end of the year 1811, a memorable period for us, the good Gavrila Gavrilovich R—— was living on his estate of Nenaradovo. He was celebrated throughout the district for his hospitality and kindheartedness. The neighbors were constantly visiting him: some to eat and drink; some to play "Boston" at five copecks with his wife, Praskovya Petrovna; and some to look at their daughter, Marya Gavrilovna, a pale, slender girl of seventeen. She was considered wealthy, and many desired her for themselves or for their sons.

Marya Gavrilovna had been brought up on French novels, and consequently was in love. The object of her choice was a poor sub-lieutenant, who was then on leave of absence in his village. It need scarcely be mentioned that the young man returned her passion with equal ardor, and that the parents of his beloved one, observing their mutual inclination, forbade their daughter to think of him, and gave him a worse reception than if he were a retired assessor.

Our lovers corresponded with each other and daily saw each other alone in the little pine wood or near the old chapel. There they exchanged vows of eternal love, lamented their cruel fate, and formed various plans. Corresponding and conversing in this way, they arrived quite naturally at the following conclusion:

If we cannot exist without each other, and the will of hard-hearted parents stands in the way of our happiness, why cannot we do without their consent?

Needless to mention that this happy idea originated in the mind of the young man, and that it was very congenial to the romantic imagination of Marya Gavrilovna.

The winter came and put a stop to their meetings, but their correspondence became all the more active. Vladimir Nikolayevich in every letter implored her to give herself up to him, to get married secretly, to hide for some time, and then throw themselves at the feet of their parents, who would, without any doubt, be touched at last by the heroic constancy and unhappiness of the lovers, and would assuredly say to them: "Children, come to our arms!"

Marya Gavrilovna hesitated for a long time, and many plans for elopement were rejected. At last she consented: on the appointed day she was not to take supper, but was to retire to her room under the pretext of a headache. Her maid was in the plot; they were both to go into the garden by the back stairs, and behind the garden, they would find ready a sledge, into which they were to get, and then drive straight to the church of Zhadrino, a village about five versts from Nenaradovo, where Vladimir would be waiting for them.

On the eve of the decisive day, Marya Gavrilovna did not sleep the whole night; she packed and tied up her linen and other articles of apparel, wrote a long letter to a sentimental young lady, a friend of hers, and another to her parents. She took leave of them in the most touching terms, urged the invincible strength of passion as an excuse for the step she was taking, and wound up with the assurance that she would consider it the happiest moment of her life, when she should be allowed to throw herself at the feet of her dear parents.

After having sealed both letters with a Tula seal, upon which were engraved two flaming hearts with a suitable inscription, she threw herself upon her bed just before daybreak, and dozed off: but even then she was constantly being awakened by terrible dreams. First it seemed to her that at the very moment when she seated herself in the sledge, in order to go and get married, her father stopped her, dragged her over the snow with agonizing rapidity, and threw her into a dark bottomless abyss, down which she fell headlong with an indescribable sinking of the heart. Then she saw Vladimir lying on the grass, pale and blood-stained. With his dying breath he implored her in a piercing voice to make haste and marry him. . . . Other abominable and absurd visions floated before her one after another. At last she arose, paler than usual, and with an unfeigned headache. Her father and mother observed her uneasiness; their tender solicitude and incessant inquiries: "What is the matter with you, Masha? Are you ill, Masha?" cut her to the heart. She tried to reassure them and to appear cheerful, but in vain.

Evening came. The thought, that this was the last day she would pass in the bosom of her family, weighed upon her heart. She was more dead than alive. In secret she took leave of everybody, of all the objects that surrounded her.

Supper was served; her heart began to beat violently. In a trembling voice she declared that she did not want any supper, and then took leave of her father and mother. They kissed her and blessed her as usual, and she could hardly restrain herself from weeping.

On reaching her own room, she threw herself into a chair and burst into tears. Her maid urged her to be calm and to take courage. Everything was ready. In half an hour Masha would leave for ever her parents' house, her room, and her peaceful girlish life. . . .

Outside a snowstorm was raging; the wind howled, the shutters shook and rattled, and everything seemed to her to portend misfortune.

Soon all was quiet in the house: everyone was asleep. Masha wrapped herself in a shawl, put on a warm cloak, took her box in her hand, and went down the back staircase. Her maid followed her with two bundles. They descended into the garden. The snowstorm had not subsided; the wind blew in their faces, as if trying to stop the young criminal. With difficulty they reached the end of the garden. On the road a sledge awaited them. The chilled horses would not keep still; Vladimir's coachman was walking up and down in front of them, trying to restrain their impatience. He helped the young lady and her maid into the sledge, stowed away the box and the bundles, seized the reins, and the horses dashed off.

Having entrusted the young lady to the care of fate and to the skill of Teryoshka the coachman, we will return to our young lover.

All day long Vladimir had been driving about. In the morning he paid a visit to the priest of Zhadrino, and having come to an agreement with him after a

great deal of difficulty, he then set out to seek for witnesses among the neighboring landowners. The first
to whom he presented himself, a retired cornet about
forty years old, whose name was Dravin, consented
with pleasure. The adventure, he declared, reminded
him of his young days and his pranks in the Hussars.
He persuaded Vladimir to stay to dinner with him,
and assured him that he would have no difficulty in
finding the other two witnesses. And, indeed, immediately after dinner, appeared the surveyor Schmidt,
wearing mustaches and spurs, and the son of the captain of police, a lad of sixteen, who had recently entered
the Uhlans. They not only accepted Vladimir's proposal, but even vowed that they were ready to sacrifice
their lives for him. Vladimir embraced them with rapture, and returned home to get everything ready.

It had been dark for some time. He dispatched his
faithful Teryoshka to Nenaradovo with his troika and
with detailed instructions, ordered for himself the one-
horse sleigh and set out alone, without any coachman,
for Zhadrino, where Marya Gavrilovna was due to arrive in about a couple of hours. He knew the road well,
and it was only a twenty-minute ride.

But Vladimir scarcely found himself on the open
road, when the wind rose and such a snowstorm came
on that he could see nothing. In one minute the road
was completely hidden; the landscape disappeared in
a thick yellow fog, through which fell white flakes of
snow; earth and sky merged into one. Vladimir found
himself off the road, and tried vainly to get back to it.
His horse went on at random, and at every moment
climbed either a snowdrift or sank into a hole, so that
the sledge kept turning over. Vladimir's one effort was
not to lose the right direction. But it seemed to him that
more than half an hour had already passed, and he had
not yet reached the Zhadrino wood. Another ten min-

utes elapsed—still no wood was to be seen. Vladimir drove across a field intersected by deep ravines. The snowstorm did not abate, the sky did not become any clearer. The horse began to grow tired, and the sweat rolled from Vladimir in great drops, in spite of the fact that he was constantly being half-buried in the snow.

At last Vladimir perceived that he was going in the wrong direction. He stopped, began to think, to recollect, and compare, and he felt convinced that he ought to have turned to the right. He turned to the right now. His horse could scarcely move forward. He had now been on the road for more than an hour. Zhadrino could not be far off. But on and on he went, and still no end to the field—nothing but snow-drifts and ravines. The sledge was constantly turning over, and as constantly being set right again. The time was passing: Vladimir began to grow seriously uneasy.

At last something dark appeared in the distance. Vladimir directed his course toward it. On drawing near, he perceived that it was a wood.

"Thank Heaven!" he thought, "I am not far off now."

He drove along by the edge of the wood, hoping by-and-by to come upon the well-known road or to pass round the wood; Zhadrino was situated just behind it. He soon found the road, and plunged among the dark trees, now denuded of leaves by the winter. The wind could not rage here; the road was smooth; the horse recovered courage, and Vladimir felt reassured.

But he drove on and on, and Zhadrino was not to be seen; there was no end to the wood. Vladimir discovered with horror that he had entered an unknown forest. Despair took possession of him. He whipped the horse; the poor animal broke into a trot, but soon slackened its pace, and in about a quarter of an hour it was scarcely able to drag one leg after the other, in spite of all the exertions of the unfortunate Vladimir.

Gradually the trees began to get sparser, and Vladimir emerged from the forest; but Zhadrino was not to be seen. It must now have been about midnight. Tears gushed from his eyes; he drove on at random. Meanwhile the storm had subsided, the clouds dispersed, and before him lay a level plain covered with a white undulating carpet. The night was tolerably clear. He saw, not far off, a little village, consisting of four or five houses. Vladimir drove toward it. At the first cottage he jumped out of the sledge, ran to the window and began to knock. After a few minutes, the wooden shutter was raised, and an old man thrust out his gray beard.

"What do you want?"

"Is Zhadrino far from here?"

"Zhadrino? Far from here?"

"Yes, yes! Is it far?"

"Not far; about ten versts."

At this reply, Vladimir clutched his hair and stood motionless, like a man condemned to death.

"Where do you come from?" continued the old man.

Vladimir had not the heart to answer the question.

"Listen, old man," said he: "can you find any horses to take me to Zhadrino?"

"How should we have such things as horses?" replied the peasant.

"Can I at least get a guide? I will pay him whatever he asks."

"Wait," said the old man, closing the shutter; "I will send my son out to you; he will direct you."

Vladimir waited. But a minute had scarcely elapsed when he began knocking again. The shutter was raised, and the beard again appeared.

"What do you want?"

"What about your son?"

"He'll be out presently; he is putting on his boots. Are you cold? Come in and warm yourself."

"Thank you; send your son out quickly."

The door creaked: a lad came out with a cudgel and led the way, now pointing out the road, now searching for it among the snow drifts.

"What time is it?" Vladimir asked him.

"It will soon be daylight," replied the young peasant. Vladimir did not say another word.

The cocks were crowing, and it was already light when they reached Zhadrino. The church was locked. Vladimir paid the guide and drove into the priest's courtyard. His troika was not there. What news awaited him! . . .

But let us return to the worthy proprietors of Nenaradovo, and see what is happening there.

Nothing.

The old people awoke and went into the parlor, Gavrila Gavrilovich in a night-cap and flannel doublet, Praskovya Petrovna in a wadded dressing-gown. The samovar was brought in, and Gavrila Gavrilovich sent a servant to ask Marya Gavrilovna how she was and how she had passed the night. The servant returned, saying that the young lady had not slept very well, but that she felt better now, and that she would come down presently into the parlor. And indeed, the door opened and Marya Gavrilovna entered the room and wished her father and mother good morning.

"How is your head, Masha?" asked Gavrila Gavrilovich.

"Better, papa," replied Masha.

"You must have gotten your headache yesterday from charcoal fumes," said Praskovya Petrovna.

"Very likely, mamma," replied Masha.

The day passed happily enough, but in the night
Masha was taken ill. They sent to town for a doctor. He arrived in the evening and found the sick
girl delirious. A violent fever ensued, and for two
weeks the poor patient hovered on the brink of the
grave.

Nobody in the house knew anything about her
intended elopement. The letters written the evening
before, had been burnt; and her maid, dreading the
wrath of her master, had not whispered a word about it
to anybody. The priest, the retired cornet, the mus-
tached surveyor, and the little Uhlan were discreet, and
not without reason. Teryoshka, the coachman, never
uttered one word too much about it, even when he was
drunk. Thus the secret was kept by more than half-a-
dozen conspirators.

But Marya Gavrilovna herself divulged her secret
during her delirious ravings. Her words were so disconnected, however, that her mother, who never left her
bedside, could only understand from them that her
daughter was deeply in love with Vladimir Nikolayevich, and that probably love was the cause of her illness. She consulted her husband and some of her
neighbors, and at last it was unanimously decided that
such was evidently Marya Gavrilovna's fate, that a
woman cannot escape her destined husband even on
horseback, that poverty is not a crime, that one does not
marry wealth, but a man, etc., etc. Moral maxims are
wonderfully useful in those cases where we can invent
little in our own justification.

In the meantime the young lady began to recover.
Vladimir had not been seen for a long time in the
house of Gavrila Gavrilovich. He was afraid of the
usual reception. It was resolved to send and announce
to him an unexpected piece of good news: the consent
of Marya's parents to his marriage with their daughter.

But what was the astonishment of the proprietor of Nenaradovo, when, in reply to their invitation, they received from him a half-insane letter. He informed them that he would never set foot in their house again, and begged them to forget an unhappy creature whose only hope was death. A few days afterwards they heard that Vladimir had joined the army again. This was in the year 1812.

For a long time they did not dare to announce this to Masha, who was now convalescent. She never mentioned the name of Vladimir. Some months afterwards, finding his name in the list of those who had distinguished themselves and been severely wounded at Borodino, she fainted away, and it was feared that she would have another attack of fever. But, Heaven be thanked! the fainting fit had no serious consequences.

Another misfortune fell upon her: Gavrila Gavrilovich died, leaving her the heiress to all his property. But the inheritance did not console her; she shared sincerely the grief of poor Praskovya Petrovna, vowing that she would never leave her. They both quitted Nenaradovo, the scene of so many sad recollections, and went to live on another estate.

Suitors crowded round the charming heiress, but she gave not the slightest hope to any of them. Her mother sometimes exhorted her to make a choice; but Marya Gavrilovna shook her head and became pensive. Vladimir no longer existed: he had died in Moscow on the eve of the entry of the French. His memory seemed to be held sacred by Masha; at least she treasured up everything that could remind her of him: books that he had once read, his drawings, his music, and verses that he had copied out for her. The neighbors, hearing of all this, were astonished at her constancy, and awaited with curiosity the hero who should at last triumph over the melancholy fidelity of this virgin Artemisia.

Meanwhile the war had ended gloriously. Our regiments returned from abroad, and the people went out to meet them. The bands played the songs of the conquered: "Vive Henri-Quatre," Tyrolese waltzes and airs from "Joconde." Officers, who had set out for the war almost mere lads, returned, grown men in the martial air, their breasts hung with crosses. The soldiers chatted gaily among themselves, constantly using French and German words in their speech. Unforgettable time! Time of glory and enthusiasm! How the Russian heart throbbed at the word "Fatherland!" How sweet were the tears of reunion! With what unanimity did we mingle feelings of national pride with love for the Czar! And for him—what a moment!

The women, the Russian women, were then incomparable. Their usual coldness disappeared. Their enthusiasm was truly intoxicating, when welcoming the conquerors they cried "Hurrah!"

"And tossed their caps into the air!"

What officer of that time does not confess that to the Russian women he was indebted for his best and most precious reward?

At this brilliant period Marya Gavrilovna was living with her mother in the province of ——, and did not see how both capitals celebrated the return of the troops. But in the districts and villages the general enthusiasm was, if possible, even greater. The appearance of an officer in those sections was for him a veritable triumph, and the lover in a frock coat fared ill in his vicinity.

We have already said that, in spite of her coldness, Marya Gavrilovna was, as before, surrounded by suitors. But all had to withdraw when the wounded Colonel Burmin of the Hussars, with the Order of St.

George in his button-hole, and with an "interesting pallor," as the young ladies of the neighborhood observed, appeared at the manor. He was about twenty-six years of age. He had obtained leave of absence to visit his estate, which was near that of Marya Gavrilovna. Marya bestowed special attention upon him. In his presence her habitual pensiveness disappeared. It cannot be said that she flirted with him, but a poet, observing her behavior, would have said:

"Se amor non è, che dunque?"

Burmin was indeed a very charming young man. He had the sort of mind which pleases women: decorous and keen, without any pretensions, and inclined to carefree mockery. His behavior toward Marya Gavrilovna was simple and frank, but whatever she said or did, both his soul and his eyes followed her. He seemed to be of a quiet and modest disposition, though it was reported that he had once been a terrible rake; but this did not injure him in the opinion of Marya Gavrilovna, who—like all young ladies—excused with pleasure follies that gave indication of boldness and ardor of temperament.

But more than everything else—more than his tenderness, more than his agreeable conversation, more than his interesting pallor, more than his arm in a sling—the silence of the young Hussar excited her curiosity and imagination. She could not but confess that he pleased her very much; probably he, too, with his intelligence and experience, had already observed that she singled him out; how was it then that she had not yet seen him at her feet or heard his declaration? What restrained him? Was it timidity, or pride, or the coquetry of a crafty ladies' man? It was a puzzle to her. After long reflection, she came to the conclusion that timidity alone was the cause of it, and she resolved to encourage him by greater attention and, if circumstances should render it necessary, even by an exhibition of tenderness. She was preparing a startling dénouement, and waited with impatience for the moment of the romantic explanation. A secret, of whatever nature it may be, always presses heavily upon the female heart. Her strategy had the desired success; at least Burmin fell into such a reverie, and his black eyes rested with such fire upon her, that the decisive moment seemed close at hand. The neighbors spoke about the marriage as if it were a settled matter, and good Praskovya Petrovna rejoiced that her daughter had at last found a worthy suitor.

On one occasion the old lady was sitting alone in the parlor, playing patience, when Burmin entered the room and immediately inquired for Marya Gavrilovna.

"She is in the garden," replied the old lady "go out to her, and I will wait here for you."

Burmin went, and the old lady made the sign of the cross and thought: "Perhaps the business will be settled today!"

Burmin found Marya Gavrilovna near the pond, under a willow-tree, with a book in her hands, and in a white dress: a veritable heroine of a novel. After the first few questions, Marya Gavrilovna purposely allowed the conversation to drop, thereby increasing their mutual embarrassment, from which there was no possible way of escape except only by a sudden and decisive declaration.

And that is what happened: Burmin, feeling the difficulty of his position, declared that he had long sought an opportunity to open his heart to her, and requested a moment's attention. Marya Gavrilovna closed her book and cast down her eyes, as a sign of consent.

"I love you," said Burmin: "I love you passionately."

Maria Gavrilovna blushed and lowered her head still further. "I have acted imprudently in indulging the sweet habit of seeing and hearing you daily. . . ." Marya Gavrilovna recalled to mind the first letter of St. Preux. "But it is now too late to resist my fate; the remembrance of you, your dear incomparable image, will henceforth be the torment and the consolation of my life, but there still remains a painful duty for me to perform—to reveal to you a terrible secret which will place between us an insurmountable barrier. . . ."

"That barrier has always existed," interrupted Marya Gavrilovna hastily: "I could never be your wife."

"I know," replied he calmly: "I know that you once loved, but death and three years of mourning. . . . Dear, kind Marya Gavrilovna, do not try to deprive me of my last consolation: the thought that you would have consented to make me happy, if . . ."

"Don't speak, for Heaven's sake, don't speak. You torture me."

"Yes, I know, I feel that you would have been mine, but—I am the most miserable creature under the sun— I am already married!"

Maria Gavrilovna looked at him in astonishment.

"I am already married," continued Burmin: "I have been married four years, and I do not know who my wife is, or where she is, or whether I shall ever see her again!'

"What are you saying?" exclaimed Marya Gavrilovna. "How very strange! Continue: I will relate to you afterwards. . . . But continue, I beg of you."

"At the beginning of the year 1812," said Burmin, "I was hastening to Vilna, where my regiment was stationed. Arriving late one evening at one of the post-stations, I ordered the horses to be got ready as quickly as possible, when suddenly a terrible snowstorm came on, and the postmaster and drivers advised me to wait till it had passed over. I followed their advice, but an unaccountable uneasiness took possession of me: it seemed as if someone were pushing me forward. Meanwhile the snowstorm did not subside; I could endure it no longer, and again ordering out the horses, I started off at the height of the storm. The driver conceived the idea of following the course of the river, which would shorten our journey by three versts. The banks were covered with snow: the driver drove past the place where we should have come out upon the road, and so we found ourselves in an unknown part of the country. . . . The storm did not abate; I saw a light in the distance, and I ordered the driver to proceed toward it. We reached a village; in the wooden church there was a light. The church was open. Outside the fence stood several sledges, and people were passing in and out through the porch.

" 'This way! this way!' cried several voices.

"I ordered the driver to proceed.

" 'In the name of Heaven, where have you been loitering?' somebody said to me. 'The bride has fainted away; the priest does not know what to do, and we were just getting ready to go back. Get out as quickly as you can.'

"I got out of the sledge without saying a word, and went into the church, which was feebly lit up by two or three tapers. A young girl was sitting on a bench in a dark corner of the church; another girl was rubbing her temples.

" 'Thank God!' said the latter, 'you have come at last. You have almost killed the young lady.'

"The old priest advanced toward me, and said:

" 'Do you wish me to begin?'

" 'Begin, begin, father,' I replied, absently.

"The young girl was raised up. She seemed to me not at all bad-looking. . . . Impelled by an incomprehensible, unpardonable levity, I placed myself by her side in front of the pulpit; the priest hurried on; three men and a maid supported the bride and only occupied themselves with her. We were married.

" 'Kiss each other!' said the witnesses to us.

"My wife turned her pale face toward me. I was about to kiss her, when she exclaimed: 'Oh! it is not he! it is not he!' and fell in a swoon.

"The witnesses gazed at me in alarm. I turned round and left the church without the least hindrance, flung myself into the *kibitka* and cried: 'Drive off!' "

"My God!" exclaimed Marya Gavrilovna. "And do you not know what became of your poor wife?"

"I do not know," replied Burmin; "neither do I know the name of the village where I was married, nor the post-station where I set out from. At that time I attached so little importance to my wicked prank, that on leaving the church, I fell asleep, and did not awake till the next morning after reaching the third station. The servant, who was then with me, died during the campaign, so that I have no hope of ever discovering the woman upon whom I played such a cruel joke, and who is now so cruelly avenged."

"My God, my God!" cried Marya Gavrilovna, seizing him by the hand: "then it was you! And you do not recognize me?"

Burmin blenched—and threw himself at her feet.

THE UNDERTAKER

Are coffins not beheld each day,
The gray hairs of an aging world?

Derzhavin

THE last of the effects of the undertaker, Adrian Prokhorov, were piled upon the hearse, and a couple of sorry-looking jades dragged themselves along for the fourth time from Basmannaya to Nikitskaya, whither the undertaker was removing with all his household. After locking up the shop, he posted upon the door a placard announcing that the house was for sale or rent, and then made his way on foot to his new abode. On approaching the little yellow house, which had so long captivated his imagination, and which at last he had bought for a considerable sum, the old undertaker was astonished to find that his heart did not rejoice. When he crossed the unfamiliar threshold and found his new home in the greatest confusion, he sighed for his old hovel, where for eighteen years the strictest order had prevailed. He began to scold his two daughters and the servants for their slowness, and then set to work to help them himself. Order was soon established; the ikon-case, the cupboard with the crockery, the table, the sofa, and the bed occupied the corners reserved for them in the back room; in the kitchen and parlor were placed the master's wares—coffins of all colors and of all sizes, together with cupboards containing mourning hats, cloaks and torches.

Over the gate was placed a sign representing a plump Cupid with an inverted torch in his hand and bearing this inscription: "Plain and colored coffins sold and upholstered here; coffins also let out on hire, and old ones repaired."

The girls retired to their bedroom; Adrian made a tour of inspection of his quarters, and then sat down by the window and ordered the samovar to be prepared.

The enlightened reader knows that Shakespeare and Walter Scott have both represented their grave-diggers as merry and facetious individuals, in order that the contrast might more forcibly strike our imagination. Out of respect for the truth, we cannot follow their example, and we are compelled to confess that the disposition of our undertaker was in perfect harmony with his gloomy métier. Adrian Prokhorov was usually sullen and pensive. He rarely opened his mouth, except to scold his daughters when he found them standing idle and gazing out of the window at the passers-by, or to ask for his wares an exorbitant price from those who had the misfortune—or sometimes the pleasure—of needing them. And so Adrian, sitting near the window and drinking his seventh cup of tea, was immersed as usual in melancholy reflections. He thought of the pouring rain which, just a week before, had commenced to beat down during the funeral of the retired brigadier. Many of the cloaks had shrunk in consequence of the downpour, and many of the hats had been put quite out of shape. He foresaw unavoidable expenses, for his old stock of funeral apparel was in a pitiable condition. He hoped to compensate himself for his losses by the burial of old Trukhina, the merchant's wife, who for more than a year had been upon the point of death. But Trukhina lay dying in Razgulyay, and Prokhorov was afraid that her heirs, in spite of their promise, would not take the trouble to send so far for him, but would make arrangements with the nearest undertaker.

These reflections were suddenly interrupted by three masonic knocks at the door.

"Who is there?" asked the undertaker.

The door opened, and a man, who at first glance could be recognized as a German artisan, entered the room, and with a jovial air advanced toward the undertaker.

"Pardon me, good neighbor," said he in that Russian dialect which to this day we cannot hear without a smile: "pardon me for disturbing you. . . . I wished to make your acquaintance as soon as possible. I am a shoemaker, my name is Gottlieb Schultz, and I live across the street, in that little house just facing your windows. To-morrow I am going to celebrate my silver wedding, and I have come to invite you and your daughters to dine with us."

The invitation was cordially accepted. The undertaker asked the shoemaker to seat himself and take a cup of tea, and thanks to the open-hearted disposition of Gottlieb Schultz, they were soon engaged in friendly conversation.

"How is business with you?" asked Adrian.

"So so," replied Schultz; "I can't complain. But my wares are not like yours: the living can do without shoes, but the dead cannot do without coffins."

"Very true," observed Adrian; "but if a living person hasn't anything to buy shoes with, he goes barefoot, and holds his peace, if you please; but a dead beggar gets his coffin for nothing."

In this manner the conversation was carried on between them for some time; at last the shoemaker rose and took leave of the undertaker, renewing his invitation.

The next day, exactly at twelve o'clock, the under-taker and his daughters issued from the wicket-door of their newly purchased residence, and went to their neighbor's. I will not stop to describe the Russian *caf-tan* of Adrian Prokhorov, nor the European toilettes of Akulina and Darya, deviating in this respect from the custom of modern novelists. But I do not think it superfluous to observe that the two girls had on the yellow hats and red shoes, which they were accustomed to don on solemn occasions only.

The shoemaker's little dwelling was filled with guests, consisting chiefly of German artisans with their wives and apprentices. Of the Russian officials there was present but one, Yurko the Finn, a constable, who, in spite of his humble calling, was the special object of the host's attention. Like Pogorelsky's postman,[1] for twenty-five years he had faithfully discharged his duties. The conflagration of 1812, which destroyed the ancient capital, destroyed also his little yellow booth. But immediately after the expulsion of the enemy, a new one appeared in its place, painted gray and with little white Doric columns, and Yurko again began to pace to and fro before it, *with his ax and armor of coarse cloth*. He was known to the greater part of the Germans who lived near the Nikitskaya Gate, and some of them had even spent Sunday night beneath his roof.

Adrian immediately made himself acquainted with him, as with a man whom, sooner or later, he might have need of, and when the guests took their places at the table, they sat down beside each other. Herr Schultz and his wife, and their daughter Lotchen, a young girl of seventeen, did the honors of the table and helped the cook to serve. The beer flowed in streams;

[1] A character in a story by Pogorelsky, a contemporary of Pushkin.
EDITOR'S NOTE

Yurko ate like four, and Adrian in no way yielded to him; his daughters, however, stood upon their dignity. The conversation, which was carried on in German, gradually grew more and more noisy. Suddenly the host requested a moment's attention, and uncorking a sealed bottle, he said loudly in Russian:

"To the health of my good Louise!"

The imitation champagne foamed. The host tenderly kissed the fresh face of his partner, and the guests drank noisily to the health of the good Louise.

"To the health of my amiable guests!" exclaimed the host, uncorking a second bottle; and the guests thanked him by draining their glasses once more.

Then followed a succession of toasts. The health of each individual guest was drunk; they drank to Moscow and to a round dozen of little German towns; they drank to the health of all guilds in general and of each in particular; they drank to the health of the masters and apprentices. Adrian drank with assiduity and became so jovial, that he proposed a facetious toast himself. Suddenly one of the guests, a fat baker, raised his glass and exclaimed:

"To the health of those for whom we work, our customers!"

This proposal like all the others, was joyously and unanimously received. The guests began to salute each other; the tailor bowed to the shoemaker, the shoemaker to the tailor, the baker to both, the whole company to the baker, and so on. In the midst of these mutual congratulations, Yurko exclaimed, turning to his neighbor:

"Come, little father! Drink to the health of your corpses!"

Everybody laughed, but the undertaker considered himself insulted, and frowned. Nobody noticed it, the guests continued to drink, and the bells had already rung for vespers when they rose from the table.

The guests dispersed at a late hour, the greater part of them in a very merry mood. The fat baker and the bookbinder, whose face seemed as if bound in red morocco, linked their arms in those of Yurko and conducted him back to his booth, thus observing the proverb: "One good turn deserves another."

The undertaker returned home drunk and angry.

"Why is it," he argued aloud, "why is it that my trade is not as honest as any other? Is an undertaker brother to the hangman? Why did those heathens laugh? Is an undertaker a buffoon? I wanted to invite them to my new house and give them a feast, but now I'll do nothing of the kind. Instead of inviting them, I will invite those for whom I work: the orthodox dead."

"What is the matter, master?" said the servant, who was engaged at that moment in taking off his boots: "why do you talk such nonsense? Make the sign of the cross! Invite the dead to your new house! What nonsense!"

"Yes, by God! I will invite them," continued Adrian, "and that, too, for tomorrow! . . . Do me the favor, my benefactors, to come and feast with me tomorrow evening; I will regale you with what God has sent me."

With these words the undertaker turned into bed and soon began to snore.

It was still dark when Adrian was roused out of his sleep. Trukhina, the merchant's wife, had died during the course of that very night, and a special messenger was sent off on horseback by her clerk to carry the news to Adrian. The undertaker gave him ten copecks to buy brandy with, dressed himself as hastily as possible, took a *droshky* and set out for Razgulyay. At the gate of the house in which the deceased lay, the police had already taken their stand, and the trades-people were busily moving back and forth, like ravens that smell a dead body. The deceased lay upon a table, yellow as wax, but not yet disfigured by decomposition. Around her stood her relatives, neighbors and domestic servants. All the windows were open; tapers were burning; and the priests were reading the prayers for the dead. Adrian went up to the nephew of Trukhina, a young shopman in a fashionable jacket, and informed him that the coffin, wax candles, pall, and the other funeral accessories would be immediately delivered in good order. The heir thanked him in an absent-minded manner, saying that he would not bargain about the price, but would rely upon his acting in everything according to his conscience. The undertaker, in accordance with his custom, swore that he would not charge him too much, exchanged significant glances with the clerk, and then departed to commence operations.

The whole day was spent in passing to and fro between Razgulyay and the Nikitskaya Gate. Toward evening everything was finished, and he returned home on foot, after having dismissed his driver. It was a moonlight night. The undertaker reached the Nikitskaya Gate in safety. Near the Church of the Ascension he was hailed by our acquaintance Yurko, who, recognizing the undertaker, wished him good night. It was late. The undertaker was just approaching his house, when suddenly he fancied he saw some one approach his gate, open the wicket, and disappear within.

"What does that mean?" thought Adrian. "Who can be wanting me again? Can it be a thief come to rob me? Or have my foolish girls got lovers coming after them? It means no good, I fear!"

And the undertaker thought of calling his friend Yurko to his assistance. But at that moment, another person approached the wicket and was about to enter, but seeing the master of the house hastening toward him, he stopped and took off his three-cornered hat. His face seemed familiar to Adrian, but in his hurry he was not able to examine it closely.

"You are favoring me with a visit," said Adrian, out of breath. "Walk in, I beg of you."

"Don't stand on ceremony, sir," replied the other, in a hollow voice; "you go first, and show your guests the way."

Adrian had no time to spend upon ceremony. The wicket was open; he ascended the steps followed by the other. Adrian thought he could hear people walking about in his rooms.

"What the devil does all this mean!" he thought to himself, and he hastened to enter. But the sight that met his eyes caused his legs to give way beneath him.

The room was full of corpses. The moon, shining through the windows, lit up their yellow and blue faces, sunken mouths, dim, half-closed eyes, and protruding noses. Adrian, with horror, recognized in them people that he himself had buried, and in the guest who had entered with him, the brigadier who had been buried during the pouring rain. They all, ladies and gentlemen, surrounded the undertaker, with bowings and salutations, except one poor man lately buried gratis, who, conscious and ashamed of his rags, did not venture to approach, but meekly kept to a corner. All the others were decently dressed: the female corpses in caps and ribbons, the officials in uniforms, but with their beards unshaven, the tradesmen in their holiday *caftans*.

"You see, Prokhorov," said the brigadier in the name of all the honorable company, "we have all risen in response to your invitation. Only those have stopped at home who were unable to come, who have crumbled to pieces and have nothing left but fleshless bones. But even of these there was one who hadn't the patience to remain behind—so much did he want to come and see you. . . ."

At this moment a little skeleton pushed his way through the crowd and approached Adrian. His skull smiled affably at the undertaker. Shreds of green and red cloth and rotten linen hung on him here and there as on a pole, and the bones of his feet rattled inside his big jackboots, like pestles in mortars.

"You do not recognize me, Prokhorov," said the skeleton. "Don't you remember the retired sergeant of the Guard, Pyotr Petrovich Kurilkin, the same to whom, in the year 1799, you sold your first coffin, and a deal one at that, instead of oak, as agreed?"

With these words the corpse stretched out his bony arms toward him; but Adrian, collecting all his strength, shrieked and pushed him away. Pyotr Petrovich staggered, fell and crumbled to pieces. Among the corpses arose a murmur of indignation; all stood up for the honor of their companion, and they overwhelmed Adrian with such threats and curses, that the poor host, deafened by their shrieks and almost crushed to death, lost his presence of mind, fell upon the bones of the retired sergeant of the Guard, and swooned away.

For some time the sun had been shining upon the bed on which the undertaker lay. At last he opened his eyes and saw before him the servant attending to the samovar. With horror, Adrian recalled all the incidents of the previous day. Trukhina, the brigadier, and the sergeant Kurilkin, rose vaguely before his imagination. He waited in silence for the servant to open the conversation and inform him of the events of the night.

"How you have slept, Adrian Prokhorovich!" said Aksinya, handing him his dressing-gown. "Your neighbor, the tailor, has been here, and the constable also called to inform you that today is his name-day; but you were so sound asleep, that we did not wish to wake you."

"Did anyone come for me from the late Trukhina?"

"The late? Is she dead, then?"

"What a fool you are! Didn't you yourself help me yesterday to prepare the things for her funeral?"

"Have you taken leave of your senses, master, or have you not yet recovered from the effects of yesterday's drinking-bout? What funeral was there yesterday? You spent the whole day feasting at the German's, and then came home drunk and threw yourself upon the bed, and have slept till this hour, when the bells have already rung for mass."

"Really!" said the undertaker, greatly relieved.

"Yes, indeed," replied the servant.

"Well, since that is the case, make tea as quickly as possible and call my daughters."

THE POSTMASTER

This tyrant, a collegiate recorder,
Still keeps the posting station in good order.

Prince Vyazemsky

W HO has not cursed postmasters, who has not quarreled with them? Who, in a moment of anger, has not demanded from them the fatal book in order to record in it unavailing complaints of their extortions, rudeness and carelessness? Who does not look upon them as monsters of the human race, equal to the attorneys of old, or, at least, the Murom highwaymen? Let us, however, be just; let us place ourselves in their position, and perhaps we shall begin to judge them with more indulgence. What is a postmaster? A veritable martyr of the fourteenth class,[1] protected by his rank from blows only, and that not always (I appeal to the conscience of my readers). What is the function of this tyrant, as Prince Vyazemsky jokingly calls him? Is he not an actual galley-slave? He has no rest either day or night. All the vexation accumulated during the course of a wearisome journey the traveler vents upon the postmaster. Should the weather prove intolerable, the road abominable, the driver obstinate, the horses stubborn—the postmaster is to blame. Entering into his poor abode, the traveler looks upon him as an enemy, and the postmaster is fortunate if he suc-

---

[1] The officials of Russia were divided into fourteen classes, the fourteenth being the lowest.   Translator's note

ceeds in soon getting rid of his unbidden guest; but if there should happen to be no horses! . . . Heavens! what volleys of abuse, what threats are showered upon his head! When it rains, when it is muddy, he is compelled to run about the village; during times of storm and bitter frost, he is glad to seek shelter in the entry, if only to enjoy a minute's repose from the shouting and jostling of incensed travelers.

A general arrives: the trembling postmaster gives him the two last *troikas*, including that intended for the courier. The general drives off without uttering a word of thanks. Five minutes afterwards—a bell! . . . and a courier throws down upon the table before him his order for fresh post-horses! . . . Let us bear all this well in mind, and, instead of anger, our hearts will be filled with sincere compassion. A few words more. During a period of twenty years I have traversed Russia in every direction; I know nearly all the post roads, and I am acquainted with several generations of drivers. There are very few postmasters that I do not know personally, and few with whom I have not had something to do. I hope shortly to publish the curious observations that I have noted down during my travels. For the present I will only say that the class of postmasters is presented to the public in a very false light. These much-calumniated officials are generally very peaceful persons, obliging by nature, disposed to be sociable, modest in their pretensions to honors and not too greedy. From their conversation (which traveling gentlemen very unreasonably scorn) much may be learnt that is both curious and instructive. For my own part, I confess that I prefer their talk to that of some official of the sixth class traveling on government business.

It may easily be supposed that I have friends among the honorable body of postmasters. Indeed, the memory of one of them is precious to me. Circumstances once brought us together, and it is of him that I now intend to tell my amiable readers.

In the month of May of the year 1816, I happened to be traveling through the X. Government, along a route that has since been abandoned. I then held an inferior rank, and I traveled by post stages, paying the fare for two horses. As a consequence, the postmasters treated me with very little ceremony, and I often had to take by force what, in my opinion, belonged to me by right. Being young and hot-tempered, I was indignant at the baseness and cowardice of the postmaster, when the latter harnessed to the coach of some gentleman of rank, the horses prepared for me. It was a long time, too, before I could get accustomed to being served out of my turn by a discriminating flunkey at the governor's dinner. Today the one and the other seem to me to be in the natural order of things. Indeed, what would become of us, if, instead of the generally observed rule: "Let rank honor rank," another were to be brought into use, as for example: "Let mind honor mind?" What disputes would arise! And whom would the butler serve first? But to return to my story.

The day was hot. About three versts from the N. station a drizzling rain came on, and in a few minutes it began to pour down in torrents and I was drenched to the skin. On arriving at the station, my first care was to change my clothes as quickly as possible, my second to ask for some tea.

"Hi! Dunya!"[1] cried the postmaster: "prepare the samovar and go and get some cream."

At these words, a young girl of about fourteen years of age appeared from behind the partition, and ran out into the entry. Her beauty struck me.

---

[1] Diminutive of Avdotya.   ·   Translator's note

"Is that your daughter?" I inquired of the post-master.

"That is my daughter," he replied, with a look of gratified pride; "and she is so sharp and sensible, just like her late mother."

Then he began to register my traveling passport, and I occupied myself with examining the pictures that adorned his humble but tidy abode. They illustrated the story of the Prodigal Son. In the first, a venerable old man, in a night-cap and dressing-gown, was taking leave of the restless lad, who was hastily accepting his blessing and a bag of money. In the next picture, the dissolute conduct of the young man was depicted in vivid colors: he was represented sitting at table surrounded by false friends and shameless women. Further on, the ruined youth, in rags and a three-cornered hat, was tending swine and sharing with them their food: his face expressed deep grief and repentance. The last picture represented his return to his father: the good old man, in the same night-cap and dressing-gown, runs forward to meet him; the prodigal son is on his knees; in the distance the cook is killing the fatted calf, and the elder brother is asking the servants the cause of all the rejoicing. Under each picture I read some suitable German verses. All this I have preserved in my memory to the present day, as well as the little pots of balsamine, the bed with gay curtains, and the other objects with which I was then surrounded. I can see, as though he were before me, the host himself, a man of about fifty years of age, healthy and vigorous, in his long green coat with three medals on faded ribbons.

I had scarcely settled my account with my old driver, when Dunya returned with the samovar. The little coquette saw at the second glance the impression she had produced upon me; she lowered her large blue eyes;

I began to talk to her; she answered me without the least timidity, like a girl who has seen the world. I offered her father a glass of punch, to Dunya herself I gave a cup of tea, and then the three of us began to converse together, as if we were old acquaintances.

The horses had long been ready, but I felt reluctant to take leave of the postmaster and his daughter. At last I bade them good-bye, the father wished me a pleasant journey, the daughter accompanied me to the coach. In the entry I stopped and asked her permission to kiss her; Dunya consented. . . . I can reckon up a great many kisses

Since first I chose this occupation,

but not one which has left behind such a long, such a pleasant recollection.

Several years passed, and circumstances led me to the same route, and to the same neighborhood.

"But," thought I, "perhaps the old postmaster has been changed, and Dunya may already be married."

The thought that one or the other of them might be dead also flashed through my mind, and I approached the N. station with a sad foreboding. The horses drew up before the little post-house. On entering the room, I immediately recognized the pictures illustrating the story of the Prodigal Son. The table and the bed stood in the same places as before, but the flowers were no longer on the window-sills, and everything around indicated decay and neglect.

The postmaster was asleep under his sheep-skin coat; my arrival awoke him, and he stood up. . . . It was certainly Samson Vyrin, but how aged! While he was preparing to register my traveling passport, I gazed at his gray hair, the deep wrinkles upon his face, that had not been shaved for a long time, his bent back, and I was astonished to see how three or four years had been able to transform a vigorous individual into a feeble old man.

"Do you recognize me?" I asked him: "we are old acquaintances."

"Maybe," replied he sullenly; "this is a high road, and many travelers have stopped here."

"Is your Dunya well?" I continued.

The old man frowned.

"God knows," he replied.

"Probably she is married?" said I.

The old man pretended not to have heard my question, and went on reading my passport in a low tone. I ceased questioning him and ordered some tea. Curiosity began to torment me, and I hoped that the punch would loosen the tongue of my old acquaintance.

I was not mistaken; the old man did not refuse the proffered glass. I observed that the rum dispelled his sullenness. At the second glass he began to talk; he remembered me, or appeared to do so, and I heard from him a story, which at the time, deeply interested and affected me.

"So you knew my Dunya?" he began. "But who did not know her? Ah, Dunya, Dunya! What a girl she was! Everybody who passed this way praised her; nobody had a word to say against her. The ladies used to give her presents—now a handkerchief, now a pair of earrings. The gentlemen used to stop on purpose, as if to dine or to take supper, but in reality only to take a longer look at her. However angry a gentleman might be, in her presence he grew calm and spoke graciously to me. Would you believe it, sir: couriers and government messengers used to talk to her for half an hour at a stretch. It was she held the home together; she put everything in order, got everything ready, and looked after everything. And I, like an old fool, could not look at her enough, could not idolize her enough. Did I not love my Dunya? Did I not indulge my child? Was not her life a happy one? But no, there is no escaping misfortune: there is no evading what has been decreed."

Then he began to tell me the story of his trouble in detail. Three years earlier, one winter evening, when the postmaster was ruling a new register, and his daughter behind the partition was sewing a dress, a *troika* drove up, and a traveler in a Circassian cap and military cloak, and enveloped in a shawl, entered the room and demanded horses. The horses were all out. On being told this, the traveler raised his voice and whip; but Dunya, accustomed to such scenes, ran out from behind the partition and graciously inquired of the traveler whether he would not like something to eat and drink.

The appearance of Dunya produced the usual effect. The traveler's anger subsided; he consented to wait for horses, and ordered supper. Having taken off his wet shaggy cap, and divested himself of his shawl and cloak, the traveler was seen to be a tall, young Hussar with a small black mustache. He settled down, and began to converse gaily with the postmaster and his daughter. Supper was served. Meanwhile the horses returned, and the postmaster ordered them, without being fed, to be harnessed immediately to the traveler's *kibitka*. But on returning to the room, he found the young man lying almost unconscious on the bench; he had been taken ill, his head ached, it was impossible for him to continue his journey. What was to be done? The postmaster gave up his own bed to him, and it was decided that if the sick man did not get better, they would send next day to S—— for the doctor.

The next day the Hussar was worse. His servant rode to town for a doctor. Dunya bound round his head a handkerchief soaked in vinegar, and sat with her needlework beside his bed. In the presence of the postmaster, the sick man groaned and scarcely uttered a word; but he drank two cups of coffee, and, groaning, ordered dinner. Dunya did not quit his side. He constantly asked for something to drink, and Dunya gave him a jug of lemonade prepared by herself. The sick man moistened his lips, and each time, on returning the jug, he feebly pressed Dunya's hand in token of gratitude.

About dinner time the doctor arrived. He felt the sick man's pulse, spoke to him in German, and declared in Russian that he only needed rest, and that in about a couple of days he would be able to set out on his journey. The Hussar gave him twenty-five rubles for his visit, and invited him to dinner; the doctor consented. They both ate with great appetite, drank a bottle of wine, and separated very well satisfied with each other.

Another day passed, and the Hussar felt quite himself again. He was extraordinarily gay, joked unceasingly, now with Dunya, now with the postmaster, whistled tunes, chatted with the travelers, copied their passports into the register, and the worthy postmaster took such a fancy to him that when the third day arrived, it was with regret that he parted with his amiable guest.

The day was Sunday; Dunya was preparing to go to mass. The Hussar's *kibitka* stood ready. He took leave of the postmaster, after having generously recompensed him for his board and lodging, bade farewell to Dunya, and offered to drive her as far as the church, which was situated at the edge of the village. Dunya hesitated.

"What are you afraid of?" asked her father. "His Excellency is not a wolf: he won't eat you. Drive with him as far as the church."

Dunya seated herself in the *kibitka* by the side of the Hussar, the servant sprang upon the box, the driver whistled, and the horses started off at a gallop.

The poor postmaster could not understand how he could have allowed his Dunya to drive off with the Hussar, how he could have been so blind, and what had become of his senses at that moment. A half-hour had not elapsed, before his heart began to ache, and uneasiness took possession of him to such a degree, that he could contain himself no longer, and started off for mass himself. On reaching the church, he saw that the people were already beginning to disperse, but Dunya was neither in the churchyard nor in the porch. He hastened into the church: the priest was leaving the chancel, the sexton was blowing out the candles, two old women were still praying in a corner, but Dunya was not in the church. The poor father was scarcely able to summon up sufficient resolution to ask the sexton if she had been to mass. The sexton replied that she had not. The postmaster returned home neither alive nor dead. One hope alone remained to him: Dunya, in the thoughtlessness of youth, might have taken it into her head to go on as far as the next station, where her godmother lived. In agonizing agitation he awaited the return of the *troika* in which he had let her set out. There was no sign of it. At last, in the evening, the driver arrived alone and intoxicated, with the terrible news: "Dunya went on with the Hussar from the next station."

The old man could not bear his misfortune: he immediately took to that very same bed where, the evening before, the young deceiver had lain. Taking all the circumstances into account, the postmaster now came to the conclusion that the illness had been a mere pretence. The poor man fell ill with a violent fever; he was removed to S——, and in his place another person was appointed for the time being. The same doctor, who had attended the Hussar, attended him also. He assured the postmaster that the young man had been perfectly well, and that at the time of his visit he had suspected him of some evil intention, but that he had kept silent through fear of his whip. Whether the German spoke the truth or only wished to boast of his perspicacity, his communication afforded no consolation to the poor invalid. Scarcely had the latter recovered from his illness, when he obtained from the postmaster of S—— two months' leave of absence, and without saying a word to anybody of his intention, he set out on foot in search of his daughter.

From the traveling passport he knew that Captain Minsky was journeying from Smolensk to St. Petersburg. The driver with whom he had gone off said that Dunya had wept the whole of the way, although she seemed to go of her own free will.

"Perhaps," thought the postmaster, "I shall bring my lost lamb home again."

With this thought he reached St. Petersburg, stopped in the neighborhood of the Izmailovsky barracks, at the house of a retired corporal, an old comrade of his, and began his search. He soon discovered that Captain Minsky was in St. Petersburg, and was living at Demoute's Inn. The postmaster resolved to call upon him.

Early in the morning he went to Minsky's antechamber, and requested that His Excellency might be informed that an old soldier wished to see him. The orderly, who was just then polishing a boot on a boot-tree, informed him that his master was still asleep, and that he never received anybody before eleven o'clock. The postmaster retired and returned at the appointed time. Minsky himself came out to him in his dressing-gown and red skull-cap.

"Well, brother, what do you want?" he asked

The old man's heart was wrung, tears started to his eyes, and he was only able to say in a trembling voice: "Your Excellency! . . . do me the great favor! . . ."

Minsky glanced quickly at him, flushed, took him by the hand, led him into his study and locked the door.

"Your Excellency!" continued the old man: "what has fallen from the load is lost; give me back at least my poor Dunya. You have had your pleasure with her; do not ruin her for nothing."

"What is done cannot be undone," said the young man, in the utmost confusion; "I am guilty before you, and am ready to ask your pardon, but do not think that I could forsake Dunya: she will be happy, I give you my word of honor. Why do you want her? She loves me; she has become unaccustomed to her former way of living. Neither you nor she will forget what has happened."

Then, pushing something into the old man's cuff, he opened the door, and the postmaster, without remembering how, found himself in the street again.

For a long time he stood motionless; at last he observed in the cuff of his sleeve a roll of papers; he drew them out and unrolled several fifty-ruble notes. Tears again filled his eyes, tears of indignation! He crushed the notes into a ball, flung them upon the ground, stamped upon them with the heel of his boot, and then walked away. . . . After having gone a few steps, he stopped, reflected, and returned . . . but the notes were no longer there. A well-dressed young man, noticing him, ran toward a *droshky*, jumped in hurriedly, and cried to the driver: "Go on!"

The postmaster did not pursue him. He resolved to return home to his station, but before doing so he wished to see his poor Dunya once more. For that purpose, he returned to Minsky's lodgings a couple of days later, but when he came the orderly told him roughly that his master received nobody, pushed him out of the ante-chamber and slammed the door in his face. The postmaster stood waiting for a long time, then he walked away.

That same day, in the evening, he was walking along Liteinaia Street, having been to a service at the Church of Our Lady of All the Sorrowing. Suddenly a smart *droshky* flew past him, and the postmaster recognized Minsky. The *droshky* stopped in front of a three-story house, close to the entrance, and the Hussar ran up the steps. A happy thought flashed through the mind of the postmaster. He returned, and, approaching the coachman:

"Whose horse is this, my friend?" asked he: "Doesn't it belong to Minsky?"

"Exactly so," replied the coachman: "what do you want?"

"Well, your master ordered me to carry a letter to his Dunya, and I have forgotten where his Dunya lives."

"She lives here, on the second floor. But you are late with your letter, my friend; he is with her himself just now."

"That doesn't matter," replied the postmaster, with an indescribable emotion. "Thanks for your information. I shall do as I was told." And with these words he ascended the staircase.

The door was locked; he rang. There was a painful delay of several seconds. The key rattled, and the door was opened.

"Does Avdotya Samsonovna live here?" he asked.

"Yes," replied a young maidservant: "what do you want with her?"

The postmaster, without replying, walked into the room.

"You mustn't go in, you mustn't go in!" the servant

cried out after him: "Avdotya Samsonovna has visitors."

But the postmaster, without heeding her, walked straight on. The first two rooms were dark; in the third there was a light. He approached the open door and paused. In the room, which was beautifully furnished, sat Minsky in deep thought. Dunya, attired in the most elegant fashion, was sitting upon the arm of his chair, like a lady rider upon her English saddle. She was gazing tenderly at Minsky, and winding his black curls round her dazzling fingers. Poor postmaster! Never had his daughter seemed to him so beautiful; he admired her against his will.

"Who is there?" she asked, without raising her head.

He remained silent. Receiving no reply, Dunya raised her head . . . and with a cry she fell upon the carpet. The alarmed Minsky hastened to pick her up, but suddenly catching sight of the old postmaster in the doorway, he left Dunya and approached him, trembling with rage.

"What do you want?" he said to him, clenching his teeth. "Why do you steal after me everywhere, like a thief? Or do you want to murder me? Be off!" and with a powerful hand he seized the old man by the collar and pushed him out onto the stairs.

The old man returned to his lodgings. His friend advised him to lodge a complaint, but the postmaster reflected, waved his hand, and resolved to abstain from taking any further steps in the matter. Two days afterward he left St. Petersburg and returned to his station to resume his duties.

"This is the third year," he concluded, "that I have been living without Dunya, and I have not heard a word about her. Whether she is alive or not—God only knows. So many things happen. She is not the first, nor yet the last, that a traveling scoundrel has seduced, kept for a little while, and then abandoned. There are many such young fools in St. Petersburg, today in satin and velvet, and tomorrow sweeping the streets along with the riff-raff of the dram-shops. Sometimes, when I think that Dunya also may come to such an end, then, in spite of myself, I sin and wish her in her grave. . . ."

Such was the story of my friend, the old postmaster, a story more than once interrupted by tears, which he picturesquely wiped away with the skirt of his coat, like the zealous Terentyich in Dmitriyev's beautiful ballad. These tears were partly induced by the punch, of which he had drunk five glasses during the course of his narrative, but for all that, they moved me deeply. After taking leave of him, it was a long time before I could forget the old postmaster, and for a long time I thought of poor Dunya. . . .

Passing through the little town of X. a short time ago, I remembered my friend. I heard that the station, over which he ruled, had been done away with. To my question: "Is the old postmaster still alive?" nobody could give me a satisfactory reply. I resolved to pay a visit to the familiar place, and having hired horses, I set out for the village of N——.

It was in the autumn. Gray clouds covered the sky; a cold wind blew across the reaped fields, carrying along with it the red and yellow leaves from the trees that it encountered. I arrived in the village at sunset, and stopped at the little post-house. In the entry (where Dunya had once kissed me) a stout woman came out to meet me, and in answer to my questions replied, that the old postmaster had been dead for about a year, that his house was occupied by a brewer, and that she was the brewer's wife. I began to regret my useless journey, and the seven rubles that I had spent in vain.

"Of what did he die?" I asked the brewer's wife.

"Of drink, sir," she replied.

"And where is he buried?"

"On the outskirts of the village, near his late wife."

"Could somebody take me to his grave?"

"To be sure! Hi, Vanka, you have played with that cat long enough. Take this gentleman to the cemetery, and show him the postmaster's grave."

At these words a ragged lad, with red hair, and blind in one eye, ran up to me and immediately began to lead the way toward the burial-ground.

"Did you know the dead man?" I asked him on the road.

"Yes, indeed! He taught me how to cut whistles. When he came out of the dram-shop (God rest his soul!) we used to run after him and call out: 'Grandfather! grandfather! some nuts!' and he used to throw nuts to us. He always used to play with us."

"And do the travelers remember him?"

"There are very few travelers now; the assessor passes this way sometimes, but he doesn't trouble himself about dead people. Last summer a lady passed through here, and she asked after the old postmaster, and went to his grave."

"What sort of a lady?" I asked with curiosity.

"A very beautiful lady," replied the lad. "She was in a carriage with six horses, and had along with her three little children, a nurse, and a little black lapdog; and when they told her that the old postmaster was dead, she began to cry, and said to the children: 'Sit still, I will go to the cemetery.' I offered to show her the way. But the lady said: 'I know the way.' And she gave me a five-copeck piece. . . . such a kind lady!"

We reached the cemetery, a bare place, with no fence around it, dotted with wooden crosses, which were not shaded by a single tree. Never in my life had I seen such a dismal cemetery.

"This is the old postmaster's grave," said the lad to me, leaping upon a heap of sand, in which was planted a black cross with a bronze ikon.

"And did the lady come here?" I asked.

"Yes," replied Vanka; "I watched her from a distance. She cast herself down here, and remained lying down for a long time. Then she went back to the village, sent for the priest, gave him some money and drove off, after giving me a five-copeck piece . . . such a kind lady!"

And I, too, gave the lad a five-copeck piece, and I no longer regretted the journey nor the seven rubles that I had spent on it.

MISTRESS INTO MAID

You're pretty, Dushenka, no matter what you wear.
Bogdanovich

IN one of our remote provinces was situated the estate
of Ivan Petrovich Berestov. In his youth he had
served in the Guards, but having quitted the service
at the beginning of the year 1797, he repaired to his
village, and since that time he had not stirred from it.
He had been married to a penniless gentlewoman, who
had died in child-bed at a time when he was absent
from home on a visit to one of the outlying fields of
his estate. He soon found consolation in attending to
his affairs. He built a house on a plan of his own,
established a textile mill, tripled his revenues, and began to consider himself the most intelligent man in the
whole country roundabout, and in this he was not
contradicted by his neighbors, who came to visit him
with their families and their dogs. On week-days he
wore a velveteen jacket, but on Sundays and holidays
he appeared in a surtout of cloth that had been manufactured on his own premises. He himself kept an account of all his expenses, and he never read anything
except the "Senate Bulletins."

In general he was liked, although he was considered
proud. There was only one person who was not on
good terms with him, and that was Grigory Ivanovich Muromsky, his nearest neighbor. This latter was a

genuine Russian gentleman. After having squandered the greater part of his fortune in Moscow, and having become a widower about the same time, he retired to his last remaining estate, where he continued to indulge in habits of extravagance, but of a new kind. He laid out an English garden, on which he expended nearly the whole of his remaining revenue. His grooms were dressed like English jockeys, his daughter had an English governess, and his fields were cultivated after the English method.

But Russian corn fares ill when foreign ways are followed,

and in spite of a considerable reduction in his expenses, the revenues of Grigory Ivanovich did not increase. He found means, even in the country, of contracting new debts. Nevertheless he was not considered a fool, for he was the first landowner in his province who conceived the idea of mortgaging his estate in the Tutorial Council—a proceeding which at that time was considered exceedingly complicated and venturesome. Of all those who censured him, Berestov showed himself the most severe. Hatred of all innovation was a distinguishing trait in his character. He could not bring himself to speak calmly of his neighbor's Anglomania, and he constantly found occasion to criticise him. If he showed his possessions to a guest, in reply to the praises bestowed upon him for his economical arrangements, he would say with a sly smile:

"Yes, sir, it is not the same with me as with my neighbor Grigory Ivanovich. What need have we to ruin ourselves in the English style, when we have enough to do to keep the wolf from the door in the Russian style?"

These, and similar sarcastic remarks, thanks to the zeal of obliging neighbors, did not fail to reach the ears of Grigory Ivanovich greatly embellished. The

Anglomaniac bore criticism as impatiently as our journalists. He became furious, and called his traducer a
boor and a country bumpkin.

Such were the relations between the two proprietors,
when Berestov's son came home. He had been educated
at the University of——, and intended to enter the military service, but to this his father would not give his
consent. For the civil service the young man had not
the slightest inclination, and as neither felt inclined to
yield to the other, the young Alexey lived in the meantime like a gentleman, and at any rate allowed his
mustache to grow.[1]

Alexey was indeed a fine young fellow, and it would
really have been a pity were his slender frame never
to be set off to advantage by a military uniform, and
were he to be compelled to spend his youth in bending
over the papers of the chancery office, instead of cutting
a figure on horseback. The neighbors, observing how
at the hunt he always dashed ahead across the fields,
agreed that he would never make a proper clerk. The
young ladies cast glances at him, and sometimes could
not leave off looking at him, but Alexey troubled himself very little about them, and they attributed this insensibility to some secret love affair. Indeed, there
passed from hand to hand a copy of the address on one
of his letters: "To Akulina Petrovna Kurochkina in
Moscow, opposite the Alexeyevsky Monastery, in the
house of the coppersmith Savelyev, with the request
that she hand this letter to A. N. R."

Those of my readers who have never lived in the
country, cannot imagine how charming these provincial young ladies are! Brought up in the pure air, under the shadow of their own apple trees, they derive
their knowledge of the world and of life from books.

[1] It was formerly the custom in Russia for military men only to
wear the mustache.   TRANSLATOR'S NOTE

Solitude, freedom, and reading develop very early
within them sentiments and passions unknown to our
town-bred beauties. For the young ladies of the country the sound of harness-bells is an event; a journey
to the nearest town marks an epoch in their lives, and
the visit of a guest leaves behind a long, and sometimes
an everlasting memory. Of course everybody is at liberty to laugh at some of their peculiarities, but the
jokes of a superficial observer cannot nullify their essential merits, the chief of which is that quality of
character, that *individualité,* without which, in Jean
Paul's opinion, there can be no human greatness. In
the capitals, women receive perhaps a better education,
but intercourse with the world soon smooths down the
character and makes their souls as uniform as their
head-dresses. This is said neither by way of judgment
nor of censure, but *"nota nostra manet,"* as one of the
old commentators writes.

It can easily be imagined what impression Alexey
produced in the circle of our young ladies. He was the
first who appeared before them gloomy and disen-
chanted, the first who spoke to them of lost happiness
and of his blighted youth; in addition to which he
wore a black ring engraved with a death's head. All
this was something quite new in that province. The
young ladies went mad over him.

But not one of them felt so much interest in him as
the daughter of our Anglomaniac, Liza, or Betsy, as
Grigory Ivanovich usually called her. As their parents
did not visit each other, she had not yet seen Alexey,
even when he had become the sole topic of conversation among all the young ladies of the neighborhood.
She was seventeen years old. Dark eyes illuminated her
swarthy and exceedingly pleasant countenance. She
was an only and consequently a spoiled child. Her
liveliness and continual pranks delighted her father

and filled with despair the heart of Miss Jackson, her governess, an affected old maid of forty, who powdered her face and darkened her eyebrows, read through *Pamela* twice a year, for which she received two thousand rubles, and was dying of boredom in this barbarous Russia.

Liza was waited upon by Nastya, who, although somewhat older, was quite as giddy as her mistress. Liza was very fond of her, confided to her all her secrets, and planned pranks together with her; in a word, Nastya was a far more important person in the village of Priluchino, than the trusted confidante in a French tragedy.

"Will you allow me to go out to-day on a visit?" said Nastya one morning, as she was dressing her mistress.

"Certainly; but where are you going to?"

"To Tugilovo, to the Berestovs'. The wife of their cook is going to celebrate her name-day to-day, and she came over yesterday to invite us to dinner."

"Well!" said Liza: "the masters are at odds with each other, but the servants entertain each other."

"What have the masters to do with us?" replied Nastya. "Besides, I belong to you, and not to your papa. You have not had any quarrel with young Berestov; let the old ones quarrel and fight, if it gives them any pleasure."

"Try and see Alexey Berestov, Nastya, and then tell me what he looks like and what sort of a person he is."

Nastya promised to do so, and all day long Liza waited with impatience for her return. In the evening Nastya made her appearance.

"Well, Lizaveta Grigoryevna," said she, on entering the room, "I have seen young Berestov, and I had ample opportunity for taking a good look at him, for we have been together all day."

"How did that happen? Tell me about it, tell me everything just as it happened."

"Very well. We set out, I, Anisya Yegorovna, Nenila, Dunka. . . ."

"Yes, yes, I know. And then?"

"With your leave, I will tell you everything in detail. We arrived just in time for dinner. The room was full of people. The folk from Kolbino were there, from Zakharyevo, the bailiff's wife and her daughters, the people from Khlupino. . . ."

"Well, and Berestov?"

"Wait a moment. We sat down to table; the bailiff's wife had the place of honor. I sat next to her . . . the daughters sulked, but I didn't care about them. . . ."

"Good heavens, Nastya, how tiresome you are with your never-ending details!"

"How impatient you are! Well, we rose from the table . . . we had been sitting down for three hours, and the dinner was excellent: pastry, blanc-mange, blue, red and striped. . . . Well, we left the table and went into the garden to have a game of tag, and it was then that the young master made his appearance."

"Well, and is it true that he is so very handsome?"

"Exceedingly handsome: tall, well-built, and with red cheeks. . . ."

"Really? And I was under the impression that he was pale. Well, and how did he seem to you? Sad, thoughtful?"

"Nothing of the kind! I have never in my life seen such a madcap. He joined in our game."

"Joined in your game of tag? Impossible!"

"Not at all impossible. And what else do you think he did? He'd catch you and kiss you!"

"With your permission, Nastya, you are fibbing."

"With your permission, I am not fibbing. I had the

greatest trouble in the world to get away from him. He spent the whole day with us."

"But they say that he is in love, and hasn't eyes for anybody."

"I don't know anything about that, but I know that he looked at me a good deal, and so he did at Tanya, the bailiff's daughter, and at Pasha from Kolbino, too. But it cannot be said that he misbehaved—the scamp!"

"That is extraordinary! And what do they say about him in the house?"

"They say that he is an excellent master—so kind, so cheerful. They have only one fault to find with him: he is too fond of running after the girls. But for my part, I don't think that is a very great fault: he will settle down with age."

"How I should like to see him!" said Liza, with a sigh.

"What is so difficult about it? Tugilovo is not far from us—only about three versts. Go and take a walk in that direction, or a ride on horseback, and you will assuredly meet him. He goes out early every morning with his gun."

"No, no, that would not do. He might think that I was running after him. Besides, our fathers are not on good terms, so that I cannot make his acquaintance. . . . Ah! Nastya, do you know what I'll do? I will dress myself up as a peasant girl!"

"Exactly! Put on a coarse blouse and a *sarafan*, and then go boldly to Tugilovo; I will answer for it that Berestov will not pass you by."

"And I know how to speak like the peasants about here. Ah, Nastya! my dear Nastya! what an excellent idea!"

And Liza went to bed, firmly resolved on putting her plan into execution.

The next morning she began to prepare to carry out

her plan. She sent to the market and bought some coarse linen, some blue nankeen and some copper buttons, and with the help of Nastya she cut out for herself a blouse and *sarafan*. She then set all the female servants to work to do the necessary sewing, so that by evening everything was ready. Liza tried on the new costume, and as she stood before the mirror, she confessed to herself that she had never looked so charming. Then she rehearsed her part. As she walked she made a low bow, and then nodded her head several times, after the manner of a clay cat, spoke in the peasants' dialect, smiled behind her sleeve, and earned Nastya's complete approval. One thing only proved irksome to her: she tried to walk barefooted across the courtyard, but the turf pricked her tender feet, and she found the sand and gravel unbearable. Nastya immediately came to her assistance. She took the measurement of Liza's foot, ran to the fields to find Trofim the shepherd, and ordered him to make a pair of bast shoes to fit.

The next morning, at crack o' dawn, Liza was already awake. Everybody in the house was still asleep. Nastya, at the gate was waiting for the shepherd. The sound of a horn was heard, and the village flock defiled past the manor-house. Trofim, as he passed Nastya, gave her a small pair of colored bast shoes, and received from her a half-ruble in exchange. Liza quietly dressed herself in the peasant's costume, whispered her instructions to Nastya with reference to Miss Jackson, descended the back staircase and made her way through the kitchen garden into the field beyond.

The eastern sky was all aglow, and the golden rows of clouds seemed to be awaiting the sun, as courtiers await their monarch. The clear sky, the freshness of the morning, the dew, the light breeze. and the singing of the birds filled the heart of Liza with childish

joy. The fear of meeting some acquaintance seemed
to give her wings, for she flew rather than walked. But
as she approached the grove which formed the boundary of her father's estate, she slackened her pace. Here
she resolved to wait for Alexey. Her heart beat violently, she knew not why; but is not the fear which accompanies our youthful escapades their greatest charm?
Liza advanced into the depth of the grove. The muffled, undulating murmur of the branches welcomed
the young girl. Her gaiety vanished. Little by little she
abandoned herself to sweet reveries. She thought—but
who can say exactly what a young lady of seventeen
thinks of, alone in a grove, at six o'clock of a spring
morning? And so she walked musingly along the path-
way, which was shaded on both sides by tall trees,
when suddenly a magnificent hunting dog barked at
her. Liza became frightened and cried out. But at the
same moment a voice called out: "*Tout beau, Sbogar,
ici!*" . . . and a young hunter emerged from behind
a clump of bushes.

"Don't be afraid, my dear," said he to Liza: "my
dog does not bite."

Liza had already recovered from her fright, and she
immediately took advantage of her opportunity.

"But, sir," said she, assuming a half-frightened, half-
bashful expression, "I am so afraid; he looks so fierce
—he might fly at me again."

Alexey—for the reader has already recognized him
—gazed fixedly at the young peasant-girl.

"I will accompany you if you are afraid," he said to
her: "will you allow me to walk along with you?"

"Who is to hinder you?" replied Liza. "A free man
may do as he likes, and the road is everybody's."

"Where do you come from?"

"From Priluchino; I am the daughter of Vassily the
blacksmith, and I am going to gather mushrooms."

(Liza carried a basket on her arm.) "And you, sir? From Tugilovo, I have no doubt."

"Exactly so," replied Alexey: "I am the young master's valet."

Alexey wanted to put himself on an equal footing with her, but Liza looked at him and laughed.

"That is a fib," said she: "I am not such a fool as you may think. I see very well that you are the young master himself."

"Why do you think so?"

"I think so for a great many reasons."

"But——"

"As if it were not possible to tell the master from the servant! You are not dressed like a servant, you do not speak like one, and you do not call your dog the way we do."

Alexey liked Liza more and more. As he was not accustomed to standing upon ceremony with pretty peasant girls, he wanted to embrace her; but Liza drew back from him, and suddenly assumed such a cold and severe look, that Alexey, although much amused, did not venture to renew the attempt.

"If you wish that we should remain good friends," said she with dignity, "be good enough not to forget yourself."

"Who taught you to be so clever?" asked Alexey, bursting into a laugh. "Can it be my friend Nastenka, the maid of your young mistress? See how enlightenment becomes diffused!"

Liza felt that she had stepped out of her rôle, and she immediately recovered herself.

"Do you think," said she, "that I have never been to the manor-house? Don't alarm yourself; I have seen and heard a great many things. . . . But," continued she, "if I talk to you, I shall not gather my mushrooms. Go your way, sir, and I will go mine. Pray excuse me."

And she was about to move off, but Alexey seized hold of her hand.

"What is your name, my dear?"

"Akulina," replied Liza, endeavoring to disengage her fingers from his grasp: "but let me go, sir; it is time for me to return home."

"Well, my friend Akulina, I will certainly pay a visit to your father, Vassily the blacksmith."

"What do you say?" exclaimed Liza quickly: "for Heaven's sake, don't think of doing such a thing! If it were known at home that I had been talking to a gentleman alone in the grove, I should fare very badly —my father, Vassily the blacksmith, would beat me to death."

"But I really must see you again."

"Well, then, I will come here again some time to gather mushrooms."

"When?"

"Well, tomorrow, if you wish it."

"My dear Akulina, I would kiss you, but I dare not. . . . Tomorrow, then, at the same time, isn't that so?"

"Yes, yes!"

"And you will not deceive me?"

"I will not deceive you."

"Swear it."

"Well, then, I swear by Holy Friday that I will come."

The young people separated. Liza emerged from the wood, crossed the field, stole into the garden and hastened to the place where Nastya awaited her. There she changed her costume, replying absently to the questions of her impatient confidante, and then she repaired to the parlor. The cloth was laid, the breakfast was ready, and Miss Jackson, already powdered and laced up, so that she looked like a wine-glass, was cutting thin slices of bread and butter.

Her father praised her for her early walk.

"There is nothing so healthy," said he, "as getting up at daybreak."

Then he cited several instances of human longevity, which he had taken from the English journals, and observed that all persons who had lived to be upwards of a hundred, abstained from brandy and rose at daybreak, winter and summer.

Liza did not listen to him. In her thoughts she was going over all the circumstances of the morning's meeting, Akulina's whole conversation with the young hunter, and her conscience began to torment her. In vain did she try to persuade herself that their talk had not gone beyond the bounds of propriety, and that the prank would be followed by no serious consequences— her conscience spoke louder than her reason. The promise given for the following day troubled her more than anything else, and she almost felt resolved not to keep her solemn oath. But then, might not Alexey, after waiting for her in vain, make his way to the village and search out the daughter of Vassily the blacksmith, the veritable Akulina—a fat, pock-marked peasant girl—and so discover the prank she had played upon him? This thought horrified Liza, and she resolved to repair to the little wood the next morning again as Akulina.

For his part, Alexey was in an ecstasy of delight. All day long he thought of his new acquaintance; and in his dreams at night the form of the dark-skinned beauty appeared before him. The morning had scarcely begun to dawn, when he was already dressed. Without giving himself time to load his gun, he set out for the fields with his faithful Sbogar, and hastened to the place of the promised rendezvous. A half-hour of intolerable waiting passed by; at last he caught a glimpse of a blue *sarafan* between the bushes, and he rushed

forward to meet his charming Akulina. She smiled at
his ecstasy of gratitude, but Alexey immediately observed upon her face traces of sadness and uneasiness.
He wished to know the cause. Liza confessed to him
that her act seemed to her very frivolous, that she repented of it, that this time she did not wish to break
her promised word, but that this meeting would be the
last, and she therefore entreated him to break off an
acquaintanceship which could not lead to any good.

All this, of course, was expressed in the language of
a peasant; but such thoughts and sentiments, so unusual in a simple girl of the lower class, struck Alexey
with astonishment. He employed all his eloquence to
divert Akulina from her purpose; he assured her that
his intentions were honorable, promised her that he
would never give her cause to repent, that he would
obey her in everything, and earnestly entreated her not
to deprive him of the joy of seeing her alone, if only
once a day, or even only twice a week. He spoke the
language of true passion, and at that moment he was
really in love. Liza listened to him in silence.

"Give me your word," said she at last, "that you will
never come to the village in search of me, and that you
will never seek a meeting with me except those that I
shall appoint myself."

Alexey swore by Holy Friday, but she stopped him
with a smile.

"I do not want you to swear," said she; "your mere
word is sufficient."

After that they began to converse together in a
friendly manner, strolling about the wood, until Liza
said to him:

"Time is up."

They separated, and when Alexey was left alone, he
could not understand how, in two meetings, a simple
peasant-girl had succeeded in acquiring such real

power over him. His relations with Akulina had for him all the charm of novelty, and although the injunctions of the strange peasant-girl appeared to him to be very severe, the thought of breaking his word never once entered his mind. The fact was that Alexey, in spite of his fateful ring, his mysterious correspondence and his gloomy disenchantment, was a good and impulsive young fellow, with a pure heart capable of innocent pleasure.

Were I to listen to my own wishes only, I would here enter into a minute description of the interviews of the young people, of their growing inclination toward each other, their confidences, occupations and conversations; but I know that the greater part of my readers would not share my interest. Such details are usually considered tedious and uninteresting, and therefore I will omit them, merely observing, that before two months had elapsed, Alexey was already hopelessly in love, and Liza equally so, though less demonstrative in revealing the fact. Both were happy in the present and troubled themselves little about the future.

The thought of indissoluble ties frequently passed through their minds, but never had they spoken to each other about the matter. The reason was plain: Alexey, however much attached he might be to his lovely Akulina, could not forget the distance that separated him from the poor peasant girl; while Liza, knowing the hatred that existed between their parents, did not dare to hope for a mutual reconciliation. Moreover, her *amour propre* was stimulated in secret by the obscure and romantic hope of seeing at last the proprietor of Tugilovo at the feet of the daughter of the Priluchino blacksmith. All at once an important event occurred which threatened to alter their mutual relations.

One bright cold morning—such a morning as is very

common during our Russian autumn—Ivan Petrovich Berestov went out for a ride on horseback, taking with him three pairs of hunting dogs, a groom and several peasant boys with clappers. At the same time, Grigory Ivanovich Muromsky, tempted by the beautiful weather, ordered his bob-tailed mare to be saddled, and started out to visit his Anglicized domains. On approaching the wood, he perceived his neighbor, sitting proudly on his horse, in his cloak lined with fox-skin, waiting for a hare which the boys, with loud cries and the rattling of their clappers, had started out of a thicket. If Grigory Ivanovich had foreseen this meeting, he would certainly have proceeded in another direction, but he came upon Berestov so unexpectedly, that he suddenly found himself no farther than the distance of a pistol-shot away from him. There was no help for it: Muromsky, like a civilized European, rode forward toward his adversary and politely saluted him. Berestov returned the salute with the zeal characteristic of a chained bear, who salutes the public in obedience to the order of his master.

At that moment the hare darted out of the wood and started off across the field. Berestov and the groom raised a loud shout, let the dogs loose, and then galloped off in pursuit. Muromsky's horse, not being accustomed to hunting, took fright and bolted. Muromsky, who prided himself on being a good horseman, gave it full rein, and inwardly rejoiced at the incident which delivered him from a disagreeable companion. But the horse, reaching a ravine which it had not previously noticed, suddenly sprang to one side, and Muromsky was thrown from the saddle. Striking the frozen ground with considerable force, he lay there cursing his bob-tailed mare, which, as if recovering itself, had suddenly come to a standstill as soon as it felt that it was without a rider.

Ivan Petrovich hastened toward him and inquired if he had injured himself. In the meantime the groom had secured the guilty horse, which he now led forward by the bridle. He helped Muromsky into the saddle, and Berestov invited him to his house. Muromsky could not refuse the invitation, for he felt indebted to him; and so Berestov returned home, covered with glory for having hunted down a hare and for bringing with him his adversary wounded and almost a prisoner of war.

The two neighbors took breakfast together and conversed with each other in a very friendly manner. Muromsky requested Berestov to lend him a *droshky*, for he was obliged to confess that, owing to his bruises, he was not in a condition to return home on horseback. Berestov conducted him to the steps, and Muromsky did not take leave of him until he had obtained a promise from him that he would come the next day in company with Alexey Ivanovich, and dine in a friendly way at Priluchino. In this way was a deeply rooted enmity of long standing apparently brought to an end by the skittishness of a bob-tailed mare.

Liza ran forward to meet Grigory Ivanovich.

"What does this mean, papa?" said she with astonishment. "Why are you limping? Where is your horse? Whose *droshky* is this?"

"You will never guess, my dear," replied Grigory Ivanovich; and then he related to her everything that had happened.

Liza could not believe her ears. Without giving her time to collect herself, Grigory Ivanovich then went on to inform her that the two Berestovs—father and son —would dine with them on the following day.

"What do you say?" she exclaimed, turning pale. "The Berestovs, father and son, will dine with us to-morrow! No, papa, you can do as you please, but I shall not show myself."

"What! Have you taken leave of your senses?" replied her father. "Since when have you been so bashful? Or do you cherish an hereditary hatred toward him like a heroine of romance? Enough, do not be a fool."

"No, papa, not for anything in the world, not for any treasure would I appear before the Berestovs."

Grigory Ivanovich shrugged his shoulders, and did not dispute with her any further, for he knew that by contradiction he would obtain nothing from her, and went to rest after his eventful ride.

Lizaveta Grigoryevna repaired to her room and summoned Nastya. They both conversed together for a long time about the impending visit. What would Alexey think if, in the well-bred young lady, he recognized his Akulina? What opinion would he have of her conduct, of her manners, of her good sense? On the other hand, Liza wished very much to see what impression would be produced upon him by a meeting so unexpected. . . . Suddenly an idea flashed through her mind. She communicated it to Nastya; both felt delighted with it, and they resolved to carry it into effect.

The next day at breakfast, Grigory Ivanovich asked his daughter if she still intended to hide from the Berestovs.

"Papa," replied Liza, "I will receive them if you wish it, but on one condition, and that is, that however I may appear before them, or whatever I may do, you will not be angry with me, or show the least sign of astonishment or displeasure."

"Some new prank!" said Grigory Ivanovich, laughing. "Very well, very well, I agree; do what you like, my dark-eyed romp."

With these words he kissed her on the forehead, and Liza ran off to put her plan into execution.

At two o'clock precisely, a carriage of domestic make, drawn by six horses, entered the courtyard and rounded the lawn. The elder Berestov mounted the steps with the assistance of two lackeys in the Muromsky livery. His son came after him on horseback, and together they entered the dining-room, where the table was already laid. Muromsky received his neighbors in the most gracious manner, proposed that they inspect his garden and menagerie before dinner, and conducted them along paths carefully kept and graveled. The elder Berestov inwardly deplored the time and labor wasted in such useless fancies, but he held his tongue out of politeness. His son shared neither the disapprobation of the economical landowner, nor the enthusiasm of the vain-glorious Anglomaniac, but waited with impatience for the appearance of his host's daughter, of whom he had heard a great deal; and although his heart, as we know, was already engaged, youthful beauty always had a claim upon his imagination.

Returning to the parlor, they all three sat down; and while the old men recalled their young days, and related anecdotes of their respective careers in the service, Alexey reflected as to what rôle he should play in the presence of Liza. He decided that an air of cold indifference would be the most becoming under the circumstances, and he prepared to act accordingly. The door opened; he turned his head with such indifference, with such haughty carelessness, that the heart of the most inveterate coquette would inevitably have quaked. Unfortunately, instead of Liza, it was old Miss Jackson, who, painted and tightly laced, entered the room with downcast eyes and with a curtsey, so that Alexey's remarkable military move was wasted. He had not succeeded in recovering from his confusion, when the door opened again, and this time it was Liza herself who entered.

All rose; her father was just beginning to introduce his guests, when suddenly he stopped short and bit his lips. . . . Liza, his dark-complexioned Liza, was painted white up to the ears, and was more heavily made up than even Miss Jackson herself; false curls, much lighter than her own hair, covered her head like the peruke of Louis the Fourteenth; her sleeves *à l'imbécile* stood out like the hooped skirts of Madame de Pompadour; her figure was pinched in like the letter X, and all her mother's jewels, which had not yet found their way to the pawnbroker's, shone upon her fingers, her neck and in her ears.

Alexey could not possibly recognize his Akulina in the grotesque and dazzling young lady. His father kissed her hand, and he followed his example, though much against his will; when he touched her little white fingers, it seemed to him that they trembled. In the meantime he succeeded in catching a glimpse of her little foot, intentionally advanced and set off to advantage by the most coquettish shoe imaginable. This reconciled him somewhat to the rest of her toilette. As for the paint and powder, it must be confessed that, in the simplicity of his heart, he had not noticed them at the first glance, and afterwards had no suspicion of them. Grigory Ivanovich remembered his promise, and endeavored not to show any astonishment; but his daughter's prank seemed to him so amusing, that he could scarcely contain himself. But the person who felt no inclination to laugh was the prim English governess. She had a shrewd suspicion that the paint and powder had been extracted from her chest of drawers, and a deep flush of anger was distinctly visible beneath the artificial whiteness of her face. She darted angry glances at the young madcap, who, reserving her explanations for another time, pretended that she did not notice them.

They sat down to table. Alexey continued to play his rôle of assumed indifference and absent-mindedness. Liza put on an air of affectation, spoke in a sing-song through her teeth, and only in French. Her father kept constantly looking at her, not understanding her object, but finding it all exceedingly amusing. The English governess fumed with rage and said not a word. Ivan Petrovich alone seemed at home: he ate like two, drank heavily, laughed at his own jokes, and grew more talkative and hilarious every moment.

At last they all rose from the table; the guests took their departure, and Grigory Ivanovich gave free vent to his laughter and to his questions.

"What put the idea into your head of fooling them like that?" he said to Liza. "But do you know what? The paint suits you admirably. I do not wish to fathom the mysteries of a lady's toilette, but if I were in your place, I would very soon begin to paint; not too much, of course, but just a little."

Liza was enchanted with the success of her stratagem. She embraced her father, promised him that she would consider his advice, and then hastened to conciliate the indignant Miss Jackson, who with great reluctance consented to open the door and listen to her explanations. Liza was ashamed to appear before strangers with her dark complexion; she had not dared to ask . . . she felt sure that dear, good Miss Jackson would pardon her, etc., etc. Miss Jackson, feeling convinced that Liza had not wished to make her a laughing-stock by imitating her, calmed down, kissed her, and as a token of reconciliation, made her a present of a small pot of English ceruse, which Liza accepted with every appearance of sincere gratitude.

The reader will readily imagine that Liza lost no

time in repairing to the rendezvous in the little wood the next morning.

"You were at our master's yesterday," she said at once to Alexey: "what do you think of our young mistress?"

Alexey replied that he had not noticed her.

"That's a pity!" replied Liza.

"Why so?" asked Alexey.

"Because I wanted to ask you if it is true what they say—"

"What do they say?"

"Is it true, as they say, that I am very much like her?"

"What nonsense! She is a perfect freak compared with you."

"Oh, sir, it is very wrong of you to speak like that. Our young mistress is so fair and so stylish! How could I be compared with her!"

Alexey vowed to her that she was more beautiful than all the fair young ladies in creation, and in order to pacify her completely, he began to describe her mistress in such comical terms, that Liza laughed heartily.

"But," said she with a sigh, "even though our young mistress may be ridiculous, I am but a poor ignorant thing in comparison with her."

"Oh!" said Alexey; "is that anything to break your heart about? If you wish it, I will soon teach you to read and write."

"Yes, indeed," said Liza, "why shouldn't I try?"

"Very well, my dear; we will commence at once."

They sat down. Alexey drew from his pocket a pencil and note-book, and Akulina learnt the alphabet with astonishing rapidity. Alexey could not sufficiently admire her intelligence. The following morning she wished to try to write. At first the pencil refused to

obey her, but after a few minutes she was able to trace
the letters with tolerable accuracy.

"It is really wonderful!" said Alexey. "Our method
certainly produces quicker results than the Lancaster
system."

And indeed, at the third lesson Akulina began to
spell through *Natalya the Boyar's Daughter,* interrupting her reading by observations which really filled
Alexey with astonishment, and she filled a whole sheet
of paper with aphorisms drawn from the same story.

A week went by, and a correspondence was established between them. Their letter-box was the hollow
of an old oak-tree, and Nastya acted as their messenger.
Thither Alexey carried his letters written in a bold
round hand, and there he found on plain blue paper
the scrawls of his beloved. Akulina perceptibly began
to acquire an elegant style of expression, and her mind
developed noticeably.

Meanwhile, the recently formed acquaintance between Ivan Petrovich Berestov and Grigory Ivanovich
Muromsky soon became transformed into a sincere
friendship, under the following circumstances. Muromsky frequently reflected that, on the death of Ivan
Petrovich, all his possessions would pass into the hands
of Alexey Ivanovich, in which case the latter would be
one of the wealthiest landed proprietors in the province, and there would be nothing to hinder him from
marrying Liza. The elder Berestov, on his side, although
recognizing in his neighbor a certain extravagance (or,
as he termed it, English folly), was perfectly ready to
admit that he possessed many excellent qualities, as
for example, his rare resourcefulness. Grigory Ivanovich was closely related to Count Pronsky, a man of
distinction and of great influence. The Count could be
of great service to Alexey, and Muromsky (so thought
Ivan Petrovich) would doubtless rejoice to see his

daughter marry so advantageously. By dint of constantly dwelling upon this idea, the two old men came at last
to communicate their thoughts to one another. They
embraced each other, both promised to do their best to
arrange the matter, and they immediately set to work,
each on his own side. Muromsky foresaw that he
would have some difficulty in persuading his Betsy to
become more intimately acquainted with Alexey,
whom she had not seen since the memorable dinner. It
seemed to him that they had not liked each other
much; at least Alexey had not paid any further visits
to Priluchino, and Liza had retired to her room every
time that Ivan Petrovich had honored them with a
visit.

"But," thought Grigory Ivanovich, "if Alexey came
to see us every day, Betsy could not help falling in love
with him. That is in the nature of things. Time will
settle everything."

Ivan Petrovich was less uneasy about the success of
his designs. That same evening he summoned his son
to his study, lit his pipe, and, after a short pause, said:

"Well, Alyosha, you have not said anything for a
long time about military service. Or has the Hussar
uniform lost its charm for you?"

"No, father," replied Alexey respectfully; "but I see
that you do not like the idea of my entering the Hussars, and it is my duty to obey you."

"Good," replied Ivan Petrovich; "I see that you are
an obedient son; that is a consolation to me. . . . On
my side, I do not wish to compel you; I do not want to
force you to enter . . . the civil service . . . at once,
but, in the meanwhile, I intend you to get married."

"To whom, father?" asked Alexey in astonishment.

"To Lizaveta Grigoryevna Muromsky," replied Ivan
Petrovich. "She is a fine bride, is she not?"

"Father, I have not thought of marriage yet."

"You have not thought of it, and therefore I have thought of it for you."

"As you please, but I do not care for Liza Muromsky in the least."

"You will get to like her afterwards. Love comes with time."

"I do not feel capable of making her happy."

"Do not fret about making her happy. What? Is this how you respect your father's wish? Very well!"

"As you choose. I do not wish to marry, and I will not marry."

"You will marry, or I will curse you; and as for my estate, as true as there is a God in heaven, I will sell it and squander the money, and not leave you a farthing. I will give you three days to think about the matter; and in the meantime, keep out of my sight."

Alexey knew that when his father once took an idea into his head, even a nail would not drive it out, as Taras Skotinin [1] says in the comedy. But Alexey took after his father, and was just as head-strong as he was. He went to his room and began to reflect upon the limits of paternal authority. Then his thoughts reverted to Lizaveta Grigoryevna, to his father's solemn vow to make him a beggar, and last of all to Akulina. For the first time he saw clearly that he was passionately in love with her; the romantic idea of marrying a peasant girl and of living by the labor of his hands came into his head, and the more he thought of such a decisive step, the more reasonable did it seem to him. For some time the interviews in the wood had ceased on account of the rainy weather. He wrote Akulina a letter in the neatest handwriting, and in the wildest style, informing her of the misfortune that threatened them, and offering her his hand. He took the letter at once to the

---

[1] A character in *The Minor*, a comedy by Denis Fonvizin.
TRANSLATOR'S NOTE

post-office in the wood, and then went to bed, well satisfied with himself.

The next day Alexey, still firm in his resolution, rode over early in the morning to visit Muromsky, in order to explain matters frankly to him. He hoped to excite his generosity and win him over to his side.

"Is Grigory Ivanovich at home?" he asked, stopping his horse in front of the steps of the Priluchino mansion.

"No, sir," replied the servant; "Grigory Ivanovich rode out early this morning, and has not yet returned."

"How annoying!" thought Alexey. . . . "Is Lizaveta Grigoryevna at home, then?" he asked.

"Yes, sir."

Alexey sprang from his horse, gave the reins to the lackey, and entered without being announced.

"Everything is going to be decided now," thought he, directing his steps toward the parlor: "I will explain everything to Lizaveta herself."

He entered . . . and then stood still as if petrified! Liza . . . no . . . Akulina, dear, dark-skinned Akulina, no longer in a *sarafan,* but in a white morning dress, was sitting in front of the window, reading his letter; she was so preoccupied that she had not heard him enter.

Alexey could not restrain an exclamation of joy. Liza started, raised her head, uttered a cry, and wished to fly from the room. But he held her back.

"Akulina! Akulina!"

Liza endeavored to free herself from his grasp.

"Mais laissez-moi donc, Monsieur! . . . Mais êtes-vous fou?" she repeated, turning away.

"Akulina! my dear Akulina!" he repeated, kissing her hands.

Miss Jackson, a witness of this scene, knew not what

to think of it. At that moment the door opened, and Grigory Ivanovich entered the room.

"Aha!" said Muromsky; "it seems that you have already arranged matters between you."

The reader will spare me the unnecessary obligation of describing the dénouement.

The End of the Tales of I. P. Belkin

[1830]

THE QUEEN OF SPADES

The Queen of Spades signifies secret ill-will.
New Fortune-Teller

I

When bleak was the weather,
The friends came together
To play.
The stakes, they were doubled;
The sly ones, untroubled,
Were gay.
They all had their innings,
And chalked up their winnings,
And so
They kept busy together
Throughout the bleak weather,
Oho!

THERE was a card party at the rooms of Narumov of the Horse Guards. The long winter night passed away imperceptibly, and it was five o'clock in the morning before the company sat down to supper. Those who had won, ate with a good appetite; the others sat staring absently at their empty plates. When the champagne appeared, however, the conversation became more animated, and all took a part in it.

"And how did you fare, Surin?" asked the host.

"Oh, I lost, as usual. I must confess that I am un-lucky: I never raise the original stakes, I always keep cool, I never allow anything to put me out, and yet I always lose!"

"And you have never been tempted? You have never staked on several cards in succession? . . . Your firm-ness astonishes me."

"But what do you think of Hermann?" said one of the guests, pointing to a young engineer: "he has never had a card in his hand in his life, he has never in his life doubled the stake, and yet he sits here till five o'clock in the morning watching our play."

"Play interests me very much," said Hermann: "but I am not in the position to sacrifice the necessary in the hope of winning the superfluous."

"Hermann is a German: he is prudent—that is all!" observed Tomsky. "But if there is one person that I cannot understand, it is my grandmother, the Countess Anna Fedotovna."

"How? What?" cried the guests.

"I cannot understand," continued Tomsky, "how it is that my grandmother does not punt."

"What is there remarkable about an old lady of eighty not gambling?" said Narumov.

"Then you know nothing about her?"

"No, really; haven't the faintest idea."

"Oh! then listen. You must know that, about sixty years ago, my grandmother went to Paris, where she created quite a sensation. People used to run after her to catch a glimpse of 'la Vénus moscovite.' Riche-lieu courted her, and my grandmother maintains that he almost blew out his brains in consequence of her cruelty. At that time ladies used to play faro. On one occasion at the Court, she lost a very considerable sum to the Duke of Orleans. On returning home, my grandmother removed the patches from her face, took off her hoops, informed my grandfather of her loss at the gaming-table, and ordered him to pay the money. My deceased grandfather, as far as I remember, was a sort of butler to my grandmother. He dreaded her like fire; but, on hearing of such a heavy loss, he almost went out of his mind; he calculated the various sums she had lost, and pointed out to her that in six months she had spent half a million, that neither their Moscow nor Saratov estates were near Paris, and finally refused point blank to pay the debt. My grandmother slapped his face and slept by herself as a sign of her displeasure. The next day she sent for her husband, hoping that this domestic punishment had produced an effect upon him, but she found him inflexible. For the first time in her life, she condescended to offer reasons and explanations. She thought she could convince him by pointing out to him that there are debts and debts, and that there is a great difference between a Prince and a coachmaker. But it was all in vain, grandfather was in revolt. He said 'no,' and that was all. My grandmother did not know what to do. She was on friendly terms with a very remarkable man. You have heard of Count St. Germain, about whom so many marvelous stories are told. You know that he represented himself as the Wandering Jew, as the discoverer of the elixir of life, of the philosopher's stone, and so forth. Some laughed at him as a charlatan; but Casanova, in his memoirs, says that he was a spy. But be that as it may, St. Germain, in spite of the mystery surrounding him, was a man of decent appearance and had an amiable manner in company. Even to this day my grandmother is in love with him, and becomes quite angry if anyone speaks disrespectfully of him. My grandmother knew that St. Germain had large sums of money at his disposal. She resolved to have recourse to him, and she wrote a letter to him asking him to come to her with-

out delay. The queer old man immediately waited upon her and found her overwhelmed with grief. She
described to him in the blackest colors the barbarity of
her husband, and ended by declaring that she placed
all her hopes in his friendship and graciousness.

"St. Germain reflected.

" 'I could advance you the sum you want,' said he;
'but I know that you would not rest easy until you had
paid me back, and I should not like to bring fresh
troubles upon you. But there is another way of getting
out of your difficulty: you can win back your money.'

" 'But, my dear Count,' replied my grandmother, 'I
tell you that we haven't any money left.'

" 'Money is not necessary,' replied St. Germain: 'be
pleased to listen to me.'

"Then he revealed to her a secret, for which each of
us would give a good deal . . ."

The young gamblers listened with increased attention. Tomsky lit his pipe, pulled at it, and continued:

"That same evening my grandmother went to Versailles *au jeu de la Reine*. The Duke of Orleans kept
the bank; my grandmother excused herself in an off-
handed manner for not having yet paid her debt, by
inventing some little story, and then began to play
against him. She chose three cards and played them
one after the other: all three won at the start and my
grandmother recovered all that she had lost."

"Mere chance!" said one of the guests.

"A fairy tale!" observed Hermann.

"Perhaps they were marked cards!" said a third.

"I do not think so," replied Tomsky gravely.

"What!" said Narumov, "you have a grandmother
who knows how to hit upon three lucky cards in succession, and you have never yet succeeded in getting
the secret of it out of her?"

"That's the deuce of it!" replied Tomsky: "she had

four sons, one of whom was my father; all four are desperate gamblers, and yet not to one of them did she ever reveal her secret, although it would not have been a bad thing either for them or for me. But this is what I heard from my uncle, Count Ivan Ilyich, and he assured me, on his honor, that it was true. The late Chaplitzky—the same who died in poverty after having squandered millions—once lost, in his youth, about three hundred thousand rubles—to Zorich, if I remember rightly. He was in despair. My grandmother, who was always very hard on extravagant young men, took pity, however, upon Chaplitzky. She mentioned to him three cards, telling him to play them one after the other, at the same time exacting from him a solemn promise that he would never play cards again as long as he lived. Chaplitzky then went to his victorious opponent, and they began a fresh game. On the first card he staked fifty thousand rubles and won at once; he doubled the stake and won again, doubled it again, and won, not only all he had lost, but something over and above that . . .

"But it is time to go to bed: it is a quarter to six already."

And indeed it was already beginning to dawn: the young men emptied their glasses and then took leave of one another.

II

—Il paraît que monsieur est
décidément pour les suivantes.
—Que voulez-vous, madame? Elles
sont plus fraîches.

Society Talk

THE OLD Countess X. was seated in her dressing-room in front of her looking-glass. Three maids stood around her. One held a small pot of rouge, another a box of hair-pins, and the third a tall cap with bright red ribbons. The Countess had no longer the slightest pretensions to beauty—hers had faded long ago—but she still preserved all the habits of her youth, dressed in strict accordance with the fashion of the 'seventies, and made as long and as careful a toilette as she would have done sixty years previously. Near the window, at an embroidery frame, sat a young lady, her ward.

"Good morning, *grand'maman,*" said a young officer, entering the room. "*Bonjour, Mademoiselle Lise. Grand'maman,* I have a favor to ask of you."

"What is it, Paul?"

"I want you to let me introduce one of my friends to you, and to allow me to bring him to the ball on Friday."

"Bring him direct to the ball and introduce him to me there. Were you at N.'s yesterday?"

"Yes; everything went off very pleasantly, and dancing kept up until five o'clock. How beautiful Mme Yeletzkaya was!"

"But, my dear, what is there beautiful about her? You should have seen her grandmother, Princess Darya Petrovna! By the way, she must have aged very much, Princess Darya Petrovna."

"How do you mean, aged?" cried Tomsky thoughtlessly; "she died seven years ago."

The young lady raised her head and made a sign to the young man. He then remembered that the old Countess was never to be informed of the death of any of her contemporaries, and he bit his lip. But the Countess heard the news with the greatest indifference.

"Died!" said she; "and I did not know it. We were appointed maids of honor at the same time, and when we were being presented, the Empress. . . ."

And the Countess for the hundredth time related the anecdote to her grandson.

"Come Paul," said she, when she had finished her story, "help me to get up. Lizanka, where is my snuff-box?"

And the Countess with her three maids went behind a screen to finish her toilette. Tomsky was left alone with the young lady.

"Who is the gentleman you wish to introduce to the Countess?" asked Lizaveta Ivanovna in a whisper.

"Narumov. Do you know him?"

"No. Is he in the army or is he a civilian?"

"In the army."

"Is he in the Engineers?"

"No, in the Cavalry. What made you think that he was in the Engineers?"

The young lady smiled, but made no reply.

"Paul," cried the Countess from behind the screen, "send me some new novel, only pray not the kind they write nowadays."

"What do you mean, *grand'maman?*"

"That is, a novel, in which the hero strangles neither his father nor his mother, and in which there are no drowned bodies. I have a great horror of them."

"There are no such novels nowadays. Would you like a Russian one?"

"Are there any Russian novels? Send me one, my dear, please send me one!"

"Good-bye, *grand'maman:* I am in a hurry. . . . Good-bye, Lizaveta Ivanovna. What, then, made you think that Narumov was in the Engineers?"

And Tomsky withdrew from the dressing-room.

Lizaveta Ivanovna was left alone: she laid aside her work and began to look out of the window. A few moments afterwards, from behind a corner house on the other side of the street, a young officer appeared. A deep blush covered her cheeks; she took up her work again and bent her head over the frame. At the same moment the Countess returned completely dressed.

"Order the carriage, Lizaveta," said she; "we will go out for a drive."

Lizaveta arose from the frame and began to put away her work.

"What is the matter with you, my dear, are you deaf?" cried the Countess. "Order the carriage to be got ready at once."

"I will do so this moment," replied the young lady, and ran into the ante-room.

A servant entered and gave the Countess some books from Prince Pavel Alexandrovich.

"Tell him that I am much obliged to him," said the Countess. "Lizaveta! Lizaveta! where are you running to?"

"I am going to dress."

"There is plenty of time, my dear. Sit down here Open the first volume and read aloud to me."

Her companion took the book and read a few lines.

"Louder," said the Countess. "What is the matter with you, my dear? Have you lost your voice? Wait— give me that footstool—a little nearer—that will do!"

Lizaveta read two more pages. The Countess yawned.

"Put the book down," said she: "what a lot of nonsense! Send it back to Prince Pavel with my thanks . . . But where is the carriage?"

"The carriage is ready," said Lizaveta, looking out into the street.

"How is it that you are not dressed?" said the Countess: "I must always wait for you. It is intolerable, my dear!"

Liza hastened to her room. She had not been there two minutes, before the Countess began to ring with all her might. The three maids came running in at one door and the valet at another.

"How is it that you don't come when I ring for you?" said the Countess. "Tell Lizaveta Ivanovna that I am waiting for her."

Lizaveta returned with her hat and cloak on.

"At last you are here!" said the Countess. "But why such an elaborate toilette? Whom do you intend to captivate? What sort of weather is it? It seems rather windy."

"No, Your Ladyship, it is very calm," replied the valet.

"You always speak thoughtlessly. Open the window. So it is: windy and bitterly cold. Unharness the horses. Lizaveta, we won't go out—there was no need for you to deck yourself out like that."

"And that's my life!" thought Lizaveta Ivanovna.

And, in truth, Lizaveta Ivanovna was a very unfortunate creature. "It is bitter to eat the bread of another," says Dante, "and hard to climb his stair." But who can know what the bitterness of dependence is so well as the poor companion of an old lady of quality? The Countess X. had by no means a bad heart, but she was capricious, like a woman who had been spoilt by the world, as well as avaricious and sunk in cold egoism, like all old people who are no longer capable of affection, and whose thoughts are with the past and not the present. She participated in all the vanities of the great world, went to balls, where she sat in a corner, painted and dressed in old-fashioned style, like an ugly but indispensable ornament of the ballroom; the guests on entering approached her and bowed profoundly, as if in accordance with a set ceremony, but after that nobody took any further notice of her. She received the whole town at her house, and observed the strictest etiquette, although she could no longer recognize people. Her numerous domestics, growing fat and old in her ante-chamber and servants' hall, did just as they liked, and vied with each other in robbing the moribund old woman. Lizaveta Ivanovna was the martyr of the household. She poured tea, and was reprimanded for using too much sugar; she read novels aloud to the Countess, and the faults of the author were visited upon her head; she accompanied the Countess in her walks, and was held answerable for the weather or the state of the pavement. A salary was attached to the post, but she very rarely received it, although she was expected to dress like everybody else, that is to say, like very few indeed. In society she played the most pitiable rôle. Everybody knew her, and nobody paid her any attention. At balls she danced only when a partner was wanted, and ladies would only take hold of her arm when it was necessary to lead her out of the room to attend to their dresses. She had a great deal of *amour propre,* and felt her position keenly, and she looked about her with impatience for a deliverer to come to her rescue; but the young men calculating in their giddiness, did not condescend to pay her any attention, although Lizaveta Ivanovna was a hundred times prettier than the bare-faced and cold-hearted marriageable girls around whom they hovered. Many a time did she quietly slink away from the dull and elegant drawing-room, to go and cry in her own poor little room, in which stood a screen, a chest of drawers, a looking-glass and a painted bedstead, and where a tallow candle burnt feebly in a copper candlestick.

One morning—this was about two days after the card party described at the beginning of this story, and a week previous to the scene at which we have just assisted—Lizaveta Ivanovna was seated near the window at her embroidery frame, when, happening to look out into the street, she caught sight of a young officer of the Engineers, standing motionless with his eyes fixed upon her window. She lowered her head and went on again with her work. About five minutes afterward she looked out again—the young officer was still standing in the same place. Not being in the habit of coquetting with passing officers, she did not continue to gaze out into the street, but went on sewing for a couple of hours, without raising her head. Dinner was announced. She rose up and began to put her embroidery away, but glancing casually out of the window, she perceived the officer again. This seemed to her very strange. After dinner she went to the window with a certain feeling of uneasiness, but the officer was no longer there—and she thought no more about him.

A couple of days afterwards, just as she was stepping into the carriage with the Countess, she saw him again. He was standing close to the entrance, with his face half-concealed by his beaver collar, his black eyes flashing beneath his hat. Lizaveta felt alarmed, though she knew not why, and she trembled as she seated herself in the carriage.

On returning home, she hastened to the window—the officer was standing in his accustomed place, with his eyes fixed upon her. She drew back, a prey to curiosity and agitated by a feeling which was quite new to her.

From that time on not a day passed without the young officer making his appearance under the window at the customary hour. A spontaneous relationship was established between them. Sitting in her place at work, she would feel his approach; and raising her head, she would look at him longer and longer each day. The young man seemed to be very grateful to her for it: she saw with the sharp eye of youth, how a sudden flush covered his pale cheeks each time that their

glances met. By the end of the week she smiled at
him. . . .

When Tomsky asked permission of his grandmother
the Countess to present one of his friends to her, the
young girl's heart beat violently. But hearing that Narumov was not an engineer, but in the Horse Guards,
she regretted that by her indiscreet question, she had
betrayed her secret to the volatile Tomsky.

Hermann was the son of a Russified German, from
whom he had inherited a small fortune. Being firmly
convinced of the necessity of ensuring his independence, Hermann did not touch even the interest on his
capital, but lived on his pay, without allowing himself
the slightest luxury. Moreover, he was reserved and
ambitious, and his companions rarely had an opportunity of making merry at the expense of his excessive
parsimony. He had strong passions and an ardent imagination, but his firmness of disposition preserved him
from the ordinary errors of youth. Thus, though a
gambler at heart, he never touched a card, for he considered his position did not allow him—as he said—
"to risk the necessary in the hope of winning the superfluous," yet he would sit for nights together at the
card table and follow with feverish excitement the
various turns of the game.

The story of the three cards had produced a powerful impression upon his imagination, and all night
long he could think of nothing else. "If only," he
thought to himself the following evening, as he wandered through St. Petersburg, "if only the old Countess
would reveal her secret to me! if she would only tell
me the names of the three winning cards! Why should
I not try my fortune? I must get introduced to her and
win her favor—perhaps become her lover. . . . But all
that will take time, and she is eighty-seven years old:
she might be dead in a week, in a couple of days even!

. . . And the story itself: is it credible? . . . No! Prudence, moderation and work: those are my three winning cards; that is what will increase my capital threefold, sevenfold, and procure for me ease and independence."

Musing in this manner, he walked on until he found himself in one of the principal streets of St. Petersburg, in front of a house of old-fashioned architecture. The street was blocked with carriages; one after the other they rolled up in front of the illuminated entrance. Every minute there emerged from the coaches the shapely foot of a young beauty, a spurred boot, a striped stocking above a diplomatic shoe. Fur coats and cloaks whisked past the majestic porter.

Hermann stopped. "Whose house is this?" he asked the watchman at the corner.

"The Countess X.'s," replied the watchman.

Hermann trembled. The strange story of the three cards again presented itself to his imagination. He began walking up and down before the house, thinking of its owner and her marvelous gift. Returning late to his modest lodging, he could not go to sleep for a long time, and when at last he did doze off, he could dream of nothing but cards, green tables, piles of banknotes and heaps of gold coins. He played card after card, firmly turning down the corners, and won uninterruptedly, raking in the gold and filling his pockets with the notes. Waking up late the next morning, he sighed over the loss of his imaginary wealth, then went out again to wander about the streets, and found himself once more in front of the Countess's house. Some unknown power seemed to draw him thither. He stopped and began to stare at the windows. In one of these he saw the head of a black-haired woman, which was bent probably over some book or handwork. The head was raised. Hermann saw a fresh-cheeked face and a pair of black eyes. That moment decided his fate.

III

Vous m'écrivez, mon ange, des lettres de quatre pages plus vite que je ne puis les lire.

A correspondence

LIZAVETA IVANOVNA had scarcely taken off her hat and cloak, when the Countess sent for her and again ordered the carriage. The vehicle drew up before the door, and they prepared to take their seats. Just at the moment when two footmen were assisting the old lady into the carriage, Lizaveta saw her engineer close beside the wheel; he grasped her hand; alarm caused her to lose her presence of mind, and the young man disappeared—but not before leaving a letter in her hand. She concealed it in her glove, and during the whole of the drive she neither saw nor heard anything. It was the custom of the Countess, when out for an airing in her carriage to be constantly asking such questions as: "Who was that person that met us just now? What is the name of this bridge? What is written on that signboard?" On this occasion, however, Lizaveta returned such vague and absurd answers, that the Countess became angry with her.

"What is the matter with you, my dear?" she exclaimed. "Have you taken leave of your senses, or what is it? Do you not hear me or understand what I say? . . . Heaven be thanked, I am still in my right mind and speak plainly enough!"

Lizaveta Ivanovna did not hear her. On returning home she ran to her room, and drew the letter out of her glove: it was not sealed. Lizaveta read it. The letter contained a declaration of love; it was tender, respectful, and copied word for word from a German novel. But Lizaveta did not know anything of the German language, and she was quite delighted with the letter.

For all that, it troubled her exceedingly. For the first time in her life she was entering into secret and intimate relations with a young man. His boldness horrified her. She reproached herself for her imprudent behavior, and knew not what to do. Should she cease to sit at the window and, by assuming an appearance of indifference toward him, put a check upon the young officer's desire to pursue her further? Should she send his letter back to him, or should she answer him in a cold and resolute manner? There was nobody to whom she could turn in her perplexity, for she had neither female friend nor adviser. . . . At length she resolved to reply to him.

She sat down at her little writing-table, took pen and paper, and began to think. Several times she began her letter, and then tore it up: the way she had expressed herself seemed to her either too indulgent or too severe. At last she succeeded in writing a few lines with which she felt satisfied.

"I am convinced," she wrote, "that your intentions are honorable, and that you do not wish to offend me by any imprudent action, but our acquaintance should not have begun in such a manner. I return you your letter, and I hope that I shall never have any cause to complain of undeserved disrespect."

The next day, as soon as Hermann made his appearance, Lizaveta rose from her embroidery, went into the drawing-room, opened the wicket and threw the letter into the street, trusting to the young officer's alertness.

Hermann hastened forward, picked it up and then repaired to a confectioner's shop. Breaking the seal of

the envelope, he found inside it his own letter and
Lizaveta's reply. He had expected this, and he returned
home, very much taken up with his intrigue.

Three days afterward, a bright-eyed young girl from
a milliner's establishment brought Lizaveta a letter.
Lizaveta opened it with great uneasiness, fearing that
it was a demand for money, when suddenly she recognized Hermann's handwriting.

"You have made a mistake, my dear," said she: "this
letter is not for me."

"Oh, yes, it is for you," replied the pert girl, without concealing a sly smile. "Have the goodness to
read it."

Lizaveta glanced at the letter. Hermann requested
an interview.

"It cannot be," said Lizaveta Ivanovna, alarmed both
at the haste with which he had made his request, and
the manner in which it had been transmitted. "This
letter is certainly not for me."

And she tore it into fragments.

"If the letter was not for you, why have you torn it
up?" said the girl. "I should have given it back to the
person who sent it."

"Be good enough, my dear," said Lizaveta, disconcerted by this remark, "not to bring me any more letters in future, and tell the person who sent you that
he ought to be ashamed. . . ."

But Hermann was not the man to be thus put off.
Every day Lizaveta received from him a letter, sent
now in this way, now in that. They were no longer
translated from the German. Hermann wrote them under the inspiration of passion, and spoke in his own
language, and they bore full testimony to the inflexi-
bility of his desire and the disordered condition of
his uncontrollable imagination. Lizaveta no longer
thought of sending them back to him: she became in-

toxicated with them and began to reply to them, and little by little her answers became longer and more affectionate. At last she threw out of the window to him the following letter:

"This evening there is going to be a ball at the X. Embassy. The Countess will be there. We shall remain until two o'clock. This is your opportunity of seeing me alone. As soon as the Countess is gone, the servants will very probably go out, and there will be nobody left but the porter, but he, too, usually retires to his lodge. Come at half-past eleven. Walk straight upstairs. If you meet anybody in the ante-room, ask if the Countess is at home. If you are told she is not, there will be nothing left for you to do but to go away and return another time. But it is most probable that you will meet nobody. The maidservants all sit together in one room. On leaving the ante-room, turn to the left, and walk straight on until you reach the Countess's bedroom. In the bedroom, behind a screen, you will find two small doors: the one on the right leads to a study, which the Countess never enters; the one on the left leads to a corridor, at the end of which is a narrow winding staircase; this leads to my room."

Hermann quivered like a tiger, as he waited for the appointed time. At ten o'clock in the evening he was already in front of the Countess's house. The weather was terrible; the wind was howling; the sleety snow fell in large flakes; the lamps emitted a feeble light, the streets were deserted; from time to time a sledge, drawn by a sorry-looking hack, passed by, the driver on the look-out for a belated fare. Hermann stood there wearing nothing but his jacket, yet he felt neither the wind nor the snow.

At last the Countess's carriage drew up. Hermann saw two footmen carry out in their arms the bent form of the old lady, wrapped in sables, and immediately behind her, clad in a light mantle, and with a wreath of fresh flowers on her head, followed Lizaveta. The door was closed. The carriage rolled away heavily through the yielding snow. The porter shut the street-door; the windows became dark.

Hermann began walking up and down near the deserted house; at length he stopped under a lamp, and glanced at his watch: it was twenty minutes past eleven. He remained standing under the lamp, his eyes fixed upon the watch, impatiently waiting for the remaining minutes to pass. At half-past eleven precisely, Hermann ascended the steps of the house, and made his way into the brightly-illuminated vestibule. The porter was not there. Hermann ran up the stairs, opened the door of the ante-room and saw a footman sitting asleep in an antique soiled armchair, under a lamp. With a light firm step Hermann walked past him. The reception-room and the drawing-room were in semi-darkness. They were lit feebly by a lamp in the ante-room.

Hermann entered the bedroom. Before an ikon-case, filled with ancient ikons, a golden sanctuary-lamp was burning. Armchairs upholstered in faded brocade, and sofas, the gilding of which was worn off and which were piled with down cushions stood in melancholy symmetry around the room, the walls of which were hung with China silk. On the wall hung two portraits painted in Paris by Madame Lebrun. One of them represented a plump, pink-cheeked man of about forty in a light-green uniform and with a star on his breast; the other—a beautiful young woman, with an aquiline nose, curls at her temples, and a rose in her powdered hair. In all the corners stood porcelain shepherds and shepherdesses, clocks from the workshop of the celebrated Leroy, boxes, roulettes, fans and the various gewgaws for ladies that were invented at the end of the last century, together with Montgolfier's balloon and Mesmer's magnetism. Hermann stepped behind the screen. Behind it stood a little iron bed; on the right was the door which led to the study; on the left— the other which led to the corridor. He opened the latter, and saw the little winding staircase which led to the room of the poor ward. . . . But he retraced his steps and entered the dark study.

The time passed slowly. All was still. The clock in the drawing-room struck twelve; in all the rooms, one clock after another marked the hour, and everything was quiet again. Hermann stood leaning against the cold stove. He was calm; his heart beat regularly, like that of a man resolved upon a dangerous but inevitable undertaking. The clock struck one, then two; and he heard the distant rumbling of carriage-wheels. In spite of himself, excitement seized him. The carriage drew near and stopped. He heard the sound of the carriage-step being let down. All was bustle within the house. The servants were running hither and thither, voices were heard, and the house was lit up. Three antiquated chamber-maids entered the bedroom, and they were shortly afterwards followed by the Countess who, more dead than alive, sank into an armchair. Hermann peeped through a chink. Lizaveta Ivanovna passed close by him, and he heard her hurried steps as she hastened up her staircase. For a moment his heart was assailed by something like remorse, but the emotion was only transitory. He stood petrified.

The Countess began to undress before her looking-glass. Her cap, decorated with roses, was unpinned, and then her powdered wig was removed from off her white and closely-cropped head. Hairpins fell in showers around her. Her yellow satin dress, embroidered with silver, fell down at her swollen feet.

Hermann witnessed the repulsive mysteries of her toilette; at last the Countess was in her night-cap and night-gown, and in this costume, more suitable to her age, she appeared less hideous and terrifying.

Like all old people in general, the Countess suffered from sleeplessness. Having undressed, she seated herself at the window in an armchair and dismissed her maids. The candles were taken away, and once more the room was lit only by the sanctuary-lamp. The Countess sat there looking quite yellow, moving her flaccid lips and swaying from side to side. Her dull eyes expressed complete vacancy of mind, and, looking at her, one would have thought that the rocking of her body was not voluntary, but was produced by the action of some concealed galvanic mechanism.

Suddenly the death-like face changed incredibly. The lips ceased to move, the eyes became animated: before the Countess stood a stranger.

"Do not be alarmed, for Heaven's sake, do not be alarmed!" said he in a low but distinct voice. "I have no intention of doing you any harm, I have only come to ask a favor of you."

The old woman looked at him in silence, as if she had not heard what he had said. Hermann thought that she was deaf, and, bending down toward her ear, he repeated what he had said. The old woman remained silent as before.

"You can insure the happiness of my life," continued Hermann, "and it will cost you nothing. I know that you can name three cards in succession——"

Hermann stopped. The Countess appeared now to understand what was asked of her; she seemed to be seeking words with which to reply.

"It was a joke," she replied at last: "I swear it was only a joke."

"This is no joking matter," replied Hermann

angrily. "Remember Chaplitzky, whom you helped to win back what he had lost."

The Countess became visibly uneasy. Her features expressed strong emotion, but she soon lapsed into her former insensibility.

"Can you not name me these three winning cards?" continued Hermann.

The Countess remained silent; Hermann continued:

"For whom are you preserving your secret? For your grandsons? They are rich enough without it; they do not know the worth of money. Your cards would be of no use to a spendthrift. He who cannot preserve his paternal inheritance, will die in want, even though he had a demon at his service. I am not a man of that sort; I know the value of money. Your three cards will not be wasted on me. Come!" . . .

He paused and tremblingly awaited her reply. The Countess remained silent; Hermann fell upon his knees.

"If your heart has ever known the feeling of love," said he, "if you remember its rapture, if you have ever smiled at the cry of your new-born child, if your breast has ever throbbed with any human feeling, I entreat you by the feelings of a wife, a lover, a mother, by all that is most sacred in life, not to reject my plea. Reveal to me your secret. Of what use is it to you? . . . Maybe it is connected with some terrible sin, the loss of eternal bliss, some bargain with the devil. . . . Consider—you are old; you have not long to live—I am ready to take your sins upon my soul. Only reveal to me your secret. Remember that the happiness of a man is in your hands, that not only I, but my children, grandchildren, and great-grandchildren, will bless your memory and reverence it as something sacred. . . ."

The old woman answered not a word.

Hermann rose to his feet.

"You old witch!" he exclaimed, clenching his teeth, "then I will make you answer!"

With these words he drew a pistol from his pocket.

At the sight of the pistol, the Countess for the second time exhibited strong emotion. She shook her head and raised her hands as if to protect herself from the shot . . . then she fell backward and remained motionless.

"Come, an end to this childish nonsense!" said Hermann, taking hold of her hand. "I ask you for the last time: will you tell me the names of your three cards, or will you not?"

The Countess made no reply. Hermann perceived that she was dead!

IV

7 mai, 18— —
Homme sans moeurs et sans religion!
A correspondence

LIZAVETA IVANOVNA was sitting in her room, still in her ball dress, lost in deep thought. On returning home, she had hastily dismissed the sleepy maid who reluctantly came forward to assist her, saying that she would undress herself, and with a trembling heart had gone up to her own room, hoping to find Hermann there, but yet desiring not to find him. At the first glance she convinced herself that he was not there, and she thanked her fate for the obstacle which had prevented their meeting. She sat down without undressing, and began to recall to mind all the circumstances which in so short a time had carried her so far. It was not three weeks since the time when she had first seen the young man from the window—and she already was in correspondence with him, and he had succeeded in inducing her to grant him a nocturnal tryst! She knew his name only through his having written it at the bottom of some of his letters; she had never spoken to him, had never heard his voice, and had never heard anything of him until that evening. But, strange to say, that very evening at the ball, Tomsky, being piqued with the young Princess Pauline N., who, contrary to her usual custom, did not flirt with him, wished to revenge himself by assuming an air of indifference: he therefore engaged Lizaveta Ivanovna and danced an endless mazurka with her. All the time he kept teasing her about her partiality for officers in the Engineers; he assured her that he knew far more than she could have supposed, and some of his jests were so happily aimed, that Lizaveta thought several times that her secret was known to him.

"From whom have you learnt all this?" she asked, smiling.

"From a friend of a person very well known to you," replied Tomsky, "from a very remarkable man."

"And who is this remarkable man?"

"His name is Hermann."

Lizaveta made no reply; but her hands and feet turned to ice.

"This Hermann," continued Tomsky, "is a truly romantic character. He has the profile of a Napoleon, and the soul of a Mephistopheles. I believe that he has at least three crimes upon his conscience. . . . How pale you are!"

"I have a headache. . . . But what did this Hermann—or whatever his name is—tell you?"

"Hermann is very much dissatisfied with his friend: he says that in his place he would act very differently. . . . I even think that Hermann himself has designs upon you; at least, he listens not indifferently to his friend's enamored exclamations."

"But where has he seen me?"

"In church, perhaps; or promenading—God alone knows where. It may have been in your room, while you were asleep, for he is capable of it."

Three ladies approaching him with the question: "*oubli ou regret?*" interrupted the conversation, which had become so tantalizingly interesting to Lizaveta.

The lady chosen by Tomsky was the Princess Pauline herself. She succeeded in effecting a reconciliation with him by making an extra turn in the dance and managing to delay resuming her seat. On returning to his place, Tomsky thought no more either of Hermann or Lizaveta. She longed to renew the interrupted conversation, but the mazurka came to an end, and shortly afterward the old Countess took her departure.

Tomsky's words were nothing more than the small talk of the mazurka, but they sank deep into the soul of the young dreamer. The portrait, sketched by Tomsky, agreed with the picture she had formed in her own mind, and that image, rendered commonplace by current novels, terrified and fascinated her imagination. She was now sitting with her bare arms crossed and her head, still adorned with flowers, was bowed over her half-uncovered breast. Suddenly the door opened and Hermann entered. She shuddered.

"Where have you been?" she asked in a frightened whisper.

"In the old Countess's bedroom," replied Hermann: "I have just left her. The Countess is dead."

"My God! What are you saying?"

"And I am afraid," added Hermann, "that I am the cause of her death."

Lizaveta looked at him, and Tomsky's words found an echo in her soul: "This man has at least three crimes upon his conscience!" Hermann sat down by the window near her, and related all that had happened.

Lizaveta listened to him in terror. So all those passionate letters, those ardent demands, this bold obstinate pursuit—all this was not love! Money—that was what his soul yearned for! She could not satisfy his desire and make him happy! The poor girl had been nothing but the blind accomplice of a robber, of the murderer of her aged benefactress! . . . She wept bitter tears of belated, agonized repentance. Hermann gazed at her in silence: his heart, too, was tormented, but neither the tears of the poor girl, nor the wonderful charm of her beauty, enhanced by her grief, could produce any impression upon his hardened soul. He felt no pricking of conscience at the thought of the dead old woman. One thing only horrified him: the irreparable loss of the secret which he had expected would bring him wealth.

"You are a monster!" said Lizaveta at last.

"I did not wish her death," replied Hermann: "my pistol is not loaded."

Both grew silent.

The day began to dawn. Lizaveta extinguished her candle: a pale light illumined her room. She wiped her tear-stained eyes and raised them toward Hermann: he was sitting on the window-sill, with his arms folded and frowning fiercely. In this attitude he bore a striking resemblance to the portrait of Napoleon. This resemblance struck even Lizaveta Ivanovna.

"How shall I get you out of the house?" said she at last. "I thought of conducting you down the secret staircase, but in that case it would be necessary to go through the Countess's bedroom, and I am afraid."

"Tell me how to find this secret staircase—I will go alone."

Lizaveta arose, took from her drawer a key, handed it to Hermann and gave him the necessary instructions.

Hermann pressed her cold, unresponsive hand, kissed her bowed head, and left the room.

He descended the winding staircase, and once more entered the Countess's bedroom. The dead old woman sat as if petrified; her face expressed profound tranquillity. Hermann stopped before her, and gazed long and earnestly at her, as if he wished to convince himself of the terrible reality; at last he entered the study, felt behind the tapestry for the door, and then began to descend the dark staircase, agitated by strange emotions. "At this very hour," thought he, "some sixty years ago, a young gallant who has long been moldering in his grave, may have stolen down this very staircase, perhaps coming from the very same bedroom, wearing an embroidered caftan, with his hair dressed à l'oiseau royal and pressing to his heart his three-cornered hat, and the heart of his aged mistress has only today ceased to beat. . . ."

At the bottom of the staircase Hermann found a door, which he opened with the same key, and found himself in a corridor which led him into the street.

V

That night the deceased Baroness von W. appeared to me. She was clad all in white and said to me: "How are you, Mr. Councilor?"

Swedenborg

THREE days after the fatal night, at nine o'clock in the morning, Hermann repaired to the Convent of ——, where the burial-service for the deceased Countess was to be held. Although feeling no remorse, he could not altogether stifle the voice of conscience, which kept repeating to him: "You are the murderer of the old woman!" While he had little true faith, he was very superstitious; and believing that the dead Countess might exercise an evil influence on his life, he resolved to be present at her funeral in order to ask her pardon.

The church was full. It was with difficulty that Hermann made his way through the crowd. The coffin stood on a sumptuous catafalque under a velvet baldachin. The deceased lay within it, her hands crossed upon her breast, and wearing a lace cap and a white satin gown. Around the catafalque stood the members of her household: the servants in black caftans, with armorial ribbons upon their shoulders, and candles in their hands; the relatives—children, grandchildren, and great-grandchildren—in deep mourning.

Nobody wept; tears would have been *une affectation*. The Countess was so old, that her death could have surprised nobody, and her relatives had long looked upon her as not among the living. A famous preacher delivered the funeral oration. In simple and touching words he described the peaceful passing away of the saintly woman whose long life had been a serene, moving preparation for a Christian end. "The angel of death found her," said the preacher, "engaged in pious meditation and waiting for the midnight bridegroom."

The service concluded in an atmosphere of melancholy decorum. The relatives went forward first to bid farewell to the deceased. Then followed the numerous acquaintances, who had come to render the last homage to her who for so many years had participated in their frivolous amusements. After these followed the members of the Countess's household. The last of these was the old housekeeper who was of the same age as the deceased. Two young women led her forward, supporting her by the arms. She had not strength enough to bow down to the ground—she was the only one to shed a few tears and kiss the cold hand of her mistress.

Hermann now resolved to approach the coffin. He bowed down to the ground and for several minutes lay on the cold floor, which was strewn with fir boughs; at last he arose, as pale as the deceased Countess herself, ascended the steps of the catafalque and bent over the corpse. . . . At that moment it seemed to him that the dead woman darted a mocking look at him and winked with one eye. Hermann started back, took a false step and fell to the ground. He was lifted up. At the same moment Lizaveta Ivanovna was carried into the vestibule of the church in a faint. This episode disturbed for some minutes the solemnity of the gloomy ceremony. Among the congregation arose a muffled murmur, and the lean chamberlain, a near relative of the deceased, whispered in the ear of an Englishman who was standing near him, that the young officer was a natural son of the Countess, to which the Englishman coldly replied: "Oh!"

During the whole of that day, Hermann was exceedingly perturbed. Dining in an out-of-the-way restaurant, he drank a great deal of wine, contrary to his usual custom, in the hope of allaying his inward agitation. But the wine only served to excite his imagination still more. On returning home, he threw himself upon his bed without undressing, and fell into a deep sleep.

When he woke up it was already night, and the moon was shining into the room. He looked at his watch: it was a quarter to three. Sleep had left him; he sat down upon his bed and thought of the funeral of the old Countess.

At that moment somebody in the street looked in at his window, and immediately passed on again. Hermann paid no attention to this incident. A few moments afterward he heard the door of the ante-room open. Hermann thought that it was his orderly, drunk as usual, returning from some nocturnal expedition, but presently he heard footsteps that were unknown to him: somebody was shuffling softly across the floor in slippers. The door opened, and a woman dressed in white, entered the room. Hermann mistook her for his old nurse, and wondered what could bring her there at that hour of the night. But the white woman glided rapidly across the room and stood before him——and Hermann recognized the Countess!

"I have come to you against my will," she said in a firm voice: "but I have been ordered to grant your request. Three, seven, ace, will win for you if played in succession, but only on these conditions: that you do not play more than one card in twenty-four hours, and that you never play again during the rest of your life. I forgive you my death, on condition that you marry my ward, Lizaveta Ivanovna."

With these words she turned round very quietly, walked with a shuffling gait toward the door and disappeared. Hermann heard the street-door bang, and he saw someone look in at him through the window again.

For a long time Hermann could not recover himself. Then he went into the next room. His orderly was asleep upon the floor, and he had much difficulty in waking him. The orderly was drunk as usual, and nothing could be got out of him. The street-door was locked. Hermann returned to his room, lit his candle, and set down an account of his vision.

VI

"Attendez!"
"How dare you say attendez *to me?"*
"Your Excellency, I said: 'Attendez, *sir.'* "

TWO FIXED ideas can no more exist together in the moral world than two bodies can occupy one and the same place in the physical world. "Three, seven, ace" soon drove out of Hermann's mind the thought of the dead Countess. "Three, seven, ace" were perpetually running through his head and continually on his lips. If he saw a young girl, he would say: "How slender she is! quite like the three of hearts." If anybody asked: "What is the time?" he would reply: "Five minutes to seven." Every stout man that he saw reminded him of the ace. "Three, seven, ace" haunted him in his sleep, and assumed all possible shapes. The three bloomed before him in the form of a magnificent flower, the seven was represented by a Gothic portal, and the ace became transformed into a gigantic spider. One thought alone occupied his whole mind—to make use of the secret which he had purchased so dearly. He thought of applying for a furlough so as to travel abroad. He wanted to go to Paris and force fortune to yield a treasure to him in the public gambling houses there. Chance spared him all this trouble.

There was in Moscow a society of wealthy gamblers, presided over by the celebrated Chekalinsky, who had passed all his life at the card-table and had amassed millions, accepting bills of exchange for his winnings and paying his losses in ready money. His long experience secured for him the confidence of his companions, and his open house, his famous cook, and his agreeable and cheerful manner gained for him the respect of the public. He came to St. Petersburg. The young men of the capital flocked to his rooms, forgetting balls for cards, and preferring the temptations of faro to the seductions of flirting. Narumov conducted Hermann to Chekalinsky's residence.

They passed through a suite of magnificent rooms, filled with courteous attendants. Several generals and privy counselors were playing whist; young men were lolling carelessly upon the velvet-covered sofas, eating ices and smoking pipes. In the drawing-room, at the head of a long table, around which crowded about a score of players, sat the master of the house keeping the bank. He was a man of about sixty years of age, of a very dignified appearance; his head was covered with silvery-white hair; his full, florid countenance expressed good-nature, and his eyes twinkled with a perpetual smile. Narumov introduced Hermann to him. Chekalinsky shook him by the hand in a friendly manner, requested him not to stand on ceremony, and then went on dealing.

The game lasted a long time. On the table lay more than thirty cards. Chekalinsky paused after each throw, in order to give the players time to arrange their cards and note down their losses, listened politely to their requests, and more politely still, straightened out the corners of cards that some absent-minded player's hand had turned down. At last the game was finished. Chekalinsky shuffled the cards and prepared to deal again.

"Allow me to play a card," said Hermann stretching out his hand from behind a stout gentleman who was punting.

Chekalinsky smiled and bowed silently, as a sign of acquiescence. Narumov laughingly congratulated Hermann on ending his long abstention from cards, and wished him a lucky beginning.

"Here goes!" said Hermann, writing the figure with chalk on the back of his card.

"How much, sir?" asked the banker, screwing up his eyes; "excuse me, I cannot see quite clearly."

"Forty-seven thousand," replied Hermann.

At these words every head in the room turned suddenly round, and all eyes were fixed upon Hermann.

"He has taken leave of his senses!" thought Narumov.

"Allow me to observe," said Chekalinsky, with his eternal smile, "that that is a very high stake; nobody here has ever staked more than two hundred and seventy-five rubles at a time."

"Well," retorted Hermann; "do you accept my card or not?"

Chekalinsky bowed with the same look of humble acquiescence.

"I only wish to inform you," said he, "that enjoying the full confidence of my partners, I can only play for ready money. For my own part, I am, of course, quite convinced that your word is sufficient, but for the sake of order, and because of the accounts, I must ask you to put the money on your card."

Hermann drew from his pocket a bank-note and handed it to Chekalinsky, who, after examining it in a cursory manner, placed it on Hermann's card.

He began to deal. On the right a nine turned up, and on the left a three.

"I win!" said Hermann, showing his card.

A murmur of astonishment arose among the players. Chekalinsky frowned, but the smile quickly returned to his face.

"Do you wish me to settle with you?" he said to Hermann.

"If you please," replied the latter.

Chekalinsky drew from his pocket a number of

bank-notes and paid up at once. Hermann took his money and left the table. Narumov could not recover from his astonishment. Hermann drank a glass of lemonade and went home.

The next evening he again appeared at Chekalinsky's. The host was dealing. Hermann walked up to the table; the punters immediately made room for him. Chekalinsky greeted him with a gracious bow.

Hermann waited for the next game, took a card and placed upon it his forty-seven thousand rubles, together with his winnings of the previous evening.

Chekalinsky began to deal. A knave turned up on the right, a seven on the left.

Hermann showed his seven.

There was a general exclamation. Chekalinsky was obviously disturbed, but he counted out the ninety-four thousand rubles and handed them over to Hermann, who pocketed them in the coolest manner possible and immediately left the house.

The next evening Hermann appeared again at the table. Everyone was expecting him. The generals and privy counselors left their whist in order to watch such extraordinary play. The young officers jumped up from their sofas, and even the servants crowded into the room. All pressed round Hermann. The other players left off punting, impatient to see how it would end. Hermann stood at the table and prepared to play alone against the pale, but still smiling Chekalinsky. Each opened a new pack of cards. Chekalinsky shuffled. Hermann took a card and covered it with a pile of bank-notes. It was like a duel. Deep silence reigned.

Chekalinsky began to deal; his hands trembled. On the right a queen turned up, and on the left an ace.

"Ace wins!" cried Hermann, showing his card.

"Your queen has lost," said Chekalinsky, sweetly.

Hermann started; instead of an ace, there lay before

him the queen of spades! He could not believe his eyes, nor could he understand how he had made such a mistake.

At that moment it seemed to him that the queen of spades screwed up her eyes and sneered. He was struck by the remarkable resemblance. . . .

"The old woman!" he exclaimed, in terror.

Chekalinsky gathered up his winnings. For some time Hermann remained perfectly motionless. When at last he left the table, the room buzzed with loud talk.

"Spendidly punted!" said the players. Chekalinsky shuffled the cards afresh, and the game went on as usual.

Conclusion

Hermann went out of his mind. He is now confined in room Number 17 of the Obukhov Hospital. He never answers any questions, but he constantly mutters with unusual rapidity: "Three, seven, ace! Three, seven, queen!"

Lizaveta Ivanovna has married a very amiable young man, a son of the former steward of the old Countess. He is a civil servant, and has a considerable fortune. Lizaveta is bringing up a poor relative.

Tomsky has been promoted to the rank of captain, and is marrying Princess Pauline.

[1833]

KIRDJALI

KIRDJALI was by birth a Bulgarian. Kirdjali, in the Turkish language, signifies a knight, a daredevil. His real name I do not know.

Kirdjali with his brigandage brought terror upon the whole of Moldavia. In order to give some idea of him, I will relate one of his exploits. One night he and the Arnaut Michaelaki fell together upon a Bulgarian village. They set it on fire at both ends, and began to go from hut to hut. Kirdjali cut throats, and Michaelaki carried off the booty. Both shouted: "Kirdjali! Kirdjali!" The whole village took to flight.

When Alexander Ypsilanti [1] proclaimed the revolt and began to collect his army, Kirdjali brought him several of his old companions. The real object of the Hetaeria was but ill understood by them, but war presented an opportunity for getting rich at the expense of the Turks, and perhaps of the Moldavians, and that was plain to them.

Alexander Ypsilanti was personally brave, but he did not possess the qualities necessary for the rôle which he had assumed with such ardor and such want of caution. He did not know how to manage the people whom he was obliged to lead. They had neither respect for him nor confidence in him. After the un-

[1] The chief of the Hetaerists, whose object was the liberation of Greece from the Turkish yoke. TRANSLATOR'S NOTE

happy battle, in which the flower of Greek youth perished, Iordaki Olimbioti persuaded him to retire, and
he himself took his place. Ypsilanti escaped to the
borders of Austria, and thence sent his curses to the
men whom he called traitors, cowards and scoundrels. These cowards and scoundrels for the most part
perished within the walls of the monastery of Seko, or
on the banks of the Pruth, desperately defending themselves against an enemy outnumbering them ten to
one.

Kirdjali found himself in the detachment of George
Kantakuzin, of whom might be repeated exactly what
has been said of Ypsilanti. On the eve of the battle of
Skulyani, Kantakuzin asked permission of the Russian
authorities to enter our territory. The detachment remained without a leader, but Kirdjali, Saphianos,
Kantagoni, and others stood in no need whatever of a
leader.

The battle of Skulyani does not seem to have been
described by anybody in all its affecting reality. Imagine seven hundred men—Arnauts, Albanians,
Greeks, Bulgarians and every kind of riff-raff—with
no idea of military art, retreating in sight of fifteen
thousand Turkish cavalry. This detachment hugged
the bank of the Pruth, and placed in front of themselves two small cannon, which they had found at
Jassy, in the courtyard of the Governor, and from
which salutes used to be fired during name-day feasts.
The Turks would have been glad to use grape-shot,
but they dared not without the permission of the
Russian authorities: the shots would infallibly have
flown over to our shore. The commander of our quarantine station (now deceased), although he had served
forty years in the army, had never in his life heard
the whistle of a bullet, but Heaven ordained that he
should hear it then. Several of them whizzed past his

ears. The old man became terribly angry, and abused the major of the Okhotsky infantry regiment, which was attached to the station. The major, not knowing what to do, ran to the river, beyond which Turkish cavalrymen were displaying their prowess, and threatened them with his finger. Seeing this, they turned round and galloped off, with the whole Turkish detachment after them. The major, who had threatened them with his finger, was called Khorchevsky. I do not know what became of him.

The next day, however, the Turks attacked the Hetaerists. Not daring to use grapeshot or cannon-balls, they resolved, contrary to their usual custom, to employ cold steel. The battle was fierce. Men slashed each other with yataghans. The Turks used lances, which they had not employed till then; these lances were Russian: Nekrassovists[1] fought in their ranks. The Hetaerists, by permission of our Emperor, were allowed to cross the Pruth and take refuge in our quarantine station. They began to cross over. Kantagoni and Saphianos remained upon the Turkish bank. Kirdjali, wounded the evening before, was already within our territory. Saphianos was killed. Kantagoni, a very stout man, was wounded in the stomach by a lance. With one hand he raised his sword, with the other he seized the hostile lance, thrust it further into himself, and in that manner was able to reach his murderer with his sword, when both fell together.

All was over. The Turks remained victorious. Moldavia was swept clear of insurrectionary bands. About six hundred Arnauts were scattered over Bessarabia; if they did not know how to support themselves, they were yet grateful to Russia for her protection. They led an idle life, but not a dissipated one. They

---

[1] Russian dissidents settled in Turkey.   EDITOR'S NOTE

could always be seen in the coffee-houses of half-Turk-
ish Bessarabia, with long pipes in their mouths, sipping
coffee grounds out of small cups. Their figured jackets and red pointed slippers were already beginning to
wear out, but their tufted skull-caps were still worn
on the side of the head, and yataghans and pistols still
protruded from their broad sashes. Nobody complained of them. It was impossible to imagine that
these poor, peaceably disposed men were the notorious
klephts of Moldavia, the companions of the ferocious
Kirdjali, and that he himself was among them.

The pasha in command at Jassy became informed of
this, and, in virtue of treaty stipulations, requested the
Russian authorities to extradite the brigand.

The police instituted a search. They discovered that
Kirdjali was really in Kishinev. They captured him in
the house of a fugitive monk in the evening, when he
was having supper, sitting in the dark with seven companions.

Kirdjali was placed under arrest. He did not try to
conceal the truth; he acknowledged that he was Kirdjali.

"But," he added, "since I crossed the Pruth, I have
not taken so much as a pin, or imposed upon even the
lowest gypsy. To the Turks, to the Moldavians and to
the Wallachians I am undoubtedly a brigand, but to
the Russians I am a guest. When Saphianos, having
fired off all his grape-shot, came here, collecting from
the wounded, for the last shots, buttons, nails, watch-
chains and the knobs of yataghans, I gave him twenty
beshliks,[1] and was left without money. God knows
that I, Kirdjali, have been living on charity. Why then
do the Russians now deliver me into the hands of my
enemies?"

---

[1] A small silver Turkish coin. EDITOR'S NOTE

After that, Kirdjali was silent, and tranquilly awaited the decision that was to determine his fate. He did
not wait long. The authorities, not being bound to look
upon brigands from their romantic side, and being
convinced of the justice of the demand, ordered Kirdjali to be sent to Jassy.

A man of heart and intellect, at that time a young
and unknown official, who is now occupying an important post, vividly described to me his departure.

At the gate of the prison stood a *caruţa*. . . . Perhaps
you do not know what a *caruţa* is. It is a low, wicker
vehicle, to which, not very long since, there were generally harnessed six or eight sorry jades. A Moldavian,
with a mustache and a sheepskin cap, sitting astride
one of them, incessantly shouted and cracked his whip,
and his wretched animals ran on at a fairly sharp trot.
If one of them began to slacken its pace, he unharnessed it with terrible oaths and left it upon the road,
little caring what might be its fate. On the return journey he was sure to find it in the same place, quietly
grazing upon the green steppe. It not unfrequently
happened that a traveler, starting from one station
with eight horses, arrived at the next with a pair only.
It used to be so about fifteen years ago. Nowadays in
Russianized Bessarabia they have adopted Russian harness and the Russian *telega*.

Such a *caruţa* stood at the gate of the prison in the
year 1821, toward the end of the month of September.
Jewesses who wore drooping sleeves and loose slippers,
Arnauts in their ragged and picturesque attire, well-pro-
portioned Moldavian women with black-eyed children
in their arms, surrounded the *caruţa*. The men preserved silence; the women were eagerly expecting
something.

The gate opened, and several police officers stepped

out into the street; behind them came two soldiers
leading the fettered Kirdjali.

He seemed about thirty years of age. The features of
his swarthy face were regular and harsh. He was tall,
broad-shouldered, and seemed endowed with unusual
physical strength. A variegated turban covered the side
of his head, and a broad sash encircled his slender
waist. A dolman of thick, dark-blue cloth, a shirt,
its broad folds falling below the knee, and handsome
slippers composed the remainder of his costume. His
look was proud and calm. . . .

One of the officials, a red-faced old man in a faded
uniform, on which dangled three buttons, pinched
with a pair of pewter spectacles the purple knob that
served him for a nose, unfolded a paper, and began to
read nasally in the Moldavian tongue. From time to
time he glanced haughtily at the fettered Kirdjali, to
whom apparently the paper referred. Kirdjali listened
to him attentively. The official finished his reading,
folded up the paper and shouted sternly at the people,
ordering them to make way and the *caruţa* to be driven
up. Then Kirdjali turned to him and said a few words
to him in Moldavian; his voice trembled, his countenance changed, he burst into tears and fell at the feet of
the police official, clanking his fetters. The police official, terrified, started back; the soldiers were about to
raise Kirdjali, but he rose up himself, gathered up his
chains, stepped into the *caruţa* and cried: "Drive on!"
A gendarme took a seat beside him, the Moldavian
cracked his whip, and the *caruţa* rolled away.

"What did Kirdjali say to you?" asked the young
official of the police officer.

"He asked me," replied the police officer, smiling, "to
look after his wife and child, who live not far from
Kilia, in a Bulgarian village: he is afraid that they may
suffer through him. Foolish fellow!"

The young official's story affected me deeply. I was sorry for poor Kirdjali. For a long time I knew nothing of his fate. Some years later I met the young official. We began to talk about the past.

"What about your friend Kirdjali?" I asked. "Do you know what became of him?"

"To be sure I do," he replied, and related to me the following.

Kirdjali, having been brought to Jassy, was taken before the Pasha, who condemned him to be impaled. The execution was deferred till some holiday. In the meantime he was confined in jail.

The prisoner was guarded by seven Turks (simple people, and at heart as much brigands as Kirdjali himself); they respected him and, like all Orientals, listened with avidity to his strange stories.

Between the guards and the prisoner an intimate acquaintance sprang up. One day Kirdjali said to them: "Brothers! my hour is near. Nobody can escape his fate. I shall soon part from you. I should like to leave you something in remembrance of me."

The Turks pricked up their ears.

"Brothers," continued Kirdjali, "three years ago, when I was engaged in plundering along with the late Milchaelaki, we buried on the steppes, not far from Jassy, a kettle filled with coins. Evidently, neither I nor he will make use of the hoard. Be it so; take it for yourselves and divide it in a friendly manner."

The Turks almost took leave of their senses. The question was, how were they to find the precious spot? They thought and thought and resolved that Kirdjali himself should conduct them to the place.

Night came on. The Turks removed the irons from the feet of the prisoner, tied his hands with a rope, and, leaving the town, set out with him for the steppe.

Kirdjali led them, walking steadily in one direction from mound to mound. They walked on for a long time. At last Kirdjali stopped near a broad stone, measured twelve paces toward the south, stamped and said: "Here."

The Turks began to make their arrangements. Four of them took out their yataghans and commenced digging. Three remained on guard. Kirdjali sat down on the stone and watched them at their work.

"Well, how much longer are you going to be?" he asked; "haven't you come to it?"

"Not yet," replied the Turks, and they worked away with such ardor, that the perspiration rolled from them in great drops.

Kirdjali began to show signs of impatience.

"What people!" he exclaimed: "they do not even know how to dig decently. I should have finished the whole business in a couple of minutes. Children! untie my hands and give me a yataghan."

The Turks reflected and began to take counsel together. "What harm would there be?" reasoned they. "Let us untie his hands and give him a yataghan. He is only one, we are seven."

And the Turks untied his hands and gave him a yataghan.

At last Kirdjali was free and armed. What must he have felt at that moment! . . . He began digging quickly, the guards helping him. . . . Suddenly he plunged his yataghan into one of them, and, leaving the blade in his breast, he snatched from his belt a couple of pistols.

The remaining six, seeing Kirdjali armed with two pistols, ran off.

Kirdjali is now operating near Jassy. Not long ago he wrote to the Governor, demanding from him five

thousand leus, and threatening, should the money not
be forthcoming, to set fire to Jassy and to get at the
Governor himself. The five thousand were delivered to
him!

Such is Kirdjali!

[1834]

THE CAPTAIN'S DAUGHTER

"Watch over your honor while you are young"
A Proverb

I

A SERGEANT OF THE GUARDS

He would have been a Captain in the Guards to-morrow.
"I do not care for that; a common soldier let him be."
A splendid thing to say! He'll have much sorrow . . .

Who is his father, then?
Knyazhnin

MY father, Andrey Petrovich Grinyov, had in his youth served under Count Münnich and retired with the rank of first major in the year 17—. From that time onward he lived on his estate in the province of Simbirsk, where he married Avdotya Vassilyevna U., daughter of a poor landowner of the district. There had been nine of us. All my brothers and sisters died in infancy. Through the kindness of Prince B., our near relative, who was a major of the Guards, I was registered as sergeant in the Semyonovsky regiment. I was supposed to be on leave until I had completed my studies. Our bringing-up in those days was very different from what it is now. At the age of five I was entrusted to the groom Savelyich, who was told off to

look after me, as a reward for the sobriety of his behavior. Under his supervision I had learned, by the
age of twelve, to read and write Russian, and could
judge very soundly the points of a borzoi dog. At that
time my father hired for me a Frenchman, Monsieur
Beaupré, who was fetched from Moscow together with
a year's supply of wine and olive oil. Savelyich very
much disliked his coming.

"The child, thank heaven, has his face washed and
his hair combed, and his food given him," he grumbled
to himself. "Much good it is to spend money on the
Frenchman, as though the master hadn't enough servants of his own on the estate!"

In his native land Beaupré had been a hairdresser;
afterward he was a soldier in Prussia, and then came
to Russia *pour être outchitel,*[1] without clearly understanding the meaning of that word. He was a good
fellow, but extremely thoughtless and flighty. His chief
weakness was his passion for the fair sex; his attentions
were often rewarded by blows, which made him groan
for hours. Besides, "he was not an enemy of the bottle,"
as he put it; that is, he liked to take a drop too much.
But since wine was only served in our house at dinner,
and then only one glass to each person, and the tutor
was generally passed over, my Beaupré soon grew accustomed to the Russian home-made brandy and, indeed, came to prefer it to the wines of his own country
as being far better for the digestion. We made friends
at once, and although he was supposed by the agreement to teach me "French, German, and all subjects,"
he preferred to pick up some Russian from me and,
after that, we each followed our own pursuits. We got
on together capitally. I wished for no other mentor.
But fate soon parted us, and this was how it happened.

---

[1] To be a teacher. TRANSLATOR'S NOTE

The laundress, Palashka, a stout pock-marked girl, and the dairymaid, one-eyed Akulka, had agreed to throw themselves together at my mother's feet, confessing their culpable weakness and tearfully complaining of the *mossoo* who had seduced their innocence. My mother did not like to trifle with such things and complained to my father. My father was not one to lose time. He sent at once for that rascal, the Frenchman. They told him *mossoo* was giving me my lesson. My father went to my room. At that time Beaupré was sleeping the sleep of innocence on the bed; I was usefully employed. I ought to mention that a map of the world had been ordered for me from Moscow. It hung on the wall; no use was made of it, and I had long felt tempted by its width and thickness. I decided to make a kite of it and, taking advantage of Beaupré's slumbers, set to work upon it. My father came in just at the moment when I was fixing a tail of tow to the Cape of Good Hope. Seeing my exercises in geography, my father pulled me by the ear, then ran up to Beaupré, roused him none too gently, and overwhelmed him with reproaches. Covered with confusion, Beaupré tried to get up but could not: the unfortunate Frenchman was dead drunk. He paid all scores at once: my father lifted him off the bed by the collar, kicked him out of the room, and sent him away that same day, to the indescribable joy of Savelyich. This was the end of my education.

I was allowed to run wild, and spent my time chasing pigeons and playing leap-frog with the boys on the estate. Meanwhile I had turned sixteen. Then there came a change in my life.

One autumn day my mother was making jam with honey in the drawing-room, and I licked my lips as I looked at the boiling scum. My father sat by the window reading the *Court Calendar,* which he received every year. This book always had a great effect on him: he never read it without agitation, and the perusal of it invariably stirred his bile. My mother, who knew all his ways by heart, always tried to stow the unfortunate book as far away as possible, and sometimes the *Court Calendar* did not catch his eye for months. When, however, he did chance to find it, he would not let it out of his hands for hours. And so my father was reading the *Court Calendar,* shrugging his shoulders from time to time and saying in an undertone:

"Lieutenant-General! . . . He was a sergeant in my company . . . a Companion of two Russian Orders! . . . And it isn't long since he and I . . . "

At last my father threw the *Calendar* on the sofa, and sank into a thoughtfulness which boded nothing good.

He suddenly turned to my mother:

"Avdotya Vassilyevna, how old is Petrusha?"

"He is going on for seventeen," my mother answered. "Petrusha was born the very year when Auntie Nastasya Gerasimovna lost her eye and when . . . "

"Very well," my father interrupted her; "it is time he went into the Service. He has been running about the servant-girls' quarters and climbing dovecots long enough."

My mother was so overwhelmed at the thought of parting from me that she dropped the spoon into the saucepan and tears flowed down her cheeks. My delight, however, could hardly be described. The idea of military service was connected in my mind with thoughts of freedom and of the pleasures of Petersburg life. I imagined myself as an officer of the Guards which, to my mind, was the height of human bliss.

My father did not like to change his plans or to put them off. The day for my departure was fixed. On the eve of it my father said that he intended sending with me a letter to my future chief and asked for paper and a pen.

"Don't forget, Andrey Petrovich, to send my greetings to Prince B.," said my mother, "and to tell him that I hope he will be kind to Petrusha."

"What nonsense!" my father answered, with a frown; "why should I write to Prince B?"

"Why, you said you were going to write to Petrusha's chief?"

"Well, what of it?"

"But Petrusha's chief is Prince B., to be sure. Petrusha is registered in the Semyonovsky regiment."

"Registered! What do I care about it? Petrusha is not going to Petersburg. What would he learn if he did his service there? To be a spendthrift and a rake? No, let him serve in the army and learn the routine of it and know the smell of powder and be a soldier and not a fop! Registered in the Guards! Where is his passport? Give it me."

My mother found my passport, which she kept put away in a chest together with my christening robe, and, with a trembling hand, gave it to my father. My father read it attentively, put it before him on the table, and began his letter.

I was consumed by curiosity. Where was I being sent if not to Petersburg? I did not take my eyes off my father's pen, which moved rather slowly. At last he finished, sealed the letter in the same envelope with the passport, took off his spectacles, called me and said:

"Here is a letter for you to Andrey Karlovich R., my old friend and comrade. You are going to Orenburg to serve under him."

And so all my brilliant hopes were dashed to the ground! Instead of the gay Petersburg life, boredom in a distant and wild part of the country awaited me. Going into the army, of which I had thought with such delight only a moment before, now seemed to me a dreadful misfortune. But it was no use protesting! Next morning a traveling-chaise drove up to the house; my bag, a box with tea-things, and bundles of pies and rolls, the last tokens of family affection, were packed into it. My parents blessed me. My father said to me:

"Good-bye, Pyotr. Carry out faithfully your oath of allegiance; obey your superiors; don't seek their favor; don't put yourself forward, and do not shirk your duty; remember the saying: 'Watch over your clothes while they are new, and over your honor while you are young.'"

My mother admonished me with tears to take care of myself, and bade Savelyich look after "the child." They dressed me in a hare-skin jacket and a fox-fur overcoat. I stepped into the chaise with Savelyich and set off on my journey weeping bitterly.

In the evening I arrived at Simbirsk, where I was to spend the next day in order to buy the things I needed; Savelyich was entrusted with the purchase of them. I put up at an inn. Savelyich went out shopping early in the morning. Bored with looking out of the window into the dirty street, I wandered about the inn. Coming into the billiard-room I saw a tall man of about thirty-five, with a long black mustache, in a dressing-gown, a billiard-cue in his hand, and a pipe in his mouth. He was playing with the marker, who drank a glass of vodka on winning and crawled under the billiard-table on all fours when he lost. I watched their game. The longer it continued, the oftener the marker had to go on all fours, till at last he remained under the table altogether. The gentleman pronounced some expressive sentences by way of a funeral oration and asked me to have a game. I refused, saying I could not play. This seemed to strike him as strange. He looked at me with something like pity; nevertheless, we entered into conversation. I learned that his name was Ivan Ivanovich Zurin, that he was captain of a Hussar regiment, that he had come to Simbirsk to receive recruits, and was staying at the inn. Zurin invited me to share his dinner, such as it was, like a fellow-soldier. I readily agreed. We sat down to dinner. Zurin drank a great deal and treated me, saying that I must get used to army ways; he told me military anecdotes, which made me rock with laughter, and we got up from table on the best of terms. Then he offered to teach me to play billiards.

"It is quite essential to us soldiers," he said. "On a march, for instance, one comes to some wretched little place; what is one to do? One can't be always beating Jews, you know. So there is nothing for it but to go to the inn and play billiards; and to do that one must be able to play!"

He convinced me completely and I set to work very diligently. Zurin encouraged me loudly, marveled at the rapid progress I was making, and after several lessons suggested we should play for money, at a penny a point, not for the sake of gain, but simply so as not to play for nothing, which, he said, was a most objectionable habit. I agreed to this, too, and Zurin ordered some punch and persuaded me to try it, repeating that I must get used to army life; what would the army be without punch! I did as he told me. We went on playing. The oftener I sipped from my glass, the more reckless I grew. My balls flew beyond the boundary every minute; I grew excited, abused the marker who did not know how to count, kept raising the stakes—in short, behaved like a silly boy who was having his first taste of freedom. I did not notice how the time passed. Zurin looked at the clock, put down his cue, and told me that I had lost a hundred rubles. I was somewha'

taken aback. My money was with Savelyich; I began
to apologize; Zurin interrupted me:

"Please do not trouble, it does not matter at all. I can
wait; and meanwhile let us go and see Arinushka."

What can I say? I finished the day as recklessly as I
had begun it. We had supper at Arinushka's. Zurin
kept filling my glass and repeating that I ought to get
used to army ways. I could hardly stand when we got
up from the table; at midnight Zurin drove me back
to the inn.

Savelyich met us on the steps. He cried out when he
saw the unmistakable signs of my zeal for the Service.

"What has come over you, sir?" he said in a shaking
voice, "wherever did you get yourself into such a state?
Good Lord! Such a dreadful thing has never happened to you before!"

"Be quiet, you old dodderer!" I mumbled. "You
must be drunk; go and lie down . . . and put me to
bed."

Next day I woke up with a headache, vaguely recalling the events of the day before. My reflections were
interrupted by Savelyich, who came in to me with a
cup of tea.

"It's early you have taken to drinking, Pyotr Andreyich," he said to me, shaking his head, "much too
early. And whom do you get it from? Neither your
father nor your grandfather were drunkards; and
your mother, it goes without saying, never tastes anything stronger than kvass. And who is at the bottom of
it all? That damned Frenchman. He kept running to
Antipyevna: 'Madame, she voo pree vodka.' Here's a
fine 'shu voo pree' for you! There is no gainsaying it,
he has taught you some good, the cur! And much need
there was to hire an infidel for a tutor! As though master had not enough servants of his own!"

I was ashamed. I turned away and said to him:

"Leave me, Savelyich, I don't want any tea." But it was not easy to stop Savelyich once he began sermonizing.

"You see now what it is to take too much, Pyotr Andreyich. Your head is heavy, and you have no appetite. A man who drinks is no good for anything. . . . Have some cucumber-brine with honey or, better still, half a glass of home-made brandy. Shall I bring you some?"

At that moment a servant-boy came in and gave me a note from Zurin.

Dear Pyotr Andreyich,
Please send me by my boy the hundred rubles you lost to me at billiards yesterday. I am in urgent need of money.
Always at your service,
                                    Ivan Zurin.

There was nothing for it. Assuming an air of indifference I turned to Savelyich, "the keeper of my money, linen, and affairs," and told him to give the boy a hundred rubles.

"What! Why should I give it him?"

"I owe it to him," I answered, as coolly as possible.

"Owe it!" repeated Savelyich, growing more and more amazed; "but when did you have time to contract a debt, sir? There's something wrong about this. You may say what you like, but I won't give the money."

I thought that if at that decisive moment I did not get the better of the obstinate old man it would be difficult for me in the future to free myself from his tutelage, and so I said, looking at him haughtily:

"I am your master, and you are my servant. The money is mine. I lost it at billiards because it was my pleasure to do so; and I advise you not to argue, but to do as you are told."

Savelyich was so startled by my words that he clasped his hands [1] and remained motionless.

"Well, why don't you go?" I cried angrily.

Savelyich began to weep.

"My dear Pyotr Andreyich," he said, in a shaking voice, "do not make me die of grief. My darling, do as I tell you, old man that I am; write to that brigand that it was all a joke, and that we have no such sum. A hundred rubles! Good Lord! Tell him that your parents have strictly forbidden you to play unless it be for nuts! . . . "

"That will do," I interrupted him sternly; "give me the money or I will turn you out."

Savelyich looked at me with profound grief and went to fetch the money. I was sorry for the poor old man, but I wanted to assert my independence and to prove that I was no longer a child.

The money was delivered to Zurin. Savelyich hastened to get me out of the accursed inn. He came to tell me that horses were ready. I left Simbirsk with an uneasy conscience and silent remorse, not saying good-bye to my teacher and not expecting ever to meet him again.

II

THE GUIDE

Thou distant land, land unknown to me!
Not of my will have I come to thee,
Nor was it my steed that brought me here.
I've been led to thee by my recklessness,
By my courage and youth and my love for drink.

An Old Song

---

[1] The gesture may more properly be described as throwing up the arms and striking the hands together.   EDITOR'S NOTE

MY REFLECTIONS on the journey were not particularly pleasant. The sum I had lost was considerable according to the standards of that time. I could not help confessing to myself that I had behaved stupidly at the Simbirsk inn, and I felt that I had been in the wrong with Savelyich. It all made me wretched. The old man sat gloomily on the coach-box, his head turned away from me; occasionally he cleared his throat but said nothing. I was determined to make peace with him, but did not know how to begin. At last I said to him:

"There, there, Savelyich, let us make it up! I am sorry; I see myself I was to blame. I got into mischief yesterday and offended you for nothing. I promise you I will be more sensible now and do as you tell me. There, don't be cross; let us make peace."

"Ah, my dear Pyotr Andreyich," he answered, with a deep sigh, "I am cross with myself—it was all my fault. How could I have left you alone at the inn! There it is—I yielded to temptation: I thought I would call on the deacon's wife, an old friend of mine. It's just as the proverb says—you go and see your friends and in jail your visit ends. It is simply dreadful! How shall I show myself before my master and mistress? What will they say when they hear that the child gambles and drinks?"

To comfort poor Savelyich I gave him my word not to dispose of a single farthing without his consent in the future. He calmed down after a time, though now and again he still muttered to himself, shaking his head: "A hundred rubles! It's no joke!"

I was approaching the place of my destination. A desolate plain intersected by hills and ravines stretched around. All was covered with snow . . . the sun was setting. The chaise was going along a narrow road, or,

rather, a track made by peasant sledges. Suddenly the
driver began looking anxiously at the horizon, and at
last, taking off his cap, he turned to me and said:

"Hadn't we better turn back, sir?"

"What for?"

"The weather is uncertain: the wind is rising; see
how it sweeps the snow."

"But what of it?"

"Do you see that?"

The driver pointed with the whip to the east.

"I see nothing but the white steppe and a clear sky."

"Why, that little cloud there."

I certainly did see at the edge of the sky a white
cloud which I had taken at first for a small hill in the
distance. The driver explained to me that the cloud betokened a snowstorm.

I had heard about snowstorms in those parts, and
knew that whole transports were sometimes buried by
them. Savelyich, like the driver, thought that we ought
to turn back. But the wind did not seem to me strong;
I hoped to arrive in time at the station, and told the
man to drive faster.

The driver set the horses at a gallop but still kept
glancing eastward. The horses went well. Meanwhile
the wind grew stronger and stronger every hour. The
little cloud grew bigger and rose heavily, gradually en-
veloping the sky. Fine snow began to fall, and then
suddenly came down in big flakes. The wind howled,
the snowstorm burst upon us. In a single moment the
dark sky melted into the sea of snow. Everything was
lost to sight.

"It's a bad look out, sir," the driver shouted. "Snowstorm!" I peeped out of the chaise: darkness and whirlwind were around us. The wind howled with such ferocious expressiveness that it seemed alive; Savelyich

and I were covered with snow; the horses walked on slowly and soon stopped altogether.

"Why don't you go on?" I asked the driver impatiently.

"What's the good?" he answered, jumping off the box. "I don't know where we are as it is; there is no road and it is dark."

I began scolding him, but Savelyich took his side.

"Why ever didn't you take his advice?" he said angrily; "you would have returned to the inn, had some tea and slept in comfort till morning, and have gone on when the storm stopped. And what's the hurry? We aren't going to a wedding."

Savelyich was right. There was nothing to be done. Snow was falling fast. A great drift of it was being heaped beside the chaise. The horses stood with their heads down and shuddered from time to time. The driver walked round them setting the harness to rights for the sake of something to do. Savelyich was grumbling; I was looking around in the hope of seeing some sign of a homestead or of the road, but I could distinguish nothing in the opaque whirlwind of snow. Suddenly I caught sight of something black.

"Hey, driver!" I cried. "Look, what is that black thing over there?"

The driver stared into the distance.

"Heaven only knows, sir," he said, climbing back on to the box; "it's not a wagon and not a tree, and it seems to be moving. It must be a wolf or a man."

I told him to go toward the unknown object, which immediately began moving toward us. In two minutes we came upon a man.

"Hey, there, good man," the driver shouted to him, "do you know where the road is?"

"The road is here," the wayfarer answered. "I am standing on hard ground, but what's the good?"

"I say, my good fellow, do you know these parts?" I asked him. "Could you guide us to a night's lodging?"

"I know the country well enough," the wayfarer answered. "I should think I have trodden every inch of it. But you see what the weather is: we should be sure to lose our way. Better stop here and wait; maybe the snowstorm will stop and when the sky is clear we can find our bearings by the stars."

His coolness gave me courage. I decided to trust to Providence and spend the night in the steppe, when the wayfarer suddenly jumped on to the box and said to the driver:

"Thank God, there's a village close by; turn to the right and make straight for it."

"And why should I go to the right?" the driver asked with annoyance; "where do you see the road? It's easy enough to drive other people's horses."

The driver seemed to me to be right.

"Indeed, how do you know that we are close to a village?" I asked the man.

"Because the wind has brought a smell of smoke from over there," he answered, "so a village must be near."

His quickness and keenness of smell astonished me. I told the driver to go on. The horses stepped with difficulty in the deep snow. The chaise moved slowly, now going into a snowdrift, now dipping into a ravine and swaying from side to side. It was like being on a ship in a stormy sea. Savelyich groaned as he kept jolting against me. I put down the front curtain, wrapped my fur coat round me and dozed, lulled to sleep by the singing of the storm and the slow swaying motion of the chaise.

I had a dream which I could never since forget and in which I still see a kind of prophecy when I reflect

upon the strange vicissitudes of my life. The reader
will forgive me, probably knowing from experience
how natural it is for man to indulge in superstition,
however great his contempt for all vain imaginings
may be.

I was in that state of mind and feeling when reality
gives way to dreams and merges into them in the shad-
owy visions of oncoming sleep. It seemed to me the
storm was still raging and we were still wandering in
the snowy desert. . . . Suddenly I saw a gateway and
drove into the courtyard of our estate. My first thought
was fear lest my father should be angry with me for my
involuntary return and regard it as an intentional disobedience. Anxious, I jumped down from the chaise
and saw my mother who came out to meet me on the
steps, with an air of profound grief.

"Don't make any noise," she said. "Your father is ill;
he is dying and wants to say good-bye to you."

Terror-stricken, I followed her to the bedroom. It
was dimly lighted; people with sad-looking faces were
standing by the bed. I approached the bed quietly; my
mother lifted the bed-curtain and said: "Andrey Petrovich! Petrusha has come; he returned when he heard
of your illness; bless him." I knelt down and looked at
the sick man. But what did I see? Instead of my father
a black-bearded peasant lay on the bed looking at me
merrily. I turned to my mother in perplexity, and said
to her: "What does it mean? This is not my father.
And why should I ask this peasant's blessing?"—
"Never mind, Petrusha," my mother answered, "he
takes your father's place for the wedding; kiss his hand
and let him bless you. . . . I would not do it. Then the
peasant jumped off the bed, seized an ax from behind
his back, and began waving it about. I wanted to run
away and could not; the room was full of dead bodies;
I stumbled against them and slipped in the pools of

blood. . . . The terrible peasant called to me kindly, saying: "Don't be afraid, come and let me bless you." Terror and confusion possessed me. . . . At that moment I woke up. The horses were standing still; Savelyich held me by the hand, saying:

"Come out, sir; we have arrived."

"Where?" I asked, rubbing my eyes.

"At the inn. With the Lord's help we stumbled right against the fence. Make haste, come and warm yourself, sir."

I stepped out of the chaise. The snowstorm was still raging though with less violence. It was pitch-dark. The landlord met us at the gate, holding a lantern under the skirt of his coat, and let us into a room that was small but clean enough; it was lighted by a burning splinter. A rifle and a tall Cossack cap hung on the wall.

The landlord, a Yaïk Cossack, was a man of about sixty, active and well preserved. Savelyich brought in the box with the tea-things and asked for a fire so that he could make tea, which had never seemed to me so welcome. The landlord went to look after things.

"Where is our guide?" I asked Savelyich.

"Here, your honor," answered a voice above me.

I looked up and on the shelf by the stove saw a black beard and two glittering eyes.

"You must have got chilled, brother?"

"I should think I did with nothing but a thin jerkin on! I did have a sheepskin coat, but I confess I pawned it yesterday in a tavern; the frost did not seem to be bad."

At that moment the landlord came in with a boiling samovar; I offered our guide a cup of tea; he climbed down from the shelf. His appearance, I thought, was striking. He was about forty, of medium height, lean and broad-shouldered. Gray was beginning to show in

his black beard; his big, lively eyes were never still. His
face had a pleasant but crafty expression. His hair was
cropped like a peasant's; he wore a ragged jerkin and
Turkish trousers. I handed him a cup of tea; he tasted
it and made a grimace.

"Be so kind, your honor . . . tell them to give me a
glass of vodka; tea is not a Cossack drink."

I readily complied with his wish. The landlord took
a glass and bottle out of the cupboard, came up to the
man, and said, glancing into his face:

"Aha! you are in our parts again! Where do you
come from?"

My guide winked significantly and answered in
riddles:

"I flew about the kitchen-garden, picking hemp
seed; granny threw a pebble but missed me. And how
are your fellows getting on?"

"Nothing much to be said of them," the landlord
said, also speaking in metaphors. "They tried to ring
the bells for vespers, but the priest's wife said they must
not: the priest is on a visit and the devils are in the
church-yard."

"Be quiet, uncle," the tramp answered; "if it rains,
there will be mushrooms, and if there are mushrooms
there will be a basket for them; and now" (he winked
again) "put the ax behind your back: the forester is
about. Your honor, here's a health to you!"

With these words he took the glass, crossed himself,
and drank it at one gulp; then he bowed to me and
returned to the shelf by the stove.

I could not at the time understand anything of this
thieves' jargon, but later on I guessed they were talking
of the affairs of the Yaïk Cossacks, who had just been
subdued after their rebellion in 1772. Savelyich listened
with an air of thorough disapproval. He looked suspi-
ciously both at the landlord and at our guide. The inn

stood in the steppe by itself, far from any village, and
looked uncommonly like a robbers' den. But there was
nothing else for it. There could be no question of con-
tinuing the journey. Savelyich's anxiety amused me
greatly. Meanwhile I made ready for the night and lay
down on the bench. Savelyich decided to sleep on the
stove; the landlord lay down on the floor. Soon the
room was full of snoring and I dropped fast asleep.

Waking up rather late in the morning I saw that the
storm had subsided. The sun was shining. The boundless steppe was wrapped in a covering of dazzling
snow. The horses were harnessed. I paid the landlord,
who charged us so little that even Savelyich did not
dispute about it or try to beat him down as was his
wont; he completely forgot his suspicions of the evening before. I called our guide, thanked him for the
help he had given us, and told Savelyich to give him
half a ruble for vodka. Savelyich frowned.

"Half a ruble!" he said. "What for? Because you
were pleased to give him a lift and bring him to the
inn? You may say what you like, sir, we have no half-
rubles to spare. If we give tips to every one we shall
soon have to starve."

I could not argue with Savelyich. I had promised
that the money was to be wholly in his charge. I was
annoyed, however, at not being able to thank the man
who had saved me from a very unpleasant situation, if
not from actual danger.

"Very well," I said calmly. "If you don't want to give
him half a ruble, give him something out of my
clothes. He is dressed much too lightly. Give him my
hareskin coat."

"Mercy on us, Pyotr Andreyich!" Savelyich cried.
"What is the good of your hareskin coat to him? He
will sell it for drink at the next pot-house, the dog."

"That's no concern of yours, old fellow, whether I

sell it for drink or not," said the tramp. "His honor gives me a fur coat of his own; it is your master's pleasure to do so, and your business, as a servant, is to obey and not to argue."

"You have no fear of God, you brigand!" Savelyich answered in an angry voice. "You see the child has no sense as yet and you are only too glad to take advantage of his good nature. What do you want with a gentleman's coat? You can't squeeze your hulking great shoulders into it, however you try!"

"Please don't argue," I said to the old man; "bring the coat at once."

"Good Lord!" my Savelyich groaned. "Why, the coat is almost new! To give it away, and not to a decent man either, but to a shameless drunkard!"

Nevertheless the hareskin coat appeared. The peasant immediately tried it on. The coat that I had slightly outgrown was certainly a little tight for him. He succeeded, however, in getting into it, bursting the seams as he did so. Savelyich almost howled when he heard the threads breaking. The tramp was extremely pleased with my present. He saw me to the chaise and said, with a low bow:

"Thank you, your honor! May God reward you for your goodness; I shall not forget your kindness so long as I live."

He went his way and I drove on, taking no notice of Savelyich, and soon forgot the snowstorm of the day before, my guide, and the hareskin coat.

Arriving in Orenburg I went straight to the General. I saw a tall man, already bent by age. His long hair was perfectly white. An old and faded uniform reminded one of the soldiers of Empress Anna's time; he spoke with a strong German accent. I gave him my father's letter. When I mentioned my name, he threw a quick glance at me.

"Du lieber Gott!" he said. "It does not seem long since Andrey Petrovich was your age, and now, see, what a big son he has! Oh, how time flies!"

He opened the letter and began reading it in an undertone, interposing his own remarks: " 'My dear Sir, Andrey Karlovich, I hope that Your Excellency' . . . Why so formal? Fie, he should be ashamed of himself! Discipline is, of course, a thing of the first importance, but is this the way to write to an old *Kamerad?* . . . 'Your Excellency has not forgotten' . . . H'm . . . 'and . . . when . . . the late Field-Marshal Münnich . . . the march . . . and also . . . Carolinchen' . . . Ehe, *Bruder!* so he still remembers our old escapades! 'Now to business . . . I am sending my young rascal to you' . . . H'm . . . 'hold him in hedgehog gloves' . . . What are hedgehog gloves! It must be a Russian saying. . . . What does it mean?" he asked me.

"That means," I answered, looking as innocent as possible, "to treat one kindly, not to be too stern, to give one plenty of freedom."

"H'm, I see . . . 'and do not give him too much rope.' No, evidently 'hedgehog gloves' means something different. . . . 'Herewith his passport' . . . Where is it? Ah, here. . . . 'Write to the Semyonovsky regiment.' . . . Very good, very good; it shall be done. . . . 'Allow me, forgetting your rank, to embrace you like an old friend and comrade' . . . Ah, at last he thought of it . . . and so on and so on. . . ."

"Well, my dear," he said, having finished the letter and put my passport aside, "it shall all be done as your father wishes; you will be transferred, with the rank of an officer, to the N. regiment, and, not to lose time, you shall go tomorrow to the Belogorsky fortress to serve under Captain Mironov, a good and honorable man. You will see real service there and learn discipline.

There is nothing for you to do at Orenburg; dissipation is bad for a young man. And tonight I shall be pleased to have you dine with me."

"I am going from bad to worse!" I thought. "What is the good of my having been a sergeant in the Guards almost before I was born! Where has it brought me? To the N. regiment and a desolate fortress on the border of the Kirghiz Steppes!"

I had dinner with Andrey Karlovich and his old aide-de-camp. Strict German economy reigned at his table, and I think the fear of seeing occasionally an additional guest at his bachelor meal had something to do with my hasty removal to the garrison. The following day I took leave of the General and set off for my destination.

III

THE FORTRESS

In this fortress fine we live;
Bread and water is our fare.
And when ferocious foes
Come to our table bare,
To a real feast we treat them.
Load the cannon and then beat them.

Soldiers' Song

Old-fashioned people, sir.

Fonvizin

THE Belogorsky fortress was twenty-five miles from Orenburg. The road ran along the steep bank of the Yaïk. The river was not yet frozen and its leaden waves looked dark and mournful between the monotonous banks covered with white snow. Beyond it the Kirghiz Steppes stretched into the distance. I was absorbed in reflections, for the most part of a melancholy nature. Life in the fortress did not attract me. I tried to picture Captain Mironov, my future chief, and thought of him as a stern, bad-tempered old man who cared for nothing but discipline and was ready to put me under arrest on a diet of bread and water for the least little trifle. Meanwhile it was growing dark. We were driving rather fast.

"Is it far to the fortress?" I asked the driver.

"No, not far," he answered; "it 's over there, you can see it."

I looked from side to side, expecting to see menacing battlements, towers, and a rampart, but saw nothing except a village surrounded by a log fence. On one side of it stood three or four haystacks, half-covered with snow, on another a tumbledown windmill with wings of bark that hung idle.

"But where is the fortress?" I asked in surprise.

"Why here," answered the driver, pointing to the village, and as he spoke we drove into it.

At the gate I saw an old cannon made of cast iron; the streets were narrow and crooked, the cottages low and, for the most part, with thatched roofs. I told the driver to take me to the Commandant's, and in another minute the chaise stopped before a wooden house built upon rising ground close to a church, also made of wood.

No one came out to meet me. I walked into the entry and opened the door into the ante-room. An old soldier was sitting on the table, sewing a blue patch on the sleeve of a green uniform. I asked him to announce me.

"Go in, my dear," he said, "our people are at home."

I stepped into a clean little room, furnished in the old-fashioned style. In the corner stood a cupboard full of crockery; an officer's diploma in a frame under glass hung on the wall; colored prints, representing

"The Taking of Ochakoff and Küstrin," "The Choosing of a Bride," and "The Cat's Funeral," made bright patches on each side of it. An elderly lady, dressed in a Russian jacket [1] and with a kerchief on her head, was sitting by the window. She was winding yarn which a one-eyed man in an officer's uniform held for her on his outstretched hands.

"What is your pleasure, sir?" she asked me, going on with her work.

I answered that I had come to serve in the army, and thought it my duty to present myself to the Captain, and with these words I turned to the one-eyed old man whom I took to be the Commandant, but the lady of the house interrupted the speech I had prepared.

"Ivan Kuzmich is not at home," she answered; "he has gone to see Father Gerasim; but it makes no difference, sir; I am his wife. You are very welcome. Please sit down."

She called the maid and asked her to call the sergeant. The old man kept looking at me inquisitively with his single eye.

"May I be so bold as to ask in what regiment you have been serving?"

I satisfied his curiosity.

"And may I ask," he continued, "why you have been transferred from the Guards to the garrison?"

I answered that such was the decision of my superiors.

"I presume it was for behavior unseemly in an officer of the Guards?" the persistent old man went on.

"That 's enough nonsense," the Captain's lady interrupted him. "You see the young man is tired after the journey; he has other things to think of . . . Hold your hands straight.

[1] *Telogreyka,* a padded or fur-lined jacket, with or without sleeves.   EDITOR'S NOTE

"And don't you worry, my dear, that you have been banished to these wilds," she went on, addressing herself to me. "You are not the first nor the last. You will like it better when you are used to it. Shvabrin, Alexey Ivanych, was transferred to us five years ago for killing a man. Heaven only knows what possessed him, but, would you believe it, he went out of town with a certain lieutenant and they both took swords and started prodding each other—and Alexey Ivanych did for the lieutenant, and before two witnesses, too! There it is—one never knows what one may do."

At that moment the sergeant, a young and well-built Cossack, came into the room.

"Maximych!" the Captain's lady said to him, "find a lodging for this gentleman and mind it is clean."

"Yes, Vasilisa Yegorovna," the Cossack answered. "Shall I get rooms for his honor at Ivan Polezhayev's?"

"Certainly not, Maximych," said the lady. "Polezhayev is crowded as it is; besides, he is a friend and always remembers that we are his superiors. Take the gentleman . . . what is your name, sir?"

"Pyotr Andreyich."

"Take Pyotr Andreyich to Semyon Kuzov's. He let his horse into my kitchen-garden, the rascal. Well, Maximych, is everything in order?"

"All is well, thank God," the Cossack answered; "only Corporal Prokhorov had a fight in the bathhouse with Ustinya Negulina about a bucket of hot water."

"Ivan Ignatyich!" said the Captain's lady to the one-eyed old man, "will you look into it and find out whether Ustinya or Prokhorov is to blame? And punish them both! Well, Maximych, you can go now. Pyotr Andreyich, Maximych will take you to your lodging."

I took leave of her. The Cossack brought me to a

cottage that stood on the high bank of the river at the very edge of the fortress. Half of the cottage was occupied by Semyon Kuzov's family, the other was allotted to me. It consisted of one fairly clean room partitioned into two. Savelyich began unpacking; I looked out of the narrow window. The melancholy steppe stretched before me. On one side I could see a few cottages; several hens strutted about the street. An old woman stood on the steps with a trough, calling to pigs that answered her with friendly grunting. And this was the place where I was doomed to spend my youth! I suddenly felt wretched; I left the window and went to bed without any supper in spite of Savelyich's entreaties. He kept repeating in distress:

"Merciful heavens; he won't eat! What will my mistress say if the child is taken ill?"

Next morning I had just begun to dress when the door opened and a young officer, short, swarthy, with a plain but extremely lively face, walked in.

"Excuse me," he said to me in French, "for coming without ceremony to make your acquaintance. Yesterday I heard of your arrival: I could not resist the desire to see at last a human face. You will understand this when you have lived here for a time."

I guessed that this was the officer who had been dismissed from the Guards on account of a duel. We made friends at once. Shvabrin was very intelligent. His conversation was witty and entertaining. He described to me in a most amusing way the Commandant's family, their friends, and the place to which fate had brought him. I was screaming with laughter when the old soldier, whom I had seen mending a uniform at the Commandant's, came in and gave me Vasilisa Yegorovna's invitation to dine with them. Shvabrin said he would go with me.

As we approached the Commandant's house we saw

in the square some twenty old garrison soldiers in
three-cornered hats and with long queues. They were
standing at attention. The Commandant, a tall, vigorous old man, wearing a night-cap and a cotton dressing-gown, stood facing them. When he saw us, he
came up, said a few kind words to me, and went on
drilling his men. We stopped to look on, but he asked
us to go to his house, promising to come soon after.

"There's nothing here worth looking at," he added.
Vasilisa Yegorovna gave us a kind and homely welcome, treating me as though she had known me all my
life. The old veteran and the maid Palasha were laying
the table.

"My Ivan Kuzmich is late with his drilling today,"
she said. "Palasha, call your master to dinner. And
where is Masha?"

At that moment a girl of eighteen, with a rosy round
face, came in; her fair hair was smoothly combed behind her ears which at that moment were burning. I
did not particularly like her at the first glance. I was
prejudiced against her: Shvabrin had described Masha,
the Captain's daughter, as quite stupid. Marya Ivanovna sat down in a corner and began sewing. Meanwhile cabbage soup was served. Not seeing her husband, Vasilisa Yegorovna sent Palasha a second time
to call him.

"Tell your master that our guests are waiting and the
soup will get cold; there is always time for drilling,
thank heaven; he can shout to his heart's content later
on."

The Captain soon appeared, accompanied by the
one-eyed old man.

"What has come over you, my dear?" his wife said
to him. "Dinner was served ages ago, and you
wouldn't come."

"But I was busy drilling soldiers, Vasilisa Yegorovna, let me tell you."

"Come, come," his wife retorted, "all this drilling is mere pretence—your soldiers don't learn anything and you are no good at it either. You had much better sit at home and say your prayers. Dear guests, come to the table."

We sat down to dinner. Vasilisa Yegorovna was never silent for a minute and bombarded me with questions: who were my parents, were they living, where did they live, how big was their estate. When she heard that my father had three hundred serfs she said: "Just fancy! to think of there being rich people in the world! And we, my dear, have only one maid, Palasha, but we are comfortable enough, thank heaven. The only trouble is Masha ought to be getting married, and all she has by way of dowry is a comb and a broom and a brass farthing, just enough to go to the baths with. If the right man turns up, all well and good, but, if not, she will die an old maid."

I glanced at Marya Ivanovna; she flushed crimson and tears dropped into her plate. I felt sorry for her and hastened to change the conversation.

"I have heard," I said, rather inappropriately, "that the Bashkirs propose to attack your fortress."

"From whom have you heard it, my good sir?" Ivan Kuzmich asked.

"I was told it at Orenburg," I answered.

"Don't you believe it!" said the Commandant, "we have not heard anything of it for years. The Bashkirs have been scared and the Kirghiz, too, have had their lesson. No fear, they won't attack us; and if they do I will give them such a fright that they will keep quiet for another ten years."

"And you are not afraid," I continued, turning to Vasilisa Yegorovna, "to remain in a fortress subject to such dangers?"

"It's a habit, my dear," she answered. "Twenty years ago when we were transferred here from the regiment

I cannot tell you how I dreaded those accursed infidels! As soon as I saw their lynx caps and heard their squealing, my heart stood still, would you believe it! And now I have grown so used to it that I don't stir when they tell us the villains are prowling round the fortress."

"Vasilisa Yegorovna is a most courageous lady," Shvabrin remarked, pompously. "Ivan Kuzmich can bear witness to it."

"Yes; she is not of the timid sort, let me tell you!" Ivan Kuzmich assented.

"And Marya Ivanovna? Is she as brave as you are?" I asked.

"Is Masha brave?" her mother answered. "No, Masha is a coward. She can't bear even now to hear a rifle-shot; it makes her all of a tremble. And when, two years ago, Ivan Kuzmich took it into his head to fire our cannon on my name-day, she nearly died of fright, poor dear. Since then we haven't fired the cursed cannon any more."

We got up from the table. The Captain and his wife went to lie down, and I went to Shvabrin's and spent the whole evening with him.

IV

THE DUEL

Oh, very well, take up then your position
And you shall see me pierce your body through.

Knyazhnin

SEVERAL weeks had passed and my life in the Belogorsky fortress had grown not merely endurable but positively pleasant. I was received in the Commandant's house as one of the family. The husband and wife were most worthy people. Ivan Kuzmich, who had risen from the ranks to be an officer, was a plain and uneducated man, but most kind and honorable. His wife ruled him, which suited his easy-going disposition. Vasilisa Yegorovna looked upon her husband's military duties as her own concern and managed the fortress as she did her own home. Marya Ivanovna soon lost her shyness with me and we became friends. I found her to be a girl of feeling and good sense. Imperceptibly I grew attached to the kind family, and even to Ivan Ignatyich, the one-eyed lieutenant of the garrison; Shvabrin had said of him that he was on improper terms with Vasilisa Yegorovna, though there was not a semblance of truth in it; but Shvabrin did not care about that.

I received my commission. My military duties were not strenuous. In our blessed fortress there were no parades, no drills, no sentry duty. Occasionally the Commandant, of his own accord, taught the soldiers, but had not yet succeeded in teaching all of them to know their left hand from their right. Shvabrin had several French books. I began reading and developed a taste for literature. In the mornings I read, practised translating, and sometimes composed verses; I almost always dined at the Commandant's and spent there the rest of the day; in the evenings, Father Gerasim and his wife, Akulina Pamfilovna, the biggest gossip in the neighborhood, sometimes came there also. Of course I saw Alexey Ivanych Shvabrin every day, but his conversation grew more and more distasteful to me as time went on. I disliked his constant jokes about the Commandant's family and, in particular, his derisive remarks about Marya Ivanovna. There was no other society in the fortress; and, indeed, I wished for no other.

In spite of the prophecies, the Bashkirs did not rise. Peace reigned around our fortress. But the peace was suddenly disturbed by an internal war.

I have already said that I tried my hand at literature. Judged by the standards of that period my attempts were quite creditable, and several years later Alexander Petrovich Sumarokov [1] thoroughly approved of them. One day I succeeded in writing a song that pleased me. Everybody knows that sometimes under the pretext of seeking advice writers try to find an appreciative listener. And so, having copied out my song, I took it to Shvabrin, who was the only person in the fortress capable of doing justice to the poet's work. After a few preliminary remarks I took my note-book out of my pocket and read the following verses to him:

> *"Thoughts of love I try to banish*
> *And her beauty to forget,*
> *And, ah me! avoiding Masha*
> *Hope I shall my freedom get.*
>
> *But the eyes that have seduced me*
> *Are before me night and day,*
> *To confusion they've reduced me,*
> *Driven rest and peace away.*
>
> *When you hear of my misfortunes*
> *Pity, Masha, pity me!*
> *You can see my cruel torments:*
> *I am captive held by thee."*

"What do you think of it?" I asked Shvabrin, expecting praise as my rightful due. But to my extreme annoyance Shvabrin, who was usually a kind critic, declared that my song was bad.

[1] Sumarokov (1718-77), an early Russian poet of the pseudo-classical school. TRANSLATOR'S NOTE

"Why so?" I asked, concealing my vexation.

"Because such lines are worthy of my teacher, Vassily Kirilych Tretyakovsky,[1] and greatly remind me of his love-verses."

He then took my note-book from me and began mercilessly criticizing every line and every word of the poem, mocking me in a most derisive manner. I could not endure it, snatched the note-book from him, and said I would never show him my verses again. Shvabrin laughed at this threat too.

"We shall see," he said, "whether you will keep your word. Poets need a listener as much as Ivan Kuzmich needs his decanter of vodka before dinner. And who is this Masha to whom you declare your tender passion and lovesickness? Is it Marya Ivanovna by any chance?"

"It's none of your business whoever she may be," I answered frowning. "I want neither your opinion nor your conjectures."

"Oho! A touchy poet and a modest lover!" Shvabrin went on, irritating me more and more. "But take a friend's advice: if you want to succeed, you must have recourse to something better than songs."

"What do you mean, sir? Please explain yourself."

"Willingly. I mean that if you want Masha Mironov to visit you at dusk, present her with a pair of earrings instead of tender verses."

My blood boiled.

"And why have you such an opinion of her?" I asked, hardly able to restrain my indignation.

"Because I know her manners and morals from experience," he answered, with a fiendish smile.

"It's a lie, you scoundrel," I cried furiously. "It's a shameless lie!"

Shvabrin changed color.

[1] One of the early Russian writers of poetry, remarkable for his unwearying zeal and utter lack of talent.   TRANSLATOR'S NOTE

"You'll have to pay for this," he said, gripping my arm; "you will give me satisfaction."

"Certainly—whenever you like," I answered, with relief. I was ready to tear him to pieces at that moment.

I went at once to Ivan Ignatyich, whom I found with a needle in his hands threading mushrooms to dry for the winter, at Vasilisa Yegorovna's request.

"Ah, Pyotr Andreyich! Pleased to see you!" he said, when he saw me. "What good fortune brings you? What business, may I ask?"

I explained to him briefly that I had quarreled with Alexey Ivanych and was asking him, Ivan Ignatyich, to be my second. Ivan Ignatyich listened to me attentively, staring at me with his solitary eye.

"You are pleased to say," he answered, "that you intend to kill Alexey Ivanych and wish me to witness it? Is that so, may I ask?"

"Quite so."

"Good heavens, Pyotr Andreyich! What are you thinking about? You have quarreled with Alexey Ivanych? What ever does it matter? Bad words are of no consequence. He abuses you—you swear back at him; he hits you in the face—you hit him on the ear, twice, three times—and then go your own way; and we shall see to it that you make it up later on. But killing a fellow-creature—is that a right thing to do, let me ask you? And, anyway, if you killed him it wouldn't matter so much; I am not very fond of Alexey Ivanych myself, for the matter of that. But what if he makes a hole in you? What will that be like? Who will be made a fool of then, may I ask?"

The sensible old man's arguments did not shake me. I stuck to my intention.

"As you like," said Ivan Ignatyich. "Do what you think best. But why should I be your witness? What for? Two men fighting each other! What is there worth seeing in it, may I ask? I've been in the Swedish War and the Turkish, and, believe me, I've seen enough."

I tried to explain to him the duties of a second, but Ivan Ignatyich simply could not understand me.

"You may say what you like," he said, "but if I am to take part in this affair it is only to go to Ivan Kuzmich and tell him, as duty bids me, that a crime contrary to the interests of the State is being planned in the fortress—and to ask if the Commandant would be pleased to take proper measures."

I was alarmed and begged Ivan Ignatyich to say nothing to the Commandant. I had difficulty in persuading him, but at last he gave me his word and I left him.

I spent the evening, as usual, at the Commandant's. I tried to appear cheerful and indifferent so as to escape inquisitive questions, and not give grounds for suspicion, but I confess I could not boast of the indifference which people in my position generally profess to feel. That evening I was inclined to be tender and emotional. Marya Ivanovna attracted me more than ever. The thought that I might be seeing her for the last time, made her seem particularly touching to me. Shvabrin was there also. I took him aside and told him of my conversation with Ivan Ignatyich.

"What do we want with seconds?" he said to me, dryly; "we will do without them."

We arranged to fight behind the corn-stacks near the fortress and to meet there the following morning between six and seven. We appeared to be talking so amicably that Ivan Ignatyich, delighted, let out the secret.

"That's right!" he said to me, looking pleased; "a bad peace is better than a good quarrel; a damaged name is better than a damaged skin."

"What's this, what's this, Ivan Ignatyich?" asked

Vasilisa Yegorovna, who was telling fortunes by cards in the corner. "I wasn't listening."

Ivan Ignatyich, seeing my look of annoyance and recalling his promise, was confused and did not know what to say. Shvabrin hastened to his assistance.

"Ivan Ignatyich approves of our making peace," he said.

"But with whom had you quarreled, my dear?"

"I had rather a serious quarrel with Pyotr Andreyich."

"What about?"

"About the merest trifle, Vasilisa Yegorovna: a song."

"That's a queer thing to quarrel about! A song! But how did it happen?"

"Why, this is how it was. Not long ago Pyotr Andreyich composed a song and today he began singing it in my presence, and I struck up my favorite:

> 'Captain's daughter, I warn you,
> Don't you go for midnight walks.'

"There was discord. Pyotr Andreyich was angry at first, but then he thought better of it, and decided that every one may sing what he likes. And that was the end of it."

Shvabrin's impudence very nearly incensed me, but no one except me understood his coarse hints, or, at any rate, no one took any notice of them. From songs the conversation turned to poets; the Commandant remarked that they were a bad lot and bitter drunkards, and advised me, as a friend, to give up writing verses, for such an occupation did not accord with military duties and brought one to no good.

Shvabrin's presence was unendurable to me. I soon said good-bye to the Captain and his family; when I came home I examined my sword, felt the point of it, and went to bed, telling Savelyich to wake me at six o'clock.

The following morning I stood behind the corn-stacks at the appointed hour waiting for my opponent. He arrived soon after me.

"We may be disturbed," he said. "We had better be quick."

We took off our uniforms and, dressed in our waist-coats only, bared our swords. At that moment Ivan Ignatyich with five soldiers of the garrison suddenly appeared from behind the stacks. He requested us to go to the Commandant's. We obeyed, vexed as we were; the soldiers surrounded us and we followed Ivan Ignatyich, who led us in triumph, stepping along with an air of extraordinary importance.

We entered the Commandant's house. Ivan Ignaty-ich opened the doors and solemnly proclaimed: "I have brought them!"

We were met by Vasilisa Yegorovna.

"Goodness me! What ever next? What? How could you? Planning murder in our fortress! Ivan Kuzmich, put them under arrest at once! Pyotr Andreyich, Alexey Ivanych! Give me your swords, give them up, give them up! Palasha, take these swords to the pantry! I did not expect this of you, Pyotr Andreyich; aren't you ashamed of yourself? It is all very well for Alexey Ivanych—he has been dismissed from the Guards for killing a man, and he does not believe in God, but fancy you doing a thing like this! Do you want to be like him?"

Ivan Kuzmich fully agreed with his wife, and kept repeating:

"Vasilisa Yegorovna is quite right; let me tell you duels are explicitly forbidden in the army regulations."

Meanwhile Palasha took our swords and carried them to the pantry. I could not help laughing; Shvabrin retained his dignity.

"With all respect for you," he said coolly, "I must observe that you give yourself unnecessary trouble in passing judgment upon us. Leave it to Ivan Kuzmich —it is his business."

"But, my dear sir, aren't husband and wife one flesh and one spirit?" the Commandant's lady retorted. "Ivan Kuzmich, what are you thinking of? Put them under arrest at once in different corners and give them nothing but bread and water till they come to their senses! And let Father Gerasim set them a penance that they may beg God to forgive them and confess their sin to the people."

Ivan Kuzmich did not know what to do. Marya Ivanovna was extremely pale. Little by little the storm subsided; Vasilisa Yegorovna calmed down and made us kiss each other. Palasha brought us back our swords. We left the Commandant's house apparently reconciled. Ivan Ignatyich accompanied us.

"Aren't you ashamed," I said to him angrily, "to have betrayed us to the Commandant when you promised me not to?"

"God is my witness, I never said anything to Ivan Kuzmich," he answered; "Vasilisa Yegorovna wormed it all out of me. And she made all the arrangements without saying a word to Ivan Kuzmich. . . . But thank Heaven that it has all ended in this way."

With these words he turned home and Shvabrin and I were left alone.

"We cannot let it end at that," I said to him.

"Of course not," Shvabrin answered; "you will answer me with your blood for your insolence, but I expect we shall be watched. We shall have to pretend to be friends for a few days. Good-bye."

And we parted as though nothing had happened. Returning to the Commandant's I sat down, as usual, by Marya Ivanovna. Ivan Kuzmich was not at home; Vasilisa Yegorovna was busy with household matters. We spoke in undertones. Marya Ivanovna tenderly reproached me for the anxiety I had caused everyone by my quarrel with Shvabrin.

"I was quite overcome," she said, "when I heard you were going to fight. How strange men are! Because of a single word which they would be sure to forget in a week's time they are ready to kill each other and to sacrifice their lives and their conscience and the welfare of those who . . . But I am sure you did not begin the quarrel. Alexey Ivanych is probably to blame."

"And why do you think so, Marya Ivanovna?"

"Oh, I don't know . . . he always jeers at people. I don't like Alexey Ivanych. He repels me and yet, strange to say, I would not, on any account, have him dislike me also. That would worry me dreadfully."

"And what do you think, Marya Ivanovna? Does he like you?"

Marya Ivanovna stammered and blushed.

"I think . . . " she said, "I believe he does like me."

"And why do you believe it?"

"Because he made me an offer of marriage."

"He made you an offer of marriage? When?"

"Last year. Some two months before you came."

"And you refused?"

"As you see. Of course, Alexey Ivanych is clever and rich, and of good family; but when I think that in church I should have to kiss him before all the people . . . not for anything! Nothing would induce me!"

Marya Ivanovna's words opened my eyes and explained a great deal to me. I understood the persistent slanders with which he pursued her. The words that gave rise to our quarrel seemed to me all the more vile

when, instead of coarse and unseemly mockery, I saw
in them deliberate calumny. My desire to punish the
impudent slanderer grew more intense, and I waited
impatiently for an opportunity.

I did not have to wait long. The following day as I
sat composing an elegy, biting my pen as I searched for
a rhyme, Shvabrin knocked at my window. I left my
pen, picked up my sword, and went out to him.

"Why wait?" Shvabrin said, "we are not watched.
Let us go down to the river. No one will disturb us
there."

We walked in silence. Descending by a steep path
we stopped at a river-bank and bared our swords.
Shvabrin was more skilled than I, but I was stronger
and more daring; Monsieur Beaupré, who had once
been a soldier, had given me a few lessons in fencing
and I made use of them. Shvabrin had not expected to
find in me so formidable an opponent. For a time we
could neither of us do the other any harm; at last, observing that Shvabrin was weakening, I began to press
him and almost drove him into the river. Suddenly I
heard someone loudly calling my name. I turned
round and saw Savelyich running toward me down
the steep path . . . at that moment I felt a stab in my
breast under the right shoulder, and fell down senseless.

V

LOVE

Ah, you young maiden, you maiden fair!
You must not marry while still so young
You must ask your father and mother first,
Your father and mother and all your kin.
You must grow in wisdom and keen good sense,
Must save up for yourself a rich dowry.

A Folk Song

If you find one better than me—you'll forget me,
If one who is worse—you 'll remember.

A Folk Song

WHEN I regained consciousness I could not grasp for a few minutes where I was, and what had happened to me. I was lying on a bed in a strange room, feeling very weak. Savelyich was standing before me with a candle in his hand. Someone was carefully unwrapping the bandages round my chest and shoulder. Gradually my thoughts cleared. I remembered my duel, and understood that I had been wounded. At that moment the door creaked.

"How is he?" whispered a voice which sent a tremor through me.

"Still the same," Savelyich answered, with a sigh. "Still unconscious. It's the fifth day."

I tried to turn my head, but could not.

"Where am I? Who is here?" I said, with an effort.

Marya Ivanovna came up to my bed and bent over me.

"Well, how do you feel?" she asked.

"God be thanked," I answered in a weak voice. "Is it you, Marya Ivanovna? Tell me . . ."

I had not the strength to go on, and broke off. Savelyich cried out. His face lit up with joy.

"He has come to his senses! Thank God! Well, my dear Pyotr Andreyich, you have given me a fright! Five days, it's no joke!"

Marya Ivanovna interrupted him.

"Don't talk to him too much, Savelyich," she said; "he is still weak." She went out and quietly closed the door.

My thoughts were in a turmoil. And so I was in the Commandant's house: Marya Ivanovna had come in to me. I wanted to ask Savelyich several questions, but the old man shook his head and stopped his ears. I closed my eyes in vexation and soon dropped asleep.

When I woke up I called Savelyich, but instead of him I saw Marya Ivanovna before me; her angelic voice greeted me. I cannot express the blissful feeling that possessed me at that moment. I seized her hand and covered it with kisses, wetting it with tears of tenderness. Masha did not withdraw her hand . . . and suddenly her lips touched my cheek and I felt their fresh and ardent kiss. A flame ran through me.

"Dear, kind Marya Ivanovna," I said to her, "be my wife, consent to make me happy."

She regained her self-possession.

"Calm yourself, for Heaven's sake," she said, taking her hand from me, "you are not out of danger yet—the wound may open. Take care of yourself, if only for my sake."

With these words she went out, leaving me in an ecstasy of delight. Happiness revived me. She would be mine! She loved me! My whole being was filled with this thought.

From that time onward I grew better every hour. I was treated by the regimental barber, for there was no other doctor in the fortress, and fortunately he did not attempt to be clever. Youth and nature hastened my recovery. The whole of the Commandant's family looked after me. Marya Ivanovna never left my side. Of course, at the first opportunity, I returned to our interrupted explanation, and Marya Ivanovna heard me out with more patience. Without any affectation she confessed her love for me and said that her parents would certainly be glad of her happiness.

"But think well," she added, "won't your parents raise objections?"

I pondered. I had no doubts of my mother's kindness; but knowing my father's views and disposition I felt that my love would not particularly touch him and that he would look upon it as a young man's whim. I candidly admitted this to Marya Ivanovna, but decided to write to my father as eloquently as possible, asking him to give us his blessing. I showed my letter to Marya Ivanovna, who found it so touching and convincing that she never doubted of its success and abandoned herself to the feelings of her tender heart with all the trustfulness of youth and love.

I made peace with Shvabrin in the first days of my convalescence. In reprimanding me for the duel Ivan Kuzmich had said to me:

"Ah, Pyotr Andreyich, I ought really to put you under arrest, but you have been punished enough already. Alexey Ivanych, though, is shut up in the storehouse and Vasilisa Yegorovna has his sword under lock and key. It is just as well he should think things over and repent."

I was much too happy to retain any hostile feeling in my heart. I interceded for Shvabrin, and the kind Commandant, with his wife's consent, decided to release him. Shvabrin called on me; he expressed a profound regret for what had passed between us; he admitted that he had been entirely to blame and asked me to forget the past. It was not in my nature to harbor malice and I sincerely forgave him both our quarrel and the wound he had inflicted on me. I ascribed his slander to the vexation of wounded vanity and rejected love, and generously excused my unhappy rival.

I was soon quite well again and able to move into my lodgings. I awaited with impatience the answer to my last letter, not daring to hope, and trying to stifle melancholy forebodings. I had not yet declared my intentions to Vasilisa Yegorovna and her husband; but my offer was not likely to surprise them. Neither Marya Ivanovna nor I attempted to conceal our feelings from them, and we were certain of their consent beforehand.

At last, one morning Savelyich came in to me holding a letter. I seized it with a tremor. The address was written in my father's hand. This prepared me for something important, for as a rule it was my mother who wrote to me and my father only added a few lines at the end of the letter. Several minutes passed before I unsealed the envelope, reading over again and again the solemnly worded address: "To my son Pyotr Andreyvich Grinyov, at the Belogorsky fortress in the Province of Orenburg." I tried to guess from the handwriting in what mood my father wrote the letter; at last I brought myself to open it and saw from the very first lines that all was lost. The letter was as follows:

My Son Pyotr!

On the 15th of this month we received the letter in which you ask for our parental blessing and consent to your marriage with Marya Ivanovna, Mironov's daughter; I do not intend to give you either my blessing or my consent, and, indeed, I mean to get at you and give you a thorough lesson as to a naughty boy for your pranks, not regarding your officer's rank, for you have proved that you are not yet worthy to wear the sword which has been given to you to defend your fatherland, and not to fight duels with scapegraces like yourself. I will write at once to Andrey Karlovich asking him to transfer you from the Belogorsky fortress to some remote place where you can get over your foolishness. When your mother heard of your duel and of your being wounded, she was taken ill with grief and is now in bed. What will become of you? I pray to God that you may be reformed although I dare not hope for this great mercy.

Your father,

A. G.

The perusal of this letter stirred various feelings in me. The cruel expressions, which my father did not stint, wounded me deeply. The contemptuous way in which he referred to Marya Ivanovna appeared to me as unseemly as it was unjust. The thought of my being transferred from the Belogorsky fortress terrified me; but most of all I was grieved by the news of my mother's illness. I felt indignant with Savelyich, never doubting it was he who had informed my parents of the duel. As I paced up and down my tiny room I stopped before him and said, looking at him angrily:

"So it's not enough for you that I have been wounded because of you, and lain for a whole month at death's door—you want to kill my mother as well."

Savelyich was thunderstruck.

"Good heavens, sir, what are you saying?" he said, almost sobbing. "You have been wounded because of me! God knows I was running to shield you with my own breast from Alexey Ivanych's sword! It was old age, curse it, that hindered me. But what have I done to your mother?"

"What have you done?" I repeated. "Who asked you to inform against me? Are you here to spy on me?"

"I informed against you?" Savelyich answered with tears. "O Lord, King of Heaven! Very well, read then what master writes to me: you will see how I informed against you."

He pulled a letter out of his pocket and I read the following:

"You should be ashamed, you old dog, not to have written to me about my son, Pyotr Andreyevich, in spite of my strict orders; strangers have to inform me of his misdoings. So this is how you carry out your duties and your master's will? I will send you to look after pigs, you old dog, for concealing the truth, and conniving with the young man. As soon as you receive this I command you to write to me at once about his health, which, I am told, is better, in what place exactly he was wounded, and whether his wound has healed properly."

It was obvious that Savelyich was innocent and I had insulted him for nothing by my reproaches and suspicion. I begged his pardon; but the old man was inconsolable.

"This is what I have come to," he kept repeating; "this is the favor my masters show me for my services! I am an old dog and a swineherd, and I am the cause of your wound! . . . No, my dear Pyotr Andreyich, not I, but the damned Frenchman is at the bottom of it: he taught you to prod people with iron spits, and to stamp with your feet, as though prodding and stamping could save one from an evil man! Much need there was to hire the Frenchman and spend money for nothing!"

But who, then, had taken the trouble to inform my father of my conduct? The General? But he did not seem to show much interest in me, and Ivan Kuzmich did not think it necessary to report my duel to him. I was lost in conjectures. My suspicions fixed upon Shvabrin. He alone could benefit by informing against me and thus causing me, perhaps, to be removed from the fortress and parted from the Commandant's family. I went to tell it all to Marya Ivanovna. She met me on the steps.

"What is the matter with you?" she said when she saw me. "How pale you are!"

"All is lost," I answered, and gave her my father's letter.

She turned pale, too. After reading the letter she returned it to me with a hand that shook, and said in a trembling voice:

"It seems it is not to be. . . . Your parents do not want me in your family. God's will be done! God knows better than we do what is good for us. There is nothing for it. Pyotr Andreyich, may you at least be happy. . . ."

"This shall not be," I cried, seizing her hand; "you love me; I am ready to face any risk. Let us go and throw ourselves at your parents' feet; they are simple-hearted people, not hard and proud . . . they will bless us; we will be married . . . and then in time I am sure we will soften my father's heart; my mother will intercede for us; he will forgive me."

"No, Pyotr Andreyich," Masha answered, "I will not marry you without your parents' blessing. Without their blessing there can be no happiness for you. Let us submit to God's will. If you find a wife, if you come to love another woman—God be with you, Pyotr Andreyich; I shall pray for you both. . . ."

She burst into tears and left me; I was about to follow her indoors, but feeling that I could not control myself, returned home.

I was sitting plunged in deep thought when Savelyich broke in upon my reflections.

"Here, sir," he said, giving me a piece of paper covered with writing, "see if I am an informer against my master and if I try to make mischief between father and son."

I took the paper from his hands: it was Savelyich's answer to my father's letter. Here it is, word for word:

Dear Sir, Andrey Petrovich, our Gracious Father!

I have received your gracious letter, in which you are pleased to be angry with me, your servant, saying that I ought to be ashamed not to obey my master's orders; I am not an old dog but your faithful servant; I obey your orders and have always served you zealously and have lived to be an old man. I have not written anything to you about Pyotr Andreyich's wound, so as not to alarm you needlessly, for I hear that, as it is, the mistress, our mother Avdotya Vlasyevna, has been taken ill with fright, and I shall pray for her health. Pyotr Andreyich was wounded in the chest under the right shoulder, just under the bone, three inches deep, and he lay in the Commandant's house where we carried him from the river-bank, and the local barber, Stepan Paramonov, treated him, and now, thank God, Pyotr Andreyich is well and there is nothing but good to be said of him. His commanders, I hear, are pleased with him and Vasilisa Yegorovna treats him as though he were her own son. And as to his having got into trouble, that is no disgrace to him: a horse has four legs, and yet it stumbles. And you are pleased to write that you will send me to herd pigs. That is for you to

decide as my master. Whereupon I humbly salute you.
Your faithful serf,
Arhip Savelyev.

I could not help smiling more than once as I read the good old man's epistle. I felt I could not answer my father, and Savelyich's letter seemed to me sufficient to relieve my mother's anxiety.

From that time my position changed. Marya Ivanovna hardly spoke to me and did her utmost to avoid me. The Commandant's house lost all its attraction for me. I gradually accustomed myself to sit at home alone. Vasilisa Yegorovna chid me for it at first, but seeing my obstinacy left me in peace. I only saw Ivan Kuzmich when my duties required it; I seldom met Shvabrin and did so reluctantly, especially as I noticed his secret dislike of me, which confirmed my suspicions. Life became unbearable to me. I sank into despondent brooding, nurtured by idleness and isolation. My love grew more ardent in solitude and oppressed me more and more. I lost the taste for reading and composition. My spirits drooped. I was afraid that I should go out of my mind or plunge into dissipation. Unexpected events that had an important influence upon my life as a whole suddenly gave my mind a powerful and beneficial shock.

VI

PUGACHOV'S REBELLION

Listen now, young men, listen,
To what we old men shall tell you.

A Folk Song

BEFORE I begin describing the strange events which I witnessed, I must say a few words about the situation in the Province of Orenburg at the end of 1773.

This vast and wealthy province was inhabited by a number of half-savage peoples who had but recently acknowledged the authority of the Russian sovereigns. Unused to the laws and habits of civilized life, cruel and reckless, they constantly rebelled, and the Government had to watch over them unremittingly to keep them in submission. Fortresses had been built in suitable places and settled for the most part with Cossacks, who had owned the shores of Yaïk for generations. But the Cossacks who were to guard the peace and safety of the place had themselves for some time past been a source of trouble and danger to the Government. In 1772 a rising took place in their chief town. It was caused by the stern measures adopted by Major-General Traubenberg in order to bring the Cossacks into due submission. The result was the barbarous assassination of Traubenberg, a mutinous change in the administration of the Cossack army, and, finally, the quelling of the mutiny by means of cannon and cruel punishments.

This had happened some time before I came to the Belogorsky fortress. All was quiet or seemed so; the authorities too easily believed the feigned repentance of the perfidious rebels, who concealed their malice and waited for an opportunity to make fresh trouble.

To return to my story.

One evening (it was at the beginning of October 1773) I sat at home alone, listening to the howling of the autumn wind, and watching through the window the clouds that raced past the moon. Someone came to call me to the Commandant's. I went at once. I found there Shvabrin, Ivan Ignatyich, and the Cossack sergeant, Maximych. Neither Vasilisa Yegorovna nor Marya Ivanovna was in the room. The Commandant looked troubled as he greeted me. He closed the doors, made us all sit down except the sergeant, who was standing by the door, pulled a letter out of his pocket and said: "Important news, gentlemen! Listen to what the General writes." He put on his spectacles and read the following:

To the Commandant of the Belogorsky Fortress,
Captain Mironov

Confidential.
*I inform you herewith that a runaway Don Cossack,
an Old Believer, Emelyan Pugachov, has perpetrated
the unpardonable outrage of assuming the name of the
deceased Emperor Peter III and, assembling a criminal
band, has caused a rising in the Yaïk settlements, and
has already taken and sacked several fortresses, committing murders and robberies everywhere. In view of
the above, you have, sir, on receipt of this, immediately
to take the necessary measures for repulsing the afore-
mentioned villain and pretender, and, if possible, for
completely destroying him, should he attack the fortress entrusted to your care.*

"Take the necessary measures," said the Commandant, removing his spectacles and folding the paper.
"That's easy enough to say, let me tell you. The villain
is evidently strong; and we have only a hundred and
thirty men, not counting the Cossacks on whom there
is no relying—no offence meant, Maximych." (The sergeant smiled.) "However, there is nothing for it,
gentlemen! Carry out your duties scrupulously, arrange for sentry duty and night patrols; in case of attack shut the gates and lead the soldiers afield. And
you, Maximych, keep a strict watch over your Cossacks. The cannon must be seen to and cleaned properly. And, above all, keep the whole thing secret so that
no one in the fortress should know as yet."

Having given us these orders, Ivan Kuzmich dismissed us. Shvabrin and I walked out together, talking of what we had just heard.

"What will be the end of it, do you think?" I asked him.

"Heaven only knows," he answered. "We shall see. So far, I don't think there is much in it. But if . . ."

He sank into thought, and began absent-mindedly whistling a French tune.

In spite of all our precautions the news of Pugachov spread throughout the fortress. Although Ivan Kuzmich greatly respected his wife, he would not for anything in the world have disclosed to her a military secret entrusted to him. Having received the General's letter, he rather skilfully got rid of Vasilisa Yegorovna by telling her that Father Gerasim had had some startling news from Orenburg, which he was guarding jealously. Vasilisa Yegorovna at once decided to go and call on the priest's wife and, on Ivan Kuzmich's advice, took Masha with her lest the girl should feel lonely at home.

Finding himself master of the house, Ivan Kuzmich at once sent for us and locked Palasha in the pantry, so that she should not listen at the door.

Vasilisa Yegorovna had not succeeded in gaining any information from the priest's wife and, coming home, she learned that, in her absence, Ivan Kuzmich had held a council, and that Palasha had been locked up. She guessed that her husband had deceived her and began questioning him. Ivan Kuzmich, however, had been prepared for attack. He was not in the least abashed and boldly answered his inquisitive consort:

"Our women, my dear, have taken to heating the stoves with straw, let me tell you; and since this may cause a fire I have given strict orders that in the future they should not use straw but wood."

"Then why did you lock up Palasha?" the Commandant's wife asked. "What had the poor girl done to have to sit in the pantry till our return?"

Ivan Kuzmich was not prepared for this question; he was confused and muttered something very incoherent. Vasilisa Yegorovna saw her husband's perfidy, but knowing that she would not succeed in learning anything from him, ceased her questions, and began talking of pickled cucumbers, which the priest's wife prepared in some very special way. Vasilisa Yegorovna could not sleep all night, trying to guess what could be in her husband's mind that she was not supposed to know.

The next day returning from Mass she saw Ivan Ignatyich pulling out of the cannon bits of rag, stones, splinters, knuckle-bones, and all kinds of rubbish that boys had thrust into it.

"What can these military preparations mean?" the Commandant's wife wondered. "Are they expecting another Kirghiz raid? But surely Ivan Kuzmich would not conceal such trifles from me!" She hailed Ivan Ignatyich with the firm intention of finding out from him the secret that tormented her feminine curiosity.

Vasilisa Yegorovna made several remarks to him about housekeeping, just as a magistrate who is cross-examining a prisoner begins with irrelevant questions so as to take him off his guard. Then, after a few moments' silence, she sighed deeply and said, shaking her head:

"Oh dear, oh dear! Just think, what news! Whatever will come of it?"

"Don't you worry, madam," Ivan Ignatyich answered; "God willing, all will be well. We have soldiers enough, plenty of gunpowder, and I have cleaned the cannon. We may yet keep Pugachov at bay. Whom God helps, nobody can harm."

"And what sort of man is this Pugachov?" she asked.

Ivan Ignatyich saw that he had made a slip and tried not to answer. But it was too late. Vasilisa Yegorovna forced him to confess everything, promising not to repeat it to anyone.

She kept her promise and did not say a word to anyone except to the priest's wife, and that was only because her cow was still grazing in the steppe and might be seized by the rebels.

Soon everyone began talking about Pugachov. The rumors differed. The Commandant sent Maximych to find out all he could in the neighboring villages and fortresses. The sergeant returned after two days' absence and said that in the steppe, some forty miles from the fortress, he had seen a lot of lights and had heard from the Bashkirs that a host of unknown size was approaching. He could not, however, say anything definite, for he had not ventured to go any farther.

The Cossacks in the fortress were obviously in a state of great agitation; in every street they stood about in groups, whispering together, dispersing as soon as they saw a dragoon or a garrison soldier. Spies were sent among them. Yulay, a Kalmuck converted to the Christian faith, brought important information to the Commandant. Yulay said that the sergeant's report was false; on his return, the sly Cossack told his comrades that he had seen the rebels, presented himself to their leader, who gave him his hand to kiss, and held a long conversation with him. The Commandant immediately arrested Maximych and put Yulay in his place. This step was received with obvious displeasure by the Cossacks. They murmured aloud and Ivan Ignatyich, who had to carry out the Commandant's order, heard with his own ears how they said: "You will catch it presently, you garrison rat!" The Commandant had intended to question his prisoner the same day, but Maximych had escaped, probably with the help of his comrades.

Another thing helped to increase the Commandant's anxiety. A Bashkir was caught carrying seditious papers. On this occasion the Commandant thought of calling his officers together once more and again wanted to send Vasilisa Yegorovna away on some pretext. But since Ivan Kuzmich was a most truthful and straightforward man, he could think of no other device than the one he had used before.

"I say, Vasilisa Yegorovna," he began, clearing his throat, "Father Gerasim, I hear, has received from town . . . "

"Don't you tell stories, Ivan Kuzmich," his wife interrupted him. "I expect you want to call a council to talk about Emelyan Pugachov without me; but you won't deceive me."

Ivan Kuzmich stared at her.

"Well, my dear," he said, "if you know all about it already, you may as well stay; we will talk before you."

"That's better, man," she answered. "You are no hand at deception; send for the officers."

We assembled again. Ivan Kuzmich read to us, in his wife's presence, Pugachov's manifesto written by some half-literate Cossack. The villain declared his intention to march against our fortress at once, invited the Cossacks and the soldiers to join his band, and exhorted the commanders not to resist him, threatening to put them to death if they did. The manifesto was written in crude but forceful language, and must have produced a strong impression upon the minds of simple people.

"The rascal!" cried Vasilisa Yegorovna. "To think of his daring to make us such offers! We are to go and meet him and lay the banners at his feet! Ah, the dog! Doesn't he know that we've been forty years in the army and have seen a thing or two? Surely no commanders have listened to the brigand?"

"I should not have thought so," Ivan Kuzmich answered, "but it appears the villain has already taken many fortresses."

"He must really be strong, then," Shvabrin remarked.

"We are just going to find out his real strength," said the Commandant. "Vasilisa Yegorovna, give me the key of the storehouse. Ivan Ignatyich, bring the Bashkir and tell Yulay to bring the whip."

"Wait, Ivan Kuzmich," said the Commandant's wife, getting up. "Let me take Masha out of the house; she will be terrified if she hears the screams. And, to tell the truth, I don't care for the business myself. Good luck to you."

In the old days torture formed so integral a part of judicial procedure that the beneficent law which abolished it long remained a dead letter. It used to be thought that the criminal's own confession was necessary for convicting him, which is both groundless and wholly opposed to judicial good sense: for if the accused person's denial of the charge is not considered a proof of his innocence, there is still less reason to regard his confession a proof of his guilt. Even now I sometimes hear old judges regretting the abolition of the barbarous custom. But in those days no one doubted the necessity of torture—neither the judges nor the accused. And so the Commandant's order did not surprise or alarm us. Ivan Ignatyich went to fetch the Bashkir, who was locked up in Vasilisa Yegorovna's storehouse, and a few minutes later the prisoner was led into the entry. The Commandant gave word for him to be brought into the room.

The Bashkir crossed the threshold with difficulty

(he was wearing fetters) and, taking off his tall cap, stood by the door. I glanced at him and shuddered. I shall never forget that man. He seemed to be over seventy. He had neither nose nor ears. His head was shaven; instead of a beard, a few gray hairs stuck out; he was small, thin and bent, but his narrow eyes still had a gleam in them.

"Aha!" said the Commandant, recognizing by the terrible marks one of the rebels punished in 1741. "I see you are an old wolf and have been in our snares. Rebelling must be an old game to you, to judge by the look of your head. Come nearer; tell me, who sent you?"

The old Bashkir was silent and gazed at the Commandant with an utterly senseless expression.

"Why don't you speak?" Ivan Kuzmich continued. "Don't you understand Russian? Yulay, ask him in your language who sent him to our fortress?"

Yulay repeated Ivan Kuzmich's question in Tatar. But the Bashkir looked at him with the same expression and did not answer a word.

"Very well!" the Commandant said. "I will make you speak! Lads, take off his stupid striped gown and streak his back. Mind you do it thoroughly, Yulay!"

Two veterans began undressing the Bashkir. The unfortunate man's face expressed anxiety. He looked about him like some wild creature caught by children. But when the old man was made to put his hands round the veteran's neck and was lifted off the ground and Yulay brandished the whip, the Bashkir groaned in a weak, imploring voice, and nodding his head, opened his mouth in which a short stump could be seen instead of a tongue.

When I recall that this happened in my lifetime and that now I have lived to see the gentle reign of the Emperor Alexander, I cannot but marvel at the rapid progress of enlightenment and the diffusion of humane principles. Young man! If my notes ever fall into your hands, remember that the best and most permanent changes are those due to the softening of manners and morals and not to any violent upheavals.

It was a shock to all of us.

"Well," said the Commandant, "we evidently cannot learn much from him. Yulay, take the Bashkir back to the storehouse. We have a few more things to talk over, gentlemen."

We began discussing our position when suddenly Vasilisa Yegorovna came into the room breathless and looking extremely alarmed.

"What is the matter with you?" the Commandant asked in surprise.

"My dear, dreadful news!" Vasilisa Yegorovna answered. "The Nizhneozerny fortress was taken this morning. Father Gerasim's servant has just returned from there. He saw it being taken. The Commandant and all the officers were hanged. All the soldiers were taken prisoners. The villains may be here any minute."

The unexpected news was a great shock to me. I knew the Commandant of the Nizhneozerny fortress, a modest and quiet young man; some two months before he had put up at Ivan Kuzmich's on his way from Orenburg with his young wife. The Nizhneozerny fortress was some fifteen miles from our fortress. Pugachov might attack us any moment now. I vividly imagined Marya Ivanovna's fate and my heart sank.

"Listen, Ivan Kuzmich," I said to the Commandant, "it is our duty to defend the fortress to our last breath; this goes without saying. But we must think of the women's safety. Send them to Orenburg if the road is still free, or to some reliable fortress farther away out of the villain's reach."

Ivan Kuzmich turned to his wife and said:

"I say, my dear, hadn't I indeed better send you and Masha away while we settle the rebels?"

"Oh, nonsense!" she replied. "No fortress is safe from bullets. What's wrong with the Belogorsky? We have lived in it for twenty-two years, thank Heaven! We have seen the Bashkirs and the Kirghiz; God willing, Pugachov won't harm us either."

"Well, my dear," Ivan Kuzmich replied, "stay if you like, since you rely on our fortress. But what are we to do about Masha? It is all very well if we ward them off or last out till reinforcements come; but what if the villains take the fortress?"

"Well, then . . . "

Vasilisa Yegorovna stopped with an air of extreme agitation.

"No, Vasilisa Yegorovna," the Commandant continued, noting that his words had produced an effect perhaps for the first time in his life, "it is not fit for Masha to stay here. Let us send her to Orenburg, to her godmother's: there are plenty of soldiers there, and enough artillery and a stone wall. And I would advise you to go with her: you may be an old woman, but you'll see what they'll do to you, if they take the fortress."

"Very well," said the Commandant's wife, "so be it, let us send Masha away. But don't you dream of asking me—I won't go; I wouldn't think of parting from you in my old age and seeking a lonely grave far away. Live together, die together."

"There is something in that," said the Commandant. "Well, we must not waste time. You had better get Masha ready for the journey. We will send her at daybreak tomorrow and give her an escort, though we have no men to spare. But where is Masha?"

"At Akulina Pamfilovna's," the Commandant's wife answered. "She fainted when she heard about the Nizhneozerny being taken; I am afraid of her falling ill."

Vasilisa Yegorovna went to see about her daughter's departure. The conversation continued, but I took no part in it, and did not listen. Marya Ivanovna came in to supper, pale and with tear-stained eyes. We ate supper in silence and rose from the table sooner than usual; saying good-bye to the family, we went to our lodgings. But I purposely left my sword behind and went back for it; I had a feeling that I should find Marya Ivanovna alone. Indeed, she met me at the door and handed me my sword.

"Good-bye, Pyotr Andreyich," she said to me with tears. "I am being sent to Orenburg. May you live and be happy; perhaps God will grant that we meet again, and if not . . ."

She broke into sobs; I embraced her.

"Good-bye, my angel," I said, "good-bye, my sweet, my darling! Whatever happens to me, believe that my last thought and my last prayer will be for you!"

Masha sobbed with her head on my shoulder. I kissed her ardently and hastened out of the room.

VII

THE ATTACK

Oh, my poor head, a soldier's head!
It served the Czar truly and faithfully
For thirty years and three years more.
It won for itself neither gold nor joy,
No word of praise and no high rank.
All it has won is a gallows high
With a cross-beam made of maple wood
And a noose of twisted silk.

A Folk Song

I DID not undress or sleep that night. I intended to go at dawn to the fortress gate from which Marya Ivanov-

na was to start on her journey, and there to say good-
bye to her for the last time. I was conscious of a great
change in myself; the agitation of my mind was much
less oppressive than the gloom in which I had but recently been plunged. The grief of parting was mingled
with vague but delicious hope, with eager expectation
of danger and a feeling of noble ambition. The night
passed imperceptibly. I was on the point of going out
when my door opened and the corporal came to tell
me that our Cossacks had left the fortress in the night,
taking Yulay with them by force, and that strange men
were riding about outside the fortress. The thought
that Marya Ivanovna might not have time to leave terrified me; I hastily gave a few instructions to the corporal and rushed off to the Commandant's.

It was already daybreak. As I ran down the street I
heard someone calling me. I stopped.

"Where are you going?" Ivan Ignatyich asked, overtaking me. "Ivan Kuzmich is on the rampart and has
sent me for you. Pugachov has come."

"Has Marya Ivanovna left?" I asked with a sinking
heart.

"She has not had time," Ivan Ignatyich answered.
"The road to Orenburg is cut off; the fortress is surrounded. It is a bad lookout, Pyotr Andreyich!"

We went to the rampart—a natural rise in the
ground reinforced by palisading. All the inhabitants of
the fortress were crowding there. The garrison stood
under arms. The cannon had been moved there the day
before. The Commandant was walking up and down
in front of his small detachment. The presence of danger inspired the old soldier with extraordinary vigor.
Some twenty men on horseback were riding to and fro
in the steppe not far from the fortress. They seemed to
be Cossacks, but there were Bashkirs among them,
easily recognized by their lynx caps and quivers. The

Commandant walked through the ranks, saying to the soldiers: "Well, children, let us stand up for our Empress and prove to all the world that we are brave and loyal men!" The soldiers loudly expressed their zeal. Shvabrin stood next to me, looking intently at the enemy. Noticing the commotion in the fortress, the horsemen in the steppe met together and began talking. The Commandant told Ivan Ignatyich to aim the cannon at the group and fired it himself. The cannonball flew with a buzzing sound over their heads without doing any damage. The horsemen dispersed and instantly galloped away, and the steppe was empty.

At that moment Vasilisa Yegorovna appeared on the rampart, followed by Masha, who would not leave her.

"Well, what's happening?" the Commandant's wife asked. "How is the battle going? Where is the enemy?"

"The enemy is not far," Ivan Kuzmich answered. "God willing, all shall be well. Well, Masha, aren't you afraid?"

"No, father," Marya Ivanovna answered. "It is worse at home by myself."

She looked at me and made an effort to smile. I clasped the hilt of my sword, remembering that the day before I had received it from her hands, as though for the protection of my lady love. My heart was glowing, I fancied myself her knight. I longed to prove that I was worthy of her trust and waited impatiently for the decisive moment.

Just then fresh crowds of horsemen appeared from behind a hill that was less than half a mile from the fortress, and soon the steppe was covered with a multitude of men armed with spears and bows and arrows. A man in a red coat, with a bare sword in his hand,

was riding among them mounted on a white horse: it
was Pugachov. He stopped; the others surrounded
him. Four men galloped at full speed, evidently at his
command, right up to the fortress. We recognized
them as our own treacherous Cossacks. One of them
was holding a sheet of paper over his cap; another carried on the point of his spear Yulay's head, which he
shook off and threw to us over the palisade. The poor
Kalmuck's head fell at the Commandant's feet; the
traitors shouted:

"Don't shoot, come out to greet the Czar! the Czar is
here!"

"I'll give it you!" Ivan Kuzmich shouted. "Shoot,
lads!"

Our soldiers fired a volley. The Cossack who held
the letter reeled and fell off his horse; others galloped
away. I glanced at Marya Ivanovna. Horrified by the
sight of Yulay's blood-stained head and stunned by the
volley, she seemed dazed. The Commandant called the
corporal and told him to take the paper out of the dead
Cossack's hands. The corporal went out into the field
and returned leading the dead man's horse by the bridle. He handed the letter to the Commandant. Ivan
Kuzmich read it to himself and then tore it to bits.
Meanwhile the rebels were evidently making ready for
action. In a few minutes bullets whizzed in our ears,
and a few arrows stuck into the ground and the palisade near us.

"Vasilisa Yegorovna," said the Commandant, "this
is no place for women, take Masha home; you see the
girl is more dead than alive."

Vasilisa Yegorovna, who had grown quiet when the
bullets began to fly, glanced at the steppe where a great
deal of movement was noticeable; then she turned to
her husband and said:

"Ivan Kuzmich, life and death are in God's hands; bless Masha. Masha, go to your father!"

Masha, pale and trembling, went up to Ivan Kuzmich, knelt before him, and bowed down to the ground. The old Commandant made the sign of the cross over her three times, then he raised her and kissing her said in a changed voice:

"Well, Masha, may you be happy. Pray to God; He will not forsake you. If you find a good man, may God give you love and concord. Live as Vasilisa Yegorovna and I have lived. Well, good-bye, Masha. Vasilisa Yegorovna, make haste and take her away!"

Masha flung her arms round his neck and sobbed.

"Let us kiss each other, too," said the Commandant's wife, bursting into tears. "Good-bye, my Ivan Kuzmich. Forgive me if I have vexed you in any way."

"Good-bye, good-bye, my dear," said the Commandant, embracing his old wife. "Well, that will do! Make haste and go home; and, if you have time, dress Masha in a sarafan."

The Commandant's wife and daughter went away. I followed Marya Ivanovna with my eyes; she looked round and nodded to me. Then Ivan Kuzmich turned to us and all his attention centered on the enemy. The rebels assembled round their leader and suddenly began dismounting.

"Now, stand firm," the Commandant said. "They are going to attack."

At that moment terrible shouting and yelling was heard; the rebels were running fast toward the fortress. Our cannon was loaded with grape-shot. The Commandant let them come quite near and then fired again. The shot fell right in the middle of the crowd; the rebels scattered and rushed back; their leader alone did not retreat. . . . He waved his saber and seemed

to be persuading them. . . . The yelling and shouting
that had stopped for a moment began again.

"Well, lads," the Commandant said, "now open the
gates, beat the drum. Forward, lads; come out, follow
me!"

The Commandant, Ivan Ignatyich, and I were instantly beyond the rampart; but the garrison lost their
nerve and did not move.

"Why do you stand still, children?" Ivan Kuzmich
shouted. "If we must die, we must—it's all in the day's
work!"

At that moment the rebels ran up to us and rushed
into the fortress. The drum stopped; the soldiers threw
down their rifles; I was knocked down, but got up
again and walked into the fortress together with the
rebels. The Commandant, wounded in the head, was
surrounded by the villains, who demanded the keys;
I rushed to his assistance; several burly Cossacks seized
me and bound me with their belts, saying: "You will
catch it presently, you enemies of the Czar!"

They dragged us along the streets; the townspeople
came out of their houses with offerings of bread and
salt. Church bells were ringing. Suddenly they shouted
in the crowd that the Czar was awaiting the prisoners
in the square and receiving the oath of allegiance. The
people rushed to the square; we were driven there also.

Pugachov was sitting in an arm-chair on the steps of
the Commandant's house. He was wearing a red Cossack *caftan* trimmed with gold braid. A tall sable cap
with golden tassels was pushed low over his glittering
eyes. His face seemed familiar to me. The Cossack elders surrounded him. Father Gerasim, pale and trembling, was standing by the steps with a cross in his
hands and seemed to be silently imploring mercy for
future victims. Gallows were being hastily put up in

the square. As we approached, the Bashkirs dispersed the crowd and brought us before Pugachov. The bells stopped ringing: there was a profound stillness.

"Which is the Commandant?" the Pretender asked.

Our Cossack sergeant stepped out of the crowd and pointed to Ivan Kuzmich. Pugachov looked at the old man menacingly and said to him:

"How did you dare resist me, your Czar?"

Exhausted by his wound the Commandant mustered his last strength and answered in a firm voice:

"You are not my Czar; you are a thief and an impostor, let me tell you!"

Pugachov frowned darkly and waved a white handkerchief. Several Cossacks seized the old Captain and dragged him to the gallows. The old Bashkir, whom we had questioned the night before, was sitting astride on the cross-beam. He was holding a rope and a minute later I saw poor Ivan Kuzmich swing in the air. Then Ivan Ignatyich was brought before Pugachov.

"Take the oath of allegiance to the Czar Peter III!" Pugachov said to him.

"You are not our monarch," Ivan Ignatyich answered, repeating his captain's words; "you are a thief and an impostor, my dear!"

Pugachov waved his handkerchief again, and the good lieutenant swung by the side of his old chief.

It was my turn next. I boldly looked at Pugachov, making ready to repeat the answer of my noble comrades. At that moment, to my extreme surprise, I saw Shvabrin among the rebellious Cossacks; he was wearing a Cossack coat and had his hair cropped like theirs. He went up to Pugachov and whispered something in his ear.

"Hang him!" said Pugachov, without looking at me.

My head was put through the noose. I began to pray silently, sincerely repenting before God of all my sins and begging Him to save all those dear to my heart. I was dragged under the gallows.

"Never you fear," the assassins repeated to me, perhaps really wishing to cheer me.

Suddenly I heard a shout: "Stop, you wretches! Wait!" The hangmen stopped. I saw Savelyich lying at Pugachov's feet.

"Dear father," the poor old man said, "what would a gentle-born child's death profit you? Let him go; they will give you a ransom for him; and as an example and a warning to others, hang me,—an old man!"

Pugachov made a sign and they instantly untied me and let go of me. "Our father pardons you," they told me.

I cannot say that at that moment I rejoiced at being saved; nor would I say that I regretted it. My feelings were too confused. I was brought before the Pretender once more and made to kneel down. Pugachov stretched out his sinewy hand to me.

"Kiss his hand, kiss his hand," people around me said. But I would have preferred the most cruel death to such vile humiliation.

"Pyotr Andreyich, my dear," Savelyich whispered, standing behind me and pushing me forward, "don't be obstinate! What does it matter? Spit and kiss the vill—— I mean, kiss his hand!"

I did not stir. Pugachov let his hand drop, saying with a laugh:

"His honor must have gone crazy with joy. Raise him!"

They pulled me up and left me in peace. I began watching the terrible comedy.

The townspeople were swearing allegiance. They came up one after another, kissed the cross and then bowed to the Pretender. The garrison soldiers were there, too. The regimental tailor, armed with his blunt scissors, was cutting off their plaits. Shaking themselves they came to kiss Pugachov's hand; he granted them his pardon and enlisted them in his gang. All this went on for about three hours. At last Pugachov got up from the arm-chair and came down the steps accompanied by his elders. A white horse in a rich harness was brought to him. Two Cossacks took him by the arms and put him on the horse. He announced to Father Gerasim that he would have dinner at his house. At that moment a woman's cry was heard. Several brigands had dragged Vasilisa Yegorovna, naked and disheveled, on to the steps. One of them had already donned her coat. Others were carrying featherbeds, boxes, crockery, linen, and all sorts of household goods.

"My dears, let me go!" the poor old lady cried. "Have mercy, let me go to Ivan Kuzmich!"

Suddenly she saw the gallows and recognized her husband.

"Villains!" she cried in a frenzy. "What have you done to him! Ivan Kuzmich, light of my eyes, soldier brave and bold! You came to no harm from Prussian swords, or from Turkish guns; you laid down your life not in a fair combat, but perished from a runaway thief!"

"Silence the old witch!" said Pugachov.

A young Cossack hit her on the head with his sabre and she fell dead on the steps. Pugachov rode away; the people rushed after him.

VIII

AN UNBIDDEN GUEST

An unbidden guest is worse than a Tatar.
                                        A Proverb

THE square emptied. I was still standing there, unable to collect my thoughts, confused by the terrible impressions of the day.

Uncertainty as to Marya Ivanovna's fate tortured me most. Where was she? What had happened to her? Had she had time to hide? Was her refuge secure? Full of anxious thoughts I entered the Commandant's house. All was empty; chairs, tables, boxes had been smashed, crockery broken; everything had been taken. I ran up the short stairway that led to the top floor and for the first time in my life entered Marya Ivanovna's room. I saw her bed pulled to pieces by the brigands; the wardrobe had been broken and pillaged; the sanctuary lamp was still burning before the empty ikonstand. The little mirror that hung between the windows had been left, too. . . . Where was the mistress of this humble virginal cell? A terrible thought flashed through my mind: I imagined her in the brigands' hands . . . my heart sank. . . . I wept bitterly and called aloud my beloved's name. . . . At that moment I heard a slight noise and Palasha, pale and trembling, appeared from behind the wardrobe.

"Ah, Pyotr Andreyich!" she cried, clasping her hands. "What a day! What horrors!"

"And Marya Ivanovna?" I asked, impatiently. "What has happened to her?"

"She is alive," Palasha answered; "she is hiding in Akulina Pamfilovna's house."

"At the priest's!" I cried, in horror. "Good God! Pu‑
gachov is there!"

I dashed out of the room, instantly found myself in
the street and ran headlong to the priest's house, not
seeing or feeling anything. Shouts, laughter, and songs
came from there. . . . Pugachov was feasting with his
comrades. Palasha followed me. I sent her to call out
Akulina Pamfilovna without attracting attention. A
minute later the priest's wife came into the entry to
speak to me with an empty bottle in her hands.

"For God's sake, where is Marya Ivanovna?" I
asked, with inexpressible anxiety.

"She is lying on my bed there, behind the partition,
poor darling," the priest's wife answered. "Well, Pyotr
Andreyich, we very nearly had trouble, but thank God,
all passed off well: the villain had just sat down to din‑
ner when she, poor thing, came to herself and groaned.
I simply gasped! He heard. 'Who is it groaning there,
old woman?' he said. I made a deep bow to the thief:
'My niece is ill, sire, she has been in bed for a fort‑
night.' 'And is your niece young?' 'She is, sire.' 'Show
me your niece, old woman.' My heart sank, but there
was nothing for it. 'Certainly, sire; only the girl cannot
get up and come into your presence.'—'Never mind,
old woman, I will go and have a look at her myself.'
And, you know, the wretch did go behind the parti‑
tion; what do you think? He drew back the curtain,
glanced at her with hawk's eyes—and nothing hap‑
pened. . . . God saved us! But, would you believe it,
both my husband and I had prepared to die a martyr's
death. Fortunately the dear girl did not know who he
was. Good Lord, what things we have lived to see!
Poor Ivan Kuzmich! Who would have thought it!
And Vasilisa Yegorovna! and Ivan Ignatyich! What
did they hang him for? How is it you were spared?

THE CAPTAIN'S DAUGHTER 667

And what do you think of Shvabrin? You know, he cropped his hair like a Cossack and is sitting here with them feasting! He is a sharp one, there's no gainsaying! And when I spoke about my sick niece, his eyes, would you believe it, went through me like a knife; but he hasn't betrayed us, and that's something to be thankful for."

At that moment the drunken shouts of the guests were heard, and Father Gerasim's voice. The guests were clamoring for more drink and the priest was calling his wife. Akulina Pamfilovna was in a flutter.

"You go home now, Pyotr Andreyich," she said. "I haven't any time for you; the villains are drinking. It might be the end of you if they met you now. Goodbye, Pyotr Andreyich. What is to be, will be; I hope God will not forsake us!"

The priest's wife left me. I set off to my lodgings feeling somewhat calmer. As I passed through the market-place I saw several Bashkirs, who crowded round the gallows, pulling the boots off the hanged men's feet; I had difficulty in suppressing my indignation, but I knew that it would have been useless to intervene. The brigands were running about the fortress, plundering the officers' quarters. The shouts of the drunken rebels resounded everywhere. I reached my lodgings. Savelyich met me at the threshold.

"Thank God!" he cried, when he saw me. "I was afraid the villains had seized you again. Well, Pyotr Andreyich, my dear! Would you believe it, the rascals have robbed us of everything: clothes, linen, crockery—they have left nothing. But there! Thank God they let you off with your life! Did you recognize their leader, sir?"

"No, I didn't; why, who is he?"

"What, sir? You have forgotten that drunkard who

took the hareskin jacket from you at the inn? The coat was as good as new, and the brute tore it along the seams as he struggled into it!"

I was surprised. Indeed, Pugachov had a striking resemblance to my guide. I felt certain Pugachov and he were the same person and understood the reason for his sparing me. I could not help marveling at the strange concatenation of circumstances: a child's coat given to a tramp had saved me from the gallows, and a drunkard who had wandered from inn to inn was besieging fortresses and shaking the foundations of the State!

"Won't you have something to eat?" asked Savelyich, true to his habit. "There is nothing at home; I will look about and prepare something for you."

Left alone, I sank into thought. What was I to do? It was not fitting for an officer to remain in a fortress that belonged to the villain or to follow his gang. It was my duty to go where my services could be of use to my country in the present trying circumstances. . . . But love prompted me to stay by Marya Ivanovna to protect and defend her. Although I had no doubt that things would soon change, I could not help shuddering at the thought of the danger she was in.

My reflections were interrupted by the arrival of a Cossack who had run to tell me that "the great Czar was asking for me."

"Where is he?" I said, making ready to obey.

"In the Commandant's house," the Cossack answered. "After dinner our father went to the bathhouse and now he is resting. Well, your honor, one can see by everything that he is a person of importance: at dinner he was pleased to eat two roast sucking-pigs, and he likes the bath-house so hot that even Taras Kurochkin could not stand it—he passed on the birch to Fomka Bikbaev, and had to have cold water poured over him. There's no denying it, all his ways are so grand. . . . And they say, in the bath-house, he showed them the royal marks on his breast: on one side the two-headed eagle, the size of a penny, and on the other his own likeness."

I did not think it necessary to dispute the Cossack's opinion and, together with him, went to the Commandant's house, trying to picture my meeting with Pugachov and wondering how it would end. The reader may well guess that I was not altogether calm.

It was growing dusk when I reached the Commandant's house. The gallows, with its victims, loomed menacingly in the dark. Poor Vasilisa Yegorovna's body was still lying at the bottom of the steps, where two Cossacks were mounting guard. The Cossack who had brought me went to announce me and returning at once, led me into the room where the night before I had taken such tender leave of Marya Ivanovna.

An extraordinary scene was before me. Pugachov and a dozen Cossack elders, wearing colored shirts and caps, were sitting round a table covered with a cloth and littered with bottles and glasses; their faces were flushed with drink and their eyes glittered. Neither Shvabrin nor our sergeant—the freshly recruited traitors—were among them.

"Ah, your honor!" said Pugachov, when he saw me, "come and be my guest; here is a place for you, you are very welcome."

The company made room for me. I sat down at the end of the table without speaking. My neighbor, a slim and good-looking young Cossack, poured out a glass of vodka for me, which I did not touch. I looked at my companions with curiosity. Pugachov sat in the place of honor leaning on the table, his black beard propped up with his broad fist. His features, regular and rather pleasant, had nothing ferocious about them. He often turned to a man of fifty, addressing him sometimes as Count, sometimes as Timofeich, and occasionally calling him uncle. They all treated one another as comrades and showed no particular deference to their leader. They talked of the morning's attack, of the success of the rising, and of the plans for the future. Everyone boasted, offered his opinion, and freely argued with Pugachov. At this strange council of war it was decided to go to Orenburg: a bold move which was very nearly crowned with disastrous success! The march was to begin the following day.

"Well, brothers," Pugachov said, "let us have my favorite song before we go to bed. Chumakov, strike up!"

My neighbor began in a high-pitched voice a mournful boatmen's song and all joined in:

"*Murmur not, mother-forest of rustling green leaves,*
Hinder not a brave lad thinking his thoughts,
For to-morrow I go before the judgment-seat,
Before the dreaded judge, our sovereign Czar,
And the Czar, our lord, will ask me:
Tell me now, good lad, tell me, peasant's son,
With whom didst thou go robbing and plundering,
And how many were thy comrades bold?
I shall tell thee the whole truth and naught but truth.
Four in number were my comrades bold:
My first trusty comrade was the dark night,
And my second true comrade—my knife of steel,
And my third one was my faithful steed,
And the fourth one was my stout bow,
And my messengers were my arrows sharp.
Then our Christian Czar will thus speak to me:
Well done, good lad, thou peasant's son!
Thou knowest how to rob and to answer for it,
And a fine reward is in store for thee—
A mansion high in the open plain,
Two pillars and a cross-beam I grant thee."

I cannot describe how affected I was by this peasant song about the gallows, sung by men doomed to the gallows. Their menacing faces, their tuneful voices, the mournful expression they gave to the words expressive enough in themselves—it all thrilled me with a feeling akin to awe.

The guests drank one more glass, got up from the table, and took leave of Pugachov. I was about to follow them when Pugachov said to me:

"Sit still, I want to talk to you."

We were left alone. We were both silent for a few minutes; Pugachov was watching me intently, occasionally screwing up his left eye with an extraordinary expression of slyness and mockery. At last he laughed with such unaffected gaiety that, as I looked at him, I laughed, too, without knowing why.

"Well, your honor?" he said to me. "Confess you had a bit of a fright, when my lads put your head in the noose? I expect the sky seemed no bigger than a sheepskin to you. . . . And you would have certainly swung if it had not been for your servant. I knew the old creature at once. Well, did you think, your honor, that the man who brought you to the inn was the great Czar himself?" (He assumed an air of mystery and importance.) "You are very much at fault," he continued, "but I have spared you for your kindness, for your having done me a service when I had to hide from my enemies. But this is nothing to what you shall see! It's not to be compared to the favor I'll show you when I obtain my kingdom! Do you promise to serve me zealously?"

The rascal's question and his impudence struck me as so amusing that I could not help smiling.

"What are you smiling at?" he asked with a frown. "Don't you believe I am the Czar? Answer me plainly."

I was confused. I felt I could not acknowledge the tramp as Czar: to do so seemed to me unpardonable cowardice. To call him an impostor to his face meant certain death; and what I was ready to do under the gallows, in sight of all the people and in the first flush of indignation, now seemed to me useless bravado. I hesitated. Pugachov gloomily awaited my reply. At last (and to this day I recall that moment with self-satisfaction) the feeling of duty triumphed over human weakness. I said to Pugachov:

"Listen, I will tell you the whole truth. Think, how can I acknowledge you as Czar? You are an intelligent man; you would see I was pretending."

"Who, then, do you think I am?"

"God only knows; but whoever you may be, you are playing a dangerous game."

Pugachov threw a swift glance at me.

"So you don't believe," he said, "that I am the Czar Peter III? Very well. But there is such a thing as success for the bold. Didn't Grishka Otrepyev [1] reign in the old days? Think of me what you like, but follow me. What does it matter to you? One master is as good as another. Serve me truly and faithfully, and I'll make you Field-Marshal and Prince. What do you say?"

"No," I answered, firmly. "I am a gentleman by birth; I swore allegiance to the Empress: I cannot serve you. If you really wish me well, let me go to Orenburg."

Pugachov was thoughtful.

"And if I let you go," he said, "will you promise, at any rate, not to fight against me?"

"How can I promise that?" I answered. "You know yourself I am not free to do as I like; if they send me against you, I shall go, there is nothing for it. You

---

[1] Pseudo-Demetrius I, an alleged impostor who ruled Russia in 1605-1606.   EDITOR'S NOTE

yourself are a leader now; you require obedience from those who serve under you. What would you call it if I refused to fight when my service was required? My life is in your hands; if you let me go, I will thank you; if you hang me, God be your judge; but I have told you the truth."

My sincerity impressed Pugachov.

"So be it," he said, clapping me on the shoulder. "I don't do things by halves. Go wherever you like and do what you think best. Come to-morrow to say good-bye to me and now go to bed; I, too, am sleepy."

I left Pugachov and went out into the street. The night was still and frostry. The moon and the stars shone brightly, shedding their light on the square and the gallows. In the fortress all was dark and quiet. Only the tavern windows were lighted and the shouts of late revelers came from there. I looked at the priest's house. The gates and shutters were closed. All seemed quiet there.

I went home and found Savelyich grieving for my absence. The news of my freedom delighted him more than I can say.

"Thanks be to God!" he said, crossing himself. "We shall leave the fortress as soon as it is light and go straight away. I have prepared some supper for you, my dear; have something to eat and then sleep peacefully till morning."

I followed his advice and having eaten my supper with great relish went to sleep on the bare floor, exhausted both in mind and body.

IX

THE PARTING

Sweet it was, O dear heart,
To meet and learn to love thee.
But sad it was from thee to part—
As though my soul fled from me.

Kheraskov

EARLY in the morning I was wakened by the drum.
I went to the square. Pugachov's crowds were already
forming into ranks by the gallows, where the victims
of the day before were still hanging. The Cossacks
were on horseback, the soldiers under arms. Banners
were flying. Several cannon, among which I recognized
ours, were placed on their carriages. All the inhabitants
were there, too, waiting for the impostor. A Cossack
stood at the steps of the Commandant's house, holding
a beautiful white Kirghiz horse by the bridle. I searched with my eyes for Vasilisa Yegorovna's body. It had
been moved a little to one side and covered with a piece
of matting. At last Pugachov appeared in the doorway.
The people took off their caps. Pugachov stood on the
steps and greeted them all. One of the elders gave him
a bag of coppers and he began throwing them down in
handfuls. The crowd rushed to pick them up, shouting; some were hurt in the scramble. Pugachov was
surrounded by his chief confederates. Shvabrin was
among them. Our eyes met; he could read contempt in
mine, and he turned away with an expression of sincere malice and feigned mockery. Catching sight of me
in the crowd, Pugachov nodded and beckoned to me.

"Listen," he said to me. "Go at once to Orenburg
and tell the Governor and all his generals from me that

they are to expect me in a week. Advise them to meet
me with childlike love and obedience, else they will not
escape a cruel death. A pleasant journey to you, your
honor!"

Then he turned to the people and said, pointing to
Shvabrin: "Here, children, is your new commandant.
Obey him in everything, and he will be answerable to
me for you and the fortress."

I heard these words with horror; Shvabrin was put
in command of the fortress; Marya Ivanovna would be
in his power! My God! what would become of her?
Pugachov came down the steps. His horse was brought
to him. He quickly jumped into the saddle without
waiting for the Cossacks to help him. At that moment
I saw my Savelyich step out of the crowd and hand
Pugachov a sheet of paper. I could not imagine what
this would lead to.

"What is this?" Pugachov asked, with an air of importance.

"Read and you will see," Savelyich answered.

Pugachov took the paper and gazed at it significantly for a few moments.

"Why do you write so illegibly?" he said at last.
"Our bright eyes can make nothing of it. Where is my
chief secretary?"

A young man in a corporal's uniform at once ran up
to Pugachov.

"Read it aloud," said the impostor, giving him the
paper. I was extremely curious to know what Savelyich could have written to Pugachov. The chief secretary began reading aloud, syllable by syllable:

"Two dressing-gowns, one cotton and one striped
silk, worth six rubles."

"What does this mean?" Pugachov asked, with a
frown.

"Tell him to read on," Savelyich answered calmly.

The chief secretary continued:

"A uniform coat of fine green cloth, worth seven rubles. White cloth trousers, worth five rubles. Twelve fine linen shirts with frilled cuffs, worth ten rubles. A tea-set worth two and a half rubles. . . ."

"What nonsense is this?" Pugachov interrupted him. "What do I care about tea-sets and frilled cuffs and trousers?"

Savelyich cleared his throat and began explaining:

"Well, you see, sir, this is a list of my master's goods stolen by the villains. . . ."

"What villains?" Pugachov said menacingly.

"I am sorry; it was a slip of the tongue," Savelyich answered. "They are not villains, of course, your men, but they rummaged about and took these things. Don't be angry: a horse has four legs and yet it stumbles. Tell him to read to the end anyway."

"Read on," Pugachov said.

The secretary continued:

"A cotton bedspread, a silk eiderdown, worth four rubles. A red cloth coat lined with fox fur, worth forty rubles. Also a hareskin jacket given to your honor at the inn, worth fifteen rubles. . . ."

"What next!" Pugachov shouted, with blazing eyes.

I confess I was alarmed for Savelyich. He was about to give more explanations, but Pugachov interrupted him.

"How dare you trouble me with such trifles!" he cried, seizing the paper from the secretary's hands and throwing it in Savelyich's face. "Stupid old man! They have been robbed—as though it mattered! Why, you old dodderer, you ought to pray for the rest of your life for me and my men, and thank your stars that you and your master are not swinging here together with those who rebelled against me. . . . Hareskin jacket, indeed!

I'll give you a hareskin jacket! Why, I'll have you flayed alive and make a jacket of your skin!"

"As you please," Savelyich answered. "But I am a bondman, and have to answer for my master's property."

Pugachov was evidently in a generous mood. He turned away and rode off without saying another word. Shvabrin and the Cossack elders followed him. The gang left the fortress in an orderly fashion. The townspeople walked out some distance after Pugachov. Savelyich and I were left alone in the square. He was holding the paper in his hands, and examining it with an air of deep regret.

Seeing that I was on good terms with Pugachov, he had decided to take advantage of it; but his wise intention did not meet with success. I tried to scold him for his misplaced zeal, but could not help laughing.

"It's all very well to laugh, sir," Savelyich answered. "It won't be so amusing when we shall have to buy everything afresh!"

I hastened to the priest's house to see Marya Ivanovna. The priest's wife had bad news for me. In the night Marya Ivanovna had developed a fever. She lay unconscious and delirious. Akulina Pamfilovna took me into her room. I walked quietly to the bedside. The change in her face struck me. She did not know me. I stood beside her for some time without listening to Father Gerasim and his kind wife who were, I think, trying to comfort me. Gloomy thoughts tormented me. The condition of the poor defenceless orphan left among the vindictive rebels, and my own helplessness, terrified me. The thought of Shvabrin tortured my imagination more than anything. Given power by the Pretender, put in charge of the fortress where the unhappy girl—the innocent object of his hatred—remained, he might do anything. What was I to do? How could I help her? How could I free her from the villain's hands? There was only one thing left me: I decided to go to Orenburg that very hour and do my utmost to hasten the relief of the Belogorsky fortress. I said good-bye to the priest and to Akulina Pamfilovna, begging them to take care of Marya Ivanovna, whom I already regarded as my wife. I took the poor girl's hand and kissed it, wetting it with my tears.

"Good-bye," said the priest's wife, taking leave of me, "good-bye, Pyotr Andreyich. I hope we shall meet in better times. Don't forget us and write to us often. Poor Marya Ivanovna has now no one to comfort and defend her but you."

Coming out into the square I stopped for a moment to look at the gallows, bowed down before it, and left the fortress by the Orenburg road, accompanied by Savelyich who kept pace with me.

I walked on, occupied with my thoughts, when I suddenly heard the sound of a horse's hoofs behind me. I turned round and saw a Cossack galloping from the fortress; he was leading a Bashkir horse by the bridle and signaling to me from a distance. I stopped and soon recognized our sergeant. Overtaking me he dismounted and said, giving me the reins of the other horse:

"Your honor, our father presents you with a horse and a fur coat of his own" (a sheepskin coat was tied to the saddle), "and he also presents you"—Maximych hesitated—"with fifty kopecks in money . . . but I lost it on the way; kindly forgive me."

Savelyich looked at him askance and grumbled: "Lost it on the way! And what is this rattling in the breast of your coat? You 've got no conscience!"

"What is rattling in the breast of my coat?" replied the sergeant, not in the least abashed. "Why, mercy on us, my good man! that's my bridle and not the fifty kopecks!"

"Very well," I said, interrupting the argument. "Thank from me him who sent you; and on your way back try to pick up the money you dropped and take it for vodka."

"Thank you very much, your honor," he answered, turning his horse; "I shall pray for you as long as I live."

With these words he galloped back, holding with one hand the breast of his coat, and in another minute was lost to sight. I put on the sheepskin and mounted the horse, making Savelyich sit behind me.

"You see now, sir," the old man said, "it was not for nothing I presented the petition to the rascal; the thief's conscience pricked him. It's true, the long-legged Bashkir nag and the sheepskin coat are not worth half of what they have stolen from us, the rascals, and what you had yourself given him, but it will come in useful; one may as well get a piece of wool off a fierce dog."

X

THE SIEGE OF THE TOWN

He pitched his camp upon the hills and meadows
And, eagle-like, he gazed upon the city;
He had a mound made beyond the camp
Concealing fire, which at night he brought to city walls.
                                                    Kheraskov

AS WE approached Orenburg we saw a crowd of convicts with shaven heads and faces disfigured by the branding iron. They were working at the fortifications under the supervision of garrison soldiers. Some were carting away the rubbish with which the moat had

been filled, others were digging; on the ramparts ma·
sons were carrying bricks, mending the town wall. At
the gates we were stopped by the sentries who asked
for our passports. As soon as the sergeant heard that I
came from the Belogorsky fortress he took me straight
to the General's house.

I found the General in the garden. He was examining the apple-trees already bared by the breath of autumn and, with the help of an old gardener, was carefully wrapping them up in warm straw. His face wore
a look of serenity, health, and good nature. He was
pleased to see me and began questioning me about the
terrible happenings I had witnessed. I told him everything. The old man listened to me attentively as he
pruned the trees.

"Poor Mironov!" he said, when I finished my sad
story. "I am sorry for him, he was a fine officer; and
Madam Mironov was an excellent woman and so good
at pickling mushrooms! And what has become of
Masha, the Captain's daughter?"

I answered that she remained at the fortress, in the
charge of the priest's wife.

"Aïe, aïe, aïe!" the General remarked, "that's bad,
very bad. There is certainly no relying on the brigands'
discipline. What will become of the poor girl?"

I answered that the Belogorsky fortress was not far
and that probably his Excellency would not delay in
sending troops to deliver its poor inhabitants. The General shook his head doubtfully. "We shall see, we shall
see," he said. "There will be time enough to talk of
this. Please come and have a cup of tea with me; I am
having a council of war today. You can give us exact
information about the rascal Pugachov and his troops.
And, meanwhile, go and have a rest!"

I went to the quarters allotted to me, where Savelyich was already setting things to rights, and waited impatiently for the appointed hour. The reader may well imagine that I did not fail to appear at the council which was of such importance to my future. At the appointed time I was at the General's.

I found there one of the town officials, the director of the customs-house, if I remember rightly, a stout, rosy-cheeked old man in a brocade coat. He asked me about the fate of Ivan Kuzmich with whom he was connected and often interrupted me with fresh questions and moral observations which proved, if not his skill in the art of war, at any rate his natural quickness and intelligence. Meanwhile other guests arrived. When all had sat down and cups of tea had been handed round, the General explained at great length and very clearly the nature of the business.

"Now, gentlemen, we must decide how we are to act against the rebels; must we take the offensive or the defensive? Each of these methods has its advantages and disadvantages. The offensive offers more hope of exterminating the enemy in the shortest time; the defensive is safer and more reliable. . . . And so let us take votes in the proper manner; that is, beginning with the youngest in rank. Ensign!" he continued, addressing himself to me, "please give us your opinion."

I got up and began by saying a few words about Pugachov and his gang; I said positively that the impostor had no means of resisting regular troops.

My opinion was received by the officials with obvious disfavor. They saw in it the defiance and rashness of youth. There was a murmur, and I clearly heard the word "greenhorn" uttered by someone in an undertone.

The General turned to me and said, with a smile: "Ensign, the first votes in councils of war are generally in favor of the offensive; this is as it should be. Now let us go on collecting votes. Mr. Collegiate Councilor! tell us your opinion."

The little old man in the brocade coat hastily finished his third cup of tea, considerably diluted with rum, and said in answer to the General:

"I think, your Excellency, we need not take either the offensive or the defensive."

"How so, sir?" the General retorted in surprise. "No other tactics are possible; one must either take the offensive or be on the defensive. . . ."

"Your Excellency, take the way of bribery."

"Ha! ha! ha! Your suggestion is very reasonable. Bribery is permitted by military tactics and we will follow your advice. We can offer seventy rubles . . . or, perhaps, a hundred for the rascal's head . . . to be paid from the secret fund."

"And then," the chief customs officer interrupted, "may I be a Kirghiz sheep and not a collegiate councilor, if those thieves do not surrender their leader to us, bound hand and foot!"

"We will think of it again and talk it over," the General answered; "but we must, in any case, take military measures. Gentlemen, please vote in the usual manner!"

All the opinions were opposed to mine. All the officials spoke of troops being unreliable and luck changeable, of caution and such like things. All thought it wiser to remain behind strong stone walls defended by cannon rather than venture into the open field. At last, when the General had heard all the opinions, he shook the ashes out of his pipe and made the following speech:

"My dear sirs! I must tell you that for my part I entirely agree with the Ensign's opinion, for it is based upon all the rules of sound military tactics, according to which it is almost always preferable to take up the offensive rather than to remain on the defensive."

At this point he stopped and began filling his pipe once more. My vanity was gratified. I proudly looked at the officials, who whispered to one another with an air of vexation and anxiety.

"But, my dear sirs," he continued, letting out, together with a deep sigh, a big whiff of tobacco smoke, "I dare not take upon myself so great a responsibility when the security of provinces entrusted to me by Her Imperial Majesty, our gracious sovereign, is at stake. And so I agree with the majority, which has decided that it is wiser and safer to await a siege within the city walls, repulsing the enemy's attacks by artillery and, if possible, by sallies."

The officials, in their turn, looked mockingly at me. The council dispersed. I could not help regetting the weakness of the venerable soldier who decided against his own conviction to follow the opinion of ignorant and inexperienced men.

Several days after this famous council we learned that Pugachov, true to his promise, was approaching Orenburg. From the top of the town hall I saw the rebels' army. It seemed to me their numbers had increased tenfold since the last attack which I witnessed. They now had artillery, brought by Pugachov from the small fortresses he had taken. Recalling the council's decision, I foresaw a prolonged confinement within the town walls and nearly wept with vexation.

I will not describe the siege of Orenburg, which belongs to history, and is not a subject for family memoirs. I will only say that, owing to the carelessness of the local authorities, the siege was disastrous for the inhabitants, who suffered famine and all sort of calamities. One may well imagine that life in Orenburg was simply unendurable. All were despondently waiting for their fate to be decided; all complained of the prices, which were, indeed, exorbitant. The inhabitants had grown used to cannon-balls falling into their back-yards; even Pugachov's assaults no longer excited general interest. I was dying of boredom. Time was passing. I received no letter from the Belogorsky fortress. All the roads were cut off. Separation from Marya Ivanovna was growing unbearable. Uncertainty about her fate tormented me. The skirmishes were my only distractions; thanks to Pugachov I had a good horse with which I shared my scanty fare, and I rode it every day to exchange shots with Pugachov's men. As a rule the advantage in these skirmishes was on the side of the villains, who were well fed, had plenty to drink, and rode good horses. The starving cavalry of the town could not get the better of them. Sometimes our hungry infantry also went afield, but the thick snow prevented it from acting successfully against the horsemen scattered all over the plain. Artillery thundered in vain from the top of the rampart, and in the field it stuck in the snow and could not move because the horses were too exhausted to pull it along. This is what our military operations were like! And this was what the Orenburg officials called being cautious and sensible.

One day when we succeeded in scattering and driving away a rather thick crowd, I overtook a Cossack who had lagged behind; I was on the point of striking him with my Turkish sword, when he suddenly took off his cap and cried:

"Good morning, Pyotr Andreyich! How are you getting on?"

I looked at him and recognized our Cossack sergeant. I was overjoyed to see him.

"How do you do, Maximych," I said to him. "Have you been in the Belogorsky lately?"

"Yes, sir, I was there only yesterday; I have a letter for you, Pyotr Andreyich."

"Where is it?" I asked, flushing all over.

"Here," said Maximych, thrusting his hand in the breast of his coat. "I promised Palasha I would manage somehow to give it to you."

He gave me a folded paper and galloped away. I opened it and read, with a tremor, the following lines:

It has pleased God to deprive me suddenly of both father and mother; I have no friends or relatives in this world. I appeal to you, knowing that you have always wished me well and that you are ready to help everyone. I pray that this letter may reach you! Maximych has promised to take it to you. Palasha has heard from Maximych that he often sees you from a distance during the sallies and that you do not take any care of yourself or think of those who pray for you with tears. I was ill for a long time, and when I recovered, Alexey Ivanovich, who is now commandant instead of my father, forced Father Gerasim to give me up to him, threatening him with Pugachov! I live in our house as a prisoner. Alexey Ivanovich is forcing me to marry him. He says he saved my life because he did not betray Akulina Pamfilovna when she told the villains I was her niece. And I would rather die than marry a man like Alexey Ivanovich. He treats me very cruelly and threatens that if I don't change my mind and marry him he will take me to the villains' camp and there the same thing will happen to me as to Lizaveta Kharlova. I have asked Alexey Ivanovich to give me time to think. He agreed to wait three more days and if I don't marry him in three days' time he will have no pity on me. Dear Pyotr Andreyich! You alone are my protector; help me in my distress. Persuade the

*General and all the commanders to make haste and
send a relief party to us, and come yourself if you can.
I remain yours obediently,*

A poor orphan,

Marya Mironov.

I almost went out of my mind when I read this letter. I galloped back to the town, spurring my poor
horse mercilessly. On the way I racked my brain for
the means of saving the poor girl, but could think of
nothing. When I reached the town I rode straight to
the General's and rushed headlong into his house.

The General was walking up and down the room,
smoking his pipe. He stopped when he saw me. He
must have been struck by my appearance; he inquired
with concern about the reason for my coming in such a
hurry.

"Your Excellency," I said to him. "I appeal to you as
to my own father; for God's sake don't refuse me, the
happiness of my whole life is at stake."

"What is it, my dear?" the old man asked in surprise. "What can I do for you? Tell me."

"Your Excellency, allow me to have a detachment of
soldiers and fifty Cossacks and let me go and clear the
Belogorsky fortress."

The General looked at me attentively, probably
thinking that I had gone out of my mind—he was not
far wrong.

"How do you mean—to clear the Belogorsky fortress?" he brought out at last.

"I vouch for success," I said eagerly, "only let me go."

"No, young man," he said, shaking his head; "at so
great a distance the enemy will find it easy to cut off
your communication with the main strategic point and
to secure a complete victory over you. Once the communication has been cut off. . . ."

I was afraid he would enter upon a military discussion and made haste to interrupt him.

"Captain Mironov's daughter," I said to him, "has sent me a letter; she begs for help; Shvabrin is forcing her to marry him."

"Really? Oh, that Shvabrin is a great *Schelm*, and if he falls into my hands I will have him court-martialed within twenty-four hours and we will shoot him on the fortress wall! But meanwhile you must have patience. . . ."

"Have patience!" I cried, beside myself. "But meanwhile he will marry Marya Ivánovna!"

"Oh, that won't be so bad," the General retorted; "it will be better for her to be Shvabrin's **wife** for the time being; he will be able to look after her **at** present, and afterwards, when we shoot him, she will find plenty of suitors, God willing. Charming widows don't remain old maids; I mean a young widow will find a husband sooner than a girl would."

"I would rather die," I cried in a rage, "than give her up to Shvabrin!"

"Oh, I see!" said the old man, "now I understand. . . . You are evidently in love with Marya Ivanovna. Oh, that's another matter! Poor boy! But all the same, I cannot possibly give you a detachment of soldiers and fifty Cossacks. Such an expedition would be unreasonable; I cannot take the responsibility for it."

I bowed my head; I was in despair. Suddenly an idea flashed through my mind. The reader will learn from the following chapter what it was—as the old-fashioned novelists put it.

XI

THE REBELS' CAMP

The lion has just had a meal;
Ferocious as he is, he asked me kindly:
"What brings you to my lair?"

Sumarokov

I LEFT the General and hastened to my lodgings.
Savelyich met me with his usual admonitions.

"Why ever do you go fighting those drunken brigands, sir? It isn't the thing for a gentleman. You may
perish for nothing any day. If at least they were Turks
or Swedes—but these wretches are not fit to be mentioned. . . ."

I interrupted him by asking how much money we
had.

"We have enough," he said, with an air of satisfaction; "the rascals rummaged everywhere, but I have
managed to hide it from them." With these words he
took out of his pocket a long knitted purse full of silver.

"Well, Savelyich," said I to him, "give me half of it
and take the rest for yourself. I am going to the Belogorsky fortress."

"My dear Pyotr Andreyich!" said the kind old man
in a shaking voice, "what are you thinking of! How
can you go at a time like this, when the brigands are
all over the place? Have pity on your parents if you
don't care about yourself. How can you go? What for?
Wait a little; troops will come and catch the rascals;
then go anywhere you like."

But my decision was firm.

"It is too late to argue," I answered; "I must go, I
cannot help it. Don't grieve, Savelyich; God willing,

we will meet again. Now don't be over-scrupulous or stint yourself. Buy everything you need, even if you have to pay three times the price. I make you a present of that money. If I don't return in three days. . . ."

"What, sir!" Savelyich interrupted me. "Do you imagine I would let you go alone? Don't you dream of asking that. Since you have decided to go, I will follow you; if I have to walk I won't leave you. To think of my sitting behind a stone wall without you! I haven't taken leave of my senses yet. Say what you like, sir, but I will go with you."

I knew it was useless to argue with Savelyich and so I allowed him to prepare for the journey. Half an hour later I mounted my good horse and Savelyich a lame and skinny nag which one of the townspeople presented to him, not having the means to feed it. We rode to the town gates; the sentries let us pass; we left Orenburg.

It was growing dusk. My way lay through the village of Berda, which was occupied by Pugachov's troops. The main road was covered with snow-drifts, but traces of horses' hoofs were all over the steppe, marked afresh each day. I was riding at a quick trot, Savelyich could hardly follow me at a distance and kept shouting:

"Not so fast, sir; for God's sake not so fast! My cursed nag cannot keep up with your long-legged devil. Where are you hurrying to? It's not to a feast we are going—more likely to our funeral! Pyotr Andreyich! . . . Pyotr Andreyich, my dear! . . . Good Lord, that child will come to grief!"

The lights of Berda soon came into sight. We rode up to the ravines that formed the natural defences of the village. Savelyich kept pace with me, never ceasing from his pitiful entreaties. I was hoping to get round the village when suddenly I saw before me in the twilight some five peasants armed with clubs: it was the advance-guard of Pugachov's camp. They called to us. Not knowing their password, I wanted to ride past them without saying anything; but they immediately surrounded me and one of them seized my horse by the bridle. I seized my sword and hit the peasant on the head; his cap saved him, but he staggered and let go the bridle. The others were confused and ran away; I took advantage of that moment, spurred my horse and galloped on. The darkness of the approaching night might have saved me from all danger, when turning round I suddenly saw that Savelyich was not with me. The poor old man could not ride away from the brigands on his lame horse. What was I to do? After waiting a few minutes and making certain that he had been detained, I turned my horse back and went to his rescue.

As I rode up to the ravine I heard a noise, shouts and my Savelyich's voice. I rode faster and soon found myself once more among the peasant watchmen who had stopped me a few minutes before. Savelyich was with them. They had pulled the old man off his nag and were preparing to bind him. My return pleased them. They rushed at me with a shout and instantly pulled me off my horse. One of them, evidently the chief, said that he would take us to the Czar at once.

"And it is for the Father Czar to decide," he added, "whether we are to hang you at once or wait till dawn."

I offered no resistance; Savelyich followed my example, and the watchmen led us along in triumph.

We crossed the ravine and entered the village. Lights were burning in all the windows. Noise and shouting came from everywhere. We met a number of people in the streets, but in the dark no one noticed us or recognized me for an officer from Orenburg. We were brought straight to a cottage that stood at the cross-roads. There were several wine-barrels and two cannon at the gate.

"Here is the palace," one of the peasants said. "I 'll go and announce you."

He went in. I glanced at Savelyich; the old man was silently repeating a prayer and crossing himself. I waited a long time; at last the peasant returned and said to me:

"Walk in, our Father says he will see the officer."

I went into the cottage or the palace as the peasants called it. It was lighted by two tallow candles and the walls were papered with gold paper; but the benches, the table, the washing arrangments, the towel on a nail, the oven-fork in the corner and the broad stove-shelf covered with pots, were just as in any other cottage. Pugachov, wearing a red coat and a tall cap, was sitting under the ikons with an air of importance, his arms akimbo. Several of his chief associates were standing by him with an expression of feigned servility: news of the arrival of an officer from Orenburg had evidently aroused the rebels' curiosity and they had prepared an impressive reception for me. Pugachov recognized me at the first glance. His assumed air of importance suddenly disappeared.

"Ah, your honor!" he said genially. "How are you? What brings you here?"

I answered that I was traveling on my own business and that his men had detained me.

"And what is your business?" he asked me.

I did not know what to say. Thinking I did not want to speak before witnesses, Pugachov turned to his comrades and ordered them to leave the room. All obeyed except two who did not stir.

"Speak boldly in their presence," Pugachov said to me, "I hide nothing from them."

I threw a sidelong glance at the impostor's confidants.

One of them, a puny, bent old man with a gray beard, had nothing remarkable about him except a blue ribbon worn across the shoulder over a gray peasant coat. But I shall never forget his comrade. He was tall, stout, and broad-shouldered, and seemed to be about forty-five. A thick red beard, gray glittering eyes, a nose without nostrils, and reddish marks on the forehead and the cheeks gave an indescribable expression to his broad, pock-marked face. He wore a red shirt, a Kirghiz gown and Cossack trousers. As I learned later, the first was a runaway corporal, Beloborodov; the second, Afanasy Sokolov, nicknamed Khlopusha, a convict who had escaped three times from the Siberian mines. In spite of the feelings which absorbed me, the company in which I so unexpectedly found myself strongly appealed to my imagination. But Pugachov brought me back to myself by repeating:

"Tell me on what business have you left Orenburg?"

A strange idea came into my head: it seemed to me that Providence which had brought me for the second time to Pugachov was giving me an opportunity to carry out my intention. I decided to take advantage of it and, without stopping to consider my decision, said in answer to Pugachov:

"I was going to the Belogorsky fortress to rescue an orphan who is being ill-treated there."

Pugachov's eyes glittered.

"Which of my men dares to ill-treat an orphan?" he cried. "He may be as clever as you please, but he won't escape my sentence. Tell me, who is the guilty man?"

"Shvabrin," I answered. "He keeps under lock and key the girl whom you saw lying ill at the priest's house, and wants to marry her by force."

"I'll teach Shvabrin!" said Pugachov, menacingly. "I'll show him what it is to take the law into his own hands and to ill-treat people. I will hang him!"

"Allow me to say a word," Khlopusha said, in a hoarse voice. "You were in a hurry to put Shvabrin in command of the fortress and now you are in a hurry to hang him. You have already offended the Cossacks by putting a gentleman over them; do not now frighten the gentry by hanging him at the first accusation."

"One need not pity them nor show them favors!" said the old man with the blue ribbon. "There is no harm in hanging Shvabrin; but it wouldn't be amiss to question this officer thoroughly, too. Why has he come here? If he doesn't recognize you as Czar he need not seek justice from you; and if he does acknowledge you, why has he sat till to-day with your enemies in Orenburg? Won't you let me take him to the office and light a fire under his toes? It seems to me his honor has been sent to us by the Orenburg commanders."

The old villain's logic struck me as rather convincing. A shiver ran down my back when I thought in whose hands I was. Pugachov noticed my confusion.

"Eh, your honor?" he said to me with a wink. "I fancy my field-marshal is talking sense. What do you think?"

Pugachov's mockery gave me back my courage. I calmly answered that I was in his power and that he was free to do what he liked with me.

"Good," said Pugachov, "and now tell me how are things going with you in the town?"

"Thank Heaven, all is well," I answered.

"All is well?" Pugachov repeated, "and people are dying of starvation?" The Pretender was right; but in accordance with my duty I began assuring him that this was an empty rumor and that there were plenty of provisions in Orenburg.

"You see," the old man chimed in, "he is deceiving you to your face. All refugees say with one voice that there is famine and pestilence in Orenburg; people eat carcasses and even that is a treat; and his honor assures you they have plenty of everything. If you want to hang Shvabrin, hang this fellow, too, on the same gallows so as to be fair to both!"

The cursed old man's words seemed to have shaken Pugachov. Fortunately Khlopusha began contradicting his comrade.

"Come, Naumych," he said to him, "you always want to be hanging and murdering. And you are not much of a man to look at—you can hardly keep body and soul together. You have one foot in the grave and yet you are destroying others. Isn't there enough blood on your conscience?"

"You are a fine saint!" Beloborodov retorted. "Why should you have pity?"

"Of course, I, too, have things on my conscience," Khlopusha answered, "and this hand" (he clenched his bony first and, turning up his sleeve, showed a hairy arm) "has been guilty of shedding Christian blood. But I destroyed enemies, not guests; on a high road and in the dark forest and not at home behind the stove; with a club and an axe and not with womanish slander."

The old man turned away and muttered: "Torn nostrils . . ."

"What are you muttering, you old wretch?" Khlopusha shouted. "I'll give you 'torn nostrils'! Wait a bit, your time will come, too; God willing, you, too, will sniff the hangman's pincers. . . . And, meanwhile, take care I don't pull out your scurvy beard!"

"My Generals!" Pugachov said pompously, "that's enough quarreling! It does not matter if all the Orenburg pack wriggle under the same gallows; but it does matter if our dogs are at one another's throats. There, make peace!"

Khlopusha and Beloborodov did not say a word and

looked at each other gloomily. I saw that it was necessary to change the subject of a conversation which might end very badly for me and, turning to Pugachov, I said to him with a cheerful air:

"Oh, I have forgotten to thank you for the horse and the sheepskin. Had it not been for you I could not have found the road and should have been frozen on the way."

My ruse succeeded. Pugachov's good humor was restored.

"One good turn deserves another," he said, with a wink. "And tell me now why are you concerned about the girl whom Shvabrin is ill-treating? Is she your sweetheart by any chance?"

"She is my betrothed!" I answered, seeing the favorable change in the weather and not thinking it necessary to conceal the truth.

"Your betrothed!" Pugachov shouted. "Why didn't you say so before? Why, we'll have you married and make merry at your wedding!"

Then he turned to Beloborodov and said: "Listen, Field-Marshal! His honor and I are old friends, so let us sit down to supper. Morning is wiser than evening; we shall see to-morrow what we are to do with him."

I should have been glad to refuse the honor, but there was nothing for it. Two young girls, daughters of the Cossack to whom the hut belonged, spread a white cloth on the table, brought bread, fish-soup, and several bottles of vodka and beer. Once more I found myself at the same table with Pugachov and his terrible comrades.

The orgy of which I was an involuntary witness lasted far into the night. At last the company were overpowered with drink. Pugachov dozed; his friends got up and made me a sign to leave him. I went with them out of the room. At Khlopusha's orders the

watchman took me into the cottage that served as office; I found Savelyich there and we were locked up together for the night. The old man was so amazed at
all that was happening that he did not ask me a single
question. He lay down in the dark and was a long time
sighing and groaning; at last he snored, and I gave myself up to thoughts which did not give me a wink of
sleep all night.

In the morning Pugachov sent for me. I went to him.
A chaise, drawn by three Tatar horses was standing at
his gate. There was a crowd in the street. I met Pugachov in the entry; he was dressed for the journey in a
fur coat and a Kirghiz cap. His comrades of the day
before surrounded him with an air of servility which
little accorded with all that I had seen the night before. Pugachov greeted me cheerfully and told me to
step into the chaise with him. We took our seats.

"To the Belogorsky fortress!" Pugachov said to the
broad-shouldered Tatar who drove the troika standing.

My heart beat violently. The horses set off, the bell
clanged, the chaise flew along . . .

"Stop! Stop!" a familiar voice called out, and I saw
Savelyich running toward us. Pugachov told the driver to stop.

"My dear Pyotr Andreyich!" Savelyich cried, "don't
abandon me in my old age among these rascals!"

"Ah, you old creature!" Pugachov said to him. "So
God has brought us together again. Well, climb on to
the box!"

"Thank you, sire, thank you, our father!" said Savelyich, climbing up. "May God let you live to be a hundred for your kindness to an old man. I will pray for
you as long as I live and will never mention the hareskin jacket again."

This hareskin jacket might anger Pugachov in earnest at last. Fortunately he had not heard or took no no-

tice of the inopportune remark. The horses set off at a
gallop; the people in the street stopped and bowed.
Pugachov nodded right and left. A minute later we left
the village and flew along the smooth road.

One may well imagine what I was feeling at that
moment. In a few hours I was to see her whom I had
already considered as lost to me. I was picturing the
moment of our meeting. . . . I was also thinking of
the man in whose hands I was and who was mysteriously connected with me through a strange combina-
tion of circumstances. I was recalling the thoughtless
cruelty, the bloodthirsty habits of the would-be rescuer
of my beloved. Pugachov did not know that she was
Captain Mironov's daughter; Shvabrin in his bitterness might tell him; or Pugachov might discover the
truth in other ways. . . . What would become of Marya Ivanovna then? A shiver ran down my back and
my hair stood on end.

Suddenly Pugachov interrupted my reflections with
a question: "What are you thinking of so deeply, your
honor?"

"How can I help thinking," I answered. "I am an
officer and a gentleman; only yesterday I was fighting
against you and today I am driving beside you and the
happiness of my whole life depends upon you."

"Well, are you afraid?" Pugachov asked.

I answered that since he had spared me once, I was
hoping he would do so again and would, indeed, help
me.

"And you are right, upon my soul, you are right!"
Pugachov said. "You saw that my men were looking
askance at you; and the old man again insisted this
morning that you were a spy and ought to be tortured
and hanged; but I did not agree," he added, lowering
his voice so that Savelyich and the Tatar should not
hear him, "remembering your glass of vodka and the

hareskin jacket. You see I am not so bloodthirsty as your people make me out."

I recalled the taking of the Belogorsky fortress but did not think it necessary to contradict him and did not answer.

"What do they say of me in Orenburg?" Pugachov asked, after a silence.

"They say it's not easy to get the better of you. There's no denying it, you've made your presence felt."

The Pretender's face assumed an expression of satisfied vanity.

"Yes!" he said cheerfully, "I am quite a hand at fighting. Do they know at Orenburg about the battle at Yuzeyeva? Forty generals were killed, four armies taken captive. What do you think? would the Prussian king be a match for me?"

The brigand's boasting amused me.

"What do you think yourself?" I asked him; "could you beat Frederick?"

"Why not? I beat your generals and they used to beat him. So far I have been lucky in war. Wait, you'll see even better things when I march on Moscow."

"Are you thinking of doing that?"

Pugachov pondered and said in a low voice:

"God only knows. I am cramped; I cannot do as I like. My men are too independent. They are thieves. I have to keep a sharp look out: at the first defeat they will ransom their necks with my head."

"That's just it!" I said. "Hadn't you better leave them yourself in good time and appeal to the Empress's mercy?"

Pugachov smiled bitterly.

"No," he said; "it is too late for me to repent. There will be no mercy for me. I will go on as I have begun.

Who knows? I may succeed after all! Grishka Otrepyev did reign over Moscow, you know."

"And do you know what his end was? They threw
him out of the window, killed him, burned his body
and fired a cannon with his ashes."

"Listen," Pugachov said, with a kind of wild inspiration, "I will tell you a fairy-tale which in my childhood an old Kalmuck woman told me. The eagle asked the raven one day: 'Tell me, raven-bird, why do you
live in the world for three hundred years and I only for
thirty-three?'—'Because, father-eagle, you drink living
blood,' the raven said, 'and I feed on things that are
dead.' The eagle thought, 'I will try and feed as he
does.' Very well. The eagle and the raven flew along.
They saw the carcass of a horse, came down and perch-
ed on it. The raven plucked and praised the food. The
eagle took a peck or two, then waved his wing and
said: 'No, brother raven, rather than feed on carrion
flesh for three hundred years, I would have one drink
of living blood—and leave the rest to God!' What do
you think of the Kalmuck tale?"

"It is clever," I answered. "But to live by murder and
brigandage is, to my mind, just pecking carrion."

Pugachov looked at me with surprise and made no
answer. We both sank into silence, each absorbed in his
own reflections. The Tatar struck up a doleful song;
Savelyich dozed as he sat, rocking to and fro on the
box. The chaise flew along the smooth winter road.
. . . Suddenly I saw on the steep bank of the Yaïk a
village with a palisade round it and a belfry rising
above it—and in another quarter of an hour we drove
into the Belogorsky fortress.

XII

AN ORPHAN

Our slender young apple-tree
Has no spreading branch nor top to it,
Our tender young bride to be
Has no father nor mother to care for her,
She has no one to see her off,
No one to bestow a blessing on her.

　　　　　　　　A Wedding Song

THE chaise drove up to the Commandant's house.
The people recognized the sound of Pugachov's bell
and ran after us in a crowd. Shvabrin met the Pretender on the steps. He was dressed like a Cossack and
had grown a beard. The traitor helped Pugachov to
step out of the chaise, speaking in servile expressions
of his delight and devotion. He was confused when he
saw me, but soon recovered and gave me his hand,
saying:

"So you, too, are one of us? Time you were!"

I turned away and made no answer.

My heart ached when we came into the familiar
room; the certificate of the late Commandant still
hung on the wall as a sad epitaph of bygone days.
Pugachov sat down on the sofa where Ivan Kuzmich
used to doze, lulled to sleep by his wife's grumbling.
Shvabrin brought him some vodka. Pugachov drank a
glass and said, pointing to me:

"Offer some to his honor, too."

Shvabrin came up to me with the tray, but I turned
away again. He was obviously very uneasy. With his
usual quickness he guessed, of course, that Pugachov
was displeased with him; he was afraid, and looked at

me with distrust. Pugachov asked about the state of the fortress, the news of the enemy's troops and such like things, and suddenly asked him:

"Tell me, brother, who is the girl you are keeping prisoner in your house? Show her to me."

Shvabrin turned white as death.

"Sire," he said in a shaking voice, "Sire, she is not a prisoner. She is ill . . . she is upstairs, in bed."

"Take me to her," the Pretender said, getting up.

It was impossible to refuse him. Shvabrin led Pugachov to Marya Ivanovna's room. I followed them.

Shvabrin stopped on the stairs.

"Sire," he said, "you may require of me whatever you wish, but do not allow a stranger to enter my wife's bedroom."

I shuddered.

"So you are married?" I said to Shvabrin, ready to tear him to pieces.

"Keep quiet!" Pugachov interrupted me. "It is my affair. And don't you try to be clever," he went on, addressing Shvabrin, "or invent excuses; wife or not, I take to her whomsoever I like. Follow me, your honor."

At Marya Ivanovna's door Shvabrin stopped again and said in a breaking voice:

"Sire, I warn you, she has brain fever and has been raving for the last three days."

"Open the door!" said Pugachov.

Shvabrin began searching in his pockets and said he had not brought the key. Pugachov pushed the door with his foot, the lock fell off, the door opened, and we went in.

I looked—and was aghast. Marya Ivanovna, pale and thin, with disheveled hair and dressed like a peasant, was sitting on the floor; a jug of water, covered with a piece of bread, stood before her. When she saw me she started and cried out. What I felt then I cannot describe.

Pugachov looked at Shvabrin and said, with a bitter smile:

"Fine hospital you have here!" Then he went up to Marya Ivanovna and said: "Tell me, my dear, what is your husband punishing you for? What wrong have you done to him?"

"My husband!" she repeated; "he is not my husband. I will never be his wife. I would rather die, and I shall die if I am not saved from him."

Pugachov looked menacingly at Shvabrin.

"And you dared to deceive me!" he said. "Do you know what you deserve, you wretch?"

Shvabrin dropped on his knees. . . . At that moment a feeling of contempt outweighed my hatred and anger. I looked with disgust upon a gentleman groveling at the feet of an escaped convict. Pugachov was softened.

"I will spare you this time," he said to Shvabrin, "but next time you are at fault, this wrong will be remembered against you."

Then he turned to Marya Ivanovna and said kindly: "Come away, my pretty maid. I set you free. I am the Czar!"

Marya Ivanovna glanced at him and understood that her parents' murderer was before her. She buried her face in her hands and fell down senseless. I rushed to her, but at that moment my old friend Palasha very boldly made her way into the room and began attending to her mistress. Pugachov walked out and the three of us went downstairs.

"Well, your honor," Pugachov said, laughing, "we've delivered the fair maiden! What do you think, hadn't we better send for the priest and tell him to marry you to his niece? I'll give her away if you like, and Shvabrin will be best man; we'll make merry and drink, and give the guests no time to think!"

The very thing that I feared happened. Shvabrin was beside himself when he heard Pugachov's suggestion.

"Sire!" he cried in a frenzy. "I am to blame; I have lied to you, but Grinyov, too, is deceiving you. This girl is not the priest's niece; she is the daughter of Captain Mironov who was hanged when the fortress was taken."

Pugachov fixed on me his fiery eye.

"What's this?" he asked, in perplexity.

"Shvabrin is right," I answered firmly.

"You hadn't told me," remarked Pugachov, and his face clouded.

"But consider," I answered him. "How could I have said in your men's presence that Mironov's daughter was living? They would have torn her to pieces. Nothing would have saved her!"

"That's true enough," Pugachov said, laughing. "My drunkards would not have spared the poor girl. The priest's wife did well to deceive them."

"Listen," I said, seeing that he was in a kind mood. "I do not know what to call you and I don't want to know. . . . But God knows I would gladly pay you with my life for what you have done for me. Only don't ask of me what is against my honor and Christian conscience. You are my benefactor. Finish as you have begun; let me go with the poor orphan whither God may lead us. And whatever happens to you and wherever you may be, we shall pray to Him every day of our lives to save your sinful soul."

It seemed that Pugachov's stern heart was touched.

"So be it!" he said. "I don't believe in stopping half

way, be it in vengeance or in mercy. Take your sweet-heart; go with her where you will and God grant you love and concord!"

Then he turned to Shvabrin and told him to give me a pass through all the villages and fortresses subject to his rule.

Shvabrin, utterly overwhelmed, stood like one dumbfounded. Pugachov went to look at the fortress. Shvabrin accompanied him and I remained behind under the pretext of making ready for the journey.

I ran upstairs. The door was locked. I knocked.

"Who is there?" Palasha asked.

I gave my name. Marya Ivanovna's sweet voice came from behind the door:

"Wait a little, Pyotr Andreyich; I am changing my dress. Go to Akulina Pamfilovna's. I shall be there directly."

I obeyed and went to Father Gerasim's house. Both he and his wife ran out to meet me. Savelyich had already given them the news.

"How do you do, Pyotr Andreyich?" the priest's wife said. "God has brought us together again! How are you? We have talked of you every day. Marya Ivanovna has been through a dreadful time without you, poor darling! . . . But tell me, my dear, how did you hit it off with Pugachov? How is it he hasn't made an end of you? It's something to the villain's credit!"

"That will do, my dear," Father Gerasim interrupted her. "Don't blurt out all you know. There is no salvation in speaking overmuch. Please come in, Pyotr Andreyich! You are very welcome. We haven't seen you for months!"

The priest's wife offered me what food there was and talked incessantly as she did so. She told me how Shvabrin had forced them to give up Marya Ivanovna; how Marya Ivanovna wept and did not want to part from them; how Marya Ivanovna always kept in touch with her through Palasha (a spirited girl who made the sergeant himself dance to her tune); how she had advised Marya Ivanovna to write a letter to me, and so on. I, in my turn, briefly told her my story. The priest and his wife crossed themselves when they heard that Pugachov knew of their deception.

"The power of the Holy Cross be with us!" said Akulina Pamfilovna. "May the Lord let the storm go by! Fancy Alexey Ivanich betraying us! He is a fine one!"

At that moment the door opened and Marya Ivanovna came in, a smile on her pale face. She had laid aside peasant clothes and was dressed as before, simply and prettily.

I clasped her hand and for some moments could not utter a word. Our hearts were too full for speech. Our hosts felt that we had no thoughts to spare for them and left us. We were alone. All was forgotten. We talked and talked. Marya Ivanovna told me all that had happened to her after the fortress was taken; she described to me the horror of her position, and all that she had had to endure at the hands of her vile pursuer. We recalled the bygone happy days. . . . We were both weeping. . . . At last I put my plans before her. It was impossible for her to stay in a fortress subject to Pugachov and ruled by Shvabrin. It was no use thinking of Orenburg where the inhabitants were suffering all the horrors of the siege. She had no one belonging to her in the world. I offered her to go to my parents' estate. She hesitated at first; she knew my father's animosity toward her and was afraid. I reassured her. I knew that my father would be happy and consider it his duty to welcome the daughter of a veteran who had died for his country.

"Darling Marya Ivanovna," I said to her, at last. "I

look upon you as my wife. Miraculous circumstances
have united us for ever; nothing in the world can part
us."

Marya Ivanovna listened to me without coyness or
feigned reluctance. She felt that her fate was united to
mine. But she repeated that she would only marry me
with my parents' consent. I did not contradict her
about it. We kissed each other sincerely and ardently
—and all was settled between us.

An hour later, Maximych brought me a pass signed
with Pugachov's hieroglyphics and said that he wanted
to see me. I found him ready for the journey. I cannot
express what I felt on parting from this terrible man, a
monster of evil to all but me. Why not confess the
truth? At that moment I was drawn to him by warm
sympathy. I longed to tear him away from the criminals whose leader he was and to save his head before it
was too late. Shvabrin and the people who crowded
round us prevented me from saying all that was in my
heart.

We parted friends. Seeing Akulina Pamfilovna in
the crowd Pugachov shook his finger at her and
winked significantly; then he stepped into the chaise,
told the driver to go to Berda, and as the horses moved
he put out his head from the chaise once more and
shouted to me:

"Good-bye, your honor! We may yet meet again."

We did meet again—but under what circumstances!

Pugachov drove away. I gazed for some time at the
white steppe where his troika was galloping. The
crowd dispersed. Shvabrin disappeared. I returned to
the priest's house. Everything was ready for our departure. I did not want to delay any longer. All our
belongings were packed in the old Commandant's carriage. The drivers harnessed the horses in a trice.
Marya Ivanovna went to say good-bye to the graves of

her parents, who were buried behind the church. I wanted to accompany her, but she asked me to let her go alone. She returned in a few minutes, silently weeping quiet tears. The carriage was brought before the house. Father Gerasim and his wife came out on to the steps. The three of us—Marya Ivanovna, Palasha, and I—sat inside the carriage and Savelyich climbed on the box.

"Good-bye, Marya Ivanovna, my darling! Good-bye, Pyotr Andreyich, our bright falcon!" kind Akulina Pamfilovna said to us. "A happy journey to you, and God grant you happiness!"

We set off. I saw Shvabrin standing at the window of the Commandant's house. His face was expressive of gloomy malice. I did not want to triumph over a defeated enemy and turned my eyes in another direction. At last we drove out of the fortress gates, and left the Belogorsky fortress for ever.

XIII

THE ARREST

"Do not be angry, sir; my duty bids me
To send you off to gaol this very day."
By all means, I am ready; but I trust
You will first allow me to have my say.

Knyazhnin

UNITED so unexpectedly to the sweet girl about whom I had been terribly anxious only that morning, I could not believe my senses and fancied that all that had happened to me was an empty dream. Marya Ivanovna gazed thoughtfully now at me and now at the road: she did not seem to have come to herself as yet. We were silent. Our hearts were much too tired. We did not notice how in a couple of hours we found ourselves at the neighboring fortress which also was in Pugachov's hands. We changed horses there. The quickness with which they were harnessed and the hurried servility of the bearded Cossack, promoted by Pugachov to the post of Commandant, proved that, owing to our driver's talkativeness, I was being taken for the Czar's favorite.

We continued our journey. Dusk was falling. We drew near a small town occupied, according to the bearded Commandant, by a strong detachment of Pugachov's supporters on their way to join him. We were stopped by the sentries. To the question, "Who goes there?" the driver answered, in a loud voice, "The Czar's friend with his lady." Suddenly a crowd of Hussars surrounded us, swearing fearfully.

"Come out, you devil's friend!" a sergeant, with a big mustache said to me. "You will get it hot presently, and that girl of yours, too."

I stepped out of the chaise and demanded to be taken to the commanding officer. Seeing my uniform, the soldiers stopped swearing. The sergeant led me to the major. Savelyich went with me, muttering to himself: "There's a fine Czar's friend for you! Out of the frying-pan into the fire. . . . Good Lord, what will the end of it be?" The chaise followed us at a walking pace. After five minutes' walk we came to a brilliantly lighted house. The sergeant left me with the sentries and went to announce me. He returned at once, saying the major had not time to see me, but that he ordered that I should be taken to jail and my lady brought to him.

"What's the meaning of this?" I cried, in a rage. "Has he gone off his head?"

"I cannot tell, your honor," the sergeant answered.

"Only his honor said that your honor was to be taken to jail and her honor brought to his honor."

I rushed up the steps. The sentries made no attempt to detain me and I ran straight into the room where six officers of the Hussars were playing cards. The major was dealing. Imagine my surprise when I recognized him for Ivan Ivanovich Zurin who had won from me at billiards at the Simbirsk inn!

"Is it possible?" I cried. "Ivan Ivanych! Is that you?"

"Why, Pyotr Andreyich! What wind brings you? Where do you come from? Glad to see you, brother. Won't you join the game?"

"Thanks. Better tell them to give me a lodging."

"What lodging? Stay with me."

"I cannot; I am not alone."

"Well, bring your comrade along."

"It's not a comrade. I am with a lady."

"A lady! Where did you pick her up? Oho, brother!" At these words, Zurin whistled so expressively that everyone laughed. I was utterly confused.

"Well," Zurin went on, "so be it! You shall have a lodging, but it's a pity. . . . We could have had a gay time, as in the old days. . . . Hey, boy! Why don't they bring along Pugachov's sweetheart? Doesn't she want to come? Tell her she need not fear, the gentleman is very kind and will do her no harm—and give her a good kick to hurry her up."

"What are you talking about?" I said to Zurin. "Pugachov's sweetheart? It is the late Captain Mironov's daughter. I have rescued her and am now seeing her off to my father's estate where I shall leave her."

"What! So it was you they have just announced? Upon my word! What does it all mean?"

"I will tell you afterward. And now for Heaven's sake reassure the poor girl whom your Hussars have frightened."

Zurin made arrangements at once. He came out into the street to apologize to Marya Ivanovna for the misunderstanding and told the sergeant to give her the best lodging in the town. I was to spend the night with him.

We had supper and when we were left alone I told him my adventures. Zurin listened with great attention. When I had finished, he shook his head and said:

"That's all very good, brother; one thing only is not good: why the devil do you want to be married? I am an honest officer; I would not deceive you; believe me, marriage is a delusion. You don't want to be bothered with a wife and be nursing babies! Throw it up! Do as I tell you: get rid of the Captain's daughter. The road to Simbirsk is safe now; I have cleared it. Send her tomorrow to your parents by herself and you stay in my detachment. There is no need for you to return to Orenburg. If you fall into the rebels' hands once more you may not escape this time. And so the love-foolishness will pass of itself and all will be well."

I did not altogether agree with him, but I felt that I was in duty bound to remain with the army. I decided to follow Zurin's advice and send Marya Ivanovna to the country while I remained in his detachment.

Savelyich came to undress me; I told him that he must be ready next day to continue the journey with Marya Ivanovna. He did not want to at first.

"What are you thinking of, sir? How can I leave you? Who will look after you? What will your parents say?"

Knowing Savelyich's obstinacy I decided to win him by affection and sincerity.

"Arhip Savelyich, my dear!" I said to him. "Don't refuse. You will be doing me a great kindness. I shall not need a servant, but I shall have no peace if Marya Ivanovna goes on her journey without you. In serving her you will be serving me, because I am determined to marry her as soon as circumstances allow."

Savelyich clasped his hands [1] with an air of indescribable amazement.

"To marry!" he replied. "The child thinks of marrying! But what will your father say; what will your mother think?"

"They will agree; I am sure they will agree when they know Marya Ivanovna," I answered. "I rely on you, too. My father and mother trust you; you will intercede for us, won't you?"

Savelyich was touched.

"Ah, Pyotr Andreyich, dear," he answered, "though it is much too early for you to think of marrying, Marya Ivanovna is such a good young lady that it would be a sin to miss the opportunity. Have it your own way! I shall go with her, angel that she is, and will tell your parents faithfully that such a bride does not need a dowry."

I thanked Savelyich and went to bed in the same room with Zurin. My mind was in a turmoil and I talked and talked. At first Zurin answered me readily, but gradually his words became few and disconnected; at last in answer to a question he gave a snore with a whistle in it. I stopped talking and soon followed his example.

Next morning I went to Marya Ivanovna and told her of my plans. She recognized their reasonableness and agreed with me at once. Zurin's detachment was to leave the town that same day. There was no time to be lost. I said good-bye to Marya Ivanovna there and then, entrusting her to Savelyich and giving her a letter to my parents. Marya Ivanovna wept.

"Good-bye, Pyotr Andreyich," she said, in a low

---

[1] See footnote on p. 608.

voice. "God only knows whether we shall meet again; but I will not forget you as long as I live; till death you alone shall remain in my heart."

I could not answer her. Other people were there. I did not want to abandon myself in their presence to the feelings that agitated me. At last she drove away. I returned to Zurin, sad and silent. He wanted to cheer me; I sought distraction; we spent the day in riotous gaiety and set out on the march in the evening.

It was the end of February. The winter, which had made military operations difficult, was coming to an end, and our generals were preparing for concerted action. Pugachov was still besieging Orenburg. Meanwhile the army detachments around him were joining forces and approaching the brigands' nest from all sides. Rebellious villages were restored to order at the sight of the soldiers, brigand bands dispersed on our approach, and everything indicated a speedy and successful end of the war.

Soon Prince Golitzyn defeated Pugachov at the Tatishcheva fortress, scattered his hordes, delivered Orenburg and dealt, it seemed, the last and decisive blow to the rebellion. Zurin was at that time sent against a gang of rebellious Bashkirs, who had dispersed before we caught sight of them. Spring found us in a Tatar village. Rivers were in flood and roads impassable. We could do nothing, but comforted ourselves with the thought that the petty and tedious war with brigands and savages would soon be over.

Pugachov was not caught, however. He appeared at the Siberian foundries, collected there fresh bands of followers and began his evil work once more. Again rumors of his success spread abroad. We heard of the fall of the Siberian fortresses. Soon afterward, the army leaders, who slumbered carefree in the hope that the contemptible rebel was powerless, were alarmed by the news of his taking Kazan and advancing toward Moscow. Zurin received an order to cross the Volga.

I will not describe our campaign and the end of the war. I shall say briefly that there was extreme misery. There was no lawful authority anywhere. The land-owners were hiding in the forests. Bands of brigands were ransacking the country. The chiefs of separate de-tachments arbitrarily meted out punishments and granted pardons; the vast region where the conflagra-tion had raged was in a terrible state. . . . God save us from seeing a Russian revolt, senseless and merciless!

Pugachov was in retreat, pursued by Ivan Ivanovich Michelson. Soon after we learned that he was utterly defeated. At last Zurin heard that he had been captured and at the same time received an order to halt. The war was over! I could go to my parents at last! The thought of embracing them and of seeing Marya Ivanovna, of whom I had had no news, delighted me. I danced with joy like a child. Zurin laughed and said, shrugging his shoulders, "No, you'll come to a bad end! You will be married and done for!"

And yet a strange feeling poisoned my joy: I could not help being troubled at the thought of the villain smeared with the blood of so many innocent victims and now awaiting his punishment. "Why didn't he fall on a bayonet? or get hit with a cannon-ball?" I thought with vexation. "He could not have done any-thing better." What will you have? I could not think of Pugachov without remembering how he had spared me at one of the awful moments of my life and saved my betrothed from the vile Shvabrin's hands.

Zurin gave me leave of absence. In a few days I was to be once more with my family and see my Marya Ivanovna. Suddenly an unexpected storm burst upon me.

On the day of my departure, at the very minute

when I was to go, Zurin came into my room with a paper in his hand, looking very much troubled. My heart sank. I was frightened without knowing why. He sent out my orderly and said he had something to tell me.

"What is it?" I asked anxiously.

"Something rather unpleasant," he answered, giving me the paper. "Read what I have just received."

I began reading it: it was a secret order to all commanding officers to arrest me wherever they might find me and to send me at once under escort to Kazan, to the Commission of Inquiry into the Pugachov rising.

The paper almost dropped out of my hands.

"There is nothing for it," Zurin said; "my duty is to obey the order. Probably the news of your friendly journeys with Pugachov has reached the authorities. I hope it will not have any consequences and that you will clear yourself before the Committee. Go, and don't be down-hearted."

My conscience was clear; I was not afraid of the trial, but the thought of putting off, perhaps for several months the sweet moment of reunion, terrified me. The carriage was ready. Zurin bade me a friendly good-bye. I stepped into the carriage. Two Hussars, with bare swords, sat down beside me and we drove along the high road.

XIV

THE TRIAL

Popular rumor is like a sea-wave.

A Proverb

I WAS certain it was all due to my leaving Orenburg without permission. I could easily justify myself: sallying out against the enemy had never been prohibited and was, indeed, encouraged in every way. I might be accused of too great rashness, but not of disobedience. My friendly relations with Pugachov, however, could be proved by a number of witnesses and must have seemed highly suspicious, to say the least of it. Throughout the journey I kept thinking of the questions I might be asked and pondering my answers; I decided to tell the plain truth at the trial, believing that this was the simplest and, at the same time, the most certain way of justifying myself.

I arrived at Kazan; it had been devastated and burnt down. Instead of houses there were heaps of cinders in the streets and remnants of charred walls without roofs or windows. Such was the trail left by Pugachov! I was brought to the fortress that had remained intact in the midst of the burnt city. The Hussars passed me on to the officer in charge. He called for the blacksmith. Shackles were put on my feet and soldered together. Then I was taken to the prison and left alone in the dark and narrow cell with bare walls and a window with iron bars.

Such a beginning boded nothing good. I did not, however, lose either hope or courage. I had recourse to the comfort of all the sorrowful and, having tasted for the first time the sweetness of prayer poured out from a pure but bleeding heart, dropped calmly asleep without caring what would happen to me.

The next morning the warder woke me up, saying I was wanted by the Commission. Two soldiers took me across the yard to the Commandant's house; they stopped in the entry and let me go into the inner room by myself.

I walked into a rather large room. Two men were sitting at a table covered with papers: an elderly general who looked cold and forbidding and a young captain of the Guards, a good-looking man of about twenty-eight, with a pleasant and easy manner. A secretary, with a pen behind his ear, sat at a separate table, bending over the paper in readiness to write down my answers. The examination began. I was asked my name and rank. The General asked whether I was the son of Andrey Petrovich Grinyov. When I said I was he remarked severely:

"It is a pity that so estimable a man has such an unworthy son!"

I calmly answered that whatever the accusation against me might be, I hoped to clear myself by candidly telling the truth. The General did not like my confidence.

"You are sharp, brother," he said to me, frowning; "but we have seen cleverer ones than you!"

Then the young man asked me:

"On what occasion and at what time did you enter Pugachov's service, and on what commissions did he employ you?"

I answered, with indignation, that as an officer and a gentleman I could not possibly have entered Pugachov's service or have carried out any commissions of his.

"How was it, then," my questioner continued, "that an officer and a gentleman was alone spared by the

Pretender while all his comrades were villainously murdered? How was it that this same officer and gentleman feasted with the rebels, as their friend, and accepted presents from the villain—a sheepskin coat, a horse, and fifty kopecks in money? How had such a strange friendship arisen and what could it be based upon except treason or, at any rate, upon base and vile cowardice?"

I was deeply offended by the officer's words and warmly began my defence. I told them how I had first met Pugachov in the steppe in the snowstorm, and how he recognized and spared me at the taking of the Belogorsky fortress. I admitted that I had not scrupled to accept from the Pretender the horse and the sheepskin coat, but said that I had defended the Belogorsky fortress against him to the last extremity. At last I referred them to my General who could testify to my zealous service during the perilous Orenburg siege.

The stern old man took an unsealed letter from the table and began reading it aloud:

"With regard to Your Excellency's inquiry concerning Ensign Grinyov, said to be involved in the present insurrection and to have had relations with the villain, contrary to the military law and to our oath of allegiance, I have the honor to report as follows: The said Ensign Grinyov served at Orenburg from the beginning of October 1773 to 24 February 1774, upon which date he left the city and returned no more to serve under my command. I have heard from refugees that he had been in Pugachov's camp and went with him to the Belogorsky fortress, where he had served before; as to his conduct, I can . . ."

At this point he interrupted his reading and said to me sternly: "What can you say for yourself now?"

I wanted to go on as I had begun and to explain my connection with Marya Ivanovna as candidly as all the rest, but I suddenly felt an overwhelming repulsion. It occurred to me that if I mentioned her, she would be summoned by the Commission; and I was so overcome at the awful thought of connecting her name with the vile slanders of the villains, and of her being confronted with them, that I became confused and hesitated.

My judges, who seemed to have been listening to me with favor, were once more prejudiced against me by my confusion. The officer of the Guards asked that I should be faced with the chief informer. The General gave word that *yesterday's villain* should be brought in. I turned to the door with interest, waiting for the appearance of my accuser. A few minutes later there was a rattle of chains, the door opened, and Shvabrin walked in. I was surprised at the change in him. He was terribly pale and thin. His hair that had a short time ago been black as pitch was now white; his long beard was unkempt. He repeated his accusations in a weak, but confident voice. According to him I had been sent by Pugachov to Orenburg as a spy; under the pretext of sallies, I had come out every day to give him written news of all that was happening in the town; at last I had openly joined the Pretender, had driven with him from fortress to fortress, doing my utmost to ruin my fellow-traitors so as to occupy their posts, and had taken presents from the Pretender. I heard him out in silence and was pleased with one thing only: Marya Ivanovna's name had not been uttered by the base villain, either because his vanity suffered at the thought of one who had scorned him, or because there lingered in his heart a spark of the same feeling which made me keep silent about her. In any case, the name of the Belogorsky Commandant's daughter was not mentioned before the Commission. I was more determined than ever not to bring it up, and when the judges asked me how I could disprove Shvabrin's accusations, I answered that I adhered to my original explanation and had nothing more to say in my defence. The General gave word for us to be led away. We went out together. I calmly looked at Shvabrin, but did not say a word to him. He gave a malignant smile and, lifting his chains, quickened his pace and left me behind. I was taken back to prison and not called for examination any more.

I have not witnessed the subsequent events of which I must inform the reader; but I had them told me so often that the least details are engraved on my memory and I feel as though I had been invisibly present.

Marya Ivanovna had been received by my parents with that sincere cordiality which distinguished people in former days. They held it to be a blessing that they had been afforded the opportunity of sheltering and comforting the poor orphan. They soon became truly attached to her, for it was impossible to know her and not to love her. My love for her no longer seemed to my father a mere whim, and my mother had but one wish—that her Petrusha should marry that dear creature, the Captain's daughter.

The news of my arrest was a shock to my family. Marya Ivanovna had told my parents of my strange acquaintance with Pugachov so simply that, so far from being troubled about it, they often laughed at it with whole-hearted amusement. My father refused to believe that I could have been implicated in vile rebellion the aim of which was to overthrow the throne and exterminate the gentry. He closely questioned Savelyich. The old man did not conceal the fact that I had been to see Pugachov and that the villain had been kind to me; but he swore that he had not heard of any treason. My parents were reassured and waited impatiently for favorable news. Marya Ivanovna was very much alarmed but said nothing, for she was extremely modest and prudent.

Several weeks passed. . . . Suddenly my father received a letter from our relative in Petersburg, Prince B. The Prince wrote about me. After beginning in the usual way he went on to say that, unfortunately, the suspicions about my complicity in the rebels' designs proved to be only too true and that I should have been put to death as an example to others had not the Empress, in consideration of my father's merits and advanced age, decided to spare the criminal son and commuted the shameful death-penalty to a mere exile for life to a remote part of Siberia.

This unexpected blow very nearly killed my father. He lost his habitual self-control, and his grief, usually silent, found expression in bitter complaints.

"What!" he repeated, beside himself. "My son is an accomplice of Pugachov's! Merciful heavens, what have I lived to see! The Empress reprieves him! Does that make it any better for me? It's not the death-penalty that is terrible. My great-grandfather died on the scaffold for what was to him a matter of conscience; my father suffered, together with Volynsky and Khrushchov.[1] But for a gentleman to betray his oath of allegiance and join brigands, murderers and runaway serfs! Shame and disgrace to our name!"

Terrified by his despair, my mother did not dare to weep in his presence and tried to cheer him by talking of the uncertainty of rumor and the small faith to be attached to people's opinions. My father was inconsolable.

[1] Leaders of the Russian party against Bühren, the German favorite of the Empress Anna. TRANSLATOR'S NOTE

Marya Ivanovna suffered most. She was certain that I could have cleared myself if I had chosen to do so, and, guessing the truth, considered herself the cause of my misfortune. She concealed her tears and sorrow from everyone, but was continually thinking of the means to save me.

One evening my father was sitting on the sofa turning over the leaves of the *Court Calendar,* but his thoughts were far away and the reading did not have its usual effect upon him. He was whistling an old march. My mother was knitting a woolen coat in silence, and now and again a tear dropped on her work. Suddenly Marya Ivanovna, who sat by her doing needlework, said that it was necessary for her to go to Petersburg, and asked for the means of traveling there. My mother was very much grieved.

"What do you want in Petersburg?" she said. "Can it be that you, too, want to leave us, Marya Ivanovna?"

Marya Ivanovna answered that her whole future depended upon this journey and that she was going to seek the help and protection of influential people, as the daughter of a man who had suffered for his loyalty.

My father bent his head: every word that reminded him of his son's alleged crime pained him and seemed to him a bitter reproach.

"Go, my dear," he said to her, with a sigh. "We don't want to stand in the way of your happiness. God grant you may have a good man for a husband and not a disgraced traitor."

He got up and walked out of the room.

Left alone with my mother, Marya Ivanovna partly explained her plan to her. My mother embraced her with tears and prayed for the success of her undertaking. Marya Ivanovna was made ready for the journey, and a few days later she set off with the faithful

Palasha and the faithful Savelyich, who in his enforced parting from me comforted himself with the thought that, at least, he was serving my betrothed.

Marya Ivanovna safely arrived at Sofia and, hearing that the Court was at Czarkoe Selo, decided to stop there. At the posting-station, a tiny recess behind the partition was assigned to her. The station-master's wife immediately got into conversation with her, said that she was the niece of the man who tended the stoves at the Palace, and initiated her into the mysteries of Court life. She told her at what time the Empress woke up in the morning, took coffee, went for walks; what courtiers were with her at the time; what she had said at dinner the day before; whom she had received in the evening. In short, Anna Vlasyevna's conversation was as good as several pages of historical memoirs and would have been precious for posterity. Marya Ivanovna listened to her attentively. They went into the gardens. Anna Vlasyevna told the history of every avenue and every bridge, and they returned to the station after a long walk, much pleased with each other.

Marya Ivanovna woke up early the next morning, dressed, and slipped out into the gardens. It was a beautiful morning; the sun was lighting the tops of the lime-trees that had already turned yellow under the fresh breath of autumn. The broad lake, without a ripple on it, glittered in the sunlight. The stately swans, just awake, came sailing out from under the bushes that covered the banks. Marya Ivanovna walked along a beautiful meadow where a monument had just been put up in honor of Count Rumyantzev's recent victories. Suddenly a little white dog of English breed ran toward her, barking. Marya Ivanovna was frightened and stood still. At that moment she heard a woman's pleasant voice.

"Don't be afraid, he won't bite."

And Marya Ivanovna saw a lady sitting on a bench opposite the monument. Marya Ivanovna sat down at the other end of the bench. The lady was looking at her attentively; Marya Ivanovna, in her turn, cast several sidelong glances at her and succeeded in examining her from head to foot. She was wearing a white morning dress, a night-cap, and a Russian jacket.[1] She seemed to be about forty. Her plump and rosy face wore an expression of calm and dignity, her blue eyes and slight smile had an indescribable charm. The lady was the first to break the silence.

"I expect you are a stranger here?" she asked.

"Yes, madam; I came from the country only yesterday."

"Have you come with your relatives?"

"No, madam; I have come alone."

"Alone! But you are so young. . . ."

"I have neither father nor mother."

"You are here on business, of course?"

"Yes, madam. I have come to present a petition to the Empress."

"You are an orphan; I suppose you are complaining of some wrong or injustice?"

"No, madam. I have come to ask for mercy, not justice."

"Allow me to ask, What is your name?"

"I am Captain Mironov's daughter."

"Captain Mironov's! The man who was Commandant in one of the Orenburg fortresses?"

"Yes, madam."

The lady was evidently touched.

"Excuse me," she said, still more kindly, "for interfering in your affairs, but I go to Court sometimes; tell me what your petition is and perhaps I may be able to help you."

[1] See footnote, p. 621.

Marya Ivanovna got up and respectfully thanked her.

Everything in the unknown lady instinctively attracted her and inspired her with confidence. Marya Ivanovna took a folded paper out of her pocket and gave it to the lady who began reading it to herself.

At first she read with an attentive and kindly air, but suddenly her expression changed, and Marya Ivanovna, who was watching her every movement, was frightened at the stern look on her face, so calm and pleasant a moment before.

"You are interceding for Grinyov?" the lady said, coldly. "The Empress cannot forgive him. He joined the Pretender not from ignorance and credulity, but as a dangerous and immoral scoundrel."

"Oh, it isn't true!" Marya Ivanovna cried.

"How, it isn't true?" the lady repeated, flushing crimson.

"It isn't true; I swear to God it isn't! I know all about it; I will tell you everything. It was solely for my sake that he went through it all. And if he hasn't cleared himself before the judges, it was only because he did not want to implicate me."

And she told, with great warmth, all that is already known to the reader.

The lady listened to her attentively.

"Where have you put up?" she asked, and hearing that it was at Anna Vlasyevna's, said, with a smile: "Ah, I know. Good-bye, do not tell anyone of our meeting. I hope you will not have long to wait for an answer to your letter."

With these words, she rose and went into a covered alley and Marya Ivanovna, full of joyous hope, returned to Anna Vlasyevna's.

Her landlady chid her for her early walk which, she said, was not good for a young girl's health, as it was autumn. She brought the samovar and just began, over a cup of tea, her endless stories about the Court, when suddenly a Court carriage stopped at the door and a footman from the Palace came into the room, saying that the Empress invited Miss Mironov to her presence.

Anna Vlasyevna was surprised and flurried.

"Dear me!" she cried. "The Empress sends for you to come to the Palace! How has she heard of you? And how are you going to appear before the Empress, my dear? I expect you know nothing about Court manners. . . . Hadn't I better go with you? I could warn you about some things, at any rate. And how can you go in your traveling dress? Hadn't we better send to the midwife for her yellow gown?"

The footman announced that it was the Empress's pleasure that Marya Ivanovna should come alone and as she was. There was nothing else for it; Marya Ivanovna stepped into the carriage and drove to the Palace accompanied by Anna Vlasyevna's admonitions and blessings.

Marya Ivanovna felt that our fate was going to be decided; her heart was throbbing. A few minutes later the carriage stopped at the Palace. Marya Ivanovna walked up the stairs, trembling. The doors were flung wide open before her. She walked through a number of deserted, luxuriously furnished rooms; the footman was pointing out the way. At last, coming to a closed door, he said he would go in and announce her, and left her alone.

The thought of seeing the Empress face to face so terrified her that she could hardly keep on her feet. In another minute the door opened and she walked into the Empress's dressing-room.

The Empress was seated in front of her dressing-table. Several courtiers were standing round her, but they respectfully made way for Marya Ivanovna. The Empress turned to her kindly and Marya Ivanovna recognized her as the lady to whom she had been talking so freely not many minutes before. The Empress called her to her side and said, with a smile:

"I am glad that I have been able to keep my promise to you and to grant your request. Your case is settled. I am convinced that your betrothed is innocent. Here is a letter which please take yourself to your future father-in-law."

Marya Ivanovna took the letter with a trembling hand and fell, weeping, at the feet of the Empress, who lifted her up, kissed her and engaged her in conversation.

"I know you are not rich," she said, "but I am in debt to Captain Mironov's daughter. Do not worry about the future. I will provide for you."

After saying many kind things to the poor orphan, the Empress dismissed her. Marya Ivanovna was driven back in the same Court carriage. Anna Vlasyevna, who had been eagerly awaiting her return, bombarded her with questions, to which Marya Ivanovna answered rather vaguely. Anna Vlasyevna was disappointed at her remembering so little, but ascribed it to provincial shyness and generously excused her. Marya Ivanovna went back to the country that same day, without troubling to have a look at Petersburg. . . .

.   .   .   .   .

The memoirs of Pyotr Andreyich Grinyov end at this point. It is known from the family tradition that he was released from confinement at the end of 1774, at the express order of the Empress; that he was present at the execution of Pugachov, who recognized him in the crowd and nodded to him a minute before his lifeless, bleeding head was held up before the people.

Soon after, Pyotr Andreyich married Marya Ivanovna. Their descendants are flourishing in the province of Simbirsk. Thirty miles from N. there is an estate belonging to ten owners. In one of the lodges a letter written by Catherine II may be seen in a frame under glass. It is addressed to Pyotr Andreyich's father; it affirms the innocence of his son and praises the heart and intelligence of Captain Mironov's daughter.

Pyotr Andreyich Grinyov's memoirs have been given to us by one of his grandchildren who had heard that we were engaged upon a work dealing with the period described by his grandfather. With the relatives' consent, we have decided to publish it separately, prefixing a suitable epigraph to each chapter and taking the liberty to change some of the proper names.

THE EDITOR.

October 19, 1836.

[1836]

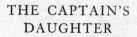

THE CAPTAIN'S DAUGHTER

OMITTED CHAPTER [1]

WE WERE approaching the banks of the Volga. Our regiment entered the village of N. and halted to spend the night there. The village headman told me that all the villages on the other side had rebelled, and that Pugachov's bands were prowling about everywhere. I was very much alarmed at this news. We were to cross the river the following morning.

Impatience possessed me and I could not rest. My father's estate was on the other side of the river, some twenty miles away. I asked if anyone would row me across. All the peasants were fishermen; there were plenty of boats. I came to Zurin and told him of my intention.

"Take care," he said, "it is dangerous for you to go alone. Wait for the morning. We will be the first to cross and will pay a visit to your parents with fifty Hussars in case of emergency."

I insisted on going. The boat was ready. I stepped into it with two boatmen. They pushed off and plied their oars.

The sky was clear. The moon was shining brightly. The air was still. The Volga flowed calmly and evenly. Swaying rhythmically, the boat glided over the dark

[1] This early variant of the latter part of Chapter XIII is offered here because of its intrinsic interest. The names of the characters have here been given as in the final version.

EDITOR'S NOTE

waves. Half an hour passed. I sank into dreaming. I thought of the calm of nature and the horrors of civil war; of love, and so on. We reached the middle of the river. . . . Suddenly the boatmen began whispering together.

"What is it?" I asked, coming to myself.

"Heaven only knows; we can't tell," the boatmen answered, looking into the distance.

I looked in the same direction and saw in the dark something floating down the river. The mysterious object was approaching us. I told the oarsmen to stop and wait.

The moon hid behind a cloud. The floating phantom seemed darker still. It was quite close to me and yet I could not distinguish it.

"Whatever can it be?" the boatmen said. "It isn't a sail nor a mast."

Suddenly the moon came out from behind the cloud and lighted a terrible sight. A gallows fixed to a raft was floating toward us. Three corpses were swinging on the cross-bar. A morbid curiosity possessed me. I wanted to look into the hanged men's faces. I told the oarsmen to hold the raft with a boat-hook, and my boat knocked against the floating gallows. I jumped out and found myself between the terrible posts. The full moon lighted the disfigured faces of the unfortunate creatures. . . . One of them was an old Chuvash, another a Russian peasant boy of about twenty, strong and healthy. I was shocked when I looked at the third and could not refrain from crying out: it was our servant Vanka—poor Vanka, who, in his foolishness, went over to Pugachov. A black board was nailed over the gallows and had written on it in white letters: "Thieves and rebels." The oarsmen waited for me unconcerned, holding the raft with the hook. I stepped into the boat. The raft floated down the river. The gallows showed black in the dim night long after we passed it. At last it disappeared and my boat landed at the high and steep bank.

I paid the oarsmen handsomely. One of them took me to the headman of the village by the landing-stage. We went into the hut together. When the headman heard that I was asking for horses he spoke to me rather rudely, but my guide whispered something to him and his sternness immediately gave way to hurried obsequiousness. The troika was ready in a minute. I stepped into the carriage and told the driver to take me to our estate.

We galloped along the high road past the sleeping villages. The only thing I feared was being stopped on the way. My night meeting on the Volga proved the presence of rebels in the district, but it also proved the strong counter-action on the part of the authorities. To meet all emergencies I had in my pocket the pass given me by Pugachov and Colonel Zurin's order. But I did not meet anyone, and, toward morning, I saw the river and the pine copse behind which lay our village. The driver whipped up the horses and in another quarter of an hour I drove into it. Our house stood at the other end. The horses were going at full speed. Suddenly in the middle of the village street the driver began pulling up.

"What is it?" I asked impatiently.

"A barrier, sir," the driver answered, with difficulty bringing the fuming horses to a standstill.

Indeed, I saw a barrier fixed across the road and a watchman with a club. The man came up to me and, taking off his hat, asked for my passport.

"What does this mean?" I asked him. "Why is this barrier here? Whom are you guarding?"

"Why, sir, we are in rebellion," he answered, scratching himself.

"And where are your masters?" I asked, with a sinking heart.

"Where are our masters?" the peasant repeated. "Master and mistress are in the granary."

"In the granary?"

"Why, Andryushka, the headman,[1] put them in stocks, you see, and wants to take them to our Father Czar."

"Good Heaven! Lift the bar, you blockhead! What are you gaping at?"

The watchman did not move. I jumped out of the carriage, gave him a box on the ear, I am sorry to say, and lifted the bar myself.

The peasant looked at me in stupid perplexity. I took my seat in the carriage once more and told the driver to drive to the house as fast as he could. Two peasants, armed with clubs, were standing by the locked doors of the granary. The carriage drew up just in front of them. I jumped out and rushed at them.

"Open the doors!" I said to them.

I must have looked formidable, for they threw down their clubs and ran away. I tried to knock the lock off the door or to pick it, but the doors were of oak and the huge lock was unbreakable. At that moment a young peasant came out of the servants' quarters and haughtily asked me how I dared to make a disturbance.

"Where is Andryushka, the headman?" I shouted to him. "Call him to me."

"I am Andrey Afanasyevich and not Andryushka," he answered proudly, with his arms akimbo. "What do you want?"

By way of an answer, I seized him by the collar, and dragging him to the granary doors told him to open them. He did not comply at once; but the "fatherly"

---

[1] "Headman," when applied to Andryushka, stands for *zemski*, an official, appointed by Pugachov.   EDITOR'S NOTE

chastisement had due effect upon him. He pulled out
the key and unlocked the granary. I rushed over the
threshold and saw in a dark corner dimly lighted by a
narrow skylight my father and mother. Their hands
were tied and their feet were in stocks. I flew to embrace them and could not utter a word. They both
looked at me with amazement: three years of military
life had so altered me that they could not recognize me.

Suddenly I heard the sweet voice I knew: "Pyotr
Andreyich! It's you?"

I turned round and saw Marya Ivanovna in another
corner, also bound hand and foot. I was dumbfounded.
My father looked at me in silence, not daring to believe his senses. His face lit up with joy.

"Welcome, Petrusha," he said, pressing me to his
heart. "Thank God, we have lived to see you!"

My mother cried out and burst into tears.

"Petrusha, my darling!" she said. "How has the Lord
brought you here? Are you well?"

I hastened to cut with my sword the ropes that
bound them and to take them out of their prison; but
when I came to the door I found that it had been locked again.

"Andryushka, open!" I shouted.

"No fear!" the man answered from behind the door.
"You may as well sit here, too! We'll teach you how
to be rowdy and drag the Czar's officials by the collar!"

I began looking round the granary to see if there
was some way of getting out.

"Don't trouble," my father said to me. "It's not my
way to have granaries into which thieves could find a
way."

My mother, who had rejoiced a moment before at
my coming, was overcome with despair at the thought
that I, too, would have to perish with the rest of the

family. But I was calmer now that I was with them and Marya Ivanovna. I had a sword and two pistols; I could withstand a siege. Zurin was due to arrive in the evening and would set us free. I told all this to my parents and succeeded in calming my mother and Marya Ivanovna. They gave themselves up completely to the joy of our meeting, and several hours passed for us imperceptibly in expressions of affection and continual conversation.

"Well, Pyotr," my father said, "you have been foolish enough, and I was quite angry with you at the time. But it's no use remembering old scores. I hope that you have sown your wild oats and are reformed. I know that you have served as an honest officer should. I thank you; you have comforted me in my old age. If I owe my deliverance to you, life will be doubly pleasant to me."

I kissed his hand with tears and gazed at Marya Ivanovna, who was so overjoyed at my presence that she seemed quite calm and happy.

About midday we heard extraordinary uproar and shouting. "What does this mean?" my father said. "Can it already be your colonel?"

"Impossible," I answered. "He won't come before evening."

The noise increased. The alarm bell was rung. We heard men on horseback galloping across the yard. At that moment Savelyich's gray head was thrust through the narrow opening cut in the wall and the poor old man said in a pitiful voice:

"Andrey Petrovich! Pyotr Andreyich, my dear! Marya Ivanovna! We are lost! The villains have come into the village. And do you know who has brought them, Pyotr Andreyich? Shvabrin, Alexey Ivanych, damnation take him!"

When Marya Ivanovna heard the hated name she clasped her hands [1] and remained motionless.

"Listen!" I said to Savelyich. "Send someone on horseback to the ferry to meet the hussar regiment and to tell the Colonel of our danger."

"But whom can I send, sir? All the boys have joined the rebels, and the horses have all been seized. Oh, dear! There they are in the yard! They are coming to the granary."

As he said this, we heard several voices behind the door. I made a sign to my mother and Marya Ivanovna to move away into a corner, bared my sword, and leaned against the wall just by the door. My father took the pistols, cocked them both, and stood beside me. The lock rattled, the door opened and Andryushka's head showed. I hit it with my sword and he fell, blocking the doorway. At the same moment my father fired the pistol. The crowd that had besieged us ran away, cursing. I dragged the wounded man across the threshold and closed the door.

The courtyard was full of armed men. I recognized Shvabrin among them.

"Don't be afraid," I said to the women, "there is hope. And don't you shoot any more, father. Let us save up the last shot."

My mother was praying silently. Marya Ivanovna stood beside her, waiting with angelic calm for her fate to be decided. Threats, abuse, and curses were heard behind the door. I was standing in the same place ready to hit the first man who dared to show himself. Suddenly the villains subsided. I heard Shvabrin's voice calling me by name.

"I am here. What do you want?"

"Surrender, Grinyov; resistance is impossible. Have

[1] See footnote on p. 608.

pity on your old people. Obstinacy will not save you. I shall get at you!"

"Try, traitor!"

"I am not going to put myself forward for nothing or waste my men; I will set the granary on fire and then we'll see what you will do, Belogorsky Don Quixote. Now it is time to have dinner. Meanwhile you can sit and think it over at leisure. Good-bye! Marya Ivanovna, I do not apologize to you: you are probably not feeling bored with your knight beside you in the dark."

Shvabrin went away, leaving sentries at the door. We were silent, each of us thinking his own thoughts, not daring to express them to the others. I was picturing to myself all that Shvabrin was capable of doing in his malice. I hardly cared about myself. Must I confess it? Even my parents' fate terrified me less than Marya Ivanovna's. I knew that my mother was adored by the peasants and the house serfs. My father, too, was loved in spite of his sternness, for he was just and knew the true needs of the men he owned. Their rebellion was a delusion, a passing intoxication, and not the expression of their resentment. It was possible that my parents would be spared. But Marya Ivanovna? What did the dissolute and unscrupulous man hold in store for her? I did not dare to dwell upon this awful thought and would have killed her (God forgive me!) sooner than see her fall once more into the hands of the cruel enemy.

Another hour passed. Drunken men could be heard singing in the village. Our sentries envied them, and in their annoyance abused us, threatening us with tortures and death. We were waiting for Shvabrin to carry out his threat. At last there was great commotion in the courtyard and we heard Shvabrin's voice once more.

"Well, have you thought better of it? Do you surrender to me of your own will?"

No one answered.

After waiting a while, Shvabrin ordered his men to bring some straw. In a few minutes flames appeared, lighting the dim granary. Smoke began to rise from under the door.

Then Marya Ivanovna came up to me and, taking me by the hand, said in a low voice:

"Come, Pyotr Andreyich, don't let both yourself and your parents perish because of me. Shvabrin will listen to me. Let me out!"

"Never!" I cried angrily. "Do you know what awaits you?"

"I will not survive dishonor," she answered calmly, "but perhaps I shall save my deliverer and the family that has so generously sheltered a poor orphan. Good-bye, Andrey Petrovich! Good-bye, Avdotya Vassily-evna! You have been more than benefactors to me. Bless me! Farewell to you, too, Pyotr Andreyich, Believe me that . . . that . . ."

She burst into tears and buried her face in her hands. . . . I was beside myself. My mother was weeping.

"Stop this nonsense, Marya Ivanovna," said my father. "Whoever would dream of letting you go alone to the brigands? Sit here and keep quiet. If we must die, we may as well die together. Listen! What is he saying now?"

"Do you surrender?" Shvabrin shouted. "You see you will be roasted in another five minutes."

"We won't surrender, you villain!" my father answered firmly.

His vigorous, deeply lined face was wonderfully animated. His eyes sparkled under the gray eyebrows. Turning to me, he said: "Now 's the time!"

He opened the door. The flames rushed in and rose

up to the beams whose chinks were stuffed with dry
moss. My father fired the pistol, stepped over the burning threshold and shouted "Follow me!" I took my
mother and Marya Ivanovna by the hands and quickly
led them out. Shvabrin, shot through by my father's
feeble hand, was lying by the threshold. The crowd of
brigands who had rushed away at our sudden sally
took courage and began closing in upon us. I succeeded
in dealing a few more blows; but a well-aimed brick
hit me right on the chest. I fell down and lost consciousness for a few moments; I was surrounded and disarmed. Coming to myself I saw Shvabrin sitting on
the blood-stained grass, with all our family standing
before him.

I was supported under the arms. A crowd of peasants, Cossacks, and Bashkirs hemmed us in. Shvabrin
was terribly pale. He was pressing one hand to his
wounded side. His face expressed malice and pain. He
slowly raised his head, glanced at me and said, in a
weak, hardly audible voice:

"Hang him . . . and all of them . . . except her."

The crowd surrounded us at once and dragged us
to the gates. But suddenly they left us and scampered
away: Zurin and a whole squadron of Hussars, with
bared swords, rode into the courtyard.

The rebels were flying as fast as they could. The Hussars pursued them, striking right and left with their
swords and taking prisoners. Zurin jumped off his
horse, bowed to my father and mother, and warmly
clasped me by the hand.

"I have come just in time," he said to me. "Ah, and
here is your betrothed!"

Marya Ivanovna flushed crimson. My father went up
to him and thanked him calmly, though he was obviously touched. My mother embraced him, calling him
an angel-deliverer.

"Welcome to our home!" my father said to him, and led him toward the house.

Zurin stopped as he passed Shvabrin.

"Who is this?" he asked, looking at the wounded man.

"It is the leader of the gang," my father answered, with a certain pride that betokened an old soldier. "God has helped my feeble hand to punish the young villain and to avenge the blood of my son."

"It is Shvabrin," I said to Zurin.

"Shvabrin! I am very glad. Hussars, take him! Tell the leech to dress his wound and to take the utmost care of him. Shvabrin must certainly be sent to the Kazan Secret Commission. He is one of the chief criminals and his evidence may be of great importance. . . ."

Shvabrin wearily opened his eyes. His face expressed nothing but physical pain. The Hussars carried him away on an outspread cloak.

We went into the house. I looked about me with a tremor, remembering the years of my childhood. Nothing had changed in the house, everything was in its usual place: Shvabrin had not allowed it to be pillaged, preserving in his very degradation an unconscious aversion to base cupidity.

The servants came into the hall. They had taken no part in the rebellion and were genuinely glad of our deliverance. Savelyich was triumphant. It must be mentioned that during the alarm produced by the brigands' arrival he ran to the stables where Shvabrin's horse had been put, saddled it, led it out quietly and, unnoticed in the confusion, galloped toward the ferry. He met the regiment having a rest this side of the Volga. When Zurin heard from him of our danger, he ordered his men to mount, cried "Off! Off! Gallop!" and, thank God, arrived in time.

Zurin insisted that Andryushka's head should be exposed for a few hours at the top of a pole by the tavern.

The Hussars returned from their pursuit bringing several prisoners with them. They were locked in the same granary where we had endured our memorable siege. We all went to our rooms. The old people needed a rest. As I had not slept the whole night, I flung myself on the bed and dropped fast asleep. Zurin went to make his arrangements.

In the evening we all met round the samovar in the drawing-room, talking gaily of the past danger. Marya Ivanovna poured out the tea. I sat down beside her and devoted myself entirely to her. My parents seemed to look with favor upon the tenderness of our relations. That evening lives in my memory to this day. I was happy, completely happy—and are there many such moments in poor human life?

The following day my father was told that the peasants had come to ask his pardon. My father went out on to the steps to talk to them. When the peasants saw him they knelt down.

"Well, you silly fools," he said to them, "whatever did you rebel for?"

"We are sorry, master," they answered as one man.

"Sorry, are you? They get into mischief and then they are sorry! I forgive you for the sake of our family joy—God has allowed me to see my son, Pyotr Andreyich, again. So be it, a sin confessed is a sin forgiven."

"We did wrong; of course we did."

"God has sent fine weather. It is time for haymaking; and what have you been doing for the last three days, you fools? Headman! send everyone to make hay; and mind that by St. John's Day all the hay is in stacks, you red-haired rascal! Begone!"

The peasants bowed and went to work as though nothing had happened. Shvabrin's wound proved not to be mortal. He was sent under escort to Kazan. I saw from the window how they laid him in a cart. Our eyes met. He bent his head and I made haste to move away from the window; I was afraid of looking as though I were triumphing over a humiliated and unhappy enemy.

Zurin had to go on farther. I decided to join him, in spite of my desire to spend a few more days with my family. On the eve of the march I came to my parents and, in accordance with the custom of the time, bowed down to the ground before them, asking their blessing on my marriage with Marya Ivanovna. The old people lifted me up, and with joyous tears gave their consent. I brought Marya Ivanovna, pale and trembling, to them. They blessed us. . . . I will not attempt to describe what I was feeling. Those who have been in my position will understand; as to those who have not, I can only pity them and advise them, while there is still time, to fall in love and receive their parents' blessing.

The following day our regiment was ready. Zurin took leave of our family. We were all certain that the military operations would soon be over. I was hoping to be married in another month's time. Marya Ivanovna kissed me in front of all as she said good-bye. I mounted my horse; Savelyich followed me again and the regiment marched off. For a long time I kept looking back at the country house that I was leaving once more. A gloomy foreboding tormented me. Something seemed to whisper to me that my misfortunes were not yet over. My heart felt that another storm was ahead.

I will not describe our campaign and the end of the Pugachov war. We passed through villages pillaged by Pugachov, and could not help taking from the poor inhabitants what the brigands had left them.

They did not know whom to obey. There was no lawful authority anywhere. The landowners were hiding in the forests. Bands of brigands were ransacking the country. The chiefs of separate detachments sent in pursuit of Pugachov, who was by then retreating toward Astrakhan, arbitrarily punished both the guilty and the innocent. The entire region where the conflagration had raged was in a terrible state. God save us from seeing a Russian revolt, senseless and merciless. Those who plot impossible upheavals among us, are either young and do not know our people or are hardhearted men who do not care a straw either about their own lives or those of other people.

Unfinished Stories

THE NEGRO OF PETER THE GREAT

I

AMONG the young men sent abroad by Peter the
Great for the acquisition of knowledge indispensable to a country in a state of transition, was his godson, the Negro, Ibrahim. After being educated in the
Military School at Paris, which he left with the rank
of Captain of Artillery, he distinguished himself in the
Spanish war and, severely wounded, returned to Paris.
The Emperor, in the midst of his vast labors, never
ceased to inquire after his favorite, and he always received flattering accounts of his progress and conduct.
Peter was exceedingly pleased with him, and repeatedly requested him to return to Russia, but Ibrahim was
in no hurry. He excused himself under various pre-
texts: now it was his wound, now it was a wish to complete his education, now a want of money; and Peter
indulgently complied with his wishes, begged him to
take care of his health, thanked him for his zeal for
study, and although extremely thrifty where his own
expenses were concerned, he did not stint his favorite
in money, adding to the ducats fatherly advice and
cautionary admonition.

According to the testimony of all the historical memoirs nothing could be compared with the frivolity, folly
and luxury of the French of that period. The last years

of the reign of Louis the Fourteenth, remarkable for the strict piety, gravity, and decorum of the Court, had left no traces behind. The Duke of Orleans, uniting many brilliant qualities with vices of every kind, unfortunately did not possess the slightest shadow of hypocrisy. The orgies of the Palais Royal were no secret in Paris; the example was infectious. At that time Law [1] appeared upon the scene; greed for money was united to the thirst for pleasure and dissipation; estates were squandered, morals perished, Frenchmen laughed and calculated, and the kingdom was falling apart to the playful refrains of satirical vaudevilles.

In the meantime society presented a most entertaining picture. Culture and the need of amusement brought all ranks together. Wealth, amiability, renown, talent, even eccentricity—everything that fed curiosity or promised pleasure, was received with the same indulgence. Literature, learning and philosophy forsook their quiet studies and appeared in the circles of the great world to render homage to fashion and to govern it. Women reigned, but no longer demanded adoration. Superficial politeness replaced the profound respect formerly shown to them. The pranks of the Duke de Richelieu, the Alcibiades of modern Athens, belong to history, and give an idea of the morals of that period.

> "*Tems fortuné, marqué par la licence,*
> *Où la folie, agitant son grelot,*
> *D'un pied léger parcourt toute la France,*
> *Où nul mortel ne daigne être dévot,*
> *Où l'on fait tout excepté pénitence.*"

The appearance of Ibrahim, his looks, culture and native intelligence excited general attention in Paris.

[1] John Law, the famous projector of financial schemes.
TRANSLATOR'S NOTE

All the ladies were anxious to see "le nègre du czar" at their houses, and vied with each other in trying to capture him. The Regent invited him more than once to his merry evening parties; he assisted at the suppers animated by the youth of Arouet, the old age of Chaulieu, and the conversations of Montesquieu and Fontenelle. He did not miss a single ball, fête or first night, and he gave himself up to the general whirl with all the ardor of his years and nature. But the thought of exchanging these distractions, these brilliant amusements for the harsh simplicity of the Petersburg Court was not the only thing that dismayed Ibrahim; other and stronger ties bound him to Paris. The young African was in love.

The Countess D——, although no longer in the first bloom of youth, was still renowned for her beauty. On leaving the convent at seventeen, she had been married to a man with whom she had not had time to fall in love, and who later on did not take the trouble to gain her affection. Rumor ascribed several lovers to her, but such was the indulgence of the world, that she enjoyed a good reputation, for nobody was able to reproach her with any ridiculous or scandalous adventure. Her house was one of the most fashionable, and the best Parisian society made it their rendezvous. Ibrahim was introducd to her by young Merville, who was generally looked upon as her latest lover—and who did all in his power to obtain credit for the report.

The Countess received Ibrahim courteously, but without any particular attention: this flattered him. Generally the young Negro was regarded in the light of a curiosity; people used to surround him and overwhelm him with compliments and questions—and this curiosity, although concealed by a show of graciousness, offended his vanity. Women's delightful attention, almost the sole aim of our exertions, not only afforded him no pleasure, but even filled him with bitterness and indignation. He felt that he was for them a kind of rare beast, a peculiar alien creature, accidentally brought into a world, with which he had nothing in common. He even envied people who remained unnoticed, and considered them fortunate in their insignificance.

The thought, that nature had not created him to enjoy requited love, saved him from self-assurance and vain pretensions, and added a rare charm to his behavior toward women. His conversation was simple and dignified; he pleased Countess D——, who had grown tired of the eternal jokes and subtle insinuations of French wits. Ibrahim frequently visited her. Little by little she became accustomed to the young Negro's appearance, and even began to find something agreeable in that curly head, that stood out so black in the midst of the powdered perukes in her reception-room (Ibrahim had been wounded in the head, and wore a bandage instead of a peruke). He was twenty-seven years of age, and was tall and slender, and more than one beauty glanced at him with a feeling more flattering than simple curiosity. But the prejudiced Ibrahim either did not observe anything of this or merely looked upon it as coquetry. But when his glances met those of the Countess, his distrust vanished. Her eyes expressed such winning kindness, her manner toward him was so simple, so unconstrained, that it was impossible to suspect her of the least shadow of coquetry or raillery.

The thought of love had not entered his head, but to see the Countess each day had become a necessity to him. He sought her out everywhere, and every meeting with her seemed an unexpected favor from heaven. The Countess guessed his feelings before he himself did. There is no denying that a love, which is without hope and which demands nothing, touches the female heart more surely than all the devices of seduction. In the presence of Ibrahim, the Countess followed all his movements, listened to every word that he said; without him she became thoughtful, and fell into her usual abstraction. Merville was the first to observe this mutual inclination, and he congratulated Ibrahim. Nothing inflames love so much as the encouraging observations of a bystander: love is blind, and, having no trust in itself, readily grasps hold of every support.

Merville's words roused Ibrahim. He had never till then imagined the possibility of possessing the woman that he loved; hope suddenly illumined his soul; he fell madly in love. In vain did the Countess, alarmed by the ardor of his passion, seek to oppose to it the admonitions of friendship and the counsels of prudence; she herself was beginning to weaken. . . . Incautious rewards swiftly followed one another. And at last, carried away by the force of the passion she had herself inspired, surrendering to its influence, she gave herself to the ravished Ibrahim. . . .

Nothing is hidden from the eyes of the observing world. The Countess's new liaison was soon known to everybody. Some ladies were amazed at her choice; to many it seemed quite natural. Some laughed; others regarded her conduct as unpardonably indiscreet. In the first intoxication of passion, Ibrahim and the Countess noticed nothing, but soon the equivocal jokes of the men and the pointed remarks of the women began to reach their ears. Ibrahim's cold and dignified manner had hitherto protected him from such attacks; he bore them with impatience, and knew not how to ward them off. The Countess, accustomed to the respect of the world, could not calmly bear to see herself an object of gossip and ridicule. With tears in her eyes she complained to Ibrahim, now bitterly reproaching him, now imploring him not to defend her, lest by some useless scandal she should be completely ruined.

A new circumstance further complicated her position: the consequence of imprudent love began to be apparent. Consolation, advice, proposals—all were exhausted and all rejected. The Countess saw that her ruin was inevitable, and in despair awaited it.

As soon as the condition of the Countess became known, tongues wagged again with fresh vigor; sentimental women gave vent to exclamations of horror; men wagered as to whether the Countess would give birth to a white or a black baby. Numerous epigrams were aimed at her husband, who alone in all Paris knew nothing and suspected nothing.

The fatal moment approached. The condition of the Countess was terrible. Ibrahim visited her every day. He saw her mental and physical strength gradually giving way. Her tears and her terror were renewed every moment. Finally she felt the first pains. Measures were hastily taken. Means were found for getting the Count out of the way. The doctor arrived. Two days before this a poor woman had been persuaded to surrender to strangers her new-born infant; a trusted person had been sent for it. Ibrahim was in the room adjoining the bedchamber where the unhappy Countess lay not daring to breathe, he heard her muffled groans, the maid's whisper, and the doctor's orders. Her sufferings lasted a long time. Her every groan lacerated his heart. Every interval of silence overwhelmed him with terror. . . . Suddenly he heard the weak cry of a baby—and, unable to repress his elation, he rushed into the Countess's room. . . . A black baby lay upon the bed at her feet. Ibrahim approached it. His heart beat violently. He blessed his son with a trembling hand. The Countess smiled faintly and stretched out to him her feeble hand, but the doctor, fearing that the excitement might be too great for the patient, dragged Ibrahim away from her bed. The new-born child was placed in a covered basket, and carried out of the house by a secret staircase. Then the other child was brought in, and its cradle placed in the bedroom. Ibrahim took his departure, feeling somewhat more at ease. The Count was expected. He returned late, heard of the happy delivery of his wife, and was much gratified. In this way the public, which had been expecting a great scandal, was deceived in its hope, and was compelled to console itself with malicious gossip alone. Everything resumed its usual course.

But Ibrahim felt that there would have to be a change in his lot, and that sooner or later his relations with the Countess would come to the knowledge of her husband. In that case, whatever might happen, the ruin of the Countess was inevitable. Ibrahim loved passionately and was passionately loved in return, but the Countess was wilful and frivolous; it was not the first time that she had loved. Disgust, and even hatred might replace in her heart the most tender feelings. Ibrahim already foresaw the moment when she would cool toward him. Hitherto he had not known jealousy, but with dread he now felt a presentiment of it; he thought that the pain of separation would be less distressing, and he resolved to break off the unhappy connection, leave Paris, and return to Russia, whither Peter and a vague sense of duty had been calling him for a long time.

II

DAYS, months passed, and the enamored Ibrahim could not resolve to leave the woman that he had seduced. The Countess grew more and more attached to him. Their son was being brought up in a distant prov-

ince. The slanders of the world were beginning to subside, and the lovers began to enjoy greater tranquillity,
silently remembering the past storm and endeavoring
not to think of the future.

One day Ibrahim attended a levee at the Duke of
Orleans' residence. The Duke, passing by him, stopped,
and handing him a letter, told him to read it at his
leisure. It was a letter from Peter the First. The Emperor, guessing the true cause of his absence, wrote to
the Duke that he had no intention of compelling Ibrahim, that he left it to his own free will to return to
Russia or not, but that in any case he would never
abandon his former foster-child. This letter touched
Ibrahim to the bottom of his heart. From that moment
his lot was settled. The next day he informed the Regent of his intention to set out immediately for Russia.

"Consider what you are doing," said the Duke to
him: "Russia is not your native country. I do not think
that you will ever again see your torrid birthplace, but
your long residence in France has made you equally a
stranger to the climate and the ways of life of half-
savage Russia. You were not born a subject of Peter.
Listen to my advice: take advantage of his magnani-
mous permission, remain in France, for which you have
already shed your blood, and rest assured that here
your services and talents will not remain unrewarded."

Ibrahim thanked the Duke sincerely, but remained
firm in his resolution.

"I am sorry," said the Regent: "but perhaps you are
right."

He promised to let him retire from the French service and wrote a full account of the matter to the Czar.

Ibrahim was soon ready for the journey. He spent
the evening before his departure at the house of the
Countess D——, as usual. She knew nothing. Ibrahim
had not the heart to inform her of his intention. The

Countess was calm and cheerful. She several times
called him to her and joked about his being so pensive.
After supper the guests departed. The Countess, her
husband, and Ibrahim were left alone in the parlor.
The unhappy man would have given everything in the
world to have been left alone with her; but Count
D—— seemed to have seated himself so comfortably
beside the fire, that there was no hope of getting him
out of the room. All three remained silent.

"*Bonne nuit!*" said the Countess at last.

Ibrahim's heart contracted and he suddenly felt all
the horrors of parting. He stood motionless.

"*Bonne nuit, messieurs!*" repeated the Countess.

Still he remained motionless. . . . At last his eyes
darkened, his head swam round, and he could scarcely walk out of the room. On reaching home, he wrote,
almost unconsciously, the following letter:

"*I am going away, dear Leonora; I am leaving you
forever. I am writing to you, because I have not the
strength to tell it to you otherwise.*

"*My happiness could not last: I have enjoyed it in
spite of fate and nature. You were bound to stop loving me; the enchantment was bound to vanish. This
thought has always pursued me, even in those moments
when I have seemed to forget everything, when at your
feet I have been intoxicated by your passionate self-
denial, by your unbounded tenderness. . . . The frivolous world unmercifully persecutes in fact that which
it permits in theory; its cold mockery sooner or later
would have vanquished you, would have humbled
your ardent soul, and at last you would have become
ashamed of your passion. . . . What would then have
become of me? No, it is better to die, better to leave
you before that terrible moment.*

"*Your peace is dearer to me than anything: you*

could not enjoy it while the eyes of the world were fixed upon us. Recall all that you have suffered, all the insults to your amour propre, all the tortures of fear; remember the terrible birth of our son. Think: ought I to expose you any longer to such agitations and dangers? Why should I endeavor to unite the fate of such a tender, beautiful creature to the miserable fate of a Negro, of a pitiable creature, scarce worthy of the name of man?

"Farewell, Leonora; farewell, my dear and only friend. I am leaving you, I am leaving the first and last joy of my life. I have neither fatherland nor kindred; I am going to gloomy Russia, where my utter solitude will be a consolation to me. Serious work, to which from now on I shall devote myself, will at least divert me from, if not stifle, painful recollections of the days of rapture and bliss. . . . Farewell, Leonora! I tear myself away from this letter, as if from your embrace. Farewell, be happy, and think sometimes of the poor Negro, of your faithful Ibrahim."

That same night he set out for Russia.

The journey did not seem to him as terrible as he had expected. His imagination triumphed over the reality. The farther he got from Paris, the more vivid and nearer rose up before him the objects he was leaving forever.

Before he was aware of it he found himself at the Russian frontier. Autumn had already set in, but the coachmen, in spite of the bad state of the roads, drove him with the speed of the wind, and on the seventeenth day of his journey he arrived at Krasnoe Selo, through which at that time the high road passed.

It was still a distance of twenty-eight versts to Petersburg. While the horses were being hitched up, Ibrahim entered the post-house. In a corner, a tall man, in a green *caftan* and with a clay pipe in his mouth, his elbows upon the table, was reading the Hamburg newspapers. Hearing somebody enter, he raised his head.

"Ah, Ibrahim!" he exclaimed, rising from the bench. "How do you do, godson?"

Ibrahim recognized Peter, and in his delight was about to rush toward him, but he respectfully paused. The Emperor approached, embraced him and kissed him upon the head.

"I was informed of your coming," said Peter, "and set off to meet you. I have been waiting for you here since yesterday."

Ibrahim could not find words to express his gratitude.

"Let your carriage follow on behind us," continued the Emperor, "and you take your place by my side and ride along with me."

The Czar's carriage was driven up; he took his seat with Ibrahim, and they set off at a gallop. In about an hour and a half they reached Petersburg. Ibrahim gazed with curiosity at the new-born city which was springing up out of the marsh at the beck of the autocrat. Bare dams, canals without embankments, wooden bridges everywhere testified to the recent triumph of the human will over the hostile elements. The houses seemed to have been built in a hurry. In the whole town there was nothing magnificent but the Neva, not yet ornamented with its granite frame, but already covered with warships and merchant vessels. The imperial carriage stopped at the palace, the so-called Czarina's Garden. On the steps Peter was met by a woman of about thirty-five years of age, handsome, and dressed in the latest Parisian fashion. Peter kissed her on the lips and, taking Ibrahim by the hand, said:

"Do you recognize my godson, Katinka? I beg you to treat him as kindly as you used to."

Catherine fixed on him her dark piercing eyes, and stretched out her hand to him in a friendly manner. Two young beauties, tall, slender, and fresh as roses, stood behind her and respectfully approached Peter.

"Liza," said he to one of them, "do you remember the little Negro who stole my apples for you at Oranienbaum? Here he is; let me introduce him to you."

The Grand Duchess laughed and blushed. They went into the dining-room. In expectation of the Czar the table had been laid. Peter sat down to dinner with all his family, and invited Ibrahim to sit down with them. During dinner the Emperor conversed with him on various subjects, questioned him about the Spanish war, the internal affairs of France, and the Regent, whom he liked, although he condemned much in him. Ibrahim possessed an exact and observant mind. Peter was very pleased with his replies. He recalled to mind some features of Ibrahim's childhood, and related them with such good-humor and gaiety, that nobody could have suspected this kind and hospitable host to be the hero of Poltava, the dread and mighty reformer of Russia.

After dinner the Emperor, according to the Russian custom, retired to rest. Ibrahim remained with the Empress and the Grand Duchesses. He tried to satisfy their curiosity, described the Parisian way of life, the holidays that were kept there, and the changeable fashions. In the meantime, some of the persons belonging to the Emperor's suite had assembled in the palace. Ibrahim recognized the magnificent Prince Menshikov, who, seeing the Negro conversing with Catherine, cast an arrogant glance at him; Prince Jacob Dolgoruky, Peter's stern counselor; the learned Bruce, who had acquired among the people the name of the "Russian Faust"; the young Raguzinsky, his former companion, and others who had come to make their reports to the Emperor and to receive his orders.

In about two hours' time the Emperor appeared.

"Let us see," said he to Ibrahim, "if you have forgotten your old duties. Take a slate and follow me."

Peter shut himself up in his turnery and busied himself with state affairs. He worked in turns with Bruce, with Prince Dolgoruky, and with the chief of police, General Devier, and dictated to Ibrahim several ukases and decisions. Ibrahim could not sufficiently admire the quickness and firmness of his understanding, the strength and flexibility of his powers of attention, and the variety of his occupations. When the work was finished, Peter drew out a notebook in order to see if all that he had proposed to do that day had been accomplished. Then, issuing from the work-room, he said to Ibrahim:

"It is late; no doubt you are tired—sleep here tonight, as you used to do in the old days; tomorrow I will wake you."

Ibrahim, on being left alone, could hardly collect his thoughts. He was in Petersburg; he saw again the great man, near whom, not yet knowing his worth, he had passed his childhood. Almost with regret he confessed to himself that the Countess D——, for the first time since their separation, had not been his sole thought during the whole of the day. He saw that the new mode of life which awaited him—the activity and constant occupation—would revive his soul, wearied by passion, idleness and secret grief. The thought of being a great man's co-worker and, together with him, influencing the fate of a great nation, aroused within him for the first time the noble feeling of ambition. In this disposition of mind he lay down upon the camp bed prepared for him, and then the usual dreams car-

ried him back to far-off Paris, to the arms of his dear
Countess.

III

THE NEXT morning, Peter, according to his promise,
woke Ibrahim and congratulated him on his elevation
to the rank of Captain-lieutenant of the Artillery company of the Preobrazhensky Regiment, in which he
himself was Captain. The courtiers surrounded Ibrahim, each in his way trying to be attentive to the new
favorite. The haughty Prince Menshikov pressed his
hand in a friendly manner; Sheremetyev inquired after
his Parisian acquaintances, and Golovin invited him to
dinner. Others followed the example of the latter, so
that Ibrahim received enough invitations to last him
at least a whole month.

Ibrahim now began to lead a monotonous but busy
life, consequently he did not feel at all dull. From day
to day he became more attached to the Emperor, and
was better able to comprehend his lofty soul. To follow
the thoughts of a great man is a most absorbing study.
Ibrahim saw Peter in the Senate arguing weighty questions of legislation with Buturlin and Dolgoruky; with
the Admiralty committee establishing the naval power
of Russia; he saw him with Feofan, Gavriil Buzhin-
sky, and Kopievich, in his free hours examining translations of foreign authors, or visiting the factory of a
merchant, the workshop of a mechanic, or the study of
a savant. Russia presented to Ibrahim the appearance
of a huge workshop, where machines alone move,
where each workman, subject to established rules, is
occupied with his own particular business. He, too,
felt obliged to work at his own bench, and he endeavored to regret as little as possible the gaieties of his Parisian life. But it was more difficult for him to drive from

his mind another and dear memory: he often thought of the Countess D——, and pictured to himself her just indignation, her tears and her despondency. . . . But sometimes a terrible thought oppressed his heart: the distractions of the great world, a new tie, another favorite—he shuddered; jealousy began to set his African blood boiling, and hot tears were ready to roll down his black face.

One morning he was sitting in his study, surrounded by business papers, when suddenly he heard a loud greeting in French. Ibrahim turned round quickly, and young Korsakov, whom he had left in Paris in the whirl of the great world, embraced him with joyful exclamations.

"I have only just arrived," said Korsakov, "and I have come straight to you. All our Parisian acquaintances send their greetings to you, and regret your absence. The Countess D—— ordered me to summon you to return without fail, and here is her letter to you."

Ibrahim seized it with a trembling hand and looked at the familiar handwriting of the address, not daring to believe his eyes.

"How glad I am," continued Korsakov, "that you have not yet died of ennui in this barbarous Petersburg! What do people do here? How do they occupy themselves? Who is your tailor? Have you opera, at least?"

Ibrahim absently replied that probably the Emperor was just then at work in the dockyard.

Korsakov laughed.

"I see," said he, "that you can't attend to me just now; some other time we will talk to our heart's content; I will go now and pay my respects to the Emperor."

With these words he turned on his heel and hastened out of the room.

Ibrahim, left alone, hastily opened the letter. The Countess tenderly complained to him, reproaching him with dissimulation and distrust.

"You say," wrote she, "that my peace is dearer to you than everything in the world. Ibrahim, if this were the truth, would you have brought me to the condition to which I was reduced by the unexpected news of your departure? You were afraid that I might have detained you. Be assured that, in spite of my love, I should have known how to sacrifice it for your happiness and for what you consider your duty."

The Countess ended the letter with passionate assurances of love, and implored him to write to her, if only now and then, even though there should be no hope of their ever seeing each other again.

Ibrahim read this letter through twenty times, kissing the priceless lines with rapture. He was burning with impatience to hear something about the Countess, and he was just preparing to set out for the Admiralty, hoping to find Korsakov still there, when the door opened, and Korsakov himself appeared once more. He had already paid his respects to the Emperor, and as was usual with him, he seemed very well satisfied with himself.

"*Entre nous,*" he said to Ibrahim, "the Emperor is a very strange person. Just fancy, I found him in a sort of linen singlet, on the mast of a new ship, whither I was compelled to climb with my dispatches. I stood on the rope ladder, and had not sufficient room to make a suitable bow, and so I became completely confused, a thing that had never happened to me in my life before. However, when the Emperor had read my letter, he looked at me from head to foot, and no doubt was agreeably struck by the taste and smartness of my attire; at any rate he smiled and invited me to tonight's assembly. But I am a perfect stranger in Petersburg; in the six years that I have been away I have quite forgotten the local customs; pray be my mentor; call for me and introduce me."

Ibrahim agreed to do so, and hastened to turn the conversation to a subject that was more interesting to him.

"Well, and how is the Countess D——?"

"The Countess? Of course, at first she was very much grieved on account of your departure; then, of course, little by little, she found solace and took a new lover: do you know whom? The lanky Marquis R——. Why are you staring at me so with your Negro eyes? Or does it seem strange to you? Don't you know that lasting grief is not in human nature, particularly in feminine nature? Chew on this, while I go and rest after my journey, and don't forget to come and call for me."

What feelings filled the soul of Ibrahim? Jealousy? Rage? Despair? No, but a deep, oppressing despondency. He repeated to himself: "I foresaw it, it had to happen." Then he opened the Countess's letter, read it again, hung his head and wept bitterly. He wept for a long time. The tears relieved his heart. Looking at the clock, he perceived that it was time to set out. Ibrahim would have been very glad to stay away, but the assembly was a matter of duty, and the Emperor strictly demanded the presence of his retainers. He dressed himself and started out to call for Korsakov.

Korsakov was sitting in his dressing-gown, reading a French book.

"So early?" he said to Ibrahim, on seeing him.

"Mercy," the latter replied; "it is already half-past five, we shall be late; make haste and dress and let us go."

Korsakov, in a flurry, rang the bell with all his

might; the servants came running in, and he began hastily to dress himself. His French valet gave him shoes with red heels, blue velvet breeches, and a pink *caftan* embroidered with spangles. His peruke was hurriedly powdered in the ante-chamber and brought in to him. Korsakov stuck his cropped head into it, asked for his sword and gloves, turned round about ten times before the glass, and then informed Ibrahim that he was ready. The footmen handed them their bearskin greatcoats, and they set out for the Winter Palace.

Korsakov overwhelmed Ibrahim with questions: Who was the greatest beauty in Petersburg? Who was supposed to be the best dancer? Which dance was just then the rage? Ibrahim very reluctantly gratified his curiosity. Meanwhile they reached the palace. A great number of long sledges, old-fashioned carriages, and gilded coaches already stood on the lawn. Near the steps were crowded liveried and mustachioed coachmen; messengers resplendent in tinsel and plumes, and bearing maces; hussars, pages, and clumsy footmen loaded with the coats and muffs of their masters—a retinue indispensable according to the notions of the gentry of that time. At the sight of Ibrahim, a general murmur arose: "The Negro, the Negro, the Czar's Negro!" He hurriedly conducted Korsakov through this motley crowd. The Court lackey opened the doors wide, and they entered the hall. Korsakov was dumbfounded. . . . In a large room, illuminated by tallow candles, which burnt dimly amidst clouds of tobacco smoke, magnates with blue ribbons across the shoulders, ambassadors, foreign merchants, officers of the Guards in green uniforms, ship-masters in jackets and striped trousers, moved backwards and forwards in crowds to the uninterrupted sound of the music of wind instruments. The ladies sat against the walls, the young ones being decked out in all the splendor of the

prevailing fashion. Gold and silver glittered upon their
gowns; out of sumptuous farthingales their slender
forms rose like flower stalks; diamonds sparkled in
their ears, in their long curls, and around their necks.
They turned gaily about to the right and to the left,
waiting for their cavaliers and for the dancing to begin. The elderly ladies craftily endeavored to combine
the new fashions with the proscribed style of the past;
their caps resembled the sable head-dress of the Czarina
Natalya Kirilovna,[1] and their gowns and capes recalled
the *sarafan* and *dushegreika*.[2] They seemed to attend
these newfangled gatherings with more astonishment
than pleasure, and cast looks of resentment at the wives
and daughters of the Dutch skippers, who, in dimity
skirts and red bodices, knitted their stockings and
laughed and chatted among themselves as if they were
at home.

Korsakov was completely bewildered. Observing
new arrivals, a servant approached them with beer and
glasses on a tray.

"*Que diable est ce que tout cela?*" he asked Ibrahim
in a whisper.

Ibrahim could not repress a smile. The Empress and
the Grand Duchesses, dazzling in their beauty and
their attire, walked through the rows of guests, conversing affably with them. The Emperor was in another room. Korsakov, wishing to show himself to
him, with difficulty succeeded in pushing his way
thither through the constantly moving crowd. In this
room were chiefly foreigners, solemnly smoking their
clay pipes and draining earthenware mugs. On the
tables were bottles of beer and wine, leather pouches
with tobacco, glasses of punch, and some chessboards.
At one of these Peter was playing draughts with a

[1] The mother of Peter the Great.   TRANSLATOR'S NOTE
[2] A fur-lined or wadded sleeveless jacket.   EDITOR'S NOTE

broad-shouldered skipper. They zealously saluted one another with whiffs of tobacco smoke, and the Emperor was so puzzled by an unexpected move that had been made by his opponent, that he did not notice Korsakov, in spite of the latter's efforts to call attention to himself. Just then a stout gentleman, with a large bouquet upon his breast, fussily entered the room, announced in a loud voice that the dancing had commenced, and immediately retired. A large number of the guests followed him, Korsakov among them.

An unexpected sight filled him with astonishment. Along the whole length of the ball-room, to the sound of the most wretched music, the ladies and gentlemen stood in two rows facing each other; the gentlemen bowed low, the ladies curtsied still lower, first forward, then to the right, then to the left, then again forward, again to the right, and so on. Korsakov, gazing at this peculiar pastime, opened his eyes wide and bit his lips. The curtseying and bowing continued for about half an hour; at last they ceased, and the stout gentleman with the bouquet announced that the ceremonial dances were ended, and ordered the musicians to play a minuet. Korsakov rejoiced, and prepared to shine. Among the young ladies was one in particular whom he was greatly charmed with. She was about sixteen years of age, was richly dressed, but with taste, and sat near an elderly gentleman of stern and dignified appearance. Korsakov approached her and asked her to do him the honor of dancing with him. The young beauty looked at him in confusion, and did not seem to know what to say to him. The gentleman sitting near her frowned still more. Korsakov awaited her decision, but the gentleman with the bouquet came up to him, led him to the middle of the room, and said in a pompous manner:

"Sir, you have done wrong. In the first place, you

approached this young person without making the
three necessary bows to her, and in the second place,
you took upon yourself to choose her, whereas, in the
minuet that right belongs to the lady, and not to the
gentleman. On that account you must be severely punished, that is to say, you must drain the goblet of the
Great Eagle."

Korsakov grew more and more astonished. In a moment the guests surrounded him, loudly demanding
the immediate payment of the penalty. Peter, hearing
the laughter and the shouting, came out of the adjoining room, as he was very fond of being present in person at such punishments. The crowd divided before
him, and he entered the circle, where stood the culprit
and before him the marshal of the assembly holding
in his hands a huge goblet filled with malmsey. He
was trying in vain to persuade the offender to comply
willingly with the law.

"Aha!" said Peter, seeing Korsakov: "you are caught,
brother. Come now, monsieur, drink and don't make
faces."

There was no help for it: the poor fop, without pausing to take breath, drained the goblet and returned it
to the marshal.

"Look here, Korsakov," said Peter to him: "those
breeches of yours are of velvet, such as I myself do not
wear, and I am far richer than you. That is extravagance; take care that I do not fall out with you."

Hearing this reprimand, Korsakov wished to make
his way out of the circle, but he staggered and almost
fell, to the indescribable delight of the Emperor and
the whole merry company. This episode not only did
not spoil the harmony and interest of the principal performance, but even enlivened it. The gentlemen began to scrape and bow, and the ladies to curtsey and
clap their heels together with great zeal, and out of

time with the music. Korsakov could not take part in the general gaiety. The lady whom he had chosen approached Ibrahim, at the command of her father, Gavrila Afanasyevich Rzhevsky, and, dropping her blue eyes, timidly gave him her hand. Ibrahim danced the minuet with her and led her back to her former place, then sought out Korsakov, led him out of the ballroom, placed him in the carriage and drove him home. On the way Korsakov began to mutter indistinctly: "Accursed assembly! . . . accursed goblet of the Great Eagle!" . . . but he soon fell into a sound sleep, and knew not how he reached home, nor how he was undressed and put into bed: and he awoke the next day with a headache, and with a dim recollection of the scraping, the curtseying, the tobacco smoke, the gentleman with the bouquet, and the goblet of the Great Eagle.

IV

I MUST now introduce the gracious reader to Gavrila Afanasyevich Rzhevsky. He was descended from an ancient noble family, possessed vast estates, was hospitable, loved falconry, and had a large number of domestics—in a word, he was a genuine Russian gentleman. To use his own expression, he could not endure the German spirit, and he endeavored to preserve in his home the ancient customs that were so dear to him. His daughter was seventeen years old. She had lost her mother while she was yet a child. She had been brought up in the old style, that is to say, she was surrounded by governesses, nurses, playmates, and maidservants, was able to embroider in gold, and could neither read nor write. Her father, notwithstanding his dislike of everything foreign, could not oppose her wish to learn German dances from a captive Swedish officer, living in their house. This deserving dancing-master was about fifty years of age; his right foot had been shot through at Narva, and consequently it was not capable of performing minuets and courantes, but the left executed with wonderful ease and agility the most difficult steps. His pupil did honor to his efforts. Natalya Gavrilovna was celebrated for being the best dancer at the assemblies, and this was partly the cause of Korsakov's transgression. He came the next day to apologize to Gavrila Afanasyevich; but the grace and elegance of the young fop did not find favor in the eyes of the proud boyar, who wittily nicknamed him the French monkey.

It was a holiday. Gavrila Afanasyevich expected some relatives and friends. In the ancient hall a long table was being laid. The guests were arriving with their wives and daughters, who had at last been set free from domestic imprisonment by the decree of the Emperor and by his own example. Natalya Gavrilovna carried round to each guest a silver tray laden with golden cups, and each man, as he drained his, regretted that the kiss, which it was customary to receive on such occasions in the olden times, had gone out of fashion.

They sat down to table. In the place of honor, next to the host, sat his father-in-law, Prince Boris Alexeyevich Lykov, a boyar of seventy years of age; the other guests ranged themselves according to the rank of their family, thus recalling the happy times when rules of precedence were generally respected. The men sat on one side, the women on the other. At the end of the table, the housekeeper in her old-fashioned jacket and head-dress, the dwarf, a thirty-year-old midget, prim and wrinkled, and the captive Swede, in his faded blue uniform, occupied their accustomed places. The table, which was loaded with a large number of dishes, was surrounded by an anxious crowd of domestics, among whom the butler was prominent, thanks to his severe look, big paunch and stately immobility. The first few minutes of the dinner were devoted entirely to the products of our old-fashioned cuisine; the noise of plates and the rattling of spoons alone disturbed the general silence. At last the host, seeing that the time had arrived for amusing the guests with agreeable conversation, turned round and asked:

"But where is Yekimovna? Call her here."

Several servants were about to rush off in different directions, but at that moment an old woman, powdered and rouged, decked out in flowers and tinsel, in a low-necked silk gown, entered, singing and dancing. All were pleased to see her.

"Good-day, Yekimovna," said Prince Lykov: "how are you?"

"Quite well and happy, gossip: still singing and dancing and looking out for suitors."

"Where have you been, fool?" asked the host.

"Decking myself out, gossip, for our dear guests, for this holy day, by the order of the Czar, at the command of the boyar, in the German style, to make you all smile."

At these words there was a loud burst of laughter, and the fool took her place behind the host's chair.

"The fool talks nonsense, but sometimes speaks the truth," said Tatyana Afanasyevna, the eldest sister of the host, for whom he entertained great respect. "Truly, the present fashions are something for all to laugh at. Since you, gentlemen, have shaved off your beards and put on short *caftans*, it is, of course, useless to talk about women's rags, but it is really a pity about the *sarafan*, the girls' ribbon, and the *povoinik!* [1] It is

---

[1] The national head-dress of the Russian women.
TRANSLATOR'S NOTE

pitiable and at the same time laughable, to see the belles of today: their hair fluffed up like tow, greased and covered with French flour; their stomachs laced so tightly that they almost break in two; their petticoats are stretched on hoops, so that they have to enter a carriage sideways, and to go through a door they have to stoop; they can neither stand, nor sit, nor breathe—real martyrs, the darlings!"

"Oh, my dear Tatyana Afanasyevna!" said Kirila Petrovich T——, a former Governor of Ryazan, where he had acquired three thousand serfs and a young wife, both by somewhat shady means, "as far as I am concerned, my wife may dress as she pleases, she may get herself up like a blowsy peasant woman or like the Chinese Emperor, provided that she does not order new dresses every month and throw away the outmoded ones that are nearly new. In former times the grandmother's *sarafan* formed part of the granddaughter's dowry, but nowadays all that is changed: the dress, that the mistress wears today, you will see the servant wearing tomorrow. What is to be done? It is the ruin of the Russian nobility; it's a calamity!"

At these words he sighed and looked at his Marya Ilyinishna, who did not seem at all to like either his praises of the past or his disparagement of the latest customs. The other young ladies shared her displeasure, but they remained silent, for modesty was then considered an indispensable attribute of a young woman.

"And who is to blame?" said Gavrila Afanasyevich, filling a tankard with foaming kvass. "Isn't it our own fault? The young women play the fool, and we encourage them."

"But what can we do, when our wishes are not consulted?" retorted Kirila Petrovich. "One would be glad to shut his wife up in the women's rooms, but with beating of drums she is summoned to appear at the assemblies. The husband goes after the whip, but the wife after frippery. Oh, those assemblies! The Lord has visited us with this punishment for our sins."

Marya Ilyinishna sat as if on needles and pins; her tongue itched to speak. At last she could restrain herself no longer, and turning to her husband, she asked him with an acid smile, what he found wrong in the assemblies.

"This is what I find wrong in them," replied the husband heatedly: "since they began, husbands have been unable to manage their wives; wives have forgotten the words of the Apostle: 'Let the wife see that she reverence her husband'; they no longer busy themselves about their households, but about finery; they do not think of how to please their husbands, but how to attract the attention of giddy officers. And is it becoming, madam, for a Russian lady to associate with tobacco-smoking Germans and their charwomen? And was ever such a thing heard of, as dancing and talking with young men till far into the night? It would be all very well if it were with relatives, but with outsiders, with strangers, with people that they are totally unacquainted with!"

"I've a word for your ear, but the wolf is prowling near," said Gavrila Afanasyevich, frowning. "I confess that I too dislike these assemblies: before you know where you are, you knock into a drunken man, or are made drunk yourself to become the laughing-stock of others. Then you must keep your eyes open for fear that some good-for-nothing fellow might be up to mischief with your daughter; the young men nowadays are so utterly spoilt. Look, for example, at the son of the late Yevgraf Sergeyevich Korsakov, who at the last assembly made such commotion over Natasha, that it brought the blood to my cheeks. The next day I

see somebody driving straight into my courtyard; I
thought to myself, who in the name of Heaven is it,
can it be Prince Alexander Danilovich? But no: it was
Ivan Yevgrafovich! He could not stop at the gate and
make his way on foot to the steps, not he! He flew in,
bowing and chattering, the Lord preserve us! The fool
Yekimovna mimics him very amusingly: by the way,
fool, give us an imitation of the foreign monkey."

The fool Yekimovna seized hold of a dish-cover,
placed it under her arm like a hat, and began twisting, scraping, and bowing in every direction, repeating: "monsieur . . . mamselle . . . assemblée . . .
pardon." General and prolonged laughter again testified to the delight of the guests.

"The very spit of Korsakov," said old Prince Lykov,
wiping away the tears of laughter when quiet was
again restored. "But why conceal the fact? He is not
the first, nor will he be the last, who has returned from
abroad to holy Russia a buffoon. What do our children
learn there? To bow and scrape with their feet, to chatter God knows what gibberish, to treat their elders
with disrespect, and to dangle after other men's wives.
Of all the young people who have been educated
abroad (the Lord forgive me!) the Czar's Negro most
resembles a man."

"Of course," observed Gavril Afanasyevich: "he is
a sober, decent man, not like that good-for-nothing
. . . But who is it that has just driven through the gate
into the courtyard? Surely it cannot be that foreign
monkey again? Why do you stand gaping there,
beasts?" he continued, turning to the servants: "run
and tell him he won't be admitted, and in future . . ."

"Old man, are you dreaming?" interrupted Yekimovna the fool, "or are you blind? It is the Emperor's
sledge—the Czar has come."

Gavrila Afanasyevich rose hastily from the table;

everybody rushed to the windows, and sure enough they saw the Emperor ascending the steps, leaning on his orderly's shoulder. There was great commotion. The host rushed to meet Peter; the servants ran hither and thither as if they had gone crazy; the guests became alarmed; some even thought how they might hasten home as quickly as possible. Suddenly the thundering voice of Peter resounded in the ante-room; all became silent, and the Czar entered, accompanied by his host, who was beside himself with joy.

"Good day, gentlemen!" said Peter, with a cheerful countenance.

All made a profound bow. The sharp eyes of the Czar sought out in the crowd the young daughter of the house; he called her to him. Natalya Gavrilovna advanced boldly enough, but she blushed not only to the ears but even to the shoulders.

"You grow prettier from hour to hour," the Emperor said to her, and as was his habit he kissed her on the head; then turning to the guests, he added: "I have disturbed you? You were dining? Pray sit down again, and give me some aniseed brandy, Gavrila Afanasyevich."

The host rushed to the stately butler, snatched from his hand a tray, filled a golden goblet himself, and gave it with a bow to the Emperor. Peter drank the brandy, ate a biscuit, and for the second time requested the guests to continue their dinner. All resumed their former places, except the dwarf and the housekeeper, who did not dare to remain at a table honored by the presence of the Czar. Peter sat down by the side of the host and asked for cabbage soup. The Emperor's orderly handed him a wooden spoon mounted with ivory, and a knife and fork with green bone handles, for Peter never used any other table implements but his own. The dinner, which a moment before had been so noisy

and merry, was now continued in silence and con-
straint. The host, in his delight and awe, ate nothing;
the guests also stood upon ceremony and listened with
respectful attention, as the Emperor spoke in German
with the captive Swede about the campaign of 1701.
The fool Yekimovna, several times questioned by the
Emperor, replied with a sort of timid indifference,
which, by the way, did not at all prove her natural
stupidity. At last the dinner came to an end. The Emperor rose, and after him all the guests.

"Gavrila Afanasyevich!" he said to the host: "I must
speak to you in private;" and, taking him by the arm,
he led him into the parlor and locked the door. The
guests remained in the dining-room, talking in whispers about the unexpected visit, and, afraid of being indiscreet, they soon drove off one after another, without
thanking the host for his hospitality. His father-in-law,
daughter, and sister conducted them very quietly to
the door, and remained alone in the dining-room,
waiting for the Emperor to emerge.

V

HALF AN HOUR later the door opened and Peter
issued forth. With a dignified inclination of the head
he responded to the threefold bow of Prince Lykov,
Tatyana Afanasyevna and Natasha, and walked
straight out into the ante-room. The host handed him
his red coat, conducted him to the sledge, and on the
steps thanked him once more for the honor he had
shown him.

Peter drove off.

Returning to the dining-room, Gavrila Afanasyevich seemed very much troubled; he angrily ordered
the servants to clear the table as quickly as possible,

sent Natasha to her own room, and, informing his sister and father-in-law that he must talk with them, he led them into the bedroom, where he usually rested after dinner. The old Prince lay down upon the oak bed; Tatyana Afanasyevna sank into the old brocaded armchair, and placed her feet upon the footstool; Gavrila Afanasyevich locked all the doors, sat down upon the bed at the feet of Prince Lykov, and in a low voice began:

"It was not for nothing that the Emperor paid me a visit today: guess what he wanted to talk to me about."

"How can we know, brother?" said Tatyana Afanasyevna.

"Has the Czar appointed you governor of some province?" said his father-in-law:—"it is high time that he did so. Or has he offered you an ambassador's post? Men of noble birth—not only plain clerks—are sent to foreign monarchs."

"No," replied his son-in-law, frowning. "I am a man of the old school, and our services nowadays are not in demand, although, perhaps, an orthodox Russian nobleman is worth more than these modern upstarts, pancake vendors [1] and heathens. But this is a different matter altogether."

"Then what was it, brother?" said Tatyana Afanasyevna, "that he was talking with you about for such a long time? Can it be that you are in trouble? The Lord save and defend us!"

"Not exactly in trouble, but I confess that it is a matter for reflection."

"Then what is it, brother? What is it all about?"

"It is about Natasha: the Czar came to speak of a match for her."

"God be praised!" said Tatyana Afanasyevna, cross-

---

[1] The allusion is to Menshikov, who is said to have sold pancakes or pies on the Moscow streets in his youth. EDITOR'S NOTE

ing herself. "The girl is of marriageable age, and as the matchmaker is, so must the bridegroom be. God give them love and counsel, the honor is great. For whom does the Czar ask her hand?"

"H'm!" exclaimed Gavrila Afanasyevich: "for whom? That's just it—for whom!"

"Who is it, then?" repeated Prince Lykov, already beginning to doze off.

"Guess," said Gavrila Afanasyevich.

"My dear brother," replied the old lady: "how can we guess? There are a great number of eligibles at Court, each of whom would be glad to take your Natasha for his wife. Is it Dolgoruky?"

"No, it is not Dolgoruky."

"It's just as well: he is much too conceited. Is it Shein? Troyekurov?"

"No, neither the one nor the other."

"I do not care for them either; they are flighty, and too much imbued with the German spirit. Well, is it Miloslavsky?"

"No, not he."

"It's just as well, he is rich and stupid. Who then? Yeletzky? Lvov? No? It cannot be Raguzinsky? I cannot think of anybody else. For whom, then, does the Czar intend Natasha?"

"For the Negro Ibrahim."

The old lady exclaimed, and struck her hands together. Prince Lykov raised his head from the pillow, and with astonishment repeated:

"For the Negro Ibrahim?"

"My dear brother!" said the old lady in a tearful voice: "do not ruin your own child, do not deliver poor little Natasha into the clutches of that black devil."

"But how," replied Gavrila Afanasyevich: "can I refuse the Emperor, who promises in return to bestow his favor upon us and all our house?"

"What!" exclaimed the old Prince, who was now wide awake: "Natasha, my granddaughter, to be married to a bought Negro!"

"He is not of common birth," said Gavrila Afanasyevich: "he is the son of a Negro Sultan. The Mussulmen took him prisoner and sold him in Constantinople, and our ambassador bought him and presented him to the Czar. The Negro's eldest brother came to Russia with a considerable ransom and——"

"My dear Gavrila Afanasyevich!" interrupted the old lady, "we have heard the fairy tale about Prince Bova and Yeruslan Lazarevich. Tell us rather what answers you made to the Emperor's proposal."

"I said that we were under his authority, and that it was our duty to obey him in all things."

At that moment a noise was heard behind the door. Gavrila Afanasyevich went to open it, but felt some obstruction. He pushed it hard, the door opened, and they saw Natasha lying in a swoon upon the blood-stained floor.

Her heart had sunk within her, when the Emperor shut himself up with her father; some presentiment had whispered to her that the matter concerned her, and when Gavrila Afanasyevitch ordered her to withdraw, saying that he wished to speak to her aunt and grandfather, she could not resist the promptings of feminine curiosity, stole quietly along through the inner rooms to the bedroom door, and did not miss a single word of the whole terrible conversation; when she heard her father's last words, the poor girl lost consciousness, and falling, struck her head against an iron-bound chest, in which her dowry was kept.

The servants hastened to the spot; Natasha was lifted up, carried to her own room, and placed in bed. After a while she regained consciousness, opened her eyes. but recognized neither father nor aunt. A violent fever set in; she spoke in her delirium about the Czar's Negro, about marriage, and suddenly cried in a plaintive and piercing voice:

"Valeryan, dear Valeryan, my life, save me! there they are, there they are. . . ."

Tatyana Afanasyevna glanced uneasily at her brother, who turned pale, bit his lips, and silently left the room. He returned to the old Prince, who, unable to mount the stairs, had remained below.

"How is Natasha?" he asked.

"Very bad," replied the grieved father: "worse than I thought; she is delirious, and raves about Valeryan."

"Who is this Valeryan?" asked the anxious old man. "Can it be that orphan, the son of a *streletz*,[1] whom you brought up in your house?"

"The same, to my misfortune!" replied Gavrila Afanasyevich. "His father, at the time of the rebellion, saved my life, and the devil put it into my head to take the accursed wolf-cub into my house. When, two years ago, he was enrolled in the regiment at his own request, Natasha, on taking leave of him, shed bitter tears, and he stood as if petrified. This seemed suspicious to me, and I spoke about it to my sister. But since that time Natasha has never mentioned his name, and nothing whatever has been heard of him. I thought that she had forgotten him, but apparently this is not the case. It's settled: she shall marry the Negro."

Prince Lykov did not contradict him: it would have been useless. He returned home; Tatyana Afanasyevna remained by the side of Natasha's bed; Gavrila Afanasyevich, having sent for the doctor, locked himself in his room, and the house grew silent and gloomy.

The unexpected proposal astonished Ibrahim quite as much as Gavrila Afanasyevich. This is how it hap-

[1] A soldier in the standing army of old Muscovy. EDITOR'S NOTE

pened. Peter, being engaged in business with Ibrahim, said to him:

"I perceive, my friend, that you are downhearted; speak frankly, what is it you want?"

Ibrahim assured the Emperor that he was very well satisfied with his lot, and wished for nothing better.

"Good," said the Emperor: "if you are dull without any cause, I know how to cheer you up."

At the conclusion of the work, Peter asked Ibrahim:

"Do you like the young lady with whom you danced the minuet at the last assembly?"

"She is very charming, Your Majesty, and seems to be a good and modest girl."

"Then I shall take it upon myself to make you better acquainted with her. Would you like to marry her?"

"I, Your Majesty?"

"Listen, Ibrahim: you are a man alone in the world, without birth and kindred, a stranger to everybody, except myself. Were I to die today, what would become of you tomorrow, my poor Negro? You must get settled while there is yet time, find support in new ties, become connected by marriage with the Russian nobility."

"Your Majesty, I am happy under your protection, and in the possession of your favor. God grant that I may not survive my Czar and benefactor—I wish for nothing more; but even if I had any idea of getting married, would the young lady and her relations consent? My appearance——"

"Your appearance? What nonsense! You are a capital fellow! A young girl must obey the will of her parents, and we will see what old Gavrila Rzhevsky will say, when I myself am your matchmaker."

With these words the Emperor ordered his sledge, and left Ibrahim sunk in deep reflection.

"Get married?" thought the African: "why not?

Am I to be condemned to pass my life in solitude, and not know the greatest pleasure and the most sacred duties of man, just because I was born in the torrid zone? I cannot hope to be loved: a childish objection! Is it possible to believe in love? Does it then exist in the frivolous heart of woman? As I have renounced for ever these sweet delusions, I choose other, more substantial attractions. The Emperor is right: I must think of my future. Marriage with the young Rzhevsky girl will connect me with the proud Russian nobility, and I shall cease to be a sojourner in my new fatherland. From my wife I shall not require love: I shall be satisfied with her fidelity; and her friendship I will acquire by constant tenderness, confidence and indulgence."

Ibrahim, according to his usual custom, wished to occupy himself with work, but his imagination was too active. He left the papers and went for a stroll along the banks of the Neva. Suddenly he heard the voice of Peter; he looked round and saw the Emperor, who, having dismissed his sledge, advanced toward him with a beaming countenance.

"It is all settled, brother!" said Peter, taking him by the arm: "I have arranged your marriage. Tomorrow, go and visit your future father-in-law, but see that you humor his boyar pride: leave the sledge at the gate, go through the courtyard on foot, talk to him about his services and distinctions, and he will be perfectly charmed with you. . . . And now," continued he, shaking his cudgel, "lead me to that rogue Danilych, with whom I must confer about his recent pranks."

Ibrahim thanked Peter heartily for his fatherly solicitude on his account, accompanied him as far as the magnificent palace of Prince Menshikov, and then returned home.

VI

A LAMP shed a soft light on the glass case in which glittered the gold and silver mountings of the old family ikons. The flickering light faintly illuminated the curtained bed and the little table set out with labeled medicine-bottles. Near the stove sat a servant-maid at her spinning-wheel, and the subdued noise of the spindle was the only sound that broke the silence of the room.

"Who is there?" asked a feeble voice.

The servant-maid rose immediately, approached the bed, and gently raised the curtain.

"Will it soon be daylight?" asked Natalya.

"It is already midday," replied the maid.

"Oh, Lord! and why is it so dark?"

"The curtains are drawn, miss."

"Help me to dress quickly."

"You must not do so, miss; the doctor has forbidden it."

"Am I ill then? How long have I been this way?"

"About a fortnight."

"Is it possible? And it seems to me as if it were only yesterday that I went to bed. . . ."

Natasha became silent; she tried to collect her scattered thoughts. Something had happened to her, but what it was she could not exactly remember. The maid stood before her, awaiting her orders. At that moment a dull noise was heard below.

"What is that?" asked the invalid.

"The gentlemen have finished dinner," replied the maid: "they are rising from the table. Tatyana Afanasyevna will be here presently."

Natasha seemed pleased at this; she waved her feeble

hand. The maid drew the curtain and seated herself again at the spinning-wheel.

A few minutes afterwards, a head in a broad white cap with dark ribbons appeared in the doorway and asked in a low voice:

"How is Natasha?"

"How do you do, auntie?" said the invalid in a faint voice, and Tatyana Afanasyevna hastened toward her.

"The young lady has come to," said the maid, carefully drawing a chair to the side of the bed. The old lady, with tears in her eyes, kissed the pale, languid face of her niece, and sat down beside her. Just behind her came a German doctor in a black *caftan* and the wig worn by the learned. He felt Natasha's pulse, and announced in Latin, and then in Russian, that the danger was over. He asked for paper and ink, wrote out a new prescription, and departed. The old lady rose, kissed Natalya once more, and immediately hurried down with the good news to Gavrila Afanasyevich.

The Czar's Negro, in uniform, wearing his sword and carrying his hat in his hand, sat in the drawing-room with Gavrila Afanasyevich. Korsakov, stretched out upon a soft couch, was listening to their conversation, and teasing a venerable greyhound. Becoming tired of this occupation, he approached the mirror, the usual refuge of the idle, and in it he saw Tatyana Afanasyevna, who through the doorway was vainly signaling to her brother.

"Someone is calling you, Gavrila Afanasyevich," said Korsakov, turning round to him and interrupting Ibrahim's speech.

Gavrila Afanasyevich immediately went to his sister and closed the door behind him.

"I am astonished at your patience," said Korsakov to

Ibrahim. "For a full hour you have been listening to a lot of nonsense about the antiquity of the Lykov and Rzhevsky lineage, and have even added your own moral observations! In your place *j'aurais planté là* the old liar and his whole tribe, including Natalya Gavrilovna, who puts on airs, and is only pretending to be ill—*une petite santé.* Tell me candidly: are you really in love with this little *mijaurée?*"

"No," replied Ibrahim, "I am not going to marry for love, I am going to make a marriage of convenience, and then only if she has no decided aversion to me."

"Listen, Ibrahim," said Korsakov, "follow my advice this time; in truth, I am more sensible than I seem. Get this foolish idea out of your head—don't marry. It seems to me that your bride has no particular liking for you. Don't all sorts of things happen in this world? For instance: I am certainly not a bad-looking fellow myself, and yet it has happened to me to deceive husbands, who, Lord knows, were in no way worse-looking than me. And you yourself . . . do you remember our Parisian friend, Count D——? There is no dependence to be placed upon a woman's fidelity; happy is he who can regard it with indifference. But you! . . . With your passionate, pensive and suspicious nature, with your flat nose, thick lips, and coarse wool, to rush into all the dangers of matrimony! . . ."

"I thank you for your friendly advice," interrupted Ibrahim coldly; "but you know the proverb: It is not your duty to rock other people's children."

"Take care, Ibrahim," replied Korsakov, laughing, "that you are not called upon some day to prove the truth of that proverb in the literal sense of the word."

Meanwhile the conversation in the next room became very heated.

"You will kill her," the old lady was saying: "she cannot bear the sight of him."

"But judge for yourself," replied her obstinate brother. "For a fortnight he has been coming here as her bridegroom, and during that time he has not once seen his bride. He may think at last that her illness is a mere invention, and that we are only seeking to gain time in order to rid ourselves of him in some way. And what will the Czar say? He has already sent three times to ask after the health of Natalya. Do as you like, but I have no intention of quarreling with him."

"Good Lord!" said Tatyana Afanasyevna: "what will become of the poor child! At least let me go and prepare her for such a visit."

Gavrila Afanasyevich consented, and then returned to the parlor.

"Thank God!" said he to Ibrahim: "the danger is over. Natalya is much better. Were it not that I do not like to leave my dear guest Ivan Yeografovich here alone, I would take you upstairs to have a glimpse of your bride."

Korsakov congratulated Gavrila Afanasyevich, asked him not to be uneasy on his account, assured him that he was compelled to go at once, and rushed out into the hall, without allowing his host to accompany him.

Meanwhile Tatyana Afanasyevna hastened to prepare the invalid for the appearance of the terrible guest. Entering the room, she sat down breathless by the side of the bed, and took Natasha by the hand; but before she was able to utter a word, the door opened.

Natasha asked: "Who has come in?"

The old lady turned faint. Gavrila Afanasyevich drew back the curtain, looked coldly at the sick girl, and asked how she was. The invalid wanted to smile at him, but could not. Her father's stern look struck her, and uneasiness took possession of her. At that moment it seemed to her that someone was standing at the head of her bed. She raised her head with an effort and suddenly recognized the Czar's Negro. Then she remembered everything, and all the horror of the future presented itself to her. But she was too exhausted to be perceptibly shocked. Natasha laid her head down again upon the pillow and closed her eyes . . . her heart beat painfully. Tatyana Afanasyevna made a sign to her brother that the invalid wanted to go to sleep, and all quitted the room very quietly, except the maid, who resumed her seat at the spinning-wheel.

The unhappy girl opened her eyes, and no longer seeing anybody by her bedside, called the maid and sent her for the dwarf. But at that moment a round, old figure rolled up to her bed, like a ball. Lastochka (for so the dwarf was called) with all the speed of her short legs had followed Gavrila Afanasyevich and Ibrahim up the stairs, and concealed herself behind the door, in accordance with the promptings of that curiosity which is inborn in the fair sex. Natasha, seeing her, sent the maid away, and the dwarf sat down upon a stool by the bedside.

Never had so small a body contained within itself so much energy. She meddled in everything, knew everything, and busied herself about everything. By cunning and insinuating ways she had succeeded in gaining the love of her masters, and the hatred of all the household, which she controlled in the most autocratic manner. Gavrila Afanasyevich listened to her tale-bearing, complaints, and petty requests. Tatyana Afanasyevna constantly asked her opinion, and followed her advice, and Natasha had the most unbounded affection for her, and confided to her all the thoughts, all the emotions of her sixteen-year-old heart.

"Do you know, Lastochka," said she, "my father is going to marry me to the Negro."

The dwarf sighed deeply, and her wrinkled face became still more wrinkled.

"Is there no hope?" continued Natasha: "will my father not take pity upon me?"

The dwarf shook her cap.

"Will not my grandfather or my aunt intercede for me?"

"No, miss; during your illness the Negro succeeded in bewitching everybody. The master dotes upon him, the Prince raves about him alone, and Tatyana Afanasyevna says it is a pity that he is a Negro, as a better bridegroom we could not wish for."

"My God, my God!" moaned poor Natasha.

"Do not grieve, my pretty one," said the dwarf, kissing her feeble hand. "If you are to marry the Negro, you will have your own way in everything. Nowadays it is not as it was in the olden times: husbands no longer keep their wives under lock and key; they say the Negro is rich; you will have a splendid house—you will lead a merry life."

"Poor Valeryan!" said Natasha, but so softly, that the dwarf could only guess what she said, rather than hear the words.

"That is just it, miss," said she, mysteriously lowering her voice; "if you thought less of the *streletz* orphan, you would not rave about him in your delirium and your father would not be angry."

"What!" said the alarmed Natasha: "I have raved about Valeryan? And my father heard it? And my father is angry?"

"That is just the trouble," replied the dwarf. "Now, if you were to ask him not to marry you to the Negro, he would think that Valeryan was the cause. There is nothing to be done; submit to the will of your parents, for what is to be, will be."

Natasha did not reply. The thought that the secret of her heart was known to her father, produced a powerful effect upon her imagination. One hope alone remained to her: to die before the consummation of the odious marriage. This thought consoled her. Weak and sad at heart she resigned herself to her fate.

VII

IN THE house of Gavrila Afanasyevich, to the right of the vestibule, was a narrow room with one window. In it stood a simple bed covered with a woolen counterpane; in front of the bed was a small deal table, on which a tallow candle was burning, and some sheets of music lay open. On the wall hung an old blue uniform and its contemporary, a three-cornered hat; above it, fastened by three nails, was a cheap print representing Charles XII. on horseback. The notes of a flute resounded through this humble abode. The captive dancing-master, its lonely occupant, in a night-cap and nankeen dressing-gown, was relieving the tedium of a winter evening, by playing some old Swedish marches which reminded him of the gay days of his youth. After devoting two whole hours to this exercise, the Swede took his flute to pieces, placed it in a box, and began to undress. . . .

Just then the latch of his door was lifted and a tall, handsome young man, in uniform, entered the room. The Swede rose, surprised.

"You do not recognize me, Gustav Adamych," said the young visitor in a moved voice. "You do not remember the boy to whom you used to give military instruction, and with whom you nearly started a fire in this very room, shooting off a toy cannon."

Gustav Adamych looked closely. . . .

"Eh, eh," he cried at last, embracing him: "Greetings! How long have you been here? Sit down, you scapegrace, let us talk."

[1827]

DUBROVSKY

I

SOME years ago, there lived on one of his estates
a Russian gentleman of the old school named
Kirila Petrovich Troyekurov. His wealth, distinguished birth, and connections gave him great weight
in the provinces where his estates were situated. The
neighbors were ready to gratify his slightest whim; the
government officials trembled at his name. Kirila
Petrovich accepted all these signs of obsequiousness as
his rightful due. His house was always full of guests,
ready to indulge his lordship in his hours of idleness
and to share his noisy and sometimes boisterous mirth.
Nobody dared to refuse his invitations or, on certain
days, omit to put in an appearance at the village of
Pokrovskoye. In his home circle, Kirila Petrovich exhibited all the vices of an uneducated man. Spoilt by
all who surrounded him, he was in the habit of giving
way to every impulse of his passionate nature, to every
caprice of his somewhat narrow mind. In spite of the
extraordinary vigor of his constitution, he suffered
two or three times a week from surfeit, and became
tipsy every evening.

Very few of the serf-girls in his household escaped

³ In the original MS. the first eight chapters are called volume I,
the rest—volume II.   EDITOR'S NOTE

the amorous attempts of this fifty-year-old satyr. Moreover, in one of the wings of his house lived sixteen
girls engaged in needlework. The windows of this
wing were protected by wooden bars, the doors were
kept locked, and the keys retained by Kirila Petrovich.
The young recluses at an appointed hour went into the
garden for a walk under the surveillance of two old
women. From time to time Kirila Petrovich married
some of them off, and newcomers took their places. He
treated his peasants and domestics in a severe and arbitrary fashion, in spite of which they were very devoted to him: they loved to boast of the wealth and influence of their master, and in their turn took many a
liberty with their neighbors, trusting to his powerful
protection.

Troyekurov's usual occupations were driving over
his vast domains, feasting at length, and playing prac-
tical jokes, invented newly every day, the victims being
generally new acquaintances, though his old friends
did not always escape, one only—Andrey Gavrilovich
Dubrovsky—excepted.

This Dubrovsky, a retired lieutenant of the Guards,
was his nearest neighbor, and the owner of seventy
serfs. Troyekurov, haughty in his dealings with people
of the highest rank, respected Dubrovsky, in spite of
his humble situation. They had been in the service together and Troyekurov knew from experience his impatient and resolute character. Circumstances separated them for a long time. Dubrovsky with his reduced
fortune, was compelled to leave the service and settle
down in the only village that remained to him. Kirila
Petrovich, hearing of this, offered him his protection;
but Dubrovsky thanked him and remained poor and independent. Some years later, Troyekurov, having retired with the rank of general, arrived at his estate. They
met again and were delighted with each other. After

that they saw each other every day, and Kirila Petrovich, who had never deigned to visit anybody in his life, came quite without ceremony to the modest house of his old comrade. In some respects their fates had been similar: both had married for love, both had soon become widowers, and both had been left with an only child. The son of Dubrovsky was being brought up in Petersburg; the daughter of Kirila Petrovich was growing up under the eyes of her father, and Troyekurov often said to Dubrovsky:

"Listen, brother Andrey Gavrilovich; if your Volodka should turn out well, I will let him have Masha for his wife, in spite of his being as poor as a church mouse."

Andrey Gavrilovich used to shake his head, and generally replied:

"No, Kirila Petrovich; my Volodka is no match for Marya Kirilovna. A penniless gentleman, such as he, would do better to marry a poor girl of the gentry, and be the head of his house, rather than become the bailiff of some spoilt baggage."

Everybody envied the good understanding existing between the haughty Troyekurov and his poor neighbor, and wondered at the boldness of the latter when, at the table of Kirila Petrovich, he expressed his own opinion frankly, and did not hesitate to maintain an opinion contrary to that of his host. Some attempted to imitate him and ventured to overstep the limits of due respect; but Kirila Petrovich taught them such a lesson, that they never afterward felt any desire to repeat the experiment. Dubrovsky alone remained beyond the range of this general law. But an accidental occurrence upset and altered all this.

One day, in the beginning of autumn, Kirila Petrovich prepared to go out hunting. Orders had been given the evening before for the whips and huntsmen to be ready at five o'clock in the morning. The tent and kitchen had been sent on beforehand to the place where Kirila Petrovich was to dine. The host and his guests went to the kennels where more than five hundred harriers and greyhounds lived in luxury and warmth, praising the generosity of Kirila Petrovich in their canine language. There was also a hospital for the sick dogs, under the care of staff-surgeon Timoshka, and a separate place where the pedigreed bitches brought forth and suckled their pups. Kirila Petrovich was proud of this magnificent establishment, and never missed an opportunity of boasting about it before his guests, each of whom had inspected it at least twenty times. He walked through the kennels, surrounded by his guests and accompanied by Timoshka and the head whips, pausing before certain kennels, either to ask after the health of some sick dog, to make some observation more or less just and severe, or to call some dog to him by name and speak tenderly to it. The guests considered it their duty to go into raptures over Kirila Petrovich's kennels; Dubrovsky alone remained silent and frowned. He was an ardent sportsman; but his modest fortune only permitted him to keep two harriers and one pack of greyhounds, and he could not restrain a certain feeling of envy at the sight of this magnificent establishment.

"Why do you frown, brother?" Kirila Petrovich asked him. "Don't you like my kennels?"

"No," replied Dubrovsky abruptly: "the kennels are marvelous, indeed I doubt whether your men live as well as your dogs."

One of the whips took offence.

"Thanks to God and our master, we don't complain of the way we live," said he; "but if the truth must be told, there is many a gentleman who would not do

badly if he exchanged his manor-house for any one of
these kennels: he would be better fed and warmer."

Kirila Petrovich burst out laughing at his servant's
insolent remark, and the guests followed his example,
although they felt that the whip's joke might apply to
them also. Dubrovsky turned pale and said not a word.
At that moment a basket, containing some new-born
puppies, was brought to Kirila Petrovich; he busied
himself with them, choosing two for himself and ordering the rest to be drowned. In the meantime Andrey Gavrilovich had disappeared without anybody
having observed it.

On returning with his guests from the kennels,
Kirila Petrovich sat down to supper, and it was only
then that he noticed the absence of Dubrovsky. His
people informed him that Andrey Gavrilovich had
gone home. Troyekurov immediately gave orders that
he was to be overtaken and brought back without fail.
He had never gone hunting without Dubrovsky, who
was a great connoisseur in all matters relating to dogs,
and an infallible umpire in all possible disputes connected with sport. The servant who had galloped after
him, returned while they were still seated at table, and
informed his master that Andrey Gavrilovich had refused to listen to him and would not return. Kirila
Petrovich, as usual, was heated with liquor, and becoming very angry, he sent the same servant a second
time to tell Andrey Gavrilovich that if he did not return at once to spend the night at Pokrovskoye, he,
Troyekurov, would never have anything further to do
with him. The servant galloped off again. Kirila Petrovich rose from the table, dismissed his guests and retired to bed.

The next day his first question was: "Is Andrey Gavrilovich here?" By way of answer, he was handed a let

ter folded in the shape of a triangle. Kirila Petrovich ordered his secretary to read it aloud and he heard the following:

"Gracious Sir!

"I do not intend to return to Pokrovskoye until you send the whip Paramoshka to me with an apology: and it shall be for me to decide whether to punish or forgive him. I do not intend to put up with jokes from your servants, or, for that matter, from you, as I am not a buffoon, but a gentleman of ancient lineage. I remain your obedient servant,

"Andrey Dubrovsky."

According to present ideas of etiquette, such a letter would be very unbecoming; yet it irritated Kirila Petrovich, not by its strange style and form, but by its substance.

"What!" thundered Troyekurov, jumping barefooted out of bed; "send my people to him with an apology! And he to decide whether to punish or pardon them! What can he be thinking of? He doesn't know with whom he is dealing! I'll show him what's what! I'll give him something to cry about! He shall know what it is to oppose Troyekurov!"

Kirila Petrovich dressed himself and set out for the hunt with his usual ostentation. But the chase was not successful; during the whole of the day one hare only was seen, and that escaped. The dinner in the field, under the tent, was also a failure, or at least it was not to the taste of Kirila Petrovich, who struck the cook, abused the guests, and on the return journey rode intentionally, with all his suite, through Dubrovsky's fields.

II

SEVERAL days passed, and the animosity between the two neighbors did not subside. Andrey Gavrilovich returned no more to Pokrovskoye, and Kirila Petrovich, bored without him, vented his spleen in the most insulting expressions, which, thanks to the zeal of the neighboring gentry, reached Dubrovsky revised and augmented. A fresh incident destroyed the last hope of a reconciliation.

One day, Dubrovsky was driving around his little property, when, on approaching a grove of birch trees, he heard the blows of an axe, and a minute afterward the crash of a falling tree; he hastened to the spot and found some of the Pokrovskoye peasants calmly stealing his timber. Seeing him, they took to flight; but Dubrovsky, with the assistance of his coachman, caught two of them, whom he brought home bound. Moreover, two horses, belonging to the enemy, fell into the hands of the victor.

Dubrovsky was exceedingly angry. Before this, Troyekurov's people, who were well-known robbers, had never dared to do any mischief within the boundaries of his property, being aware of the friendship which existed between him and their master. Dubrovsky now perceived that they were taking advantage of the rupture which had occurred between him and his neighbor, and he resolved, contrary to all ideas of the rules of war, to teach his prisoners a lesson with the rods which they themselves had collected in his grove, and to send the horses to work, adding them to his own live-stock.

The news of these proceedings reached the ears of Kirila Petrovich that very day. He was almost beside himself, and in the first moment of his rage, he wanted to take all of his domestics and make an attack upon Kistenyovka (for such was the name of his neighbor's village), raze it to the ground, and besiege the landholder in his own manor. Such exploits were not rare with him; but his thoughts soon took another direction. Pacing with heavy steps up and down the hall, he glanced casually out of the window, and saw a *troika* stopping at his gate. A little man in a leather traveling-cap and a frieze cloak stepped out of the carriage and proceeded toward the wing occupied by the bailiff. Troyekurov recognized the assessor Shabashkin, and gave orders for him to be sent in to him. A minute afterward Shabashkin stood before Kirila Petrovich, and bowing repeatedly, waited respectfully to hear his orders.

"Good day—what is your name anyway?" said Troyekurov. "What has brought you here?"

"I was going to town, Your Excellency," replied Shabashkin, "and I called on Ivan Demyanov to find out if there were any orders from Your Excellency."

"You have come just at the right time—whatever your name is. I have need of you. Have some vodka and listen to me."

Such a friendly welcome agreeably surprised the assessor: he declined the vodka, and listened to Kirila Petrovich with all possible attention.

"I have a neighbor," said Troyekurov, "a small proprietor, a rude fellow, and I want to take his property away from him. . . . What do you think of that?"

"Your Excellency, are there any documents, or . . . ?"

"Don't talk nonsense, brother, what documents are you talking about? Ukases will take care of them. The point is to take his property away from him, in spite of the law. But stop! This estate belonged to us at one time. It was bought from a certain Spitzyn, and then

sold to Dubrovsky's father. Can't you make a case out
of that?"

"It would be difficult, Your Excellency: probably the
sale was effected in strict accordance with the law."

"Think, brother; try your hardest."

"If, for example, Your Excellency could in some way
obtain from your neighbor the deed, in virtue of which
he holds possession of his estate, then, of course . . ."

"I understand, but that is the trouble: all his papers
were burnt at the time of the fire."

"What! Your Excellency, his papers were burnt?
What could be better? In that case, take proceedings
according to law; without the slightest doubt you will
receive complete satisfaction."

"You think so? Well, see to it; I rely upon your zeal,
and you can rest assured of my gratitude."

Shabashkin, bowing almost to the ground, took his
departure; at once he began to occupy himself with the
business intrusted to him and, thanks to his prompt action, exactly a fortnight afterward Dubrovsky received
from town a summons to appear in court and to produce the documents, in virtue of which he held possession of the village of Kistenyovka.

Andrey Gavrilovich, greatly astonished by this unexpected request, wrote that very same day a somewhat
rude reply, in which he explained that the village of
Kistenyovka became his on the death of his father, that
he held it by right of inheritance, that Troyekurov had
nothing to do with the matter, and that anyone else's
claim to this property of his was nothing but chicanery and fraud.

This letter produced a very agreeable impression on
the mind of Shabashkin; he saw, in the first place, that
Dubrovsky knew very little about legal matters; and,
in the second, that it would not be difficult to place

such a rash and hot-tempered man in a very disadvantageous position.

Andrey Gavrilovich, after a more careful consideration of the questions addressed to him, saw the necessity of replying more circumstantially. He wrote a sufficiently businesslike letter, but this ultimately proved insufficient also. Dubrovsky had no experience in litigation. He generally followed the dictates of common sense, a guide rarely safe, and nearly always insufficient.

The business dragged on. Confident of being in the right, Andrey Gavrilovich troubled himself very little about the matter; he had neither the inclination nor the means to scatter money about, and although he was always the first to poke fun at the venality of the scribbling fraternity, the idea of being made the victim of chicanery never entered his head. Troyekurov, on his side, thought as little of winning the case he had started. Shabashkin took the matter in hand for him, acting in his name, intimidating and bribing the judges and quoting and interpreting various ukases in the most distorted manner possible.

At last, on the 9th day of February, in the year 18—, Dubrovsky received, through the town police, an invitation to appear at the district Court to hear the decision in the matter of the disputed property between himself—Lieutenant Dubrovsky—and General Troyekurov, and to signify his approval or disapproval of the verdict. That same day Dubrovsky set out for town. On the road he was overtaken by Troyekurov. They glared haughtily at each other, and Dubrovsky observed a malicious smile upon the face of his adversary.

Arriving in town, Andrey Gavrilovich stopped at the house of an acquaintance, a merchant, where he spent the night, and the next morning he appeared before the Court. Nobody paid any attention to him. After him arrived Kirila Petrovich. The clerks rose and stuck their pens behind their ears, while the members of the Court received him with every sign of abject obsequiousness, and an arm-chair was offered him out of consideration for his rank, years and corpulence. He sat down; Andrey Gavrilovich stood leaning against the wall. A deep silence ensued, and the secretary began in a sonorous voice to read the decree of the Court.

We cite it in full, believing that everyone will be pleased to see one of the ways in which we in Russia may lose an estate to which we have an indisputable right.[1]

When the secretary had ceased reading, the assessor arose and, with a low bow, turned to Troyekurov, inviting him to sign the paper which he held out to him. Troyekurov, quite triumphant, took the pen and wrote beneath the decision of the Court a statement signifying his complete satisfaction with it.

It was now Dubrovsky's turn. The secretary handed the paper to him, but Dubrovsky stood immovable, with his head bowed. The secretary repeated his invitation: "To signify his full and complete satisfaction, or his manifest dissatisfaction, if he felt in his conscience that his case was just, and intended, at the time stipulated by law, to appeal against the decision of the Court."

Dubrovsky remained silent . . . Suddenly he raised his head, his eyes flashed, he stamped his foot, pushed back the secretary with such force that he fell, seized the inkstand, and hurled it at the assessor. Everyone was horrified.

"What!" Dubrovsky shouted, "Not to respect the Church of God! Out with you, you spawn of Ham!"

Then turning to Kirila Petrovich:

[1] The lengthy court decree, which abounds in all the technicalities of a legal document, is omitted here.   EDITOR'S NOTE

"Has such a thing ever been heard of, Your Excellency?" he continued. "The whips bring dogs into the
Church of God! The dogs are running about the
church! I will teach you a lesson!"

The guards rushed in on hearing the noise, and with
difficulty overpowered him. They led him out and
placed him in a sledge. Troyekurov went out after
him, accompanied by the whole Court. Dubrovsky's
sudden madness had produced a deep impression upon his imagination and poisoned his triumph. The
judges, who had counted upon his gratitude, did not
receive a single affable word from him. He returned
immediately to Pokrovskoye. Dubrovsky, in the meantime, lay in bed. The district doctor—not altogether a
blockhead—bled him and applied leeches and fly-blis-
ters to him. Toward evening he began to feel better,
and the next day he was taken to Kistenyovka, which
scarcely belonged to him any longer.

III

SOME time elapsed, but poor Dubrovsky's health
showed no signs of improvement. It was true that the
fits of madness did not recur, but his strength was visibly failing. He abandoned his former occupations,
rarely left his room, and for days together remained
absorbed in his own reflections. Yegorovna, a kind-
hearted old woman who had once tended his son, now
became his nurse. She waited upon him as though he
were a child, reminded him when it was time to eat
and sleep, fed him and put him to bed. Andrey Gavrilovich obeyed her, and had no dealings with anybody
else. He was not in a condition to think about his affairs or to look after his property, and Yegorovna saw
the necessity of informing young Dubrovsky, who was

then serving in one of the regiments of Foot Guards stationed in St. Petersburg, of everything that had happened. And so, tearing a leaf from the account-book, she dictated to Khariton the cook, the only literate person in Kistenyovka, a letter, which she sent off that same day to town to be posted.

But it is time to acquaint the reader with the real hero of our story.

Vladimir Dubrovsky had been educated at the cadet school and, on leaving it, had entered the Guards as sub-lieutenant. His father spared nothing that was necessary to enable him to live in a becoming manner, and the young man received from home a great deal more than he had any right to expect. Being imprudent and ambitious, he indulged in extravagant habits, played cards, ran into debt, and troubled himself very little about the future. Occasionally the thought crossed his mind that sooner or later he would be obliged to take to himself a rich bride, the dream of every poverty-stricken youth.

One evening, when several officers were visiting him, lolling on couches and smoking his amber pipes, Grisha, his valet, handed him a letter, the address and seal of which immediately struck the young man. He hastily opened it and read the following:

"*Our Master Vladimir Andreyevich, I, your old nurse, have decided to report to you regarding your father's health. He is very poorly, sometimes he wanders in his talk, and the whole day long he sits like a foolish child—but life and death are in the hands of God. Come to us, my bright little falcon, and we will send horses to meet you at Pesochnoye. We hear that the Court is going to hand us over to Kirila Petrovich Troyekurov, because it is said that we belong to him, although we have always belonged to you, and have always heard so ever since we can remember. You might, living in St. Petersburg, inform our father the Czar of this, and he will not allow us to be wronged. I remain your faithful servant, nurse Arina Yegorovna Buzireva.*

"*I send my maternal blessing to Grisha, does he serve you well? It has been raining here for the last fortnight and Rodya the shepherd died about St. Nicholas' day.*"

Vladimir Dubrovsky read these somewhat confused lines several times with great agitation. He had lost his mother during his childhood, and, hardly knowing his father, had been taken to St. Petersburg when he was eight years of age. In spite of that, he was romantically attached to his father, and having had but little opportunity of enjoying the pleasures of family life, he loved it all the more in consequence.

The thought of losing his father pained him exceedingly, and the condition of the poor invalid, which he guessed from his nurse's letter, horrified him. He imagined his father, left in an out-of-the-way village in the hands of a stupid old woman and the domestics, threatened with some misfortune, and fading away helplessly in the midst of mental and physical tortures. Vladimir reproached himself with criminal neglect. Not having received any news of his father for a long time, he had not thought of making inquiries about him, supposing him to be traveling about or absorbed in the management of his estate. He decided to go to him and even to retire from the army, should his father's condition require his presence at his side. Seeing that he was upset, his friends left. Once alone, Vladimir wrote an application for leave of absence, lit his pipe, and sank into deep thought. That same evening he began to take further steps for obtaining leave of absence, and two days afterward he set out in a stage coach, accompanied by his faithful Grisha.

Vladimir Andreyevich neared the post station at which he was to take the turning for Kistenyovka. His heart was filled with sad forebodings; he feared that he would no longer find his father alive. He pictured to himself the dreary kind of life that awaited him in the village: the desolation, solitude, poverty and cares connected with business of which he did not understand a thing. Arriving at the station, he went to the postmaster and asked for horses. The postmaster, having inquired where he was going, informed him that horses sent from Kistenyovka had been waiting for him for the last four days. Before Vladimir Andreyevich there soon appeared the old coachman Anton, who used formerly to take him over the stables and look after his pony. Anton's eyes filled with tears on seeing his young master, and bowing to the ground, he told him that his old master was still alive, and then rushed off to harness the horses. Vladimir Andreyevich declined the proffered meal, and hastened to depart. Anton drove him along the cross-country roads, and conversation began between them.

"Tell me, if you please, Anton, what is this business between my father and Troyekurov?"

"God knows, little father Vladimir Andreyevich; the master, they say, fell out with Kirila Petrovich, and the latter went to law about it, though often he takes the law into his own hands. It is not the business of us servants to have a say about what our masters please to do, but God knows that your father had no business to go against the will of Kirila Petrovich: it's no use butting your head against a wall."

"It seems, then, that this Kirila Petrovich does just what he pleases with you?"

"He certainly does, master: he does not care a rap for the assessor, and the police officer is his errand boy. The gentry kowtow to him, for as the proverb says: 'Where there is a trough, there will the pigs be also.'"

"Is it true that he is taking our estate from us?"

"Oh, master, that is what we have heard. The other day, the sexton from Pokrovskoye said at the christening held at the house of our overseer: 'You've had it easy long enough; Kirila Petrovich will soon take you in hand;' and Mikita the blacksmith said to him: 'Savelich, don't distress the godfather, don't disturb the guests. Kirila Petrovich is for himself, and Andrey Gavrilovich is for himself—and we are all God's and the Czar's.' But you cannot sew a button upon another person's mouth."

"Then you do not wish to pass into the possession of Troyekurov?"

"Into the possession of Kirila Petrovich! The Lord save and preserve us! His own people fare badly enough, and if he got possession of strangers, he would strip off, not only the skin, but the flesh also. No, may God grant long life to Andrey Gavrilovich; and if God should take him to Himself, we want nobody but you, our provider. Do not give us up, and we will stand by you."

With these words, Anton flourished his whip, shook the reins, and the horses broke into a brisk trot.

Touched by the devotion of the old coachman, Dubrovsky became silent and gave himself up to his own reflections. More than an hour passed; suddenly Grisha roused him by exclaiming: "There is Pokrovskoye!" Dubrovsky raised his head. They were just then driving along the bank of a broad lake, out of which flowed a small stream which was lost to sight among the hills. On one of these, above a thick green wood, rose the green roof and belvedere of a huge stone house, and on another a church with five cupolas and an ancient belfry; round about were scattered the village huts with their kitchen gardens and wells. Dubrovsky recognized these places; he remembered that on that very hill he had played with little Masha Troyekurov, who was two years younger than he, and who even then gave promise of being a beauty. He wanted to make inquiries of Anton about her, but a certain bashfulness restrained him.

As they drove past the manor house, he noticed a white dress flitting among the trees in the garden. At that moment Anton whipped the horses, and impelled by that vanity, common to village coachmen as to drivers in general, he drove at full speed over the bridge and past the village. On emerging from the village, they ascended the hill, and Vladimir perceived the little birch grove, and to the left, in an open place, a small gray house with a red roof. His heart began to beat—before him was Kistenyovka, and the humble house of his father.

About ten minutes afterwards he drove into the courtyard. He looked around him with indescribable emotion: it was twelve years since he had last seen his birthplace. The little birches, which had just then been planted near the wooden fence, had now become tall, spreading trees. The courtyard, formerly ornamented with three regular flower-beds, between which ran a broad path carefully swept, had been converted into a meadow, in which was grazing a tethered horse. The dogs began to bark, but recognizing Anton, they stopped and wagged their shaggy tails. The servants came rushing out of the house and surrounded the young master with loud manifestations of joy. It was with difficulty that he was able to make his way through the enthusiastic crowd. He ran up the rickety steps; in the vestibule he was met by Yegorovna, who tearfully embraced him.

"How do you do, how do you do, nurse?" he re-

peated, pressing the good old woman to his heart.
"And father? Where is he? How is he?"

At that moment a tall old man, pale and thin, in a
dressing-gown and cap, entered the room, dragging
one foot after the other with difficulty.

"How are you Volodka?" said he in a weak voice,
and Vladimir embraced his father warmly.

The joy proved too much for the sick man; he grew
weak, his legs gave way beneath him, and he would
have fallen, if his son had not held him up.

"Why did you get out of bed?" said Yegorovna to
him. "He cannot keep on his feet, and yet he wants to
behave just like anybody."

The old man was carried back to his bedroom. He
tried to converse with his son, but he could not collect
his thoughts, and his words were incoherent. He became silent and fell into a kind of doze. Vladimir was
struck by his condition. He installed himself in the
bedroom and requested to be left alone with his father.
The household obeyed, and then all turned toward
Grisha and led him away to the servants' hall, where
they regaled him with a hearty meal according to the
rustic custom, and entertained him hospitably, weary-
ing him with questions and greetings.

IV

There is a coffin where the festive board was spread.

A FEW days after his arrival, young Dubrovsky wished to turn his attention to business, but his father was
not in a condition to give him the necessary explanations, and there was no one in charge of Andrey Gavrilovich's affairs. Examining his papers, Vladimir only
found the first letter of the assessor and a rough copy

of his father's reply to it. From these he could not obtain any clear idea of the lawsuit, and he determined to await the result, trusting in the justice of their cause.

Meanwhile the health of Andrey Gavrilovich grew worse from hour to hour. Vladimir foresaw that his end was not far off, and he never left the old man, who was now in his second childhood.

In the meantime the term for appealing the case had elapsed and nothing had been done. Kistenyovka now belonged to Troyekurov. Shabashkin came to him, and with a profusion of salutations and congratulations, inquired when His Excellency intended to enter into possession of his newly acquired property—would he go and do so himself, or would he deign to commission somebody else to act as his representative?

Kirila Petrovich was troubled. By nature he was not avaricious; his desire for revenge had carried him too far, and now his conscience pricked him. He knew in what condition his adversary, the old comrade of his youth, was, and his victory brought no joy to his heart. He glared sternly at Shabashkin, seeking for some pretext to give him a dressing-down, but not finding a suitable one, he said to him in an angry tone:

"Get out! I'm in no mood to see you!"

Shabashkin, seeing that he was in a bad humor, bowed and hastened to withdraw, and Kirila Petrovich, left alone, began to pace up and down, whistling: "Thunder of victory resound!" which, with him, was always a sure sign of unusual agitation of mind.

At last he gave orders for the droshky to be got ready, wrapped himself up warmly (it was already the end of September), and, himself holding the reins, drove away.

He soon caught sight of Andrey Gavrilovich's little house. Contradictory feelings filled his soul. Satisfied vengeance and love of power had, to a certain extent, deadened his more noble sentiments, but at last these latter prevailed. He resolved to effect a reconciliation with his old neighbor, to efface the traces of the quarrel and restore to him his property. Having eased his soul with this good intention, Kirila Petrovich set off at a gallop toward the residence of his neighbor and drove straight into the courtyard.

At that moment the invalid was sitting at his bedroom window. He recognized Kirila Petrovich—and his face assumed a look of violent agitation: a livid flush replaced his usual pallor, his eyes gleamed and he uttered unintelligible sounds. His son, who was sitting there examining the account books, raised his head and was struck by the change in his father's condition. The sick man pointed with his finger toward the courtyard with an expression of rage and horror. At that moment the voice and heavy tread of Yegorovna were heard:

"Master, master! Kirila Petrovich has come! Kirila Petrovich is on the steps!" she cried. . . . "Good God! What is the matter? What has happened to him?"

Andrey Gavrilovich had hastily gathered up the skirts of his dressing-gown and was preparing to rise from his arm-chair. He succeeded in getting upon his feet—and then suddenly collapsed. His son rushed toward him; the old man lay insensible and without breathing: he had had a stroke.

"Quick, quick! send to town for a doctor!" cried Vladimir.

"Kirila Petrovich is asking for you," said a servant, entering the room.

Vladimir gave him a terrible look.

"Tell Kirila Petrovich to take himself off as quickly as possible, before I have him turned out—go!"

The servant gladly left the room to execute his master's orders. Yegorovna struck her hands together.

"Master," she exclaimed in a piping voice, "you will

do for yourself! Kirila Petrovich will devour us all."

"Silence, nurse," said Vladimir angrily: "send Anton to town at once for a doctor."

Yegorovna left the room. There was nobody in the ante-chamber; all the domestics had run out into the courtyard to look at Kirila Petrovich. She went out on the steps and heard the servant deliver his young master's word. Kirila Petrovich heard it, seated in the droshky; his face became darker than night; he smiled contemptuously, looked threateningly at the assembled domestics, and then drove slowly out of the courtyard. He glanced up at the window where, a minute before, Andrey Gavrilovich had been sitting, but he was no longer there. The nurse remained standing on the steps, forgetful of her master's order. The domestics were noisily talking of what had just occurred. Suddenly Vladimir appeared in the midst of them, and said abruptly:

"There is no need for a doctor—father is dead!"

General consternation followed. The domestics rushed to the room of their old master. He was lying in the arm-chair in which Vladimir had placed him; his right arm hung down to the floor, his head was sunk on his chest—there was not the least sign of life in his body, which, although not yet cold, was already disfigured by death. Yegorovna set up a wail. The domestics surrounded the corpse, which was left to their care, washed it, dressed it in a uniform made in the year 1797, and laid it out on the same table at which for so many years they had waited upon their master.

V

THE funeral took place on the third day. The body of the poor old man lay in the coffin, covered with a

shroud and surrounded by candles. The dining-room
was filled with domestics, ready to carry out the corpse.
Vladimir and three servants raised the coffin. The priest
went in front, followed by the deacon, chanting the
prayers for the dead. The master of Kistenyovka crossed
the threshold of his house for the last time. The coffin
was carried through the wood—the church lay just behind it. The day was clear and cold; the autumn
leaves were falling from the trees. On emerging from
the wood, they saw before them the wooden church of
Kistenyovka and the cemetery shaded by old lime trees.
There reposed the body of Vladimir's mother; there,
beside her tomb, a new grave had been dug the day
before.

The church was full of the Kistenyovka peasantry,
come to render the last homage to their master. Young
Dubrovsky stood in the chancel; he neither wept nor
prayed, but the expression on his face was terrible. The
sad ceremony came to an end. Vladimir approached
first to take leave of the corpse, after him came the
domestics. The lid was brought and nailed upon the
coffin. The women wailed loudly, and the men frequently wiped away their tears with their fists. Vladimir and three of the servants carried the coffin to the
cemetery, accompanied by the whole village. The coffin was lowered into the grave, all present threw upon
it a handful of earth, the pit was filled up, the crowd
saluted for the last time and then dispersed. Vladimir
hastily departed, got ahead of everybody, and disappeared into the Kistenyovka wood.

Yegorovna, in her master's name, invited the priest
and all the clergy to a funeral feast, informing them
that her young master did not intend being present.

Then Father Anton, his wife Fedotovna and the
deacon set out on foot for the manor-house, discours-
ing with Yegorovna upon the virtues of the deceased

and upon what, in all probability, awaited his heir. The visit of Troyekurov and the reception given to him were already known to the whole neighborhood, and the local politicians predicted that it would have serious consequences.

"What is to be, will be," said the priest's wife: "but it will be a pity if Vladimir Andreyevich does not become our master. He is a fine young fellow, there is no denying that."

"And who is to be our master if he is not to be?" interrupted Yegorovna. "Kirila Petrovich is storming to no purpose—it's no timid soul he has to deal with. My young falcon will know how to stand up for his rights, and with God's help, his friends in high places will stick up for him. Kirila Petrovich is too proud; and yet he did put his tail between his legs when my Grishka cried out to him: 'Be off, you old cur! Clear out of the place!'"

"Oh! Yegorovna," said the deacon, "however could he bring his tongue to utter such words? I think I could more easily bring myself to gainsay the bishop than look askance at Kirila Petrovich. I shiver and shake at the very sight of him, and my back bends of itself, of itself!"

"Vanity of vanities!" said the priest: "the service for the dead will some day be chanted for Kirila Petrovich, as it was today for Andrey Gavrilovich; the funeral will perhaps be more imposing, and more guests will be invited; but is it not all the same to God?"

"Oh, father, we wanted to invite all the neighborhood, but Vladimir Andreyevich forbade it. To be sure, we have plenty to entertain people with. . . . but what would you have had us do? At all events, if there are not many people I will treat you well, our dear guests."

This friendly promise and the hope of finding a toothsome pie, caused the talkers to quicken their steps and they safely reached the manor-house, where the table was already laid and vodka served.

Meanwhile Vladimir advanced further into the depth of the wood, trying to deaden his grief by tiring himself out. He walked on without troubling to keep to the road; the branches constantly caught at and scratched him, and his feet continually sank into the swamp —he observed nothing. At last he reached a small glade surrounded by trees on every side; a little stream wound silently through the trees, half-stripped of their leaves by the autumn. Vladimir stopped, sat down upon the cold turf, and thoughts, each more gloomy than the other, crowded his mind. . . . He felt his loneliness very keenly; the future appeared to him enveloped in threatening clouds. Troyekurov's enmity foreboded fresh misfortunes for him. His modest heritage might pass from him into the hands of another, in which case destitution awaited him. For a long time he sat quite motionless, observing the gentle flow of the stream, bearing along on its surface a few withered leaves, and vividly presenting to him a true image of life. At last he noticed that it was growing dark; he arose and began to look for the road home, but for a long time he wandered about the unknown forest before he stumbled upon the path which led straight up to the gate of his house.

There he saw the priest and his companions coming toward him. The thought immediately occurred to him that this foreboded misfortune. He automatically turned aside and disappeared behind the trees. They had not caught sight of him, and they continued talking heatedly among themselves as they passed him.

"Fly from evil and do good," said the priest to his wife. "There is no need for us to remain here; it does not concern us, however the business may end."

The priest's wife made some reply, but Vladimir could not hear what she said.

Approaching the house, he saw a crowd of people; peasants and house serfs filled the courtyard. In the distance Vladimir could hear an unusual noise and the sound of voices. Near the shed stood two *troikas*. On the steps several unknown men in uniform were seemingly engaged in conversation.

"What does this mean?" he asked angrily of Anton, who ran forward to meet him. "Who are these people, and what do they want?"

"Oh, father Vladimir Andreyevich," replied Anton, out of breath, "the magistrates have come. They are handing us over to Troyekurov, they are taking us from your honor! . . ."

Vladimir hung his head; his people surrounded their unhappy master.

"You are our father," they cried, kissing his hands. "We want no other master but you. We will die, but we will not leave you. Give us the order, and we will settle the officials."

Vladimir looked at them, and strange feelings moved him.

"Keep quiet," he said to them: "I will speak to the officers."

"That's it — speak to them, father," shouted the crowd: "bring the accursed wretches to reason!"

Vladimir approached the officials. Shabashkin, with his cap on his head, stood with his arms akimbo, looking proudly around him. The sheriff, a tall stout man, of about fifty years of age, with a red face and a mustache, seeing Dubrovsky approach, cleared his throat and called out in a hoarse voice:

"And therefore I repeat to you what I have already said: by the decision of the district Court, you now belong to Kirila Petrovich Troyekurov, who is here represented by Mr. Shabashkin. Obey all his orders; and you, women, love and honor him, for he is certainly fond of you."

At this coarse joke the sheriff guffawed, Shabashkin and the other officials following his example. Vladimir was boiling with indignation.

"Allow me to ask, what does all this mean?" he inquired, with pretended calmness, of the jocular police officer.

"It means," replied the witty official, "that we have come to place Kirila Petrovich Troyekurov in possession of this property, and to request certain others to take themselves off while they can do it in peace."

"But I think that you could have communicated all this to me first, rather than to my peasants, and announced to the landowner the decision of the authorities——"

"The former landowner, Andrey Gavrilovich Dubrovsky, died by the will of God; and who are you anyway?" said Shabashkin, with an insolent look. "We do not know you, and we don't want to know you."

"Your honor, that is our young master, Vladimir Andreyevich," said a voice in the crowd.

"Who dared to open his mouth?" said the sheriff ferociously. "What master? What Vladimir Andreyevich? Your master is Kirila Petrovich Troyekurov. . . . do you hear, you blockheads?"

"Not quite!" said the same voice.

"But this is a revolt!" shrieked the police officer. "Hi, bailiff, come here!"

The bailiff stepped forward.

"Find out immediately who it was that dared to answer me. I'll teach him a lesson!"

The bailiff turned toward the crowd and asked who had spoken. But all remained silent. Soon a murmur was heard at the back; it gradually grew louder, and in a minute it broke out into a terrible clamor. The sheriff lowered his voice and was about to try to persuade them to be calm.

"Don't pay attention to him!" cried the house serfs; "Lay on, lads!" And the crowd lurched forward.

Shabashkin and the others rushed into the vestibule, and locked the door behind them.

"Break in, lads!" cried the same voice, and the crowd pressed forward.

"Hold!" cried Dubrovsky: "idiots! what are you doing? You will ruin yourselves and me, too. Go home all of you, and leave me to myself. Don't fear, the Czar is merciful: I will present a petition to him—he will not let us be wronged. We are all his children. But how can he stand up for you, if you begin acting like rebels and brigands?"

This speech of young Dubrovsky's, his resonant voice and imposing appearance, produced the desired effect. The crowd grew quiet and dispersed; the courtyard became empty, the officials kept indoors. Vladimir sadly ascended the steps. Shabashkin cautiously unlocked the door, came out on to the steps and with obsequious bows began to thank Dubrovsky for his kind intervention.

Vladimir listened to him with contempt and made no reply.

"We have decided," continued the assessor, "with your permission, to remain here for the night, as it is already dark, and your peasants might attack us on the road. Be kind enough to order some hay to be put down for us on the parlor floor; as soon as it is daylight, we will leave."

"Do what you please," replied Dubrovsky drily: "I am no longer master here."

With these words he retired to his father's room and locked the door behind him.

VI

"AND SO, I'm done for!" said Vladimir to himself. "This morning I had a corner and a piece of bread; tomorrow I must leave the house where I was born. My father, with the ground where he reposes, will belong to that hateful man, the cause of his death and of my ruin!" . . . Vladimir clenched his teeth and fixed his eyes upon the portrait of his mother. The artist had represented her leaning upon a balustrade, in a white morning dress, with a rose in her hair.

"And that portrait will fall into the hands of the enemy of my family," thought Vladimir. "It will be thrown into a lumber room together with broken chairs, or hung up in the ante-room, to become an object of derision for his whips; and in her bedroom, in the room where my father died, will be installed his bailiff, or his harem. No, no! he shall not have possession of the house of mourning, from which he is driving me."

Vladimir clenched his teeth again; terrible thoughts rose up in his mind. The voices of the officials reached him; they were giving orders, demanding first one thing and then another, and disagreeably disturbing him in the midst of his sad meditations.

At last all became quiet.

Vladimir unlocked the chests and boxes and began to examine the papers of the deceased. They consisted for the most part of accounts and business letters. Vladimir tore them up without reading them. Among them he came across a packet with the inscription: "Letters from my wife." A prey to deep emotion, Vladimir began to read them. They had been written during the Turkish campaign, and were addressed to the army from Kistenyovka. She described to her husband her

lonely life and the affairs of the farm, complained with
tenderness of the separation, and implored him to return home as soon as possible to the arms of his good
wife. In one of these letters, she expressed to him her
anxiety concerning the health of little Vladimir; in another she rejoiced over his early intelligence, and predicted for him a happy and brilliant future. Vladimir
was so absorbed in his reading, that he forgot everything else in the world as his mind conjured up visions
of domestic happiness, and he did not observe how the
time was passing: the clock upon the wall struck elev-
en. Vladimir placed the letters in his pocket, took a
candle and left the room. In the parlor the officials
were sleeping on the floor. Upon the table were tumblers which they had emptied, and a strong smell of
rum pervaded the entire room. Vladimir turned from
them with disgust, and passed into the ante-room. The
doors were locked. Not finding the key, Vladimir returned to the parlor; the key was lying on the table.
Vladimir unlocked the door and stumbled on a man
who was crouching in a corner. An ax glistened in
his hands. Turning the candle on him, Vladimir recognized Arkhip the blacksmith.

"Why are you here?" he asked.

"Oh, Vladimir Andreyevich, it's you!" Arkhip answered in a whisper. "The Lord save and preserve us!
It's a good thing that you had a candle with you."

Vladimir looked at him in amazement.

"Why are you hiding here?" he asked the blacksmith.

"I wanted—I came to find out if they were all in the
house," replied Arkhip, in a low faltering voice.

"And why have you got your ax?"

"Why have I got my ax? Can anybody go about
nowadays without an ax? These officials are such impudent knaves, that one never knows——"

"You are drunk; drop the ax and go sleep it off."

"I drunk? Master Vladimir Andreyevich, God is my witness that not a single drop of brandy has passed my lips, nor has the thought of such a thing entered my mind. Would the thought of drink enter my mind at a time like this? Was ever such a thing heard of? These clerks have taken it into their heads to rule over us and to drive our master out of the manor-house. . . . How they snore, the wretches! I 'd put an end to the lot and be done with it."

Dubrovsky frowned.

"Listen, Arkhip," said he, after a short pause: "Get such ideas out of your head. It is not the fault of the officials. Light the lantern and follow me."

Arkhip took the candle out of his master's hand, found the lantern behind the stove, lit it, and then both of them softly descended the steps and proceeded down the courtyard. The watchman began beating upon an iron plate; the dogs commenced to bark.

"Who is on the watch?" asked Dubrovsky.

"We, master," replied a thin voice: "Vasilisa and Lukerya."

"Go home," said Dubrovsky to them, "you are not wanted."

"You can quit," added Arkhip.

"Thank you, kind sir," replied the women, and they immediately went home.

Dubrovsky walked on further. Two men approached him: they challenged him, and Dubrovsky recognized the voices of Anton and Grisha.

"Why are you not in bed and asleep?" he asked them.

"This is no time for us to think of sleep," replied Anton. "Who would have thought that we should ever have come to this?"

"Softly," interrupted Dubrovsky. "Where is Yego-rovna?"

"In the manor-house, in her room," replied Grisha.

"Go and bring her here, and make all our people get out of the house; let not a soul remain in it except the officials; and you, Anton, get the cart ready."

Grisha departed; a minute afterward he returned with his mother. The old woman had not undressed that night; with the exception of the officials, nobody in the house had closed an eye.

"Are all here?" asked Dubrovsky. "Has anybody been left in the house?"

"Nobody, except the clerks," replied Grisha.

"Bring some hay or some straw," said Dubrovsky.

The servants ran to the stables and returned with armfuls of hay.

"Put it under the steps—that's it. Now, my lads, a light!"

Arkhip opened the lantern and Dubrovsky kindled a torch.

"Wait a minute," said he to Arkhip: "I think, in my hurry, that I locked the doors of the hall. Go quickly and open them."

Arkhip ran to the vestibule: the doors were open. He locked them, muttering in an undertone: "It's likely that I'll leave them open!" and then returned to Dubrovsky.

Dubrovsky applied the torch to the hay, which burst into a blaze, the flames rising to a great height and illuminating the whole courtyard.

"Oh, dear me!" cried Yegorovna plaintively: "Vladimir Andreyevich, what are you doing?"

"Silence!" said Dubrovsky. "Now, children, fare-well! I am going where God may direct me. Be happy with your new master."

"Our father, our provider!" cried the peasants, "we will die—but we will not leave you, we will go with you."

The horses were ready. Dubrovsky took his seat in the cart with Grisha; Anton whipped the horses and they drove out of the courtyard.

A wind rose. In one moment the whole house was enveloped in flames. The panes cracked and splintered; the burning beams began to crash; a red smoke rose above the roof, and there were piteous groans and cries of "Help, help!"

"Shout away!" said Arkhip, with a malicious smile, contemplating the fire.

"Dear Arkhip," said Yegorovna to him, "save them, the scoundrels, and God will reward you."

"Not a chance," replied the blacksmith.

At that moment the officials appeared at the window, endeavoring to burst the double sash. But at the same instant the roof caved in with a crash—and the cries ceased.

Soon all the peasants came pouring into the courtyard. The women, screaming wildly, hastened to save their effects; the children danced about admiring the conflagration. The sparks flew up in a fiery shower, setting the huts on fire.

"Now everything is right!" said Arkhip. "How it burns! It must be a grand sight from Pokrovskoye."

At that moment a new sight attracted his attention. A cat ran along the roof of a burning barn, without knowing where to leap down. Flames surrounded it on every side. The poor creature cried for help with plaintive mewings; the children screamed with laughter on seeing its despair.

"What are you laughing at, you imps?" said the blacksmith, angrily. "Do you not fear God? One of God's creatures is perishing, and you rejoice over it."

Then placing a ladder against the burning roof, he climbed up to fetch the cat. She understood his intention, and, with grateful eagerness, clutched hold of his sleeve. The half-burnt blacksmith descended with his burden.

"And now, lads, good-bye," he said to the dismayed peasants: "there is nothing more for me to do here. May you be happy. Do not think too badly of me."

The blacksmith went away. The fire raged for some time longer, and at last went out. Piles of red-hot embers glowed brightly in the darkness of the night, while round about them wandered the burnt-out inhabitants of Kistenyovka.

VII

THE next day the news of the fire spread through all the neighborhood. All discussed it and made various guesses about it. Some maintained that Dubrovsky's servants, having got drunk at the funeral, had set fire to the house through carelessness; others blamed the officials, who were drunk also in their new quarters. Many maintained that he had himself perished in the flames with the officials and all his servants. Some guessed the truth, and affirmed that the author of the terrible calamity was Dubrovsky himself, urged on by resentment and despair.

Troyekurov came the next day to the scene of the conflagration, and conducted the inquest himself. It transpired that the sheriff, the assessor of the district Court, a solicitor and a clerk, as well as Vladimir Dubrovsky, the nurse Yegorovna, the servant Grisha, the coachman Anton, and the blacksmith Arkhip had disappeared—nobody knew where. All the servants declared that the officials perished at the moment when the roof fell in. Their charred remains in fact were discovered. Vasilisa and Lukerya, said that they had seen Dubrovsky and Arkhip the blacksmith a few minutes before the fire. The blacksmith Arkhip, all asserted, was alive, and was probably the principal, if not the sole author of the fire. Strong suspicions fell upon Dubrovsky. Kirila Petrovich sent to the Governor a detailed account of all that had happened, and a new suit was commenced.

Soon other reports furnished fresh food for curiosity and gossip. Brigands appeared at X. and spread terror throughout the neighborhood. The measures taken against them proved unavailing. Robberies, each more startling than the last, followed one after another. There was no security either on the roads or in the villages. Several *troikas*, filled with brigands, traversed the whole province in open daylight, stopping travelers and the mail. The villages were visited by them, and the manor-houses were attacked and set on fire. The chief of the band had acquired a great reputation for intelligence, daring, and a sort of generosity. Wonders were related of him. The name of Dubrovsky was upon every tongue. Everybody was convinced that it was he, and nobody else, who commanded the daring robbers. One thing was remarkable: the domains and property of Troyekurov were spared. The brigands had not attacked a single barn of his, nor stopped a single cart belonging to him. With his usual arrogance, Troyekurov attributed this exception to the fear which he had inspired throughout the whole province, as well as to the excellent police which he had organized in his villages. At first the neighbors smiled at the presumption of Troyekurov, and everyone expected that the uninvited guests would visit Pokrovskoye, where they would find something worth having, but at last they were compelled to agree and confess that the

brigands showed him unaccountable respect. Troyekurov triumphed, and at the news of each fresh exploit on the part of Dubrovsky, he indulged in ironical
remarks at the expense of the Governor, the police, and
the company commanders, from whom Dubrovsky invariably escaped with impunity.

Meanwhile the 1st of October arrived, the day of the
annual church festival in Troyekurov's village. But before we proceed to describe this solemn occasion, as
well as further events, we must acquaint the reader
with some characters who are new to him, or whom
we merely mentioned at the beginning of our story.

VIII

THE reader has probably already guessed that Kirila
Petrovich's daughter, of whom we have as yet said but
very little, is the heroine of our story. At the period
about which we are writing, she was seventeen years
old, and in the full bloom of her beauty. Her father
loved her to distraction, but treated her with his characteristic wilfulness, at one time endeavoring to gratify
her slightest whims, at another terrifying her by his
stern and sometimes brutal behavior. Convinced of her
attachment, he could yet never gain her confidence.
She was accustomed to conceal from him her thoughts
and feelings, because she never knew in what manner
they would be received. She had no companions, and
had grown up in solitude. The wives and daughters of
the neighbors rarely visited Kirila Petrovich, whose
usual conversation and amusements demanded the
companionship of men, and not the presence of ladies.
Our beauty rarely appeared among the guests who
feasted at her father's house. The extensive library, consisting for the most part of works of French writers of

the eighteenth century, was put at her disposal. Her father, who never read anything except *The Perfect Cook*, could not guide her in the choice of books, and Masha, after having rummaged through works of various kinds, had naturally given her preference to romances. In this manner she went on completing her education, first begun under the direction of Mademoiselle Mimi, in whom Kirila Petrovich reposed great confidence, and whom he was at last obliged to send away secretly to another estate, when the results of this friendship became too apparent.

Mademoiselle Mimi left behind her a rather agreeable recollection. She was a good-natured girl, and had never misused the influence that she evidently exercised over Kirila Petrovich, in which she differed from the other favorites, whom he constantly kept changing. Kirila Petrovich himself seemed to like her more than the others, and a dark-eyed, roguish-looking little fellow of nine, recalling the Southern features of Mademoiselle Mimi, was being brought up by him and was recognized as his son, in spite of the fact that quite a number of bare-footed lads ran about in front of his windows, who were the very spit of Kirila Petrovich, and who were considered house serfs. Kirila Petrovich had sent to Moscow for a French tutor for his little son, Sasha, and this tutor came to Pokrovskoye at the time of the events that we are now describing.

This tutor, by his pleasant appearance and simple manner, produced an agreeable impression upon Kirila Petrovich. He presented to the latter his diplomas, and a letter from one of Troyekurov's relations, with whom he had lived as tutor for four years. Kirila Petrovich examined all these, and was dissatisfied only with the youthfulness of the Frenchman, not because he considered this agreeable defect incompatible with the patience and experience necessary for the unhappy calling of a tutor, but because he had doubts of his own, which he immediately resolved to have cleared up. For this purpose he ordered Masha to be sent to him. Kirila Petrovich did not speak French, and she acted as interpreter for him.

"Come here, Masha: tell this Monsieur that I accept him only on condition that he does not venture to run after my girls, for if he should do so, the son of a dog, I'll . . . Translate that to him, Masha."

Masha blushed, and turning to the tutor, told him in French that her father counted upon his modesty and orderly conduct.

The Frenchman bowed to her, and replied that he hoped to merit esteem, even if favor were not shown to him.

Masha translated his reply word for word.

"Very well, very well," said Kirila Petrovich, "he needs neither favor nor esteem. His business is to look after Sasha and teach him grammar and geography—translate that to him."

Masha softened the rude expressions of her father in translating them, and Kirila Petrovich dismissed his Frenchman to the wing of the house where a room had been assigned to him.

Masha had not given a thought to the young Frenchman. Brought up with aristocratic prejudices, a tutor, in her eyes, was only a sort of servant or artisan; and a servant or an artisan did not seem to her to be a man. Nor did she observe the impression that she had produced upon Monsieur Deforges, his confusion, his agitation, his changed voice. For several days in succession, she met him fairly often, but without deigning to pay him much attention. In an unexpected manner, however, she formed quite a new idea of him.

In Kirila Petrovich's courtyard there were usually kept several bear-cubs, and they formed one of the chief amusements of the master of Pokrovskoye. While they were young, they were brought every day into the parlor, where Kirila Petrovich used to spend whole hours in amusing himself with them, setting them at cats and puppies. When they were grown up, they were put on a chain, being baited in earnest. Sometimes they were brought out in front of the windows of the manor-house, and an empty wine-cask, studded with nails, was put before them. The bear would sniff it, then touch it gently, and getting its paws pricked, it would become angry and push the cask with greater force, and so wound itself still more. The beast would then work itself into a perfect frenzy, and fling itself upon the cask, growling furiously, until they removed from the poor animal the object of its vain rage. Sometimes a pair of bears were harnessed to a *telega*, then, willingly or unwillingly, guests were placed in it, and the bears were allowed to gallop wherever chance might direct them. But the favorite joke of Kirila Petrovich's was as follows:

A starved bear used to be locked up in an empty room and fastened by a rope to a ring screwed into the wall. The rope was nearly the length of the room, so that only the opposite corner was out of the reach of the ferocious beast. A novice was generally brought to the door of this room, and, as if by accident, pushed in where the bear was; the door was then locked, and the unhappy **victim was** left alone with the shaggy hermit. The poor guest, with torn skirt and scratched hands, soon sought the safe corner, but he was sometimes compelled to stand for three whole hours, pressed against the wall, watching the savage beast, two steps from him, leaping and standing on its hind legs, growling, tugging at the rope and endeavoring to reach him. Such were the noble amusements of a Russian gentleman!

Some days after the arrival of the French tutor, Troyekurov thought of him, and resolved to give him a
taste of the bear's room. For this purpose, he summoned him one morning, and conducted him along several
dark corridors; suddenly a side door opened—two servants pushed the Frenchman into the room and locked
the door after him. Recovering from his surprise, the
tutor perceived the chained bear. The animal began to
snort and to sniff at his visitor from a distance, and
suddenly raising himself upon his hind legs, he advanced toward him. . . . The Frenchman did not lose
his head; he did not run away but awaited the attack.
The bear approached; Deforges drew from his pocket
a small pistol, inserted it in the ear of the hungry animal, and fired. The bear rolled over. All ran to the
spot, the door was opened, and Kirila Petrovich entered, astonished at the outcome of his joke.

Kirila Petrovich wanted an explanation of the whole
affair. Who had warned Deforges of the joke, or how
came he to have a loaded pistol in his pocket? He sent
for Masha. Masha came and interpreted her father's
questions to the Frenchman.

"I never heard of the bear," replied Deforges, "but
I always carry a pistol about with me, because I do not
intend to put up with an offence for which, on account
of my calling, I cannot demand satisfaction."

Masha looked at him in astonishment and translated
his words to Kirila Petrovich. Kirila Petrovich made
no reply; he ordered the bear to be removed and
skinned; then turning to his people, he said:

"A capital fellow! There is nothing of the coward
about him. By the Lord, he is certainly no coward!"

From that moment he took a liking to Deforges, and
never thought again of putting him to the proof.

But this incident produced a still greater impression
upon Masha. Her imagination had been struck: she

had seen the dead bear, and Deforges standing calmly over it and talking tranquilly to her. She saw that bravery and proud self-respect did not belong exclusively to one class, and from that moment she began to show the young man a respect which increased from hour to hour. A certain intimacy sprang up between them. Masha had a beautiful voice and great musical ability; Deforges volunteered to give her lessons. After that it will not be difficult for the reader to guess that Masha fell in love with him without acknowledging it to herself.

IX

ON THE eve of the festival, of which we have already spoken, the guests began to arrive at Pokrovskoye. Some were accommodated at the manor-house and in the wings; others in the house of the bailiff; a third party was quartered upon the priest; and the remainder upon the better class of peasants. The stables were filled with the horses of the visitors, and the yards and coach-houses were crowded with vehicles of every sort. At nine o'clock in the morning the bells rang for mass, and everybody repaired to the new stone church, built by Kirila Petrovich and annually embellished, thanks to his contributions. The church was soon crowded with such a number of distinguished worshipers, that the simple peasants could find no room within the edifice, and had to stand on the porch and within the enclosure. The mass had not yet begun: they were waiting for Kirila Petrovich. He arrived at last in a calèche drawn by six horses, and solemnly walked to his place, accompanied by Marya Kirilovna. The eyes of both men and women were turned upon her—the former were astonished at her beauty, the latter examined her dress with great attention.

The mass began. The home-trained choristers sang
in the choir, and Kirila Petrovich joined in with them.
He prayed without looking either to the right or to the
left, and with proud humility he bowed himself to the
ground when the deacon in a loud voice mentioned
the name of the builder of *this temple*.

The mass came to an end. Kirila Petrovich was the
first to go up to kiss the crucifix. All the others followed him; the neighbors approached him with deference,
the ladies surrounded Masha. Kirila Petrovich, on leaving the church, invited everybody to dine with him,
then he seated himself in his coach and drove home.
All the guests followed him.

The rooms began to fill with the visitors; every moment new faces appeared, and it was with difficulty that
the host could be approached. The ladies sat decorous-
ly in a semicircle, dressed in antiquated fashion, in
gowns of faded but expensive material, and were be-
decked with pearls and diamonds. The men crowded
round the caviar and the vodka, conversing among
themselves with great animation. In the dining-room
the table was laid for eighty; the servants were bustling
about, arranging the bottles and decanters and adjusting the table-cloths.

At last the house-steward announced that dinner was
ready. Kirila Petrovich went in first to take his seat at
the table; the ladies followed him, and took their places
with an air of great dignity, obeying, to some extent,
the rule of seniority. The young ladies crowded together like a timid flock of kids, and took their places
next to one another. Opposite to them sat the men. At
the end of the table sat the tutor by the side of little
Sasha.

The servants began to serve the guests according to
rank; in case of doubt, they were guided by Lavater's
theories, and almost never made a mistake. The noise

of the plates and spoons mingled with the loud talk of the guests. Kirila Petrovich looked gaily round his table and thoroughly enjoyed the pleasure of being so hospitable a host. At that moment a carriage, drawn by six horses, drove into the yard.

"Who is that?" asked the host.

"Anton Pafnutyich," replied several voices.

The doors opened, and Anton Pafnutyich Spitzyn, a stout man of about fifty years of age, with a round pock-marked face, adorned with a treble chin, rolled into the dining-room, bowing, smiling, and preparing to make his excuses.

"A cover here!" cried Kirila Petrovich. "Pray sit down, Anton Pafnutyich, and tell us what this means: you were not at my mass, and you are late for dinner. This is not like you. You are devout, and you love good cheer."

"Pardon me," replied Anton Pafnutyich, fastening his serviette in the button-hole of his coat: "pardon me, my dear Kirila Petrovich, I started out early, but I had not gone ten versts, when suddenly the tire of the front wheel snapped in two. What was to be done? Fortunately it was not far from the village. But by the time we had arrived there, and had found a blacksmith, and had got everything put to rights, three hours had elapsed. It could not be helped. To take the shortest route through the Kistenyovka woods, I did not dare, so we came the longest way round."

"Ah, ah!" interrupted Kirila Petrovich, "it is evident that you are no dare-devil. What are you afraid of?"

"How, what am I afraid of, my dear Kirila Petrovich? And Dubrovsky? I might have fallen into his clutches. He is a young man who never misses his aim —he lets nobody off; and I am afraid he would have flayed *me* twice over, had he got hold of me."

"Why, brother, such a distinction?"

"Why, dear Kirila Petrovich? Have you forgotten the lawsui. of the late Andrey Gavrilovich? Was it not I who, to please you, that is to say, according to conscience and justice, showed that Dubrovsky held possession of Kistenyovka without having any right to it, and solely through your condescension; and did not the deceased—God rest his soul!—vow that he would settle with me in his own way, and might not the son keep his father's word? Hitherto the Lord has been merciful to me. Up to the present they have only plundered one of my barns, but one of these days they may find their way to the manor-house."

"Where they would find rich booty," observed Kirila Petrovich: "I have no doubt that the little red cash-box is as full as it can be."

"Not so, dear Kirila Petrovich; there was a time when it was full, but now it is quite empty."

"Don't you fib, Anton Pafnutyich. We know you. Where do you spend money? At home you live like a pig, you never receive anybody, and you fleece your peasants. You do nothing with your money but hoard it."

"You are only joking, dear Kirila Petrovich," murmured Anton Pafnutyich, smiling; "but I swear to you that we are ruined," and Anton Pafnutyich began to chew a greasy piece of pie, to take away the sting of his host's joke.

Kirila Petrovich left him and turned to the new sheriff, who was his guest for the first time and who was sitting at the other end of the table, near the tutor.

"Well, Mr. Sheriff, will *you* catch Dubrovsky?"

The sheriff was frightened, bowed, smiled, stammered, and said at last:

"We will do our best, Your Excellency."

"H 'm! 'we will do our best!' You have been doing

your best for a long time and to no purpose. And, after
all, why try to catch him? Dubrovsky's robberies are
a blessing to the sheriffs: what with trips and investiga-
tions, the money gets into one's pocket. Why do away
with such a godsend? Isn't that true, Mr. Sheriff?"

"Perfectly true, Your Excellency," replied the sheriff,
in utter confusion.

The guests roared with laughter.

"I like the fellow for his frankness," said Kirila Petrovich: "but it is a pity that our late sheriff is no longer
with us. If he had not been burnt, the neighborhood
would have been quieter. And what news of Dubrovsky? Where was he last seen?"

"At my house, Kirila Petrovich," said a female voice:
"last Tuesday he dined with me."

All eyes were turned toward Anna Savishna Glob-
ova, a widow, a rather simple person, beloved by everybody for her kind and cheerful disposition. Everyone
prepared to listen to her story with curiosity.

"You must know that three weeks ago I sent my
steward to the post with a letter for my Vanyusha. I
do not spoil my son, and moreover I haven't the means
of spoiling him, even if I wished to do so. However,
you know very well that an officer of the Guards must
live in suitable style, and I share my income with Vanyusha as well as I can. Well, I sent two thousand rubles to him; and although the thought of Dubrovsky
came more than once into my mind, I thought to myself: the town is not far off—only seven versts altogether, please God all will be well. But what happens? In the evening my steward returns, pale, tattered, and on foot. 'What is the matter? What has happened to you!' I exclaimed. 'The brigands have robbed and almost killed me,' he answered. 'Dubrovsky
himself was there, and he wanted to hang me, but he
afterwards had pity upon me and let me go. But he

took away everything I had—money, horse, and cart.'
A faintness came over me. Heavenly Lord! What will
become of my Vanyusha? There was nothing to be
done. I wrote him a letter, telling him all that had happened, and sent him my blessing without a groat.
One week passed, and then another. Suddenly, one
day, a coach drove into my courtyard. Some general
asked to see me: I gave orders for him to be shown in.
He entered the room, and I saw before me a man of
about thirty-five years of age, dark, with black hair,
mustache and beard—the exact portrait of Kulnev.
He introduced himself to me as a friend and colleague
of my late husband, Ivan Andreyevich. He happened
to be passing by, he said, and he could not resist paying
a visit to his old friend's widow, knowing that I lived
there. I invited him to dine, and I set before him what
God had sent me. We spoke of this and that, and at
last we began to talk about Dubrovsky. I told him of
my trouble. My general frowned. 'That is strange,' said
he: 'I have heard that Dubrovsky does not attack everybody, but only people who are well known to be rich,
and that even then he leaves them a part of their possessions and does not rob them of everything. As for
murdering people, nobody has yet accused him of that.
Is there not some knavery here? Oblige me by sending
for your steward.'

"The steward was sent for, and quickly made his appearance. But as soon as he caught sight of the general
he stood as if petrified.

" 'Tell me, brother, in what manner did Dubrovsky
rob you, and how was it that he wanted to hang you?'
My steward began to tremble and fell at the general's
feet.

" 'Sir, I am guilty. The evil one led me astray. I have
lied.'

" 'If that is so,' replied the general, 'have the goodness to relate to your mistress how it all happened, and I will listen.'

"My steward could not recover himself.

" 'Well, then,' continued the general, 'tell us where you met Dubrovsky.'

" 'At the two pine trees, sir, at the two pine trees.'

" 'What did he say to you?'

" 'He asked me who I was, where I was going, and why.'

" 'Well, and after that?'

" 'After that he demanded the letter and the money from me, and I gave them to him.'

" 'And he?'

" 'Well, and he . . . forgive me, sir!'

" 'Well, what did he do?'

" 'He returned me the money and the letter, and said: "Go in peace, and post this." '

" 'Well!'

" 'Forgive me, sir!"

" 'I will settle with you, my dear fellow,' said the general sternly. 'And you, madam, order this scoundrel's trunk to be searched, and then give him into my hands; I will teach him a lesson. Remember that Dubrovsky himself was once an officer in the Guards, and would not wish to take advantage of a comrade.'

"I guessed who His Excellency was, but there was no use saying anything. The coachmen tied the steward to the carriage-box; the money was found; the general dined with me, and departed immediately afterwards, taking with him my steward. The steward was found the next day in the wood, tied to an oak, and stripped bare."

Everybody listened in silence to Anna Savishna's story, especially the young ladies. Many of them secretly wished well to Dubrovsky, seeing in him a romantic hero, particularly Marya Kirilovna, an ardent dreamer, steeped in the mysteries and horrors of Mrs. Anne Radcliffe.

"And do you think, Anna Savishna, that it was Dubrovsky himself who visited you?" asked Kirila Petrovich. "You are very much mistaken. I do not know who your guest may have been, but I feel quite sure that it was not Dubrovsky."

"Not Dubrovsky? How can that be, my dear sir? But who else would stop travelers on the high road and search them?"

"I don't know; but certainly not Dubrovsky. I remember him as a child; I do not know whether his hair has turned black, but in those days his hair was fair and curly. But I do know for a positive fact, that Dubrovsky is five years older than my Masha, and that consequently he is not thirty-five, but about twenty-three."

"Exactly, Your Excellency," observed the sheriff: "I have in my pocket the description of Vladimir Dubrovsky. There it is distinctly stated that he is twenty-three years of age."

"Ah!" said Kirila Petrovich. "By the way, read it, and we will listen: it will not be a bad thing for us to know what he looks like. Perhaps we may catch a glimpse of him, and if so, he will not escape in a hurry."

The sheriff drew from his pocket a rather dirty sheet of paper, unfolded it with an air of importance, and began to read in a sing-song manner:

"Description of Vladimir Dubrovsky, based upon the depositions of his former house-serfs:

"*Age:* twenty-two; *height:* medium; *complexion:* clear; *beard:* shaven; *eyes:* hazel; *hair:* light; *nose:* straight; *special marks:* none."

"And is that all?" said Kirila Petrovich.

"That is all," replied the sheriff, folding up the paper.

"I congratulate you, Mr. Sheriff. A very valuable document! With that description it will not be difficult for you to find Dubrovsky! Who is not of medium height? Who has not light hair, a straight nose and hazel eyes? I would wager that you would talk for three hours at a stretch to Dubrovsky himself, and you would never guess in whose company you were. There is no denying that these officials are clever fellows."

The sheriff, meekly replacing the paper in his pocket, silently attacked his goose and cabbage. Meanwhile the servants had already gone the round of the guests several times, filling up each one's glass. Several bottles of Don and Caucasian wine had been opened with a great deal of noise, and had been favorably received under the name of champagne. Faces began to glow, and the conversation grew louder, more incoherent and more lively.

"No," continued Kirila Petrovich, "we shall never see another sheriff like the late Taras Alexeyevich! He was no blunderhead, no simpleton. It is a pity that the fellow was burnt, for otherwise not one of the band would have got away from him. He would have laid his hands upon the whole lot of them, and not even Dubrovsky himself would have escaped, or bribed his way out. Taras Alexeyevich would surely have taken his money, but he would not have let him go. That was the man's way. Evidently there is nothing else to be done but for me to take the matter in hand and go after the brigands with my people. I will begin by sending out twenty men to scour the wood. My people are not cowards. Each of them would attack a bear single-handed, and they certainly would not fall back before a brigand."

"How is your bear, Kirila Petrovich?" asked Anton Pafnutyich, being reminded by these words of his shaggy acquaintance and of certain pleasantries of which he had once been the victim.

"Misha has departed this life," replied Kirila Petrovich: "he died a glorious death at the hands of the enemy. There is his conqueror!" Kirila Petrovich pointed to the French tutor. "You should have an image of the Frenchman's patron saint. He has avenged you—if you will allow me to say so—do you remember?"

"How should I not remember?" said Anton Pafnutyich, scratching his head: "I remember it only too well. So Misha is dead. I am very sorry for Misha—upon my word, I am very sorry! How amusing he was! How intelligent! You will not find another bear like him. And why did *mossoo* kill him?"

Kirila Petrovich began, with great satisfaction, to relate the exploit of his Frenchman, for he possessed the happy faculty of boasting of all that belonged to his entourage. The guests listened with great attention to the story of Misha's death, and gazed in astonishment at Deforges, who, not suspecting that his bravery was the subject of the conversation, calmly sat in his place, occasionally rebuking his restive pupil.

The dinner, which had lasted about three hours, came to an end; the host placed his napkin upon the table, and everybody rose and repaired to the parlor, where coffee and cards were awaiting them, and a continuation of the drinking so famously begun in the dining-room.

X

ABOUT seven o'clock in the evening, some of the guests wished to depart, but the host, merry with

punch, ordered the gates to be locked, and declared
that he would let no one leave the house until the next
morning. Music soon resounded, the doors of the ballroom were thrown open and the dancing began. The
host and his intimates sat in a corner, draining glass
after glass, and admiring the gaiety of the young
people. The old ladies played cards. There were fewer
men than women, as is always the case, except where a
brigade of Uhlans is stationed, and all the men, suitable
for partners, were soon pressed into service. The tutor
particularly distinguished himself; he danced more
than anyone else; all the young ladies wanted to have
him as a partner, finding it very pleasant to waltz with
him. He danced several times with Marya Kirilovna,
and the young ladies observed them mockingly. At
last, about midnight, the tired host stopped the dancing, ordered supper to be served, while he betook himself to bed.

The retirement of Kirila Petrovich allowed the company more freedom and animation. The gentlemen
ventured to sit near the ladies; the girls laughed and
whispered to their neighbors; the ladies spoke in loud
voices across the table; the gentlemen drank, disputed,
and laughed boisterously. In a word, the supper was
exceedingly merry, and left behind it many agreeable
memories.

One man only did not share in the general joy. Anton Pafnutyich sat gloomy and silent in his place, ate
absently, and seemed extremely uneasy. The conversation about the brigands had worked upon his imagination. We shall soon see that he had good cause to fear
them.

Anton Pafnutyich, in invoking God as a witness that
the little red cash-box was empty, had not lied and
sinned. The little red cash-box was really empty. The
money which it had at one time contained had been

transferred to a leather pouch, which he carried on his breast under his shirt. This precaution alone quieted his distrust of everybody and his constant fear. Being compelled to spend the night in a strange house, he was afraid that he might be lodged in some solitary room, where thieves could easily break in. He looked round in search of a trustworthy companion, and at last his choice fell upon Deforges. His appearance—indicative of strength—but especially the bravery shown by him in his encounter with the bear, which poor Anton Pafnutyich could never think of without a shudder, decided his choice. When they rose from the table, Anton Pafnutyich began to circle round the young French man, clearing his throat and coughing, and at last he turned to him and addressed him:

"Hm! hm! Couldn't I spend the night in your room, *mossoo,* because you see——"

"*Que désire monsieur?*" asked Deforges, with a polite bow.

"Ah! what a pity, *mossoo,* that you have not yet learnt Russian. *Je vais moa chez vous coucher.* Do you understand?"

"*Monsieur, très volontiers,*" replied Deforges "*veuillez donner des ordres en conséquence.*"

Anton Pafnutyich, well satisfied with his knowledge of the French language, went off at once to make the necessary arrangements.

The guests began to wish each other good night, and each retired to the room assigned to him, while Anton Pafnutyich went with the tutor to the wing. The night was dark. Deforges lighted the way with a lantern. Anton Pafnutyich followed him boldly enough, pressing the hidden treasure occasionally against his breast, in order to convince himself that his money was still there.

On arriving at the wing, the tutor lit a candle and

both began to undress; in the meantime Anton Pafnutyich was walking about the room, examining the locks
and windows, and shaking his head at the disquieting
results of his inspection. The doors fastened with only
a bolt, and the windows had not yet their double
frames. He tried to complain to Deforges, but his
knowledge of the French language was too limited for
so elaborate an explanation. The Frenchman did not
understand him, and Anton Pafnutyich was obliged to
cease his complaints. Their beds stood opposite each
other; they both lay down, and the tutor extinguished
the light.

"*Pourquoi vous extinguishez; pourquoi vous extinguishez?*" cried Anton Pafnutyich, conjugating the
verb to extinguish, after the French manner. "I cannot
dormir in the dark."

Deforges did not understand his exclamation, and
wished him good night.

"Accursed heathen!" muttered Spitzyn, wrapping
himself up in the bedclothes: "he couldn't do without
extinguishing the light. So much the worse for him. I
cannot sleep without a light—*Mossoo, mossoo,*" he continued: "*Je vé avec vous parler.*"

But the Frenchman did not reply, and soon began to
snore.

"He is snoring, the French brute," thought Anton
Pafnutyich, "while I can't even think of sleep. Thieves
might walk in at any moment through the open doors
or climb in through the window, and the firing of a
cannon would not wake him, the beast!"

"*Mossoo! mossoo!*—the devil take you!"

Anton Pafnutyich became silent. Fatigue and the
effect of the wine gradually overcame his fear. He began to doze, and soon fell into a deep sleep. A strange
sensation aroused him. He felt in his sleep that someone was gently pulling him by the collar of his shirt.

Anton Pafnutyich opened his eyes and, by the pale
light of an autumn morning, he saw Deforges standing before him. In one hand the Frenchman held a
pocket pistol, and with the other he was unfastening
the strings of the precious leather pouch. Anton Pafnutyich felt faint.

"*Qu'est ce que c'est, Mossoo, qu'est ce que c'est?*"
said he, in a trembling voice.

"Hush! Silence!" replied the tutor in pure Russian.
"Silence! or you are lost. I am Dubrovsky."

XI

WE WILL now ask the reader's permission to explain
the last incidents of our story, by referring to the circumstances that preceded them, and which we have
not yet had time to relate.

At the station, in the house of the postmaster, of
whom we have already spoken, sat a traveler in a corner, looking very meek and patient, which showed him
to be a man without rank or a foreigner, that is, a person unable to assert his rights on the post road. His
carriage stood in the courtyard, waiting for the wheels
to be greased. Within it lay a small portmanteau, evidence of a very modest fortune. The traveler ordered
neither tea nor coffee, but sat looking out of the window and whistling, to the great annoyance of the
postmistress sitting behind the partition.

"The Lord has sent us a whistler," said she, in a low
voice. "How he does whistle! I wish he would burst,
the accursed heathen!"

"What does it matter?" said her husband. "Let him
whistle!"

"What does it matter?" retorted his angry spouse;
"don't you know the saying?"

"What saying? That whistling drives money away? Oh, Pakhomovna, whether he whistles or not, we shall have precious little money anyway."

"Then let him go, Sidorych. What pleasure have you in keeping him here? Give him the horses, and let him go to the devil."

"He can wait, Pakhomovna. I have only three troikas in the stable, the fourth is resting. Travelers of more importance may arrive at any moment, and I don't wish to risk my neck for a Frenchman. . . . Listen! there you are! Someone is driving up! And at what a rate! Can it be a general?"

A coach stopped in front of the steps. The servant jumped down from the box, opened the door, and a moment afterwards a young man in a military cloak and white cap entered the station. Behind him followed his servant, carrying a small box which he placed upon the window-ledge.

"Horses!" said the officer, in an imperious voice.

"Directly!" replied the postmaster: "your pass, if you please."

"I have no pass: I am not going to take the main road. . . . Don't you recognize me?"

The postmaster began to bustle about and rushed out to hurry the drivers. The young man began to pace up and down the room, went behind the partition, and inquired in a low voice of the postmaster's wife:

"Who is that traveler?"

"God knows!" she replied: "some Frenchman or other. He has been five hours waiting for horses, and has done nothing but whistle the whole time. I am tired of him, drat him!"

The young man spoke to the traveler in French.

"Where are you bound for, sir?" he asked.

"For the neighboring town," replied the Frenchman: "and from there I am going to a landed proprietor who has engaged me as tutor without ever having seen me. I thought I should have reached the place to-day, but the postmaster has evidently decided other-wise. In this country it is difficult to procure horses, Mr. Officer."

"And who is the landed proprietor about here with whom you have found a position?" asked the officer.

"Mr. Troyekurov," replied the Frenchman.

"Troyekurov? Who is this Troyekurov?"

"*Ma foi, monsieur.* I have heard very little good of him. They say that he is a proud and wilful gentleman, and so harsh toward the members of his household, that nobody can live on good terms with him: that all tremble at his name, and that with his tutors he stands upon no ceremony whatever, indeed, that he has flogged two of them to death."

"Good Lord! And you have decided to take a posi-tion with such a monster?"

"What can I do, Mr. Officer? He offers me a good salary: three thousand rubles a year and all found. Perhaps I shall be more fortunate than the others. I have an aged mother: one half of my salary I will send to her for her support, and out of the rest of my money I shall be able in five years to save a small capital suffi-cient to make me independent for the rest of my life. Then, *bon soir,* I return to Paris and set up in busi-ness."

"Does anybody at Troyekurov's know you?" asked the officer.

"Nobody," replied the tutor. "He engaged me at Moscow, through one of his friends, whose cook is a countryman of mine, and who recommended me. I must tell you that I did not intend to be a tutor, but a confectioner; but I was told that in your country the profession of tutor is more lucrative."

The officer reflected.

"Listen to me," he said to the Frenchman: "What would you say if, instead of this position, you were offered ten thousand rubles, ready money, on condition that you returned immediately to Paris?"

The Frenchman looked at the officer in astonishment, smiled, and shook his head.

"The horses are ready," said the postmaster, entering the room at that moment.

The servant confirmed this statement.

"Presently," replied the officer: "leave the room for a moment." The postmaster and the servant withdrew. "I am not joking," he continued in French. "I can give you ten thousand rubles; I only want your absence and your papers."

So saying, he opened his small box and took out of it several bank notes. The Frenchman stared. He did not know what to think.

"My absence . . . my papers!" he repeated in astonishment. "Here are my papers . . . but you are surely joking. What do you want my papers for?"

"That does not concern you. I ask you, do you consent or not?"

The Frenchman, still unable to believe his own ears, handed his papers to the young officer, who rapidly examined them.

"Your passport . . . very well; your letter of recommendation . . . let us see; your birth certificate . . . capital! Well, here is your money; return home. Farewell."

The Frenchman stood as if glued to the spot. The officer came back.

"I had almost forgotten the most important thing of all. Give me your word of honor that all this will remain between you and me. . . . Your word of honor."

"My word of honor," replied the Frenchman. "But my papers? What shall I do without them?"

"In the first town you come to, announce that you have been robbed by Dubrovsky. They will believe you, and give you the necessary documents. Farewell: God grant you a safe and speedy return to Paris, and may you find your mother in good health."

Dubrovsky left the room, got into the coach and dashed off.

The postmaster stood looking out of the window, and when the coach had driven off, he turned to his wife, exclaiming:

"Pakhomovna, do you know who that was? That was Dubrovsky!"

The postmaster's wife rushed toward the window, but it was too late. Dubrovsky was already a long way off. Then she began to scold her husband.

"You have no fear of God, Sidorych. Why did you not tell me sooner, I should at least have had a glimpse of Dubrovsky. But now I shall have to wait long enough before he looks in on us again. You have no conscience—that's what it is, no conscience!"

The Frenchman stood as if petrified. The agreement with the officer, the money—everything seemed like a dream to him. But the bundle of bank notes was there in his pocket, eloquently confirming the reality of the wonderful adventure.

He resolved to hire horses to take him to the next town. He was driven very slowly, and he reached the town at nightfall.

Just before they reached the gates where, in place of a sentinel, stood a dilapidated sentry-box, the Frenchman told the driver to stop, got out of the carriage and proceeded on foot, explaining by signs to the driver that he might keep the vehicle and the portmanteau as a tip. The driver was as much astonished at his generosity as the Frenchman himself had been at Dubrovsky's proposal. But concluding that the foreigner had taken leave of his senses, the driver thanked him with a very profound bow, and not caring about entering the town, he made his way to a house of entertainment which was well known to him, and the proprietor of which was a friend of his. There he passed the whole night, and the next morning he started back on his return journey with the troika, without the carriage and without the portmanteau, but with a swollen face and red eyes.

Dubrovsky, having possessed himself of the Frenchman's papers, boldly presented himself to Troyekurov, as we have already seen, and settled in the house. Whatever were his secret intentions—we shall know them later on—there was nothing at all objectionable in his behavior. It is true that he did not occupy himself very much with the education of little Sasha, to whom he allowed full liberty, nor was he very exacting in the matter of the boy's lessons, which were only given as a matter of form, but he paid great attention to the musical studies of his fair pupil, and frequently sat for hours beside her at the piano.

Everybody liked the young tutor: Kirila Petrovich, for his boldness and dexterity in the hunting-field; Marya Kirilovna, for his unbounded zeal and slavish attentiveness; Sasha, for his tolerance; and the members of the household for his kindness and generosity, apparently incompatible with his station. He himself seemed to be attached to the whole family, and already regarded himself as a member of it.

Between the time that he entered upon a tutor's calling and the date of the memorable fête, about a month had elapsed and nobody suspected that the modest young Frenchman was in reality the terrible brigand whose name was a source of terror to all the landed proprietors of the neighborhood. During all this time,

Dubrovsky had never quitted Pokrovskoye, but the reports of his depredations did not cease for all that, thanks to the inventive imagination of the country people. It is possible, too, that his band may have continued their exploits during their chief's absence.

Passing the night in the same room with a man whom he could only regard as a personal enemy, and one of the principal authors of his misfortune, Dubrovsky had not been able to resist temptation. He knew of the existence of the pouch, and had resolved to take possession of it.

We have seen how he astounded poor Anton Pafnutyich by his unexpected transformation from a tutor into a brigand.

At nine o'clock in the morning, the guests who had passed the night at Pokrovskoye repaired one after the other to the sitting-room, where the samovar was already boiling, while before it sat Marya Kirilovna in a morning frock, and Kirila Petrovich in a frieze coat and slippers, drinking his tea out of a large cup like a slop-basin.

The last to appear was Anton Pafnutyich; he was so pale, and seemed so troubled, that everybody was struck by his appearance, and Kirila Petrovich inquired after his health. In reply Spitzyn said something unintelligible, glaring with horror at the tutor, who sat there as if nothing had happened. A few minutes afterward a servant entered and announced to Spitzyn that his carriage was ready. Anton Pafnutyich hastened to take his leave of the company, and then hurried out of the room and, in spite of the host's efforts to detain him, drove off immediately. No one could understand what had happened to him, and Kirila Petrovich came to the conclusion that he had over-eaten.

After tea and the farewell breakfast, the other guests began to take their leave, and soon Pokrovskoye grew empty, and life there resumed its ordinary course.

XII

SEVERAL days passed, and nothing remarkable had happened. The life of the inhabitants of Pokrovskoye was monotonous. Kirila Petrovich went out hunting every day; while Marya Kirilovna devoted her time to reading, walking, and especially to music lessons. She was beginning to understand her own heart, and acknowledged to herself with involuntary vexation that she was not indifferent to the good qualities of the young Frenchman. He, on his side, never overstepped the limits of respect and strict decorum, and thereby quieted her pride and her timid doubts. With more and more confidence she gave herself up to the alluring habit of seeing him. She felt dull without Deforges, and in his presence she was constantly occupied with him, wishing to know his opinion of everything, and always agreeing with him. She was not yet in love with him perhaps; but at the first accidental obstacle or sudden adverse move of Fate, the flame of passion was sure to burst forth within her heart.

One day, on entering the parlor, where the tutor awaited her, Marya Kirilovna observed with astonishment that he looked pale and troubled. She opened the piano and sang a few notes; but Dubrovsky, under the pretext of a headache, apologized, interrupted the lesson, and, closing the music-book, immediately slipped a note into her hand. Marya Kirilovna, without pausing to reflect, took it, and immediately repented. But Dubrovsky had gone. Marya Kirilovna went to her room, unfolded the note, and read as follows:

"Be in the arbor near the brook this evening, at seven o'clock: I must speak to you."

Her curiosity was strongly excited. She had long expected a declaration, both desiring it and dreading it. It would have been agreeable to her to hear the confirmation of what she divined; but she felt that it would have been unbecoming to hear such a declaration from a man who, on account of his position, ought never to aspire to win her hand. She resolved to keep the tryst, but she hesitated about one thing: in what manner she ought to receive the tutor's declaration—with aristocratic indignation, with friendly admonition, with good-humored banter, or with silent sympathy. In the meantime she kept constantly looking at the clock. It grew dark: candles were brought in. Kirila Petrovich sat down to play at Boston with some of his neighbors who had come to pay him a visit. The clock struck a quarter to seven, and Marya Kirilovna walked quietly out on to the steps, looked round on every side, and then ran into the garden.

The night was dark, the sky was covered with clouds, and it was impossible to see anything at a distance of two paces; but Marya Kirilovna went forward in the darkness along paths that were quite familiar to her, and in a few minutes she reached the arbor. There she paused in order to draw breath and to present herself before Deforges with an air of unhurried indifference. But Deforges already stood before her.

"I thank you," he said in a low, sad voice, "for having granted my request. I should have been in despair if you had not complied with it."

Marya Kirilovna answered him in the words she had prepared beforehand.

"I hope you will not cause me to repent of my condescension."

He was silent, and seemed to be collecting himself.

"Circumstances demand—I am obliged to leave you," he said at last. "It may be that you will soon hear —but before going away, I must have an explanation with you."

Marya Kirilovna made no reply. In these words she saw the preface to the expected declaration.

"I am not what you suppose," he continued, lowering his head: "I am not the Frenchman Deforges—I am Dubrovsky."

Marya Kirilovna uttered a cry.

"Do not be alarmed, for God's sake! You need not be afraid of my name. Yes, I am that unhappy man, whom your father, after depriving him of his last crust of bread, drove out of his paternal home and sent on to the highway to rob. But you need not be afraid, either on your own account or on your father's. All is over. . . . I have forgiven him; you have saved him. My first bloody deed was to have had him for its victim. I prowled round his house, determining where the fire was to burst out, where I should enter his bedroom, and how I should cut him off from all means of escape; at that moment you passed by me like a heavenly vision, and my heart was subdued. I understood that the house, in which you dwelt, was sacred; that not a single being, connected with you by the ties of blood, could be subject to my curse. I repudiated vengeance as though it were madness. For days on end I wandered around the gardens of Pokrovskoye, in the hope of seeing your white dress in the distance. On your incautious walks I followed you, stealing from bush to bush, happy in the thought that I was protecting you, that for you there was no danger, where I was secretly present. At last an opportunity presented itself. . . . I came to live in your house. Those three weeks were for me days of happiness; the recollection of them will be the joy of my sad life. . . . To-day I received news which renders it impossible for me to remain here any longer. I part from you to-day—at this very moment. . . . But before doing so, I felt that it was necessary that I should reveal myself to you, so that you might not curse me nor despise me. Think sometimes of Dubrovsky. Know that he was born for another fate, that his soul was capable of loving you, that never——"

Just then a low whistle sounded, and Dubrovsky stopped. He seized her hand and pressed it to his burning lips. The whistle was repeated.

"Farewell," said Dubrovsky: "they are calling me. A moment's delay may undo me."

He moved away. . . . Marya Kirilovna stood motionless. Dubrovsky returned and once more took her hand.

"If misfortune should ever overtake you," he said, in a tender and moving voice, "and you are unable to obtain help or protection from anybody, will you promise to apply to me, to demand from me everything that may be necessary for your happiness? Will you promise not to reject my devotion?"

Marya Kirilovna wept silently. The whistle sounded for the third time.

"You are ruining me!" cried Dubrovsky: "but I will not leave you until you give me a reply. Do you promise me or not?"

"I promise!" murmured the poor girl.

Greatly agitated by her interview with Dubrovsky, Marya Kirilovna returned from the garden. As she approached the house, she perceived a great crowd of people in the courtyard; a troika was standing in front of the steps, the servants were running hither and thither, and the whole house was in a commotion. In the distance she heard the voice of Kirila Petrovich, and she hastened to reach her room, fearing that her absence might be noticed. Kirila Petrovich met her in the hall. The visitors were pressing round our old acquaintance the sheriff, and were overwhelming him with questions. The sheriff, in traveling clothes, and armed to the teeth, answered them with a mysterious and anxious air.

"Where have you been, Masha?" asked Kirila Petrovich. "Have you seen Monsieur Deforges?"

Masha could scarcely answer in the negative.

"Just imagine," continued Kirila Petrovich: "the sheriff has come to arrest nim, and assures me that he is Dubrovsky."

"He answers the description in every respect, Your Excellency," said the sheriff respectfully.

"Oh! brother," interrupted Kirila Petrovich, "go to —you know where—with your description. I will not surrender my Frenchman to you until I have investigated the matter myself. How can anyone believe the word of Anton Pafnutyich, a coward and a liar? He must have dreamt that the tutor wanted to rob him. Why didn't he tell me about it the next morning? He never said a word about the matter."

"The Frenchman scared him, Your Excellency," replied the sheriff, "and made him swear that he would preserve silence."

"A pack of lies!" exclaimed Kirila Petrovich: "I will clear the matter up immediately. Where is the tutor?" he asked of a servant who entered at that moment.

"He cannot be found anywhere, sir," replied the servant.

"Then search for him!" cried Troyekurov, beginning to entertain doubts.

"Show me your vaunted description," he said to the sheriff, who immediately handed him the paper.

"Hm! hm! twenty-three years old, etc., etc. That is so, but yet that does not prove anything. Well, what about the tutor?"

"He is not to be found," was again the answer.

Kirila Petrovich began to be uneasy; Marya Kirilovna was neither dead nor alive.

"You are pale, Masha," her father remarked to her "they have frightened you."

"No, papa," replied Masha; "I have a headache."

"Go to your own room, Masha, and don't be alarmed."

Masha kissed his hand and retired hastily to her room. There she threw herself upon her bed and burst into tears, and a fit of hysterics. The maids hastened to her assistance, undressed her with difficulty, and with difficulty succeeded in calming her by means of cold water and all kinds of smelling salts. They put her to bed and she dozed off.

In the meantime the Frenchman could not be found. Kirila Petrovich paced up and down the room, loudly whistling "Thunder of Victory Resound." The visitors whispered among themselves; the sheriff looked foolish; the Frenchman was not to be found. Probably he had managed to escape through being warned beforehand. But by whom and how? That remained a mystery.

It was eleven o'clock, but nobody thought of sleep. At last Kirila Petrovich said angrily to the sheriff:

"Well, do you wish to stop here till daylight? My house is not an inn. You are not quick enough, brother, to catch Dubrovsky—if he is Dubrovsky. Go home, and in future be a little quicker. And it is time for you to go home, too," he continued, addressing his guests. "Order the horses to be hitched up. I want to go to bed."

In this ungracious manner did Troyekurov take leave of his guests.

XIII

SOME TIME elapsed without anything remarkable happening. But at the beginning of the following summer, many changes occurred in the family life of Kirila Petrovich.

About thirty versts from Pokrovskoye was the wealthy estate of Prince Vereysky. The Prince had lived abroad for a long time, and his estate was managed by a retired major. No intercourse existed between Pokrovskoye and Arbatovo. But at the end of the month of May, the Prince returned from abroad and took up residence in his own village, which he had never seen since he was born. Accustomed to social pleasures, he could not endure solitude, and the third day after his arrival, he set out to dine with Troyekurov, with whom he had formerly been acquainted. The Prince was about fifty years of age, but he looked much older. Excesses of every kind had ruined his health, and had placed upon him their indelible stamp. In spite of that, his appearance was agreeable and distinguished, and his having always been accustomed to society gave him a certain adroitness, especially with women. He had a constant need of amusement, and he was a constant victim of ennui.

Kirila Petrovich was exceedingly gratified by this visit, which he regarded as a mark of respect from a man who knew the world. In accordance with his usual custom, he began to entertain his visitor by conducting him to inspect his out-buildings and kennels. But the Prince could hardly breathe in the atmosphere of the kennels, and he hurried out, holding a scented handkerchief to his nose. The old garden, with its clipped limes, square pond and regular walks, did not please him; he liked English gardens and so-called nature; but he praised and admired everything. The servant came to announce that dinner was served, and they went in to dine. The Prince limped, being fatigued after his walk, and already repenting his visit.

But in the reception room Marya Kirilovna met

them—and the old roué was struck by her beauty. Troyekurov placed his guest beside her. The Prince was revived by her presence; he became quite cheerful, and succeeded several times in arresting her attention by his curious stories. After dinner Kirila Petrovich proposed a ride on horseback, but the Prince excused himself, pointing to his velvet boots and joking about his gout. He preferred a drive in a carriage; so that he should not be separated from his charming neighbor. The carriage was got ready. The two old men and the beautiful young girl took their seats in it, and they drove off. The conversation did not flag. Marya Kirilovna listened with pleasure to the flattering compliments and witty remarks of the man of the world, when suddenly Vereysky, turning to Kirila Petrovich, asked him what that burnt building was, and whether it belonged to him.

Kirila Petrovich frowned: the memories awakened by the burnt manor-house were disagreeable to him. He replied that the land was his now, but that formerly it had belonged to Dubrovsky.

"To Dubrovsky?" repeated Vereysky. "What! to the famous brigand?"

"To his father," replied Troyekurov: "and the father himself was something of a brigand, too."

"And what has become of our Rinaldo? Have they caught him? Is he still alive?"

"He is still alive and at liberty, and as long as our sheriffs are in league with thieves he will not be caught. By the way, Prince, Dubrovsky paid you a visit at Arbatovo."

"Yes, last year, I think, he burnt something down or got away with some loot. Don't you think, Marya Kirilovna, that it would be very interesting to make a closer acquaintance with this romantic hero?"

"Interesting!" said Troyekurov: "she knows him already. He taught her music for three whole weeks, and thank God, took nothing for his lessons."

Then Kirila Petrovich began to relate the story of his French tutor. Marya Kirilovna was on pins and needles. Vereysky, listening with deep attention, found it all very strange, and changed the subject. On returning from the drive, he ordered his carriage to be brought, and in spite of the earnest requests of Kirila Petrovich to spend the night, he took his departure immediately after tea. Before setting out, however, he invited Kirila Petrovich to pay him a visit and to bring Marya Kirilovna with him, and the proud Troyekurov promised to do so; for taking into consideration his princely dignity, his two stars, and the three thousand serfs belonging to his ancestral estate, he regarded Prince Vereysky in some degree as his equal.

Two days after this visit, Kirila Petrovich set out with his daughter to call on Prince Vereysky. On approaching Arbatovo, he could not sufficiently admire the clean and cheerful-looking huts of the peasants, and the stone manor-house built in the style of an English castle. In front of the house stretched a green lawn, upon which were grazing some Swiss cows tinkling their bells. A spacious park surrounded the house on every side. The master met the guests on the steps, and gave his arm to the young beauty. She was then conducted into a magnificent hall, where the table was laid for three. The Prince led his guests to a window, and a charming view opened out before them. The Volga flowed past the windows, and upon its bosom floated laden barges under full sail, and small fishing-boats known by the expressive name of "murderers." Beyond the river stretched hills and fields, and several villages animated the landscape.

Then they proceeded to inspect the pictures bought by the Prince in foreign countries. The Prince explained to Marya Kirilovna their subjects, related the history of the painters, and pointed out the merits and defects of their canvases. He did not speak of pictures in the conventional language of the pedantic connoisseur, but with feeling and imagination. Marya Kirilovna listened to him with pleasure.

They went in to dine. Troyekurov rendered full justice to his host's wines, and to the skill of his cook; while Marya Kirilovna did not feel at all confused or constrained in her conversation with a man whom she now saw for the second time in her life. After dinner the host proposed a walk in the garden. They drank coffee in the arbor on the bank of a broad lake studded with little islands. Suddenly music was heard, and a boat with six oars drew up before the arbor. They rowed on the lake, round the islands, and visited some of them. On one they found a marble statue; on another, a lonely grotto; on a third, a monument with a mysterious inscription, which awakened within Marya Kirilovna a girlish curiosity not completely satisfied by the polite but reticent explanations of the Prince. Time passed imperceptibly. It began to grow dark. The Prince, under the pretext of the chill and the dew, hastened to return to the house, where the samovar awaited them. The Prince requested Marya Kirilovna to discharge the functions of hostess in this home of an old bachelor. She poured out the tea, listening to the inexhaustible stories of the charming talker. Suddenly a shot was heard, and a rocket illuminated the sky. The Prince gave Marya Kirilovna a shawl, and led her and Troyekurov onto the balcony. In front of the house, in the darkness, different colored fires blazed up, whirled round, rose up in sheaves, poured out in fountains, fell in showers of rain and stars, went out and then burst into a blaze again. Marya Kirilovna was happy as a child. Prince Vereysky was delighted with her enjoyment, and Troyekurov was very well satisfied with him, for he accepted *tous les frais* of the Prince as signs of respect and a desire to please him.

The supper was quite equal to the dinner in every respect. Then the guests retired to the rooms assigned to them, and the next morning took leave of their amiable host, promising each other soon to·meet again.

XIV

MARYA KIRILOVNA was sitting in her room, bent over her embroidery frame before the open window. She did not mistake one skein for another, like Conrad's mistress, who, in her amorous distraction, embroidered a rose in green silk. Under her needle, the canvas repeated unerringly the design of the original; but in spite of that, her thoughts did not follow her work—they were far away.

Suddenly a hand was thrust silently through the window, placed a letter upon the embroidery frame and disappeared before Marya Kirilovna could recover herself. At the same moment a servant entered to call her to Kirila Petrovich. Trembling, she hid the letter under her fichu and hastened to her father in his study.

Kirila Petrovich was not alone. Prince Vereysky was in the room with him. On the appearance of Marya Kirilovna, the Prince rose and silently bowed, with a confusion that was quite unusual in him.

"Come here, Masha," said Kirila Petrovich: "I have a piece of news to tell you which I hope will gladden you. Here is a suitor for you: the Prince seeks you in marriage."

Masha was dumbfounded; her face grew deathly pale. She was silent. The Prince approached her, took her hand, and with a tender look, asked her if she would consent to make him happy. Masha remained silent.

"Consent? Of course she consents," said Kirila Petrovich; "but you know, Prince, it is difficult for a girl to say the word. Well, children, kiss one another and be happy."

Masha stood motionless; the old Prince kissed her hand. Suddenly the tears began to stream down her pale cheeks. The Prince frowned slightly.

"Go, go, go!" said Kirila Petrovich: "dry your tears and come back to us in a merry mood. They all weep when they are betrothed," he continued, turning to Vereysky; "it is their custom. Now, Prince, let us talk business, that is to say, about the dowry."

Marya Kirilovna eagerly took advantage of the permission to retire. She ran to her room, locked herself in and gave way to her tears, already imagining herself the wife of the old Prince. He had suddenly become repugnant and hateful to her. Marriage terrified her, like the block, like the grave.

"No, no," she repeated in despair; "I would rather go into a convent, I would rather marry Dubrovsky . . ."

Then she remembered the letter and eagerly began to read it, having a presentiment that it was from him. In fact, it was written by him, and contained only the following words:

"This evening, at ten o'clock, at the same place."

XV

THE MOON was shining; the July night was calm; the wind rose now and then, and a gentle rustle ran over the garden.

Like a light shadow, the beautiful young girl drew

near to the appointed meeting-place. Nobody was yet to be seen. Suddenly, from behind the arbor, Dubrovsky appeared before her.

"I know all," he said to her in a low, sad voice; "remember your promise."

"You offer me your protection," replied Masha; "do not be angry—but it alarms me. In what way can you help me?"

"I can deliver you from the man you detest. . . ."

"For God's sake, do not touch him, do not dare to touch him, if you love me. I do not wish to be the cause of any horror . . ."

"I will not touch him: your wish is sacred to me. He owes his life to you. Never shall a crime be committed in your name. You must be pure, even though I commit crimes. But how can I save you from a cruel father?"

"There is still hope; perhaps I shall touch him by my tears—my despair. He is obstinate, but he loves me very dearly."

"Do not put your trust in a vain hope. In those tears he will see only the usual timidity and aversion common to all young girls, when they make a marriage of convenience instead of marrying for love. But what if he takes it into his head to bring about your happiness in spite of yourself? What if you are conducted to the altar by force, in order that your life may be placed for ever in the power of an old man?"

"Then—then there will be nothing else to do. Come for me—I will be your wife."

Dubrovsky trembled; his pale face flushed, deeply, and the next minute he became paler than before. He remained silent for a long time, with his head bent down.

"Muster the full strength of your soul, implore your father, throw yourself at his feet; represent to him all the horror of the future that he is preparing for you, your youth fading away by the side of a decrepit and dissipated old man. Tell him that riches will not procure for you a single moment of happiness. Luxury consoles poverty alone, and at that only for a short time, until one becomes accustomed to it. Do not be put off by him, and do not be frightened either by his anger or by his threats, as long as there remains the least shadow of hope. For God's sake do not stop pleading with him. If, however, you have no other resource left, decide upon a cruel explanation; tell him that if he remains inexorable, then—then you will find a terrible protector."

Here Dubrovsky covered his face with his hands; he seemed to be choking. Masha wept.

"My miserable, miserable fate!" said he, with a bitter sigh. "For you I would have given my life. To see you from afar, to touch your hand was for me happiness beyond expression; and when I see before me the possibility of pressing you to my agitated heart, and saying to you: 'Angel, let us die'—miserable creature that I am! I must fly from such happiness, I must put it from me with all my strength. I dare not throw myself at your feet and thank Heaven for an unthinkable, unmerited reward. Oh! how I ought to hate him who— but I feel that now there is no place in my heart for hatred."

He gently passed his arm round her slender figure and pressed her tenderly to his heart. Confidingly she leaned her head upon the young brigand's shoulder. Both were silent. . . . Time flew.

"I must go," said Masha at last.

Dubrovsky seemed to awaken from a dream. He took her hand and placed a ring on her finger.

"If you decide upon having recourse to me," said he, "then bring the ring here and place it in the hollow of this oak. I shall know what to do."

Dubrovsky kissed her hand and disappeared among the trees.

XVI

PRINCE VEREYSKY'S intention of getting married was no longer a secret to the neighbors. Kirila Petrovich was receiving congratulations and preparations were being made for the wedding. Masha postponed from day to day the decisive explanation. In the meantime her manner toward her elderly fiancé was cold and constrained. The Prince did not trouble himself about that; the question of love gave him no concern; her silent consent was quite sufficient for him.

But time was passing. Masha at last decided to act, and wrote a letter to Prince Vereysky. She tried to awaken within his heart a feeling of magnanimity, candidly confessing that she had not the least attachment for him, and entreating him to renounce her hand and even to protect her from the tyranny of her father. She furtively handed the letter to Prince Vereysky. The latter read it alone, but was not in the least moved by the candor of his betrothed. On the contrary, he perceived the necessity of hastening the marriage, and therefore he showed the letter to his future father-in-law.

Kirila Petrovich was furious, and it was with difficulty that the Prince succeeded in persuading him not to let Masha see that he knew of the letter. Kirila Petrovich agreed not to speak about the matter to her, but he resolved to lose no time and fixed the wedding for the next day. The Prince found this very reasonable, and he went to his betrothed and told her that her letter had grieved him very much, but that he hoped in time to gain her affection; that the thought of resigning her was too much for him to bear, and that he had not the strength to consent to his own death sentence. Then he kissed her hand respectfully and took his departure, without saying a word to her about Kirila Petrovich's decision.

But scarcely had he left the house, when her father entered and peremptorily ordered her to be ready for the next day. Marya Kirilovna, already agitated by the interview with Prince Vereysky, burst into tears and threw herself at her father's feet.

"Papa!" she cried in a plaintive voice, "papa! do not destroy me. I do not love the Prince, I do not wish to be his wife."

"What does this mean?" said Kirila Petrovich, fiercely. "All this time you have kept silent as though you consented, and now, when everything is settled you become capricious and refuse to accept him. Don't play the fool; you will gain nothing from me that way."

"Do not destroy me!" repeated poor Masha. "Why are you sending me away from you and giving me to a man that I do not love? Are you tired of me? I want to stay with you as before. Papa, you will be sad without me, and sadder still when you know that I am unhappy. Papa, do not force me: I do not wish to marry."

Kirila Petrovich was touched, but he concealed his emotion, and pushing her away from him, said harshly:

"That is all nonsense, do you hear? I know better than you what is necessary for your happiness. Tears will not help you. The day after tomorrow your wedding will take place."

"The day after tomorrow!" exclaimed Masha. "My God! No, no, impossible; it cannot be! Papa, hear me; if you have resolved to destroy me, then I will find a protector that you do not dream of. You will see, and then you will regret having driven me to despair."

"What? What?" said Troyekurov. "Threats! You threaten me? Insolent girl! You will see that I will do something to you that you little imagine. You dare to threaten me! Let us see, who will this protector be?"

"Vladimir Dubrovsky," replied Masha, in despair.

Kirila Petrovich thought that she had gone out of her mind, and looked at her in astonishment.

"Very well!" he said to her, after an interval of silence; "expect whom you please to deliver you, but, in the meantime, remain in this room—you shall not leave it till the very moment of the wedding."

With these words Kirila Petrovich went out, locking the door behind him.

For a long time the poor girl wept, imagining all that awaited her. But the stormy interview had eased her soul, and she could more calmly consider the question of her future and what it behoved her to do. The principal thing was—to escape this odious marriage. The lot of a brigand's wife seemed paradise to her in comparison with the fate prepared for her. She glanced at the ring given to her by Dubrovsky. Ardently did she long to see him alone once more and take counsel with him before the decisive moment. A presentiment told her that in the evening she would find Dubrovsky in the garden, near the arbor; she resolved to go and wait for him there.

As soon as it began to grow dark, Masha prepared to carry out her intention, but the door of her room was locked. Her maid told her from the other side of the door, that Kirila Petrovich had given orders that she was not to be let out. She was under arrest. Deeply hurt, she sat down by the window and remained there till late in the night, without undressing, gazing fixedly at the dark sky. Toward dawn she dozed off, but her light sleep was disturbed by sad visions, and she was soon awakened by the rays of the rising sun.

XVII

SHE AWOKE, and all the horror of her position rose up in her mind. She rang. The maid entered, and in answer to her questions, replied that Kirila Petrovich had been to Arbatovo the previous evening, and had returned very late; that he had given strict orders that she was not to be allowed out of her room and that nobody was to be permitted to speak to her; that otherwise, there were no signs of any particular preparations for the wedding, except that the priest had been ordered not to leave the village under any pretext whatever. After giving her this news, the maid left Marya Kirilovna and again locked the door.

Her words hardened the young prisoner. Her head burned, her blood boiled. She resolved to inform Dubrovsky of everything, and she began to think of some means by which she could get the ring conveyed to the hollow in the chosen oak. At that moment a stone struck against her window; the glass rattled, and Marya Kirilovna, looking out into the courtyard, saw little Sasha making signs to her. She knew that he was attached to her, and she was pleased to see him. She opened the window.

"Good morning, Sasha; why do you call me?"

"I came, sister, to know if you wanted anything. Papa is angry, and has forbidden the whole house to do anything for you; but order me to do whatever you like, and I will do it for you."

"Thank you, my dear Sasha. Listen; you know the old hollow oak near the arbor?"

"Yes, I know it, sister."

"Then, if you love me, run there as quickly as you can and put this ring in the hollow; but take care that nobody sees you."

With these words, she threw the ring to him and closed the window.

The lad picked up the ring, and ran off with all his might, and in three minutes he arrived at the chosen tree. There he paused, quite out of breath, and after looking round on every side, placed the ring in the hollow. Having successfully accomplished his mission, he wanted to inform Marya Kirilovna of the fact at once, when suddenly a red-haired, cross-eyed boy in rags darted out from behind the arbor, dashed toward the oak and thrust his hand into the hole. Sasha, quicker than a squirrel, threw himself upon him and seized him with both hands.

"What are you doing here?" said he sternly.

"What business is that of yours?" said the boy, trying to disengage himself.

"Leave that ring alone, red head," cried Sasha, "or I will teach you a lesson in my own style."

Instead of replying, the boy gave him a blow in the face with his fist; but Sasha still held him firmly in his grasp, and cried out at the top of his voice:

"Thieves! thieves! help! help!"

The boy tried to get away from him. He seemed to be about two years older than Sasha, and very much stronger; but Sasha was more agile. They struggled together for some minutes; at last the red-headed boy gained the advantage. He threw Sasha upon the ground and seized him by the throat. But at that moment a strong hand grasped hold of his shaggy red hair, and Stepan, the gardener, lifted him half a yard from the ground.

"Ah! you red-headed beast!" said the gardener. "How dare you strike the young gentleman?"

In the meantime, Sasha had jumped to his feet and recovered himself.

"You caught me under the arm-pits," said he, "or

you would never have thrown me. Give me the ring at once and be off."

"It's likely!" replied the red-headed one, and suddenly twisting himself round, he freed his mop from Stepan's hand.

Then he started off running, but Sasha overtook him, gave him a blow in the back, and the boy fell. The gardener again seized him and bound him with his belt.

"Give me the ring!" cried Sasha.

"Wait a moment, young master," said Stepan; "we will take him to the bailiff to be questioned."

The gardener led the captive into the courtyard of the manor-house, accompanied by Sasha, who glanced uneasily at his torn and grass-stained trousers. Suddenly all three found themselves face to face with Kirila Petrovich, who was going to inspect his stables.

"What is the meaning of this?" he said to Stepan.

Stepan in a few words related all that had happened. Kirila Petrovich listened to him with attention.

"You rascal," said he, turning to Sasha: "why did you get into a fight with him?"

"He stole a ring from the hollow, papa; make him give up the ring."

"What ring? From what hollow?"

"The one that Marya Kirilovna . . . that ring. . . ." Sasha stammered and became confused. Kirila Petrovich frowned and said, shaking his head:

"Ah! Marya Kirilovna is mixed up in this. Confess everything, or I will give you such a thrashing as you have never had in your life."

"As true as Heaven, papa, I . . . papa . . . Marya Kirilovna never told me to do anything, papa."

"Stepan, go and cut me some fine, fresh birch switches."

"Stop, papa, I will tell you all. I was running about

the courtyard today, when sister opened the window. I
ran toward her, and she opened the window and
dropped a ring, not on purpose, and I went and hid it
in the hollow, and . . . and this red-headed fellow
wanted to steal the ring."

"She dropped it, not on purpose—you wanted to
hide it . . . Stepan, go and get the switches."

"Papa, wait, I will tell you everything. Sister told me
to run to the oak tree and put the ring in the hollow; I
ran and did so, but this nasty fellow——"

Kirila Petrovich turned to the "nasty fellow" and
said to him sternly:

"To whom do you belong?"

"I am a house-serf of the Dubrovsky's," answered the
red-headed boy.

Kirila Petrovich's face darkened.

"It seems, then, that you do not recognize me as your
master. Very well. What were you doing in my garden?"

"Stealing raspberries," the boy answered with complete indifference.

"Aha! like master, like servant. As the priest is, so is
his parish. And do my raspberries grow upon oak
trees?"

The boy made no reply.

"Papa, make him give up the ring," said Sasha.

"Silence, Alexander!" replied Kirila Petrovich;
"don't forget that I intend to settle with you presently.
Go to your room. And you, squint-eyes, you seem a
clever lad; if you confess everything to me, I will not
whip you, but will give you a five-copeck piece to buy
nuts with. Give up the ring and go home."

The boy opened his fist and showed that there was
nothing in his hand.

"If you don't, I shall do something to you that you
little expect. Now!"

The boy did not answer a word, but stood with his head bent, looking like a perfect simpleton.

"Very well!" said Kirila Petrovich: "lock him up somewhere, and see that he does not escape, or I'll flay everyone of you."

Stepan conducted the boy to the pigeon-house, locked him in there, and ordered the old poultry woman, Agafya, to keep a watch upon him.

"There is no doubt about it: she has been in touch with that accursed Dubrovsky. But can it be that she has really asked his help?" thought Kirila Petrovich, pacing up and down the room, and whistling "Thunder of Victory," angrily—"Perhaps I am hot upon his track, and he will not escape us. We shall take advantage of this opportunity. . . . Hark! a bell; thank God, that is the sheriff. Bring here the boy that is locked up."

Meanwhile, a small carriage drove into the court-yard, and our old acquaintance, the sheriff, entered the room, all covered with dust.

"Glorious news!" said Kirila Petrovich: "I have caught Dubrovsky."

"Thank God, Your Excellency!" said the sheriff, his face beaming with delight. "Where is he?"

"That is to say, not Dubrovsky himself, but one of his band. He will be here presently. He will help us to catch his chief. Here he is."

The sheriff, who expected to see some fierce-looking brigand, was astonished to perceive a thirteen-year-old lad, of somewhat delicate appearance. He turned to Kirila Petrovich with an incredulous look, and awaited an explanation. Kirila Petrovich then began to relate the events of the morning, without, however, mentioning the name of Marya Kirilovna.

The sheriff listened to him attentively, glancing from time to time at the young rogue, who, assuming a look of imbecility, seemed to be paying no attention to all that was going on around him.

"Will Your Excellency allow me to speak to you privately?" said the sheriff at last.

Kirila Petrovich took him into another room and locked the door after him.

Half an hour afterwards they returned to the hall, where the captive was awaiting the decision respecting his fate.

"The master wished," the sheriff said to him, "to have you locked up in the town gaol, to be whipped, and then deported as a convict; but I interceded for you and have obtained your pardon. Untie him!"

The lad was unbound.

"Thank the master," said the sheriff.

The lad went up to Kirila Petrovich and kissed his hand.

"Run away home," Kirila Petrovich said to him, "and in future do not steal raspberries from oak trees."

The lad went out, ran merrily down the steps, and without looking behind him, dashed off across the fields in the direction of Kistenyovka. On reaching the village, he stopped at a ramshackle hut, on the edge of the settlement, and tapped at the window. The window was opened, and an old woman appeared.

"Grandmother, some bread!" said the boy: "I have eaten nothing since this morning; I am dying of hunger."

"Ah! it is you, Mitya; but where have you been all this time, you imp?" asked the old woman.

"I will tell you afterwards, grandmother. For God's sake, some bread!"

"Come into the hut, then."

"I haven't the time, grandmother; I've got to run on to another place. Bread, for the Lord's sake, bread!"

"What a fidget!" grumbled the old woman: "there's a piece for you," and she pushed through the window a slice of black bread.

The boy bit into it greedily, and went on slowly, chewing as he walked.

It was beginning to grow dark. Mitya made his way along past the barns and kitchen gardens toward the Kistenyovka grove. On arriving at the two pine trees, standing like advance guards before the grove, he paused, looked round on every side, gave a shrill, abrupt whistle, and then listened. A faint and prolonged whistle was heard in reply, and somebody came out of the grove and advanced toward him.

XVIII

KIRILA PETROVICH was pacing up and down the hall, whistling his favorite air louder than usual. The whole house was in commotion; the servants were running about, and the maids were busy. In the coach-house horses were being hitched up to a carriage. In the courtyard there was a crowd of people. In Marya Kirilovna's dressing-room, before the looking-glass, a lady, surrounded by maidservants, was attiring the pale, motionless young bride. Her head bent languidly beneath the weight of her diamonds; she started slightly when a careless hand pricked her, but she remained silent, gazing absently into the mirror.

"Will you soon be ready?" the voice of Kirila Petrovich was heard at the door.

"In a minute!" replied the lady. "Marya Kirilovna, get up and look at yourself. Is everything right?"

Marya Kirilovna rose, but made no reply. The door was opened.

"The bride is ready," said the lady to Kirila Petrovich; "order the carriage."

"May God be with us!" replied Kirila Petrovich, and taking a sacred ikon from the table, "Approach, Masha," he said, with emotion; "I bless you . . ."

The poor girl fell at his feet and began to sob.

"Papa . . . papa . . ." she said through her tears, and then her voice failed her.

Kirila Petrovich hastened to give her his blessing. She was lifted up and almost carried into the carriage. The matron of honor and one of the maidservants got in with her, and they drove off to the church. There the bridegroom was already waiting for them. He came forward to meet the bride, and was struck by her pallor and her strange look. They entered the cold deserted church together, and the door was locked behind them. The priest came out of the chancel, and the ceremony at once began.

Marya Kirilovna saw nothing, heard nothing; she had been thinking of but one thing the whole morning: she expected Dubrovsky; nor did her hope abandon her for one moment. When the priest turned to her with the usual question, she started and felt faint; but still she hesitated, still she expected. The priest, receiving no reply from her, pronounced the irrevocable words.

The ceremony was over. She felt the cold kiss of her unloved husband; she heard the flattering congratulations of those present; and yet she could not believe that her life was bound for ever, that Dubrovsky had not arrived to deliver her. The Prince turned to her with tender words—she did not understand them. They left the church; in the porch was a crowd of peasants from Pokrovskoye. Her glance rapidly scanned them, and again she seemed unaware of what was going on around her. The newly married couple seated themselves in the carriage and drove off to Arbatovo, whither Kirila Petrovich had already gone on before, in order to welcome the wedded pair there.

Alone with his young wife, the Prince was not in the least piqued by her cold manner. He did not begin to weary her with amorous protestations and ridiculous enthusiasm; his words were simple and required no answer. In this way they traveled about ten versts. The horses dashed rapidly along the uneven country roads, and the carriage scarcely shook upon its English springs. Suddenly shouts of pursuit were heard. The carriage stopped, and a crowd of armed men surrounded it. A man in a half mask opened the door on the side where the young Princess sat, and said to her:

"You are free! Alight."

"What does this mean?" cried the Prince. "Who are you that——"

"It is Dubrovsky," replied the Princess.

The Prince, without losing his presence of mind, drew from his side pocket a traveler's pistol and fired at the masked brigand. The Princess shrieked, and, in horror, covered her face with both hands. Dubrovsky was wounded in the shoulder; the blood was flowing. The Prince, without losing a moment, drew another pistol; but he was not allowed time to fire; the door was opened, and several strong hands dragged him out of the carriage and snatched the pistol from him. Above him flashed several knives.

"Do not touch him!" cried Dubrovsky, and his somber companions drew back.

"You are free!" continued Dubrovsky, turning to the pale Princess.

"No!" she replied; "it is too late! I am married. I am the wife of Prince Vereysky."

"What are you saying?" cried Dubrovsky in despair. "No! you are not his wife. You were forced, you could never have consented."

"I did consent, I took the oath," she answered with firmness. "The Prince is my husband; give orders for him to be set at liberty, and leave me with him. I have not deceived you. I waited for you till the last moment . . . but now, I tell you, now, it is too late. Let us go."

But Dubrovsky no longer heard her. The pain of his
wound, and his violent emotion had deprived him of
his strength. He fell against the wheel; the brigands
surrounded him. He managed to say a few words to
them. They placed him on horseback; two of them
supported him, a third took the horse by the bridle,
and all withdrew from the spot, leaving the carriage
in the middle of the road, the servants bound, the
horses unharnessed, but without having done any pil-
laging, and without having shed one drop of blood in
revenge for the blood of their chief.

XIX

IN THE MIDST of a dense forest, in a narrow clearing, rose a small fort, consisting of earthworks and a
ditch, behind which were some shacks and mud-huts.
Within the inclosed space, a crowd of men who, by
their varied garments and by their arms, could at once
be recognized as brigands, were having their dinner,
seated bareheaded around a common cauldron. On the
earthworks, by the side of a small cannon, squatted a
sentinel, with his legs crossed under him. He was sewing a patch upon a certain part of his garment, plying
his needle with a dexterity that bespoke the experienced
tailor, and every now and then glancing round on
every side.

Although a certain mug had passed from hand to
hand several times, a strange silence reigned among
this crowd. The brigands finished their dinner; one
after another rose and said a prayer; some dispersed
among the shacks, others strolled away into the forest
or lay down to sleep, according to the Russian custom.

The sentinel finished his work, shook his garment,
gazed admiringly at the patch, stuck the needle in his
sleeve, sat astride the cannon, and began to sing a melancholy old song at the top of his lungs:

"Green boughs, do not murmur, be still, Mother
  Forest,
Hinder me not from thinking my thoughts."

At that moment the door of one of the shacks opened, and an old woman in a white cap, neatly and even .
primly dressed, appeared upon the threshold,

"Enough of that, Styopka," she said angrily. "The
master is resting, and yet you must go on bawling like
that; you have neither conscience nor pity."

"I beg pardon, Yegorovna," replied Styopka. "I won't
do it any more. Let our good master rest and get well."

The old woman withdrew into the hut, and Styopka
began to pace to and fro upon the earthworks.

Within the shack, from which the old woman had
emerged, lay the wounded Dubrovsky upon an army
cot behind a partition. Before him, upon a small table,
lay his pistols, and a sword above the head of the bed.
Rich carpets covered the floor and walls of the mud-
hut. In the corner was a lady's silver toilet set and mirror. Dubrovsky held in his hand an open book, but his
eyes were closed, and the old woman, peeping at him
from behind the partition, could not tell whether he
was asleep or only lost in thought.

Suddenly Dubrovsky started. The fort was roused by
an alarm, and Styopka thrust his head in through the
window.

"Vladimir Andreyevich!" he cried; "our men are
signaling—they are on our track!"

Dubrovsky leaped from his bed, seized his arms and
came out of the shack. The brigands were noisily
crowding together in the inclosure, but when he appeared a deep silence fell.

"Is everyone here?" asked Dubrovsky.

"Everyone except the sentries," was the reply.

"To your places!" cried Dubrovsky, and each of the
brigands took his appointed place.

At that moment, three of the sentries ran up to the gate of the fort. Dubrovsky went to meet them.

"What is it?" he asked.

"The soldiers are in the forest," was the reply; "they are surrounding us."

Dubrovsky ordered the gate to be locked, and then went himself to examine the cannon. In the wood could be heard the sound of several voices, every moment drawing nearer and nearer. The brigands waited in silence. Suddenly three or four soldiers appeared out of the forest, but immediately fell back again, firing their guns as a signal to their comrades.

"Prepare for battle!" cried Dubrovsky. There was a movement among the brigands, then all was silent again.

Then the noise of an approaching column was heard; arms glittered among the trees, and about a hundred and fifty soldiers dashed out of the forest and rushed with a wild shout toward the earthworks. Dubrovsky applied the match to the cannon; the shot was successful—one soldier had his head torn off, and two others were wounded. The troops were thrown into confusion, but the officer in command rushed forward, the soldiers followed him and jumped down into the ditch. The brigands fired down at them with muskets and pistols, and then, with axes in their hands, they began to defend the earthworks, up which the infuriated soldiers were now climbing, leaving twenty of their comrades wounded in the ditch below. A hand to hand struggle began. The soldiers were already upon the earthworks, the brigands were beginning to give way; but Dubrovsky advanced toward the officer in command, placed his pistol at his breast, and fired. The officer fell over backward. Several soldiers raised him in their arms and hastened to carry him into the forest; the others, having lost their chief, stopped fighting.

The emboldened brigands took advantage of this moment of hesitation, and surging forward, hurled their
assailants back into the ditch. The besiegers began to
run; the brigands with fierce yells started in pursuit of
them. The victory was decisive. Dubrovsky, trusting to
the complete confusion of the enemy, stopped his men
and shut himself up in the fortress, doubled the sen-
tinels, forbade anyone to absent himself, and ordered
the wounded to be picked up.

This last event drew the serious attention of the government to Dubrovsky's exploits. Information was obtained of his whereabouts, and a detachment of soldiers
was sent to take him, dead or alive. Several of his band
were captured, and from these it was ascertained that
Dubrovsky was no longer among them. A few days
after the battle we have just described, he had collected
all his followers and informed them that it was his intention to leave them for ever, and advised them, too,
to change their mode of life:

"You have become rich under my command. Each
of you has a passport with which he will be able to
make his way safely to some distant province, where
he can pass the rest of his life in ease and honest labor.
But you are all rascals, and probably do not wish to
abandon your trade."

Thereupon he had left them, taking with him only
one of his men. Nobody knew what became of him.
At first the truth of this account was doubted, for the
devotion of the brigands to their chief was well known,
and it was supposed that they had concocted the story
to secure his safety; but after events confirmed their
statement. The terrible visits, burnings, and robberies
ceased; the roads again became safe. According to another report, Dubrovsky had escaped abroad.

[1832-33]
[Published posthumously, 1841]

EGYPTIAN NIGHTS

I

Quel est cet homme?—Ha, c'est un bien grand talent,
il fait de sa voix tout ce qu'il veut.—Il devroit bien, ma-
dame, s'en faire une culotte.

CHARSKY was one of the native-born inhabitants of St. Petersburg. He was not yet thirty years of age; he was not married; the service did not burden him. His late uncle, having been a vice-governor in the good old days, had left him a respectable estate. His life was a very agreeable one, but he had the misfortune to write and print verse. In the journals he was called "poet," and in the servants' quarters "scribbler."

In spite of the great privileges which versifiers enjoy (we must confess that, except the right of using the accusative instead of the genitive, and other so-called poetical licenses, we fail to see what are the particular privileges of Russian poets), in spite of their every possible privilege, these persons are compelled to suffer a great many disadvantages and much unpleasantness. The bitterest misfortune of all, the most intolerable for the poet, is the appellation with which he is branded, and which always clings to him. The public look upon him as their own property; in their opinion, he was created for their especial benefit and pleasure. Should he return from the country, the first person who meets him accosts him with:

"Haven't you brought anything new for us?"

Should the derangement of his affairs, or the illness of some being dear to him, cause him to become lost in reflection, immediately a trite smile accompanies the trite exclamation:

"No doubt you are composing something!"

Should he happen to fall in love, his fair one purchases an album at the English shop, and expects a poem.

Should he call upon a man whom he hardly knows, to talk about serious matters of business, the latter quickly calls his son and compels him to read some of the verses of so-and-so, and the lad regales the poet with some of his lame productions. And these are but the flowers of the calling; what then must be the thorns! Charsky acknowledged that the compliments, the questions, the albums, and the little boys bored him to such an extent, that he was constantly compelled to restrain himself from committing some act of rudeness.

Charsky endeavored in every possible way to rid himself of the intolerable appellation. He avoided the society of his literary brethren, and preferred to them men of the world, even the most shallow-minded. His conversation was of the most commonplace character, and never turned upon literature. In his dress he always observed the very latest fashion, with the timidity and superstition of a young Moscovite arriving in St. Petersburg for the first time in his life. In his study, furnished like a lady's bedroom, nothing recalled the writer; no books littered the tables; the divan was not stained with ink; there was none of that disorder which denotes the presence of the Muse and the absence of broom and brush. Charsky was in despair if any of his society friends found him with a pen in his hand. It is difficult to believe to what trifles a man, otherwise endowed with talent and soul, can descend. At one time he pretended to be a passionate lover of horses, at another a desperate gambler, and at another a refined gourmet, although he was never able to distinguish the mountain breed from the Arab, could never remember the trump cards, and in secret preferred a baked potato to all the inventions of the French cuisine. He led a life of dissipation, was seen at all the balls, over-ate at all the diplomatic dinners, and at all the soirées was as inevitable as the Rezanov ices. For all that, he was a poet, and his passion was invincible. When the "silly fit" (thus he called inspiration) came upon him, Charsky would lock himself up in his study, and write from morning till late into the night. He confessed to his genuine friends that only then did he know what real happiness was. The rest of his time he strolled about, dissembled, and was assailed at every step by the eternal question:

"Haven't you written anything new?"

One morning, Charsky felt that happy disposition of the spirit when the dreams shape themselves clearly before your eyes, and you find vivid, unexpected words to body forth your visions, when verses flow easily from the pen, and sonorous rhythms fly to meet harmonious thoughts. Charsky was mentally plunged into sweet oblivion . . . and the world, and the opinions of the world, and his own particular whims no longer existed for him. He was writing verse.

Suddenly the door of his study creaked, and a strange head appeared. Charsky started and frowned.

"Who is there?" he asked with vexation, inwardly cursing his servants, who were never in the ante-room when they were wanted.

The stranger entered. He was tall and spare, and ap-

peared to be about thirty years of age. The features of
his swarthy face were very expressive: his pale, lofty
forehead, shaded by locks of black hair, his sparkling
black eyes, aquiline nose, and thick beard surrounding
his sunken, tawny cheeks, showed him to be a foreigner. He wore a black dress-coat, already whitened
at the seams, and summer trousers (although the sea
son was well into the autumn); under his threadbare
black cravat, upon a yellowish shirt-front, glittered an
imitation diamond; his shaggy hat seemed to have seen
good and bad weather. Meeting such a man in a wood,
you would have taken him for a robber; in society—
for a political conspirator; in an ante-room—for a charlatan, a seller of elixirs and arsenic.

"What do you wish?" Charsky asked him in French.

"Signor," replied the foreigner, with profound bows:
"*Lei voglia perdonarmi se . . .*"

Charsky did not offer him a chair, and he rose himself: the conversation was continued in Italian.

"I am a Neapolitan artist," said the stranger: "circumstances compelled me to leave my native land; I
have come to Russia, trusting to my talent."

Charsky thought that the Neapolitan was preparing
to give some violoncello concerts and was disposing of
his tickets from house to house. He was just about to
give him twenty-five rubles in order to get rid of him
as quickly as possible, when the stranger added:

"I hope, signor, that you will give friendly support
to your confrère, and introduce me into the houses to
which you have entrée."

It was impossible to offer a greater affront to Charsky's vanity. He glanced haughtily at the individual
who called himself his confrère.

"Allow me to ask, what are you, and for whom do
you take me?" he said, with difficulty restraining his
indignation.

The Neapolitan observed his vexation.

"Signor," he replied, stammering: "*Ho creduto . . . ho sentito . . . la vostra Eccelenza . . . mi perdonera . . .*"

"What do you wish?" repeated Charsky drily.

"I have heard a great deal of your wonderful talent; I am sure that the gentlemen of this place esteem it an honor to extend every possible protection to such an excellent poet," replied the Italian: "and that is why I have ventured to present myself to you. . . ."

"You are mistaken, signor," interrupted Charsky. "The calling of poet does not exist among us. Our poets do not solicit the protection of gentlemen; our poets are gentlemen themselves, and if our Mæcenases (devil take them!) do not know that, so much the worse for them. Among us there are no ragged abbés, whom a musician would take off the streets to write him a libretto. Among us, poets do not go on foot from house to house, begging for help. Moreover, they must have been joking, when they told you that I was a great poet. It is true that I once wrote some wretched epigrams, but thank God, I haven't anything in common with versifiers, and do not wish to have."

The poor Italian became disconcerted. He looked around him. The pictures, marble statues, bronzes, and the costly baubles on Gothic what-nots, struck him. He understood that between the haughty dandy, standing before him in a tufted brocaded cap, gold-colored Chinese dressing-gown and Turkish sash—and himself, a poor wandering artist, in threadbare cravat and shabby dress-coat—there was nothing in common. He stammered out some unintelligible excuses, bowed, and wished to retire. His pitiable appearance touched Charsky, who, in spite of the pettiness of his character, had a good and noble heart. He felt ashamed of the irritability caused by the wound to his vanity.

"Where are you going?" he said to the Italian.

"Wait . . . I was compelled to decline an unmerited title and confess to you that I was not a poet. Now let us speak about your business. I am ready to serve you, if it be in my power to do so. Are you a musician?"

"No, Eccelenza," replied the Italian; "I am a poor improviser."

"An improviser!" cried Charsky, feeling all the cruelty of his reception. "Why didn't you say sooner that you were an improviser?"

And Charsky pressed his hand with a feeling of sincere regret.

His friendly manner encouraged the Italian. He spoke naïvely of his plans. His exterior was not deceptive. He was in need of money, and he hoped somehow in Russia to improve his domestic circumstances. Charsky listened to him with attention.

"I hope," said he to the poor artist, "that you will have success; society here has never heard an improviser. Curiosity will be aroused. It is true that the Italian language is not in use among us; you will not be understood, but that will be no great misfortune; the chief thing is that you should be in the fashion."

"But if nobody among you understands Italian," said the improviser, becoming thoughtful, "who will come to hear me?"

"Have no fear about that—they will come: some out of curiosity, others to pass away the evening somehow or other, others to show that they understand Italian. I repeat, it is only necessary that you should be in the fashion, and you will be in the fashion—here is my hand."

Charsky dismissed the improviser very cordially, after having taken his address, and the same evening he set to work to do what he could for him.

II

I am both king and slave, both worm and god.
Derzhavin.

THE next day, in the dark and dirty corridor of a tavern, Charsky found number 35. He stopped at the door and knocked. It was opened by the Italian.

"Victory!" Charsky said to him: "your affairs are in a good way. The Princess N—— offers you her salon; yesterday, at the rout, I succeeded in enlisting half of St. Petersburg; get your tickets and announcements printed. If I cannot guarantee a triumph for you, I'll answer for it that you will at least be a gainer in pocket. . . ."

"And that is the chief thing," cried the Italian showing his delight in lively gestures characteristic of his Southern origin. "I knew that you would help me. *Corpo di Bacco!* You are a poet like myself, and there is no denying that poets are excellent fellows! How can I show my gratitude to you? Wait. . . . Would you like to hear an improvisation?"

"An improvisation! . . . Can you then do without public, without music, and without sounds of applause?"

"Nonsense, nonsense! Where could I find a better public? You are a poet: you will understand me better than they, and your quiet approbation will be dearer to me than a whole storm of applause. . . . Sit down somewhere and give me a theme."

Charsky sat down on a suitcase (of the two chairs in the narrow cubicle, one was broken and the other piled with papers and linen). The improviser took a guitar from a chair, and stood before Charsky touching the strings with bony fingers and awaiting his order.

"Here is your theme, then," Charsky said to him: *"the poet himself chooses the subject of his songs; the crowd has not the right to command his inspiration."*

The eyes of the Italian began to sparkle: he tried a few chords, raised his head proudly, and passionate strophes—the expression of instantaneous feeling—fell rhythmically from his lips. . . .

> *With open eyes the poet marches,*
> *But seeing no one, seeming blind,*
> *Now someone clutches at his garment,*
> *And pulls him gently from behind!*
>
> *"The fool! Where to? He must be dreaming."*
> *They cry: "This way—the road is clear."*
> *It is in vain they seek to guide him,*
> *The heedless poet does not hear.*
>
> *Such is the poet: like the wind*
> *That man can neither call nor bind—*
> *His flight is free as any eagle's,*
> *He asks no counsel in his art,*
> *But like another Desdemona*
> *Chooses the idol of his heart.*

The Italian ceased. . . . Charsky was silent, amazed and touched.

"Well?" asked the improviser.

Charsky seized his hand and pressed it firmly.

"Well, how was it?" asked the improviser.

"Wonderful!" replied the poet. "Another's thought has scarcely reached your ears, and already it has become your own, as if you had nursed, fondled and developed it for a long time. And so for you there exists neither toil nor disenchantment, nor that uneasiness which precedes inspiration? Wonderful, wonderful!"

The improviser replied: "Every talent is inexplicable. How does the sculptor see, in a block of Carrara marble, the hidden Jupiter, and how does he bring it to light with hammer and chisel by chipping off its envelope? Why does the idea issue from the poet's head already equipped with four rhymes, and measured off in ordered, regular feet? Thus, nobody, except the improviser himself, can understand that rapidity of impression, that close connection between his own inspiration proper and the will of another; I myself would try in vain to explain it. But . . . I must think of my first evening. What is your opinion? What price could I charge for the tickets, so that it may not be too much for the public, and so that, at the same time, I may not be out of pocket? They say that La Signora Catalani [1] charged twenty-five rubles. It's a good price. . . ."

It was very disagreeable for Charsky to fall suddenly from the heights of poesy down to the bookkeeper's desk, but he understood wordly necessities very well, and he plunged into commercial calculations with the Italian. The latter, during this part of the business, exhibited such savage greed, such an artless love of gain, that he disgusted Charsky, who hastened to take leave of him, so that he might not lose altogether the feeling of ecstasy awakened within him by the brilliant improvisation. The preoccupied Italian did not observe this change, and he conducted Charsky into the corridor and out to the steps, with profound bows and assurances of eternal gratitude.

[1] A celebrated Italian singer, fl. 1779-1849.   EDITOR'S NOTE

III

The price of a ticket is 10 *rubles; the performance starts at seven o'clock.*

Play-bill.

THE ballroom of Princess N—— had been placed at the disposal of the improviser; a platform had been erected, and the chairs were arranged in twelve rows. On the appointed day, at seven o'clock in the evening, the room was illuminated; at the door, before a small table, to sell and receive tickets, sat a long-nosed old woman, in a gray hat with broken feathers, and with rings on all her fingers. Near the entrance to the house stood gendarmes.

The public began to assemble. Charsky was one of the first to arrive. He had played a large part in arranging for the performance, and wished to see the improviser, in order to learn if he was satisfied with everything. He found the Italian in a side room, looking at his watch with impatience. The improviser was attired in a theatrical costume. He was dressed in black from head to foot. The lace collar of his shirt was thrown open; his bare neck, by its strange whiteness, offered a striking contrast to his thick black beard; his hair was combed forward, and overshadowed his forehead and eyebrows.

All this was not very gratifying to Charsky, who did not care to see a poet in the dress of a wandering juggler. After a short conversation, he returned to the ballroom, which was now rapidly beginning to fill up. Soon all the rows of seats were occupied by brilliant ladies: the gentlemen crowded round the sides of the platform, along the walls, and behind the chairs at the back; the musicians, with their stands, occupied two sides of the platform. In the middle, upon a table, stood a porcelain vase.

The audience was a large one. Everybody awaited the commencement with impatience. At last, at half-past seven, the musicians made a stir, prepared their bows, and played the overture from "Tancredi." All took their places and became silent. The last sounds of the overture ceased. . . . The improviser, welcomed by deafening applause which rose from all sides, advanced with profound bows to the very edge of the platform.

Charsky waited with uneasiness to see what would be the first impression created, but he perceived that the costume, which had seemed to him so unseemly, did not produce the same effect upon the audience; even Charsky himself found nothing ridiculous in the Italian, when he saw him upon the platform, with his pale face brightly illuminated by a multitude of lamps and candles. The applause subsided; the sound of voices ceased . . .

The Italian, expressing himself in bad French, requested the gentlemen present to indicate some themes, by writing them upon separate pieces of paper. At this unexpected invitation, all looked at one another in silence and nobody responded. The Italian, after waiting a little while, repeated his request in a timid and humble voice. Charsky was standing right under the platform; a feeling of uneasiness took possession of him; he had a presentiment that the business would not be able to go on without him, and that he would be compelled to write his theme. Indeed, several ladies turned their faces toward him and began to pronounce his name, at first in a low tone, then louder and louder. Hearing his name, the improviser sought him out with his eyes, and perceiving him at his feet, he handed him a pencil and a piece of paper with a friendly smile. To

play a rôle in this comedy seemed very disagreeable to
Charsky, but there was no help for it: he took the pencil and paper from the hands of the Italian and wrote
some words. The Italian, taking the vase from the table, descended from the platform and presented the
urn to Charsky, who dropped his theme into it. His
example produced an effect: two journalists, in their
capacity as literary men, considered it incumbent upon
them to write each his theme; the secretary of the
Neapolitan embassy, and a young diplomat recently returned from a journey and in ecstasies over Florence,
placed in the vase their folded papers. At last, a very
plain-looking girl, at the command of her mother, with
tears in her eyes, wrote a few lines in Italian and,
blushing to the ears, gave them to the improviser,
the ladies in the meantime regarding her in silence,
with a scarcely perceptible smile. Returning to the platform, the improviser placed the urn upon the table,
and began to take out the papers one after the other,
reading each aloud:

"*La famiglia dei Cenci. . . . L'ultimo giorno di
Pompeia. . . . Cleopatra e i suoi amanti. . . . La pri-
mavera veduta da una prigione. . . . Il trionfo di
Tasso.*"

"What does the honorable company command?"
asked the Italian humbly. "Will it indicate itself one
of the subjects proposed, or let the matter be decided
by lot?"

"By lot!" said a voice in the crowd. . . . "By lot, by
lot!" repeated the audience.

The improviser again descended from the platform, holding the urn in his hands, and casting an imploring glance along the first row of chairs, asked:

"Who will be kind enough to draw out the theme?"

Not one of the brilliant ladies, who were sitting
there, stirred. The improviser, not accustomed to

Northern indifference, was obviously in distress. . . .
Suddenly he perceived on one side of the room a small
white-gloved hand held up: he turned quickly and advanced toward a majestic young beauty, seated at the
end of the second row. She rose without the slightest
embarrassment, and, with the greatest simplicity in the
world, plunged her aristocratic hand into the urn and
drew out a rolled slip of paper.

"Will you please unfold it and read," said the improviser to her.

The young lady unrolled the paper and read aloud:
"*Cleopatra e i suoi amanti.*"

These words were uttered in a low voice, but such a
complete silence reigned in the room, that everybody
heard them. The improviser bowed profoundly to the
young lady, with an air of the deepest gratitude, and
returned to his platform.

"Gentlemen," said he, turning to the audience: "the
lot has indicated as the subject of improvisation: 'Cleopatra and her lovers.' I humbly request the person who
has chosen this theme, to explain to me his idea: what
lovers are in question, *perchè la grande regina aveva
molto?*"

At these words, several gentlemen burst out laughing. The improviser was somewhat embarrassed.

"I should like to know," he continued, "to what historical topic does the person, who has chosen this
theme, allude? . . . I should feel very grateful if this
person would kindly explain."

Nobody hastened to reply. Several ladies directed
their glances toward the plain-looking girl who had
written a theme at the command of her mother. The
poor girl observed this hostile attention, and became so
embarrassed, that the tears came into her eyes. . . .
Charsky could not endure this, and turning to the improviser, he said to him in Italian:

"It was I who proposed the theme. I had in view a passage in Aurelius Victor, who alleges that Cleopatra named death as the price of her love, and that there were found adorers whom such a condition neither frightened nor repelled. It seems to me, however, that the subject is somewhat difficult. . . . Could you not choose another?"

But the improviser already felt the approach of the god. . . . He gave a sign to the musicians to play. His face became terribly pale; he trembled as if in a fever; his eyes sparkled with a strange fire; he pushed his dark hair off his forehead with his hand, wiped his lofty brow, covered with beads of perspiration, with his handkerchief . . . then suddenly stepped forward and folded his arms across his breast. . . . The music ceased. . . . The improvisation began:

> The palace shone. Sweet songs resounded
> To lyres and flutes. The dazzling queen
> With voice and look inspired the feasters
> And kindled the resplendent scene;
> Her throne drew all men's hearts and glances.
> But suddenly her fervor fled;
> Pensive, she held the golden goblet,
> And o'er it bent her wondrous head. . . .
>
> The regal feast seems hushed in slumber,
> The guests, the choir, are still. But she
> Now lifts her head up to address them
> With an assured serenity:
> "My love brings bliss, have you not sworn it?
> That bliss the man who wills may buy;
> Attend me: I shall make you equal,
> Bid if you dare, the boon am I.
> Who starts the auction-sale of passion?
> I sell my love; but at a fee;
> Who, at the cost of life, will purchase
> The guerdon of a night with me?"

She spoke—and all are seized with horror,
Each heart with passion waxes bold;
Unmoved, she hears the troubled murmur,
Her face is insolent and cold,
Her gaze contemptuously circles
The thronged admirers gathered there . . .
Now one steps forth, two others follow,
Who greatly love and greatly dare.
As they approach her throne she rises—
Their eyes are clear, their step is free.
The bargain's sealed: three nights are purchased,
And death will take the lovers three.

The hall is frozen into silence,
Still as a statue sits each guest,
As lots are drawn in slow succession
From the dread urn the priests have blessed.
First Flavius, face sternly chiseled,
Who in the legions had grown grizzled—
Not readily the Roman bore
Affront: was life so dear a treasure?
The cost he did not stop to measure,
Accepting, as in time of war,
The challenge that was flung by pleasure.
Next Crito came, a sage though young,
Born in the groves of Epicurus;
The Graces he had loved and sung,
And Aphrodite too, and Eros . . .
The last, who charmed both heart and eye,
Was like a flower scarce unfolded;
It was his lot to love and die
Unknown, alas; his cheeks were shaded
With tender down, his eyes were bright,
With youthful ecstasy alight;
The violence of virgin passion
Was surging in his boyish breast . . .
Or him the scornful queen permitted
Briefly a grieving look to rest.

"I vow . . . Mother of joy, to serve you,
And strangely, since for man and boy
I play the harlot, and surrender
Myself unto a purchased joy.
Then hear my vow, great Aphrodite,
Kings of the nether regions, hear,
You gods who govern dreadful Hades,
I vow—till dawn's first rays appear
I shall delight my masters wholly
And show them every shape of bliss
That satisfies the lover's ardor
With soft caress and curious kiss—
But when eternal Eos enters
In morning purple, then—I vow—
The lucky ones will greet the headsman,
And to his ax their necks will bow."
And lo! the fevered day has passed,
The golden-hornèd moon is rising.
About the Alexandrian palace
The tender shade of night is cast.
Rare incense smokes, the lamps burn softly,
The fountains play with sounds of mirth,
The darkness brings voluptuous coolness
For those who shall be gods on earth.
'Midst marvels of a queen's designing,
In a luxurious dim room,
Behind the curtains' purple gloom,
The aureate couch is softly shining. . . .

[1835]
[Published posthumously, 1837]

POSTSCRIPT

THE TEXT

In the preparation of this volume the original Pushkin text followed has been that edited by B. Tomashevsky and published in Leningrad in 1935. In the case of the posthumously published tale, "Dubrovsky," of which only a rough draft is extant, a compromise was effected between the text as it appears in S. A. Vengerov's edition of Pushkin's works (St. Petersburg, 1910, v. 4) and the more recent one made by Y. G. Oxman (v. 4 of the six-volume edition of Pushkin's works, Moscow, 1932). Vengerov's edition has also been relied upon for the final stanza of the poem which concludes "Egyptian Nights."

Maurice Baring's translation of "I've Lived To Bury My Desires" first appeared in *The Slavonic and East European Review,* London, July, 1935. Thomas B. Shaw's version, revised by the editor, of "The Lay of the Wise Oleg," was published in *Blackwood's Magazine,* Edinburgh, 1845, v. 58. Constance Garnett's translation of "To The Poet" was taken from *The Nation,* London, June 13, 1908. The following lyrics are reprinted from *Russian Poetry, An Anthology,* chosen and translated by Babette Deutsch and Avrahm Yarmolinsky, New York, International Publishers: "A Nereid," "The Coach of Life," "For One Last Time," "With Freedom's Seed," "The Prophet," "Message to Siberia" (translated by Max Eastman), "Three Springs," "Casual Gift," "Antiar," "Madonna," "Verses Written During a Sleepless Night," "Work," "Autumn." The first three, as well as "Antiar," have been slightly revised for the present volume. Oliver Elton's translation of "The Bronze Horseman" and of "The Tale of the Pope and his Workman Baldà," originally appeared in *The Slavonic Review*, London, 1934-35, v. 13, and were reprinted in his volume: *Verse from Pushkin and Others,* Edward Arnold & Co., London, 1935. Alfred Hayes's version of "Boris Godunov" appeared in a volume published in London by Kegan Paul, and in New York by Dutton. The text has been revised for the present edition. A. F. B. Clark's translation of "Mozart and Salieri" first appeared in *The University of Toronto Quarterly*, July, 1933. The translator wishes to express his indebtedness to Prof. G. R. Noyes, Dr. Isabel MacInness, Mr. Jacob Biely, and the editor of this volume for valuable corrections and emendations, most of which have been incorporated in the text as revised for this volume. T. Keane's translations of the stories (from *The Prose Tales of Alexander Pushkin*, London) have been subjected to a thorough revision by the editor. The verse in "Egyptian Nights" was translated by Babette Deutsch. The present edition of Natalie Duddington's rendering of "The Captain's Daughter" differs from the earlier ones in that the so-called Omitted Chapter, instead of being incorporated in the text, is printed separately, in order to give the reader the story as Pushkin himself prepared it for the press. In Chapter XIV a paragraph left out by the translator was restored to its proper place; for the translation of this paragraph the editor alone is responsible.

The editor wishes to thank the translators whose work appears in these pages, particularly Babette Deutsch, as well as Messrs. Alfred Hayes and A. F. B. Clark.

A. Y.